Guide to estimatin small wor

19th edition 2013

struction

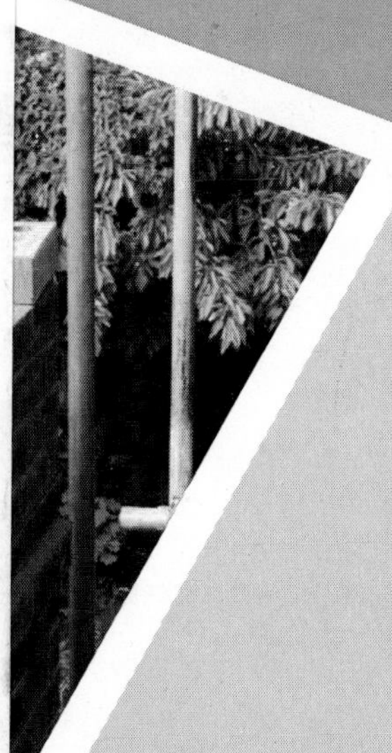

BCIS is the Building Cost Information Service of RICS

Preface

BCIS GUIDE TO ESTIMATING FOR SMALL WORKS 2013

Preface to the 19th Edition - February 2013

We appreciate that for many firms estimating can be a headache, conventional building price books being too expensive, too complex and generally intended for larger projects. They also contain unit rates which are not relevant and perhaps not easily understood.

For many years BCIS had received persistent requests for a building price book aimed specifically at the smaller builder who is chiefly engaged in the construction of small extensions to existing buildings using traditional methods and materials, with the result that the Guide to Estimating for Small Works was produced. This book has established itself and is very popular with the small builder.

Such work represents a significant part of the total volume of construction undertaken in the UK and is generally carried out by small firms typically having less than 20 employees, often as few as one or two, with some trades sub-contracted out.

The smaller builder is more likely to build up his estimate in recognised building sections or elements using just the total costs of the foundations, walls, roof etc. Certainly our research shows that most smaller builders are happier with this approach.

The book follows the method of estimating in sections or elements by providing:-

a) A comprehensive selection of fully priced standard estimates for the most common type, style and size of building extension with the total cost of each section or element clearly shown.

b) A separate detailed price build up for each section or element included in the standard estimates showing how the cost of the foundations, walls, roof etc. have been built up.

Drawings and specifications are also included together with essential pricing information such as labour hourly rates, gang rates, plant hire rates and basic material prices. In addition, measured rates are given for alteration works and external works including paving and drainage. The pricing information is completed with a fully detailed estimate for a roof space conversion.

An important feature of this book is that in addition to providing prices and estimates, it explains in a clear and straightforward manner how to adjust and manipulate the standard estimates to suit the builder's particular project. By this means we aim to enhance the value of the book, increase the confidence of the user and promote a greater understanding of building estimating.

Although this book has been published with the smaller builder in mind, it will nevertheless be of immense value to larger builders engaged in the construction of small building extensions as well as building owners and consultants. The book is now also easier to use with a comprehensive index to take you straight to the place where you need to be and a far superior layout providing clearer and more concise information.

We believe that this publication bridges the gap between the estimating text book and the building price book, providing answers to the questions and solutions to many of the problems of estimating for small extension works.

N.P. Barnett BSc (Hons)
Head of Resource Data
BCIS/IPG

BCIS GUIDE TO ESTIMATING FOR SMALL WORKS 2013

COPYRIGHT

It is the Publishers' policy to continue to improve and develop the BCIS Databases and we invite your suggestions for improvements to the book.

ISBN: 978 1 907196 37 9

BCIS
Parliament Square
London
SW1P 3AD

Telephone:	+44 (0)24 7686 8555
Fax:	+44 (0)20 7695 1501
Web Site:	www.bcis.co.uk
E-Mail	contact@bcis.co.uk

February 2013

BCIS GUIDE TO ESTIMATING FOR SMALL WORKS 2013

19TH EDITION

BCIS would like to thank our members of staff together with all those who assisted in the preparation and production of the 19th Edition of the BCIS Guide to Estimating for Small Works. We also wish to acknowledge the invaluable assistance given by the following individuals, including those who have given their kind permission for the reproduction and publication of copyright material.

Technical Editor:

N P Barnett BSc (Hons)

Editorial staff and contributors to original material:
C A Rowe MRICS
Robert C Murphy MSc, DipBE, FRICS
Carl F Isgar FRICS
Alan J Hobbs DMS, FRICS, FBIM
Mrs M Damon-De Waele

Editorial Assistants:
Mrs C Barnett
Mrs R Read

Drawings:

T M Wood MBIAT

A Note about the Book:

This publication represents one, in a range of construction price books, from BCIS, designed to assist in the preparation and pricing of estimates and contracts from small extensions right up to multi-million pound projects. All the pricing information within this book has been extracted from the BCIS Building Price Database, which contains over 500,000 pricing elements. All extracted prices were then tailored to reflect the needs of the smaller builder, enabling a fast and reliable estimate to be produced.

Contents

Contents

Index

(Bold italic numbers refer to chapter numbers, plain numbers are page numbers)

-W-

TABLE OF REFERENCE NUMBERS (**all chapter 4**)

Projection x Width	SPECIFICATION A (see Chapter 4 Page 1)								SPECIFICATION B (see Chapter 4 page 1)							
	Single Storey				Two Storey				Single Storey				Two Storey			
	Flat Roof		Pitched Roof		Flat Roof		Pitched Roof		Flat Roof		Pitched Roof		Flat Roof		Pitched Roof	
	Ref	Page	Ref	Page	Ref	Page	Ref	Page	Ref	Page	Ref	Page	Ref	Page	Ref	Page
2.00 x 2.00 m	A/1F 2x2	**12**	A/1P 2x2	**50**	A/2F 2x2	**88**	A/2P 2x2	**128**	B/1F 2x2	**168**	B/1P 2x2	**206**	B/2F 2x2	**244**	B/2P 2x2	**284**
2.00 x 3.00 m	A/1F 2x3	**12**	A/1P 2x3	**50**	A/2F 2x3	**88**	A/2P 2x3	**128**	B/1F 2x3	**168**	B/1P 2x3	**206**	B/2F 2x3	**244**	B/2P 2x3	**284**
2.00 x 4.00 m	A/1F 2x4	**12**	A/1P 2x4	**50**	A/2F 2x4	**88**	A/2P 2x4	**128**	B/1F 2x4	**168**	B/1P 2x4	**206**	B/2F 2x4	**244**	B/2P 2x4	**284**
2.00 x 5.00 m	A/1F 2x5	**12**	A/1P 2x5	**50**	A/2F 2x5	**88**	A/2P 2x5	**128**	B/1F 2x5	**168**	B/1P 2x5	**206**	B/2F 2x5	**244**	B/2P 2x5	**284**
2.00 x 6.00 m	A/1F 2x6	**13**	A/1P 2x6	**51**	A/2F 2x6	**89**	A/2P 2x6	**129**	B/1F 2x6	**169**	B/1P 2x6	**207**	B/2F 2x6	**245**	B/2P 2x6	**285**
2.00 x 7.00 m	A/1F 2x7	**13**	A/1P 2x7	**51**	A/2F 2x7	**89**	A/2P 2x7	**129**	B/1F 2x7	**169**	B/1P 2x7	**207**	B/2F 2x7	**245**	B/2P 2x7	**285**
2.00 x 8.00 m	A/1F 2x8	**13**	A/1P 2x8	**51**	A/2F 2x8	**89**	A/2P 2x8	**129**	B/1F 2x8	**169**	B/1P 2x8	**207**	B/2F 2x8	**245**	B/2P 2x8	**285**
2.00 x 9.00 m	A/1F 2x9	**13**	A/1P 2x9	**51**	A/2F 2x9	**89**	A/2P 2x9	**129**	B/1F 2x9	**169**	B/1P 2x9	**207**	B/2F 2x9	**245**	B/2P 2x9	**285**
3.00 x 2.00 m	A/1F 3x2	**20**	A/1P 3x2	**58**	A/2F 3x2	**96**	A/2P 3x2	**136**	B/1F 3x2	**176**	B/1P 3x2	**214**	B/2F 3x2	**252**	B/2P 3x2	**292**
3.00 x 3.00 m	A/1F 3x3	**20**	A/1P 3x3	**58**	A/2F 3x3	**96**	A/2P 3x3	**136**	B/1F 3x3	**176**	B/1P 3x3	**214**	B/2F 3x3	**252**	B/2P 3x3	**292**
3.00 x 4.00 m	A/1F 3x4	**20**	A/1P 3x4	**58**	A/2F 3x4	**96**	A/2P 3x4	**136**	B/1F 3x4	**176**	B/1P 3x4	**214**	B/2F 3x4	**252**	B/2P 3x4	**292**
3.00 x 5.00 m	A/1F 3x5	**20**	A/1P 3x5	**58**	A/2F 3x5	**96**	A/2P 3x5	**136**	B/1F 3x5	**176**	B/1P 3x5	**214**	B/2F 3x5	**252**	B/2P 3x5	**292**
3.00 x 6.00 m	A/1F 3x6	**21**	A/1P 3x6	**59**	A/2F 3x6	**97**	A/2P 3x6	**137**	B/1F 3x6	**177**	B/1P 3x6	**215**	B/2F 3x6	**253**	B/2P 3x6	**293**
3.00 x 7.00 m	A/1F 3x7	**21**	A/1P 3x7	**59**	A/2F 3x7	**97**	A/2P 3x7	**137**	B/1F 3x7	**177**	B/1P 3x7	**215**	B/2F 3x7	**253**	B/2P 3x7	**293**
3.00 x 8.00 m	A/1F 3x8	**21**	A/1P 3x8	**59**	A/2F 3x8	**97**	A/2P 3x8	**137**	B/1F 3x8	**177**	B/1P 3x8	**215**	B/2F 3x8	**253**	B/2P 3x8	**293**
3.00 x 9.00 m	A/1F 3x9	**21**	A/1P 3x9	**59**	A/2F 3x9	**97**	A/2P 3x9	**137**	B/1F 3x9	**177**	B/1P 3x9	**215**	B/2F 3x9	**253**	B/2P 3x9	**293**
4.00 x 2.00 m	A/1F 4x2	**28**	A/1P 4x2	**66**	A/2F 4x2	**104**	A/2P 4x2	**144**	B/1F 4x2	**184**	B/1P 4x2	**222**	B/2F 4x2	**260**	B/2P 4x2	**300**
4.00 x 3.00 m	A/1F 4x3	**28**	A/1P 4x3	**66**	A/2F 4x3	**104**	A/2P 4x3	**144**	B/1F 4x3	**184**	B/1P 4x3	**222**	B/2F 4x3	**260**	B/2P 4x3	**300**
4.00 x 4.00 m	A/1F 4x4	**28**	A/1P 4x4	**66**	A/2F 4x4	**104**	A/2P 4x4	**144**	B/1F 4x4	**184**	B/1P 4x4	**222**	B/2F 4x4	**260**	B/2P 4x4	**300**
4.00 x 5.00 m	A/1F 4x5	**28**	A/1P 4x5	**66**	A/2F 4x5	**104**	A/2P 4x5	**144**	B/1F 4x5	**184**	B/1P 4x5	**222**	B/2F 4x5	**260**	B/2P 4x5	**300**
4.00 x 6.00 m	A/1F 4x6	**29**	A/1P 4x6	**67**	A/2F 4x6	**105**	A/2P 4x6	**145**	B/1F 4x6	**185**	B/1P 4x6	**223**	B/2F 4x6	**261**	B/2P 4x6	**301**
4.00 x 7.00 m	A/1F 4x7	**29**	A/1P 4x7	**67**	A/2F 4x7	**105**	A/2P 4x7	**145**	B/1F 4x7	**185**	B/1P 4x7	**223**	B/2F 4x7	**261**	B/2P 4x7	**301**
4.00 x 8.00 m	A/1F 4x8	**29**	A/1P 4x8	**67**	A/2F 4x8	**105**	A/2P 4x8	**145**	B/1F 4x8	**185**	B/1P 4x8	**223**	B/2F 4x8	**261**	B/2P 4x8	**301**
4.00 x 9.00 m	A/1F 4x9	**29**	A/1P 4x9	**67**	A/2F 4x9	**105**	A/2P 4x9	**145**	B/1F 4x9	**185**	B/1P 4x9	**223**	B/2F 4x9	**261**	B/2P 4x9	**301**
5.00 x 2.00 m	A/1F 5x2	**36**	A/1P 5x2	**74**	A/2F 5x2	**112**	A/2P 5x2	**152**	B/1F 5x2	**192**	B/1P 5x2	**230**	B/2F 5x2	**268**	B/2P 5x2	**308**
5.00 x 3.00 m	A/1F 5x3	**36**	A/1P 5x3	**74**	A/2F 5x3	**112**	A/2P 5x3	**152**	B/1F 5x3	**192**	B/1P 5x3	**230**	B/2F 5x3	**268**	B/2P 5x3	**308**
5.00 x 4.00 m	A/1F 5x4	**36**	A/1P 5x4	**74**	A/2F 5x4	**112**	A/2P 5x4	**152**	B/1F 5x4	**192**	B/1P 5x4	**230**	B/2F 5x4	**268**	B/2P 5x4	**308**
5.00 x 5.00 m	A/1F 5x5	**36**	A/1P 5x5	**74**	A/2F 5x5	**112**	A/2P 5x5	**152**	B/1F 5x5	**192**	B/1P 5x5	**230**	B/2F 5x5	**268**	B/2P 5x5	**308**
5.00 x 6.00 m	A/1F 5x6	**37**	A/1P 5x6	**75**	A/2F 5x6	**113**	A/2P 5x6	**153**	B/1F 5x6	**193**	B/1P 5x6	**231**	B/2F 5x6	**269**	B/2P 5x6	**309**
5.00 x 7.00 m	A/1F 5x7	**37**	A/1P 5x7	**75**	A/2F 5x7	**113**	A/2P 5x7	**153**	B/1F 5x7	**193**	B/1P 5x7	**231**	B/2F 5x7	**269**	B/2P 5x7	**309**
5.00 x 8.00 m	A/1F 5x8	**37**	A/1P 5x8	**75**	A/2F 5x8	**113**	A/2P 5x8	**153**	B/1F 5x8	**193**	B/1P 5x8	**231**	B/2F 5x8	**269**	B/2P 5x8	**309**
5.00 x 9.00 m	A/1F 5x9	**37**	A/1P 5x9	**75**	A/2F 5x9	**113**	A/2P 5x9	**153**	B/1F 5x9	**193**	B/1P 5x9	**231**	B/2F 5x9	**269**	B/2P 5x9	**309**

N.B Projection is the length of the side of the extension.

1

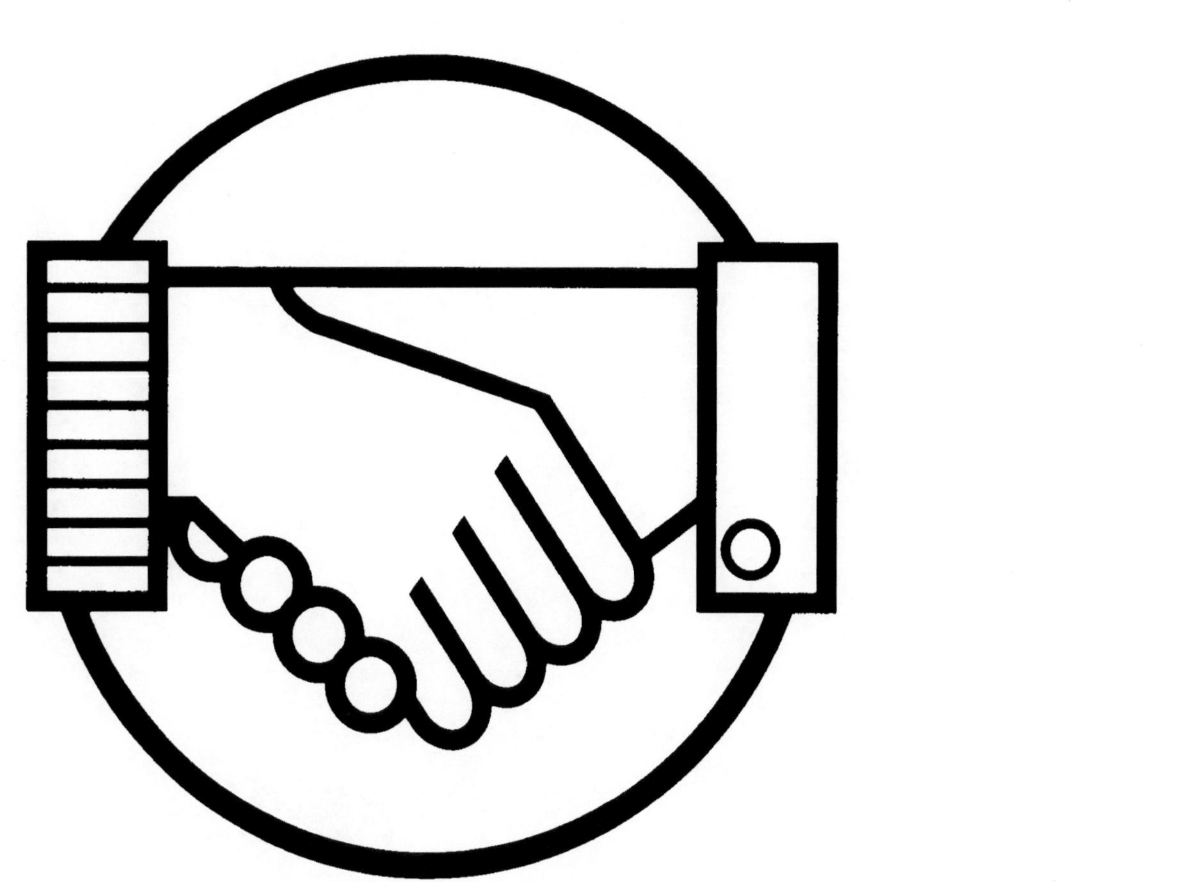

Introduction

CHAPTER 1

INTRODUCTION

Generally
The objective of this book is to assist the smaller builder to estimate the cost of building construction work swiftly and accurately with the minimum of complication. Since most builders have to bid in competition for their work, it follows that a greater understanding of straightforward estimating methods coupled with reliable cost information will increase the builder's chances of winning contracts and building a successful business. This book aims to provide both the understanding and the cost information.

Most conventional building price books give unit rates for measured work, however, it is recognised that the majority of smaller builders do not estimate this way. Instead they simply break the building down into sections or elements and calculate the total cost of the foundations, walls, roof etc.

This book gives the cost of each building section or element and provides a comprehensive selection of standard estimates priced in sections for a range of traditionally constructed building extensions of various types and sizes.

The building sections or elements used are:-

- Substructure
- Frame
- Upper Floors
- Roofs
- Stairs
- External Walls
- External Doors and Windows
- Internal Walls and Partitions
- Internal Doors
- Wall Finishes
- Floor Finishes
- Ceiling Finishes
- Fittings and Furnishings
- Services
- Site works
- Drainage
- Manholes
- Alterations to Existing Building

These building elements are in common use and are recognised by Builders and Professionals alike.

To provide an insight into the scope of this book and its usefulness to the smaller builder, the contents are summarised below.

Chapter 1	Introduction	In addition to the foregoing notes, this chapter outlines the basis of the prices including the criteria followed in the calculation of both net and gross rates together with the breakdown of the labour hourly rates.
Chapter 2	Contract	This useful chapter highlights the importance of using a written contract and provides a check list of points which any contract should cover.
Chapter 3	Preliminaries	This chapter identifies those items which should be included in Preliminaries and provides a worked example of a calculation of the Cost of Preliminaries for a contract having a value of £40,000.
Chapter 4	Standard Estimates	Outlines the building extension types and sizes, the specifications used and provides 256 separate fully priced estimates.
Chapter 5	Cost Details and Adjustments	This chapter provides the detailed cost breakdown of all the items used in the estimates. It includes worked examples of how to adjust prices and modify the standard estimates.
Chapter 6	Alteration Work	This chapter provides an extensive selection of rates for alteration work and includes a fully priced estimate for a roof space conversion.
Chapter 7	External Works	Provides a selection of rates for paving, drainage and manholes.
Chapter 8	Basic Prices, Labour, Plant and Materials	Provides details of which labour rates have been used in the prices and shows the calculation of gang rates. Also provides plant hire rates and an extensive selection of basic material prices.
Chapter 9	Planning and Building Regulation Fees	Provides guidance for the application and cost of the Town and Country Planning Regulations and The Building (Prescribed Fees etc.) Regulations

Chapter 10	Memoranda	Contains metric conversion tables, weights of materials, covering capacities, number of bricks and tiles per square metre etc.

The standard estimates in Chapter 4 are related to items of completed work and prices have already been built up from detailed labour, plant and materials cost information. By selecting the estimate nearest to that required a total cost can be obtained very quickly.

Should the standard estimate need to be modified, then the builder can measure 'finished' work from drawings and relate this to the detailed breakdown of the items given in Chapter 5. The standard details can be compared with the required specification and repriced if necessary - an example is given in Chapter 5. As can be seen from that example, labour times, labour costs and materials costs can easily be obtained for each element of the building. Labour times can be checked against the builders own assessment of time for each element.

The standard estimates not only provide a framework for a fast and efficient estimate but they also enable a sound basis to be established for the contract which may follow. The builder can refer to the detailed breakdown of rates and prove exactly what is included in his contract price.

Successful estimates, which have been produced in this methodical way, will form good records which can be checked against work done. The builder can then use the information to modify future estimates and continue to improve his efficiency.

Basis of Pricing
The aim of the BCIS Guide to Estimating for Small Works is to provide builders with a guide to current net cost unit prices for building work at competitive rates.

In calculating the hours required for each separate operation, and in seeking prices for materials; contracts of alterations and extensions to an existing house, of up to two storeys, with a tender price up to £60,000 have been assumed.

The prices have been created on a nationally averaged 'best price' basis. For an indication of regional differentials, see the last paragraph of this Chapter.

The prices represent the net cost of labour, plant and materials, without additions for site overheads (examples of which are shown separately in Chapter 3 - Preliminaries), or for off-site office overheads or profit, as such additions fluctuate with market conditions.

Prices for work which is normally under the Builder's direct control, whether employing in-house labour or labour only sub-contractors, are broken down into 'Net Labour', 'Net Plant' and 'Net Materials', with the total of these separate prices giving the 'NET UNIT PRICE'.

Work is generally measured as composite items which relate to a particular operation on site. These composites are made up of unit prices. This system enables the Builder to make a quick assessment of the work and modify the content of a composite item without the need to build up all the detail.

Work normally undertaken by specialist sub-contract firms has been priced by specialist firms and the prices given are total 'Net Unit Prices' inclusive of labour, plant, materials and the specialists' overheads and profit. The prices are inclusive of 2.5% cash discount to the Builder but are exclusive of the Builder's own overheads and profit.

Guide Prices
It must be stressed that the prices in the book are **guide prices.** Quotations for materials and specialists' work should be obtained for particular projects as the prices cannot be guaranteed. The nature of the publication, which is intended to be a guide to building prices throughout the United Kingdom, precludes the possibility of firm prices for all situations. Regional price variations, qualities and quantities of materials and work, availability of skilled labour, location of sites and individual project requirements all have a bearing on prices for building work.

Descriptions
Descriptions of work are generally based upon the Sixth Edition of the Standard Method of Measurement for Building Works (SMM6) but have been simplified for ease of understanding and to reflect the scale of work covered by this book.

Value Added Tax
The prices throughout the book are EXCLUSIVE of Value Added Tax.

MATERIAL PRICES

Base date of prices
The supply prices of materials, as shown in 'Basic Prices of Materials' at the beginning of each work section were current during the last quarter of 2012.

Trade and quantity discounts
The supply prices of materials generally are Trade prices delivered to site unless otherwise stated. The prices generally are for part loads or small quantities.

Waste factors
Waste percentages added to the supply prices of materials are generally for handling wastage, for such materials as cement, sand and lime. The percentages added to other materials are generally for waste in use and in order to simplify the computation of the material constants used in the calculations of the Net Unit Prices.

Unloading Costs
Where materials are not supplied crated or palletised, the cost of site labour and plant in unloading materials has been calculated, where applicable, and added to the supply prices.

Crates and pallets
Surcharges for returnable crates and pallets have been excluded from the supply prices of the materials

PLANT COSTS

Plant hire charges are applicable to the last quarter of 2012 and are typical rates obtained from plant hire companies.

Idle time
Allowances have been made against the hire charges to allow for idle or standing time so that the hourly constants shown in the build-up of prices are for the actual working time of the plant.

Operators
Weekly hire charges for mechanical equipment are exclusive of operators. The costs of operators are shown separately and are calculated in accordance with the build-up of labour rates shown in this Chapter. Daily or hourly hire charges for mechanical equipment are inclusive of operators where indicated.

Fuel etc.
The hire charges for mechanical equipment exclude the provision of fuel but include maintenance and services charges. Unit rate build-ups include for fuel costs.

Constants
The constants, in the form of hours, against the items of plant have been rounded off to two decimal places after calculation.

LABOUR COSTS

Generally
Labour costs have been calculated in accordance with the recommendations of the Code of Estimating Practice published by the Chartered Institute of Building.

Base date of pricing
Labour costs are based upon the rates of wages and allowances payable to operatives from 12th September 2011.

The Total Cost per Hour figures have been corrected to the nearest whole penny and are based on a 39 hour working week. However, the detailed calculations have been made using several places of decimals which may give rise to apparent 1p differences in some of the printed figures.

Plus rates
An enhanced 'plus rates' has been inserted in the calculation to suit the nature of Small Works Contracts.

The hourly rates used for the calculations are as follows:-

Craftsman	**BATJIC**	**£15.43 per hour**
Labourer	**BATJIC**	**£11.39 per hour**
Labourer	**BATJIC (skill rate A)**	**£12.01 per hour**
Labourer	**BATJIC (skill rate B)**	**£12.31 per hour**
Labourer	**BATJIC (skill rate C)**	**£12.65 per hour**
Labourer	**BATJIC (semi-skilled A)**	**£14.24 per hour**
Labourer	**BATJIC (semi-skilled B)**	**£14.60 per hour**
Labourer	**BATJIC (semi-skilled C)**	**£14.97 per hour**
Technician PHMES Operative	**JIBPMES**	**£22.11 per hour**
Advanced PHMES Operative	**JIBPMES**	**£19.86 per hour**
PHMES Operative	**JIBPMES**	**£16.97 per hour**
Apprentice Plumber (3rd year)	**JIBPMES**	**£12.17 per hour**

NOTE: National Insurance rates have been based on those applicable from 6 April 2012

Travelling Allowances
As travelling allowances vary with the distance of building sites from the Builder's office they have been excluded from the calculation of the hourly labour costs. Allowances for travelling time and/or expenses should be made in Preliminaries.

Trade Supervision
Trade supervision has been excluded from the calculation of the hourly labour costs. Where trade supervision is required, separate allowances should be made in Preliminaries.

Overtime
Allowance for overtime in the calculation of the hourly labour costs has been based on an average of 5 hours overtime per operative per week during British Summer Time. The non-productive element in the overtime amounts to an average of 65.5 hours per operative per annum.

Training Allowance
The CITB advise a levy of 0.50% of PAYE payroll and 1.50% of labour-only sub-contract costs. The training allowance below was agreed in November 2000 and each variation of £20 per annum would equate to approximately 1p variation of the total hourly cost.

Constants
The constants, in the form of hours, against each item in the price book have been rounded off to two decimal places after calculation.

Calculation of hours worked per annum: Craftsmen and Labourers

	Hours	Hours	Hours
(a) Summertime working: 30 weeks of British Summertime at 44 hours per week Monday to Friday			
30 weeks at 44 hours		1320.0	
Less annual holidays (14 days)	123.2		
public holidays (5 days)	44.0	167.2	1152.8
(b) Winter working: 22 weeks at 39 hours per week			
22 weeks at 39 hours		858.0	
Less annual holidays (7 days)	54.6		
public holidays (3 days)	23.4		
sick leave (8 days NB 3 days unpaid)	39.0	117.0	741.0
Total number of paid working hours during year			1893.8
Less allowance for inclement weather (2%)			37.8
TOTAL NUMBER OF PRODUCTIVE HOURS WORKED PER ANNUM			**1856.0**

Calculation of Labour Costs - BATJIC award

The hourly cost of wages based upon the rates of wages and allowances agreed by the Building and Allied Trades Joint Industry Council is calculated as follows:

Annual cost of wages		**Craftsman**		**Labourer**
		£		£
Flat time	1893.8 hours at 10.73	20320.47	at 7.96	15074.65
Non-productive overtime	65.5 hours at 10.73	702.82	at 7.96	521.38
Public holidays	63.0 hours at 10.73	675.99	at 7.96	501.48
Sick Pay	5.0 days at 23.61	118.05	at 23. 61	118.05
Plus rate (See notes below)	2022.3 hours at 0.10	202.23	at 0.10	202.23
		-------		-------
		22019.56		16417.79
Holiday credits	12.6%	2774.46	12.6%	2068.64
		-------		-------
		24794.02		**18486.43**
Employer's National Insurance Contribution – Above ST	13.80%	2388.23	13.80%	1517.78
Training Allowance	(0.50% of PAYE)	123.97		92.43
Retirement benefit	52.0 weeks at 3.00	156.00	at 3.00	156.00
Death benefit	12.0 months at 6.02	72.28	at 6.02	72.28
		-------		-------
		27534.50		20324.92
Severance pay and other statutory costs	2.00%	550.69	2.00%	406.50
		-------		-------
		28085.19		20731.42
Employer's liability insurance	2.00%	561.70	2.00%	414.63
		-------		-------
TOTAL COST OF 1856 PRODUCTIVE HOURS		28046.89		21146.05
		-------		-------
Total Labour Cost per hour		**15.43**		**11.39**
		=======		=======
Effect of 10p/hr plus rate on total cost per hour (see note 2 below)		0.1459		0.1459

Notes:

1 Sources - BATJIC Agreement effective from 12th September 2011.

2 As previously stated, a 10p plus rate has been allowed and the effect of a further 10p variation is shown above

3 Travelling, subsistence and trade supervision should be calculated as project overhead or preliminary items.

4 USERS OF THIS GUIDE SHOULD SATISFY THEMSELVES AS TO THE BASIS OF CALCULATION OF PAYMENTS TO OPERATIVES, RELATED COSTS, WORKING AND PRODUCTIVE TIME ETC., WITHIN THEIR OWN ORGANISATION AND REGION, BEFORE APPLYING ANY LABOUR RATES WITHIN THIS GUIDE. PARTICULAR ATTENTION IS DRAWN TO THE CHANGE IN RULES CONCERNING RECOVERY OF STATUTORY SICK PAY. ALTHOUGH NO ALLOWANCE HAS BEEN MADE IN THESE CALCULATIONS FOR RECOVERY OF SSP, IT SHOULD BE NOTED THAT THE RATES OF NATIONAL INSURANCE CONTRIBUTION WERE REDUCED FOR 1994/5 IN ORDER TO ALLOW FOR POSSIBLE INCREASED OVERALL SICKNESS COSTS, AND THAT THESE REDUCTIONS **ARE** INCORPORATED IN THE CALCULATION.

5 With effect from 15th June 1998 tool allowances have been consolidated into the basic rate of pay.

6 With effect from 11th June 2001 the Holiday Credit and Retirement Benefit System ceased and was replaced with the Building and Civil Engineering Benefits Scheme. Holiday Pay Scheme - This sets out the percentage of PAYE to allow for holiday pay. The retirement benefit is accrued according to the stake-holders' pension scheme using the recommended allowance of £3 per week. However, if the employee chooses to pay a higher amount, up to £13.50, then this must be matched by the employer.

Calculation of Labour Costs - JIBPMES award

The hourly cost of wages for Plumbers based upon the rates of wages and allowances agreed by the Joint Industry Board for Plumbing and Mechanical Engineering Services in England and Wales is calculated as follows:

Annual Cost of Wages			**Technican PHMES Operative** £		**Advanced PHMES Operative** £		**PHMES Operative** £		**Apprentice Plumber 3rd Year** £
Flat time	1870.4 hours at	14.99	28037.30	13.50	25250.40	11.58	21659.23	7.26	13579.10
Non-productive overtime	65.5 hours at	14.99	981.84	13.50	884.25	11.58	758.49	0.00	0.00
Non-productive overtime	41.0 hours at	0.00	0.00	0.00	0.00	0.00	0.00	0.00	0.00
Sick pay	0.00 days at	0.00	0.00	0.00	0.00	0.00	0.00	0.00	0.00
Plus rate	2025.6 hours at	0.10	202.56	0.10	202.56	0.10	202.56	0.10	202.56
Holiday credit (Public &	60 weeks at	59	3540.00	53.10	3186.00	45.55	2733.00	25.55	1533.00
			-------		-------		-------		-------
			32761.70		29523.21		25353.28		15314.66
National Insurance Employers Contribution – Above ST		13.80%	3487.77	13.80%	3040.86	13.80%	2465.41	13.80%	1080.08
Training Allowance annual)	(0.50% of PAYE)		163.81	0.50%	147.62	0.50%	126.77	0.00%	0.00
			-------		-------		------		-------
			36413.28		32711.69		27945.46		16394.74
Severance pay and other statutory costs		1.50%	546.20	1.50%	490.67	1.50%	419.18	1.50%	245.92
			------		-------		-------		-------
			36959.48		33202.36		28364.64		16640.66
Employers liability etc.		2.00%	739.19	2.00%	664.05	2.00%	567.29	2.00%	332.81
			-----		-------		------		-------
			37698.67		33866.41		28931.93		16973.47
Industry Pension Scheme		7.50%	2827.40	7.50%	2539.98	7.50%	2169.89	7.50%	1273.01
			-------		-------		-------		-------
TOTAL COST OF 1832.99 PRODUCTIVE HOURS			40526.07		36406.39		31101.82		
TOTAL COST OF 1499.79 PRODUCTIVE HOURS									18246.48
Total labour cost per hour			**22.11**		**19.86**		**16.97**		**12.17**
			=========		=========		=========		========

Notes:

1. The operative date for the wages and allowances is 2nd January 2012.
2. NI revisions as at 6th April 2012.
3. For Trade supervision see Preliminaries.
4. For travelling expenses and allowances see Preliminaries.
5. For every 10p variation in the basic hourly rate of pay for Technican PHMES Operative, Advanced PHMES Operative and PHMES Operative, add or deduct approximately 14p from the total cost per hour.
6. For every 10p variation in the basic hourly rate of pay for Apprentice Plumbers, Third Year, add or deduct approximately 17p from the total cost per hour
7. The Tool Allowance has now been incorporated as part of the hourly rate of pay as at 23rd August 1999.
8. A plus Rate of 10p has been allowed in the labour cost to reflect the nature of Small Works Contracts.

UNITS USED IN THE PRICING SECTIONS OF THIS BOOK

The Units have been abbreviated as follows:-

Abbr.	Unit	Abbr.	Unit	Abbr.	Unit
m	linear metre	kg	kilogramme	Nr	number
m2	square metre	t	tonne	Ft	feet
m3	cubic metre	ltr	litre		
mm	millimetre	ml	millilitre		

REGIONAL VARIATIONS

The prices generally are based upon average national price levels.

Individual prices may be calculated by applying the relevant local rates obtained for labour and plant, to the hourly constants indicated against each item, together with the local cost of materials, using the methods described in this book.

In order to provide some guidance on regional pricing levels and adjustment the BCIS Location study can be found below. This information is based on the Tender Price Indices, which relate to tenders for new construction work, but may also be used as an indicator for adjustment of maintenance and repair works.

It is stressed that this can only provide an approximate overall guide to the level of pricing of complete projects and will not necessarily be applicable to individual trades or items.

Scotland	0.97
Northern Ireland	0.58
Northern	0.92
Yorkshire and Humberside	0.98
North West	0.91
West Midlands	0.98
East Midlands	0.97
Wales	0.94
East Anglia	1.05
South East	1.07
South West	1.03
Greater London	1.12
Islands (Man, Scilly and Channel)	1.74

However, as the BCIS Quarterly Review is based upon total tender prices, it is stressed that this can only provide an **approximate overall guide** to the level of pricing and the figures in the guide should **never** be applied to individual prices under any circumstances.

2

Contracts

CHAPTER 2

THE CONTRACT

GENERALLY

In order to form a legally binding contract it is normally only necessary for one party to make a firm 'offer' and for the other party to accept the 'offer'. This offer and acceptance need not be in writing and, indeed, many small builders simply enter into an oral agreement to do certain work for a specified sum of money. Frequently, they will make an offer by letter and the client will then accept by letter. Whether the agreement is by word of mouth or by letter, a legally binding contract will come into existence. However, using such agreements, it is often not clear precisely what has actually been agreed.

WRITTEN CONTRACTS

Detailed terms of the contract should be set down in writing, if not, disputes may arise as to the scope, quantity and quality of the work to be done. Such disputes usually occur after work has started and can result in costly delays and bad relationships between builder and client. A written contract will prevent many problems from arising and substantially reduce the possibility of having to go to the courts in order to decide on the terms intended by both parties.

A written contract to provide a clear statement of the intentions and obligations of client and builder requires careful preparation. It is generally not advisable for either party to draw up the contract if allegations of bias are to be avoided and if the Unfair Contract Terms Act 1977 is to be met.

Fortunately, there are a number of standard forms of contract already in existence and it is usually a straightforward procedure to select one of these and fill-in the appropriate information relating to a particular contract. The small builder can obtain advice from a Chartered Quantity Surveyor on selecting the appropriate standard form and inserting the necessary information. The time and cost involved in preparing proper contract documents is quite small and can prevent misunderstanding and difficulties from arising later.

CONTRACT DOCUMENTS

The basic contract document, usually referred to as "the Contract" is the written agreement and list of Conditions of Contract which both the builder and the client will sign in the presence of witnesses. The provisions of the Contract will then be binding on both parties and they will be deemed to be aware of each others' intentions, rights and obligations. Should any disputes arise, they can be referred to arbitration and a judgement can be made without the need to go to court.

The contract should contain at least the following:-

1. The contract price
2. A list of all the contract documents such as drawings, specifications etc.
3. Start date, contract period and any other critical dates
4. Arrangements in event of delays
5. Variations
6. Payments
7. Special Conditions, e.g. site access, protection of adjacent buildings etc.
8. Insurances
9. Planning and Building Regulations approval
10. Names and addresses of both parties.

These items are considered in the following paragraphs.

1. The Contract Price

The Contract Price is the lump sum given in the builder's quotation and which has been accepted by the client. Provided that the builder exercises all reasonable skill and care and the completed Works are suitable for the intended purpose, then the client is obliged to pay the Contract Price. However, most disputes arise due to differences of opinion as to the scope and quality of the work to be done. Therefore, the Contract Price must be accompanied by a clear definition of the work.

2. Contract Documents

The Work is normally defined by detailed drawings and specification (or bills of quantities on larger jobs). Drawings which have been submitted for Building Regulation approval often become the Contract Drawings and will normally incorporate specification notes. They should be examined carefully to ensure that the work is fully designed and that both builder and client understand and agree the extent of the work to be done. Any amendments should be marked on the drawings and they should be signed by both parties and dated.

Note - Design Responsibility

Builders frequently have to make decisions on the construction of details which are not shown on drawings.

e.g.

Drawings will show typical sections through the roof and give sizes of structural timbers etc., but may not fully detail the arrangement of timbers where changes in plan shape occur. The builder may therefore have to decide on the design of the details not shown on the drawings - consequently he is taking on some design responsibility and the legal obligations that go with it.

Therefore it is in the builder's interest to ensure that the Contract Drawings adequately cover the full extent of the work. The designer should be responsible for all calculation of the sizes and layout of the building components. The builder must then exercise all reasonable skill and care in carrying out and completing the works.

When defects occur in completed work, it is not always easy to ascertain whether they have developed as a result of poor design or poor workmanship or a combination of both. Therefore, it is advisable to take some simple precautions before the work is done. If the builder thinks that the design is inadequate, he has a duty to point this out to the designer who should then issue further drawings or instructions. This will help to clarify the extent of the builder's obligations under the contract.

Builders are reminded that many clients will have difficulty in visualising the completed works and therefore it may be helpful if a visit to a similar project is arranged. A little time spent in clarifying what is represented on the drawings may save much time and recrimination later.

3. Start Date and Contract Period

Dates may not be an essential part of the contract but it is worth considering the effects of any delays by either the builder or the client. For example, if alteration works are being carried out, the client may arrange to move into temporary accommodation and any delay may cause inconvenience and expense to the client. On the other hand, it may be necessary for the client to vacate the premises by a specified date to allow work to start - if he does not, the builder may suffer inconvenience and expense. It is therefore useful to state critical dates in the contract when delay or disruption to the programme is likely to cause difficulties for either party.

It is generally not advisable to make the construction programme part of the contract since it may change due to variations in delivery times for materials, timing of sub-contractor work etc. Generally, it will only be start and finish dates which are significant.

4. Delays

If delays do occur, the completion date can be amended and agreed by both parties. However, there may be difficulties when one party suffers loss as a result of delays by the other party.

Standard Contracts often contain a Liquidated and Ascertained Damages Clause which specifies the amount of damages to be paid by the builder. Any amount stated must be a realistic assessment of loss, otherwise payment will not be legally enforceable.

On larger contracts there may be provision for the builder to claim Direct Loss and Expense arising from delays or variations etc. but there is generally no such provision in standard contracts for small works (e.g. J.C.T. Agreement for Minor Building Works 1998 or Building Contract for the Home Owner/Occupier 2000). Builders should therefore make provision in their tender price for possible expenses arising from delays such as late instructions from the architect or client, postponement of work etc.

This is a complex area of law and readers requiring more detailed information are referred to the many publications on Contract Law. In cases of specific problems, advice should be obtained from a Chartered Quantity Surveyor.

5. Variations

A Variation Clause is essential to enable the almost inevitable changes to be dealt with. If there is no Variation Clause and the client asks for a change in the works, a dispute could ensue. Technically, such a change could invalidate the contract and it may require a new contract to include it. Clearly, an arrangement is needed to cover small changes required as the work proceeds.

The Variation Clause is intended to cover small changes which do not alter the scope of the contract (e.g. a change in the size of a window would be covered but a change from a single storey house extension to a two storey house extension would not). The latter case would change the scope of the work from that originally undertaken and would therefore require a new contract to be drawn up.

If there is a Bill of Quantities or Schedule of Rates it may be used as a basis for valuation of the variation. On most small contracts there will be no such basis for valuation, therefore the builder should agree a price with the client **before** the work is done and this price will be added to or subtracted from the Contract Price as appropriate. It is bad policy to present the client with a bill for 'extras' after the Works are complete as this can often generate disputes and damage reputations.

6. Payments

Payment of the Contract Sum becomes due to the builder on completion of the works (subject to any retention provision in the contract). The agreed amounts for variations will be added to, or deducted from, the contract sum.

On very small contracts, one payment at the end of the job is normal. Where the contract extends for several weeks or months there may be a need for interim payments - the work being valued at regular intervals, agreed between the builder and the client, and payment made accordingly. The payment intervals should be written into the contract (standard contracts do not specify an exact period).

- Building Contract for the Home Owner/Occupier 2000 suggest that agreement on interim payments be included if necessary.

- J.C.T. Minor Building Works 1998 states that intervals should be "not less than four weeks".

An alternative to payment at regular intervals is for "stage payments", wherein the Contract sum is divided up in accordance with the approximate value of work at each stage (e.g. up to dpc level; up to roof level etc.). Payments become due on completion of each stage. From the client's viewpoint this system provides an incentive for the builder to maintain regular progress and from the builder's viewpoint it ensures a cash flow in line with his estimate and expenditure.

The amount to be paid is known in advance and there should be no disputing it. Of course, the stage payments must be set at a realistic level and the client may wish to take advice from a Chartered Quantity Surveyor before agreeing to the amount.

Payments are always subject to the work being properly executed and a deduction may be made from an interim valuation in respect of work which is defective.

7. Special Conditions

A standard form of contract cannot cover every possibility for all building works, therefore special conditions applicable to each particular site must be considered. For example, it is important that the client allows the builder full access to the site - any restrictions on access should be stated in the contract. Other matters, such as reinstatement of driveways or gardens should also be detailed.

Most builders will have experience of problems arising from matters such as those mentioned above. The builder should therefore give careful thought to site layout, access etc. and tell the client about the method and timing of operation. Most small contracts involving house alterations or extensions are carried out while the client is still in residence. Many clients may not appreciate the extent to which their use of the premises may be restricted by building operations and it is prudent for the builder to ensure that clients understand how they will be affected. Any special contract conditions required can then be taken into consideration in the Contract price.

8. Insurances

Building work involves potentially dangerous operations and there is always the risk of injury to persons or damage to property. In lump sum contracts the risks are generally shared between the builder and the client. The responsibilities of each party to the contract must be clearly defined and the insurance requirements included in the conditions of contract. Insurance is essential, since the sums of money, which may be payable in damages in the event of an accident, may be far in excess of the resources of either the builder or the client.

Generally, the builder would be liable for injury or death of persons caused by the building works. These persons may be the builder's employees or other people off the site. The builder would not be liable if the injury or death is caused by the client's negligence.

The builder would also be liable for damage to property caused by the works. This includes work on the site and property outside the site which may be damaged by the works. Again, the builder would not be liable if the damage is caused by the client's negligence.

In his own interests, as well as the client's, the builder should insure against the above risks.

Where damage occurs due to causes not related to the building work, then the client is generally liable, e.g. fire, flood etc. These events may be covered by the normal domestic building insurance policy but the extent of cover should be checked and extra cover obtained if necessary.

Insurance is a complex subject requiring careful consideration. Generally, standard contract conditions will define the liabilities of each party but a great deal of care is needed if the wording of these standard clauses is to be changed. These clauses have been carefully considered in order to convey precise legal meanings and should not be modified without expert advice.

A common arrangement, used in contracts of extension works, is for the client to fully insure the existing buildings with the builder accepting responsibility for the new construction.

The essential point is that a contract should define the obligations of each party to insure against the various risks. Failure to take out proper insurance may result in the builder losing his business or the client losing his home.

9. Planning and Building Regulations

When an architect is employed by the client to prepare drawings for Planning and Building Regulation approval, then he should ensure that all fees are paid and approvals obtained. These drawings will usually become contract drawings and will be used by the builder as a guide to the construction works. The builder is required to submit notices of commencement and completion, of certain stages of the work, to the Local Authority. However, the builder's obligations can extend much further than submitting notices.

The builder has a duty to comply with the legal requirements detailed in the many Acts of Parliament and Statutory Instruments. (The Building Regulations is a statutory instrument). Standard contracts will cover many of the legal requirements. Usually it will be sufficient to check that contract documents are in order and drawings comply with Building Regulations. If the works do not comply with Building Regulations then the builder may be held liable unless he has notified the architect that the drawings failed to comply.

On very small jobs, the client may simply tell the builder what is required and the builder carries out the work. There may be no architect, no drawings and no planning or Building Regulation approval. Nevertheless, the builder has an obligation to comply with legal requirements. If he carries out work which does not comply with Building Regulations, he is liable. The builder may also have liability for design defects as previously mentioned under Section 2 Contract Documents - Design Responsibility.

The contract conditions may contain a clause to the effect that the Employer (client) warrants that full planning and Building Regulation approval has been obtained. However, the builder should take the precaution of checking Regulations, especially where no architect or other consultant is involved.

It should be remembered that, in the absence of an architect or other professional adviser, the builder would be held to be the "expert" in all matters appertaining to the building works and would be expected to exercise his knowledge and expertise in ensuring that statutory requirements are met.

10. Names and Addresses of Parties

This may seem self evident but nevertheless must be stated. The situation is not unknown where a householder has work done by a builder and his only means of contact is a telephone number. If the number is unobtainable there may be difficulties. On the other hand, the occupier of a property may ask for work to be done, without the authority of the owner, and is then unable to pay. In one case, known to the author, the occupier went away and the owner refused to pay the builder. Clear identification of the parties is therefore essential.

CONCLUSION

The written contract will not necessarily eliminate all possible problems but it will certainly help to avoid the vast majority. The essential point is that both parties must be clear as to the scope and quality of the work to be done and how much is to be paid for it. The main aim is to avoid misunderstandings where possible but if they do occur, good contract documentation avoids a complicated legal dispute.

3

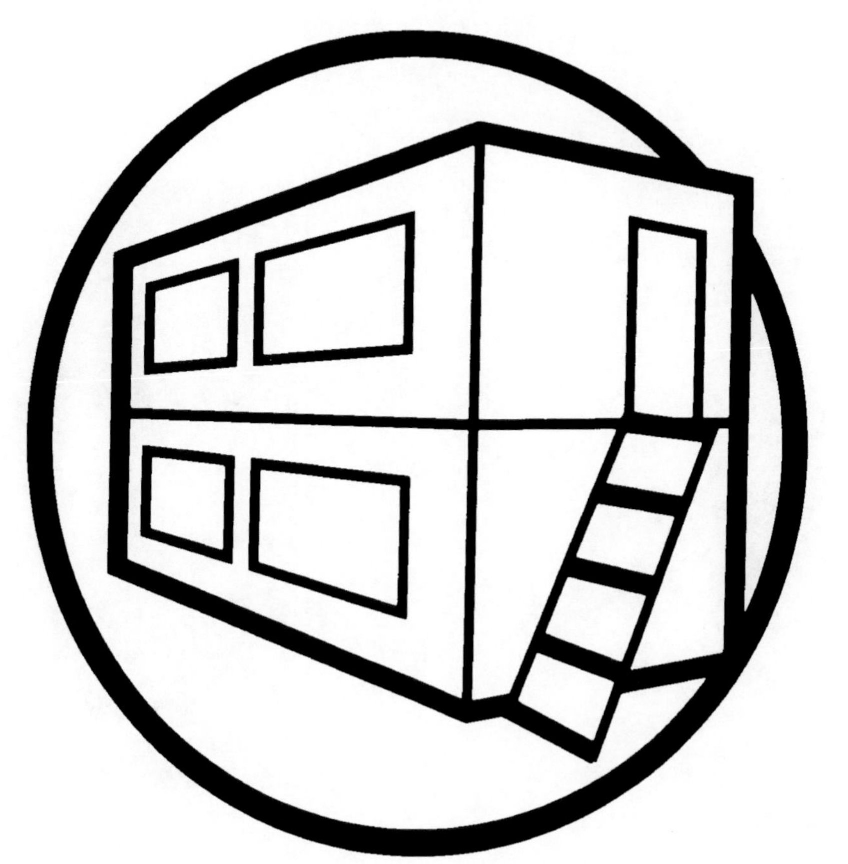

Preliminaries

CHAPTER 3

PRELIMINARIES

THE GENERAL ITEMS
In any building project, the Contractor must include for and price a number of general items not related to any one specific item of work but required in order to carry out the project as a whole.

Typical examples of such items are:-

- Site Supervision
- Insurances
- Cost Fluctuations
- Transport and Haulage
- Plant and Small Tools
- Scaffolding
- Temporary Buildings
- Temporary Services
- Removal of Debris from Site
- Cleaning
- Temporary Fencing and Screens

These items are collectively known as 'PRELIMINARIES'. With some projects the Preliminaries will be listed in the Contract Document, usually in the Specification. Where a Bill of Quantities has been prepared, the Preliminaries will be itemised in the first part of the Bill.

The foregoing list is not exhaustive, other circumstances may cause additional costs, for example, where the site is in a difficult location with, say, restrictions on the method or timing of access, or where hours of work are restricted due to constraints on noise, activity etc. When these situations exist, an item should be included and priced in the Preliminaries to allow for the additional time (and hence, costs) which would be required to execute the work. Such situations are common in small alteration/extension works and must be carefully considered.

The following is a priced example of the Preliminaries for a small works project. A total value of £40,000 and a contract period of 4 weeks has been assumed.

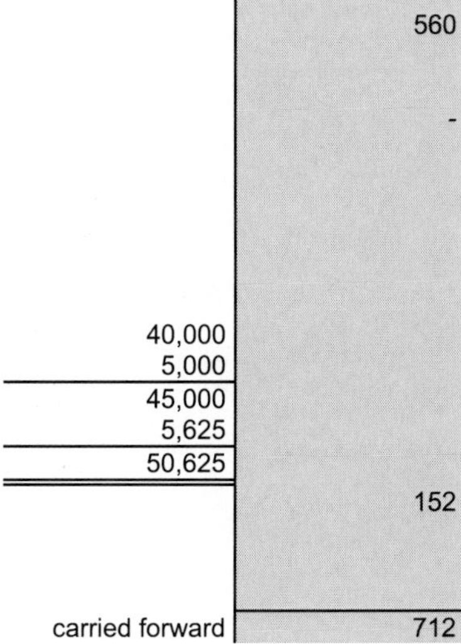

	£	£
Supervision and administration		
A full time foreman may not be economic and some jobs will not even have a working foreman. The leading tradesman on the site may be required to supervise from time to time. Otherwise, supervision and administration is organised by office personnel.		
A possible allowance could be an average of one day per week for the entire contract period by office personnel.		
4 weeks at £140.00		560
Insurances		
Building Employer's Liability and Public Liability will be allowed for in the calculation of the total hourly labour rate and does not need to be priced separately.		-
The building owner will normally undertake the responsibility for insuring the existing buildings in contracts of the type considered in this book. However, in extension works it is essential that the responsibility for insuring the existing building is firmly established, for it is likely that the building owner's existing policies will need endorsement to cover the additional risks during the period of the contract.		
a) If the builder is required to insure the new building works only, then an allowance would be made as follows:		
Contract Value	40,000	
Allowance for associated demolitions and clearance	5,000	
	45,000	
Professional fees (say) 12.5%	5,625	
	50,625	
Premium allowance (say) 0.3% of £50,625 = £151.88		152
carried forward		712

		£	£
		brought forward	712

Insurances (cont/...)
b) If the contract requires the builder to fully insure, then the replacement value of the existing building must be obtained from the building owner (or by independent valuation) and added to the cost of the improvements, with increased allowances for demolition and fees as the following example:

	£	£
Value of existing buildings	110,000	
Contract Value	40,000	
Allowance for demolitions and clearance	5,000	
	155,000	
Professional fees (say) 15%	23,250	
	178,250	
Premium allowance (say) 0.3% of £166,750 = £500.00 would need to be included in lieu of (a) above.		-

Increased costs
Increased costs may result from changes in wage rates or increases in construction materials prices and plant hire rates whilst work is being carried out.
If the contract is for a short period of a few weeks, as in this example, then increased costs will not be significant, but any longer period may see increases which could be more important especially if, for example, a large increase in brick prices was to occur on a project constructed mostly of brickwork.

The contract duration will be the governing factor in determining whether or not to allow for this item. An overall allowance based on 4% per annum would not be unreasonable in the current economic climate.

		£	£
Transport and haulage			
500 kg van and driver:	4 weeks at £400	1600	
Running expenses say 40 miles per day for 4 weeks	40 x 5 x 4 £0.35	280	
			1,880
Plant and small tools			
Concrete mixer:	4 weeks at £22	88	
Small tools allowance:	4 weeks at £35	140	
Sundry haulage of plant not covered in unit rates (say)		150	
			378
Scaffolding			
Scaffolding to new extension:			
externally:	(say):	1000	
internally:	(say):	250	
			1250

Temporary buildings
Site offices are not usually required on extension work but may be needed on all new work.

Storage sheds, if required, should be allowed at lump sums of (say) £175 each. -

No cost has been included in this priced example as it is considered likely that the contractor would be permitted to use the existing building.

Temporary Services
Connections are not normally required on extension work but water charges may be imposed at rates per £100 on the cost of the new building work.

If existing services are not available, then allowance for connections should be made, a typical charge for each service is shown:

water	£250	
electricity	£350	
telephone	£125	-
	carried forward	4,220

	£	£
	brought forward	4,220

Temporary Services (cont/...)
(NOTE: A minimum of 4 quarters' rental is required by British Telecom).
No cost has been included in this priced example as it is considered likely that temporary services will be provided by the building owner.

Allowances for the consumption costs of services should be made when separately metered:

		£
4 x (say) £50 per week		200

Removal of debris from site
Prices for 'removing' in the standard estimates are for getting out of the building and loading into skips. The cost of the skips is not included in the removing prices but should be calculated separately from the following data:

	£	£
Hire of 4.5 m3 skip, including delivery to site, removing when full, disposal of contents and payment of tipping charges, for each hiring	160.00	
Add rental for each day on site, £0.50 per day, say 5 days x £0.50	2.50	
	162.50	
Total cost of 4.5 m3 skip Say 4 skips required = 4 x £162.50		650

Cleaning
Sundry cleaning up of building and surrounds during the contract:

	£	£
4 weeks at: (approximately 1-2 hours) (say) £12	48	
cleaning up on completion (say)	40	
		88

Temporary fencing and screens
Such temporary fencing and screens as are required should be allowed:

fencing at:	(say) £11 per m	
temporary screens at:	(say) £16.50 per m	

No cost has been included in this priced example as it is considered unlikely that such fencing and screens would be required. -

SUMMARY OF PRELIMINARY COSTS

Total estimated cost of foregoing example **£5,158**

Having calculated the foregoing, the final summary of a contractor's bid might be as follows:

		£
Total value of work shown on the drawings and specification	(say)	30,306
Add for contractor's profit and off-site overheads	say 15%	4,546
	Sub Total	34,852
Add PRELIMINARIES as calculated above		5,158
Overall cost of project excluding VAT		**£40,000**

The Preliminaries of £5,158 on the net cost of the work gives a percentage of :-

$\frac{5,158}{30,306} \times 100 =$ 17.02% which would be a guide to the level of Preliminary costs for building projects of this size and type.

4

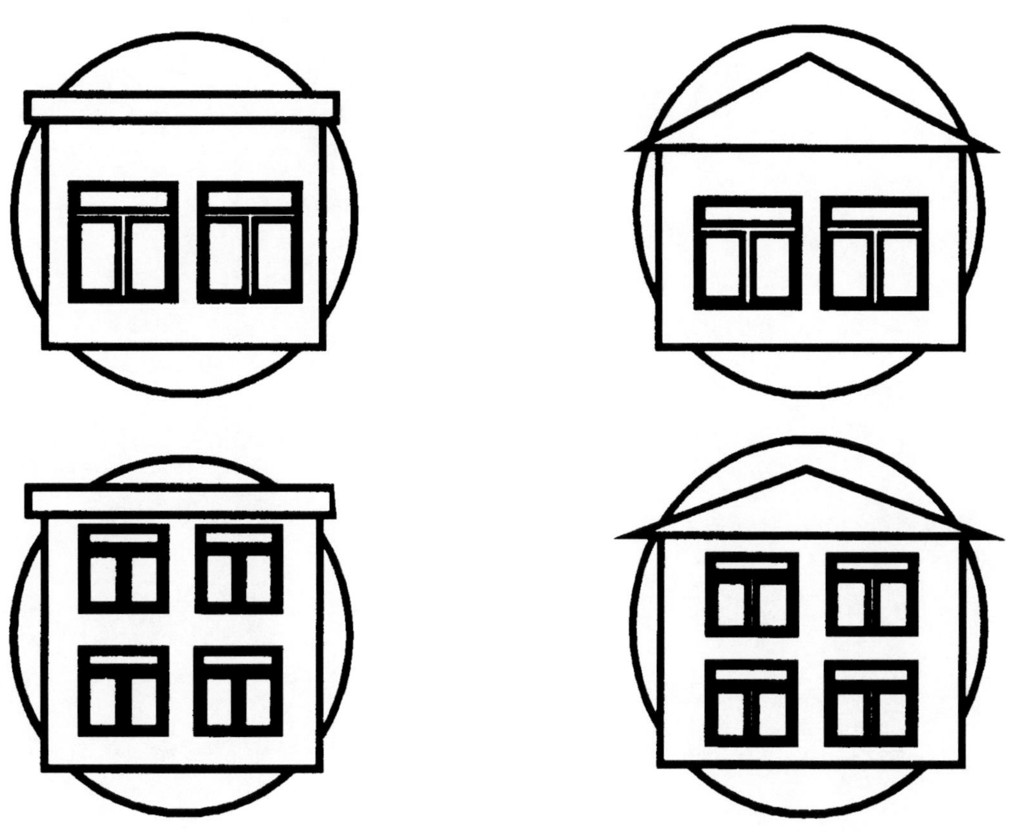

Standard Estimates

STANDARD ESTIMATES

EXPLANATION

This chapter contains no less than 256 fully priced estimates for a range of traditionally constructed building extensions. These building extensions may be used for domestic, commercial or professional purposes.

Two specifications have been used, i.e.

Specification A	A high quality finish with hardwood windows, doors and skirtings.
Specification B	A standard quality finish with PVCu windows, external doors and painted softwood skirtings.

The two specifications are fully detailed in the following pages.

For each of the two specifications, four types of building extension are provided:-

Single storey with flat roof

Single storey with pitched roof

Two storey with flat roof

Two storey with pitched roof

For each building extension, 32 separate plan sizes have been measured and priced and are given as a standard estimate. These standard estimates are tabled on the pages following the specification in groups by building type. Each group of standard estimates includes a plan, front and side elevation. Detailed drawings are included in Chapter 5, where the detailed costs will be found.

Each standard estimate has been given a simple reference number which is based on the specification, building type and plan size. The references are tabled in the index, but generally you should identify your needs with regard to :-

1. Specification A or B
2. Single or Two storey
3. Flat or Pitched roof
4. Locating the plan size

For example, an estimate for a standard quality, two storey flat roofed extension will be found within the pages referenced B/2F, you merely need to locate the plan size required.

SPECIFICATIONS

Two specifications have been used, they are similar in construction but have a differing level of finish. Specification A has a high quality finish including hardwood windows, doors and skirtings, Specification B has a standard quality finish including painted softwood windows, doors and skirtings.

The two specifications are detailed together so that they may be easily compared.

Section	SPECIFICATION A	SPECIFICATION B
SUBSTRUCTURE	Strip footings, hand excavation, concrete foundations 300 mm thick, brick and block cavity wall of Class A Engineering bricks PC £493.42/1000, 75 mm cavity with 5 Nr stainless steel housing wall ties per m2, 140 mm solid concrete blocks, all in cement mortar 1:3, cavity filled with plain concrete, polyethylene damp proof course.	Strip footings, hand excavation, concrete foundations 300 mm thick, brick and block cavity wall of common bricks PC £311.01/1000, 75 mm cavity with 5 Nr stainless steel housing wall ties per m2, 100 mm solid concrete blocks, all in cement mortar 1:3, cavity filled with plain concrete, polyethylene damp proof course.
	Hollow ground floor, hardcore filling 100 mm thick, concrete bed 150 mm thick, half brick honeycomb wall in common bricks PC £311.01 per 1000, polyethylene damp proof course, sawn softwood wall plate, sawn softwood floor joists, 19 mm wrought softwood tongued and grooved floor boarding. 70 mm Rockwool insulation.	Solid ground floor, hardcore filling 150 mm thick, concrete bed 100 mm thick, 1200 gauge polythene sheet, Polyfoam insulation.
UPPER FLOORS	Sawn softwood floor joists on B.A.T SWP joist hangers built in, 50 x 50 mm herring-bone strutting, 25 mm wrought softwood tongued and grooved floor boarding on 15mm wallboard. Insulated with 100 mm Isover APR 1200 between joists.	Sawn softwood floor joists on B.A.T. SWP joist hangers built in, 50 x 50 mm herring-bone strutting, 22 mm tongued and grooved chipboard flooring.
ROOFS	Flat roof construction of sawn softwood roof joists, 50 x 50 mm herring-bone strutting, 18 mm exterior grade plywood.	Flat roof construction of sawn softwood roof joists, 50 x 50 mm herring-bone strutting, chipboard tongued and grooved decking.
	Pitched roof construction 35 degree pitch of sawn softwood wall plates, rafters, joists, binders, hangers, ties, struts, purlins and ridge board.	Pitched roof construction 35 degree pitch of sawn softwood wall plates, rafters, joists, binders, hangers, ties, struts, purlins and ridge board.
	Close top of external wall with Supalux cavity closer, sawn softwood wall plate bedded in cement mortar 1:3, galvanised mild steel strap.	Close top of external wall with Supalux cavity closer, sawn softwood wall plate bedded in cement mortar 1:3, galvanised mild steel strap.
	Three layer built-up felt roofing with Ruberglas GP120 finished with solar reflective paint.	Three layer built-up felt roofing with Ruberglas GP120.
	Redland concrete plain tiles 265 x 165 mm 100 gauge, 65 mm lap, sawn softwood battens, Starex reinforced slaters felt, verge tiles, hip tiles bedded and pointed in cement mortar 1:3, double course at eaves, Redvent eaves ventilator.	Redland Renown granular faced tiles 418 x 330 mm, 75 mm lap, sawn softwood battens, Starex reinforced slaters felt, verge tiles, hip tiles bedded and pointed in cement mortar 1:3, Redvent eaves ventilator.

ROOFS (cont)	Fascia and eaves soffit of 25 mm exterior plywood fascia, 12 mm Supalux soffit, sawn softwood bearers, alkyd based painted finish.	Fascia and eaves soffit of 25 mm wrought softwood fascia, 12 mm exterior plywood soffit, sawn softwood bearers, alkyd based gloss painted finish.
	112 mm half round PVCu gutter fixed with standard bracket.	112 mm half round PVCu gutter fixed with standard bracket.
	Code 4 milled lead flashings.	Code 4 milled lead flashings.
	Cut out brick course, insert cavity tray, replace bricks and make good where new flat roof abuts existing external wall.	Cut out brick course, insert cavity tray, replace bricks and make good where new flat roof abuts existing external wall.
EXTERNAL WALLS	Brick and block cavity wall of facing bricks PC £351.38/1000, 75 mm cavity with 5 Nr stainless steel housing wall ties per m2, Thermalite shield blocks 140 mm thick, all in gauged mortar 1:2:9, 75 mm Dritherm cavity insulation	Brick and block cavity wall of facing bricks PC £351.38/1000, 75 mm cavity with 5 Nr stainless steel housing wall ties per m2, Thermalite shield blocks 100 mm thick, all in gauged mortar 1:2:9, 35 mm cavity insulation.
EXTERNAL DOORS AND WINDOWS	Premdor 44 mm hardwood four-panel pre-glazed door in hardwood frame with hardwood weatherboard, finished 2 coats polyurethane varnish internally, 2 coats external grade polyurethane varnish externally, fixing ironmongery PC £65.00 for ironmongery.	Solid PVCu white doorset with weatherboard, including lock and lever furniture.
	Standard hardwood window 1200 x 1200 mm factory double glazed with stays and fasteners, hardwood window board, galvanised steel frame ties, finished 2 coats polyurethane varnish internally, 2 coats external grade varnish externally.	Standard PVCu window 1200 x 1200 mm double glazed with stays and fasteners, softwood window board, galvanised steel frame ties, finished alkyd based gloss paint.
	Opening in cavity wall for door, Catnic lintel, cavity gutter, close cavity at jambs and sills, horizontal and vertical DPC, plaster finish to reveals.	Opening in cavity wall for door, Catnic lintel, cavity gutter, close cavity at jambs and sills, horizontal and vertical DPC, plaster finish to reveals.
	Opening in cavity wall for window, Catnic lintel, cavity gutter, close cavity at jambs and sills, brick-on-edge sill in facings, horizontal and vertical DPC, plaster finish to reveals.	Opening in cavity wall for window, Catnic lintel, cavity gutter, close cavity at jambs and sills, brick-on-edge sill in facings, horizontal and vertical DPC, plaster finish to reveals.
INTERNAL WALLS AND PARTITIONS	Stud partition, sawn softwood studding and noggings, gypsum plasterboard both sides.	Stud partition, sawn softwood studding and noggings, gypsum plasterboard both sides.
	Premdor hardwood factory finished flush door and hardwood frame and lining, finished 2 coats polyurethane varnish, fixing ironmongery, PC £55.00 for ironmongery.	Premdor softwood factory primed flush door and softwood frame and lining, finished oil gloss paint, fixing ironmongery, PC £55.00 for ironmongery.
WALL FINISHES	Thistle plaster 13 mm thick in two coats; 1 mist coat, 2 full coats vinyl silk emulsion paint.	Thistle plaster 13 mm thick in two coats; 1 mist coat, 2 full coats vinyl silk emulsion paint.

FLOOR FINISHES	10mm laminate flooring, oak plank, microbevelled edges, lacquared finish on and including 5mm thick underlay Moulded hardwood skirting finished 2 coats polyurethane varnish.	Marleyflex (Series 4) thermoplastic tiles on 38 mm cement and sand screed. Wrought softwood bullnose skirting finished alkyd based gloss paint.
CEILING FINISHES	Gypsum plasterboard fixed with nails, 5 mm Thistle board finish plaster. 1 mist coat, 2 full coats vinyl silk emulsion.	Gypsum plasterboard fixed with nails, one coat Artex sealer and one coat Artex stipple finish.
SERVICES	68 mm diameter PVCu rainwater pipes fixed with standard bracket.	68 mm diameter PVCu rainwater pipes fixed with standard bracket.
	Cold water service point, hot water service point and central heating service point in 22 mm copper pipes BS EN1057, Table X. Capillary fittings including pipe fittings, bends, elbows, tees, stop valves and draw-off cock.	Cold water service point, hot water service point and central heating service point in 22 mm copper pipes BS EN1057, Table X. Capillary fittings including pipe fittings, bends, elbows, tees, stop valves and draw-off cock.
	Electrical installation in concealed wiring including cable, switchplates, socket and cooker outlet.	Electrical installation in concealed wiring including cable, switchplates, socket and cooker outlet.
ALTERATION TO EXISTING BUILDING	Cut opening in existing cavity wall including needling and propping, insert prestressed concrete lintel, cavity tray, make good joints, DPC, work to reveals and make good plasterwork.	Cut opening in existing cavity wall including needling and propping, insert prestressed concrete lintel, cavity tray, make good joints, DPC, work to reveals and make good plasterwork.

Specification A

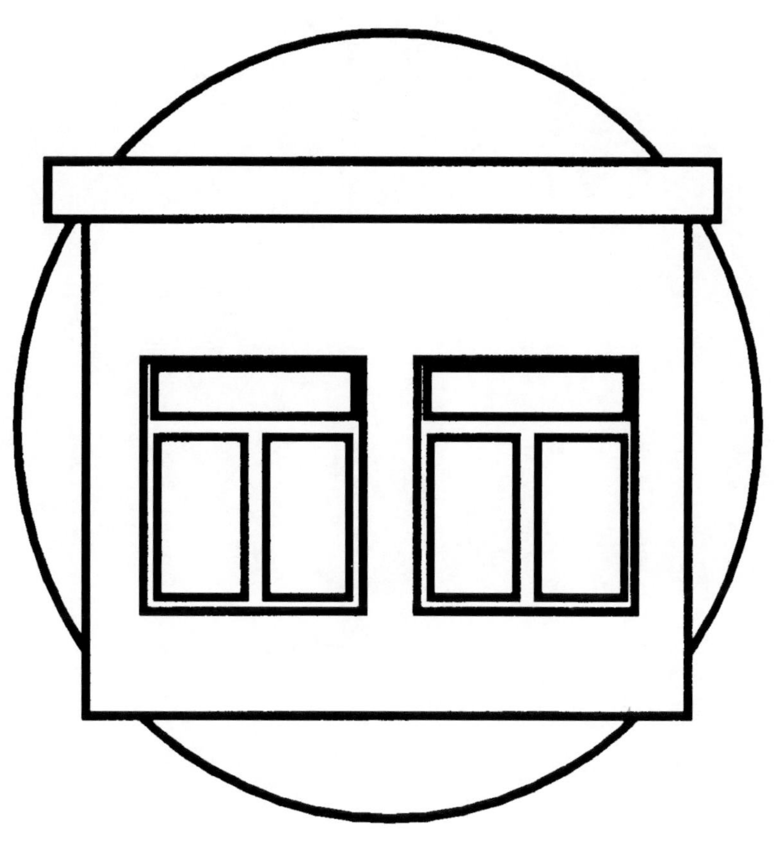

Single storey flat roof

[1F] 2×2/3/4/5.

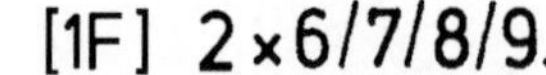
[1F] 2×6/7/8/9.

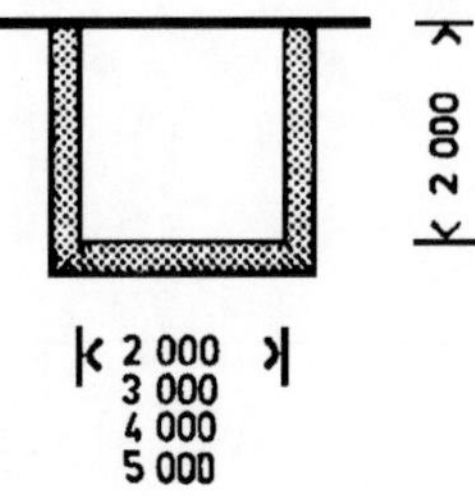
2 000
2 000
3 000
4 000
5 000

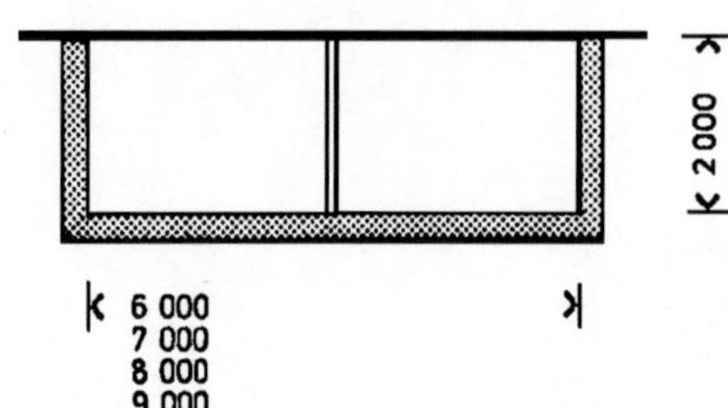
2 000
6 000
7 000
8 000
9 000

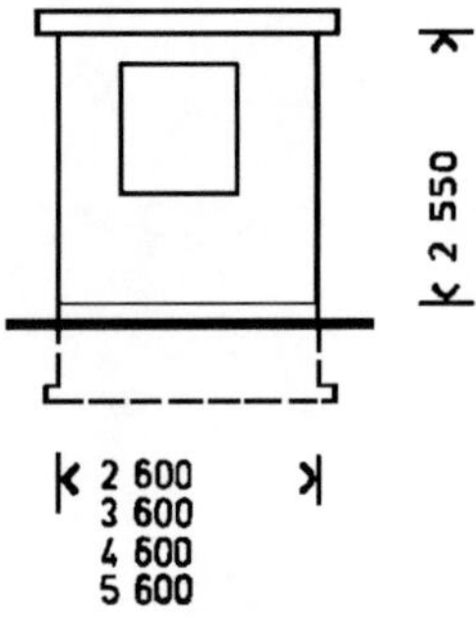
2 550
2 600
3 600
4 600
5 600

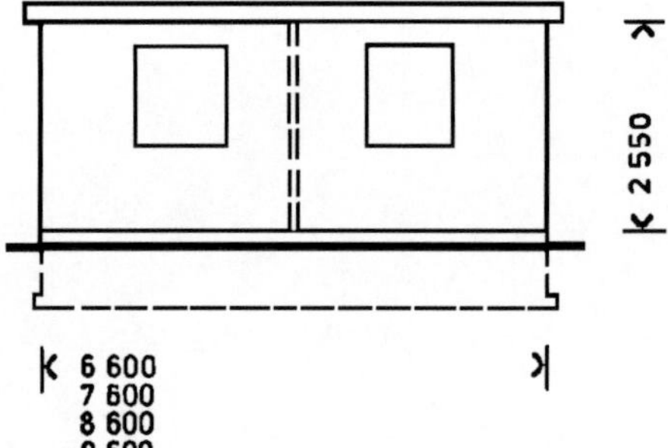
2 550
6 600
7 600
8 600
9 600

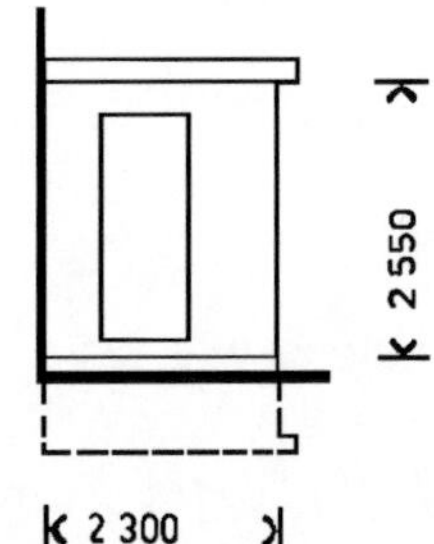
2 550
2 300

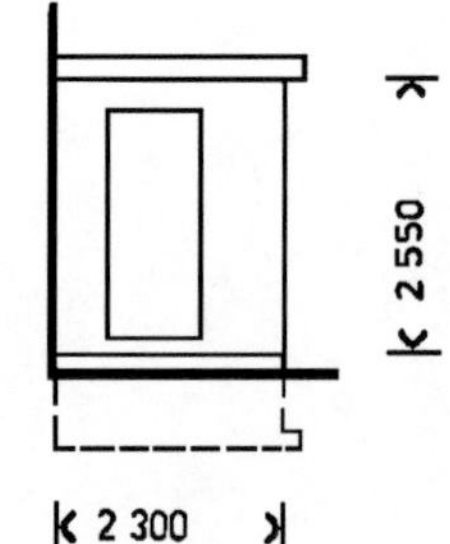
2 550
2 300

[1F] 3×2/3/4/5.

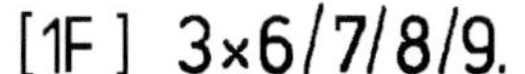
[1F] 3×6/7/8/9.

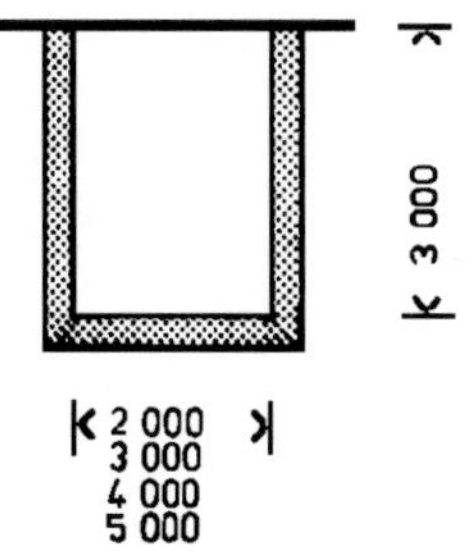
3 000
2 000
3 000
4 000
5 000

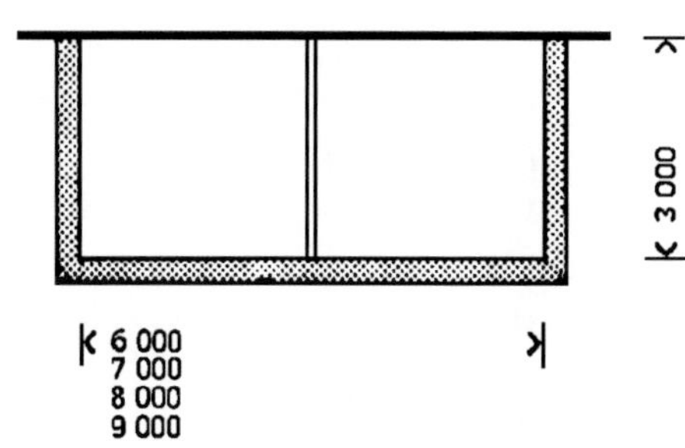
3 000
6 000
7 000
8 000
9 000

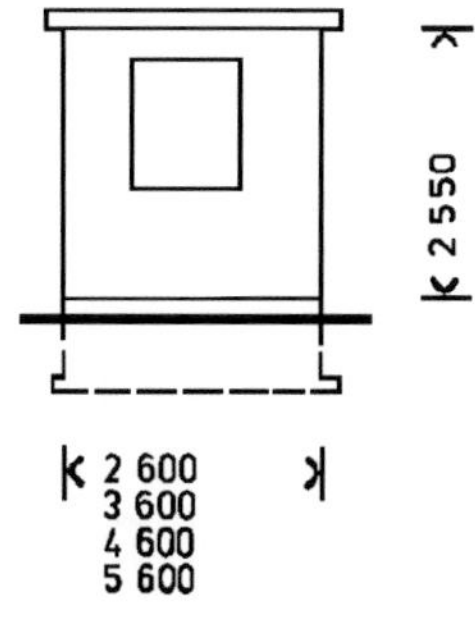
2 550
2 600
3 600
4 600
5 600

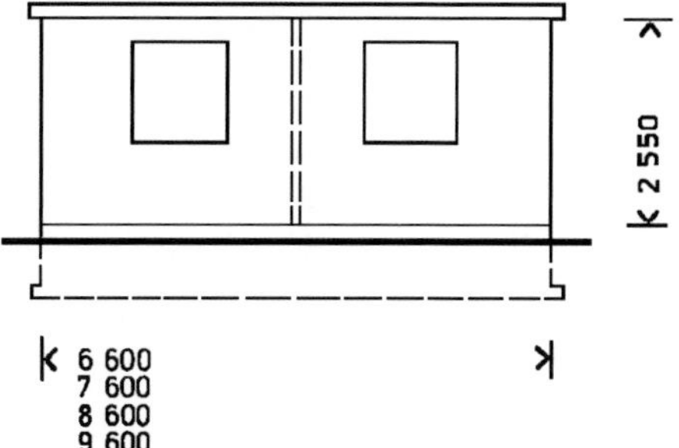
2 550
6 600
7 600
8 600
9 600

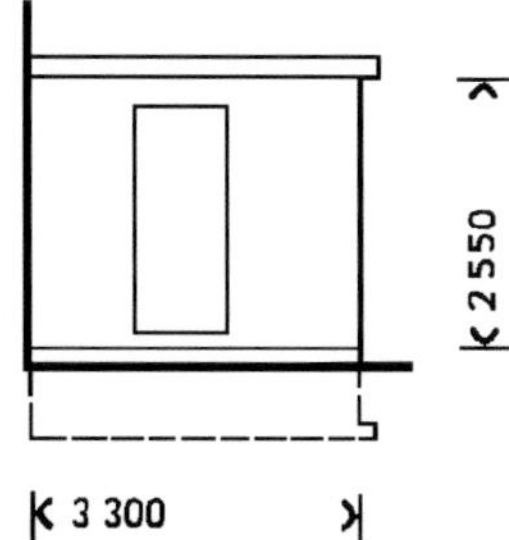
2 550
3 300

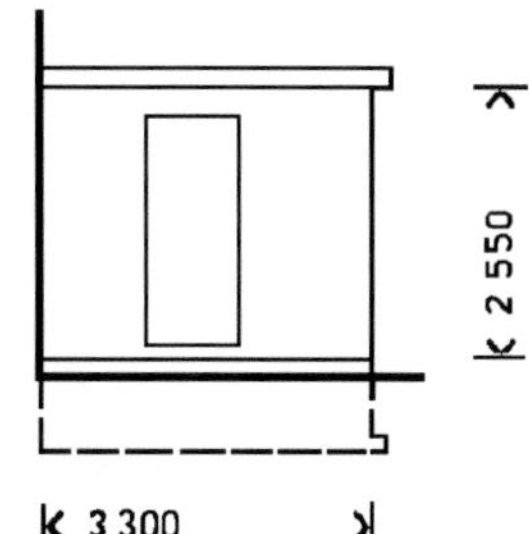
2 550
3 300

[1F] 4×2/3/4/5.

[1F] 4×6/7/8/9.

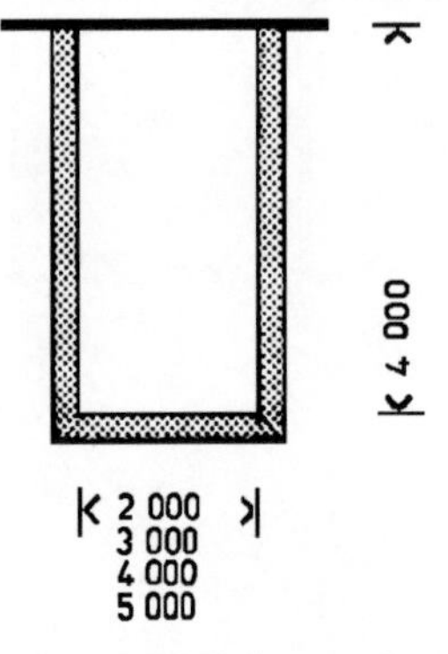
4 000
2 000
3 000
4 000
5 000

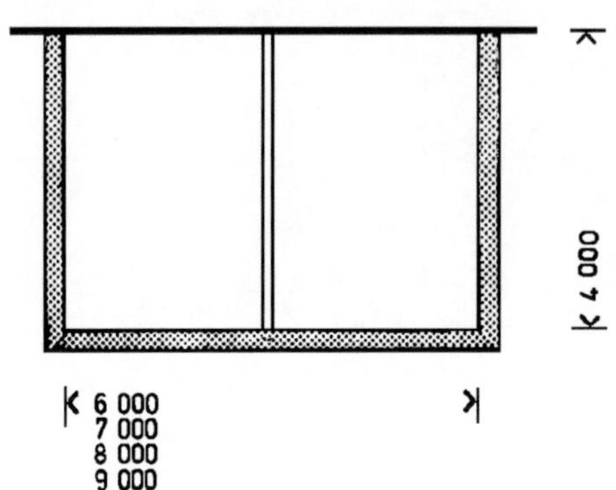
4 000
6 000
7 000
8 000
9 000

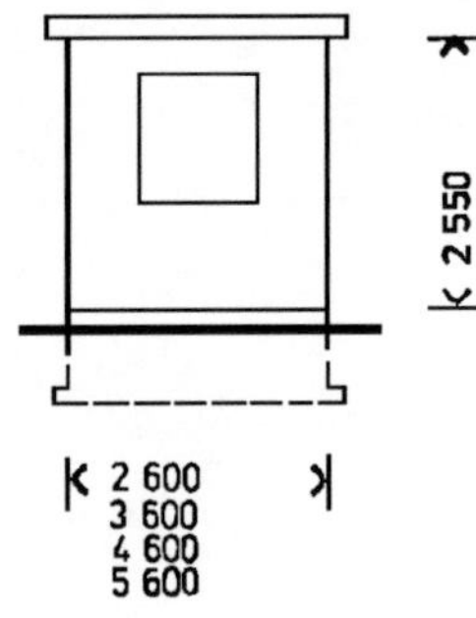
2 550
2 600
3 600
4 600
5 600

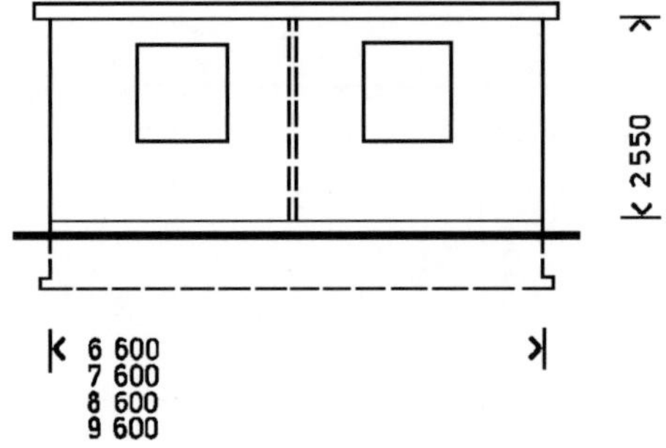
2 550
6 600
7 600
8 600
9 600

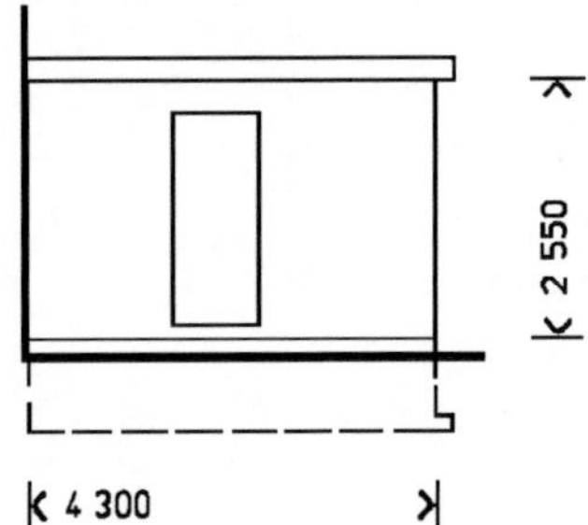
2 550
4 300

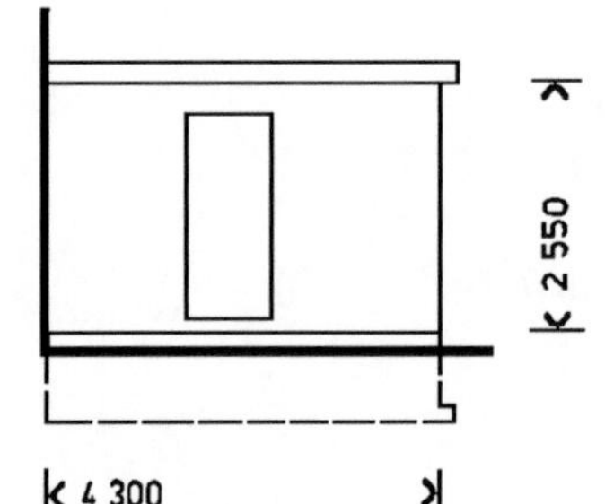
2 550
4 300

[1F] 5×2/3/4/5.

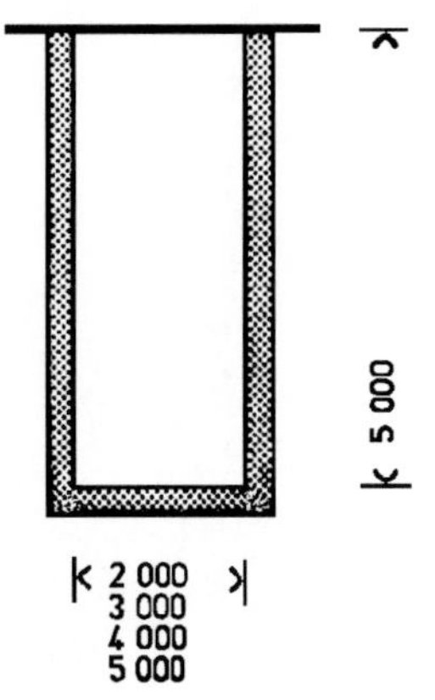

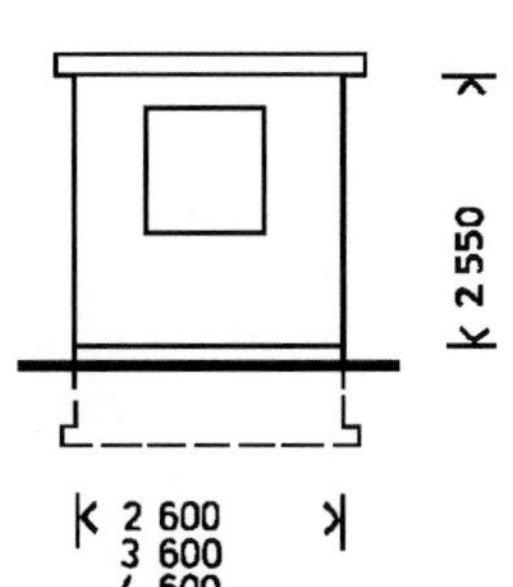

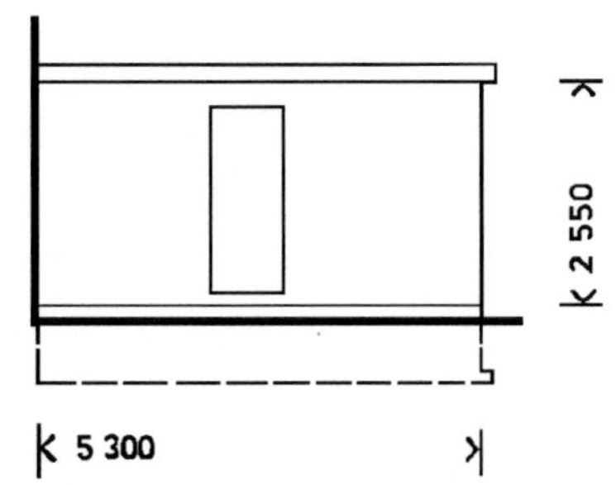

[1F] 5×6/7/8/9.

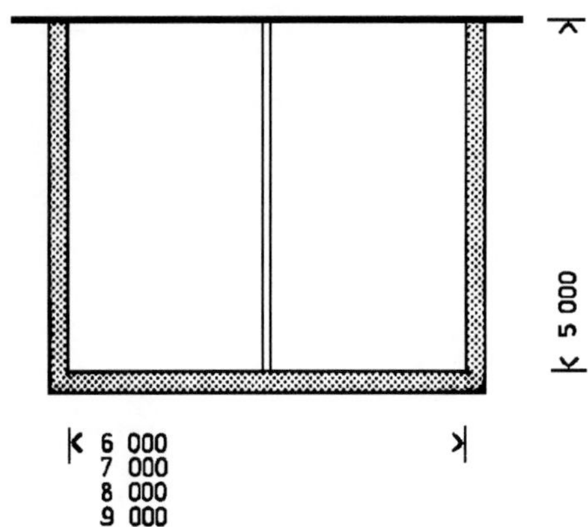

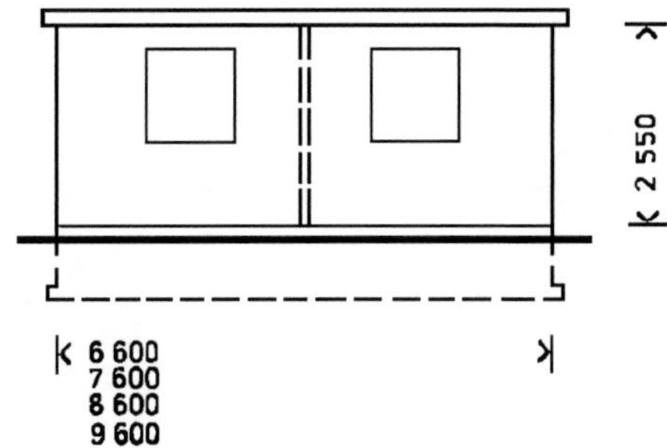

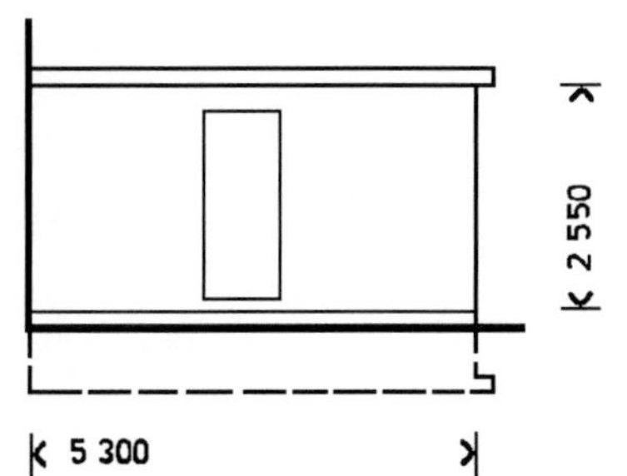

Specification A
4 m2 - 10 m2

Element	Unit	Unit Rate £	Ref A/1F 2x2 Size 2.00 x 2.00 m Area 4 m2 Qty	Total £	Element Total £	Ref A/1F 2x3 Size 2.00 x 3.00 m Area 6 m2 Qty	Total £	Element Total £	Ref A/1F 2x4 Size 2.00 x 4.00 m Area 8 m2 Qty	Total £	Element Total £	Ref A/1F 2x5 Size 2.00 x 5.00 m Area 10 m2 Qty	Total £	Element Total £
SINGLE STOREY														
FLAT ROOF														
SUBSTRUCTURE														
Strip footings	M	144.41	7M	1010.87		8M	1155.28		9M	1299.69		10M	1444.10	
Hollow ground floor	M2	91.57	4M2	366.28	**1377.15**	6M2	549.42	**1704.70**	8M2	732.56	**2032.25**	10M2	915.70	**2359.80**
ROOF														
Flat roof construction 50 x 150 mm joists	M2	66.28	8M2	530.24		10M2	662.80		13M2	861.64		15M2	994.20	
Work to top of external wall	M	23.71	7M	165.97		8M	189.68		9M	213.39		10M	237.10	
Three layer felt roofing	M2	51.19	8M2	409.52		10M2	511.90		13M2	665.47		15M2	767.85	
Fascia and eaves soffit	M	48.01	8M	384.08		9M	432.09		10M	480.10		11M	528.11	
Gutters and fittings	M	18.68	3M	56.04		4M	74.72		5M	93.40		6M	112.08	
Flashings	M	24.70	3M	74.10		4M	98.80		5M	123.50		6M	148.20	
Abutment to existing wall	M	61.52	3M	184.56	**1804.51**	4M	246.08	**2216.07**	5M	307.60	**2745.10**	6M	369.12	**3156.66**
EXTERNAL WALLS														
Brick and block cavity wall	M2	114.25	13M2	1485.25	**1485.25**	15M2	1713.75	**1713.75**	18M2	2056.50	**2056.50**	20M2	2285.00	**2285.00**

Specification A 12 m2 - 18 m2			Ref A/1F 2x6 Size 2.00 x 6.00 m Area 12 m2			Ref A/1F 2x7 Size 2.00 x 7.00 m Area 14 m2			Ref A/1F 2x8 Size 2.00 x 8.00 m Area 16 m2			Ref A/1F 2x9 Size 2.00 x 9.00 m Area 18 m2		
			Qty	Total £	Element Total £	Qty	Total £	Element Total £	Qty	Total £	Element Total £	Qty	Total £	Element Total £
SINGLE STOREY FLAT ROOF continued/.....														
Element	Unit	Unit Rate £												
	M	144.41	11M	1588.51		12M	1732.92		13M	1877.33		14M	2021.74	
	M2	91.57	12M2	1098.84	**2687.35**	14M2	1281.98	**3014.90**	16M2	1465.12	**3342.45**	18M2	1648.26	**3670.00**
	M2	66.28	18M2	1193.04		20M2	1325.60		23M2	1524.44		25M2	1657.00	
	M	23.71	11M	260.81		12M	284.52		13M	308.23		14M	331.94	
	M2	51.19	18M2	921.42		20M2	1023.80		23M2	1177.37		25M2	1279.75	
	M	48.01	12M	576.12		13M	624.13		14M	672.14		15M	720.15	
	M	18.68	7M	130.76		8M	149.44		9M	168.12		10M	186.80	
	M	24.70	7M	172.90		8M	197.60		9M	222.30		10M	247.00	
	M	61.52	7M	430.64	**3685.69**	8M	492.16	**4097.25**	9M	553.68	**4626.28**	10M	615.20	**5037.84**
	M2	114.25	21M2	2399.25	**2399.25**	23M2	2627.75	**2627.75**	26M2	2970.50	**2970.50**	28M2	3199.00	**3199.00**

Specification A 4 m2 - 10 m2

SINGLE STOREY FLAT ROOF			Ref A/1F 2x2 Size 2.00 x 2.00 m Area 4 m2			Ref A/1F 2x3 Size 2.00 x 3.00 m Area 6 m2			Ref A/1F 2x4 Size 2.00 x 4.00 m Area 8 m2			Ref A/1F 2x5 Size 2.00 x 5.00 m Area 10 m2		
Element	Unit	Unit Rate £	Qty	Total £	Element Total £	Qty	Total £	Element Total £	Qty	Total £	Element Total £	Qty	Total £	Element Total £
EXTERNAL DOORS AND WINDOWS														
External door	NR	655.02	1NR	655.02		1NR	655.02		1NR	655.02		1NR	655.02	
Windows	NR	672.89	1NR	672.89		1NR	672.89		1NR	672.89		1NR	672.89	
Opening in cavity wall for door	NR	144.37	1NR	144.37		1NR	144.37		1NR	144.37		1NR	144.37	
Opening in cavity wall for window	NR	162.98	1NR	162.98	**1635.26**	1NR	162.98	**1635.26**	1NR	162.98	**1635.26**	1NR	162.98	**1635.26**
INTERNAL WALLS AND PARTITIONS														
Stud partitions	M2	51.63												
INTERNAL DOORS														
Hardwood flush door	NR	412.45												
WALL FINISHES														
Plaster & decoration	M2	19.58	20M2	391.60	**391.60**	25M2	489.50	**489.50**	30M2	587.40	**587.40**	35M2	685.30	**685.30**
FLOOR FINISHES														
Laminate	M2	30.30	4M2	121.20		6M2	181.80		8M2	242.40		10M2	303.00	
Hardwood skirting	M	19.52	8M	156.16	**277.36**	10M	195.20	**377.00**	12M	234.24	**476.64**	14M	273.28	**576.28**
CEILING FINISHES														
Plasterboard, plaster and decoration	M2	26.68	4M2	106.72	**106.72**	6M2	160.08	**160.08**	8M2	213.44	**213.44**	10M2	266.80	**266.80**

Specification A
12 m2 - 18 m2

SINGLE STOREY

FLAT ROOF continued/.....

Element	Unit	Unit Rate £	Ref A/1F 2x6 Size 2.00 x 6.00 m Area 12 m2			Ref A/1F 2x7 Size 2.00 x 7.00 m Area 14 m2			Ref A/1F 2x8 Size 2.00 x 8.00 m Area 16 m2			Ref A/1F 2x9 Size 2.00 x 9.00 m Area 18 m2		
			Qty	Total £	Element Total £	Qty	Total £	Element Total £	Qty	Total £	Element Total £	Qty	Total £	Element Total £
	NR	655.02	1NR	655.02		1NR	655.02		1NR	655.02		1NR	655.02	
	NR	672.89	2NR	1345.78		2NR	1345.78		2NR	1345.78		2NR	1345.78	
	NR	144.37	1NR	144.37		1NR	144.37		1NR	144.37		1NR	144.37	
	NR	162.98	2NR	325.96	**2471.13**	2NR	325.96	**2471.13**	2NR	325.96	**2471.13**	2NR	325.96	**2471.13**
	M2	51.63	5M2	258.15	**258.15**	5M2	258.15	**258.15**	5M2	258.15	**258.15**	5M2	258.15	**258.15**
	NR	412.45	1NR	412.45	**412.45**	1NR	412.45	**412.45**	1NR	412.45	**412.45**	1NR	412.45	**412.45**
	M2	19.58	40M2	783.20	**783.20**	45M2	881.10	**881.10**	50M2	979.00	**979.00**	55M2	1076.90	**1076.90**
	M2	30.30	12M2	363.60		14M2	424.20		16M2	484.80		18M2	545.40	
	M	19.52	16M	312.32	**675.92**	18M	351.36	**775.56**	20M	390.40	**875.20**	22M	429.44	**974.84**
	M2	26.68	12M2	320.16	**320.16**	14M2	373.52	**373.52**	16M2	426.88	**426.88**	18M2	480.24	**480.24**

Specification A 4 m2 - 10 m2

SINGLE STOREY

FLAT ROOF

Element	Unit	Unit Rate £	Ref A/1F 2x2 Size 2.00 x 2.00 m Area 4 m2 Qty	Total £	Element Total £	Ref A/1F 2x3 Size 2.00 x 3.00 m Area 6 m2 Qty	Total £	Element Total £	Ref A/1F 2x4 Size 2.00 x 4.00 m Area 8 m2 Qty	Total £	Element Total £	Ref A/1F 2x5 Size 2.00 x 5.00 m Area 10 m2 Qty	Total £	Element Total £
SERVICES														
Rainwater pipes	M	26.64	3M	79.92		3M	79.92		3M	79.92		3M	79.92	
Cold water service point	NR	110.52	1NR	110.52		1NR	110.52		1NR	110.52		1NR	110.52	
Hot water service point	NR	191.67	1NR	191.67		1NR	191.67		1NR	191.67		1NR	191.67	
Central heating service point	NR	386.51	1NR	386.51		1NR	386.51		1NR	386.51		1NR	386.51	
Electrical installation	NR	286.50	1NR	286.50	**1055.12**	1NR	286.50	**1055.12**	1NR	286.50	**1055.12**	1NR	286.50	**1055.12**
ALTERATIONS TO EXISTING BUILDINGS														
Opening in existing wall 1.80 m wide 2.00 m high	NR	689.44	1NR	689.44	**689.44**									
Opening in existing wall 2.40 m wide 2.00 m high	NR	865.59												
Opening in existing wall 3.00 m wide 2.00 m high	NR	921.26				1NR	921.26	**921.26**						
Opening in existing wall 4.00 m wide 2.00 m high	NR	1131.22							1NR	1131.22	**1131.22**			
Opening in existing wall 5.00 m wide 2.00 m high	NR	1341.19										1NR	1341.19	**1341.19**

Specification A 12 m2 - 18 m2			Ref A/1F 2x6 Size 2.00 x 6.00 m Area 12 m2			Ref A/1F 2x7 Size 2.00 x 7.00 m Area 14 m2			Ref A/1F 2x8 Size 2.00 x 8.00 m Area 16 m2			Ref A/1F 2x9 Size 2.00 x 9.00 m Area 18 m2		
SINGLE STOREY FLAT ROOF continued/.....			Qty	Total £	Element Total £	Qty	Total £	Element Total £	Qty	Total £	Element Total £	Qty	Total £	Element Total £
Element	Unit	Unit Rate £												
	M	26.64	3M	79.92		3M	79.92		3M	79.92		3M	79.92	
	NR	110.52	1NR	110.52		1NR	110.52		1NR	110.52		1NR	110.52	
	NR	191.67	1NR	191.67		1NR	191.67		1NR	191.67		1NR	191.67	
	NR	386.51	2NR	773.02		2NR	773.02		2NR	773.02		2NR	773.02	
	NR	286.50	2NR	573.00	**1728.13**	2NR	573.00	**1728.13**	2NR	573.00	**1728.13**	2NR	573.00	**1728.13**
	NR	689.44												
	NR	865.59	2NR	1731.18	**1731.18**									
	NR	921.26				2NR	1842.52	**1842.52**	2NR	1842.52	**1842.52**			
	NR	1131.22										2NR	2262.44	**2262.44**
	NR	1341.19												

Specification A 4 m2 - 10 m2	Ref A/1F 2x2 Size 2.00 x 2.00 m Area 4 m2	Ref A/1F 2x3 Size 2.00 x 3.00 m Area 6 m2	Ref A/1F 2x4 Size 2.00 x 4.00 m Area 8 m2	Ref A/1F 2x5 Size 2.00 x 5.00 m Area 10 m2
	Element Total £	**Element Total £**	**Element Total £**	**Element Total £**
SINGLE STOREY				
FLAT ROOF				
SUMMARY				
SUBSTRUCTURE	1377.15	1704.70	2032.25	2359.80
UPPER FLOORS	-	-	-	-
ROOF	1804.51	2216.07	2745.10	3156.66
EXTERNAL WALLS	1485.25	1713.75	2056.50	2285.00
EXTERNAL DOORS AND WINDOWS	1635.26	1635.26	1635.26	1635.26
INTERNAL WALLS AND PARTITIONS	-	-	-	-
INTERNAL DOORS	-	-	-	-
WALL FINISHES	391.60	489.50	587.40	685.30
FLOOR FINISHES	277.36	377.00	476.64	576.28
CEILING FINISHES	106.72	160.08	213.44	266.80
SERVICES	1055.12	1055.12	1055.12	1055.12
ALTERATIONS TO EXISTING BUILDINGS	689.44	921.26	1131.22	1341.19
Sub Total	8822.41	10272.74	11932.93	13361.41
Allowance for unmeasured items and sundries 5%	441.12	513.64	596.65	668.07
NET TOTAL excluding Preliminaries, Profit and Overheads	**9263.53**	**10786.38**	**12529.58**	**14029.48**

Specification A 12 m2 - 18 m2	Ref A/1F 2x6 Size 2.00 x 6.00 m Area 12 m2 Element Total £	Ref A/1F 2x7 Size 2.00 x 7.00 m Area 14 m2 Element Total £	Ref A/1F 2x8 Size 2.00 x 8.00 m Area 16 m2 Element Total £	Ref A/1F 2x9 Size 2.00 x 9.00 m Area 18 m2 Element Total £
SINGLE STOREY				
FLAT ROOF				
SUMMARY Continued/.....				
	2687.35	3014.90	3342.45	3670.00
	-	-	-	-
	3685.69	4097.25	4626.28	5037.84
	2399.25	2627.75	2970.50	3199.00
	2471.13	2471.13	2471.13	2471.13
	258.15	258.15	258.15	258.15
	412.45	412.45	412.45	412.45
	783.20	881.10	979.00	1076.90
	675.92	775.56	875.20	974.84
	320.16	373.52	426.88	480.24
	1728.13	1728.13	1728.13	1728.13
	1731.18	1842.52	1842.52	2262.44
Sub Total	17152.61	18482.46	19932.69	21571.12
Allowance for unmeasured items and sundries 5%	857.63	924.12	996.63	1078.56
NET TOTAL excluding Preliminaries, Profit and Overheads	**18010.24**	**19406.58**	**20929.32**	**22649.68**

Specification A 6 m2 - 15 m2

			Ref A/1F 3x2 Size 3.00 x 2.00 m Area 6 m2			Ref A/1F 3x3 Size 3.00 x 3.00 m Area 9 m2			Ref A/1F 3x4 Size 3.00 x 4.00 m Area 12 m2			Ref A/1F 3x5 Size 3.00 x 5.00 m Area 15 m2		
SINGLE STOREY FLAT ROOF			Qty	Total £	Element Total £	Qty	Total £	Element Total £	Qty	Total £	Element Total £	Qty	Total £	Element Total £
Element	Unit	Unit Rate £												
SUBSTRUCTURE														
Strip footings	M	144.41	9M	1299.69		10M	1444.10		11M	1588.51		12M	1732.92	
Hollow ground floor	M2	91.57	6M2	549.42	**1849.11**	9M2	824.13	**2268.23**	12M2	1098.84	**2687.35**	15M2	1373.55	**3106.47**
ROOF														
Flat roof construction 50 x 150 mm joists	M2	66.28	11M2	729.08		14M2	927.92		18M2	1193.04		21M2	1391.88	
Work to top of external wall	M	23.71	9M	213.39		10M	237.10		11M	260.81		12M	284.52	
Three layer felt roofing	M2	51.19	11M2	563.09		14M2	716.66		18M2	921.42		21M2	1074.99	
Fascia and eaves soffit	M	48.01	10M	480.10		11M	528.11		12M	576.12		13M	624.13	
Gutters and fittings	M	18.68	3M	56.04		4M	74.72		5M	93.40		6M	112.08	
Flashings	M	24.70	3M	74.10		4M	98.80		5M	123.50		6M	148.20	
Abutment to existing wall	M	61.52	3M	184.56	**2300.36**	4M	246.08	**2829.39**	5M	307.60	**3475.89**	6M	369.12	**4004.92**
EXTERNAL WALLS														
Brick and block cavity wall	M2	114.25	18M2	2056.50	**2056.50**	20M2	2285.00	**2285.00**	23M2	2627.75	**2627.75**	25M2	2856.25	**2856.25**

Specification A 18 m2 - 27 m2

			Ref A/1F 3x6 Size 3.00 x 6.00 m Area 18 m2			Ref A/1F 3x7 Size 3.00 x 7.00 m Area 21 m2			Ref A/1F 3x8 Size 3.00 x 8.00 m Area 24 m2			Ref A/1F 3x9 Size 3.00 x 9.00 m Area 27 m2		
SINGLE STOREY FLAT ROOF continued/.....			Qty	Total £	Element Total £	Qty	Total £	Element Total £	Qty	Total £	Element Total £	Qty	Total £	Element Total £
Element	Unit	Unit Rate £												
	M	144.41	13M	1877.33		14M	2021.74		15M	2166.15		16M	2310.56	
	M2	91.57	18M2	1648.26	**3525.59**	21M2	1922.97	**3944.71**	24M2	2197.68	**4363.83**	27M2	2472.39	**4782.95**
	M2	66.28	25M2	1657.00		28M2	1855.84		32M2	2120.96		35M2	2319.80	
	M	23.71	13M	308.23		14M	331.94		15M	355.65		16M	379.36	
	M2	51.19	25M2	1279.75		28M2	1433.32		32M2	1638.08		35M2	1791.65	
	M	48.01	14M	672.14		15M	720.15		16M	768.16		17M	816.17	
	M	18.68	7M	130.76		8M	149.44		9M	168.12		10M	186.80	
	M	24.70	7M	172.90		8M	197.60		9M	222.30		10M	247.00	
	M	61.52	7M	430.64	**4651.42**	8M	492.16	**5180.45**	9M	553.68	**5826.95**	10M	615.20	**6355.98**
	M2	114.25	26M2	2970.50	**2970.50**	27M2	3084.75	**3084.75**	31M2	3541.75	**3541.75**	33M2	3770.25	**3770.25**

Specification A
6 m2 - 15 m2

SINGLE STOREY

FLAT ROOF

Element	Unit	Unit Rate £	Ref A/1F 3x2 Size 3.00 x 2.00 m Area 6 m2 Qty	Total £	Element Total £	Ref A/1F 3x3 Size 3.00 x 3.00 m Area 9 m2 Qty	Total £	Element Total £	Ref A/1F 3x4 Size 3.00 x 4.00 m Area 12 m2 Qty	Total £	Element Total £	Ref A/1F 3x5 Size 3.00 x 5.00 m Area 15 m2 Qty	Total £	Element Total £
EXTERNAL DOORS AND WINDOWS														
External door	NR	655.02	1NR	655.02		1NR	655.02		1NR	655.02		1NR	655.02	
Windows	NR	672.89	1NR	672.89		1NR	672.89		1NR	672.89		1NR	672.89	
Opening in cavity wall for door	NR	144.37	1NR	144.37		1NR	144.37		1NR	144.37		1NR	144.37	
Opening in cavity wall for window	NR	162.98	1NR	162.98	**1635.26**	1NR	162.98	**1635.26**	1NR	162.98	**1635.26**	1NR	162.98	**1635.26**
INTERNAL WALLS AND PARTITIONS														
Stud partitions	M2	51.63												
INTERNAL DOORS														
Hardwood flush door	NR	412.45												
WALL FINISHES														
Plaster & decoration	M2	19.58	25M2	489.50	**489.50**	30M2	587.40	**587.40**	35M2	685.30	**685.30**	40M2	783.20	**783.20**
FLOOR FINISHES														
Laminate	M2	30.30	6M2	181.80		9M2	272.70		12M2	363.60		15M2	454.50	
Hardwood skirting	M	19.52	10M	195.20	**377.00**	12M	234.24	**506.94**	14M	273.28	**636.88**	16M	312.32	**766.82**
CEILING FINISHES														
Plasterboard, plaster and decoration	M2	26.68	6M2	160.08	**160.08**	9M2	240.12	**240.12**	12M2	320.16	**320.16**	15M2	400.20	**400.20**

Specification A
18 m2 - 27 m2

SINGLE STOREY

FLAT ROOF continued/.....

Element	Unit	Unit Rate £	Ref A/1F 3x6 Size 3.00 x 6.00 m Area 18 m2 Qty	Total £	Element Total £	Ref A/1F 3x7 Size 3.00 x 7.00 m Area 21 m2 Qty	Total £	Element Total £	Ref A/1F 3x8 Size 3.00 x 8.00 m Area 24 m2 Qty	Total £	Element Total £	Ref A/1F 3x9 Size 3.00 x 9.00 m Area 27 m2 Qty	Total £	Element Total £
	NR	655.02	1NR	655.02		1NR	655.02		1NR	655.02		1NR	655.02	
	NR	672.89	2NR	1345.78		2NR	1345.78		2NR	1345.78		2NR	1345.78	
	NR	144.37	1NR	144.37		1NR	144.37		1NR	144.37		1NR	144.37	
	NR	162.98	2NR	325.96	**2471.13**	2NR	325.96	**2471.13**	2NR	325.96	**2471.13**	2NR	325.96	**2471.13**
	M2	51.63	8M2	413.04	**413.04**	8M2	413.04	**413.04**	8M2	413.04	**413.04**	8M2	413.04	**413.04**
	NR	412.45	1NR	412.45	**412.45**	1NR	412.45	**412.45**	1NR	412.45	**412.45**	1NR	412.45	**412.45**
	M2	19.58	45M2	881.10	**881.10**	50M2	979.00	**979.00**	55M2	1076.90	**1076.90**	60M2	1174.80	**1174.80**
	M2	30.30	18M2	545.40		21M2	636.30		24M2	727.20		27M2	818.10	
	M	19.52	18M	351.36	**896.76**	20M	390.40	**1026.70**	22M	429.44	**1156.64**	24M	468.48	**1286.58**
	M2	26.68	18M2	480.24	**480.24**	21M2	560.28	**560.28**	24M2	640.32	**640.32**	27M2	720.36	**720.36**

Specification A 6 m2 - 15 m2			**Ref A/1F 3x2 Size 3.00 x 2.00 m Area 6 m2**			**Ref A/1F 3x3 Size 3.00 x 3.00 m Area 9 m2**			**Ref A/1F 3x4 Size 3.00 x 4.00 m Area 12 m2**			**Ref A/1F 3x5 Size 3.00 x 5.00 m Area 15 m2**		
			Qty	**Total £**	**Element Total £**	**Qty**	**Total £**	**Element Total £**	**Qty**	**Total £**	**Element Total £**	**Qty**	**Total £**	**Element Total £**
SINGLE STOREY														
FLAT ROOF														
Element	Unit	Unit Rate £												
SERVICES														
Rainwater pipes	M	26.64	3M	79.92		3M	79.92		3M	79.92		3M	79.92	
Cold water service point	NR	110.52	1NR	110.52		1NR	110.52		1NR	110.52		1NR	110.52	
Hot water service point	NR	191.67	1NR	191.67		1NR	191.67		1NR	191.67		1NR	191.67	
Central heating service point	NR	386.51	1NR	386.51		1NR	386.51		1NR	386.51		1NR	386.51	
Electrical installation	NR	286.50	1NR	286.50	**1055.12**	1NR	286.50	**1055.12**	1NR	286.50	**1055.12**	1NR	286.50	**1055.12**
ALTERATIONS TO EXISTING BUILDINGS														
Opening in existing wall 1.80 m wide 2.00 m high	NR	689.44	1NR	689.44	**689.44**									
Opening in existing wall 2.40 m wide 2.00 m high	NR	865.59												
Opening in existing wall 3.00 m wide 2.00 m high	NR	921.26				1NR	921.26	**921.26**						
Opening in existing wall 4.00 m wide 2.00 m high	NR	1131.22							1NR	1131.22	**1131.22**			
Opening in existing wall 5.00 m wide 2.00 m high	NR	1341.19										1NR	1341.19	**1341.19**

Specification A
18 m2 - 27 m2

SINGLE STOREY

FLAT ROOF continued/.....

Element	Unit	Unit Rate £	Ref A/1F 3x6 Size 3.00 x 6.00 m Area 18 m2 Qty	Total £	Element Total £	Ref A/1F 3x7 Size 3.00 x 7.00 m Area 21 m2 Qty	Total £	Element Total £	Ref A/1F 3x8 Size 3.00 x 8.00 m Area 24 m2 Qty	Total £	Element Total £	Ref A/1F 3x9 Size 3.00 x 9.00 m Area 27 m2 Qty	Total £	Element Total £
	M	26.64	3M	79.92		3M	79.92		3M	79.92		3M	79.92	
	NR	110.52	1NR	110.52		1NR	110.52		1NR	110.52		1NR	110.52	
	NR	191.67	1NR	191.67		1NR	191.67		1NR	191.67		1NR	191.67	
	NR	386.51	2NR	773.02		2NR	773.02		2NR	773.02		2NR	773.02	
	NR	286.50	2NR	573.00	**1728.13**	2NR	573.00	**1728.13**	2NR	573.00	**1728.13**	2NR	573.00	**1728.13**
	NR	689.44												
	NR	865.59	2NR	1731.18	**1731.18**									
	NR	921.26				2NR	1842.52	**1842.52**	2NR	1842.52	**1842.52**			
	NR	1131.22										2NR	2262.44	**2262.44**
	NR	1341.19												

Specification A 6 m2 - 15 m2	Ref A/1F 3x2 Size 3.00 x 2.00 m Area 6 m2	Ref A/1F 3x3 Size 3.00 x 3.00 m Area 9 m2	Ref A/1F 3x4 Size 3.00 x 4.00 m Area 12 m2	Ref A/1F 3x5 Size 3.00 x 5.00 m Area 15 m2
	Element Total £	**Element Total £**	**Element Total £**	**Element Total £**
SINGLE STOREY				
FLAT ROOF				
SUMMARY				
SUBSTRUCTURE	1849.11	2268.23	2687.35	3106.47
UPPER FLOORS	-	-	-	-
ROOF	2300.36	2829.39	3475.89	4004.92
EXTERNAL WALLS	2056.50	2285.00	2627.75	2856.25
EXTERNAL DOORS AND WINDOWS	1635.26	1635.26	1635.26	1635.26
INTERNAL WALLS AND PARTITIONS	-	-	-	-
INTERNAL DOORS	-	-	-	-
WALL FINISHES	489.50	587.40	685.30	783.20
FLOOR FINISHES	377.00	506.94	636.88	766.82
CEILING FINISHES	160.08	240.12	320.16	400.20
SERVICES	1055.12	1055.12	1055.12	1055.12
ALTERATIONS TO EXISTING BUILDINGS	689.44	921.26	1131.22	1341.19
Sub Total	10612.37	12328.72	14254.93	15949.43
Allowance for unmeasured items and sundries 5%	530.62	616.44	712.75	797.47
NET TOTAL excluding Preliminaries, Profit and Overheads	**11142.99**	**12945.16**	**14967.68**	**16746.90**

Specification A 18 m2 - 27 m2	Ref A/1F 3x6 Size 3.00 x 6.00 m Area 18 m2 Element Total £	Ref A/1F 3x7 Size 3.00 x 7.00 m Area 21 m2 Element Total £	Ref A/1F 3x8 Size 3.00 x 8.00 m Area 24 m2 Element Total £	Ref A/1F 3x9 Size 3.00 x 9.00 m Area 27 m2 Element Total £
SINGLE STOREY				
FLAT ROOF				
SUMMARY Continued/.....				
	3525.59	3944.71	4363.83	4782.95
	-	-	-	-
	4651.42	5180.45	5826.95	6355.98
	2970.50	3084.75	3541.75	3770.25
	2471.13	2471.13	2471.13	2471.13
	413.04	413.04	413.04	413.04
	412.45	412.45	412.45	412.45
	881.10	979.00	1076.90	1174.80
	896.76	1026.70	1156.64	1286.58
	480.24	560.28	640.32	720.36
	1728.13	1728.13	1728.13	1728.13
	1731.18	1842.52	1842.52	2262.44
Sub Total	20161.54	21643.16	23473.66	25378.11
Allowance for unmeasured items and sundries 5%	1008.08	1082.16	1173.68	1268.91
NET TOTAL excluding Preliminaries, Profit and Overheads	**21169.62**	**22725.32**	**24647.34**	**26647.02**

Specification A 8 m2 - 20 m2

SINGLE STOREY

FLAT ROOF

Element	Unit	Unit Rate £	Ref A/1F 4x2 Size 4.00 x 2.00 m Area 8 m2 Qty	Total £	Element Total £	Ref A/1F 4x3 Size 4.00 x 3.00 m Area 12 m2 Qty	Total £	Element Total £	Ref A/1F 4x4 Size 4.00 x 4.00 m Area 16 m2 Qty	Total £	Element Total £	Ref A/1F 4x5 Size 4.00 x 5.00 m Area 20 m2 Qty	Total £	Element Total £
SUBSTRUCTURE														
Strip footings	M	144.41	11M	1588.51		12M	1732.92		13M	1877.33		14M	2021.74	
Hollow ground floor	M2	91.57	8M2	732.56	**2321.07**	12M2	1098.84	**2831.76**	16M2	1465.12	**3342.45**	20M2	1831.40	**3853.14**
ROOF														
Flat roof construction 50 x 150 mm joists	M2	66.28	14M2	927.92		18M2	1193.04							
Flat roof construction 50 x 200 mm joists	M2	68.48							23M2	1575.04		27M2	1848.96	
Work to top of external wall	M	23.71	11M	260.81		12M	284.52		13M	308.23		14M	331.94	
Three layer felt roofing	M2	51.19	14M2	716.66		18M2	921.42		23M2	1177.37		27M2	1382.13	
Fascia and eaves soffit	M	48.01	12M	576.12		13M	624.13		14M	672.14		15M	720.15	
Gutters and fittings	M	18.68	3M	56.04		4M	74.72		5M	93.40		6M	112.08	
Flashings	M	24.70	3M	74.10		4M	98.80		5M	123.50		6M	148.20	
Abutment to existing wall	M	61.52	3M	184.56	**2796.21**	4M	246.08	**3442.71**	5M	307.60	**4257.28**	6M	369.12	**4912.58**
EXTERNAL WALLS														
Brick and block cavity wall	M2	114.25	23M2	2627.75	**2627.75**	25M2	2856.25	**2856.25**	28M2	3199.00	**3199.00**	29M2	3313.25	**3313.25**

Specification A
24 m2 - 36 m2

SINGLE STOREY

FLAT ROOF continued/.....

Element	Unit	Unit Rate £	Ref A/1F 4x6 Size 4.00 x 6.00 m Area 24 m2 Qty	Total £	Element Total £	Ref A/1F 4x7 Size 4.00 x 7.00 m Area 28 m2 Qty	Total £	Element Total £	Ref A/1F 4x8 Size 4.00 x 8.00 m Area 32 m2 Qty	Total £	Element Total £	Ref A/1F 4x9 Size 4.00 x 9.00 m Area 36 m2 Qty	Total £	Element Total £
	M	144.41	15M	2166.15		16M	2310.56		17M	2454.97		18M	2599.38	
	M2	91.57	24M2	2197.68	**4363.83**	28M2	2563.96	**4874.52**	32M2	2930.24	**5385.21**	36M2	3296.52	**5895.90**
	M2	66.28	32M2	2120.96		36M2	2386.08							
	M2	68.48							41M2	2807.68		45M2	3081.60	
	M	23.71	15M	355.65		16M	379.36		17M	403.07		18M	426.78	
	M2	51.19	32M2	1638.08		36M2	1842.84		41M2	2098.79		45M2	2303.55	
	M	48.01	16M	768.16		17M	816.17		18M	864.18		19M	912.19	
	M	18.68	7M	130.76		8M	149.44		9M	168.12		10M	186.80	
	M	24.70	7M	172.90		8M	197.60		9M	222.30		10M	247.00	
	M	61.52	7M	430.64	**5617.15**	8M	492.16	**6263.65**	9M	553.68	**7117.82**	10M	615.20	**7773.12**
	M2	114.25	31M2	3541.75	**3541.75**	33M2	3770.25	**3770.25**	36M2	4113.00	**4113.00**	38M2	4341.50	**4341.50**

Specification A 8 m2 - 20 m2

SINGLE STOREY

FLAT ROOF

Element	Unit	Unit Rate £	Ref A/1F 4x2 Size 4.00 x 2.00 m Area 8 m2 Qty	Total £	Element Total £	Ref A/1F 4x3 Size 4.00 x 3.00 m Area 12 m2 Qty	Total £	Element Total £	Ref A/1F 4x4 Size 4.00 x 4.00 m Area 16 m2 Qty	Total £	Element Total £	Ref A/1F 4x5 Size 4.00 x 5.00 m Area 20 m2 Qty	Total £	Element Total £
EXTERNAL DOORS AND WINDOWS														
External door	NR	655.02	1NR	655.02		1NR	655.02		1NR	655.02		1NR	655.02	
Windows	NR	672.89	1NR	672.89		1NR	672.89		1NR	672.89		1NR	672.89	
Opening in cavity wall for door	NR	144.37	1NR	144.37		1NR	144.37		1NR	144.37		1NR	144.37	
Opening in cavity wall for window	NR	162.98	1NR	162.98	**1635.26**	1NR	162.98	**1635.26**	1NR	162.98	**1635.26**	1NR	162.98	**1635.26**
INTERNAL WALLS AND PARTITIONS														
Stud partitions	M2	51.63												
INTERNAL DOORS														
Hardwood flush door	NR	412.45												
WALL FINISHES														
Plaster & decoration	M2	19.58	30M2	587.40	**587.40**	35M2	685.30	**685.30**	40M2	783.20	**783.20**	45M2	881.10	**881.10**
FLOOR FINISHES														
Laminate	M2	30.30	8M2	242.40		12M2	363.60		16M2	484.80		20M2	606.00	
Hardwood skirting	M	19.52	12M	234.24	**476.64**	14M	273.28	**636.88**	16M	312.32	**797.12**	18M	351.36	**957.36**
CEILING FINISHES														
Plasterboard, plaster and decoration	M2	26.68	8M2	213.44	**213.44**	12M2	320.16	**320.16**	16M2	426.88	**426.88**	20M2	533.60	**533.60**

Specification A 24 m2 - 36 m2			Ref A/1F 4x6 Size 4.00 x 6.00 m Area 24 m2			Ref A/1F 4x7 Size 4.00 x 7.00 m Area 28 m2			Ref A/1F 4x8 Size 4.00 x 8.00 m Area 32 m2			Ref A/1F 4x9 Size 4.00 x 9.00 m Area 36 m2		
			Qty	Total £	Element Total £	Qty	Total £	Element Total £	Qty	Total £	Element Total £	Qty	Total £	Element Total £
SINGLE STOREY FLAT ROOF continued/.....														
Element	Unit	Unit Rate £												
	NR	655.02	1NR	655.02		1NR	655.02		1NR	655.02		1NR	655.02	
	NR	672.89	2NR	1345.78		2NR	1345.78		2NR	1345.78		2NR	1345.78	
	NR	144.37	1NR	144.37		1NR	144.37		1NR	144.37		1NR	144.37	
	NR	162.98	2NR	325.96	**2471.13**	2NR	325.96	**2471.13**	2NR	325.96	**2471.13**	2NR	325.96	**2471.13**
	M2	51.63	10M2	516.30	**516.30**	10M2	516.30	**516.30**	10M2	516.30	**516.30**	10M2	516.30	**516.30**
	NR	412.45	1NR	412.45	**412.45**	1NR	412.45	**412.45**	1NR	412.45	**412.45**	1NR	412.45	**412.45**
	M2	19.58	50M2	979.00	**979.00**	55M2	1076.90	**1076.90**	60M2	1174.80	**1174.80**	65M2	1272.70	**1272.70**
	M2	30.30	24M2	727.20		28M2	848.40		32M2	969.60		36M2	1090.80	
	M	19.52	20M	390.40	**1117.60**	22M	429.44	**1277.84**	24M	468.48	**1438.08**	26M	507.52	**1598.32**
	M2	26.68	24M2	640.32	**640.32**	28M2	747.04	**747.04**	32M2	853.76	**853.76**	36M2	960.48	**960.48**

Specification A 8 m2 - 20 m2

SINGLE STOREY FLAT ROOF			Ref A/1F 4x2 Size 4.00 x 2.00 m Area 8 m2			Ref A/1F 4x3 Size 4.00 x 3.00 m Area 12 m2			Ref A/1F 4x4 Size 4.00 x 4.00 m Area 16 m2			Ref A/1F 4x5 Size 4.00 x 5.00 m Area 20 m2		
Element	Unit	Unit Rate £	Qty	Total £	Element Total £	Qty	Total £	Element Total £	Qty	Total £	Element Total £	Qty	Total £	Element Total £
SERVICES														
Rainwater pipes	M	26.64	3M	79.92		3M	79.92		3M	79.92		3M	79.92	
Cold water service point	NR	110.52	1NR	110.52		1NR	110.52		1NR	110.52		1NR	110.52	
Hot water service point	NR	191.67	1NR	191.67		1NR	191.67		1NR	191.67		1NR	191.67	
Central heating service point	NR	386.51	1NR	386.51		1NR	386.51		1NR	386.51		1NR	386.51	
Electrical installation	NR	286.50	1NR	286.50	**1055.12**	1NR	286.50	**1055.12**	1NR	286.50	**1055.12**	1NR	286.50	**1055.12**
ALTERATIONS TO EXISTING BUILDINGS														
Opening in existing wall 1.80 m wide 2.00 m high	NR	689.44	1NR	689.44	**689.44**									
Opening in existing wall 2.40 m wide 2.00 m high	NR	865.59												
Opening in existing wall 3.00 m wide 2.00 m high	NR	921.26				1NR	921.26	**921.26**						
Opening in existing wall 4.00 m wide 2.00 m high	NR	1131.22							1NR	1131.22	**1131.22**			
Opening in existing wall 5.00 m wide 2.00 m high	NR	1341.19										1NR	1341.19	**1341.19**

Specification A 24 m2 - 36 m2

SINGLE STOREY

FLAT ROOF continued/.....

Element	Unit	Unit Rate £	Ref A/1F 4x6 Size 4.00 x 6.00 m Area 24 m2 Qty	Total £	Element Total £	Ref A/1F 4x7 Size 4.00 x 7.00 m Area 28 m2 Qty	Total £	Element Total £	Ref A/1F 4x8 Size 4.00 x 8.00 m Area 32 m2 Qty	Total £	Element Total £	Ref A/1F 4x9 Size 4.00 x 9.00 m Area 36 m2 Qty	Total £	Element Total £
	M	26.64	3M	79.92		3M	79.92		3M	79.92		3M	79.92	
	NR	110.52	1NR	110.52		1NR	110.52		1NR	110.52		1NR	110.52	
	NR	191.67	1NR	191.67		1NR	191.67		1NR	191.67		1NR	191.67	
	NR	386.51	2NR	773.02		2NR	773.02		2NR	773.02		2NR	773.02	
	NR	286.50	2NR	573.00	**1728.13**	2NR	573.00	**1728.13**	2NR	573.00	**1728.13**	2NR	573.00	**1728.13**
	NR	689.44												
	NR	865.59	2NR	1731.18	**1731.18**									
	NR	921.26				2NR	1842.52	**1842.52**	2NR	1842.52	**1842.52**			
	NR	1131.22										2NR	2262.44	**2262.44**
	NR	1341.19												

Specification A 8 m2 - 20 m2	Ref A/1F 4x2 Size 4.00 x 2.00 m Area 8 m2	Ref A/1F 4x3 Size 4.00 x 3.00 m Area 12 m2	Ref A/1F 4x4 Size 4.00 x 4.00 m Area 16 m2	Ref A/1F 4x5 Size 4.00 x 5.00 m Area 20 m2
	Element Total £	Element Total £	Element Total £	Element Total £
SINGLE STOREY				
FLAT ROOF				
SUMMARY				
SUBSTRUCTURE	2321.07	2831.76	3342.45	3853.14
UPPER FLOORS	-	-	-	-
ROOF	2796.21	3442.71	4257.28	4912.58
EXTERNAL WALLS	2627.75	2856.25	3199.00	3313.25
EXTERNAL DOORS AND WINDOWS	1635.26	1635.26	1635.26	1635.26
INTERNAL WALLS AND PARTITIONS	-	-	-	-
INTERNAL DOORS	-	-	-	-
WALL FINISHES	587.40	685.30	783.20	881.10
FLOOR FINISHES	476.64	636.88	797.12	957.36
CEILING FINISHES	213.44	320.16	426.88	533.60
SERVICES	1055.12	1055.12	1055.12	1055.12
ALTERATIONS TO EXISTING BUILDINGS	689.44	921.26	1131.22	1341.19
Sub Total	12402.33	14384.70	16627.53	18482.60
Allowance for unmeasured items and sundries 5%	620.12	719.24	831.38	924.13
NET TOTAL excluding Preliminaries, Profit and Overheads	**13022.45**	**15103.94**	**17458.91**	**19406.73**

Specification A 24 m2 - 36 m2	Ref A/1F 4x6 Size 4.00 x 6.00 m Area 24 m2 Element Total £	Ref A/1F 4x7 Size 4.00 x 7.00 m Area 28 m2 Element Total £	Ref A/1F 4x8 Size 4.00 x 8.00 m Area 32 m2 Element Total £	Ref A/1F 4x9 Size 4.00 x 9.00 m Area 36 m2 Element Total £
SINGLE STOREY				
FLAT ROOF				
SUMMARY Continued/.....				
	4363.83	4874.52	5385.21	5895.90
	-	-	-	-
	5617.15	6263.65	7117.82	7773.12
	3541.75	3770.25	4113.00	4341.50
	2471.13	2471.13	2471.13	2471.13
	516.30	516.30	516.30	516.30
	412.45	412.45	412.45	412.45
	979.00	1076.90	1174.80	1272.70
	1117.60	1277.84	1438.08	1598.32
	640.32	747.04	853.76	960.48
	1728.13	1728.13	1728.13	1728.13
	1731.18	1842.52	1842.52	2262.44
Sub Total	23118.84	24980.73	27053.20	29232.47
Allowance for unmeasured items and sundries 5%	1155.94	1249.04	1352.66	1461.62
NET TOTAL excluding Preliminaries, Profit and Overheads	**24274.78**	**26229.77**	**28405.86**	**30694.09**

Specification A 10 m2 - 25 m2

SINGLE STOREY

FLAT ROOF

Element	Unit	Unit Rate £	Ref A/1F 5x2 Size 5.00 x 2.00 m Area 10 m2 Qty	Total £	Element Total £	Ref A/1F 5x3 Size 5.00 x 3.00 m Area 15 m2 Qty	Total £	Element Total £	Ref A/1F 5x4 Size 5.00 x 4.00 m Area 20 m2 Qty	Total £	Element Total £	Ref A/1F 5x5 Size 5.00 x 5.00 m Area 25 m2 Qty	Total £	Element Total £
SUBSTRUCTURE														
Strip footings	M	144.41	13M	1877.33		14M	2021.74		15M	2166.15		16M	2310.56	
Hollow ground floor	M2	91.57	10M2	915.70	**2793.03**	15M2	1373.55	**3395.29**	20M2	1831.40	**3997.55**	25M2	2289.25	**4599.81**
ROOF														
Flat roof construction 50 x 150 mm joists	M2	66.28	17M2	1126.76		22M2	1458.16							
Flat roof construction 50 x 200 mm joists	M2	68.48							28M2	1917.44		33M2	2259.84	
Work to top of external wall	M	23.71	13M	308.23		14M	331.94		15M	355.65		16M	379.36	
Three layer felt roofing	M2	51.19	17M2	870.23		22M2	1126.18		28M2	1433.32		33M2	1689.27	
Fascia and eaves soffit	M	48.01	14M	672.14		15M	720.15		16M	768.16		17M	816.17	
Gutters and fittings	M	18.68	3M	56.04		4M	74.72		5M	93.40		6M	112.08	
Flashings	M	24.70	3M	74.10		4M	98.80		5M	123.50		6M	148.20	
Abutment to existing wall	M	61.52	3M	184.56	**3292.06**	4M	246.08	**4056.03**	5M	307.60	**4999.07**	6M	369.12	**5774.04**
EXTERNAL WALLS														
Brick and block cavity wall	M2	114.25	28M2	3199.00	**3199.00**	30M2	3427.50	**3427.50**	33M2	3770.25	**3770.25**	35M2	3998.75	**3998.75**

Specification A 30 m2 - 45 m2

SINGLE STOREY FLAT ROOF continued/.....			Ref A/1F 5x6 Size 5.00 x 6.00 m Area 30 m2			Ref A/1F 5x7 Size 5.00 x 7.00 m Area 35 m2			Ref A/1F 5x8 Size 5.00 x 8.00 m Area 40 m2			Ref A/1F 5x9 Size 5.00 x 9.00 m Area 45 m2		
Element	Unit	Unit Rate £	Qty	Total £	Element Total £	Qty	Total £	Element Total £	Qty	Total £	Element Total £	Qty	Total £	Element Total £
	M	144.41	17M	2454.97		18M	2599.38		19M	2743.79		20M	2888.20	
	M2	91.57	30M2	2747.10	**5202.07**	35M2	3204.95	**5804.33**	40M2	3662.80	**6406.59**	45M2	4120.65	**7008.85**
	M2	66.28	39M2	2584.92		44M2	2916.32							
	M2	68.48							50M2	3424.00		55M2	3766.40	
	M	23.71	17M	403.07		18M	426.78		19M	450.49		20M	474.20	
	M2	51.19	39M2	1996.41		44M2	2252.36		50M2	2559.50		55M2	2815.45	
	M	48.01	18M	864.18		19M	912.19		20M	960.20		21M	1008.21	
	M	18.68	7M	130.76		8M	149.44		9M	168.12		10M	186.80	
	M	24.70	7M	172.90		8M	197.60		9M	222.30		10M	247.00	
	M	61.52	7M	430.64	**6582.88**	8M	492.16	**7346.85**	9M	553.68	**8338.29**	10M	615.20	**9113.26**
	M2	114.25	36M2	4113.00	**4113.00**	38M2	4341.50	**4341.50**	41M2	4684.25	**4684.25**	45M2	5141.25	**5141.25**

Specification A 10 m2 - 25 m2

SINGLE STOREY

FLAT ROOF

Element	Unit	Unit Rate £	Ref A/1F 5x2 Size 5.00 x 2.00 m Area 10 m2			Ref A/1F 5x3 Size 5.00 x 3.00 m Area 15 m2			Ref A/1F 5x4 Size 5.00 x 4.00 m Area 20 m2			Ref A/1F 5x5 Size 5.00 x 5.00 m Area 25 m2		
			Qty	Total £	Element Total £	Qty	Total £	Element Total £	Qty	Total £	Element Total £	Qty	Total £	Element Total £
EXTERNAL DOORS AND WINDOWS														
External door	NR	655.02	1NR	655.02		1NR	655.02		1NR	655.02		1NR	655.02	
Windows	NR	672.89	1NR	672.89		1NR	672.89		1NR	672.89		1NR	672.89	
Opening in cavity wall for door	NR	144.37	1NR	144.37		1NR	144.37		1NR	144.37		1NR	144.37	
Opening in cavity wall for window	NR	162.98	1NR	162.98	**1635.26**	1NR	162.98	**1635.26**	1NR	162.98	**1635.26**	1NR	162.98	**1635.26**
INTERNAL WALLS AND PARTITIONS														
Stud partitions	M2	51.63												
INTERNAL DOORS														
Hardwood flush door	NR	412.45												
WALL FINISHES														
Plaster & decoration	M2	19.58	35M2	685.30	**685.30**	40M2	783.20	**783.20**	45M2	881.10	**881.10**	50M2	979.00	**979.00**
FLOOR FINISHES														
Laminate	M2	30.30	10M2	303.00		15M2	454.50		20M2	606.00		25M2	757.50	
Hardwood skirting	M	19.52	14M	273.28	**576.28**	16M	312.32	**766.82**	18M	351.36	**957.36**	20M	390.40	**1147.90**
CEILING FINISHES														
Plasterboard, plaster and decoration	M2	26.68	10M2	266.80	**266.80**	15M2	400.20	**400.20**	20M2	533.60	**533.60**	25M2	667.00	**667.00**

Specification A 30 m2 - 45 m2

SINGLE STOREY

FLAT ROOF continued/.....

Element	Unit	Unit Rate £	Ref A/1F 5x6 Size 5.00 x 6.00 m Area 30 m2 Qty	Total £	Element Total £	Ref A/1F 5x7 Size 5.00 x 7.00 m Area 35 m2 Qty	Total £	Element Total £	Ref A/1F 5x8 Size 5.00 x 8.00 m Area 40 m2 Qty	Total £	Element Total £	Ref A/1F 5x9 Size 5.00 x 9.00 m Area 45 m2 Qty	Total £	Element Total £
	NR	655.02	1NR	655.02		1NR	655.02		1NR	655.02		1NR	655.02	
	NR	672.89	2NR	1345.78		2NR	1345.78		2NR	1345.78		2NR	1345.78	
	NR	144.37	1NR	144.37		1NR	144.37		1NR	144.37		1NR	144.37	
	NR	162.98	2NR	325.96	**2471.13**	2NR	325.96	**2471.13**	2NR	325.96	**2471.13**	2NR	325.96	**2471.13**
	M2	51.63	17M2	877.71	**877.71**	17M2	877.71	**877.71**	17M2	877.71	**877.71**	17M2	877.71	**877.71**
	NR	412.45	1NR	412.45	**412.45**	1NR	412.45	**412.45**	1NR	412.45	**412.45**	1NR	412.45	**412.45**
	M2	19.58	55M2	1076.90	**1076.90**	60M2	1174.80	**1174.80**	65M2	1272.70	**1272.70**	70M2	1370.60	**1370.60**
	M2	30.30	30M2	909.00		35M2	1060.50		40M2	1212.00		45M2	1363.50	
	M	19.52	22M	429.44	**1338.44**	24M	468.48	**1528.98**	26M	507.52	**1719.52**	28M	546.56	**1910.06**
	M2	26.68	30M2	800.40	**800.40**	35M2	933.80	**933.80**	40M2	1067.20	**1067.20**	45M2	1200.60	**1200.60**

Specification A 10 m2 - 25 m2

SINGLE STOREY

FLAT ROOF

Element	Unit	Unit Rate £	Ref A/1F 5x2 Size 5.00 x 2.00 m Area 10 m2 Qty	Total £	Element Total £	Ref A/1F 5x3 Size 5.00 x 3.00 m Area 15 m2 Qty	Total £	Element Total £	Ref A/1F 5x4 Size 5.00 x 4.00 m Area 20 m2 Qty	Total £	Element Total £	Ref A/1F 5x5 Size 5.00 x 5.00 m Area 25 m2 Qty	Total £	Element Total £
SERVICES														
Rainwater pipes	M	26.64	3M	79.92		3M	79.92		3M	79.92		3M	79.92	
Cold water service point	NR	110.52	1NR	110.52		1NR	110.52		1NR	110.52		1NR	110.52	
Hot water service point	NR	191.67	1NR	191.67		1NR	191.67		1NR	191.67		1NR	191.67	
Central heating service point	NR	386.51	1NR	386.51		1NR	386.51		1NR	386.51		1NR	386.51	
Electrical installation	NR	286.50	1NR	286.50	**1055.12**	1NR	286.50	**1055.12**	1NR	286.50	**1055.12**	1NR	286.50	**1055.12**
ALTERATIONS TO EXISTING BUILDINGS														
Opening in existing wall 1.80 m wide 2.00 m high	NR	689.44	1NR	689.44	**689.44**									
Opening in existing wall 2.40 m wide 2.00 m high	NR	865.59												
Opening in existing wall 3.00 m wide 2.00 m high	NR	921.26				1NR	921.26	**921.26**						
Opening in existing wall 4.00 m wide 2.00 m high	NR	1131.22							1NR	1131.22	**1131.22**			
Opening in existing wall 5.00 m wide 2.00 m high	NR	1341.19										1NR	1341.19	**1341.19**

Specification A 30 m2 - 45 m2

			Ref A/1F 5x6 Size 5.00 x 6.00 m Area 30 m2			Ref A/1F 5x7 Size 5.00 x 7.00 m Area 35 m2			Ref A/1F 5x8 Size 5.00 x 8.00 m Area 40 m2			Ref A/1F 5x9 Size 5.00 x 9.00 m Area 45 m2		
SINGLE STOREY FLAT ROOF continued/.....			Qty	Total £	Element Total £	Qty	Total £	Element Total £	Qty	Total £	Element Total £	Qty	Total £	Element Total £
Element	Unit	Unit Rate £												
	M	26.64	3M	79.92		3M	79.92		3M	79.92		3M	79.92	
	NR	110.52	1NR	110.52		1NR	110.52		1NR	110.52		1NR	110.52	
	NR	191.67	1NR	191.67		1NR	191.67		1NR	191.67		1NR	191.67	
	NR	386.51	2NR	773.02		2NR	773.02		2NR	773.02		2NR	773.02	
	NR	286.50	2NR	573.00	**1728.13**	2NR	573.00	**1728.13**	2NR	573.00	**1728.13**	2NR	573.00	**1728.13**
	NR	689.44												
	NR	865.59	2NR	1731.18	**1731.18**									
	NR	921.26				2NR	1842.52	**1842.52**	2NR	1842.52	**1842.52**			
	NR	1131.22										2NR	2262.44	**2262.44**
	NR	1341.19												

Specification A 10 m2 - 25 m2	Ref A/1F 5x2 Size 5.00 x 2.00 m Area 10 m2	Ref A/1F 5x3 Size 5.00 x 3.00 m Area 15 m2	Ref A/1F 5x4 Size 5.00 x 4.00 m Area 20 m2	Ref A/1F 5x5 Size 5.00 x 5.00 m Area 25 m2
	Element Total £	Element Total £	Element Total £	Element Total £
SINGLE STOREY				
FLAT ROOF				
SUMMARY				
SUBSTRUCTURE	2793.03	3395.29	3997.55	4599.81
UPPER FLOORS	-	-	-	-
ROOF	3292.06	4056.03	4999.07	5774.04
EXTERNAL WALLS	3199.00	3427.50	3770.25	3998.75
EXTERNAL DOORS AND WINDOWS	1635.26	1635.26	1635.26	1635.26
INTERNAL WALLS AND PARTITIONS	-	-	-	-
INTERNAL DOORS	-	-	-	-
WALL FINISHES	685.30	783.20	881.10	979.00
FLOOR FINISHES	576.28	766.82	957.36	1147.90
CEILING FINISHES	266.80	400.20	533.60	667.00
SERVICES	1055.12	1055.12	1055.12	1055.12
ALTERATIONS TO EXISTING BUILDINGS	689.44	921.26	1131.22	1341.19
Sub Total	14192.29	16440.68	18960.53	21198.07
Allowance for unmeasured items and sundries 5%	709.61	822.03	948.03	1059.90
NET TOTAL excluding Preliminaries, Profit and Overheads	**14901.90**	**17262.71**	**19908.56**	**22257.97**

Specification A 30 m2 - 45 m2	Ref A/1F 5x6 Size 5.00 x 6.00 m Area 30 m2 Element Total £	Ref A/1F 5x7 Size 5.00 x 7.00 m Area 35 m2 Element Total £	Ref A/1F 5x8 Size 5.00 x 8.00 m Area 40 m2 Element Total £	Ref A/1F 5x9 Size 5.00 x 9.00 m Area 45 m2 Element Total £
SINGLE STOREY				
FLAT ROOF				
SUMMARY Continued/.....				
	5202.07	5804.33	6406.59	7008.85
	-	-	-	-
	6582.88	7346.85	8338.29	9113.26
	4113.00	4341.50	4684.25	5141.25
	2471.13	2471.13	2471.13	2471.13
	877.71	877.71	877.71	877.71
	412.45	412.45	412.45	412.45
	1076.90	1174.80	1272.70	1370.60
	1338.44	1528.98	1719.52	1910.06
	800.40	933.80	1067.20	1200.60
	1728.13	1728.13	1728.13	1728.13
	1731.18	1842.52	1842.52	2262.44
Sub Total	26334.29	28462.20	30820.49	33496.48
Allowance for unmeasured items and sundries 5%	1316.71	1423.11	1541.02	1674.82
NET TOTAL excluding Preliminaries, Profit and Overheads	**27651.00**	**29885.31**	**32361.51**	**35171.30**

Specification A

Single storey pitch roof

[1P] 2×2/3/4.

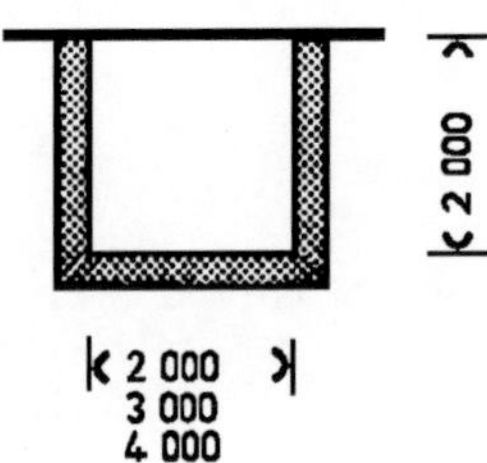

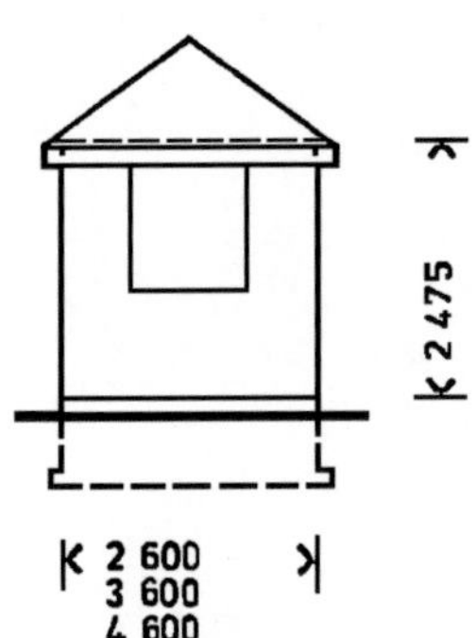

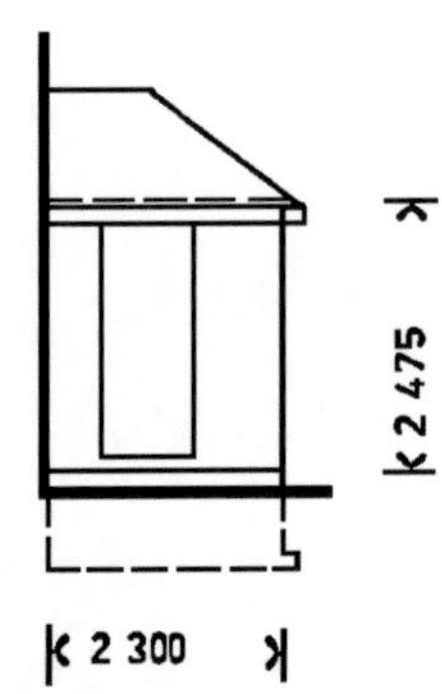

[1P] 2×5.

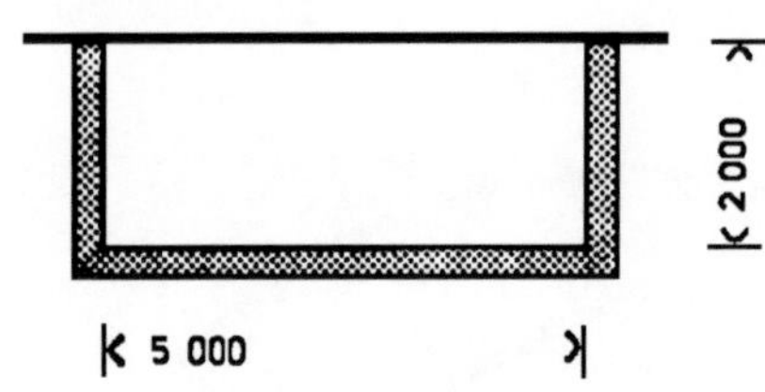

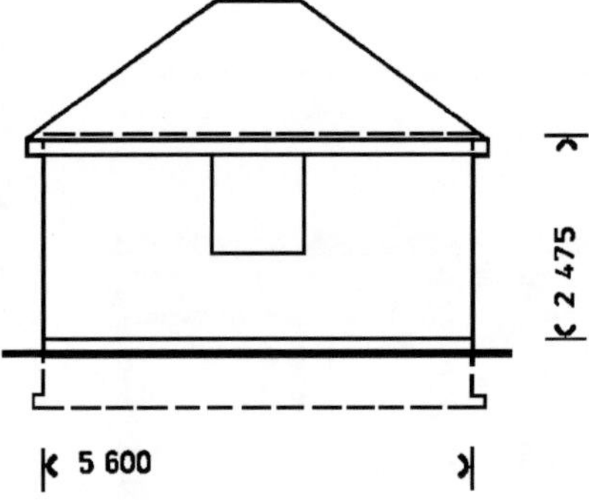

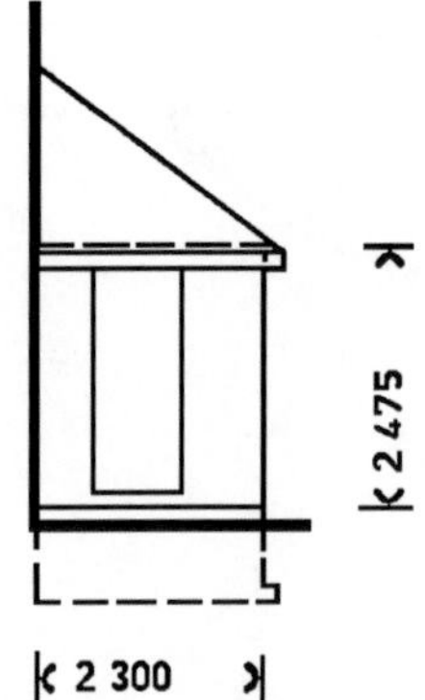

[1P] 2×6/7/8/9.

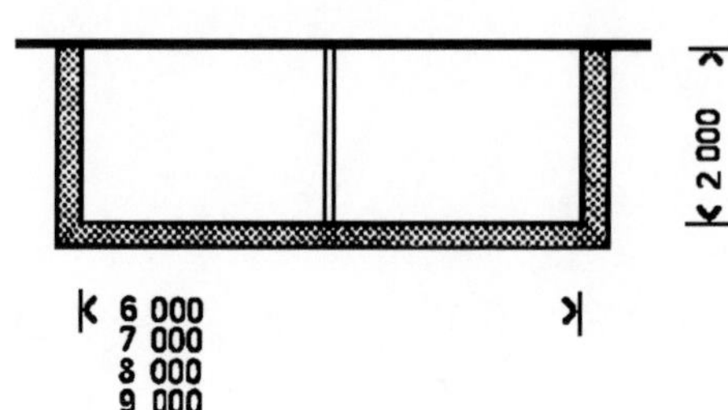

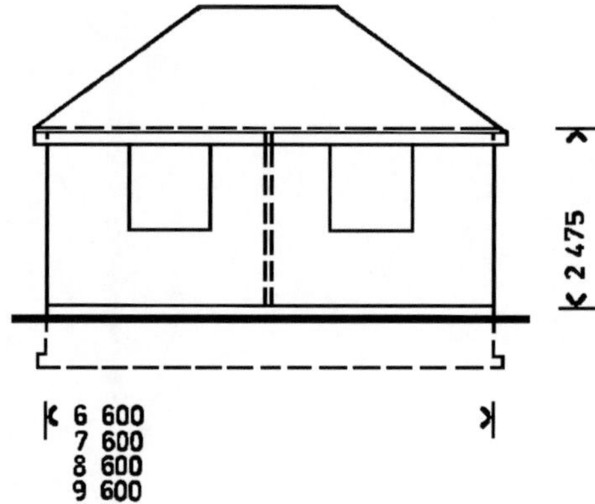

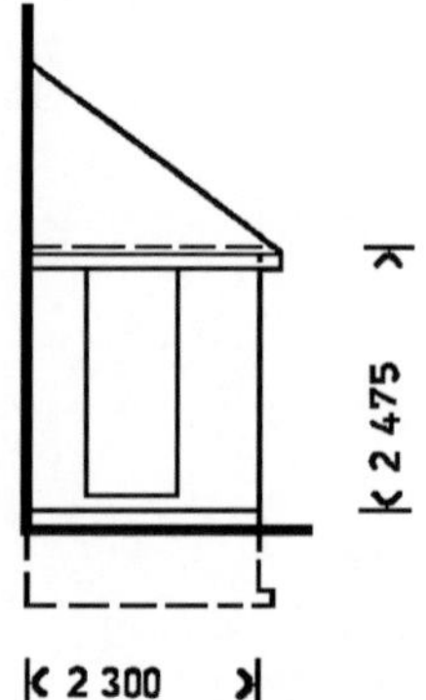

[1P] 3×2/3/4/5.

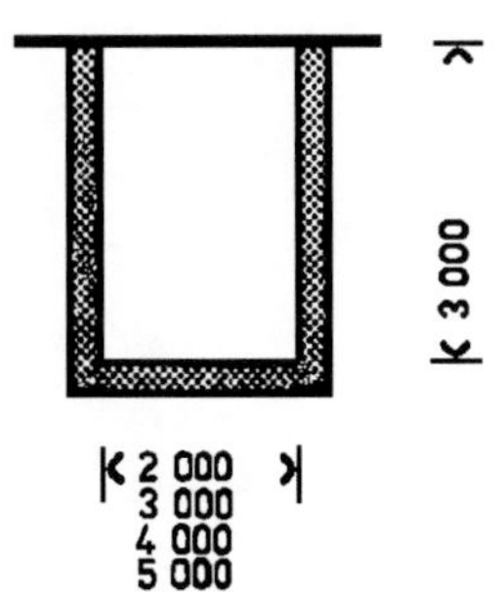

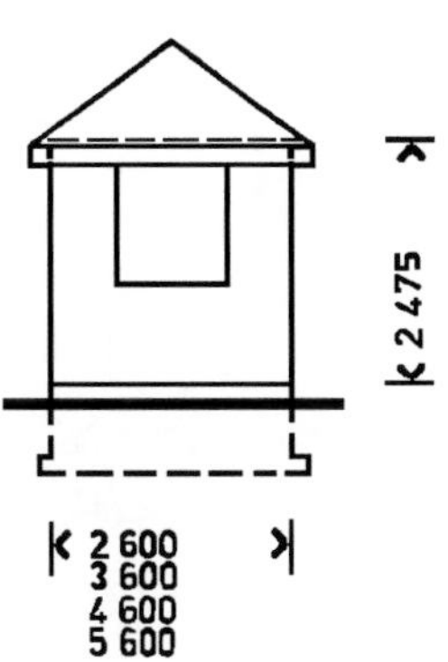

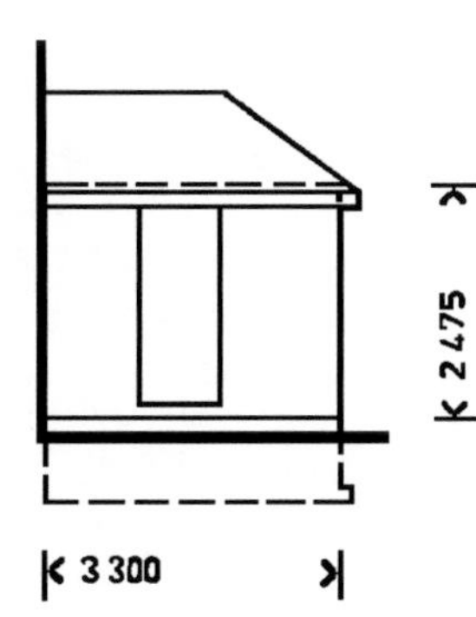

[1P] 3×6.

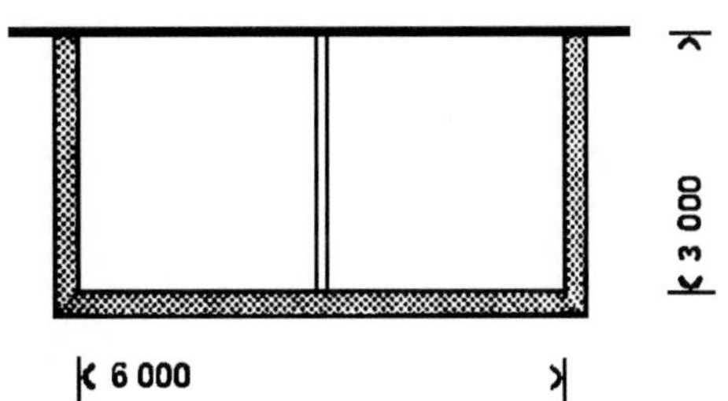

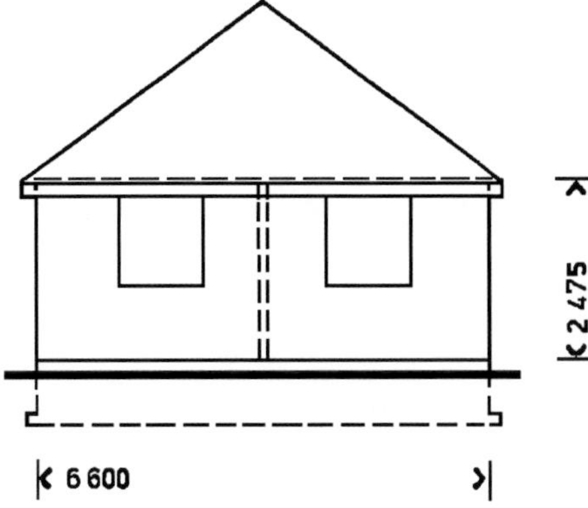

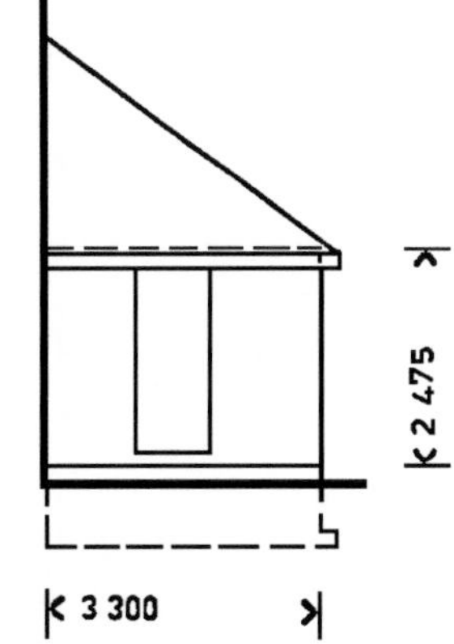

[1P] 3×7/8/9.

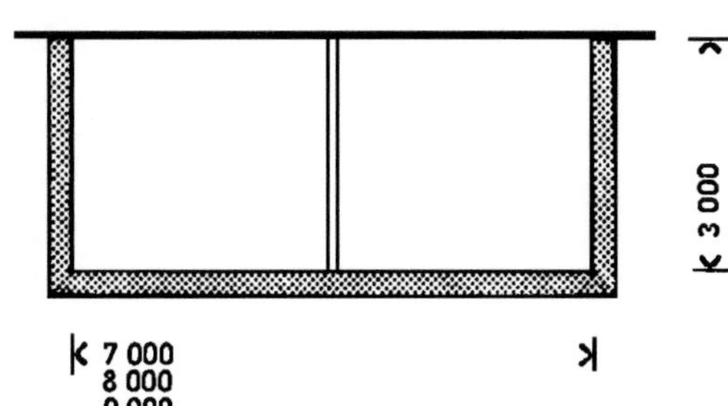

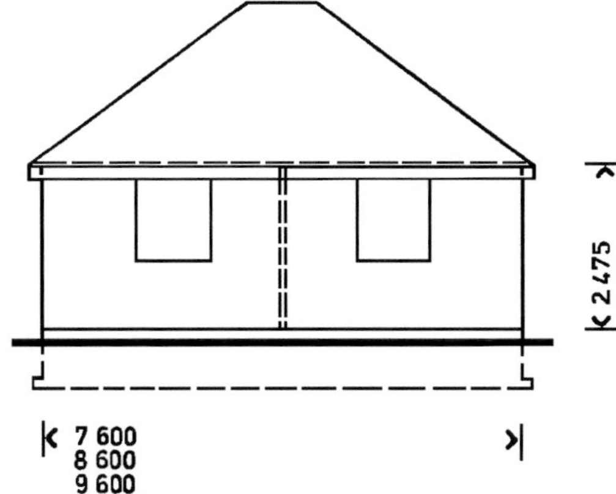

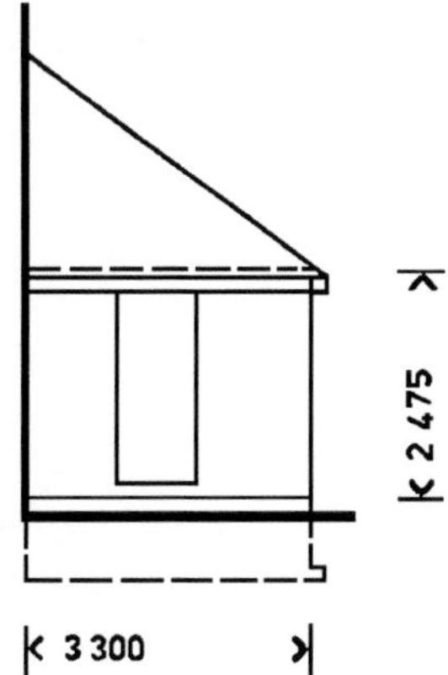

[1P] 4 × 2/3/4/5.

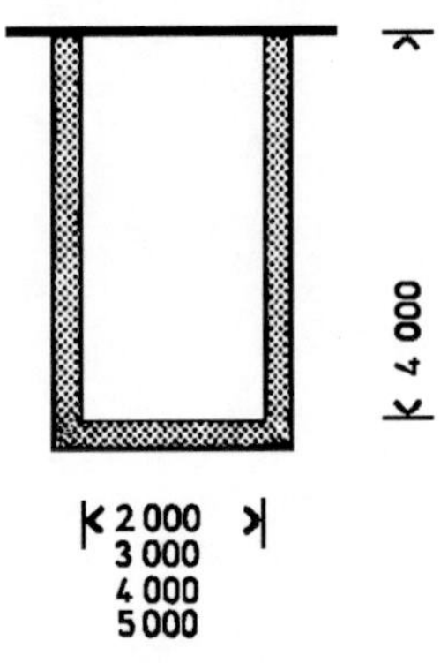

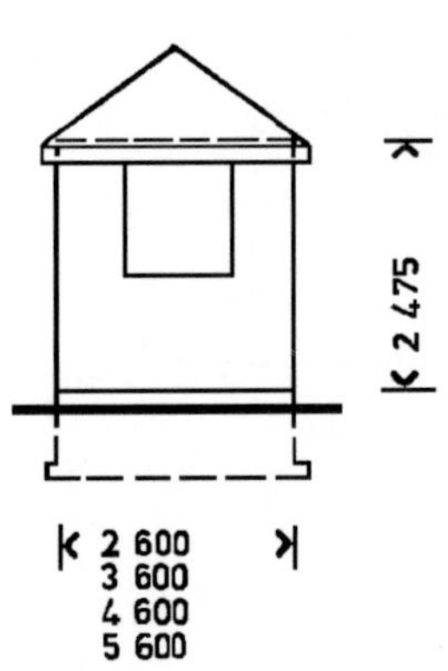

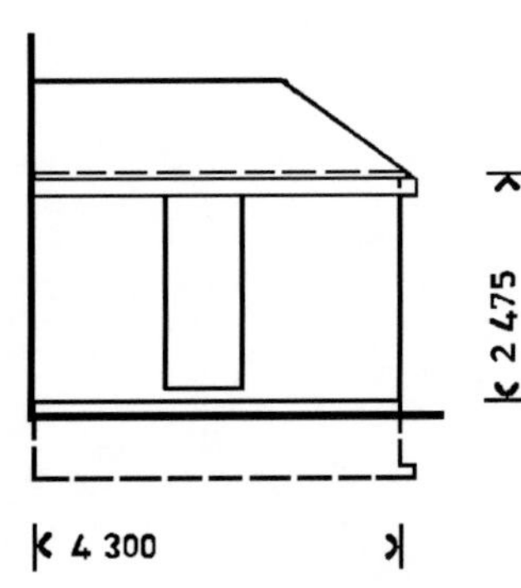

[1P] 4 × 6/7/8.

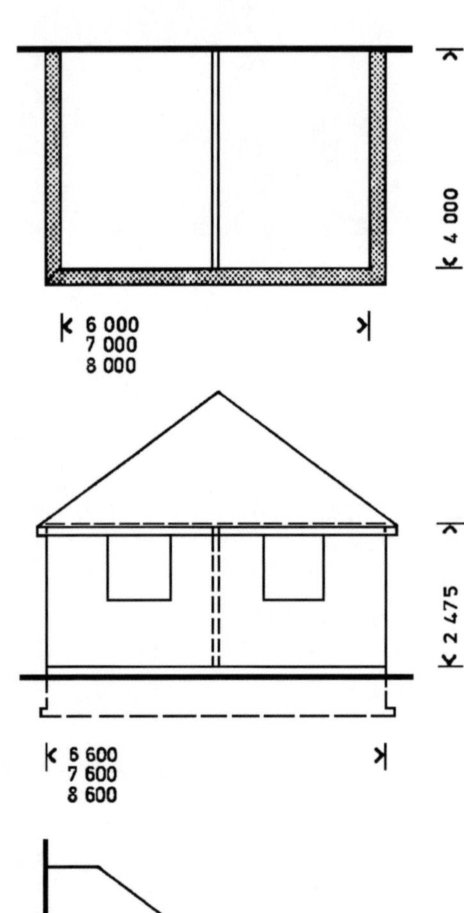

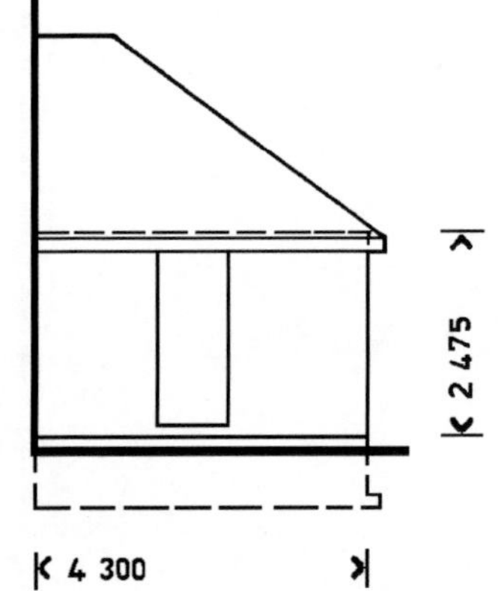

[1P] 4 × 9.

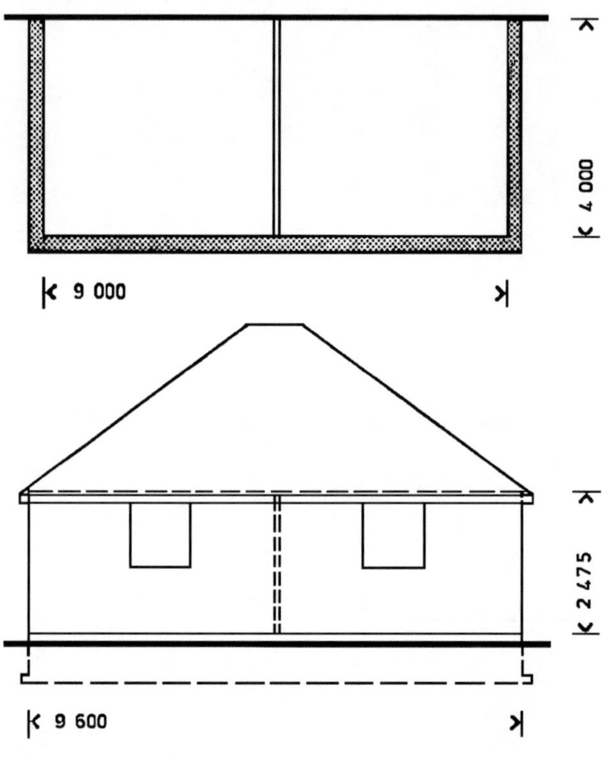

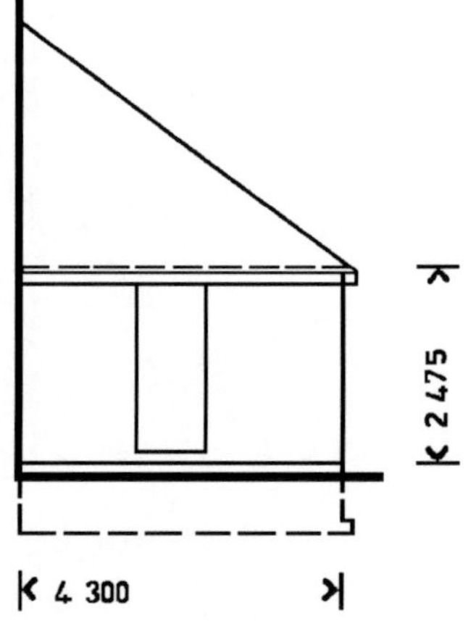

[1P] 5×2/3/4/5.

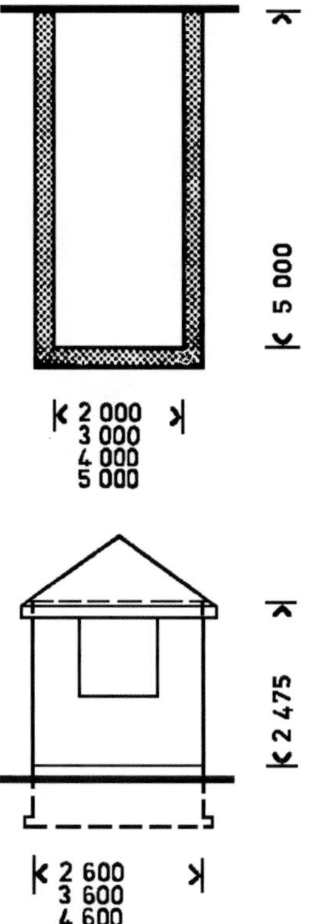

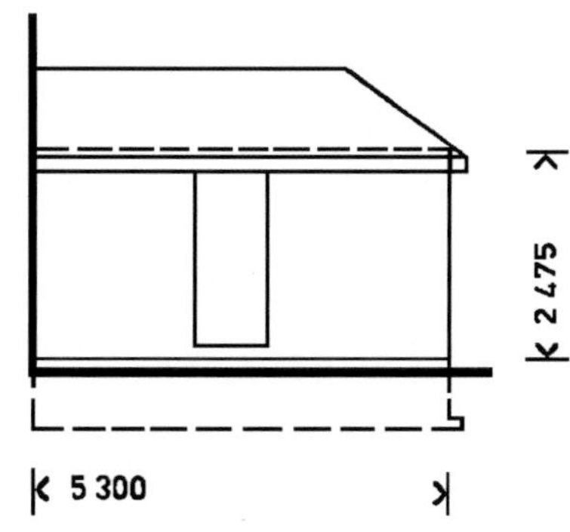

[1P] 5×6/7/8/9.

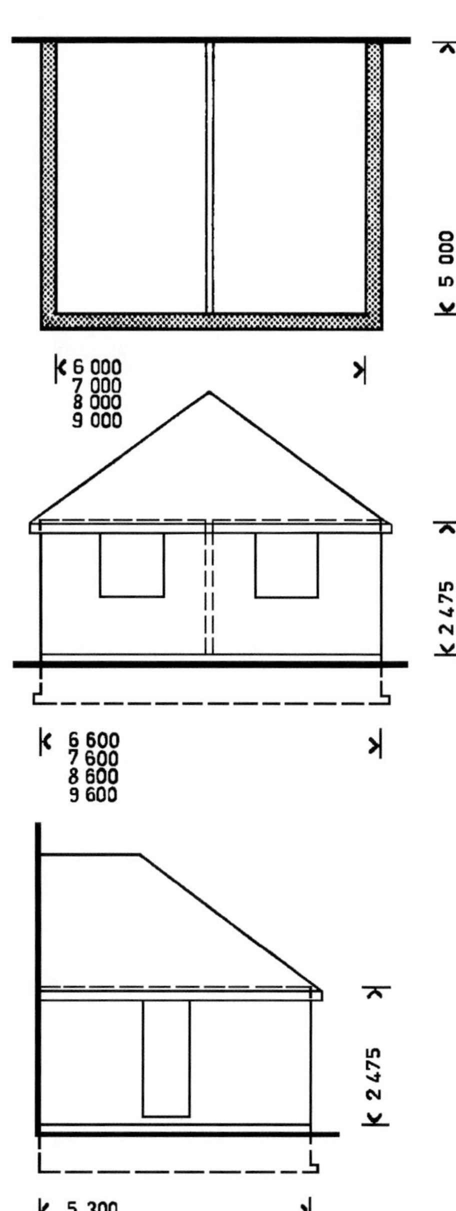

Specification A 4 m2 - 10 m2

SINGLE STOREY

PITCHED ROOF

Element	Unit	Unit Rate £	Ref A/1P 2x2 Size 2.00 x 2.00 m Area 4 m2 Qty	Total £	Element Total £	Ref A/1P 2x3 Size 2.00 x 3.00 m Area 6 m2 Qty	Total £	Element Total £	Ref A/1P 2x4 Size 2.00 x 4.00 m Area 8 m2 Qty	Total £	Element Total £	Ref A/1P 2x5 Size 2.00 x 5.00 m Area 10 m2 Qty	Total £	Element Total £
SUBSTRUCTURE														
Strip footings	M	144.41	7M	1010.87		8M	1155.28		9M	1299.69		10M	1444.10	
Hollow ground floor	M2	91.57	4M2	366.28	**1377.15**	6M2	549.42	**1704.70**	8M2	732.56	**2032.25**	10M2	915.70	**2359.80**
ROOF														
Pitched roof construction	M2	55.42	8M2	443.36		10M2	554.20		13M2	720.46		15M2	831.30	
Work to top of external wall	M	23.71	7M	165.97		8M	189.68		9M	213.39		10M	237.10	
Plain tile roofing	M2	69.30	9M2	623.70		12M2	831.60		15M2	1039.50		18M2	1247.40	
Work to verge	M	11.58	4M	46.32		5M	57.90		6M	69.48		7M	81.06	
Work to hip	M	41.73	6M	250.38		7M	292.11		8M	333.84		8M	333.84	
Work to eaves	M	22.73	8M	181.84		9M	204.57		10M	227.30		11M	250.03	
Fascia and eaves soffit	M	48.01	8M	384.08		9M	432.09		10M	480.10		11M	528.11	
Gutters and fittings	M	18.68	8M	149.44		9M	168.12		10M	186.80		11M	205.48	
Flashings	M	69.52	4M	278.08	**2523.17**	5M	347.60	**3077.87**	6M	417.12	**3687.99**	7M	486.64	**4200.96**
EXTERNAL WALLS														
Brick and block cavity wall	M2	114.25	13M2	1485.25	**1485.25**	15M2	1713.75	**1713.75**	18M2	2056.50	**2056.50**	20M2	2285.00	**2285.00**

Specification A 12 m2 - 18 m2			Ref A/1P 2x6 Size 2.00 x 6.00 m Area 12 m2			Ref A/1P 2x7 Size 2.00 x 7.00 m Area 14 m2			Ref A/1P 2x8 Size 2.00 x 8.00 m Area 16 m2			Ref A/1P 2x9 Size 2.00 x 9.00 m Area 18 m2		
			Qty	Total £	Element Total £	Qty	Total £	Element Total £	Qty	Total £	Element Total £	Qty	Total £	Element Total £
SINGLE STOREY														
PITCHED ROOF Continued/.....														
Element	Unit	Unit Rate £												
	M	144.41	11M	1588.51		12M	1732.92		13M	1877.33		14M	2021.74	
	M2	91.57	12M2	1098.84	**2687.35**	14M2	1281.98	**3014.90**	16M2	1465.12	**3342.45**	18M2	1648.26	**3670.00**
	M2	55.42	18M2	997.56		20M2	1108.40		23M2	1274.66		25M2	1385.50	
	M	23.71	11M	260.81		12M	284.52		13M	308.23		14M	331.94	
	M2	69.30	22M2	1524.60		25M2	1732.50		28M2	1940.40		31M2	2148.30	
	M	11.58	8M	92.64		9M	104.22		10M	115.80		11M	127.38	
	M	41.73	8M	333.84		8M	333.84		8M	333.84		8M	333.84	
	M	22.73	12M	272.76		13M	295.49		14M	318.22		15M	340.95	
	M	48.01	12M	576.12		13M	624.13		14M	672.14		15M	720.15	
	M	18.68	12M	224.16		13M	242.84		14M	261.52		15M	280.20	
	M	69.52	8M	556.16	**4838.65**	9M	625.68	**5351.62**	10M	695.20	**5920.01**	11M	764.72	**6432.98**
	M2	114.25	21M2	2399.25	**2399.25**	23M2	2627.75	**2627.75**	26M2	2970.50	**2970.50**	28M2	3199.00	**3199.00**

Specification A 4 m2 - 10 m2

SINGLE STOREY

PITCHED ROOF

Element	Unit	Unit Rate £	Ref A/1P 2x2 Size 2.00 x 2.00 m Area 4 m2 Qty	Total £	Element Total £	Ref A/1P 2x3 Size 2.00 x 3.00 m Area 6 m2 Qty	Total £	Element Total £	Ref A/1P 2x4 Size 2.00 x 4.00 m Area 8 m2 Qty	Total £	Element Total £	Ref A/1P 2x5 Size 2.00 x 5.00 m Area 10 m2 Qty	Total £	Element Total £
EXTERNAL DOORS AND WINDOWS														
External door	NR	655.02	1NR	655.02		1NR	655.02		1NR	655.02		1NR	655.02	
Windows	NR	672.89	1NR	672.89		1NR	672.89		1NR	672.89		1NR	672.89	
Opening in cavity wall for door	NR	144.37	1NR	144.37		1NR	144.37		1NR	144.37		1NR	144.37	
Opening in cavity wall for window	NR	162.98	1NR	162.98	**1635.26**	1NR	162.98	**1635.26**	1NR	162.98	**1635.26**	1NR	162.98	**1635.26**
INTERNAL WALLS AND PARTITIONS														
Stud partitions	M2	51.63												
INTERNAL DOORS														
Hardwood flush door	NR	412.45												
WALL FINISHES														
Plaster & decoration	M2	19.58	20M2	391.60	**391.60**	25M2	489.50	**489.50**	30M2	587.40	**587.40**	35M2	685.30	**685.30**
FLOOR FINISHES														
Laminate	M2	30.30	4M2	121.20		6M2	181.80		8M2	242.40		10M2	303.00	
Hardwood skirting	M	19.52	8M	156.16	**277.36**	10M	195.20	**377.00**	12M	234.24	**476.64**	14M	273.28	**576.28**
CEILING FINISHES														
Plasterboard, plaster and decoration	M2	26.68	4M2	106.72	**106.72**	6M2	160.08	**160.08**	8M2	213.44	**213.44**	10M2	266.80	**266.80**

Specification A 12 m2 - 18 m2

			Ref A/1P 2x6 Size 2.00 x 6.00 m Area 12 m2			Ref A/1P 2x7 Size 2.00 x 7.00 m Area 14 m2			Ref A/1P 2x8 Size 2.00 x 8.00 m Area 16 m2			Ref A/1P 2x9 Size 2.00 x 9.00 m Area 18 m2		
SINGLE STOREY PITCHED ROOF Continued/.....			Qty	Total £	Element Total £	Qty	Total £	Element Total £	Qty	Total £	Element Total £	Qty	Total £	Element Total £
Element	Unit	Unit Rate £												
	NR	655.02	1NR	655.02		1NR	655.02		1NR	655.02		1NR	655.02	
	NR	672.89	2NR	1345.78		2NR	1345.78		2NR	1345.78		2NR	1345.78	
	NR	144.37	1NR	144.37		1NR	144.37		1NR	144.37		1NR	144.37	
	NR	162.98	2NR	325.96	**2471.13**	2NR	325.96	**2471.13**	2NR	325.96	**2471.13**	2NR	325.96	**2471.13**
	M2	51.63	5M2	258.15	**258.15**	5M2	258.15	**258.15**	5M2	258.15	**258.15**	5M2	258.15	**258.15**
	NR	412.45	1NR	412.45	**412.45**	1NR	412.45	**412.45**	1NR	412.45	**412.45**	1NR	412.45	**412.45**
	M2	19.58	40M2	783.20	**783.20**	45M2	881.10	**881.10**	50M2	979.00	**979.00**	55M2	1076.90	**1076.90**
	M2	30.30	12M2	363.60		14M2	424.20		16M2	484.80		18M2	545.40	
	M	19.52	16M	312.32	**675.92**	18M	351.36	**775.56**	20M	390.40	**875.20**	22M	429.44	**974.84**
	M2	26.68	12M2	320.16	**320.16**	14M2	373.52	**373.52**	16M2	426.88	**426.88**	18M2	480.24	**480.24**

Specification A 4 m2 - 10 m2			Ref A/1P 2x2 Size 2.00 x 2.00 m Area 4 m2			Ref A/1P 2x3 Size 2.00 x 3.00 m Area 6 m2			Ref A/1P 2x4 Size 2.00 x 4.00 m Area 8 m2			Ref A/1P 2x5 Size 2.00 x 5.00 m Area 10 m2		
			Qty	Total £	Element Total £	Qty	Total £	Element Total £	Qty	Total £	Element Total £	Qty	Total £	Element Total £
SINGLE STOREY														
PITCHED ROOF														
Element	Unit	Unit Rate £												
SERVICES														
Rainwater pipes	M	26.64	3M	79.92		3M	79.92		3M	79.92		3M	79.92	
Cold water service point	NR	110.52	1NR	110.52		1NR	110.52		1NR	110.52		1NR	110.52	
Hot water service point	NR	191.67	1NR	191.67		1NR	191.67		1NR	191.67		1NR	191.67	
Central heating service point	NR	386.51	1NR	386.51		1NR	386.51		1NR	386.51		1NR	386.51	
Electrical installation	NR	286.50	1NR	286.50	**1055.12**	1NR	286.50	**1055.12**	1NR	286.50	**1055.12**	1NR	286.50	**1055.12**
ALTERATIONS TO EXISTING BUILDINGS														
Opening in existing wall 1.80 m wide 2.00 m high	NR	689.44	1NR	689.44	**689.44**									
Opening in existing wall 2.40 m wide 2.00 m high	NR	865.59												
Opening in existing wall 3.00 m wide 2.00 m high	NR	921.26				1NR	921.26	**921.26**						
Opening in existing wall 4.00 m wide 2.00 m high	NR	1131.22							1NR	1131.22	**1131.22**			
Opening in existing wall 5.00 m wide 2.00 m high	NR	1341.19										1NR	1341.19	**1341.19**

Specification A 12 m2 - 18 m2

SINGLE STOREY

PITCHED ROOF Continued/.....

Element	Unit	Unit Rate £	Ref A/1P 2x6 Size 2.00 x 6.00 m Area 12 m2 Qty	Total £	Element Total £	Ref A/1P 2x7 Size 2.00 x 7.00 m Area 14 m2 Qty	Total £	Element Total £	Ref A/1P 2x8 Size 2.00 x 8.00 m Area 16 m2 Qty	Total £	Element Total £	Ref A/1P 2x9 Size 2.00 x 9.00 m Area 18 m2 Qty	Total £	Element Total £
	M	26.64	3M	79.92		3M	79.92		3M	79.92		3M	79.92	
	NR	110.52	1NR	110.52		1NR	110.52		1NR	110.52		1NR	110.52	
	NR	191.67	1NR	191.67		1NR	191.67		1NR	191.67		1NR	191.67	
	NR	386.51	2NR	773.02		2NR	773.02		2NR	773.02		2NR	773.02	
	NR	286.50	2NR	573.00	**1728.13**	2NR	573.00	**1728.13**	2NR	573.00	**1728.13**	2NR	573.00	**1728.13**
	NR	689.44												
	NR	865.59	2NR	1731.18	**1731.18**									
	NR	921.26				2NR	1842.52	**1842.52**	2NR	1842.52	**1842.52**			
	NR	1131.22										2NR	2262.44	**2262.44**
	NR	1341.19												

Specification A 4 m2 - 10 m2	Ref A/1P 2x2 Size 2.00 x 2.00 m Area 4 m2 Element Total £	Ref A/1P 2x3 Size 2.00 x 3.00 m Area 6 m2 Element Total £	Ref A/1P 2x4 Size 2.00 x 4.00 m Area 8 m2 Element Total £	Ref A/1P 2x5 Size 2.00 x 5.00 m Area 10 m2 Element Total £
SINGLE STOREY				
PITCHED ROOF				
SUMMARY				
SUBSTRUCTURE	1377.15	1704.70	2032.25	2359.80
UPPER FLOORS	-	-	-	-
ROOF	2523.17	3077.87	3687.99	4200.96
EXTERNAL WALLS	1485.25	1713.75	2056.50	2285.00
EXTERNAL DOORS AND WINDOWS	1635.26	1635.26	1635.26	1635.26
INTERNAL WALLS AND PARTITIONS	-	-	-	-
INTERNAL DOORS	-	-	-	-
WALL FINISHES	391.60	489.50	587.40	685.30
FLOOR FINISHES	277.36	377.00	476.64	576.28
CEILING FINISHES	106.72	160.08	213.44	266.80
SERVICES	1055.12	1055.12	1055.12	1055.12
ALTERATIONS TO EXISTING BUILDINGS	689.44	921.26	1131.22	1341.19
Sub Total	9541.07	11134.54	12875.82	14405.71
Allowance for unmeasured items and sundries 5%	477.05	556.73	643.79	720.29
NET TOTAL excluding Preliminaries, Profit and Overheads	**10018.12**	**11691.27**	**13519.61**	**15126.00**

Specification A 12 m2 - 18 m2	Ref A/1P 2x6 Size 2.00 x 6.00 m Area 12 m2	Ref A/1P 2x7 Size 2.00 x 7.00 m Area 14 m2	Ref A/1P 2x8 Size 2.00 x 8.00 m Area 16 m2	Ref A/1P 2x9 Size 2.00 x 9.00 m Area 18 m2
	Element Total £	Element Total £	Element Total £	Element Total £
SINGLE STOREY				
PITCHED ROOF				
SUMMARY Continued/.....				
	2687.35	3014.90	3342.45	3670.00
	-	-	-	-
	4838.65	5351.62	5920.01	6432.98
	2399.25	2627.75	2970.50	3199.00
	2471.13	2471.13	2471.13	2471.13
	258.15	258.15	258.15	258.15
	412.45	412.45	412.45	412.45
	783.20	881.10	979.00	1076.90
	675.92	775.56	875.20	974.84
	320.16	373.52	426.88	480.24
	1728.13	1728.13	1728.13	1728.13
	1731.18	1842.52	1842.52	2262.44
Sub Total	18305.57	19736.83	21226.42	22966.26
Allowance for unmeasured items and sundries 5%	915.28	986.84	1061.32	1148.31
NET TOTAL excluding Preliminaries, Profit and Overheads	**19220.85**	**20723.67**	**22287.74**	**24114.57**

Specification A 6 m2 - 15 m2			Ref A/1P 3x2 Size 3.00 x 2.00 m Area 6 m2			Ref A/1P 3x3 Size 3.00 x 3.00 m Area 9 m2			Ref A/1P 3x4 Size 3.00 x 4.00 m Area 12 m2			Ref A/1P 3x5 Size 3.00 x 5.00 m Area 15 m2		
			Qty	Total £	Element Total £	Qty	Total £	Element Total £	Qty	Total £	Element Total £	Qty	Total £	Element Total £
SINGLE STOREY														
PITCHED ROOF														
Element	Unit	Unit Rate £												
SUBSTRUCTURE														
Strip footings	M	144.41	9M	1299.69		10M	1444.10		11M	1588.51		12M	1732.92	
Hollow ground floor	M2	91.57	6M2	549.42	**1849.11**	9M2	824.13	**2268.23**	12M2	1098.84	**2687.35**	15M2	1373.55	**3106.47**
ROOF														
Pitched roof construction	M2	55.42	11M2	609.62		14M2	775.88		18M2	997.56		21M2	1163.82	
Work to top of external wall	M	23.71	9M	213.39		10M	237.10		11M	260.81		12M	284.52	
Plain tile roofing	M2	69.30	13M2	900.90		17M2	1178.10		22M2	1524.60		26M2	1801.80	
Work to verge	M	11.58	4M	46.32		5M	57.90		6M	69.48		7M	81.06	
Work to hip	M	41.73	7M	292.11		8M	333.84		9M	375.57		10M	417.30	
Work to eaves	M	22.73	10M	227.30		11M	250.03		12M	272.76		13M	295.49	
Fascia and eaves soffit	M	48.01	10M	480.10		11M	528.11		12M	576.12		13M	624.13	
Gutters and fittings	M	18.68	10M	186.80		11M	205.48		12M	224.16		13M	242.84	
Flashings	M	69.52	4M	278.08	**3234.62**	5M	347.60	**3914.04**	6M	417.12	**4718.18**	7M	486.64	**5397.60**
EXTERNAL WALLS														
Brick and block cavity wall	M2	114.25	18M2	2056.50	**2056.50**	20M2	2285.00	**2285.00**	23M2	2627.75	**2627.75**	25M2	2856.25	**2856.25**

Specification A
18 m2 - 27 m2

SINGLE STOREY

PITCHED ROOF Continued/.....

Element	Unit	Unit Rate £	Ref A/1P 3x6 Size 3.00 x 6.00 m Area 18 m2			Ref A/1P 3x7 Size 3.00 x 7.00 m Area 21 m2			Ref A/1P 3x8 Size 3.00 x 8.00 m Area 24 m2			Ref A/1P 3x9 Size 3.00 x 9.00 m Area 27 m2		
			Qty	Total £	Element Total £	Qty	Total £	Element Total £	Qty	Total £	Element Total £	Qty	Total £	Element Total £
	M	144.41	13M	1877.33		14M	2021.74		15M	2166.15		16M	2310.56	
	M2	91.57	18M2	1648.26	**3525.59**	21M2	1922.97	**3944.71**	24M2	2197.68	**4363.83**	27M2	2472.39	**4782.95**
	M2	55.42	25M2	1385.50		28M2	1551.76		32M2	1773.44		35M2	1939.70	
	M	23.71	13M	308.23		14M	331.94		15M	355.65		16M	379.36	
	M2	69.30	30M2	2079.00		34M2	2356.20		39M2	2702.70		43M2	2979.90	
	M	11.58	9M	104.22		10M	115.80		11M	127.38		12M	138.96	
	M	41.73	11M	459.03		11M	459.03		11M	459.03		11M	459.03	
	M	22.73	14M	318.22		15M	340.95		16M	363.68		17M	386.41	
	M	48.01	14M	672.14		15M	720.15		16M	768.16		17M	816.17	
	M	18.68	14M	261.52		15M	280.20		16M	298.88		17M	317.56	
	M	69.52	9M	625.68	**6213.54**	10M	695.20	**6851.23**	11M	764.72	**7613.64**	12M	834.24	**8251.33**
	M2	114.25	26M2	2970.50	**2970.50**	27M2	3084.75	**3084.75**	31M2	3541.75	**3541.75**	33M2	3770.25	**3770.25**

Specification A 6 m2 - 15 m2

SINGLE STOREY

PITCHED ROOF

Element	Unit	Unit Rate £	Ref A/1P 3x2 Size 3.00 x 2.00 m Area 6 m2 Qty	Total £	Element Total £	Ref A/1P 3x3 Size 3.00 x 3.00 m Area 9 m2 Qty	Total £	Element Total £	Ref A/1P 3x4 Size 3.00 x 4.00 m Area 12 m2 Qty	Total £	Element Total £	Ref A/1P 3x5 Size 3.00 x 5.00 m Area 15 m2 Qty	Total £	Element Total £
EXTERNAL DOORS AND WINDOWS														
External door	NR	655.02	1NR	655.02		1NR	655.02		1NR	655.02		1NR	655.02	
Windows	NR	672.89	1NR	672.89		1NR	672.89		1NR	672.89		1NR	672.89	
Opening in cavity wall for door	NR	144.37	1NR	144.37		1NR	144.37		1NR	144.37		1NR	144.37	
Opening in cavity wall for window	NR	162.98	1NR	162.98	**1635.26**	1NR	162.98	**1635.26**	1NR	162.98	**1635.26**	1NR	162.98	**1635.26**
INTERNAL WALLS AND PARTITIONS														
Stud partitions	M2	51.63												
INTERNAL DOORS														
Hardwood flush door	NR	412.45												
WALL FINISHES														
Plaster & decoration	M2	19.58	25M2	489.50	**489.50**	30M2	587.40	**587.40**	35M2	685.30	**685.30**	40M2	783.20	**783.20**
FLOOR FINISHES														
Laminate	M2	30.30	6M2	181.80		9M2	272.70		12M2	363.60		15M2	454.50	
Hardwood skirting	M	19.52	10M	195.20	**377.00**	12M	234.24	**506.94**	14M	273.28	**636.88**	16M	312.32	**766.82**
CEILING FINISHES														
Plasterboard, plaster and decoration	M2	26.68	6M2	160.08	**160.08**	9M2	240.12	**240.12**	12M2	320.16	**320.16**	15M2	400.20	**400.20**

Specification A
18 m2 - 27 m2

SINGLE STOREY

PITCHED ROOF Continued/.....

Element	Unit	Unit Rate £	Ref A/1P 3x6 Size 3.00 x 6.00 m Area 18 m2			Ref A/1P 3x7 Size 3.00 x 7.00 m Area 21 m2			Ref A/1P 3x8 Size 3.00 x 8.00 m Area 24 m2			Ref A/1P 3x9 Size 3.00 x 9.00 m Area 27 m2		
			Qty	Total £	Element Total £	Qty	Total £	Element Total £	Qty	Total £	Element Total £	Qty	Total £	Element Total £
	NR	655.02	1NR	655.02		1NR	655.02		1NR	655.02		1NR	655.02	
	NR	672.89	2NR	1345.78		2NR	1345.78		2NR	1345.78		2NR	1345.78	
	NR	144.37	1NR	144.37		1NR	144.37		1NR	144.37		1NR	144.37	
	NR	162.98	2NR	325.96	**2471.13**	2NR	325.96	**2471.13**	2NR	325.96	**2471.13**	2NR	325.96	**2471.13**
	M2	51.63	8M2	413.04	**413.04**	8M2	413.04	**413.04**	8M2	413.04	**413.04**	8M2	413.04	**413.04**
	NR	412.45	1NR	412.45	**412.45**	1NR	412.45	**412.45**	1NR	412.45	**412.45**	1NR	412.45	**412.45**
	M2	19.58	45M2	881.10	**881.10**	50M2	979.00	**979.00**	55M2	1076.90	**1076.90**	60M2	1174.80	**1174.80**
	M2	30.30	18M2	545.40		21M2	636.30		24M2	727.20		27M2	818.10	
	M	19.52	18M	351.36	**896.76**	20M	390.40	**1026.70**	22M	429.44	**1156.64**	24M	468.48	**1286.58**
	M2	26.68	18M2	480.24	**480.24**	21M2	560.28	**560.28**	24M2	640.32	**640.32**	27M2	720.36	**720.36**

Specification A
6 m2 - 15 m2

SINGLE STOREY

PITCHED ROOF

Element	Unit	Unit Rate £	Ref A/1P 3x2 Size 3.00 x 2.00 m Area 6 m2 Qty	Total £	Element Total £	Ref A/1P 3x3 Size 3.00 x 3.00 m Area 9 m2 Qty	Total £	Element Total £	Ref A/1P 3x4 Size 3.00 x 4.00 m Area 12 m2 Qty	Total £	Element Total £	Ref A/1P 3x5 Size 3.00 x 5.00 m Area 15 m2 Qty	Total £	Element Total £
SERVICES														
Rainwater pipes	M	26.64	3M	79.92		3M	79.92		3M	79.92		3M	79.92	
Cold water service point	NR	110.52	1NR	110.52		1NR	110.52		1NR	110.52		1NR	110.52	
Hot water service point	NR	191.67	1NR	191.67		1NR	191.67		1NR	191.67		1NR	191.67	
Central heating service point	NR	386.51	1NR	386.51		1NR	386.51		1NR	386.51		1NR	386.51	
Electrical installation	NR	286.50	1NR	286.50	**1055.12**	1NR	286.50	**1055.12**	1NR	286.50	**1055.12**	1NR	286.50	**1055.12**
ALTERATIONS TO EXISTING BUILDINGS														
Opening in existing wall 1.80 m wide 2.00 m high	NR	689.44	1NR	689.44	**689.44**									
Opening in existing wall 2.40 m wide 2.00 m high	NR	865.59												
Opening in existing wall 3.00 m wide 2.00 m high	NR	921.26				1NR	921.26	**921.26**						
Opening in existing wall 4.00 m wide 2.00 m high	NR	1131.22							1NR	1131.22	**1131.22**			
Opening in existing wall 5.00 m wide 2.00 m high	NR	1341.19										1NR	1341.19	**1341.19**

Specification A
18 m2 - 27 m2

SINGLE STOREY

PITCHED ROOF Continued/.....

Element	Unit	Unit Rate £	Ref A/1P 3x6 Size 3.00 x 6.00 m Area 18 m2 Qty	Total £	Element Total £	Ref A/1P 3x7 Size 3.00 x 7.00 m Area 21 m2 Qty	Total £	Element Total £	Ref A/1P 3x8 Size 3.00 x 8.00 m Area 24 m2 Qty	Total £	Element Total £	Ref A/1P 3x9 Size 3.00 x 9.00 m Area 27 m2 Qty	Total £	Element Total £
	M	26.64	3M	79.92		3M	79.92		3M	79.92		3M	79.92	
	NR	110.52	1NR	110.52		1NR	110.52		1NR	110.52		1NR	110.52	
	NR	191.67	1NR	191.67		1NR	191.67		1NR	191.67		1NR	191.67	
	NR	386.51	2NR	773.02		2NR	773.02		2NR	773.02		2NR	773.02	
	NR	286.50	2NR	573.00	**1728.13**	2NR	573.00	**1728.13**	2NR	573.00	**1728.13**	2NR	573.00	**1728.13**
	NR	689.44												
	NR	865.59	2NR	1731.18	**1731.18**									
	NR	921.26				2NR	1842.52	**1842.52**	2NR	1842.52	**1842.52**			
	NR	1131.22										2NR	2262.44	**2262.44**
	NR	1341.19												

Specification A 6 m2 - 15 m2	Ref A/1P 3x2 Size 3.00 x 2.00 m Area 6 m2	Ref A/1P 3x3 Size 3.00 x 3.00 m Area 9 m2	Ref A/1P 3x4 Size 3.00 x 4.00 m Area 12 m2	Ref A/1P 3x5 Size 3.00 x 5.00 m Area 15 m2
	Element Total £	Element Total £	Element Total £	Element Total £
SINGLE STOREY				
PITCHED ROOF				
SUMMARY				
SUBSTRUCTURE	1849.11	2268.23	2687.35	3106.47
UPPER FLOORS	-	-	-	-
ROOF	3234.62	3914.04	4718.18	5397.60
EXTERNAL WALLS	2056.50	2285.00	2627.75	2856.25
EXTERNAL DOORS AND WINDOWS	1635.26	1635.26	1635.26	1635.26
INTERNAL WALLS AND PARTITIONS	-	-	-	-
INTERNAL DOORS	-	-	-	-
WALL FINISHES	489.50	587.40	685.30	783.20
FLOOR FINISHES	377.00	506.94	636.88	766.82
CEILING FINISHES	160.08	240.12	320.16	400.20
SERVICES	1055.12	1055.12	1055.12	1055.12
ALTERATIONS TO EXISTING BUILDINGS	689.44	921.26	1131.22	1341.19
Sub Total	11546.63	13413.37	15497.22	17342.11
Allowance for unmeasured items and sundries 5%	577.33	670.67	774.86	867.11
NET TOTAL excluding Preliminaries, Profit and Overheads	**12123.96**	**14084.04**	**16272.08**	**18209.22**

Specification A 18 m2 - 27 m2	Ref A/1P 3x6 Size 3.00 x 6.00 m Area 18 m2	Ref A/1P 3x7 Size 3.00 x 7.00 m Area 21 m2	Ref A/1P 3x8 Size 3.00 x 8.00 m Area 24 m2	Ref A/1P 3x9 Size 3.00 x 9.00 m Area 27 m2
	Element Total £	**Element Total £**	**Element Total £**	**Element Total £**
SINGLE STOREY				
PITCHED ROOF				
SUMMARY Continued/.....				
	3525.59	3944.71	4363.83	4782.95
	-	-	-	-
	6213.54	6851.23	7613.64	8251.33
	2970.50	3084.75	3541.75	3770.25
	2471.13	2471.13	2471.13	2471.13
	413.04	413.04	413.04	413.04
	412.45	412.45	412.45	412.45
	881.10	979.00	1076.90	1174.80
	896.76	1026.70	1156.64	1286.58
	480.24	560.28	640.32	720.36
	1728.13	1728.13	1728.13	1728.13
	1731.18	1842.52	1842.52	2262.44
Sub Total	21723.66	23313.94	25260.35	27273.46
Allowance for unmeasured items and sundries 5%	1086.18	1165.70	1263.02	1363.67
NET TOTAL excluding Preliminaries, Profit and Overheads	**22809.84**	**24479.64**	**26523.37**	**28637.13**

Specification A
8 m2 - 20 m2

SINGLE STOREY

PITCHED ROOF

Element	Unit	Unit Rate £	Ref A/1P 4x2 Size 4.00 x 2.00 m Area 8 m2 Qty	Total £	Element Total £	Ref A/1P 4x3 Size 4.00 x 3.00 m Area 12 m2 Qty	Total £	Element Total £	Ref A/1P 4x4 Size 4.00 x 4.00 m Area 16 m2 Qty	Total £	Element Total £	Ref A/1P 4x5 Size 4.00 x 5.00 m Area 20 m2 Qty	Total £	Element Total £
SUBSTRUCTURE														
Strip footings	M	144.41	11M	1588.51		12M	1732.92		13M	1877.33		14M	2021.74	
Hollow ground floor	M2	91.57	8M2	732.56	**2321.07**	12M2	1098.84	**2831.76**	16M2	1465.12	**3342.45**	20M2	1831.40	**3853.14**
ROOF														
Pitched roof construction	M2	55.42	14M2	775.88		18M2	997.56		23M2	1274.66		27M2	1496.34	
Work to top of external wall	M	23.71	11M	260.81		12M	284.52		13M	308.23		14M	331.94	
Plain tile roofing	M2	69.30	17M2	1178.10		22M2	1524.60		28M2	1940.40		33M2	2286.90	
Work to verge	M	11.58	4M	46.32		5M	57.90		6M	69.48		7M	81.06	
Work to hip	M	41.73	8M	333.84		9M	375.57		10M	417.30		11M	459.03	
Work to eaves	M	22.73	12M	272.76		13M	295.49		14M	318.22		15M	340.95	
Fascia and eaves soffit	M	48.01	12M	576.12		13M	624.13		14M	672.14		15M	720.15	
Gutters and fittings	M	18.68	12M	224.16		13M	242.84		14M	261.52		15M	280.20	
Flashings	M	69.52	4M	278.08	**3946.07**	5M	347.60	**4750.21**	6M	417.12	**5679.07**	7M	486.64	**6483.21**
EXTERNAL WALLS														
Brick and block cavity wall	M2	114.25	23M2	2627.75	**2627.75**	25M2	2856.25	**2856.25**	28M2	3199.00	**3199.00**	29M2	3313.25	**3313.25**

Specification A
24 m2 - 36 m2

			Ref A/1P 4x6 Size 4.00 x 6.00 m Area 24 m2			Ref A/1P 4x7 Size 4.00 x 7.00 m Area 28 m2			Ref A/1P 4x8 Size 4.00 x 8.00 m Area 32 m2			Ref A/1P 4x9 Size 4.00 x 9.00 m Area 36 m2		
SINGLE STOREY PITCHED ROOF Continued/.....			Qty	Total £	Element Total £	Qty	Total £	Element Total £	Qty	Total £	Element Total £	Qty	Total £	Element Total £
Element	Unit	Unit Rate £												
	M	144.41	15M	2166.15		16M	2310.56		17M	2454.97		18M	2599.38	
	M2	91.57	24M2	2197.68	**4363.83**	28M2	2563.96	**4874.52**	32M2	2930.24	**5385.21**	36M2	3296.52	**5895.90**
	M2	55.42	32M2	1773.44		36M2	1995.12		41M2	2272.22		45M2	2493.90	
	M	23.71	15M	355.65		16M	379.36		17M	403.07		18M	426.78	
	M2	69.30	39M2	2702.70		44M2	3049.20		50M2	3465.00		55M2	3811.50	
	M	11.58	9M	104.22		10M	115.80		11M	127.38		12M	138.96	
	M	41.73	12M	500.76		13M	542.49		14M	584.22		14M	584.22	
	M	22.73	16M	363.68		17M	386.41		18M	409.14		19M	431.87	
	M	48.01	16M	768.16		17M	816.17		18M	864.18		19M	912.19	
	M	18.68	16M	298.88		17M	317.56		18M	336.24		19M	354.92	
	M	69.52	9M	625.68	**7493.17**	10M	695.20	**8297.31**	11M	764.72	**9226.17**	12M	834.24	**9988.58**
	M2	114.25	31M2	3541.75	**3541.75**	33M2	3770.25	**3770.25**	36M2	4113.00	**4113.00**	38M2	4341.50	**4341.50**

Specification A
8 m2 - 20 m2

SINGLE STOREY PITCHED ROOF			Ref A/1P 4x2 Size 4.00 x 2.00 m Area 8 m2			Ref A/1P 4x3 Size 4.00 x 3.00 m Area 12 m2			Ref A/1P 4x4 Size 4.00 x 4.00 m Area 16 m2			Ref A/1P 4x5 Size 4.00 x 5.00 m Area 20 m2		
Element	Unit	Unit Rate £	Qty	Total £	Element Total £	Qty	Total £	Element Total £	Qty	Total £	Element Total £	Qty	Total £	Element Total £
EXTERNAL DOORS AND WINDOWS														
External door	NR	655.02	1NR	655.02		1NR	655.02		1NR	655.02		1NR	655.02	
Windows	NR	672.89	1NR	672.89		1NR	672.89		1NR	672.89		1NR	672.89	
Opening in cavity wall for door	NR	144.37	1NR	144.37		1NR	144.37		1NR	144.37		1NR	144.37	
Opening in cavity wall for window	NR	162.98	1NR	162.98	**1635.26**	1NR	162.98	**1635.26**	1NR	162.98	**1635.26**	1NR	162.98	**1635.26**
INTERNAL WALLS AND PARTITIONS														
Stud partitions	M2	51.63												
INTERNAL DOORS														
Hardwood flush door	NR	412.45												
WALL FINISHES														
Plaster & decoration	M2	19.58	30M2	587.40	**587.40**	35M2	685.30	**685.30**	40M2	783.20	**783.20**	45M2	881.10	**881.10**
FLOOR FINISHES														
Laminate	M2	30.30	8M2	242.40		12M2	363.60		16M2	484.80		20M2	606.00	
Hardwood skirting	M	19.52	12M	234.24	**476.64**	14M	273.28	**636.88**	16M	312.32	**797.12**	18M	351.36	**957.36**
CEILING FINISHES														
Plasterboard, plaster and decoration	M2	26.68	8M2	213.44	**213.44**	12M2	320.16	**320.16**	16M2	426.88	**426.88**	20M2	533.60	**533.60**

Specification A 24 m2 - 36 m2

SINGLE STOREY

PITCHED ROOF Continued/.....

Element	Unit	Unit Rate £	Ref A/1P 4x6 Size 4.00 x 6.00 m Area 24 m2			Ref A/1P 4x7 Size 4.00 x 7.00 m Area 28 m2			Ref A/1P 4x8 Size 4.00 x 8.00 m Area 32 m2			Ref A/1P 4x9 Size 4.00 x 9.00 m Area 36 m2		
			Qty	Total £	Element Total £	Qty	Total £	Element Total £	Qty	Total £	Element Total £	Qty	Total £	Element Total £
	NR	655.02	1NR	655.02		1NR	655.02		1NR	655.02		1NR	655.02	
	NR	672.89	2NR	1345.78		2NR	1345.78		2NR	1345.78		2NR	1345.78	
	NR	144.37	1NR	144.37		1NR	144.37		1NR	144.37		1NR	144.37	
	NR	162.98	2NR	325.96	**2471.13**	2NR	325.96	**2471.13**	2NR	325.96	**2471.13**	2NR	325.96	**2471.13**
	M2	51.63	10M2	516.30	**516.30**	10M2	516.30	**516.30**	10M2	516.30	**516.30**	10M2	516.30	**516.30**
	NR	412.45	1NR	412.45	**412.45**	1NR	412.45	**412.45**	1NR	412.45	**412.45**	1NR	412.45	**412.45**
	M2	19.58	50M2	979.00	**979.00**	55M2	1076.90	**1076.90**	60M2	1174.80	**1174.80**	65M2	1272.70	**1272.70**
	M2	30.30	24M2	727.20		28M2	848.40		32M2	969.60		36M2	1090.80	
	M	19.52	20M	390.40	**1117.60**	22M	429.44	**1277.84**	24M	468.48	**1438.08**	26M	507.52	**1598.32**
	M2	26.68	24M2	640.32	**640.32**	28M2	747.04	**747.04**	32M2	853.76	**853.76**	36M2	960.48	**960.48**

Specification A 8 m2 - 20 m2

Element	Unit	Unit Rate £	Ref A/1P 4x2 Size 4.00 x 2.00 m Area 8 m2 Qty	Total £	Element Total £	Ref A/1P 4x3 Size 4.00 x 3.00 m Area 12 m2 Qty	Total £	Element Total £	Ref A/1P 4x4 Size 4.00 x 4.00 m Area 16 m2 Qty	Total £	Element Total £	Ref A/1P 4x5 Size 4.00 x 5.00 m Area 20 m2 Qty	Total £	Element Total £
SINGLE STOREY														
PITCHED ROOF														
SERVICES														
Rainwater pipes	M	26.64	3M	79.92		3M	79.92		3M	79.92		3M	79.92	
Cold water service point	NR	110.52	1NR	110.52		1NR	110.52		1NR	110.52		1NR	110.52	
Hot water service point	NR	191.67	1NR	191.67		1NR	191.67		1NR	191.67		1NR	191.67	
Central heating service point	NR	386.51	1NR	386.51		1NR	386.51		1NR	386.51		1NR	386.51	
Electrical installation	NR	286.50	1NR	286.50	**1055.12**	1NR	286.50	**1055.12**	1NR	286.50	**1055.12**	1NR	286.50	**1055.12**
ALTERATIONS TO EXISTING BUILDINGS														
Opening in existing wall 1.80 m wide 2.00 m high	NR	689.44	1NR	689.44	**689.44**									
Opening in existing wall 2.40 m wide 2.00 m high	NR	865.59												
Opening in existing wall 3.00 m wide 2.00 m high	NR	921.26				1NR	921.26	**921.26**						
Opening in existing wall 4.00 m wide 2.00 m high	NR	1131.22							1NR	1131.22	**1131.22**			
Opening in existing wall 5.00 m wide 2.00 m high	NR	1341.19										1NR	1341.19	**1341.19**

Specification A 24 m2 - 36 m2

SINGLE STOREY

PITCHED ROOF Continued/.....

Element	Unit	Unit Rate £	Ref A/1P 4x6 Size 4.00 x 6.00 m Area 24 m2			Ref A/1P 4x7 Size 4.00 x 7.00 m Area 28 m2			Ref A/1P 4x8 Size 4.00 x 8.00 m Area 32 m2			Ref A/1P 4x9 Size 4.00 x 9.00 m Area 36 m2		
			Qty	**Total £**	**Element Total £**	**Qty**	**Total £**	**Element Total £**	**Qty**	**Total £**	**Element Total £**	**Qty**	**Total £**	**Element Total £**
	M	26.64	3M	79.92		3M	79.92		3M	79.92		3M	79.92	
	NR	110.52	1NR	110.52		1NR	110.52		1NR	110.52		1NR	110.52	
	NR	191.67	1NR	191.67		1NR	191.67		1NR	191.67		1NR	191.67	
	NR	386.51	2NR	773.02		2NR	773.02		2NR	773.02		2NR	773.02	
	NR	286.50	2NR	573.00	**1728.13**	2NR	573.00	**1728.13**	2NR	573.00	**1728.13**	2NR	573.00	**1728.13**
	NR	689.44												
	NR	865.59	2NR	1731.18	**1731.18**									
	NR	921.26				2NR	1842.52	**1842.52**	2NR	1842.52	**1842.52**			
	NR	1131.22										2NR	2262.44	**2262.44**
	NR	1341.19												

Specification A 8 m2 - 20 m2	Ref A/1P 4x2 Size 4.00 x 2.00 m Area 8 m2	Ref A/1P 4x3 Size 4.00 x 3.00 m Area 12 m2	Ref A/1P 4x4 Size 4.00 x 4.00 m Area 16 m2	Ref A/1P 4x5 Size 4.00 x 5.00 m Area 20 m2
	Element Total £	Element Total £	Element Total £	Element Total £
SINGLE STOREY				
PITCHED ROOF				
SUMMARY				
SUBSTRUCTURE	2321.07	2831.76	3342.45	3853.14
UPPER FLOORS	-	-	-	-
ROOF	3946.07	4750.21	5679.07	6483.21
EXTERNAL WALLS	2627.75	2856.25	3199.00	3313.25
EXTERNAL DOORS AND WINDOWS	1635.26	1635.26	1635.26	1635.26
INTERNAL WALLS AND PARTITIONS	-	-	-	-
INTERNAL DOORS	-	-	-	-
WALL FINISHES	587.40	685.30	783.20	881.10
FLOOR FINISHES	476.64	636.88	797.12	957.36
CEILING FINISHES	213.44	320.16	426.88	533.60
SERVICES	1055.12	1055.12	1055.12	1055.12
ALTERATIONS TO EXISTING BUILDINGS	689.44	921.26	1131.22	1341.19
Sub Total	13552.19	15692.20	18049.32	20053.23
Allowance for unmeasured items and sundries 5%	677.61	784.61	902.47	1002.66
NET TOTAL excluding Preliminaries, Profit and Overheads	**14229.80**	**16476.81**	**18951.79**	**21055.89**

Specification A 24 m2 - 36 m2	Ref A/1P 4x6 Size 4.00 x 6.00 m Area 24 m2	Ref A/1P 4x7 Size 4.00 x 7.00 m Area 28 m2	Ref A/1P 4x8 Size 4.00 x 8.00 m Area 32 m2	Ref A/1P 4x9 Size 4.00 x 9.00 m Area 36 m2
	Element Total £	**Element Total £**	**Element Total £**	**Element Total £**
SINGLE STOREY				
PITCHED ROOF				
SUMMARY Continued/.....				
	4363.83	4874.52	5385.21	5895.90
	-	-	-	-
	7493.17	8297.31	9226.17	9988.58
	3541.75	3770.25	4113.00	4341.50
	2471.13	2471.13	2471.13	2471.13
	516.30	516.30	516.30	516.30
	412.45	412.45	412.45	412.45
	979.00	1076.90	1174.80	1272.70
	1117.60	1277.84	1438.08	1598.32
	640.32	747.04	853.76	960.48
	1728.13	1728.13	1728.13	1728.13
	1731.18	1842.52	1842.52	2262.44
Sub Total	24994.86	27014.39	29161.55	31447.93
Allowance for unmeasured items and sundries 5%	1249.74	1350.72	1458.08	1572.40
NET TOTAL excluding Preliminaries, Profit and Overheads	**26244.60**	**28365.11**	**30619.63**	**33020.33**

Specification A
10 m2 - 25 m2

SINGLE STOREY

PITCHED ROOF

Element	Unit	Unit Rate £	Ref A/1P 5x2 Size 5.00 x 2.00 m Area 10 m2 Qty	Total £	Element Total £	Ref A/1P 5x3 Size 5.00 x 3.00 m Area 15 m2 Qty	Total £	Element Total £	Ref A/1P 5x4 Size 5.00 x 4.00 m Area 20 m2 Qty	Total £	Element Total £	Ref A/1P 5x5 Size 5.00 x 5.00 m Area 25 m2 Qty	Total £	Element Total £
SUBSTRUCTURE														
Strip footings	M	144.41	13M	1877.33		14M	2021.74		15M	2166.15		16M	2310.56	
Hollow ground floor	M2	91.57	10M2	915.70	**2793.03**	15M2	1373.55	**3395.29**	20M2	1831.40	**3997.55**	25M2	2289.25	**4599.81**
ROOF														
Pitched roof construction	M2	55.42	17M2	942.14		22M2	1219.24		28M2	1551.76		33M2	1828.86	
Work to top of external wall	M	23.71	13M	308.23		14M	331.94		15M	355.65		16M	379.36	
Plain tile roofing	M2	69.30	20M2	1386.00		27M2	1871.10		34M2	2356.20		41M2	2841.30	
Work to verge	M	11.58	4M	46.32		5M	57.90		6M	69.48		7M	81.06	
Work to hip	M	41.73	9M	375.57		10M	417.30		11M	459.03		12M	500.76	
Work to eaves	M	22.73	14M	318.22		15M	340.95		16M	363.68		17M	386.41	
Fascia and eaves soffit	M	48.01	14M	672.14		15M	720.15		16M	768.16		17M	816.17	
Gutters and fittings	M	18.68	14M	261.52		15M	280.20		16M	298.88		17M	317.56	
Flashings	M	69.52	4M	278.08	**4588.22**	5M	347.60	**5586.38**	6M	417.12	**6639.96**	7M	486.64	**7638.12**
EXTERNAL WALLS														
Brick and block cavity wall	M2	114.25	28M2	3199.00	**3199.00**	30M2	3427.50	**3427.50**	33M2	3770.25	**3770.25**	35M2	3998.75	**3998.75**

Specification A
30 m2 - 45 m2

SINGLE STOREY

PITCHED ROOF Continued/.....

Element	Unit	Unit Rate £	Ref A/1P 5x6 Size 5.00 x 6.00 m Area 30 m2 Qty	Total £	Element Total £	Ref A/1P 5x7 Size 5.00 x 7.00 m Area 35 m2 Qty	Total £	Element Total £	Ref A/1P 5x8 Size 5.00 x 8.00 m Area 40 m2 Qty	Total £	Element Total £	Ref A/1P 5x9 Size 5.00 x 9.00 m Area 45 m2 Qty	Total £	Element Total £
	M	144.41	17M	2454.97		18M	2599.38		19M	2743.79		20M	2888.20	
	M2	91.57	30M2	2747.10	**5202.07**	35M2	3204.95	**5804.33**	40M2	3662.80	**6406.59**	45M2	4120.65	**7008.85**
	M2	55.42	39M2	2161.38		44M2	2438.48		50M2	2771.00		55M2	3048.10	
	M	23.71	17M	403.07		18M	426.78		19M	450.49		20M	474.20	
	M2	69.30	47M2	3257.10		54M2	3742.20		61M2	4227.30		68M2	4712.40	
	M	11.58	9M	104.22		10M	115.80		11M	127.38		12M	138.96	
	M	41.73	13M	542.49		14M	584.22		15M	625.95		16M	667.68	
	M	22.73	18M	409.14		19M	431.87		20M	454.60		21M	477.33	
	M	48.01	18M	864.18		19M	912.19		20M	960.20		21M	1008.21	
	M	18.68	18M	336.24		19M	354.92		20M	373.60		21M	392.28	
	M	69.52	9M	625.68	**8703.50**	10M	695.20	**9701.66**	11M	764.72	**10755.24**	12M	834.24	**11753.40**
	M2	114.25	36M2	4113.00	**4113.00**	38M2	4341.50	**4341.50**	41M2	4684.25	**4684.25**	43M2	4912.75	**4912.75**

Specification A
10 m2 - 25 m2

			Ref A/1P 5x2 Size 5.00 x 2.00 m Area 10 m2			Ref A/1P 5x3 Size 5.00 x 3.00 m Area 15 m2			Ref A/1P 5x4 Size 5.00 x 4.00 m Area 20 m2			Ref A/1P 5x5 Size 5.00 x 5.00 m Area 25 m2		
SINGLE STOREY PITCHED ROOF			Qty	Total £	Element Total £	Qty	Total £	Element Total £	Qty	Total £	Element Total £	Qty	Total £	Element Total £
Element	Unit	Unit Rate £												
EXTERNAL DOORS AND WINDOWS														
External door	NR	655.02	1NR	655.02		1NR	655.02		1NR	655.02		1NR	655.02	
Windows	NR	672.89	1NR	672.89		1NR	672.89		1NR	672.89		1NR	672.89	
Opening in cavity wall for door	NR	144.37	1NR	144.37		1NR	144.37		1NR	144.37		1NR	144.37	
Opening in cavity wall for window	NR	162.98	1NR	162.98	**1635.26**	1NR	162.98	**1635.26**	1NR	162.98	**1635.26**	1NR	162.98	**1635.26**
INTERNAL WALLS AND PARTITIONS														
Stud partitions	M2	51.63												
INTERNAL DOORS														
Hardwood flush door	NR	412.45												
WALL FINISHES														
Plaster & decoration	M2	19.58	35M2	685.30	**685.30**	40M2	783.20	**783.20**	45M2	881.10	**881.10**	50M2	979.00	**979.00**
FLOOR FINISHES														
Laminate	M2	30.30	10M2	303.00		15M2	454.50		20M2	606.00		25M2	757.50	
Hardwood skirting	M	19.52	14M	273.28	**576.28**	16M	312.32	**766.82**	18M	351.36	**957.36**	20M	390.40	**1147.90**
CEILING FINISHES														
Plasterboard, plaster and decoration	M2	26.68	10M2	266.80	**266.80**	15M2	400.20	**400.20**	20M2	533.60	**533.60**	25M2	667.00	**667.00**

Specification A 30 m2 - 45 m2

SINGLE STOREY

PITCHED ROOF Continued/.....

Element	Unit	Unit Rate £	Ref A/1P 5x6 Size 5.00 x 6.00 m Area 30 m2 Qty	Total £	Element Total £	Ref A/1P 5x7 Size 5.00 x 7.00 m Area 35 m2 Qty	Total £	Element Total £	Ref A/1P 5x8 Size 5.00 x 8.00 m Area 40 m2 Qty	Total £	Element Total £	Ref A/1P 5x9 Size 5.00 x 9.00 m Area 45 m2 Qty	Total £	Element Total £
	NR	655.02	1NR	655.02		1NR	655.02		1NR	655.02		1NR	655.02	
	NR	672.89	2NR	1345.78		2NR	1345.78		2NR	1345.78		2NR	1345.78	
	NR	144.37	1NR	144.37		1NR	144.37		1NR	144.37		1NR	144.37	
	NR	162.98	2NR	325.96	**2471.13**	2NR	325.96	**2471.13**	2NR	325.96	**2471.13**	2NR	325.96	**2471.13**
	M2	51.63	13M2	671.19	**671.19**	13M2	671.19	**671.19**	13M2	671.19	**671.19**	13M2	671.19	**671.19**
	NR	412.45	1NR	412.45	**412.45**	1NR	412.45	**412.45**	1NR	412.45	**412.45**	1NR	412.45	**412.45**
	M2	19.58	55M2	1076.90	**1076.90**	60M2	1174.80	**1174.80**	65M2	1272.70	**1272.70**	70M2	1370.60	**1370.60**
	M2	30.30	30M2	909.00		35M2	1060.50		40M2	1212.00		45M2	1363.50	
	M	19.52	22M	429.44	**1338.44**	24M	468.48	**1528.98**	26M	507.52	**1719.52**	28M	546.56	**1910.06**
	M2	26.68	30M2	800.40	**800.40**	35M2	933.80	**933.80**	40M2	1067.20	**1067.20**	45M2	1200.60	**1200.60**

Specification A
10 m2 - 25 m2

SINGLE STOREY

PITCHED ROOF

Element	Unit	Unit Rate £	Ref A/1P 5x2 Size 5.00 x 2.00 m Area 10 m2 Qty	Total £	Element Total £	Ref A/1P 5x3 Size 5.00 x 3.00 m Area 15 m2 Qty	Total £	Element Total £	Ref A/1P 5x4 Size 5.00 x 4.00 m Area 20 m2 Qty	Total £	Element Total £	Ref A/1P 5x5 Size 5.00 x 5.00 m Area 25 m2 Qty	Total £	Element Total £
SERVICES														
Rainwater pipes	M	26.64	3M	79.92		3M	79.92		3M	79.92		3M	79.92	
Cold water service point	NR	110.52	1NR	110.52		1NR	110.52		1NR	110.52		1NR	110.52	
Hot water service point	NR	191.67	1NR	191.67		1NR	191.67		1NR	191.67		1NR	191.67	
Central heating service point	NR	386.51	1NR	386.51		1NR	386.51		1NR	386.51		1NR	386.51	
Electrical installation	NR	286.50	1NR	286.50	**1055.12**	1NR	286.50	**1055.12**	1NR	286.50	**1055.12**	1NR	286.50	**1055.12**
ALTERATIONS TO EXISTING BUILDINGS														
Opening in existing wall 1.80 m wide 2.00 m high	NR	689.44	1NR	689.44	**689.44**									
Opening in existing wall 2.40 m wide 2.00 m high	NR	865.59												
Opening in existing wall 3.00 m wide 2.00 m high	NR	921.26				1NR	921.26	**921.26**						
Opening in existing wall 4.00 m wide 2.00 m high	NR	1131.22							1NR	1131.22	**1131.22**			
Opening in existing wall 5.00 m wide 2.00 m high	NR	1341.19										1NR	1341.19	**1341.19**

Specification A
30 m2 - 45 m2

SINGLE STOREY

PITCHED ROOF Continued/.....

Element	Unit	Unit Rate £	Ref A/1P 5x6 Size 5.00 x 6.00 m Area 30 m2 Qty	Total £	Element Total £	Ref A/1P 5x7 Size 5.00 x 7.00 m Area 35 m2 Qty	Total £	Element Total £	Ref A/1P 5x8 Size 5.00 x 8.00 m Area 40 m2 Qty	Total £	Element Total £	Ref A/1P 5x9 Size 5.00 x 9.00 m Area 45 m2 Qty	Total £	Element Total £
	M	26.64	3M	79.92		3M	79.92		3M	79.92		3M	79.92	
	NR	110.52	1NR	110.52		1NR	110.52		1NR	110.52		1NR	110.52	
	NR	191.67	1NR	191.67		1NR	191.67		1NR	191.67		1NR	191.67	
	NR	386.51	2NR	773.02		2NR	773.02		2NR	773.02		2NR	773.02	
	NR	286.50	2NR	573.00	**1728.13**	2NR	573.00	**1728.13**	2NR	573.00	**1728.13**	2NR	573.00	**1728.13**
	NR	689.44												
	NR	865.59	2NR	1731.18	**1731.18**									
	NR	921.26				2NR	1842.52	**1842.52**	2NR	1842.52	**1842.52**			
	NR	1131.22										2NR	2262.44	**2262.44**
	NR	1341.19												

Specification A 10 m2 - 25 m2	Ref A/1P 5x2 Size 5.00 x 2.00 m Area 10 m2	Ref A/1P 5x3 Size 5.00 x 3.00 m Area 15 m2	Ref A/1P 5x4 Size 5.00 x 4.00 m Area 20 m2	Ref A/1P 5x5 Size 5.00 x 5.00 m Area 25 m2
	Element Total £	Element Total £	Element Total £	Element Total £
SINGLE STOREY				
PITCHED ROOF				
SUMMARY				
SUBSTRUCTURE	2793.03	3395.29	3997.55	4599.81
UPPER FLOORS	-	-	-	-
ROOF	4588.22	5586.38	6639.96	7638.12
EXTERNAL WALLS	3199.00	3427.50	3770.25	3998.75
EXTERNAL DOORS AND WINDOWS	1635.26	1635.26	1635.26	1635.26
INTERNAL WALLS AND PARTITIONS	-	-	-	-
INTERNAL DOORS	-	-	-	-
WALL FINISHES	685.30	783.20	881.10	979.00
FLOOR FINISHES	576.28	766.82	957.36	1147.90
CEILING FINISHES	266.80	400.20	533.60	667.00
SERVICES	1055.12	1055.12	1055.12	1055.12
ALTERATIONS TO EXISTING BUILDINGS	689.44	921.26	1131.22	1341.19
Sub Total	15488.45	17971.03	20601.42	23062.15
Allowance for unmeasured items and sundries 5%	774.42	898.55	1030.07	1153.11
NET TOTAL excluding Preliminaries, Profit and Overheads	**16262.87**	**18869.58**	**21631.49**	**24215.26**

Specification A 30 m2 - 45 m2	Ref A/1P 5x6 Size 5.00 x 6.00 m Area 30 m2	Ref A/1P 5x7 Size 5.00 x 7.00 m Area 35 m2	Ref A/1P 5x8 Size 5.00 x 8.00 m Area 40 m2	Ref A/1P 5x9 Size 5.00 x 9.00 m Area 45 m2
	Element Total £	Element Total £	Element Total £	Element Total £
SINGLE STOREY				
PITCHED ROOF				
SUMMARY Continued/.....				
	5202.07	5804.33	6406.59	7008.85
	-	-	-	-
	8703.50	9701.66	10755.24	11753.40
	4113.00	4341.50	4684.25	4912.75
	2471.13	2471.13	2471.13	2471.13
	671.19	671.19	671.19	671.19
	412.45	412.45	412.45	412.45
	1076.90	1174.80	1272.70	1370.60
	1338.44	1528.98	1719.52	1910.06
	800.40	933.80	1067.20	1200.60
	1728.13	1728.13	1728.13	1728.13
	1731.18	1842.52	1842.52	2262.44
Sub Total	28248.39	30610.49	33030.92	35701.60
Allowance for unmeasured items and sundries 5%	1412.42	1530.52	1651.55	1785.08
NET TOTAL excluding Preliminaries, Profit and Overheads	**29660.81**	**32141.01**	**34682.47**	**37486.68**

Specification A

Two storey flat roof

[2F] 2×2/3/4/5.

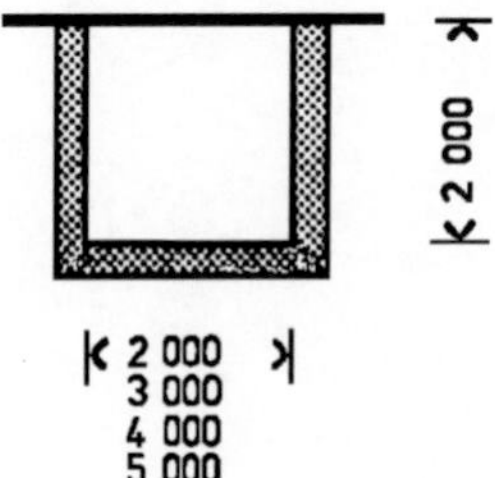

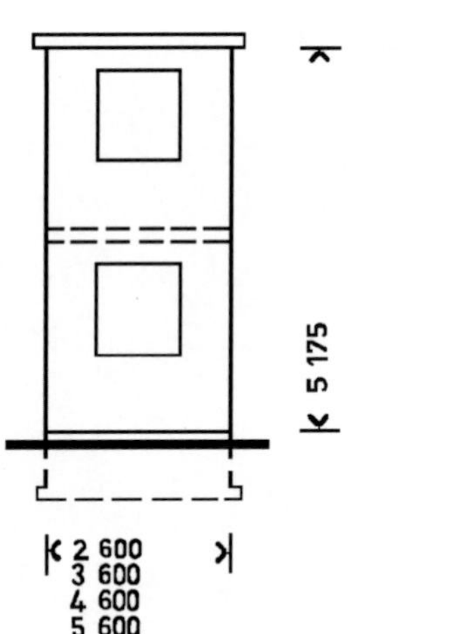

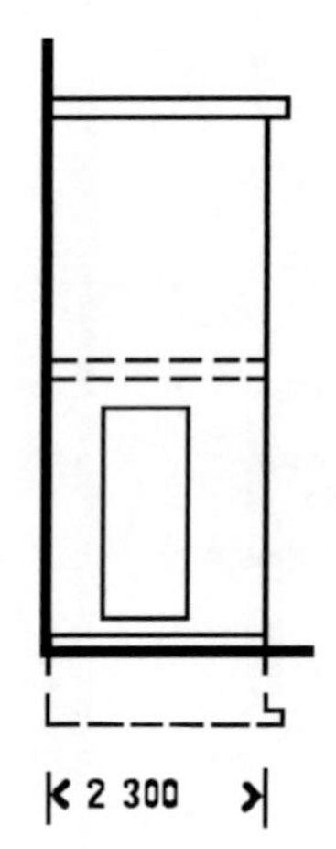

[2F] 2×6/7/8/9.

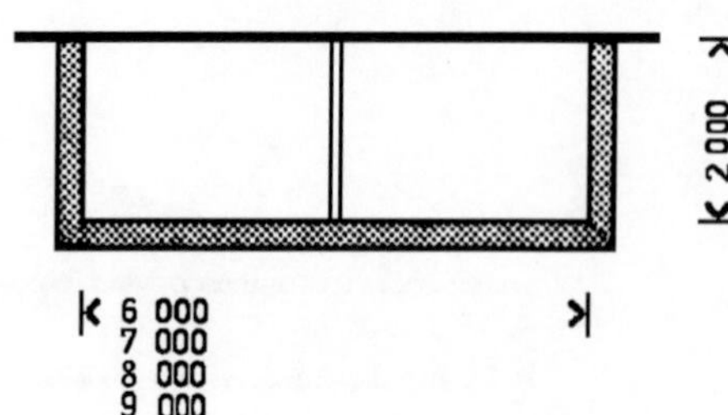

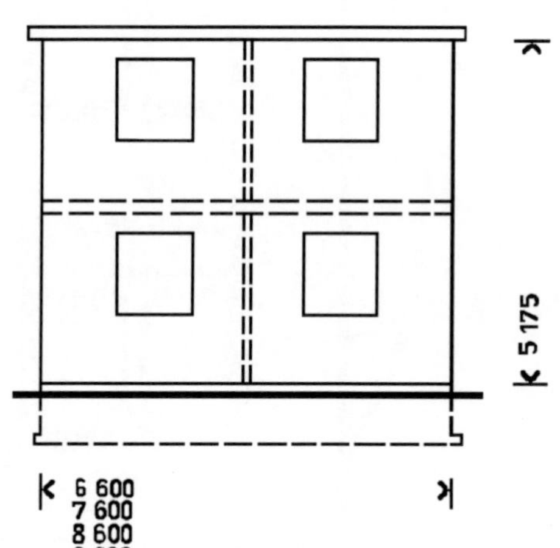

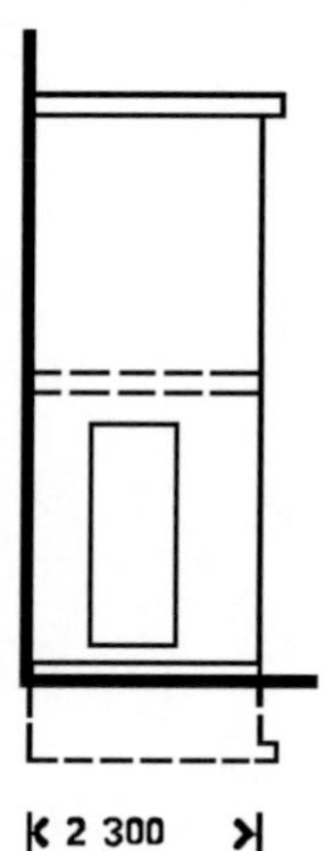

[2F] 3×2/3/4/5.

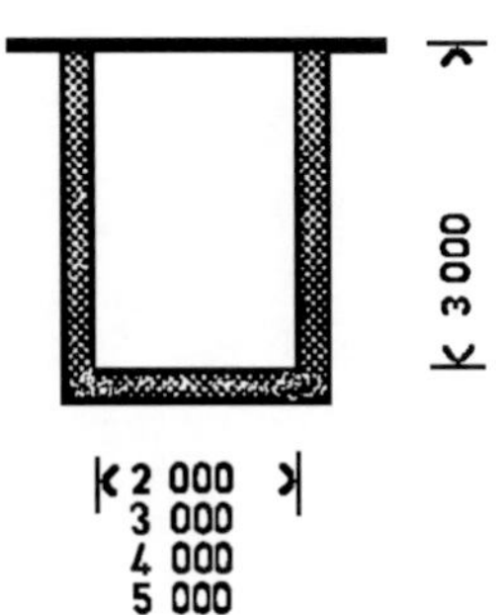

[2F] 3×6/7/8/9.

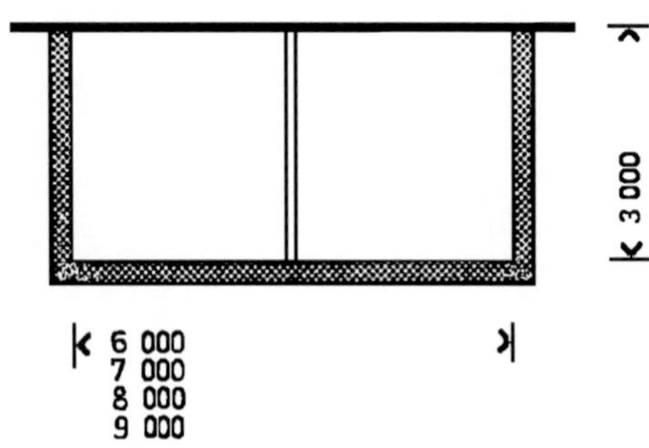

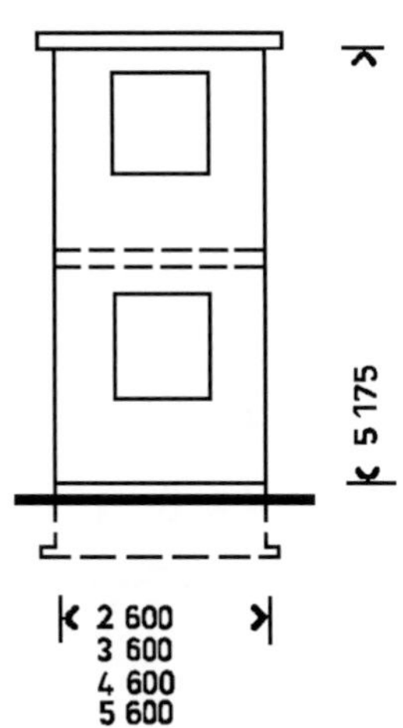

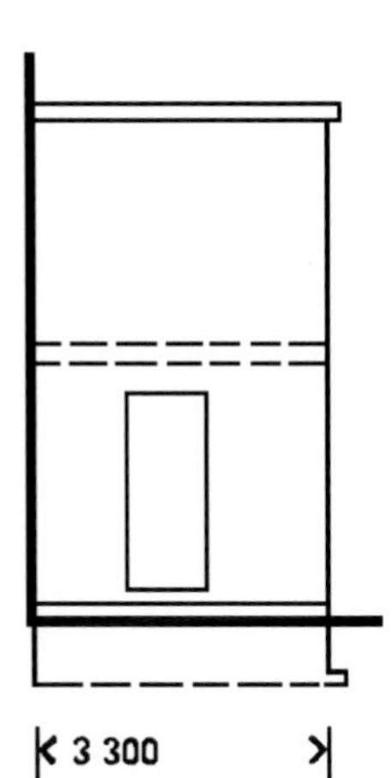

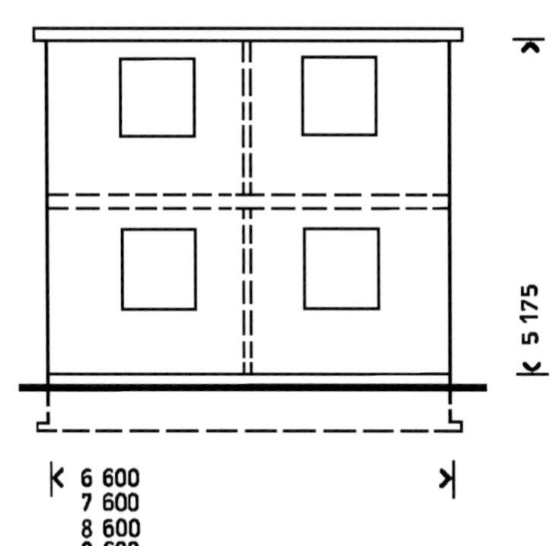

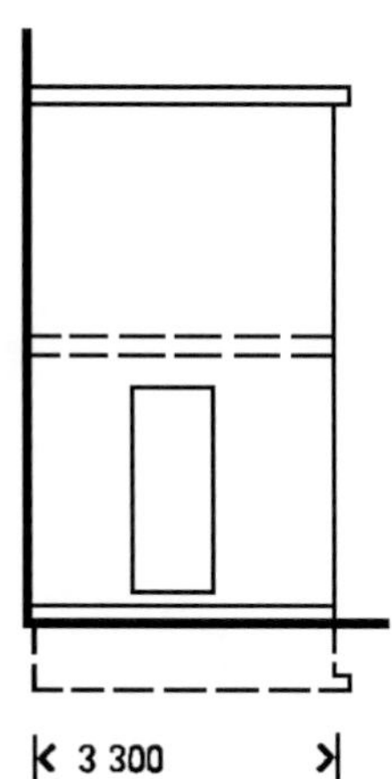

[2F] 4×2/3/4/5.

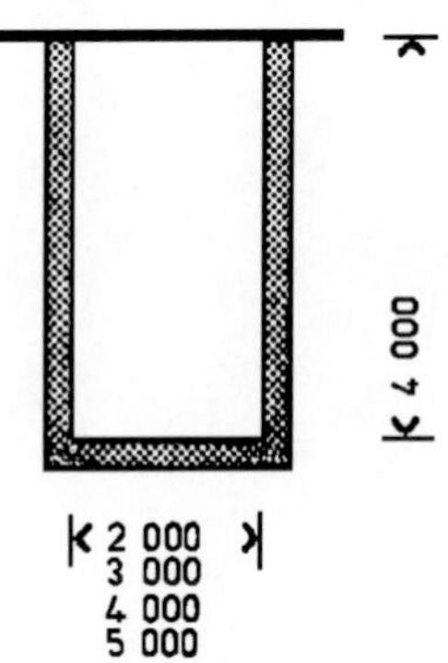

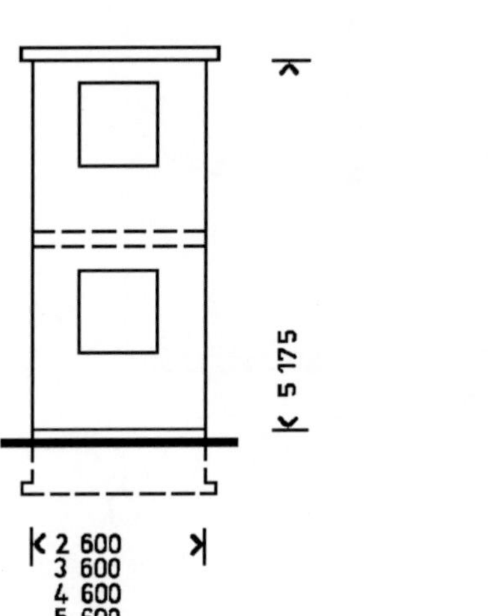

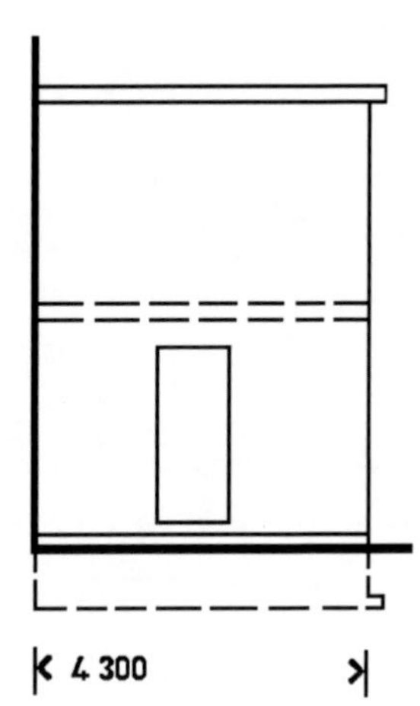

[2F] 4×6/7/8/9.

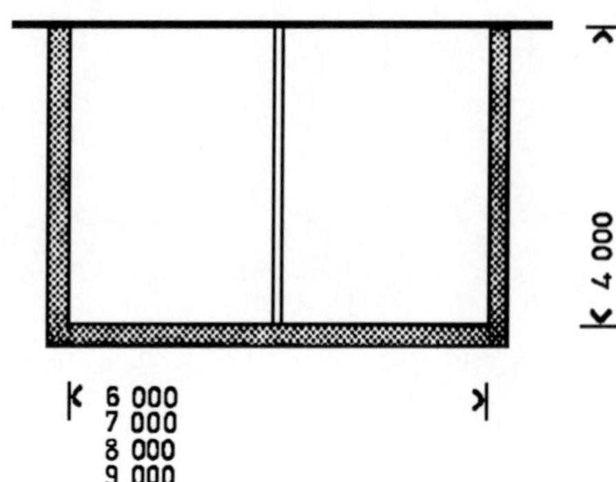

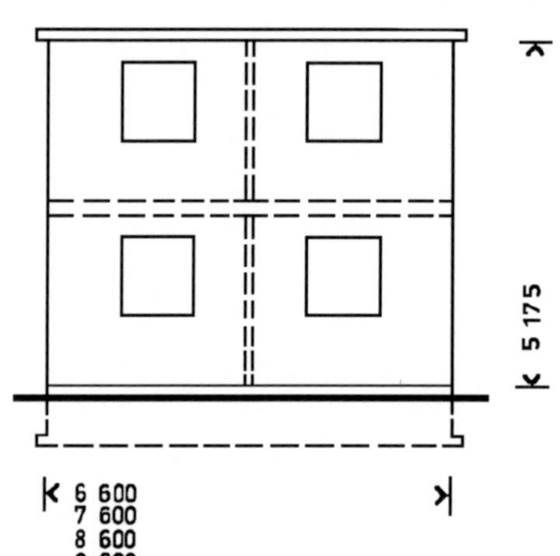

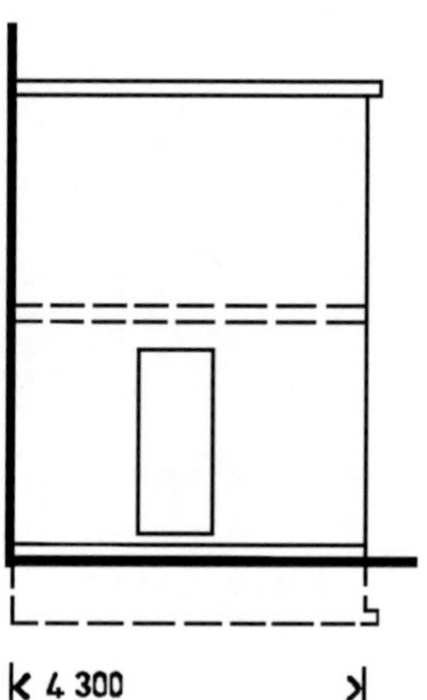

[2F] 5×2/3/4/5.

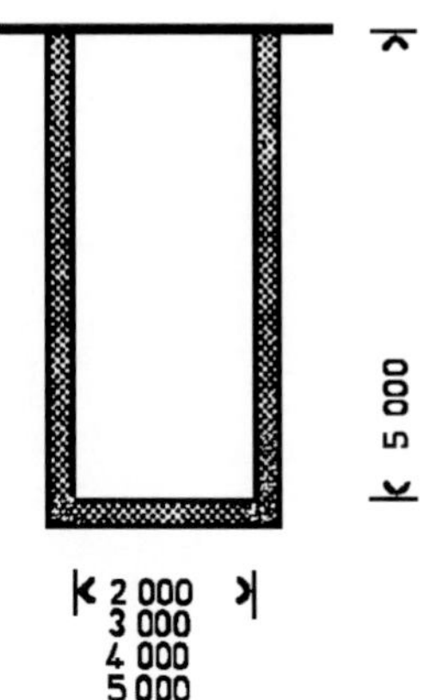

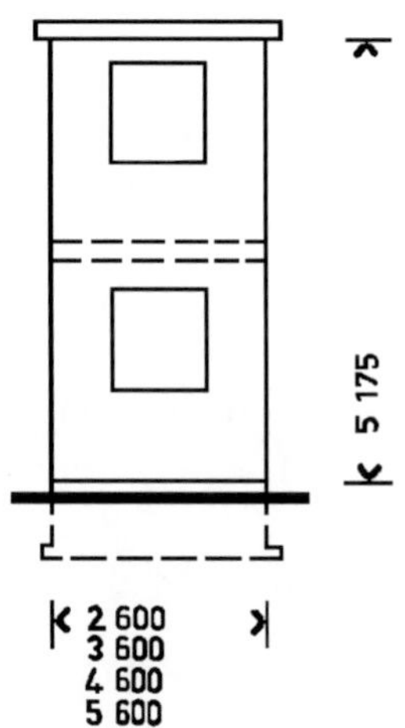

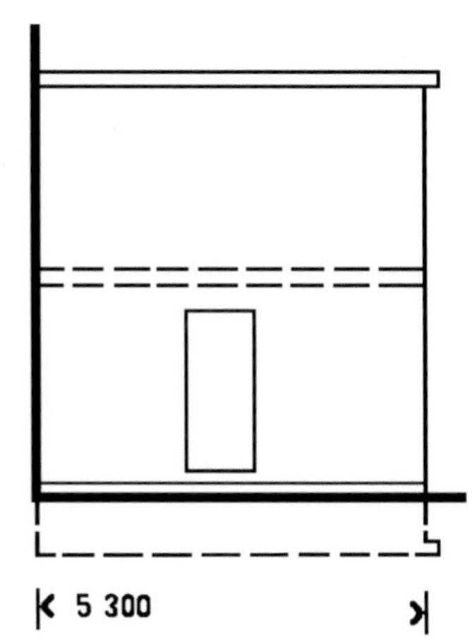

[2F] 5×6/7/8/9.

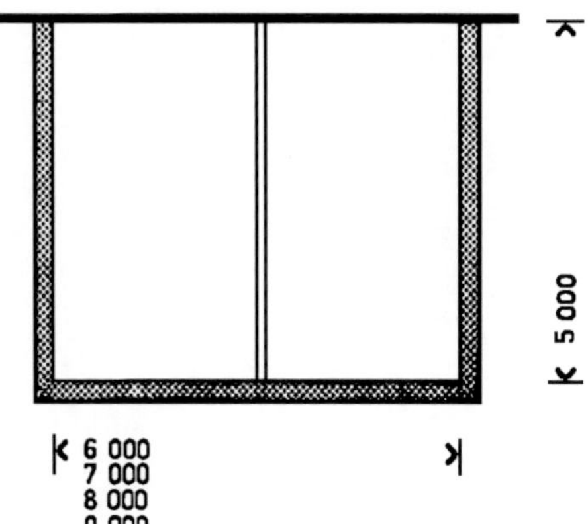

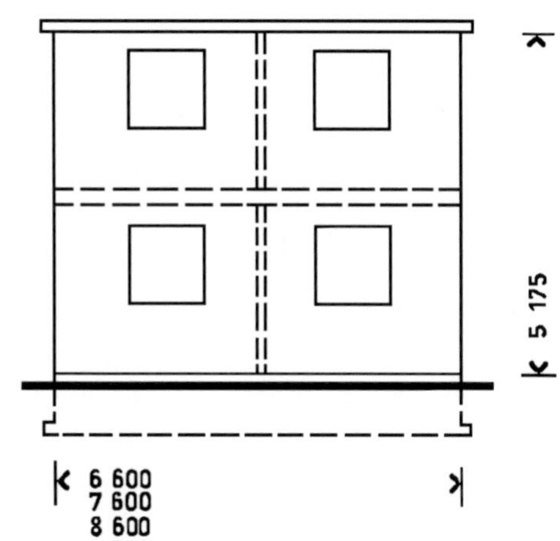

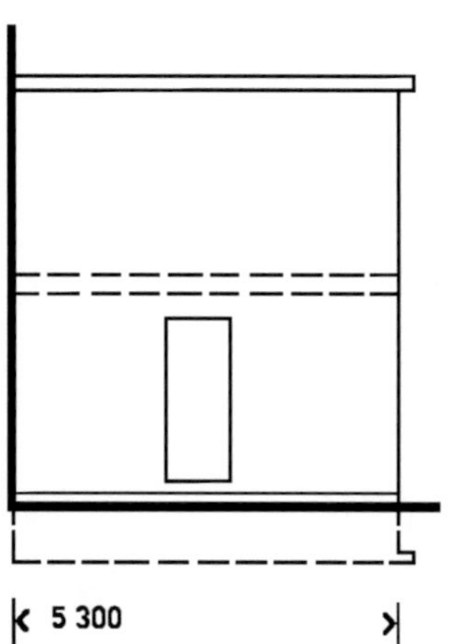

Specification A
4 m2 - 10 m2

TWO STOREY

FLAT ROOF

Element	Unit	Unit Rate £	Ref A/2F 2x2 Size 2.00 x 2.00 m Area 4 m2 Qty	Total £	Element Total £	Ref A/2F 2x3 Size 2.00 x 3.00 m Area 6 m2 Qty	Total £	Element Total £	Ref A/2F 2x4 Size 2.00 x 4.00 m Area 8 m2 Qty	Total £	Element Total £	Ref A/2F 2x5 Size 2.00 x 5.00 m Area 10 m2 Qty	Total £	Element Total £
SUBSTRUCTURE														
Strip footings	M	144.41	7M	1010.87		8M	1155.28		9M	1299.69		10M	1444.10	
Hollow ground floor	M2	91.57	4M2	366.28	**1377.15**	6M2	549.42	**1704.70**	8M2	732.56	**2032.25**	10M2	915.70	**2359.80**
UPPER FLOORS														
Timber floor construction 50 x 150 mm joists	M2	77.86	4M2	311.44	**311.44**	6M2	467.16	**467.16**	8M2	622.88	**622.88**	10M2	778.60	**778.60**
ROOF														
Flat roof construction 50 x 150 mm joists	M2	66.28	8M2	530.24		10M2	662.80		13M2	861.64		15M2	994.20	
Work to top of external wall	M	23.71	7M	165.97		8M	189.68		9M	213.39		10M	237.10	
Three layer felt roofing	M2	51.19	8M2	409.52		10M2	511.90		13M2	665.47		15M2	767.85	
Fascia and eaves soffit	M	48.01	8M	384.08		9M	432.09		10M	480.10		11M	528.11	
Gutters and fittings	M	18.68	3M	56.04		4M	74.72		5M	93.40		6M	112.08	
Flashings	M	24.70	3M	74.10		4M	98.80		5M	123.50		6M	148.20	
Abutment to existing wall	M	61.52	3M	184.56	**1804.51**	4M	246.08	**2216.07**	5M	307.60	**2745.10**	6M	369.12	**3156.66**
EXTERNAL WALLS														
Brick and block cavity wall	M2	114.25	27M2	3084.75	**3084.75**	32M2	3656.00	**3656.00**	37M2	4227.25	**4227.25**	42M2	4798.50	**4798.50**

Specification A
12 m2 - 18 m2

TWO STOREY

FLAT ROOF Continued/.....

Element	Unit	Unit Rate £	Ref A/2F 2x6 Size 2.00 x 6.00 m Area 12 m2 Qty	Total £	Element Total £	Ref A/2F 2x7 Size 2.00 x 7.00 m Area 14 m2 Qty	Total £	Element Total £	Ref A/2F 2x8 Size 2.00 x 8.00 m Area 16 m2 Qty	Total £	Element Total £	Ref A/2F 2x9 Size 2.00 x 9.00 m Area 18 m2 Qty	Total £	Element Total £
	M	144.41	11M	1588.51		12M	1732.92		13M	1877.33		14M	2021.74	
	M2	91.57	12M2	1098.84	**2687.35**	14M2	1281.98	**3014.90**	16M2	1465.12	**3342.45**	18M2	1648.26	**3670.00**
	M2	77.86	12M2	934.32	**934.32**	14M2	1090.04	**1090.04**	16M2	1245.76	**1245.76**	18M2	1401.48	**1401.48**
	M2	66.28	18M2	1193.04		20M2	1325.60		23M2	1524.44		25M2	1657.00	
	M	23.71	11M	260.81		12M	284.52		13M	308.23		14M	331.94	
	M2	51.19	18M2	921.42		20M2	1023.80		23M2	1177.37		25M2	1279.75	
	M	48.01	12M	576.12		13M	624.13		14M	672.14		15M	720.15	
	M	18.68	7M	130.76		8M	149.44		9M	168.12		10M	186.80	
	M	24.70	7M	172.90		8M	197.60		9M	222.30		10M	247.00	
	M	61.52	7M	430.64	**3685.69**	8M	492.16	**4097.25**	9M	553.68	**4626.28**	10M	615.20	**5037.84**
	M2	114.25	43M2	4912.75	**4912.75**	48M2	5484.00	**5484.00**	53M2	6055.25	**6055.25**	58M2	6626.50	**6626.50**

Specification A
4 m2 - 10 m2

TWO STOREY

FLAT ROOF

Element	Unit	Unit Rate £	Ref A/2F 2x2 Size 2.00 x 2.00 m Area 4 m2 Qty	Total £	Element Total £	Ref A/2F 2x3 Size 2.00 x 3.00 m Area 6 m2 Qty	Total £	Element Total £	Ref A/2F 2x4 Size 2.00 x 4.00 m Area 8 m2 Qty	Total £	Element Total £	Ref A/2F 2x5 Size 2.00 x 5.00 m Area 10 m2 Qty	Total £	Element Total £
EXTERNAL DOORS AND WINDOWS														
External door	NR	655.02	1NR	655.02		1NR	655.02		1NR	655.02		1NR	655.02	
Windows	NR	672.89	2NR	1345.78		2NR	1345.78		2NR	1345.78		2NR	1345.78	
Opening in cavity wall for door	NR	144.37	1NR	144.37		1NR	144.37		1NR	144.37		1NR	144.37	
Opening in cavity wall for window	NR	162.98	2NR	325.96	**2471.13**	2NR	325.96	**2471.13**	2NR	325.96	**2471.13**	2NR	325.96	**2471.13**
INTERNAL WALLS AND PARTITIONS														
Stud partitions	M2	51.63												
INTERNAL DOORS														
Hardwood flush door	NR	412.45												
WALL FINISHES														
Plaster & decoration	M2	19.58	40M2	783.20	**783.20**	50M2	979.00	**979.00**	60M2	1174.80	**1174.80**	70M2	1370.60	**1370.60**
FLOOR FINISHES														
Laminate	M2	30.30	4M2	121.20		6M2	181.80		8M2	242.40		10M2	303.00	
Hardwood skirting	M	19.52	16M	312.32	**433.52**	20M	390.40	**572.20**	24M	468.48	**710.88**	28M	546.56	**849.56**
CEILING FINISHES														
Plasterboard, plaster and decoration	M2	26.68	8M2	213.44	**213.44**	12M2	320.16	**320.16**	16M2	426.88	**426.88**	20M2	533.60	**533.60**

Specification A
12 m2 - 18 m2

TWO STOREY

FLAT ROOF Continued/.....

Element	Unit	Unit Rate £	Ref A/2F 2x6 Size 2.00 x 6.00 m Area 12 m2			Ref A/2F 2x7 Size 2.00 x 7.00 m Area 14 m2			Ref A/2F 2x8 Size 2.00 x 8.00 m Area 16 m2			Ref A/2F 2x9 Size 2.00 x 9.00 m Area 18 m2		
			Qty	Total £	Element Total £	Qty	Total £	Element Total £	Qty	Total £	Element Total £	Qty	Total £	Element Total £
	NR	655.02	1NR	655.02		1NR	655.02		1NR	655.02		1NR	655.02	
	NR	672.89	4NR	2691.56		4NR	2691.56		4NR	2691.56		4NR	2691.56	
	NR	144.37	1NR	144.37		1NR	144.37		1NR	144.37		1NR	144.37	
	NR	162.98	4NR	651.92	**4142.87**	4NR	651.92	**4142.87**	4NR	651.92	**4142.87**	4NR	651.92	**4142.87**
	M2	51.63	10M2	516.30	**516.30**	10M2	516.30	**516.30**	10M2	516.30	**516.30**	10M2	516.30	**516.30**
	NR	412.45	2NR	824.90	**824.90**	2NR	824.90	**824.90**	2NR	824.90	**824.90**	2NR	824.90	**824.90**
	M2	19.58	80M2	1566.40	**1566.40**	90M2	1762.20	**1762.20**	100M2	1958.00	**1958.00**	110M2	2153.80	**2153.80**
	M2	30.30	12M2	363.60		14M2	424.20		16M2	484.80		18M2	545.40	
	M	19.52	32M	624.64	**988.24**	36M	702.72	**1126.92**	40M	780.80	**1265.60**	44M	858.88	**1404.28**
	M2	26.68	24M2	640.32	**640.32**	28M2	747.04	**747.04**	32M2	853.76	**853.76**	36M2	960.48	**960.48**

Specification A 4 m2 - 10 m2

TWO STOREY

FLAT ROOF

Element	Unit	Unit Rate £	Ref A/2F 2x2 Size 2.00 x 2.00 m Area 4 m2 Qty	Total £	Element Total £	Ref A/2F 2x3 Size 2.00 x 3.00 m Area 6 m2 Qty	Total £	Element Total £	Ref A/2F 2x4 Size 2.00 x 4.00 m Area 8 m2 Qty	Total £	Element Total £	Ref A/2F 2x5 Size 2.00 x 5.00 m Area 10 m2 Qty	Total £	Element Total £
SERVICES														
Rainwater pipes	M	26.64	6M	159.84		6M	159.84		6M	159.84		6M	159.84	
Cold water service point	NR	110.52	1NR	110.52		1NR	110.52		1NR	110.52		1NR	110.52	
Hot water service point	NR	191.67	1NR	191.67		1NR	191.67		1NR	191.67		1NR	191.67	
Central heating service point	NR	386.51	2NR	773.02		2NR	773.02		2NR	773.02		2NR	773.02	
Electrical installation	NR	286.50	2NR	573.00	**1808.05**	2NR	573.00	**1808.05**	2NR	573.00	**1808.05**	2NR	573.00	**1808.05**
ALTERATIONS TO EXISTING BUILDINGS														
Opening in existing wall 1.80 m wide 2.00 m high	NR	689.44	2NR	1378.88	**1378.88**									
Opening in existing wall 2.40 m wide 2.00 m high	NR	865.59												
Opening in existing wall 3.00 m wide 2.00 m high	NR	921.26				2NR	1842.52	**1842.52**						
Opening in existing wall 4.00 m wide 2.00 m high	NR	1131.22							2NR	2262.44	**2262.44**			
Opening in existing wall 5.00 m wide 2.00 m high	NR	1341.19										2NR	2682.38	**2682.38**

Specification A
12 m2 - 18 m2

TWO STOREY

Element	Unit	Unit Rate £	Ref A/2F 2x6 Size 2.00 x 6.00 m Area 12 m2 Qty	Total £	Element Total £	Ref A/2F 2x7 Size 2.00 x 7.00 m Area 14 m2 Qty	Total £	Element Total £	Ref A/2F 2x8 Size 2.00 x 8.00 m Area 16 m2 Qty	Total £	Element Total £	Ref A/2F 2x9 Size 2.00 x 9.00 m Area 18 m2 Qty	Total £	Element Total £
	M	26.64	6M	159.84		6M	159.84		6M	159.84		6M	159.84	
	NR	110.52	1NR	110.52		1NR	110.52		1NR	110.52		1NR	110.52	
	NR	191.67	1NR	191.67		1NR	191.67		1NR	191.67		1NR	191.67	
	NR	386.51	4NR	1546.04		4NR	1546.04		4NR	1546.04		4NR	1546.04	
	NR	286.50	4NR	1146.00	**3154.07**	4NR	1146.00	**3154.07**	4NR	1146.00	**3154.07**	4NR	1146.00	**3154.07**
	NR	689.44												
	NR	865.59	4NR	3462.36	**3462.36**									
	NR	921.26				4NR	3685.04	**3685.04**	4NR	3685.04	**3685.04**			
	NR	1131.22										4NR	4524.88	**4524.88**
	NR	1341.19												

Specification A 4 m2 - 10 m2	Ref A/2F 2x2 Size 2.00 x 2.00 m Area 4 m2 Element Total £	Ref A/2F 2x3 Size 2.00 x 3.00 m Area 6 m2 Element Total £	Ref A/2F 2x4 Size 2.00 x 4.00 m Area 8 m2 Element Total £	Ref A/2F 2x5 Size 2.00 x 5.00 m Area 10 m2 Element Total £
TWO STOREY				
FLAT ROOF				
SUMMARY				
SUBSTRUCTURE	1377.15	1704.70	2032.25	2359.80
UPPER FLOORS	311.44	467.16	622.88	778.60
ROOF	1804.51	2216.07	2745.10	3156.66
EXTERNAL WALLS	3084.75	3656.00	4227.25	4798.50
EXTERNAL DOORS AND WINDOWS	2471.13	2471.13	2471.13	2471.13
INTERNAL WALLS AND PARTITIONS	-	-	-	-
INTERNAL DOORS	-	-	-	-
WALL FINISHES	783.20	979.00	1174.80	1370.60
FLOOR FINISHES	433.52	572.20	710.88	849.56
CEILING FINISHES	213.44	320.16	426.88	533.60
SERVICES	1808.05	1808.05	1808.05	1808.05
ALTERATIONS TO EXISTING BUILDINGS	1378.88	1842.52	2262.44	2682.38
Sub Total	13666.07	16036.99	18481.66	20808.88
Allowance for unmeasured items and sundries 5%	683.30	801.85	924.08	1040.44
NET TOTAL excluding Preliminaries, Profit and Overheads	**14349.37**	**16838.84**	**19405.74**	**21849.32**

Specification A 12 m2 - 18 m2	Ref A/2F 2x6 Size 2.00 x 6.00 m Area 12 m2	Ref A/2F 2x7 Size 2.00 x 7.00 m Area 14 m2	Ref A/2F 2x8 Size 2.00 x 8.00 m Area 16 m2	Ref A/2F 2x9 Size 2.00 x 9.00 m Area 18 m2
	Element Total £	Element Total £	Element Total £	Element Total £
TWO STOREY				
FLAT ROOF				
SUMMARY Continued/.....				
	2687.35	3014.90	3342.45	3670.00
	934.32	1090.04	1245.76	1401.48
	3685.69	4097.25	4626.28	5037.84
	4912.75	5484.00	6055.25	6626.50
	4142.87	4142.87	4142.87	4142.87
	516.30	516.30	516.30	516.30
	824.90	824.90	824.90	824.90
	1566.40	1762.20	1958.00	2153.80
	988.24	1126.92	1265.60	1404.28
	640.32	747.04	853.76	960.48
	3154.07	3154.07	3154.07	3154.07
	3462.36	3685.04	3685.04	4524.88
Sub Total	27515.57	29645.53	31670.28	34417.40
Allowance for unmeasured items and sundries 5%	1375.78	1482.28	1583.51	1720.87
NET TOTAL excluding Preliminaries, Profit and Overheads	**28891.35**	**31127.81**	**33253.79**	**36138.27**

Specification A 6 m2 - 15 m2

TWO STOREY

FLAT ROOF

Element	Unit	Unit Rate £	Ref A/2F 3x2 Size 3.00 x 2.00 m Area 6 m2 Qty	Total £	Element Total £	Ref A/2F 3x3 Size 3.00 x 3.00 m Area 9 m2 Qty	Total £	Element Total £	Ref A/2F 3x4 Size 3.00 x 4.00 m Area 12 m2 Qty	Total £	Element Total £	Ref A/2F 3x5 Size 3.00 x 5.00 m Area 15 m2 Qty	Total £	Element Total £
SUBSTRUCTURE														
Strip footings	M	144.41	9M	1299.69		10M	1444.10		11M	1588.51		12M	1732.92	
Hollow ground floor	M2	91.57	6M2	549.42	**1849.11**	9M2	824.13	**2268.23**	12M2	1098.84	**2687.35**	15M2	1373.55	**3106.47**
UPPER FLOORS														
Timber floor construction 50 x 150 mm joists	M2	77.86	6M2	467.16	**467.16**									
Timber floor construction 50 x 200 mm joists	M2	81.38				9M2	732.42	**732.42**	12M2	976.56	**976.56**	15M2	1220.70	**1220.70**
ROOF														
Flat roof construction 50 x 150 mm joists	M2	66.28	11M2	729.08		14M2	927.92		18M2	1193.04		21M2	1391.88	
Work to top of external wall	M	23.71	9M	213.39		10M	237.10		11M	260.81		12M	284.52	
Three layer felt roofing	M2	51.19	11M2	563.09		14M2	716.66		18M2	921.42		21M2	1074.99	
Fascia and eaves soffit	M	48.01	10M	480.10		11M	528.11		12M	576.12		13M	624.13	
Gutters and fittings	M	18.68	3M	56.04		4M	74.72		5M	93.40		6M	112.08	
Flashings	M	24.70	3M	74.10		4M	98.80		5M	123.50		6M	148.20	
Abutment to existing wall	M	61.52	3M	184.56	**2300.36**	4M	246.08	**2829.39**	5M	307.60	**3475.89**	6M	369.12	**4004.92**
EXTERNAL WALLS														
Brick and block cavity wall	M2	114.25	37M2	4227.25	**4227.25**	42M2	4798.50	**4798.50**	47M2	5369.75	**5369.75**	52M2	5941.00	**5941.00**

Specification A
18 m2 - 27 m2

TWO STOREY

FLAT ROOF Continued/.....

Element	Unit	Unit Rate £	Ref A/2F 3x6 Size 3.00 x 6.00 m Area 18 m2 Qty	Total £	Element Total £	Ref A/2F 3x7 Size 3.00 x 7.00 m Area 21 m2 Qty	Total £	Element Total £	Ref A/2F 3x8 Size 3.00 x 8.00 m Area 24 m2 Qty	Total £	Element Total £	Ref A/2F 3x9 Size 3.00 x 9.00 m Area 27 m2 Qty	Total £	Element Total £
	M	144.41	13M	1877.33		14M	2021.74		15M	2166.15		16M	2310.56	
	M2	91.57	18M2	1648.26	**3525.59**	21M2	1922.97	**3944.71**	24M2	2197.68	**4363.83**	27M2	2472.39	**4782.95**
	M2	77.86												
	M2	81.38	18M2	1464.84	**1464.84**	21M2	1708.98	**1708.98**	24M2	1953.12	**1953.12**	27M2	2197.26	**2197.26**
	M2	66.28	25M2	1657.00		28M2	1855.84		32M2	2120.96		35M2	2319.80	
	M	23.71	13M	308.23		14M	331.94		15M	355.65		16M	379.36	
	M2	51.19	25M2	1279.75		28M2	1433.32		32M2	1638.08		35M2	1791.65	
	M	48.01	14M	672.14		15M	720.15		16M	768.16		17M	816.17	
	M	18.68	7M	130.76		8M	149.44		9M	168.12		10M	186.80	
	M	24.70	7M	172.90		8M	197.60		9M	222.30		10M	247.00	
	M	61.52	7M	430.64	**4651.42**	8M	492.16	**5180.45**	9M	553.68	**5826.95**	10M	615.20	**6355.98**
	M2	114.25	53M2	6055.25	**6055.25**	55M2	6283.75	**6283.75**	63M2	7197.75	**7197.75**	68M2	7769.00	**7769.00**

Specification A
6 m2 - 15 m2

TWO STOREY

FLAT ROOF

Element	Unit	Unit Rate £	Ref A/2F 3x2 Size 3.00 x 2.00 m Area 6 m2 Qty	Total £	Element Total £	Ref A/2F 3x3 Size 3.00 x 3.00 m Area 9 m2 Qty	Total £	Element Total £
EXTERNAL DOORS AND WINDOWS								
External door	NR	655.02	1NR	655.02		1NR	655.02	
Windows	NR	672.89	2NR	1345.78		2NR	1345.78	
Opening in cavity wall for door	NR	144.37	1NR	144.37		1NR	144.37	
Opening in cavity wall for window	NR	162.98	2NR	325.96	**2471.13**	2NR	325.96	**2471.13**
INTERNAL WALLS AND PARTITIONS								
Stud partitions	M2	51.63						
INTERNAL DOORS								
Hardwood flush door	NR	412.45						
WALL FINISHES								
Plaster & decoration	M2	19.58	50M2	979.00	**979.00**	60M2	1174.80	**1174.80**
FLOOR FINISHES								
Laminate	M2	30.30	6M2	181.80		9M2	272.70	
Hardwood skirting	M	19.52	20M	390.40	**572.20**	24M	468.48	**741.18**
CEILING FINISHES								
Plasterboard, plaster and decoration	M2	26.68	12M2	320.16	**320.16**	18M2	480.24	**480.24**

Element	Ref A/2F 3x4 Size 3.00 x 4.00 m Area 12 m2 Qty	Total £	Element Total £	Ref A/2F 3x5 Size 3.00 x 5.00 m Area 15 m2 Qty	Total £	Element Total £
EXTERNAL DOORS AND WINDOWS						
External door	1NR	655.02		1NR	655.02	
Windows	2NR	1345.78		2NR	1345.78	
Opening in cavity wall for door	1NR	144.37		1NR	144.37	
Opening in cavity wall for window	2NR	325.96	**2471.13**	2NR	325.96	**2471.13**
INTERNAL WALLS AND PARTITIONS						
Stud partitions						
INTERNAL DOORS						
Hardwood flush door						
WALL FINISHES						
Plaster & decoration	70M2	1370.60	**1370.60**	80M2	1566.40	**1566.40**
FLOOR FINISHES						
Laminate	12M2	363.60		15M2	454.50	
Hardwood skirting	28M	546.56	**910.16**	32M	624.64	**1079.14**
CEILING FINISHES						
Plasterboard, plaster and decoration	24M2	640.32	**640.32**	30M2	800.40	**800.40**

Specification A
18 m2 - 27 m2

Element	Unit	Unit Rate £	Ref A/2F 3x6 Size 3.00 x 6.00 m Area 18 m2 Qty	Total £	Element Total £	Ref A/2F 3x7 Size 3.00 x 7.00 m Area 21 m2 Qty	Total £	Element Total £	Ref A/2F 3x8 Size 3.00 x 8.00 m Area 24 m2 Qty	Total £	Element Total £	Ref A/2F 3x9 Size 3.00 x 9.00 m Area 27 m2 Qty	Total £	Element Total £
TWO STOREY FLAT ROOF Continued/.....														
	NR	655.02	1NR	655.02		1NR	655.02		1NR	655.02		1NR	655.02	
	NR	672.89	4NR	2691.56		4NR	2691.56		4NR	2691.56		4NR	2691.56	
	NR	144.37	1NR	144.37		1NR	144.37		1NR	144.37		1NR	144.37	
	NR	162.98	4NR	651.92	**4142.87**	4NR	651.92	**4142.87**	4NR	651.92	**4142.87**	4NR	651.92	**4142.87**
	M2	51.63	16M2	826.08	**826.08**	16M2	826.08	**826.08**	16M2	826.08	**826.08**	16M2	826.08	**826.08**
	NR	412.45	2NR	824.90	**824.90**	2NR	824.90	**824.90**	2NR	824.90	**824.90**	2NR	824.90	**824.90**
	M2	19.58	90M2	1762.20	**1762.20**	100M2	1958.00	**1958.00**	110M2	2153.80	**2153.80**	120M2	2349.60	**2349.60**
	M2	30.30	18M2	545.40		21M2	636.30		24M2	727.20		27M2	818.10	
	M	19.52	36M	702.72	**1248.12**	40M	780.80	**1417.10**	44M	858.88	**1586.08**	48M	936.96	**1755.06**
	M2	26.68	36M2	960.48	**960.48**	42M2	1120.56	**1120.56**	48M2	1280.64	**1280.64**	54M2	1440.72	**1440.72**

Specification A 6 m2 - 15 m2

TWO STOREY FLAT ROOF			Ref A/2F 3x2 Size 3.00 x 2.00 m Area 6 m2			Ref A/2F 3x3 Size 3.00 x 3.00 m Area 9 m2			Ref A/2F 3x4 Size 3.00 x 4.00 m Area 12 m2			Ref A/2F 3x5 Size 3.00 x 5.00 m Area 15 m2		
Element	Unit	Unit Rate £	Qty	Total £	Element Total £	Qty	Total £	Element Total £	Qty	Total £	Element Total £	Qty	Total £	Element Total £
SERVICES														
Rainwater pipes	M	26.64	6M	159.84		6M	159.84		6M	159.84		6M	159.84	
Cold water service point	NR	110.52	1NR	110.52		1NR	110.52		1NR	110.52		1NR	110.52	
Hot water service point	NR	191.67	1NR	191.67		1NR	191.67		1NR	191.67		1NR	191.67	
Central heating service point	NR	386.51	2NR	773.02		2NR	773.02		2NR	773.02		2NR	773.02	
Electrical installation	NR	286.50	2NR	573.00	**1808.05**	2NR	573.00	**1808.05**	2NR	573.00	**1808.05**	2NR	573.00	**1808.05**
ALTERATIONS TO EXISTING BUILDINGS														
Opening in existing wall 1.80 m wide 2.00 m high	NR	689.44	2NR	1378.88	**1378.88**									
Opening in existing wall 2.40 m wide 2.00 m high	NR	865.59												
Opening in existing wall 3.00 m wide 2.00 m high	NR	921.26				2NR	1842.52	**1842.52**						
Opening in existing wall 4.00 m wide 2.00 m high	NR	1131.22							2NR	2262.44	**2262.44**			
Opening in existing wall 5.00 m wide 2.00 m high	NR	1341.19										2NR	2682.38	**2682.38**

Specification A 18 m2 - 27 m2			Ref A/2F 3x6 Size 3.00 x 6.00 m Area 18 m2			Ref A/2F 3x7 Size 3.00 x 7.00 m Area 21 m2			Ref A/2F 3x8 Size 3.00 x 8.00 m Area 24 m2			Ref A/2F 3x9 Size 3.00 x 9.00 m Area 27 m2		
TWO STOREY FLAT ROOF Continued/.....			Qty	Total £	Element Total £	Qty	Total £	Element Total £	Qty	Total £	Element Total £	Qty	Total £	Element Total £
Element	Unit	Unit Rate £												
	M	26.64	6M	159.84		6M	159.84		6M	159.84		6M	159.84	
	NR	110.52	1NR	110.52		1NR	110.52		1NR	110.52		1NR	110.52	
	NR	191.67	1NR	191.67		1NR	191.67		1NR	191.67		1NR	191.67	
	NR	386.51	4NR	1546.04		4NR	1546.04		4NR	1546.04		4NR	1546.04	
	NR	286.50	4NR	1146.00	**3154.07**	4NR	1146.00	**3154.07**	4NR	1146.00	**3154.07**	4NR	1146.00	**3154.07**
	NR	689.44												
	NR	865.59	4NR	3462.36	**3462.36**									
	NR	921.26				4NR	3685.04	**3685.04**	4NR	3685.04	**3685.04**			
	NR	1131.22										4NR	4524.88	**4524.88**
	NR	1341.19												

Specification A 6 m2 - 15 m2	Ref A/2F 3x2 Size 3.00 x 2.00 m Area 6 m2 Element Total £	Ref A/2F 3x3 Size 3.00 x 3.00 m Area 9 m2 Element Total £	Ref A/2F 3x4 Size 3.00 x 4.00 m Area 12 m2 Element Total £	Ref A/2F 3x5 Size 3.00 x 5.00 m Area 15 m2 Element Total £
TWO STOREY				
FLAT ROOF				
SUMMARY				
SUBSTRUCTURE	1849.11	2268.23	2687.35	3106.47
UPPER FLOORS	467.16	732.42	976.56	1220.70
ROOF	2300.36	2829.39	3475.89	4004.92
EXTERNAL WALLS	4227.25	4798.50	5369.75	5941.00
EXTERNAL DOORS AND WINDOWS	2471.13	2471.13	2471.13	2471.13
INTERNAL WALLS AND PARTITIONS	-	-	-	-
INTERNAL DOORS	-	-	-	-
WALL FINISHES	979.00	1174.80	1370.60	1566.40
FLOOR FINISHES	572.20	741.18	910.16	1079.14
CEILING FINISHES	320.16	480.24	640.32	800.40
SERVICES	1808.05	1808.05	1808.05	1808.05
ALTERATIONS TO EXISTING BUILDINGS	1378.88	1842.52	2262.44	2682.38
Sub Total	16373.30	19146.46	21972.25	24680.59
Allowance for unmeasured items and sundries 5%	818.67	957.32	1098.61	1234.03
NET TOTAL excluding Preliminaries, Profit and Overheads	**17191.97**	**20103.78**	**23070.86**	**25914.62**

Specification A 18 m2 - 27 m2	Ref A/2F 3x6 Size 3.00 x 6.00 m Area 18 m2 Element Total £	Ref A/2F 3x7 Size 3.00 x 7.00 m Area 21 m2 Element Total £	Ref A/2F 3x8 Size 3.00 x 8.00 m Area 24 m2 Element Total £	Ref A/2F 3x9 Size 3.00 x 9.00 m Area 27 m2 Element Total £
TWO STOREY				
FLAT ROOF				
SUMMARY Continued/.....				
	3525.59	3944.71	4363.83	4782.95
	1464.84	1708.98	1953.12	2197.26
	4651.42	5180.45	5826.95	6355.98
	6055.25	6283.75	7197.75	7769.00
	4142.87	4142.87	4142.87	4142.87
	826.08	826.08	826.08	826.08
	824.90	824.90	824.90	824.90
	1762.20	1958.00	2153.80	2349.60
	1248.12	1417.10	1586.08	1755.06
	960.48	1120.56	1280.64	1440.72
	3154.07	3154.07	3154.07	3154.07
	3462.36	3685.04	3685.04	4524.88
Sub Total	32078.18	34246.51	36995.13	40123.37
Allowance for unmeasured items and sundries 5%	1603.91	1712.33	1849.76	2006.17
NET TOTAL excluding Preliminaries, Profit and Overheads	**33682.09**	**35958.84**	**38844.89**	**42129.54**

Specification A 8 m2 - 20 m2

TWO STOREY

FLAT ROOF

Element	Unit	Unit Rate £	Ref A/2F 4x2 Size 4.00 x 2.00 m Area 8 m2 Qty	Total £	Element Total £	Ref A/2F 4x3 Size 4.00 x 3.00 m Area 12 m2 Qty	Total £	Element Total £	Ref A/2F 4x4 Size 4.00 x 4.00 m Area 16 m2 Qty	Total £	Element Total £	Ref A/2F 4x5 Size 4.00 x 5.00 m Area 20 m2 Qty	Total £	Element Total £
SUBSTRUCTURE														
Strip footings	M	144.41	11M	1588.51		12M	1732.92		13M	1877.33		14M	2021.74	
Hollow ground floor	M2	91.57	8M2	732.56	**2321.07**	12M2	1098.84	**2831.76**	16M2	1465.12	**3342.45**	20M2	1831.40	**3853.14**
UPPER FLOORS														
Timber floor construction 50 x 150 mm joists	M2	77.86	8M2	622.88	**622.88**									
Timber floor construction 50 x 200 mm joists	M2	81.38				12M2	976.56	**976.56**	16M2	1302.08	**1302.08**	20M2	1627.60	**1627.60**
ROOF														
Flat roof construction 50 x 150 mm joists	M2	66.28	14M2	927.92		18M2	1193.04							
Flat roof construction 50 x 200 mm joists	M2	68.48							23M2	1575.04		27M2	1848.96	
Work to top of external wall	M	23.71	11M	260.81		12M	284.52		13M	308.23		14M	331.94	
Three layer felt roofing	M2	51.19	14M2	716.66		18M2	921.42		23M2	1177.37		27M2	1382.13	
Fascia and eaves soffit	M	48.01	12M	576.12		13M	624.13		14M	672.14		15M	720.15	
Gutters and fittings	M	18.68	3M	56.04		4M	74.72		5M	93.40		6M	112.08	
Flashings	M	24.70	3M	74.10		4M	98.80		5M	123.50		6M	148.20	
Abutment to existing wall	M	61.52	3M	184.56	**2796.21**	4M	246.08	**3442.71**	5M	307.60	**4257.28**	6M	369.12	**4912.58**

Specification A
24 m2 - 36 m2

TWO STOREY

FLAT ROOF Continued/.....

Element	Unit	Unit Rate £	Ref A/2F 4x6 Size 4.00 x 6.00 m Area 24 m2 Qty	Total £	Element Total £	Ref A/2F 4x7 Size 4.00 x 7.00 m Area 28 m2 Qty	Total £	Element Total £	Ref A/2F 4x8 Size 4.00 x 8.00 m Area 32 m2 Qty	Total £	Element Total £	Ref A/2F 4x9 Size 4.00 x 9.00 m Area 36 m2 Qty	Total £	Element Total £
	M	144.41	15M	2166.15		16M	2310.56		17M	2454.97		18M	2599.38	
	M2	91.57	24M2	2197.68	**4363.83**	28M2	2563.96	**4874.52**	32M2	2930.24	**5385.21**	36M2	3296.52	**5895.90**
	M2	77.86												
	M2	81.38	24M2	1953.12	**1953.12**	28M2	2278.64	**2278.64**	32M2	2604.16	**2604.16**	36M2	2929.68	**2929.68**
	M2	66.28	32M2	2120.96		36M2	2386.08							
	M2	68.48							41M2	2807.68		45M2	3081.60	
	M	23.71	15M	355.65		16M	379.36		17M	403.07		18M	426.78	
	M2	51.19	32M2	1638.08		36M2	1842.84		41M2	2098.79		45M2	2303.55	
	M	48.01	16M	768.16		17M	816.17		18M	864.18		19M	912.19	
	M	18.68	7M	130.76		8M	149.44		9M	168.12		10M	186.80	
	M	24.70	7M	172.90		8M	197.60		9M	222.30		10M	247.00	
	M	61.52	7M	430.64	**5617.15**	8M	492.16	**6263.65**	9M	553.68	**7117.82**	10M	615.20	**7773.12**

Specification A 8 m2 - 20 m2

TWO STOREY

FLAT ROOF

Element	Unit	Unit Rate £	Ref A/2F 4x2 Size 4.00 x 2.00 m Area 8 m2 Qty	Total £	Element Total £	Ref A/2F 4x3 Size 4.00 x 3.00 m Area 12 m2 Qty	Total £	Element Total £	Ref A/2F 4x4 Size 4.00 x 4.00 m Area 16 m2 Qty	Total £	Element Total £	Ref A/2F 4x5 Size 4.00 x 5.00 m Area 20 m2 Qty	Total £	Element Total £
EXTERNAL WALLS														
Brick and block cavity wall	M2	114.25	47M2	5369.75	**5369.75**	52M2	5941.00	**5941.00**	57M2	6512.25	**6512.25**	59M2	6740.75	**6740.75**
EXTERNAL DOORS AND WINDOWS														
External door	NR	655.02	1NR	655.02		1NR	655.02		1NR	655.02		1NR	655.02	
Windows	NR	672.89	2NR	1345.78		2NR	1345.78		2NR	1345.78		2NR	1345.78	
Opening in cavity wall for door	NR	144.37	1NR	144.37		1NR	144.37		1NR	144.37		1NR	144.37	
Opening in cavity wall for window	NR	162.98	2NR	325.96	**2471.13**	2NR	325.96	**2471.13**	2NR	325.96	**2471.13**	2NR	325.96	**2471.13**
INTERNAL WALLS AND PARTITIONS														
Stud partitions	M2	51.63												
INTERNAL DOORS														
Hardwood flush door	NR	412.45												
WALL FINISHES														
Plaster & decoration	M2	19.58	60M2	1174.80	**1174.80**	70M2	1370.60	**1370.60**	80M2	1566.40	**1566.40**	90M2	1762.20	**1762.20**
FLOOR FINISHES														
Laminate	M2	30.30	8M2	242.40		12M2	363.60		16M2	484.80		20M2	606.00	
Hardwood skirting	M	19.52	24M	468.48	**710.88**	28M	546.56	**910.16**	32M	624.64	**1109.44**	36M	702.72	**1308.72**

Specification A
24 m2 - 36 m2

TWO STOREY

FLAT ROOF Continued/.....

Element	Unit	Unit Rate £	Ref A/2F 4x6 Size 4.00 x 6.00 m Area 24 m2			Ref A/2F 4x7 Size 4.00 x 7.00 m Area 28 m2			Ref A/2F 4x8 Size 4.00 x 8.00 m Area 32 m2			Ref A/2F 4x9 Size 4.00 x 9.00 m Area 36 m2		
			Qty	Total £	Element Total £	Qty	Total £	Element Total £	Qty	Total £	Element Total £	Qty	Total £	Element Total £
	M2	114.25	63M2	7197.75	**7197.75**	68M2	7769.00	**7769.00**	73M2	8340.25	**8340.25**	78M2	8911.50	**8911.50**
	NR	655.02	1NR	655.02		1NR	655.02		1NR	655.02		1NR	655.02	
	NR	672.89	4NR	2691.56		4NR	2691.56		4NR	2691.56		4NR	2691.56	
	NR	144.37	1NR	144.37		1NR	144.37		1NR	144.37		1NR	144.37	
	NR	162.98	4NR	651.92	**4142.87**	4NR	651.92	**4142.87**	4NR	651.92	**4142.87**	4NR	651.92	**4142.87**
	M2	51.63	20M2	1032.60	**1032.60**	20M2	1032.60	**1032.60**	20M2	1032.60	**1032.60**	20M2	1032.60	**1032.60**
	NR	412.45	2NR	824.90	**824.90**	2NR	824.90	**824.90**	2NR	824.90	**824.90**	2NR	824.90	**824.90**
	M2	19.58	100M2	1958.00	**1958.00**	110M2	2153.80	**2153.80**	120M2	2349.60	**2349.60**	130M2	2545.40	**2545.40**
	M2	30.30	24M2	727.20		28M2	848.40		32M2	969.60		36M2	1090.80	
	M	19.52	40M	780.80	**1508.00**	44M	858.88	**1707.28**	48M	936.96	**1906.56**	52M	1015.04	**2105.84**

Specification A 8 m2 - 20 m2			Ref A/2F 4x2 Size 4.00 x 2.00 m Area 8 m2			Ref A/2F 4x3 Size 4.00 x 3.00 m Area 12 m2			Ref A/2F 4x4 Size 4.00 x 4.00 m Area 16 m2			Ref A/2F 4x5 Size 4.00 x 5.00 m Area 20 m2		
TWO STOREY FLAT ROOF			Qty	Total £	Element Total £	Qty	Total £	Element Total £	Qty	Total £	Element Total £	Qty	Total £	Element Total £
Element	Unit	Unit Rate £												
CEILING FINISHES														
Plasterboard, plaster and decoration	M2	26.68	16M2	426.88	**426.88**	24M2	640.32	**640.32**	32M2	853.76	**853.76**	40M2	1067.20	**1067.20**
SERVICES														
Rainwater pipes	M	26.64	6M	159.84		6M	159.84		6M	159.84		6M	159.84	
Cold water service point	NR	110.52	1NR	110.52		1NR	110.52		1NR	110.52		1NR	110.52	
Hot water service point	NR	191.67	1NR	191.67		1NR	191.67		1NR	191.67		1NR	191.67	
Central heating service point	NR	386.51	2NR	773.02		2NR	773.02		2NR	773.02		2NR	773.02	
Electrical installation	NR	286.50	2NR	573.00	**1808.05**	2NR	573.00	**1808.05**	2NR	573.00	**1808.05**	2NR	573.00	**1808.05**
ALTERATIONS TO EXISTING BUILDINGS														
Opening in existing wall 1.80 m wide 2.00 m high	NR	689.44	2NR	1378.88	**1378.88**									
Opening in existing wall 2.40 m wide 2.00 m high	NR	865.59												
Opening in existing wall 3.00 m wide 2.00 m high	NR	921.26				2NR	1842.52	**1842.52**						
Opening in existing wall 4.00 m wide 2.00 m high	NR	1131.22							2NR	2262.44	**2262.44**			
Opening in existing wall 5.00 m wide 2.00 m high	NR	1341.19										2NR	2682.38	**2682.38**

Specification A 24 m2 - 36 m2

TWO STOREY

FLAT ROOF Continued/.....

Element	Unit	Unit Rate £	Ref A/2F 4x6 Size 4.00 x 6.00 m Area 24 m2 Qty	Total £	Element Total £	Ref A/2F 4x7 Size 4.00 x 7.00 m Area 28 m2 Qty	Total £	Element Total £	Ref A/2F 4x8 Size 4.00 x 8.00 m Area 32 m2 Qty	Total £	Element Total £	Ref A/2F 4x9 Size 4.00 x 9.00 m Area 36 m2 Qty	Total £	Element Total £
	M2	26.68	48M2	1280.64	**1280.64**	56M2	1494.08	**1494.08**	64M2	1707.52	**1707.52**	72M2	1920.96	**1920.96**
	M	26.64	6M	159.84		6M	159.84		6M	159.84		6M	159.84	
	NR	110.52	1NR	110.52		1NR	110.52		1NR	110.52		1NR	110.52	
	NR	191.67	1NR	191.67		1NR	191.67		1NR	191.67		1NR	191.67	
	NR	386.51	4NR	1546.04		4NR	1546.04		4NR	1546.04		4NR	1546.04	
	NR	286.50	4NR	1146.00	**3154.07**	4NR	1146.00	**3154.07**	4NR	1146.00	**3154.07**	4NR	1146.00	**3154.07**
	NR	689.44												
	NR	865.59	4NR	3462.36	**3462.36**									
	NR	921.26				4NR	3685.04	**3685.04**	4NR	3685.04	**3685.04**			
	NR	1131.22										4NR	4524.88	**4524.88**
	NR	1341.19												

Specification A 8 m2 - 20 m2	Ref A/2F 4x2 Size 4.00 x 2.00 m Area 8 m2 Element Total £	Ref A/2F 4x3 Size 4.00 x 3.00 m Area 12 m2 Element Total £	Ref A/2F 4x4 Size 4.00 x 4.00 m Area 16 m2 Element Total £	Ref A/2F 4x5 Size 4.00 x 5.00 m Area 20 m2 Element Total £
TWO STOREY				
FLAT ROOF				
SUMMARY				
SUBSTRUCTURE	2321.07	2831.76	3342.45	3853.14
UPPER FLOORS	622.88	976.56	1302.08	1627.60
ROOF	2796.21	3442.71	4257.28	4912.58
EXTERNAL WALLS	5369.75	5941.00	6512.25	6740.75
EXTERNAL DOORS AND WINDOWS	2471.13	2471.13	2471.13	2471.13
INTERNAL WALLS AND PARTITIONS	-	-	-	-
INTERNAL DOORS	-	-	-	-
WALL FINISHES	1174.80	1370.60	1566.40	1762.20
FLOOR FINISHES	710.88	910.16	1109.44	1308.72
CEILING FINISHES	426.88	640.32	853.76	1067.20
SERVICES	1808.05	1808.05	1808.05	1808.05
ALTERATIONS TO EXISTING BUILDINGS	1378.88	1842.52	2262.44	2682.38
Sub Total	19080.53	22234.81	25485.28	28233.75
Allowance for unmeasured items and sundries 5%	954.03	1111.74	1274.26	1411.69
NET TOTAL excluding Preliminaries, Profit and Overheads	**20034.56**	**23346.55**	**26759.54**	**29645.44**

Specification A 24 m2 - 36 m2	Ref A/2F 4x6 Size 4.00 x 6.00 m Area 24 m2	Ref A/2F 4x7 Size 4.00 x 7.00 m Area 28 m2	Ref A/2F 4x8 Size 4.00 x 8.00 m Area 32 m2	Ref A/2F 4x9 Size 4.00 x 9.00 m Area 36 m2
	Element Total £	Element Total £	Element Total £	Element Total £
TWO STOREY				
FLAT ROOF				
SUMMARY Continued/.....				
	4363.83	4874.52	5385.21	5895.90
	1953.12	2278.64	2604.16	2929.68
	5617.15	6263.65	7117.82	7773.12
	7197.75	7769.00	8340.25	8911.50
	4142.87	4142.87	4142.87	4142.87
	1032.60	1032.60	1032.60	1032.60
	824.90	824.90	824.90	824.90
	1958.00	2153.80	2349.60	2545.40
	1508.00	1707.28	1906.56	2105.84
	1280.64	1494.08	1707.52	1920.96
	3154.07	3154.07	3154.07	3154.07
	3462.36	3685.04	3685.04	4524.88
Sub Total	36495.29	39380.45	42250.60	45761.72
Allowance for unmeasured items and sundries 5%	1824.76	1969.02	2112.53	2288.09
NET TOTAL excluding Preliminaries, Profit and Overheads	**38320.05**	**41349.47**	**44363.13**	**48049.81**

Specification A 10 m2 - 25 m2

TWO STOREY

FLAT ROOF

Element	Unit	Unit Rate £	Ref A/2F 5x2 Size 5.00 x 2.00 m Area 10 m2 Qty	Total £	Element Total £	Ref A/2F 5x3 Size 5.00 x 3.00 m Area 15 m2 Qty	Total £	Element Total £	Ref A/2F 5x4 Size 5.00 x 4.00 m Area 20 m2 Qty	Total £	Element Total £	Ref A/2F 5x5 Size 5.00 x 5.00 m Area 25 m2 Qty	Total £	Element Total £
SUBSTRUCTURE														
Strip footings	M	144.41	13M	1877.33		14M	2021.74		15M	2166.15		16M	2310.56	
Hollow ground floor	M2	91.57	10M2	915.70	**2793.03**	15M2	1373.55	**3395.29**	20M2	1831.40	**3997.55**	25M2	2289.25	**4599.81**
UPPER FLOORS														
Timber floor construction 50 x 150 mm joists	M2	77.86	10M2	778.60	**778.60**									
Timber floor construction 50 x 200 mm joists	M2	81.38				15M2	1220.70	**1220.70**	20M2	1627.60	**1627.60**			
Timber floor construction75 x 250 mm joists	M2	103.03										25M2	2575.75	**2575.75**
ROOF														
Flat roof construction 50 x 150 mm joists	M2	66.28	17M2	1126.76		22M2	1458.16							
Flat roof construction 50 x 200 mm joists	M2	68.48							28M2	1917.44		33M2	2259.84	
Work to top of external wall	M	23.71	13M	308.23		14M	331.94		15M	355.65		16M	379.36	
Three layer felt roofing	M2	51.19	17M2	870.23		22M2	1126.18		28M2	1433.32		33M2	1689.27	
Fascia and eaves soffit	M	48.01	14M	672.14		15M	720.15		16M	768.16		17M	816.17	
Gutters and fittings	M	18.68	3M	56.04		4M	74.72		5M	93.40		6M	112.08	
Flashings	M	24.70	3M	74.10		4M	98.80		5M	123.50		6M	148.20	
Abutment to existing wall	M	61.52	3M	184.56	**3292.06**	4M	246.08	**4056.03**	5M	307.60	**4999.07**	6M	369.12	**5774.04**

Specification A 30 m2 - 45 m2

TWO STOREY

FLAT ROOF Continued/.....

Element	Unit	Unit Rate £	Ref A/2F 5x6 Size 5.00 x 6.00 m Area 30 m2			Ref A/2F 5x7 Size 5.00 x 7.00 m Area 35 m2			Ref A/2F 5x8 Size 5.00 x 8.00 m Area 40 m2			Ref A/2F 5x9 Size 5.00 x 9.00 m Area 45 m2		
			Qty	Total £	Element Total £	Qty	Total £	Element Total £	Qty	Total £	Element Total £	Qty	Total £	Element Total £
	M	144.41	17M	2454.97		18M	2599.38		19M	2743.79		20M	2888.20	
	M2	91.57	30M2	2747.10	**5202.07**	35M2	3204.95	**5804.33**	40M2	3662.80	**6406.59**	45M2	4120.65	**7008.85**
	M2	77.86												
	M2	81.38	30M2	2441.40	**2441.40**	35M2	2848.30	**2848.30**	40M2	3255.20	**3255.20**			
	M2	103.03										45M2	4636.35	**4636.35**
	M2	66.28	39M2	2584.92		44M2	2916.32							
	M2	68.48							50M2	3424.00		55M2	3766.40	
	M	23.71	17M	403.07		18M	426.78		19M	450.49		20M	474.20	
	M2	51.19	39M2	1996.41		44M2	2252.36		50M2	2559.50		55M2	2815.45	
	M	48.01	18M	864.18		19M	912.19		20M	960.20		21M	1008.21	
	M	18.68	7M	130.76		8M	149.44		9M	168.12		10M	186.80	
	M	24.70	7M	172.90		8M	197.60		9M	222.30		10M	247.00	
	M	61.52	7M	430.64	**6582.88**	8M	492.16	**7346.85**	9M	553.68	**8338.29**	10M	615.20	**9113.26**

Specification A
10 m2 - 25 m2

TWO STOREY

FLAT ROOF

Element	Unit	Unit Rate £	Ref A/2F 5x2 Size 5.00 x 2.00 m Area 10 m2 Qty	Total £	Element Total £	Ref A/2F 5x3 Size 5.00 x 3.00 m Area 15 m2 Qty	Total £	Element Total £	Ref A/2F 5x4 Size 5.00 x 4.00 m Area 20 m2 Qty	Total £	Element Total £	Ref A/2F 5x5 Size 5.00 x 5.00 m Area 25 m2 Qty	Total £	Element Total £
EXTERNAL WALLS														
Brick and block cavity wall	M2	114.25	57M2	6512.25	**6512.25**	62M2	7083.50	**7083.50**	67M2	7654.75	**7654.75**	72M2	8226.00	**8226.00**
EXTERNAL DOORS AND WINDOWS														
External door	NR	655.02	1NR	655.02		1NR	655.02		1NR	655.02		1NR	655.02	
Windows	NR	672.89	2NR	1345.78		2NR	1345.78		2NR	1345.78		2NR	1345.78	
Opening in cavity wall for door	NR	144.37	1NR	144.37		1NR	144.37		1NR	144.37		1NR	144.37	
Opening in cavity wall for window	NR	162.98	2NR	325.96	**2471.13**	2NR	325.96	**2471.13**	2NR	325.96	**2471.13**	2NR	325.96	**2471.13**
INTERNAL WALLS AND PARTITIONS														
Stud partitions	M2	51.63												
INTERNAL DOORS														
Hardwood flush door	NR	412.45												
WALL FINISHES														
Plaster & decoration	M2	19.58	70M2	1370.60	**1370.60**	80M2	1566.40	**1566.40**	90M2	1762.20	**1762.20**	100M2	1958.00	**1958.00**

Specification A 30 m2 - 45 m2

TWO STOREY

FLAT ROOF Continued/.....

Element	Unit	Unit Rate £	Ref A/2F 5x6 Size 5.00 x 6.00 m Area 30 m2 Qty	Total £	Element Total £	Ref A/2F 5x7 Size 5.00 x 7.00 m Area 35 m2 Qty	Total £	Element Total £	Ref A/2F 5x8 Size 5.00 x 8.00 m Area 40 m2 Qty	Total £	Element Total £	Ref A/2F 5x9 Size 5.00 x 9.00 m Area 45 m2 Qty	Total £	Element Total £
	M2	114.25	73M2	8340.25	**8340.25**	78M2	8911.50	**8911.50**	83M2	9482.75	**9482.75**	88M2	10054.00	**10054.00**
	NR	655.02	1NR	655.02		1NR	655.02		1NR	655.02		1NR	655.02	
	NR	672.89	4NR	2691.56		4NR	2691.56		4NR	2691.56		4NR	2691.56	
	NR	144.37	1NR	144.37		1NR	144.37		1NR	144.37		1NR	144.37	
	NR	162.98	4NR	651.92	**4142.87**	4NR	651.92	**4142.87**	4NR	651.92	**4142.87**	4NR	651.92	**4142.87**
	M2	51.63	26M2	1342.38	**1342.38**	26M2	1342.38	**1342.38**	26M2	1342.38	**1342.38**	26M2	1342.38	**1342.38**
	NR	412.45	2NR	824.90	**824.90**	2NR	824.90	**824.90**	2NR	824.90	**824.90**	2NR	824.90	**824.90**
	M2	19.58	110M2	2153.80	**2153.80**	120M2	2349.60	**2349.60**	130M2	2545.40	**2545.40**	140M2	2741.20	**2741.20**

Specification A 10 m2 - 25 m2			Ref A/2F 5x2 Size 5.00 x 2.00 m Area 10 m2			Ref A/2F 5x3 Size 5.00 x 3.00 m Area 15 m2			Ref A/2F 5x4 Size 5.00 x 4.00 m Area 20 m2			Ref A/2F 5x5 Size 5.00 x 5.00 m Area 25 m2		
			Qty	Total £	Element Total £	Qty	Total £	Element Total £	Qty	Total £	Element Total £	Qty	Total £	Element Total £
TWO STOREY														
FLAT ROOF														
Element	Unit	Unit Rate £												
FLOOR FINISHES														
Laminate	M2	30.30	10M2	303.00		15M2	454.50		20M2	606.00		25M2	757.50	
Hardwood skirting	M	19.52	28M	546.56	**849.56**	32M	624.64	**1079.14**	36M	702.72	**1308.72**	40M	780.80	**1538.30**
CEILING FINISHES														
Plasterboard, plaster and decoration	M2	26.68	20M2	533.60	**533.60**	30M2	800.40	**800.40**	40M2	1067.20	**1067.20**	50M2	1334.00	**1334.00**
SERVICES														
Rainwater pipes	M	26.64	6M	159.84		6M	159.84		6M	159.84		6M	159.84	
Cold water service point	NR	110.52	1NR	110.52		1NR	110.52		1NR	110.52		1NR	110.52	
Hot water service point	NR	191.67	1NR	191.67		1NR	191.67		1NR	191.67		1NR	191.67	
Central heating service point	NR	386.51	2NR	773.02		2NR	773.02		2NR	773.02		2NR	773.02	
Electrical installation	NR	286.50	2NR	573.00	**1808.05**	2NR	573.00	**1808.05**	2NR	573.00	**1808.05**	2NR	573.00	**1808.05**

Specification A 30 m2 - 45 m2

TWO STOREY

FLAT ROOF Continued/.....

Element	Unit	Unit Rate £	Ref A/2F 5x6 Size 5.00 x 6.00 m Area 30 m2 Qty	Total £	Element Total £	Ref A/2F 5x7 Size 5.00 x 7.00 m Area 35 m2 Qty	Total £	Element Total £	Ref A/2F 5x8 Size 5.00 x 8.00 m Area 40 m2 Qty	Total £	Element Total £	Ref A/2F 5x9 Size 5.00 x 9.00 m Area 45 m2 Qty	Total £	Element Total £
	M2	30.30	30M2	909.00		35M2	1060.50		40M2	1212.00		45M2	1363.50	
	M	19.52	44M	858.88	**1767.88**	48M	936.96	**1997.46**	52M	1015.04	**2227.04**	56M	1093.12	**2456.62**
	M2	26.68	60M2	1600.80	**1600.80**	70M2	1867.60	**1867.60**	80M2	2134.40	**2134.40**	90M2	2401.20	**2401.20**
	M	26.64	6M	159.84		6M	159.84		6M	159.84		6M	159.84	
	NR	110.52	1NR	110.52		1NR	110.52		1NR	110.52		1NR	110.52	
	NR	191.67	1NR	191.67		1NR	191.67		1NR	191.67		1NR	191.67	
	NR	386.51	4NR	1546.04		4NR	1546.04		4NR	1546.04		4NR	1546.04	
	NR	286.50	4NR	1146.00	**3154.07**	4NR	1146.00	**3154.07**	4NR	1146.00	**3154.07**	4NR	1146.00	**3154.07**

Specification A
10 m2 - 25 m2

TWO STOREY

FLAT ROOF

Element	Unit	Unit Rate £	Ref A/2F 5x2 Size 5.00 x 2.00 m Area 10 m2 Qty	Total £	Element Total £	Ref A/2F 5x3 Size 5.00 x 3.00 m Area 15 m2 Qty	Total £	Element Total £	Ref A/2F 5x4 Size 5.00 x 4.00 m Area 20 m2 Qty	Total £	Element Total £	Ref A/2F 5x5 Size 5.00 x 5.00 m Area 25 m2 Qty	Total £	Element Total £
ALTERATIONS TO EXISTING BUILDINGS														
Opening in existing wall 1.80 m wide 2.00 m high	NR	689.44	2NR	1378.88	**1378.88**									
Opening in existing wall 2.40 m wide 2.00 m high	NR	865.59												
Opening in existing wall 3.00 m wide 2.00 m high	NR	921.26				2NR	1842.52	**1842.52**						
Opening in existing wall 4.00 m wide 2.00 m high	NR	1131.22							2NR	2262.44	**2262.44**			
Opening in existing wall 5.00 m wide 2.00 m high	NR	1341.19										2NR	2682.38	**2682.38**

Specification A 30 m2 - 45 m2			**Ref A/2F 5x6 Size 5.00 x 6.00 m Area 30 m2**			**Ref A/2F 5x7 Size 5.00 x 7.00 m Area 35 m2**			**Ref A/2F 5x8 Size 5.00 x 8.00 m Area 40 m2**			**Ref A/2F 5x9 Size 5.00 x 9.00 m Area 45 m2**		
			Qty	**Total £**	**Element Total £**	**Qty**	**Total £**	**Element Total £**	**Qty**	**Total £**	**Element Total £**	**Qty**	**Total £**	**Element Total £**
TWO STOREY FLAT ROOF Continued/.....														
Element	Unit	Unit Rate £												
	NR	689.44												
	NR	865.59	4NR	3462.36	**3462.36**									
	NR	921.26				4NR	3685.04	**3685.04**	4NR	3685.04	**3685.04**			
	NR	1131.22										4NR	4524.88	**4524.88**
	NR	1341.19												

Specification A 10 m2 - 25 m2	Ref A/2F 5x2 Size 5.00 x 2.00 m Area 10 m2 Element Total £	Ref A/2F 5x3 Size 5.00 x 3.00 m Area 15 m2 Element Total £	Ref A/2F 5x4 Size 5.00 x 4.00 m Area 20 m2 Element Total £	Ref A/2F 5x5 Size 5.00 x 5.00 m Area 25 m2 Element Total £
TWO STOREY				
FLAT ROOF				
SUMMARY				
SUBSTRUCTURE	2793.03	3395.29	3997.55	4599.81
UPPER FLOORS	778.60	1220.70	1627.60	2575.75
ROOF	3292.06	4056.03	4999.07	5774.04
EXTERNAL WALLS	6512.25	7083.50	7654.75	8226.00
EXTERNAL DOORS AND WINDOWS	2471.13	2471.13	2471.13	2471.13
INTERNAL WALLS AND PARTITIONS	-	-	-	-
INTERNAL DOORS	-	-	-	-
WALL FINISHES	1370.60	1566.40	1762.20	1958.00
FLOOR FINISHES	849.56	1079.14	1308.72	1538.30
CEILING FINISHES	533.60	800.40	1067.20	1334.00
SERVICES	1808.05	1808.05	1808.05	1808.05
ALTERATIONS TO EXISTING BUILDINGS	1378.88	1842.52	2262.44	2682.38
Sub Total	21787.76	25323.16	28958.71	32967.46
Allowance for unmeasured items and sundries 5%	1089.39	1266.16	1447.94	1648.37
NET TOTAL excluding Preliminaries, Profit and Overheads	**22877.15**	**26589.32**	**30406.65**	**34615.83**

Specification A 30 m2 - 45 m2

	Ref A/2F 5x6 Size 5.00 x 6.00 m Area 30 m2			Ref A/2F 5x7 Size 5.00 x 7.00 m Area 35 m2			Ref A/2F 5x8 Size 5.00 x 8.00 m Area 40 m2			Ref A/2F 5x9 Size 5.00 x 9.00 m Area 45 m2		
	Qty	Total £	Element Total £	Qty	Total £	Element Total £	Qty	Total £	Element Total £	Qty	Total £	Element Total £
TWO STOREY												
FLAT ROOF												
SUMMARY Continued/.....												
			5202.07			5804.33			6406.59			7008.85
			2441.40			2848.30			3255.20			4636.35
			6582.88			7346.85			8338.29			9113.26
			8340.25			8911.50			9482.75			10054.00
			4142.87			4142.87			4142.87			4142.87
			1342.38			1342.38			1342.38			1342.38
			824.90			824.90			824.90			824.90
			2153.80			2349.60			2545.40			2741.20
			1767.88			1997.46			2227.04			2456.62
			1600.80			1867.60			2134.40			2401.20
			3154.07			3154.07			3154.07			3154.07
			3462.36			3685.04			3685.04			4524.88
Sub Total			41015.66			44274.90			47538.93			52400.58
Allowance for unmeasured items and sundries 5%			2050.78			2213.75			2376.95			2620.03
NET TOTAL excluding Preliminaries, Profit and Overheads			**43066.44**			**46488.65**			**49915.88**			**55020.61**

Specification A

Two storey pitch roof

[2P] 2×2/3/4/5.

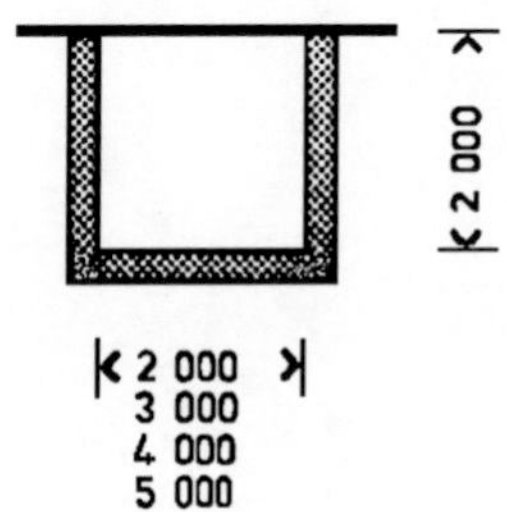

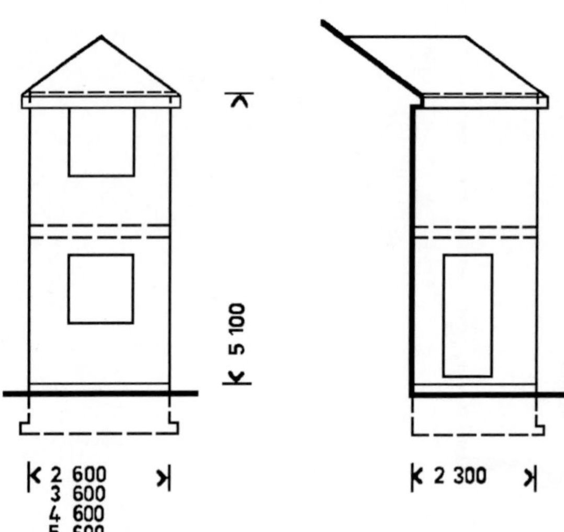

[2P] 2×6/7/8/9.

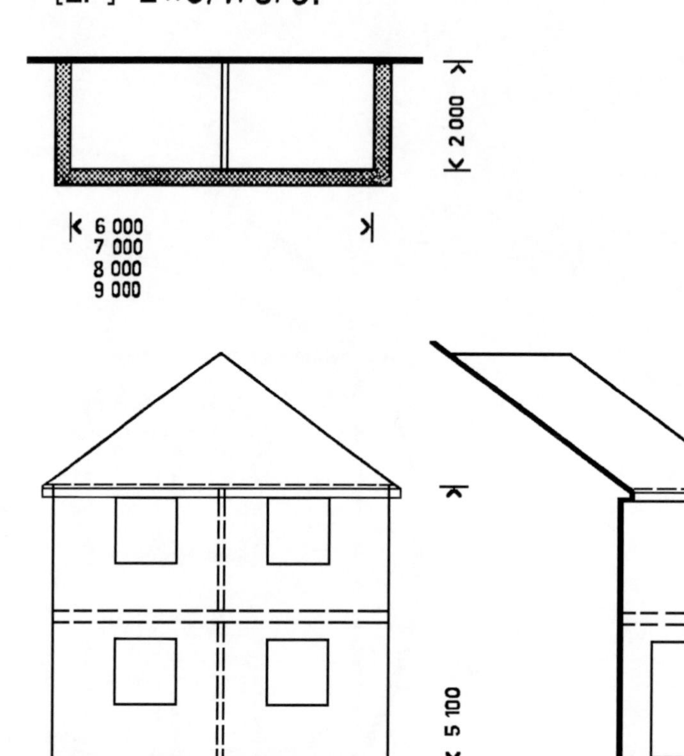

6 600
7 600
8 600
9 600

2 300

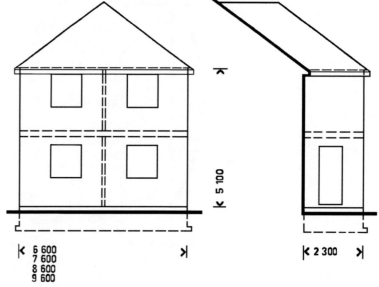

[2P] 3 × 2/3/4/5.

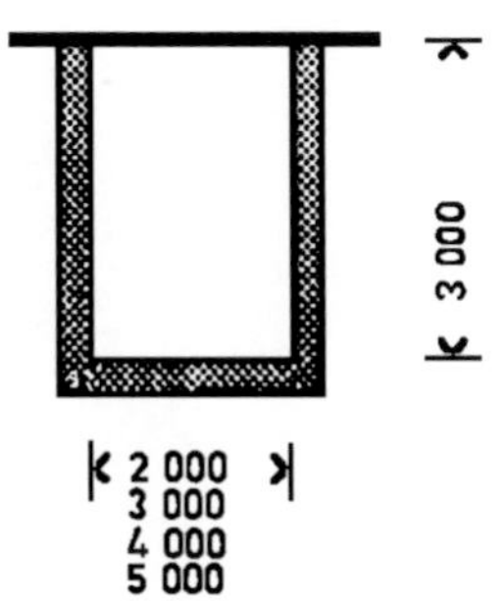

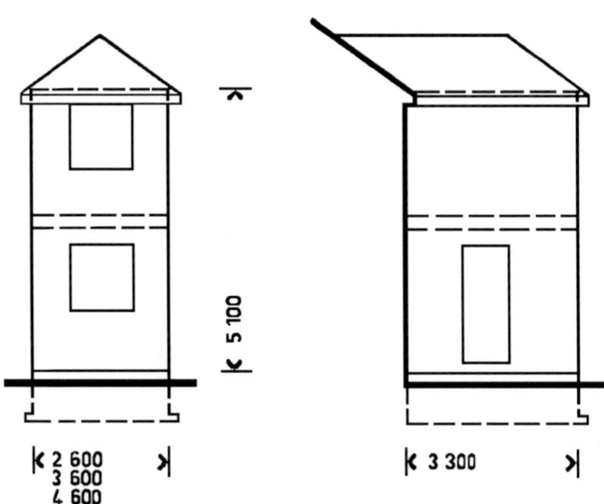

[2P] 3 × 6/7/8/9.

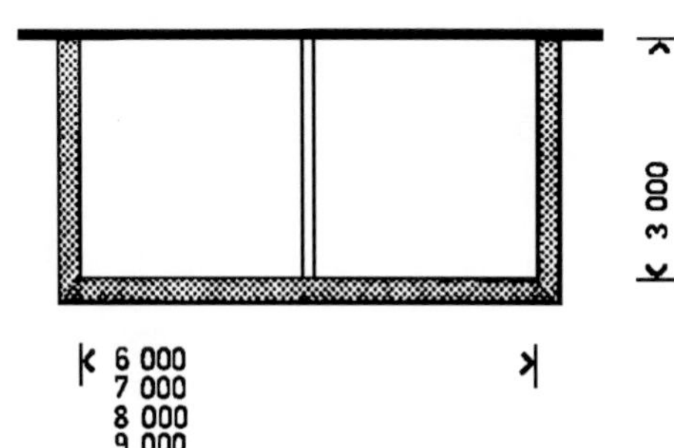

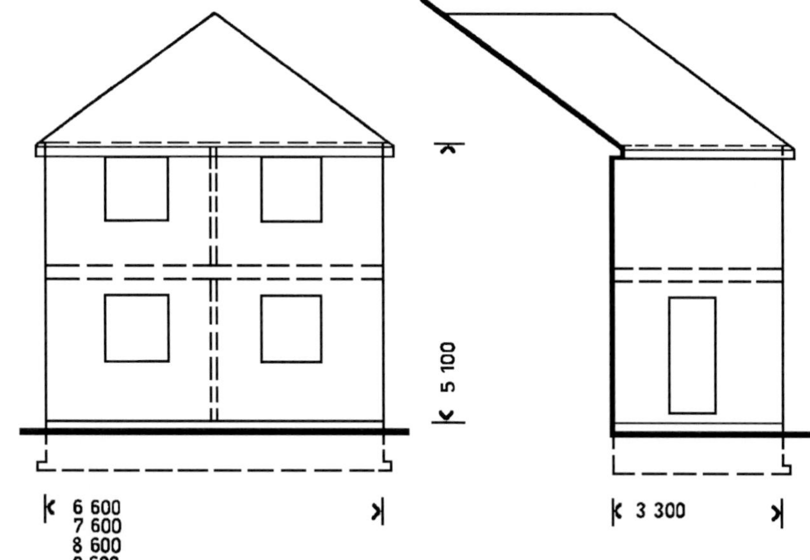

[2P] 4×2/3/4/5.

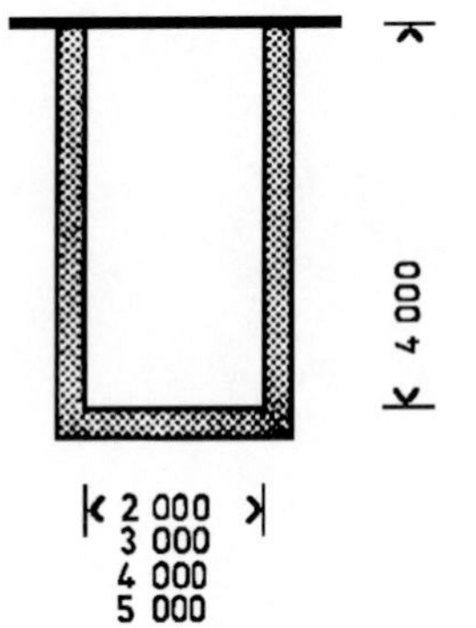

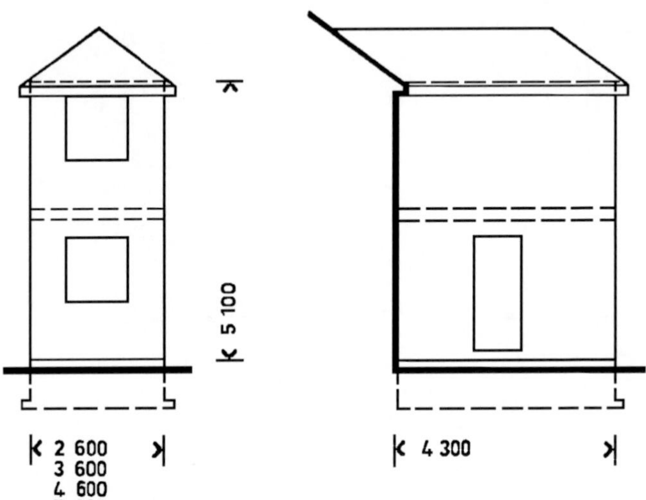

[2P] 4×6/7/8/9.

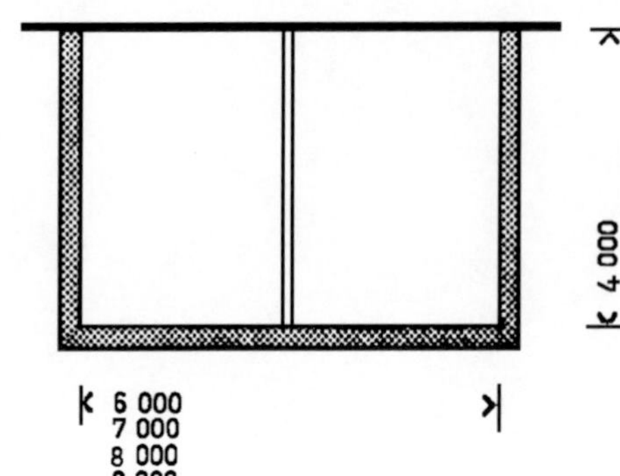

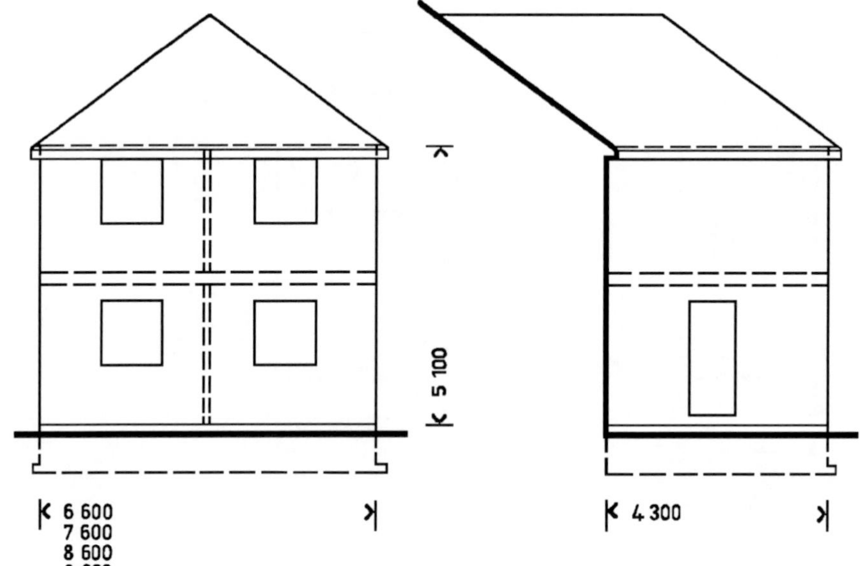

[2P] 5 × 2/3/4/5.

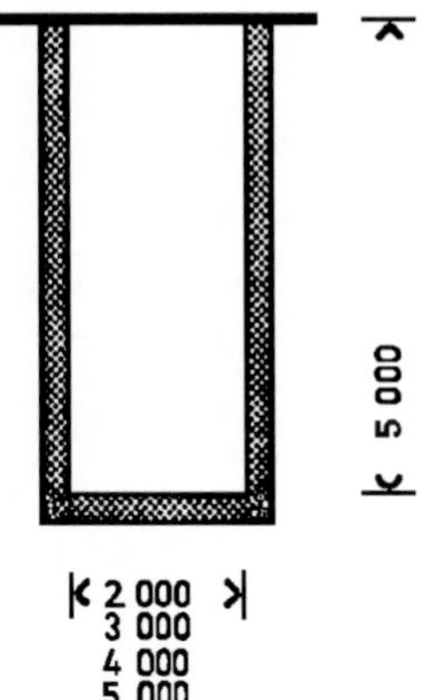

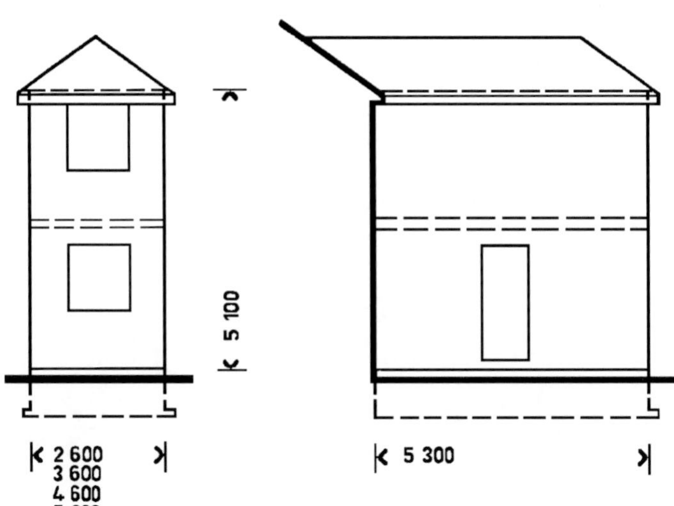

[2P] 5 × 6/7/8/9.

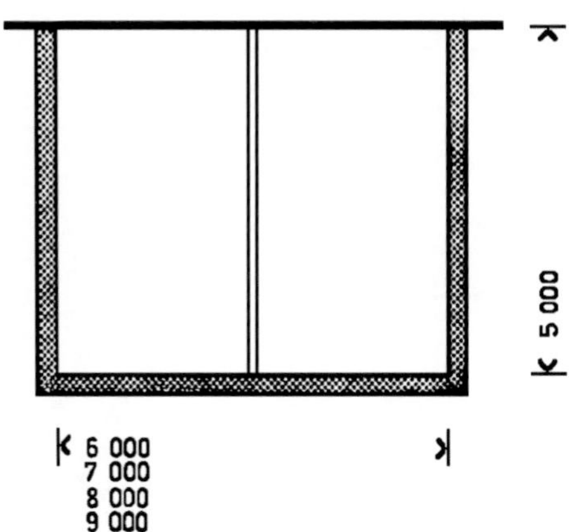

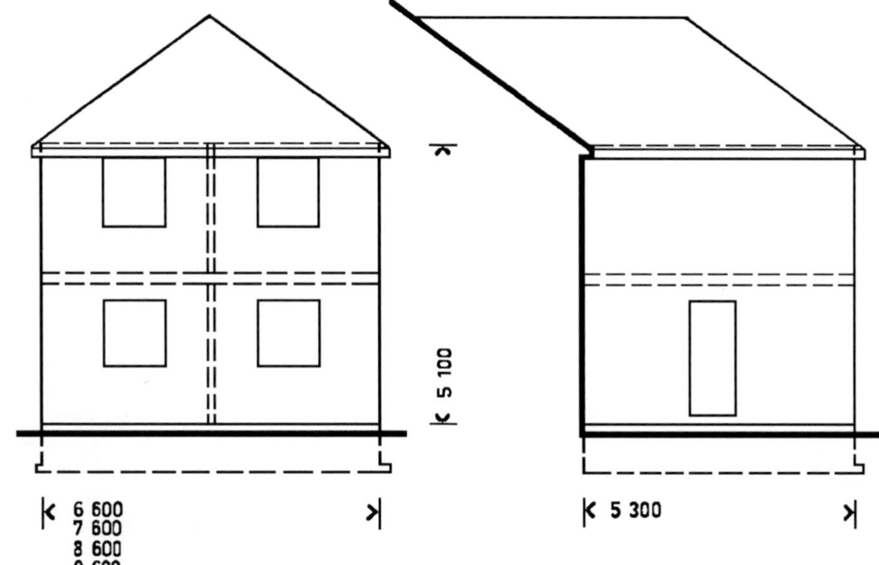

Specification A
4 m2 - 10 m2

TWO STOREY

PITCHED ROOF

Element	Unit	Unit Rate £	Ref A/2P 2x2 Size 2.00 x 2.00 m Area 4 m2 Qty	Total £	Element Total £	Ref A/2P 2x3 Size 2.00 x 3.00 m Area 6 m2 Qty	Total £	Element Total £	Ref A/2P 2x4 Size 2.00 x 4.00 m Area 8 m2 Qty	Total £	Element Total £	Ref A/2P 2x5 Size 2.00 x 5.00 m Area 10 m2 Qty	Total £	Element Total £
SUBSTRUCTURE														
Strip footings	M	144.41	7M	1010.87		8M	1155.28		9M	1299.69		10M	1444.10	
Hollow ground floor	M2	91.57	4M2	366.28	**1377.15**	6M2	549.42	**1704.70**	8M2	732.56	**2032.25**	10M2	915.70	**2359.80**
UPPER FLOORS														
Timber floor construction 50 x 150 mm joists	M2	77.86	4M2	311.44	**311.44**	6M2	467.16	**467.16**	8M2	622.88	**622.88**	10M2	778.60	**778.60**
ROOF														
Pitched roof construction	M2	55.42	10M2	554.20		14M2	775.88		19M2	1052.98		24M2	1330.08	
Work to top of external wall	M	23.71	7M	165.97		8M	189.68		9M	213.39		10M	237.10	
Plain tile roofing	M2	69.30	12M2	831.60		17M2	1178.10		23M2	1593.90		29M2	2009.70	
Work to hip	M	41.73	7M	292.11		9M	375.57		11M	459.03		11M	459.03	
Work to eaves	M	22.73	8M	181.84		9M	204.57		10M	227.30		11M	250.03	
Fascia and eaves soffit	M	48.01	8M	384.08		9M	432.09		10M	480.10		11M	528.11	
Gutters and fittings	M	18.68	8M	149.44	**2559.24**	9M	168.12	**3324.01**	10M	186.80	**4213.50**	11M	205.48	**5019.53**
EXTERNAL WALLS														
Brick and block cavity wall	M2	114.25	27M2	3084.75	**3084.75**	32M2	3656.00	**3656.00**	37M2	4227.25	**4227.25**	42M2	4798.50	**4798.50**

Specification A
12 m2 - 18 m2

TWO STOREY PITCHED ROOF Continued/.....			Ref A/2P 2x6 Size 2.00 x 6.00 m Area 12 m2			Ref A/2P 2x7 Size 2.00 x 7.00 m Area 14 m2			Ref A/2P 2x8 Size 2.00 x 8.00 m Area 16 m2			Ref A/2P 2x9 Size 2.00 x 9.00 m Area 18 m2		
Element	Unit	Unit Rate £	Qty	Total £	Element Total £	Qty	Total £	Element Total £	Qty	Total £	Element Total £	Qty	Total £	Element Total £
	M	144.41	11M	1588.51		12M	1732.92		13M	1877.33		14M	2021.74	
	M2	91.57	12M2	1098.84	**2687.35**	14M2	1281.98	**3014.90**	16M2	1465.12	**3342.45**	18M2	1648.26	**3670.00**
	M2	77.86	12M2	934.32	**934.32**	14M2	1090.04	**1090.04**	16M2	1245.76	**1245.76**	18M2	1401.48	**1401.48**
	M2	55.42	30M2	1662.60		36M2	1995.12		43M2	2383.06		50M2	2771.00	
	M	23.71	11M	260.81		12M	284.52		13M	308.23		14M	331.94	
	M2	69.30	37M2	2564.10		45M2	3118.50		53M2	3672.90		62M2	4296.60	
	M	41.73	13M	542.49		15M	625.95		16M	667.68		19M	792.87	
	M	22.73	12M	272.76		13M	295.49		14M	318.22		15M	340.95	
	M	48.01	12M	576.12		13M	624.13		14M	672.14		15M	720.15	
	M	18.68	12M	224.16	**6103.04**	13M	242.84	**7186.55**	14M	261.52	**8283.75**	15M	280.20	**9533.71**
	M2	114.25	43M2	4912.75	**4912.75**	48M2	5484.00	**5484.00**	53M2	6055.25	**6055.25**	58M2	6626.50	**6626.50**

Specification A
4 m2 - 10 m2

			Ref A/2P 2x2 Size 2.00 x 2.00 m Area 4 m2			Ref A/2P 2x3 Size 2.00 x 3.00 m Area 6 m2			Ref A/2P 2x4 Size 2.00 x 4.00 m Area 8 m2			Ref A/2P 2x5 Size 2.00 x 5.00 m Area 10 m2		
			Qty	Total £	Element Total £	Qty	Total £	Element Total £	Qty	Total £	Element Total £	Qty	Total £	Element Total £
TWO STOREY														
PITCHED ROOF														
Element	Unit	Unit Rate £												
EXTERNAL DOORS AND WINDOWS														
External door	NR	655.02	1NR	655.02		1NR	655.02		1NR	655.02		1NR	655.02	
Windows	NR	672.89	2NR	1345.78		2NR	1345.78		2NR	1345.78		2NR	1345.78	
Opening in cavity wall for door	NR	144.37	1NR	144.37		1NR	144.37		1NR	144.37		1NR	144.37	
Opening in cavity wall for window	NR	162.98	2NR	325.96	**2471.13**	2NR	325.96	**2471.13**	2NR	325.96	**2471.13**	2NR	325.96	**2471.13**
INTERNAL WALLS AND PARTITIONS														
Stud partitions	M2	51.63												
INTERNAL DOORS														
Hardwood flush door	NR	412.45												
WALL FINISHES														
Plaster & decoration	M2	19.58	40M2	783.20	**783.20**	50M2	979.00	**979.00**	60M2	1174.80	**1174.80**	70M2	1370.60	**1370.60**
FLOOR FINISHES														
Laminate	M2	30.30	4M2	121.20		6M2	181.80		8M2	242.40		10M2	303.00	
Hardwood skirting	M	19.52	16M	312.32	**433.52**	20M	390.40	**572.20**	24M	468.48	**710.88**	28M	546.56	**849.56**
CEILING FINISHES														
Plasterboard, plaster and decoration	M2	26.68	8M2	213.44	**213.44**	12M2	320.16	**320.16**	16M2	426.88	**426.88**	20M2	533.60	**533.60**

Specification A 12 m2 - 18 m2

TWO STOREY

PITCHED ROOF Continued/.....

Element	Unit	Unit Rate £	Ref A/2P 2x6 Size 2.00 x 6.00 m Area 12 m2			Ref A/2P 2x7 Size 2.00 x 7.00 m Area 14 m2			Ref A/2P 2x8 Size 2.00 x 8.00 m Area 16 m2			Ref A/2P 2x9 Size 2.00 x 9.00 m Area 18 m2		
			Qty	Total £	Element Total £	Qty	Total £	Element Total £	Qty	Total £	Element Total £	Qty	Total £	Element Total £
	NR	655.02	1NR	655.02		1NR	655.02		1NR	655.02		1NR	655.02	
	NR	672.89	4NR	2691.56		4NR	2691.56		4NR	2691.56		4NR	2691.56	
	NR	144.37	1NR	144.37		1NR	144.37		1NR	144.37		1NR	144.37	
	NR	162.98	4NR	651.92	**4142.87**	4NR	651.92	**4142.87**	4NR	651.92	**4142.87**	4NR	651.92	**4142.87**
	M2	51.63	10M2	516.30	**516.30**	10M2	516.30	**516.30**	10M2	516.30	**516.30**	10M2	516.30	**516.30**
	NR	412.45	2NR	824.90	**824.90**	2NR	824.90	**824.90**	2NR	824.90	**824.90**	2NR	824.90	**824.90**
	M2	19.58	80M2	1566.40	**1566.40**	90M2	1762.20	**1762.20**	100M2	1958.00	**1958.00**	110M2	2153.80	**2153.80**
	M2	30.30	12M2	363.60		14M2	424.20		16M2	484.80		18M2	545.40	
	M	19.52	32M	624.64	**988.24**	36M	702.72	**1126.92**	40M	780.80	**1265.60**	44M	858.88	**1404.28**
	M2	26.68	24M2	640.32	**640.32**	28M2	747.04	**747.04**	32M2	853.76	**853.76**	36M2	960.48	**960.48**

Specification A 4 m2 - 10 m2

			Ref A/2P 2x2 Size 2.00 x 2.00 m Area 4 m2			Ref A/2P 2x3 Size 2.00 x 3.00 m Area 6 m2			Ref A/2P 2x4 Size 2.00 x 4.00 m Area 8 m2			Ref A/2P 2x5 Size 2.00 x 5.00 m Area 10 m2		
TWO STOREY PITCHED ROOF			Qty	Total £	Element Total £	Qty	Total £	Element Total £	Qty	Total £	Element Total £	Qty	Total £	Element Total £
Element	Unit	Unit Rate £												
SERVICES														
Rainwater pipes	M	26.64	6M	159.84		6M	159.84		6M	159.84		6M	159.84	
Cold water service point	NR	110.52	1NR	110.52		1NR	110.52		1NR	110.52		1NR	110.52	
Hot water service point	NR	191.67	1NR	191.67		1NR	191.67		1NR	191.67		1NR	191.67	
Central heating service point	NR	386.51	2NR	773.02		2NR	773.02		2NR	773.02		2NR	773.02	
Electrical installation	NR	286.50	2NR	573.00	**1808.05**	2NR	573.00	**1808.05**	2NR	573.00	**1808.05**	2NR	573.00	**1808.05**
ALTERATIONS TO EXISTING BUILDINGS														
Opening in existing wall 1.80 m wide 2.00 m high	NR	689.44	2NR	1378.88	**1378.88**									
Opening in existing wall 2.40 m wide 2.00 m high	NR	865.59												
Opening in existing wall 3.00 m wide 2.00 m high	NR	921.26				2NR	1842.52	**1842.52**						
Opening in existing wall 4.00 m wide 2.00 m high	NR	1131.22							2NR	2262.44	**2262.44**			
Opening in existing wall 5.00 m wide 2.00 m high	NR	1341.19										2NR	2682.38	**2682.38**

Specification A 12 m2 - 18 m2

TWO STOREY

PITCHED ROOF Continued/.....

Element	Unit	Unit Rate £	Ref A/2P 2x6 Size 2.00 x 6.00 m Area 12 m2 Qty	Total £	Element Total £	Ref A/2P 2x7 Size 2.00 x 7.00 m Area 14 m2 Qty	Total £	Element Total £	Ref A/2P 2x8 Size 2.00 x 8.00 m Area 16 m2 Qty	Total £	Element Total £	Ref A/2P 2x9 Size 2.00 x 9.00 m Area 18 m2 Qty	Total £	Element Total £
	M	26.64	6M	159.84		6M	159.84		6M	159.84		6M	159.84	
	NR	110.52	1NR	110.52		1NR	110.52		1NR	110.52		1NR	110.52	
	NR	191.67	1NR	191.67		1NR	191.67		1NR	191.67		1NR	191.67	
	NR	386.51	4NR	1546.04		4NR	1546.04		4NR	1546.04		4NR	1546.04	
	NR	286.50	4NR	1146.00	**3154.07**	4NR	1146.00	**3154.07**	4NR	1146.00	**3154.07**	4NR	1146.00	**3154.07**
	NR	689.44												
	NR	865.59	4NR	3462.36	**3462.36**									
	NR	921.26				4NR	3685.04	**3685.04**	4NR	3685.04	**3685.04**			
	NR	1131.22										4NR	4524.88	**4524.88**
	NR	1341.19												

Specification A 4 m2 - 10 m2	Ref A/2P 2x2 Size 2.00 x 2.00 m Area 4 m2 Element Total £	Ref A/2P 2x3 Size 2.00 x 3.00 m Area 6 m2 Element Total £	Ref A/2P 2x4 Size 2.00 x 4.00 m Area 8 m2 Element Total £	Ref A/2P 2x5 Size 2.00 x 5.00 m Area 10 m2 Element Total £
TWO STOREY				
PITCHED ROOF				
SUMMARY				
SUBSTRUCTURE	1377.15	1704.70	2032.25	2359.80
UPPER FLOORS	311.44	467.16	622.88	778.60
ROOF	2559.24	3324.01	4213.50	5019.53
EXTERNAL WALLS	3084.75	3656.00	4227.25	4798.50
EXTERNAL DOORS AND WINDOWS	2471.13	2471.13	2471.13	2471.13
INTERNAL WALLS AND PARTITIONS	-	-	-	-
INTERNAL DOORS	-	-	-	-
WALL FINISHES	783.20	979.00	1174.80	1370.60
FLOOR FINISHES	433.52	572.20	710.88	849.56
CEILING FINISHES	213.44	320.16	426.88	533.60
SERVICES	1808.05	1808.05	1808.05	1808.05
ALTERATIONS TO EXISTING BUILDINGS	1378.88	1842.52	2262.44	2682.38
Sub Total	14420.80	17144.93	19950.06	22671.75
Allowance for unmeasured items and sundries 5%	721.04	857.25	997.50	1133.59
NET TOTAL excluding Preliminaries, Profit and Overheads	**15141.84**	**18002.18**	**20947.56**	**23805.34**

Specification A 12 m2 - 18 m2	Ref A/2P 2x6 Size 2.00 x 6.00 m Area 12 m2 Element Total £	Ref A/2P 2x7 Size 2.00 x 7.00 m Area 14 m2 Element Total £	Ref A/2P 2x8 Size 2.00 x 8.00 m Area 16 m2 Element Total £	Ref A/2P 2x9 Size 2.00 x 9.00 m Area 18 m2 Element Total £
TWO STOREY				
PITCHED ROOF				
SUMMARY Continued/.....				
	2687.35	3014.90	3342.45	3670.00
	934.32	1090.04	1245.76	1401.48
	6103.04	7186.55	8283.75	9533.71
	4912.75	5484.00	6055.25	6626.50
	4142.87	4142.87	4142.87	4142.87
	516.30	516.30	516.30	516.30
	824.90	824.90	824.90	824.90
	1566.40	1762.20	1958.00	2153.80
	988.24	1126.92	1265.60	1404.28
	640.32	747.04	853.76	960.48
	3154.07	3154.07	3154.07	3154.07
	3462.36	3685.04	3685.04	4524.88
Sub Total	29932.92	32734.83	35327.75	38913.27
Allowance for unmeasured items and sundries 5%	1496.65	1636.74	1766.39	1945.66
NET TOTAL excluding Preliminaries, Profit and Overheads	**31429.57**	**34371.57**	**37094.14**	**40858.93**

Specification A 6 m2 - 15 m2

TWO STOREY

PITCHED ROOF

Element	Unit	Unit Rate £	Ref A/2P 3x2 Size 3.00 x 2.00 m Area 6 m2 Qty	Total £	Element Total £	Ref A/2P 3x3 Size 3.00 x 3.00 m Area 9 m2 Qty	Total £	Element Total £	Ref A/2P 3x4 Size 3.00 x 4.00 m Area 12 m2 Qty	Total £	Element Total £	Ref A/2P 3x5 Size 3.00 x 5.00 m Area 15 m2 Qty	Total £	Element Total £
SUBSTRUCTURE														
Strip footings	M	144.41	9M	1299.69		10M	1444.10		11M	1588.51		12M	1732.92	
Hollow ground floor	M2	91.57	6M2	549.42	**1849.11**	9M2	824.13	**2268.23**	12M2	1098.84	**2687.35**	15M2	1373.55	**3106.47**
UPPER FLOORS														
Timber floor construction 50 x 150 mm joists	M2	77.86	6M2	467.16	**467.16**									
Timber floor construction 50 x 200 mm joists	M2	81.38				9M2	732.42	**732.42**	12M2	976.56	**976.56**	15M2	1220.70	**1220.70**
ROOF														
Pitched roof construction	M2	55.42	13M2	720.46		18M2	997.56		24M2	1330.08		30M2	1662.60	
Work to top of external wall	M	23.71	9M	213.39		10M	237.10		11M	260.81		12M	284.52	
Plain tile roofing	M2	69.30	16M2	1108.80		22M2	1524.60		30M2	2079.00		37M2	2564.10	
Work to hip	M	41.73	9M	375.57		10M	417.30		11M	459.03		13M	542.49	
Work to eaves	M	22.73	10M	227.30		11M	250.03		12M	272.76		13M	295.49	
Fascia and eaves soffit	M	48.01	10M	480.10		11M	528.11		12M	576.12		13M	624.13	
Gutters and fittings	M	18.68	10M	186.80	**3312.42**	11M	205.48	**4160.18**	12M	224.16	**5201.96**	13M	242.84	**6216.17**
EXTERNAL WALLS														
Brick and block cavity wall	M2	114.25	37M2	4227.25	**4227.25**	42M2	4798.50	**4798.50**	47M2	5369.75	**5369.75**	52M2	5941.00	**5941.00**

Specification A
18 m2 - 27 m2

TWO STOREY

PITCHED ROOF Continued/.....

Element	Unit	Unit Rate £	Ref A/2P 3x6 Size 3.00 x 6.00 m Area 18 m2 Qty	Total £	Element Total £	Ref A/2P 3x7 Size 3.00 x 7.00 m Area 21 m2 Qty	Total £	Element Total £	Ref A/2P 3x8 Size 3.00 x 8.00 m Area 24 m2 Qty	Total £	Element Total £	Ref A/2P 3x9 Size 3.00 x 9.00 m Area 27 m2 Qty	Total £	Element Total £
	M	144.41	13M	1877.33		14M	2021.74		15M	2166.15		16M	2310.56	
	M2	91.57	18M2	1648.26	**3525.59**	21M2	1922.97	**3944.71**	24M2	2197.68	**4363.83**	27M2	2472.39	**4782.95**
	M2	77.86												
	M2	81.38	18M2	1464.84	**1464.84**	21M2	1708.98	**1708.98**	24M2	1953.12	**1953.12**	27M2	2197.26	**2197.26**
	M2	55.42	37M2	2050.54		44M2	2438.48		52M2	2881.84		60M2	3325.20	
	M	23.71	13M	308.23		14M	331.94		15M	355.65		16M	379.36	
	M2	69.30	45M2	3118.50		54M2	3742.20		64M2	4435.20		74M2	5128.20	
	M	41.73	15M	625.95		16M	667.68		17M	709.41		19M	792.87	
	M	22.73	14M	318.22		15M	340.95		16M	363.68		17M	386.41	
	M	48.01	14M	672.14		15M	720.15		16M	768.16		17M	816.17	
	M	18.68	14M	261.52	**7355.10**	15M	280.20	**8521.60**	16M	298.88	**9812.82**	17M	317.56	**11145.77**
	M2	114.25	53M2	6055.25	**6055.25**	55M2	6283.75	**6283.75**	63M2	7197.75	**7197.75**	68M2	7769.00	**7769.00**

Specification A
6 m2 - 15 m2

TWO STOREY

PITCHED ROOF

Element	Unit	Unit Rate £	Ref A/2P 3x2 Size 3.00 x 2.00 m Area 6 m2 Qty	Total £	Element Total £	Ref A/2P 3x3 Size 3.00 x 3.00 m Area 9 m2 Qty	Total £	Element Total £	Ref A/2P 3x4 Size 3.00 x 4.00 m Area 12 m2 Qty	Total £	Element Total £	Ref A/2P 3x5 Size 3.00 x 5.00 m Area 15 m2 Qty	Total £	Element Total £
EXTERNAL DOORS AND WINDOWS														
External door	NR	655.02	1NR	655.02		1NR	655.02		1NR	655.02		1NR	655.02	
Windows	NR	672.89	2NR	1345.78		2NR	1345.78		2NR	1345.78		2NR	1345.78	
Opening in cavity wall for door	NR	144.37	1NR	144.37		1NR	144.37		1NR	144.37		1NR	144.37	
Opening in cavity wall for window	NR	162.98	2NR	325.96	**2471.13**	2NR	325.96	**2471.13**	2NR	325.96	**2471.13**	2NR	325.96	**2471.13**
INTERNAL WALLS AND PARTITIONS														
Stud partitions	M2	51.63												
INTERNAL DOORS														
Hardwood flush door	NR	412.45												
WALL FINISHES														
Plaster & decoration	M2	19.58	50M2	979.00	**979.00**	60M2	1174.80	**1174.80**	70M2	1370.60	**1370.60**	80M2	1566.40	**1566.40**
FLOOR FINISHES														
Laminate	M2	30.30	6M2	181.80		9M2	272.70		12M2	363.60		15M2	454.50	
Hardwood skirting	M	19.52	20M	390.40	**572.20**	24M	468.48	**741.18**	28M	546.56	**910.16**	32M	624.64	**1079.14**
CEILING FINISHES														
Plasterboard, plaster and decoration	M2	26.68	12M2	320.16	**320.16**	18M2	480.24	**480.24**	24M2	640.32	**640.32**	30M2	800.40	**800.40**

Specification A 18 m2 - 27 m2

			Ref A/2P 3x6 Size 3.00 x 6.00 m Area 18 m2			Ref A/2P 3x7 Size 3.00 x 7.00 m Area 21 m2			Ref A/2P 3x8 Size 3.00 x 8.00 m Area 24 m2			Ref A/2P 3x9 Size 3.00 x 9.00 m Area 27 m2		
			Qty	Total £	Element Total £	Qty	Total £	Element Total £	Qty	Total £	Element Total £	Qty	Total £	Element Total £
TWO STOREY PITCHED ROOF Continued/.....														
Element	Unit	Unit Rate £												
	NR	655.02	1NR	655.02		1NR	655.02		1NR	655.02		1NR	655.02	
	NR	672.89	4NR	2691.56		4NR	2691.56		4NR	2691.56		4NR	2691.56	
	NR	144.37	1NR	144.37		1NR	144.37		1NR	144.37		1NR	144.37	
	NR	162.98	4NR	651.92	**4142.87**	4NR	651.92	**4142.87**	4NR	651.92	**4142.87**	4NR	651.92	**4142.87**
	M2	51.63	16M2	826.08	**826.08**	16M2	826.08	**826.08**	16M2	826.08	**826.08**	16M2	826.08	**826.08**
	NR	412.45	2NR	824.90	**824.90**	2NR	824.90	**824.90**	2NR	824.90	**824.90**	2NR	824.90	**824.90**
	M2	19.58	90M2	1762.20	**1762.20**	100M2	1958.00	**1958.00**	110M2	2153.80	**2153.80**	120M2	2349.60	**2349.60**
	M2	30.30	18M2	545.40		21M2	636.30		24M2	727.20		27M2	818.10	
	M	19.52	36M	702.72	**1248.12**	40M	780.80	**1417.10**	44M	858.88	**1586.08**	48M	936.96	**1755.06**
	M2	26.68	36M2	960.48	**960.48**	42M2	1120.56	**1120.56**	48M2	1280.64	**1280.64**	54M2	1440.72	**1440.72**

Specification A
6 m2 - 15 m2

TWO STOREY

PITCHED ROOF

Element	Unit	Unit Rate £	Ref A/2P 3x2 Size 3.00 x 2.00 m Area 6 m2 Qty	Total £	Element Total £	Ref A/2P 3x3 Size 3.00 x 3.00 m Area 9 m2 Qty	Total £	Element Total £	Ref A/2P 3x4 Size 3.00 x 4.00 m Area 12 m2 Qty	Total £	Element Total £	Ref A/2P 3x5 Size 3.00 x 5.00 m Area 15 m2 Qty	Total £	Element Total £
SERVICES														
Rainwater pipes	M	26.64	6M	159.84		6M	159.84		6M	159.84		6M	159.84	
Cold water service point	NR	110.52	1NR	110.52		1NR	110.52		1NR	110.52		1NR	110.52	
Hot water service point	NR	191.67	1NR	191.67		1NR	191.67		1NR	191.67		1NR	191.67	
Central heating service point	NR	386.51	2NR	773.02		2NR	773.02		2NR	773.02		2NR	773.02	
Electrical installation	NR	286.50	2NR	573.00	**1808.05**	2NR	573.00	**1808.05**	2NR	573.00	**1808.05**	2NR	573.00	**1808.05**
ALTERATIONS TO EXISTING BUILDINGS														
Opening in existing wall 1.80 m wide 2.00 m high	NR	689.44	2NR	1378.88	**1378.88**									
Opening in existing wall 2.40 m wide 2.00 m high	NR	865.59												
Opening in existing wall 3.00 m wide 2.00 m high	NR	921.26				2NR	1842.52	**1842.52**						
Opening in existing wall 4.00 m wide 2.00 m high	NR	1131.22							2NR	2262.44	**2262.44**			
Opening in existing wall 5.00 m wide 2.0 0m high	NR	1341.19										2NR	2682.38	**2682.38**

Specification A
18 m2 - 27 m2

TWO STOREY

PITCHED ROOF Continued/.....

Element	Unit	Unit Rate £	Ref A/2P 3x6 Size 3.00 x 6.00 m Area 18 m2 Qty	Total £	Element Total £	Ref A/2P 3x7 Size 3.00 x 7.00 m Area 21 m2 Qty	Total £	Element Total £	Ref A/2P 3x8 Size 3.00 x 8.00 m Area 24 m2 Qty	Total £	Element Total £	Ref A/2P 3x9 Size 3.00 x 9.00 m Area 27 m2 Qty	Total £	Element Total £
	M	26.64	6M	159.84		6M	159.84		6M	159.84		6M	159.84	
	NR	110.52	1NR	110.52		1NR	110.52		1NR	110.52		1NR	110.52	
	NR	191.67	1NR	191.67		1NR	191.67		1NR	191.67		1NR	191.67	
	NR	386.51	4NR	1546.04		4NR	1546.04		4NR	1546.04		4NR	1546.04	
	NR	286.50	4NR	1146.00	**3154.07**	4NR	1146.00	**3154.07**	4NR	1146.00	**3154.07**	4NR	1146.00	**3154.07**
	NR	689.44												
	NR	865.59	4NR	3462.36	**3462.36**									
	NR	921.26				4NR	3685.04	**3685.04**	4NR	3685.04	**3685.04**			
	NR	1131.22										4NR	4524.88	**4524.88**
	NR	1341.19												

Specification A 6 m2 - 15 m2	Ref A/2P 3x2 Size 3.00 x 2.00 m Area 6 m2 Element Total £	Ref A/2P 3x3 Size 3.00 x 3.00 m Area 9 m2 Element Total £	Ref A/2P 3x4 Size 3.00 x 4.00 m Area 12 m2 Element Total £	Ref A/2P 3x5 Size 3.00 x 5.00 m Area 15 m2 Element Total £
TWO STOREY				
PITCHED ROOF				
SUMMARY				
SUBSTRUCTURE	1849.11	2268.23	2687.35	3106.47
UPPER FLOORS	467.16	732.42	976.56	1220.70
ROOF	3312.42	4160.18	5201.96	6216.17
EXTERNAL WALLS	4227.25	4798.50	5369.75	5941.00
EXTERNAL DOORS AND WINDOWS	2471.13	2471.13	2471.13	2471.13
INTERNAL WALLS AND PARTITIONS	-	-	-	-
INTERNAL DOORS	-	-	-	-
WALL FINISHES	979.00	1174.80	1370.60	1566.40
FLOOR FINISHES	572.20	741.18	910.16	1079.14
CEILING FINISHES	320.16	480.24	640.32	800.40
SERVICES	1808.05	1808.05	1808.05	1808.05
ALTERATIONS TO EXISTING BUILDINGS	1378.88	1842.52	2262.44	2682.38
Sub Total	17385.36	20477.25	23698.32	26891.84
Allowance for unmeasured items and sundries 5%	869.27	1023.86	1184.92	1344.59
NET TOTAL excluding Preliminaries, Profit and Overheads	**18254.63**	**21501.11**	**24883.24**	**28236.43**

Specification A 18 m2 - 27 m2	Ref A/2P 3x6 Size 3.00 x 6.00 m Area 18 m2	Ref A/2P 3x7 Size 3.00 x 7.00 m Area 21 m2	Ref A/2P 3x8 Size 3.00 x 8.00 m Area 24 m2	Ref A/2P 3x9 Size 3.00 x 9.00 m Area 27 m2
	Element Total £	Element Total £	Element Total £	Element Total £
TWO STOREY				
PITCHED ROOF				
SUMMARY Continued/.....				
	3525.59	3944.71	4363.83	4782.95
	1464.84	1708.98	1953.12	2197.26
	7355.10	8521.60	9812.82	11145.77
	6055.25	6283.75	7197.75	7769.00
	4142.87	4142.87	4142.87	4142.87
	826.08	826.08	826.08	826.08
	824.90	824.90	824.90	824.90
	1762.20	1958.00	2153.80	2349.60
	1248.12	1417.10	1586.08	1755.06
	960.48	1120.56	1280.64	1440.72
	3154.07	3154.07	3154.07	3154.07
	3462.36	3685.04	3685.04	4524.88
Sub Total	34781.86	37587.66	40981.00	44913.16
Allowance for unmeasured items and sundries 5%	1739.09	1879.38	2049.05	2245.66
NET TOTAL excluding Preliminaries, Profit and Overheads	**36520.95**	**39467.04**	**43030.05**	**47158.82**

Specification A 8 m2 - 20 m2			Ref A/2P 4x2 Size 4.00 x 2.00 m Area 8 m2			Ref A/2P 4x3 Size 4.00 x 3.00 m Area 12 m2			Ref A/2P 4x4 Size 4.00 x 4.00 m Area 16 m2			Ref A/2P 4x5 Size 4.00 x 5.00 m Area 20 m2		
			Qty	Total £	Element Total £	Qty	Total £	Element Total £	Qty	Total £	Element Total £	Qty	Total £	Element Total £
TWO STOREY														
PITCHED ROOF														
Element	Unit	Unit Rate £												
SUBSTRUCTURE														
Strip footings	M	144.41	11M	1588.51		12M	1732.92		13M	1877.33		14M	2021.74	
Hollow ground floor	M2	91.57	8M2	732.56	**2321.07**	12M2	1098.84	**2831.76**	16M2	1465.12	**3342.45**	20M2	1831.40	**3853.14**
UPPER FLOORS														
Timber floor construction 50 x 150 mm joists	M2	77.86	8M2	622.88	**622.88**									
Timber floor construction 50 x 200 mm joists	M2	81.38				12M2	976.56	**976.56**	16M2	1302.08	**1302.08**	20M2	1627.60	**1627.60**
ROOF														
Pitched roof construction	M2	55.42	16M2	886.72		22M2	1219.24		29M2	1607.18		36M2	1995.12	
Work to top of external wall	M	23.71	11M	260.81		12M	284.52		13M	308.23		14M	331.94	
Plain tile roofing	M2	69.30	20M2	1386.00		27M2	1871.10		34M2	2356.20		44M2	3049.20	
Work to hip	M	41.73	9M	375.57		11M	459.03		13M	542.49		14M	584.22	
Work to eaves	M	22.73	12M	272.76		13M	295.49		14M	318.22		15M	340.95	
Fascia and eaves soffit	M	48.01	12M	576.12		13M	624.13		14M	672.14		15M	720.15	
Gutters and fittings	M	18.68	12M	224.16	**3982.14**	13M	242.84	**4996.35**	14M	261.52	**6065.98**	15M	280.20	**7301.78**
EXTERNAL WALLS														
Brick and block cavity wall	M2	114.25	47M2	5369.75	**5369.75**	52M2	5941.00	**5941.00**	57M2	6512.25	**6512.25**	59M2	6740.75	**6740.75**

Specification A 24 m2 - 36 m2			Ref A/2P 4x6 Size 4.00 x 6.00 m Area 24 m2			Ref A/2P 4x7 Size 4.00 x 7.00 m Area 28 m2			Ref A/2P 4x8 Size 4.00 x 8.00 m Area 32 m2			Ref A/2P 4x9 Size 4.00 x 9.00 m Area 36 m2		
TWO STOREY PITCHED ROOF Continued/.....														
Element	Unit	Unit Rate £	Qty	Total £	Element Total £	Qty	Total £	Element Total £	Qty	Total £	Element Total £	Qty	Total £	Element Total £
	M	144.41	15M	2166.15		16M	2310.56		17M	2454.97		18M	2599.38	
	M2	91.57	24M2	2197.68	**4363.83**	28M2	2563.96	**4874.52**	32M2	2930.24	**5385.21**	36M2	3296.52	**5895.90**
	M2	77.86												
	M2	81.38	24M2	1953.12	**1953.12**	28M2	2278.64	**2278.64**	32M2	2604.16	**2604.16**	36M2	2929.68	**2929.68**
	M2	55.42	44M2	2438.48		52M2	2881.84		61M2	3380.62		70M2	3879.40	
	M	23.71	15M	355.65		16M	379.36		17M	403.07		18M	426.78	
	M2	69.30	54M2	3742.20		64M2	4435.20		75M2	5197.50		86M2	5959.80	
	M	41.73	16M	667.68		17M	709.41		19M	792.87		20M	834.60	
	M	22.73	16M	363.68		17M	386.41		18M	409.14		19M	431.87	
	M	48.01	16M	768.16		17M	816.17		18M	864.18		19M	912.19	
	M	18.68	16M	298.88	**8634.73**	17M	317.56	**9925.95**	18M	336.24	**11383.62**	19M	354.92	**12799.56**
	M2	114.25	63M2	7197.75	**7197.75**	68M2	7769.00	**7769.00**	73M2	8340.25	**8340.25**	78M2	8911.50	**8911.50**

Specification A 8 m2 - 20 m2			Ref A/2P 4x2 Size 4.00 x 2.00 m Area 8 m2			Ref A/2P 4x3 Size 4.00 x 3.00 m Area 12 m2			Ref A/2P 4x4 Size 4.00 x 4.00 m Area 16 m2			Ref A/2P 4x5 Size 4.00 x 5.00 m Area 20 m2		
TWO STOREY PITCHED ROOF			Qty	Total £	Element Total £	Qty	Total £	Element Total £	Qty	Total £	Element Total £	Qty	Total £	Element Total £
Element	Unit	Unit Rate £												
EXTERNAL DOORS AND WINDOWS														
External door	NR	655.02	1NR	655.02		1NR	655.02		1NR	655.02		1NR	655.02	
Windows	NR	672.89	2NR	1345.78		2NR	1345.78		2NR	1345.78		2NR	1345.78	
Opening in cavity wall for door	NR	144.37	1NR	144.37		1NR	144.37		1NR	144.37		1NR	144.37	
Opening in cavity wall for window	NR	162.98	2NR	325.96	**2471.13**	2NR	325.96	**2471.13**	2NR	325.96	**2471.13**	2NR	325.96	**2471.13**
INTERNAL WALLS AND PARTITIONS														
Stud partitions	M2	51.63												
INTERNAL DOORS														
Hardwood flush door	NR	412.45												
WALL FINISHES														
Plaster & decoration	M2	19.58	60M2	1174.80	**1174.80**	70M2	1370.60	**1370.60**	80M2	1566.40	**1566.40**	90M2	1762.20	**1762.20**
FLOOR FINISHES														
Laminate	M2	30.30	8M2	242.40		12M2	363.60		16M2	484.80		20M2	606.00	
Hardwood skirting	M	19.52	24M	468.48	**710.88**	28M	546.56	**910.16**	32M	624.64	**1109.44**	36M	702.72	**1308.72**
CEILING FINISHES														
Plasterboard, plaster and decoration	M2	26.68	16M2	426.88	**426.88**	24M2	640.32	**640.32**	32M2	853.76	**853.76**	40M2	1067.20	**1067.20**

Specification A 24 m2 - 36 m2

TWO STOREY

PITCHED ROOF Continued/.....

Element	Unit	Unit Rate £	Ref A/2P 4x6 Size 4.00 x 6.00 m Area 24 m2 Qty	Total £	Element Total £	Ref A/2P 4x7 Size 4.00 x 7.00 m Area 28 m2 Qty	Total £	Element Total £	Ref A/2P 4x8 Size 4.00 x 8.00 m Area 32 m2 Qty	Total £	Element Total £	Ref A/2P 4x9 Size 4.00 x 9.00 m Area 36 m2 Qty	Total £	Element Total £
	NR	655.02	1NR	655.02		1NR	655.02		1NR	655.02		1NR	655.02	
	NR	672.89	4NR	2691.56		4NR	2691.56		4NR	2691.56		4NR	2691.56	
	NR	144.37	1NR	144.37		1NR	144.37		1NR	144.37		1NR	144.37	
	NR	162.98	4NR	651.92	**4142.87**	4NR	651.92	**4142.87**	4NR	651.92	**4142.87**	4NR	651.92	**4142.87**
	M2	51.63	20M2	1032.60	**1032.60**	20M2	1032.60	**1032.60**	20M2	1032.60	**1032.60**	20M2	1032.60	**1032.60**
	NR	412.45	2NR	824.90	**824.90**	2NR	824.90	**824.90**	2NR	824.90	**824.90**	2NR	824.90	**824.90**
	M2	19.58	100M2	1958.00	**1958.00**	110M2	2153.80	**2153.80**	120M2	2349.60	**2349.60**	130M2	2545.40	**2545.40**
	M2	30.30	24M2	727.20		28M2	848.40		32M2	969.60		36M2	1090.80	
	M	19.52	40M	780.80	**1508.00**	44M	858.88	**1707.28**	48M	936.96	**1906.56**	52M	1015.04	**2105.84**
	M2	26.68	48M2	1280.64	**1280.64**	56M2	1494.08	**1494.08**	64M2	1707.52	**1707.52**	72M2	1920.96	**1920.96**

Specification A 8 m2 - 20 m2			Ref A/2P 4x2 Size 4.00 x 2.00 m Area 8 m2			Ref A/2P 4x3 Size 4.00 x 3.00 m Area 12 m2			Ref A/2P 4x4 Size 4.00 x 4.00 m Area 16 m2			Ref A/2P 4x5 Size 4.00 x 5.00 m Area 20 m2		
TWO STOREY PITCHED ROOF			Qty	Total £	Element Total £	Qty	Total £	Element Total £	Qty	Total £	Element Total £	Qty	Total £	Element Total £
Element	Unit	Unit Rate £												
SERVICES														
Rainwater pipes	M	26.64	6M	159.84		6M	159.84		6M	159.84		6M	159.84	
Cold water service point	NR	110.52	1NR	110.52		1NR	110.52		1NR	110.52		1NR	110.52	
Hot water service point	NR	191.67	1NR	191.67		1NR	191.67		1NR	191.67		1NR	191.67	
Central heating service point	NR	386.51	2NR	773.02		2NR	773.02		2NR	773.02		2NR	773.02	
Electrical installation	NR	286.50	2NR	573.00	**1808.05**	2NR	573.00	**1808.05**	2NR	573.00	**1808.05**	2NR	573.00	**1808.05**
ALTERATIONS TO EXISTING BUILDINGS														
Opening in existing wall 1.80 m wide 2.00 m high	NR	689.44	2NR	1378.88	**1378.88**									
Opening in existing wall 2.40 m wide 2.00 m high	NR	865.59												
Opening in existing wall 3.00 m wide 2.00 m high	NR	921.26				2NR	1842.52	**1842.52**						
Opening in existing wall 4.00 m wide 2.00 m high	NR	1131.22							2NR	2262.44	**2262.44**			
Opening in existing wall 5.00 m wide 2.00 m high	NR	1341.19										2NR	2682.38	**2682.38**

Specification A
24 m2 - 36 m2

TWO STOREY

PITCHED ROOF Continued/.....

Element	Unit	Unit Rate £	Ref A/2P 4x6 Size 4.00 x 6.00 m Area 24 m2 Qty	Total £	Element Total £	Ref A/2P 4x7 Size 4.00 x 7.00 m Area 28 m2 Qty	Total £	Element Total £	Ref A/2P 4x8 Size 4.00 x 8.00 m Area 32 m2 Qty	Total £	Element Total £	Ref A/2P 4x9 Size 4.00 x 9.00 m Area 36 m2 Qty	Total £	Element Total £
	M	26.64	6M	159.84		6M	159.84		6M	159.84		6M	159.84	
	NR	110.52	1NR	110.52		1NR	110.52		1NR	110.52		1NR	110.52	
	NR	191.67	1NR	191.67		1NR	191.67		1NR	191.67		1NR	191.67	
	NR	386.51	4NR	1546.04		4NR	1546.04		4NR	1546.04		4NR	1546.04	
	NR	286.50	4NR	1146.00	**3154.07**	4NR	1146.00	**3154.07**	4NR	1146.00	**3154.07**	4NR	1146.00	**3154.07**
	NR	689.44												
	NR	865.59	4NR	3462.36	**3462.36**									
	NR	921.26				4NR	3685.04	**3685.04**	4NR	3685.04	**3685.04**			
	NR	1131.22										4NR	4524.88	**4524.88**
	NR	1341.19												

Specification A **8 m2 - 20 m2**	Ref A/2P 4x2 Size 4.00 x 2.00 m Area 8 m2 Element Total £	Ref A/2P 4x3 Size 4.00 x 3.00 m Area 12 m2 Element Total £	Ref A/2P 4x4 Size 4.00 x 4.00 m Area 16 m2 Element Total £	Ref A/2P 4x5 Size 4.00 x 5.00 m Area 20 m2 Element Total £
TWO STOREY				
PITCHED ROOF				
SUMMARY				
SUBSTRUCTURE	2321.07	2831.76	3342.45	3853.14
UPPER FLOORS	622.88	976.56	1302.08	1627.60
ROOF	3982.14	4996.35	6065.98	7301.78
EXTERNAL WALLS	5369.75	5941.00	6512.25	6740.75
EXTERNAL DOORS AND WINDOWS	2471.13	2471.13	2471.13	2471.13
INTERNAL WALLS AND PARTITIONS	-	-	-	-
INTERNAL DOORS	-	-	-	-
WALL FINISHES	1174.80	1370.60	1566.40	1762.20
FLOOR FINISHES	710.88	910.16	1109.44	1308.72
CEILING FINISHES	426.88	640.32	853.76	1067.20
SERVICES	1808.05	1808.05	1808.05	1808.05
ALTERATIONS TO EXISTING BUILDINGS	1378.88	1842.52	2262.44	2682.38
Sub Total	20266.46	23788.45	27293.98	30622.95
Allowance for unmeasured items and sundries 5%	1013.32	1189.42	1364.70	1531.15
NET TOTAL excluding Preliminaries, Profit and Overheads	**21279.78**	**24977.87**	**28658.68**	**32154.10**

Specification A 24 m2 - 36 m2	Ref A/2P 4x6 Size 4.00 x 6.00 m Area 24 m2 Element Total £	Ref A/2P 4x7 Size 4.00 x 7.00 m Area 28 m2 Element Total £	Ref A/2P 4x8 Size 4.00 x 8.00 m Area 32 m2 Element Total £	Ref A/2P 4x9 Size 4.00 x 9.00 m Area 36 m2 Element Total £
TWO STOREY				
PITCHED ROOF				
SUMMARY Continued/.....				
	4363.83	4874.52	5385.21	5895.90
	1953.12	2278.64	2604.16	2929.68
	8634.73	9925.95	11383.62	12799.56
	7197.75	7769.00	8340.25	8911.50
	4142.87	4142.87	4142.87	4142.87
	1032.60	1032.60	1032.60	1032.60
	824.90	824.90	824.90	824.90
	1958.00	2153.80	2349.60	2545.40
	1508.00	1707.28	1906.56	2105.84
	1280.64	1494.08	1707.52	1920.96
	3154.07	3154.07	3154.07	3154.07
	3462.36	3685.04	3685.04	4524.88
Sub Total	39512.87	43042.75	46516.40	50788.16
Allowance for unmeasured items and sundries 5%	1975.64	2152.14	2325.82	2539.41
NET TOTAL excluding Preliminaries, Profit and Overheads	**41488.51**	**45194.89**	**48842.22**	**53327.57**

Specification A 10 m2 - 25 m2

TWO STOREY

PITCHED ROOF

Element	Unit	Unit Rate £	Ref A/2P 5x2 Size 5.00 x 2.00 m Area 10 m2 Qty	Total £	Element Total £	Ref A/2P 5x3 Size 5.00 x 3.00 m Area 15 m2 Qty	Total £	Element Total £	Ref A/2P 5x4 Size 5.00 x 4.00 m Area 20 m2 Qty	Total £	Element Total £	Ref A/2P 5x5 Size 5.00 x 5.00 m Area 25 m2 Qty	Total £	Element Total £
SUBSTRUCTURE														
Strip footings	M	144.41	13M	1877.33		14M	2021.74		15M	2166.15		16M	2310.56	
Hollow ground floor	M2	91.57	10M2	915.70	**2793.03**	15M2	1373.55	**3395.29**	20M2	1831.40	**3997.55**	25M2	2289.25	**4599.81**
UPPER FLOORS														
Timber floor construction 50 x 150 mm joists	M2	77.86	10M2	778.60	**778.60**									
Timber floor construction 50 x 200 mm joists	M2	81.38				15M2	1220.70	**1220.70**	20M2	1627.60	**1627.60**			
Timber floor construction 75 x 250 mm joists	M2	103.03										25M2	2575.75	**2575.75**
ROOF														
Pitched roof construction	M2	55.42	19M2	1052.98		26M2	1440.92		34M2	1884.28		42M2	2327.64	
Work to top of external wall	M	23.71	13M	308.23		14M	331.94		15M	355.65		16M	379.36	
Plain tile roofing	M2	69.30	23M2	1593.90		32M2	2217.60		44M2	3049.20		52M2	3603.60	
Work to hip	M	41.73	10M	417.30		12M	500.76		14M	584.22		15M	625.95	
Work to eaves	M	22.73	14M	318.22		15M	340.95		16M	363.68		17M	386.41	
Fascia and eaves soffit	M	48.01	14M	672.14		15M	720.15		16M	768.16		17M	816.17	
Gutters and fittings	M	18.68	14M	261.52	**4624.29**	15M	280.20	**5832.52**	16M	298.88	**7304.07**	17M	317.56	**8456.69**

Specification A 30 m2 - 45 m2

TWO STOREY

PITCHED ROOF Continued/.....

Element	Unit	Unit Rate £	Ref A/2P 5x6 Size 5.00 x 6.00 m Area 30 m2 Qty	Total £	Element Total £	Ref A/2P 5x7 Size 5.00 x 7.00 m Area 35 m2 Qty	Total £	Element Total £	Ref A/2P 5x8 Size 5.00 x 8.00 m Area 40 m2 Qty	Total £	Element Total £	Ref A/2P 5x9 Size 5.00 x 9.00 m Area 45 m2 Qty	Total £	Element Total £
	M	144.41	17M	2454.97		18M	2599.38		19M	2743.79		20M	2888.20	
	M2	91.57	30M2	2747.10	**5202.07**	35M2	3204.95	**5804.33**	40M2	3662.80	**6406.59**	45M2	4120.65	**7008.85**
	M2	77.86												
	M2	81.38	30M2	2441.40	**2441.40**	35M2	2848.30	**2848.30**	40M2	3255.20	**3255.20**			
	M2	103.03										45M2	4636.35	**4636.35**
	M2	55.42	51M2	2826.42		60M2	3325.20		70M2	3879.40		80M2	4433.60	
	M	23.71	17M	403.07		18M	426.78		19M	450.49		20M	474.20	
	M2	69.30	62M2	4296.60		74M2	5128.20		86M2	5959.80		99M2	6860.70	
	M	41.73	17M	709.41		18M	751.14		20M	834.60		21M	876.33	
	M	22.73	18M	409.14		19M	431.87		20M	454.60		21M	477.33	
	M	48.01	18M	864.18		19M	912.19		20M	960.20		21M	1008.21	
	M	18.68	18M	336.24	**9845.06**	19M	354.92	**11330.30**	20M	373.60	**12912.69**	21M	392.28	**14522.65**

Specification A
10 m2 - 25 m2

TWO STOREY

PITCHED ROOF

Element	Unit	Unit Rate £	Ref A/2P 5x2 Size 5.00 x 2.00 m Area 10 m2			Ref A/2P 5x3 Size 5.00 x 3.00 m Area 15 m2			Ref A/2P 5x4 Size 5.00 x 4.00 m Area 20 m2			Ref A/2P 5x5 Size 5.00 x 5.00 m Area 25 m2		
			Qty	Total £	Element Total £	Qty	Total £	Element Total £	Qty	Total £	Element Total £	Qty	Total £	Element Total £
EXTERNAL WALLS														
Brick and block cavity wall	M2	114.25	57M2	6512.25	**6512.25**	62M2	7083.50	**7083.50**	67M2	7654.75	**7654.75**	72M2	8226.00	**8226.00**
EXTERNAL DOORS AND WINDOWS														
External door	NR	655.02	1NR	655.02		1NR	655.02		1NR	655.02		1NR	655.02	
Windows	NR	672.89	2NR	1345.78		2NR	1345.78		2NR	1345.78		2NR	1345.78	
Opening in cavity wall for door	NR	144.37	1NR	144.37		1NR	144.37		1NR	144.37		1NR	144.37	
Opening in cavity wall for window	NR	162.98	2NR	325.96	**2471.13**	2NR	325.96	**2471.13**	2NR	325.96	**2471.13**	2NR	325.96	**2471.13**
INTERNAL WALLS AND PARTITIONS														
Stud partitions	M2	51.63												
INTERNAL DOORS														
Hardwood flush door	NR	412.45												
WALL FINISHES														
Plaster & decoration	M2	19.58	70M2	1370.60	**1370.60**	80M2	1566.40	**1566.40**	90M2	1762.20	**1762.20**	100M2	1958.00	**1958.00**

Specification A 30 m2 - 45 m2

TWO STOREY

PITCHED ROOF Continued/.....

Element	Unit	Unit Rate £	Ref A/2P 5x6 Size 5.00 x 6.00 m Area 30 m2 Qty	Total £	Element Total £	Ref A/2P 5x7 Size 5.00 x 7.00 m Area 35 m2 Qty	Total £	Element Total £	Ref A/2P 5x8 Size 5.00 x 8.00 m Area 40 m2 Qty	Total £	Element Total £	Ref A/2P 5x9 Size 5.00 x 9.00 m Area 45 m2 Qty	Total £	Element Total £
	M2	114.25	73M2	8340.25	**8340.25**	78M2	8911.50	**8911.50**	83M2	9482.75	**9482.75**	88M2	10054.00	**10054.00**
	NR	655.02	1NR	655.02		1NR	655.02		1NR	655.02		1NR	655.02	
	NR	672.89	4NR	2691.56		4NR	2691.56		4NR	2691.56		4NR	2691.56	
	NR	144.37	1NR	144.37		1NR	144.37		1NR	144.37		1NR	144.37	
	NR	162.98	4NR	651.92	**4142.87**	4NR	651.92	**4142.87**	4NR	651.92	**4142.87**	4NR	651.92	**4142.87**
	M2	51.63	26M2	1342.38	**1342.38**	26M2	1342.38	**1342.38**	26M2	1342.38	**1342.38**	26M2	1342.38	**1342.38**
	NR	412.45	2NR	824.90	**824.90**	2NR	824.90	**824.90**	2NR	824.90	**824.90**	2NR	824.90	**824.90**
	M2	19.58	110M2	2153.80	**2153.80**	120M2	2349.60	**2349.60**	130M2	2545.40	**2545.40**	140M2	2741.20	**2741.20**

Specification A
10 m2 - 25 m2

Element	Unit	Unit Rate £	Ref A/2P 5x2 Size 5.00 x 2.00 m Area 10 m2 Qty	Total £	Element Total £	Ref A/2P 5x3 Size 5.00 x 3.00 m Area 15 m2 Qty	Total £	Element Total £	Ref A/2P 5x4 Size 5.00 x 4.00 m Area 20 m2 Qty	Total £	Element Total £	Ref A/2P 5x5 Size 5.00 x 5.00 m Area 25 m2 Qty	Total £	Element Total £
TWO STOREY														
PITCHED ROOF														
FLOOR FINISHES														
Laminate	M2	30.30	10M2	303.00		15M2	454.50		20M2	606.00		25M2	757.50	
Hardwood skirting	M	19.52	28M	546.56	**849.56**	32M	624.64	**1079.14**	36M	702.72	**1308.72**	40M	780.80	**1538.30**
CEILING FINISHES														
Plasterboard, plaster and decoration	M2	26.68	20M2	533.60	**533.60**	30M2	800.40	**800.40**	40M2	1067.20	**1067.20**	50M2	1334.00	**1334.00**
SERVICES														
Rainwater pipes	M	26.64	6M	159.84		6M	159.84		6M	159.84		6M	159.84	
Cold water service point	NR	110.52	1NR	110.52		1NR	110.52		1NR	110.52		1NR	110.52	
Hot water service point	NR	191.67	1NR	191.67		1NR	191.67		1NR	191.67		1NR	191.67	
Central heating service point	NR	386.51	2NR	773.02		2NR	773.02		2NR	773.02		2NR	773.02	
Electrical installation	NR	286.50	2NR	573.00	**1808.05**	2NR	573.00	**1808.05**	2NR	573.00	**1808.05**	2NR	573.00	**1808.05**

Specification A 30 m2 - 45 m2

TWO STOREY

PITCHED ROOF Continued/.....

Element	Unit	Unit Rate £	Ref A/2P 5x6 Size 5.00 x 6.00 m Area 30 m2 Qty	Total £	Element Total £	Ref A/2P 5x7 Size 5.00 x 7.00 m Area 35 m2 Qty	Total £	Element Total £	Ref A/2P 5x8 Size 5.00 x 8.00 m Area 40 m2 Qty	Total £	Element Total £	Ref A/2P 5x9 Size 5.00 x 9.00 m Area 45 m2 Qty	Total £	Element Total £
	M2	30.30	30M2	909.00		35M2	1060.50		40M2	1212.00		45M2	1363.50	
	M	19.52	44M	858.88	**1767.88**	48M	936.96	**1997.46**	52M	1015.04	**2227.04**	56M	1093.12	**2456.62**
	M2	26.68	60M2	1600.80	**1600.80**	70M2	1867.60	**1867.60**	80M2	2134.40	**2134.40**	90M2	2401.20	**2401.20**
	M	26.64	6M	159.84		6M	159.84		6M	159.84		6M	159.84	
	NR	110.52	1NR	110.52		1NR	110.52		1NR	110.52		1NR	110.52	
	NR	191.67	1NR	191.67		1NR	191.67		1NR	191.67		1NR	191.67	
	NR	386.51	4NR	1546.04		4NR	1546.04		4NR	1546.04		4NR	1546.04	
	NR	286.50	4NR	1146.00	**3154.07**	4NR	1146.00	**3154.07**	4NR	1146.00	**3154.07**	4NR	1146.00	**3154.07**

Specification A 10 m2 - 25 m2

TWO STOREY

PITCHED ROOF

Element	Unit	Unit Rate £	Ref A/2P 5x2 Size 5.00 x 2.00 m Area 10 m2 Qty	Total £	Element Total £	Ref A/2P 5x3 Size 5.00 x 3.00 m Area 15 m2 Qty	Total £	Element Total £	Ref A/2P 5x4 Size 5.00 x 4.00 m Area 20 m2 Qty	Total £	Element Total £	Ref A/2P 5x5 Size 5.00 x 5.00 m Area 25 m2 Qty	Total £	Element Total £
ALTERATIONS TO EXISTING BUILDINGS														
Opening in existing wall 1.80 m wide 2.00 m high	NR	689.44	2NR	1378.88	**1378.88**									
Opening in existing wall 2.40 m wide 2.00 m high	NR	865.59												
Opening in existing wall 3.00 m wide 2.00 m high	NR	921.26				2NR	1842.52	**1842.52**						
Opening in existing wall 4.00 m wide 2.00 m high	NR	1131.22							2NR	2262.44	**2262.44**			
Opening in existing wall 5.00 m wide 2.00 m high	NR	1341.19										2NR	2682.38	**2682.38**

Specification A 30 m2 - 45 m2

TWO STOREY

PITCHED ROOF Continued/.....

Element	Unit	Unit Rate £	Ref A/2P 5x6 Size 5.00 x 6.00 m Area 30 m2 Qty	Total £	Element Total £	Ref A/2P 5x7 Size 5.00 x 7.00 m Area 35 m2 Qty	Total £	Element Total £	Ref A/2P 5x8 Size 5.00 x 8.00 m Area 40 m2 Qty	Total £	Element Total £	Ref A/2P 5x9 Size 5.00 x 9.00 m Area 45 m2 Qty	Total £	Element Total £
	NR	689.44												
	NR	865.59	4NR	3462.36	**3462.36**									
	NR	921.26				4NR	3685.04	**3685.04**	4NR	3685.04	**3685.04**			
	NR	1131.22										4NR	4524.88	**4524.88**
	NR	1341.19												

Specification A 10 m2 - 25 m2	Ref A/2P 5x2 Size 5.00 x 2.00 m Area 10 m2	Ref A/2P 5x3 Size 5.00 x 3.00 m Area 15 m2	Ref A/2P 5x4 Size 5.00 x 4.00 m Area 20 m2	Ref A/2P 5x5 Size 5.00 x 5.00 m Area 25 m2
	Element Total £	Element Total £	Element Total £	Element Total £
TWO STOREY				
PITCHED ROOF				
SUMMARY				
SUBSTRUCTURE	2793.03	3395.29	3997.55	4599.81
UPPER FLOORS	778.60	1220.70	1627.60	2575.75
ROOF	4624.29	5832.52	7304.07	8456.69
EXTERNAL WALLS	6512.25	7083.50	7654.75	8226.00
EXTERNAL DOORS AND WINDOWS	2471.13	2471.13	2471.13	2471.13
INTERNAL WALLS AND PARTITIONS	-	-	-	-
INTERNAL DOORS	-	-	-	-
WALL FINISHES	1370.60	1566.40	1762.20	1958.00
FLOOR FINISHES	849.56	1079.14	1308.72	1538.30
CEILING FINISHES	533.60	800.40	1067.20	1334.00
SERVICES	1808.05	1808.05	1808.05	1808.05
ALTERATIONS TO EXISTING BUILDINGS	1378.88	1842.52	2262.44	2682.38
Sub Total	23119.99	27099.65	31263.71	35650.11
Allowance for unmeasured items and sundries 5%	1156.00	1354.98	1563.19	1782.51
NET TOTAL excluding Preliminaries, Profit and Overheads	**24275.99**	**28454.63**	**32826.90**	**37432.62**

Specification A 30 m2 - 45 m2	Ref A/2P 5x6 Size 5.00 x 6.00 m Area 30 m2	Ref A/2P 5x7 Size 5.00 x 7.00 m Area 35 m2	Ref A/2P 5x8 Size 5.00 x 8.00 m Area 40 m2	Ref A/2P 5x9 Size 5.00 x 9.00 m Area 45 m2
	Element Total £	Element Total £	Element Total £	Element Total £
TWO STOREY				
PITCHED ROOF				
SUMMARY Continued/.....				
	5202.07	5804.33	6406.59	7008.85
	2441.40	2848.30	3255.20	4636.35
	9845.06	11330.30	12912.69	14522.65
	8340.25	8911.50	9482.75	10054.00
	4142.87	4142.87	4142.87	4142.87
	1342.38	1342.38	1342.38	1342.38
	824.90	824.90	824.90	824.90
	2153.80	2349.60	2545.40	2741.20
	1767.88	1997.46	2227.04	2456.62
	1600.80	1867.60	2134.40	2401.20
	3154.07	3154.07	3154.07	3154.07
	3462.36	3685.04	3685.04	4524.88
Sub Total	44277.84	48258.35	52113.33	57809.97
Allowance for unmeasured items and sundries 5%	2213.89	2412.92	2605.67	2890.50
NET TOTAL excluding Preliminaries, Profit and Overheads	**46491.73**	**50671.27**	**54719.00**	**60700.47**

Specification B

Single storey flat roof

[1F] 2×2/3/4/5.

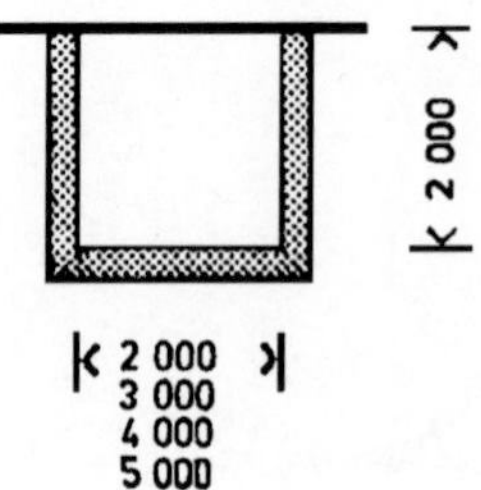

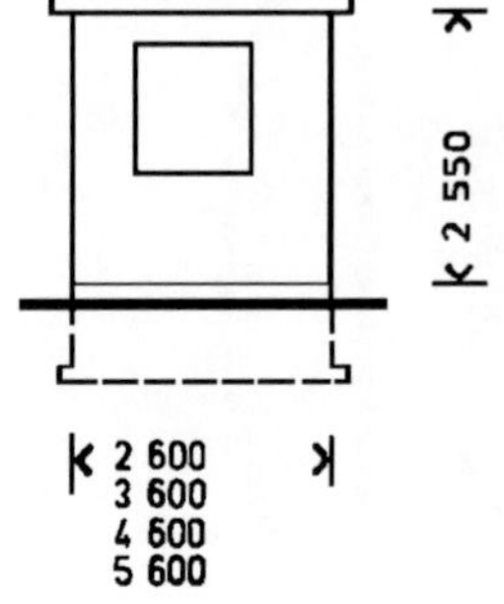

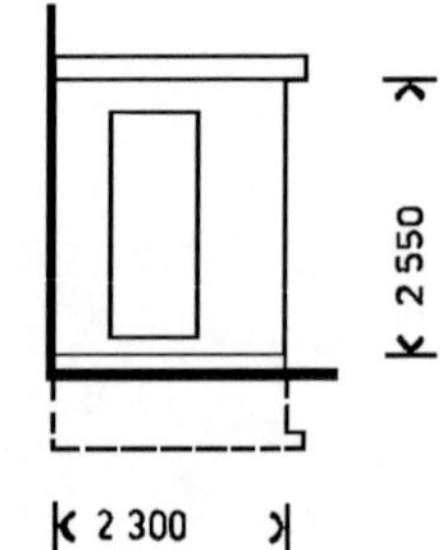

[1F] 2×6/7/8/9.

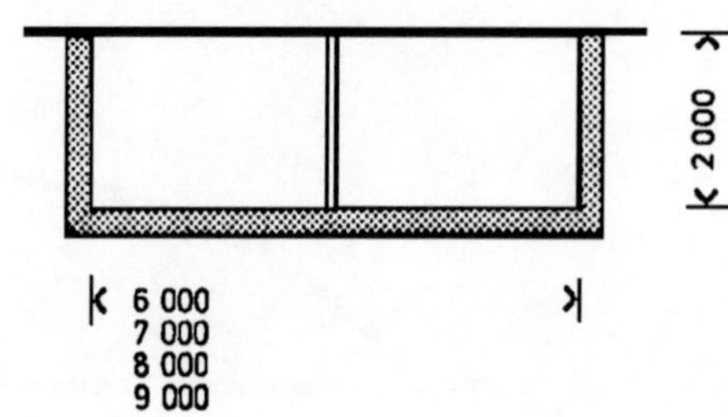

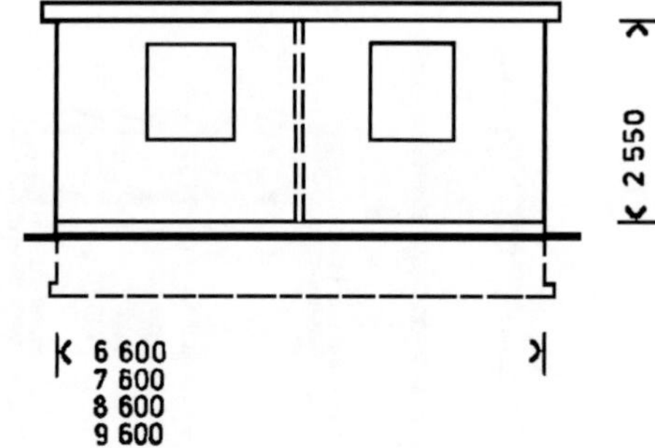

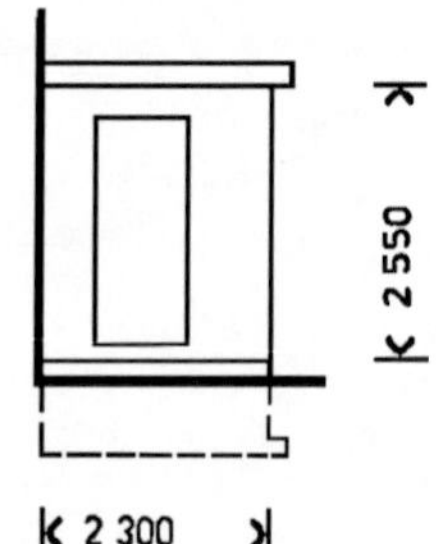

[1F] 3×2/3/4/5.

[1F] 3×6/7/8/9.

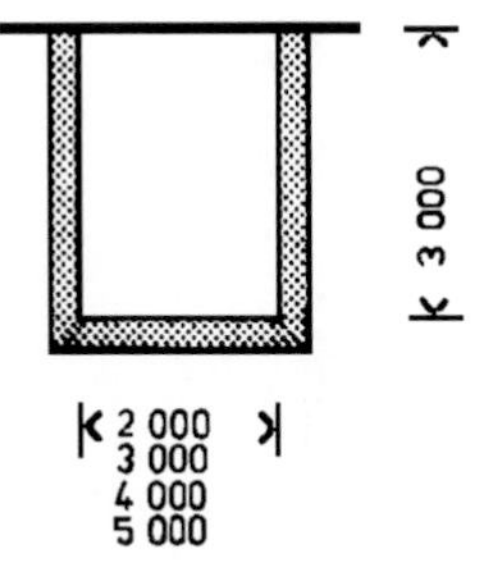

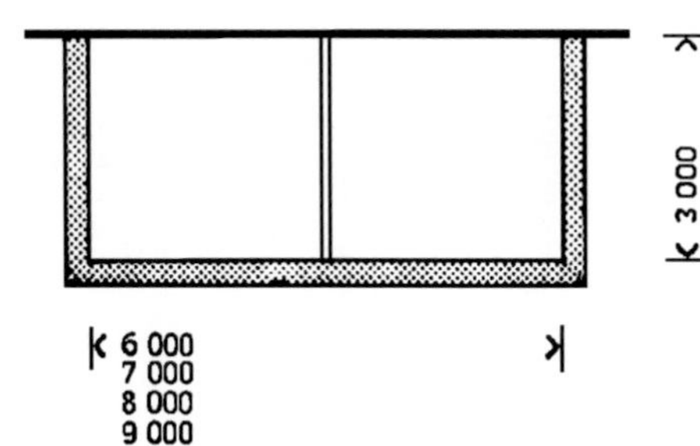

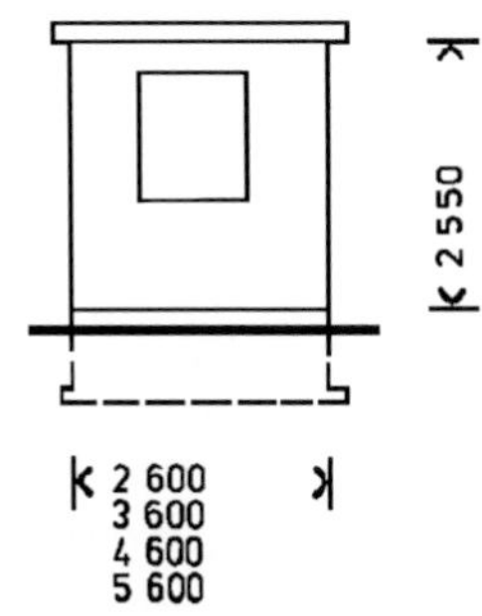

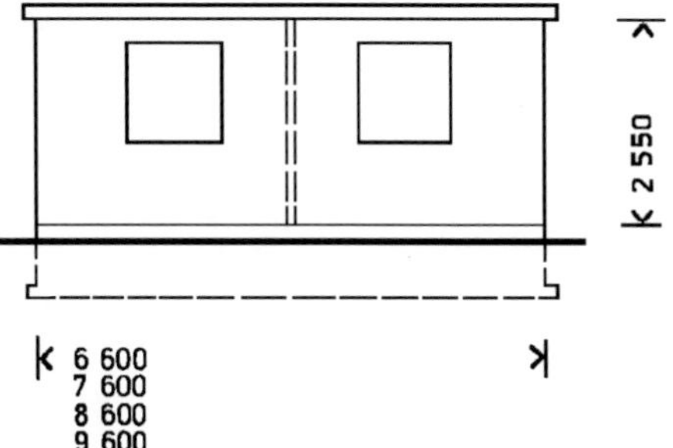

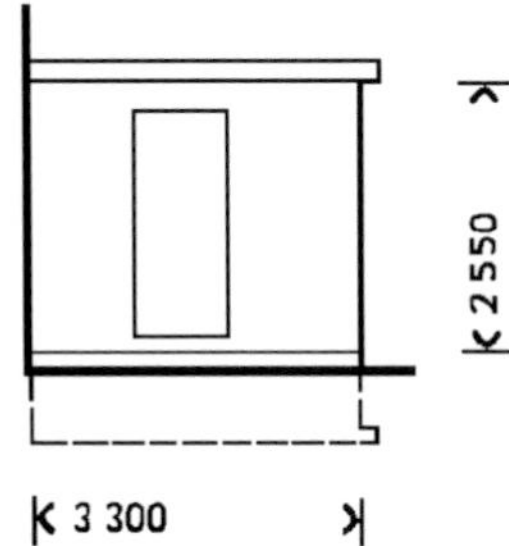

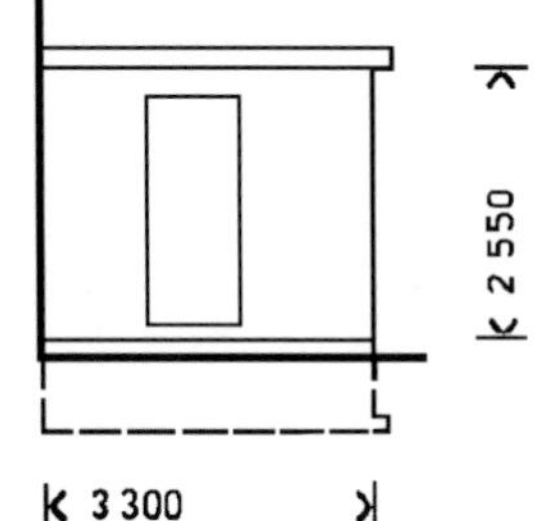

[1F] 4×2/3/4/5.

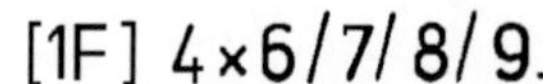
[1F] 4×6/7/8/9.

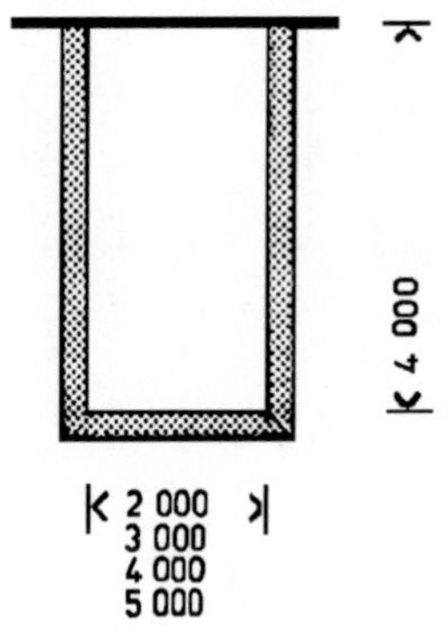
4 000
2 000
3 000
4 000
5 000

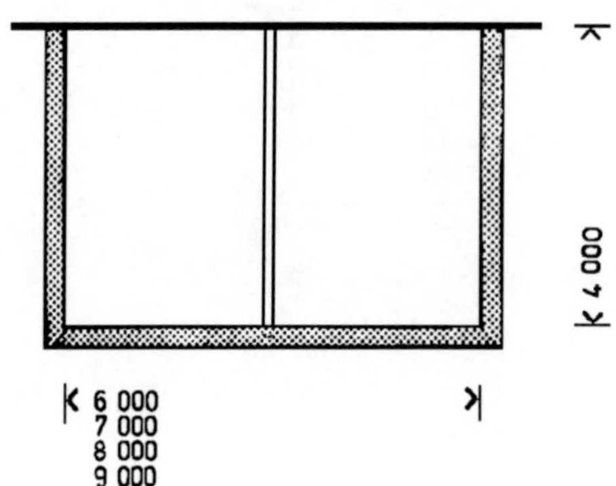
4 000
6 000
7 000
8 000
9 000

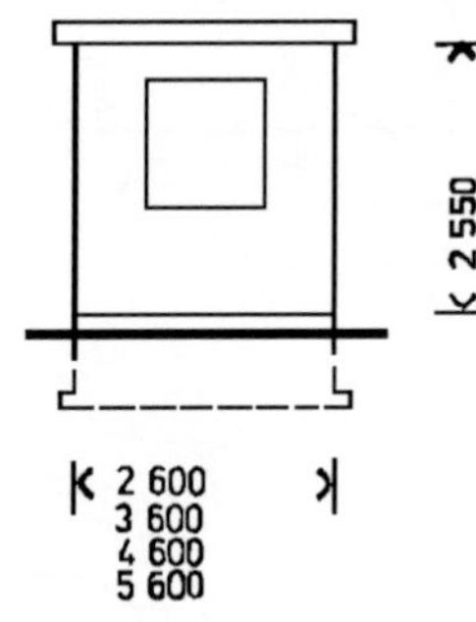
2 550
2 600
3 600
4 600
5 600

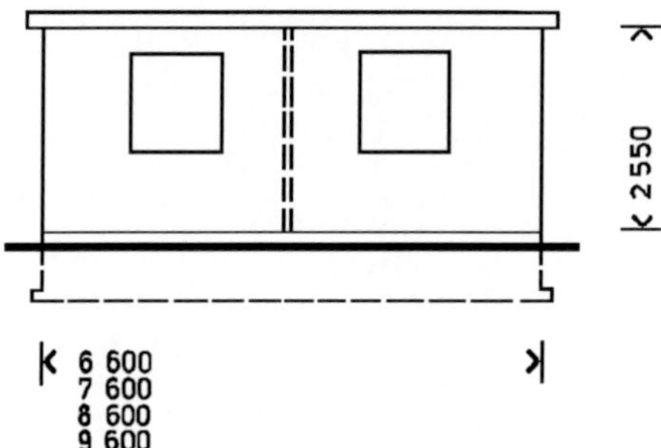
2 550
6 600
7 600
8 600
9 600

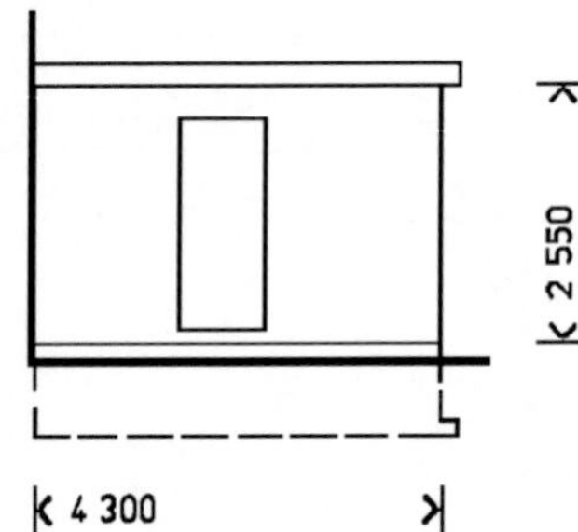
2 550
4 300

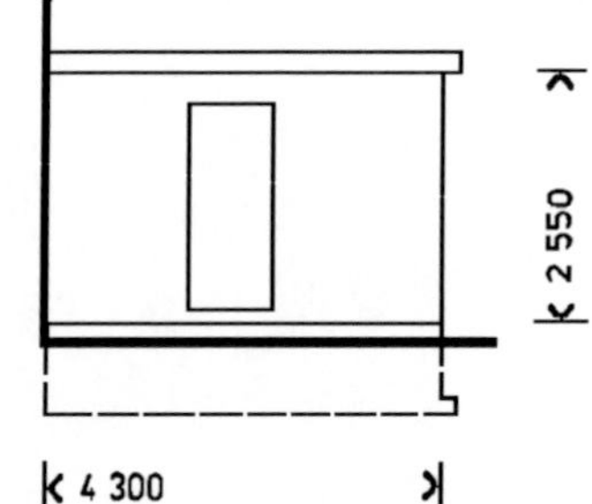
2 550
4 300

[1F] 5×2/3/4/5.

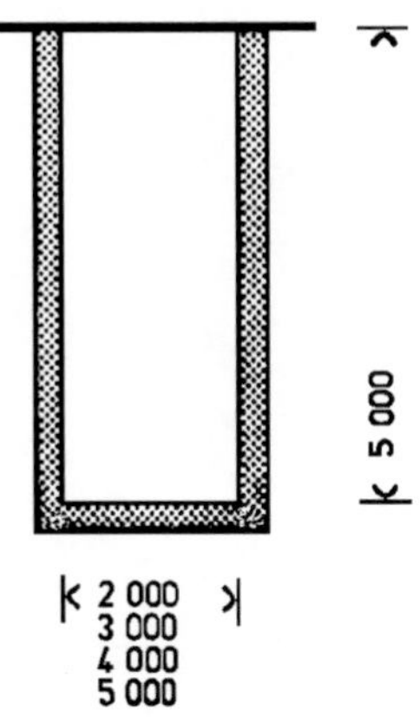

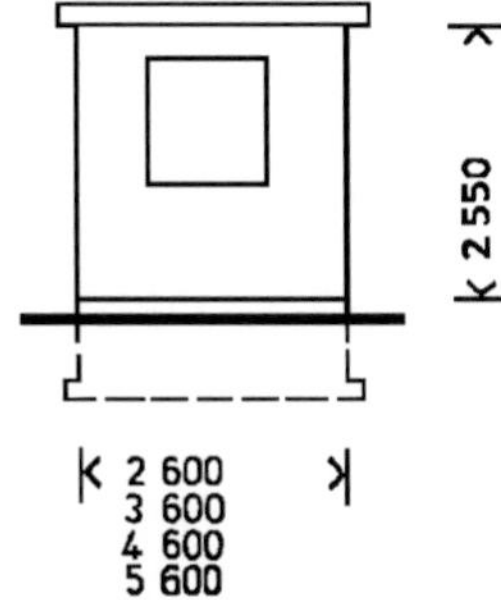

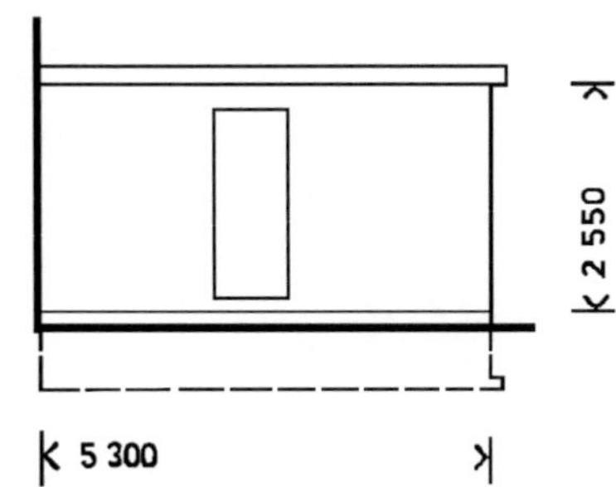

[1F] 5×6/7/8/9.

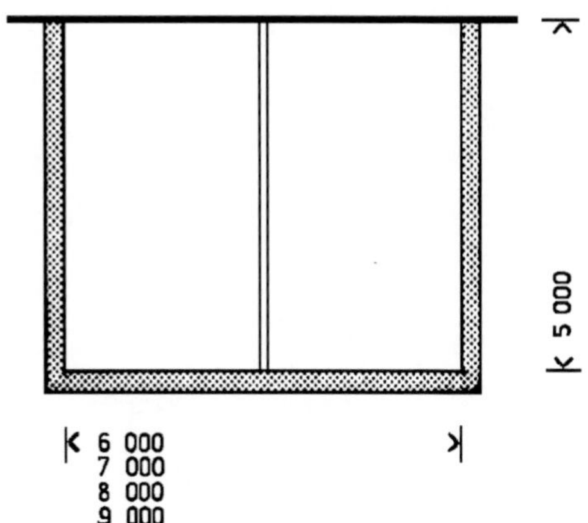

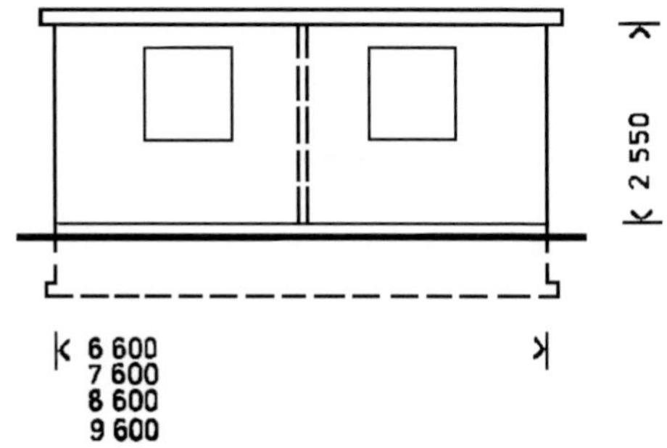

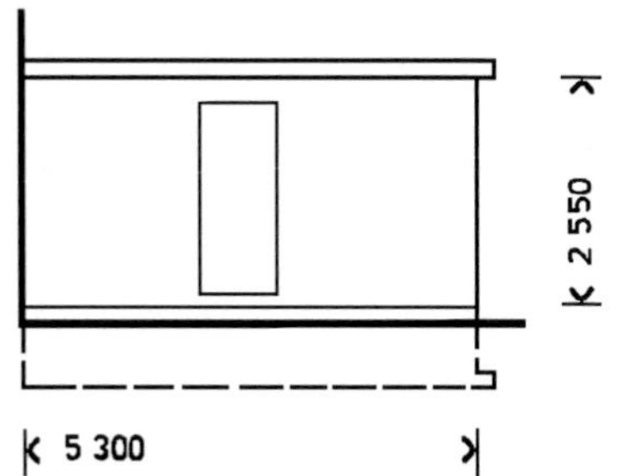

Specification B 4 m2 - 10 m2

SINGLE STOREY FLAT ROOF			Ref B/1F 2x2 Size 2.00 x 2.00 m Area 4 m2			Ref B/1F 2x3 Size 2.00 x 3.00 m Area 6 m2			Ref B/1F 2x4 Size 2.00 x 4.00 m Area 8 m2			Ref B/1F 2x5 Size 2.00 x 5.00 m Area 10 m2		
Element	Unit	Unit Rate £	Qty	Total £	Element Total £	Qty	Total £	Element Total £	Qty	Total £	Element Total £	Qty	Total £	Element Total £
SUBSTRUCTURE														
Strip footings	M	124.73	7M	873.11		8M	997.84		9M	1122.57		10M	1247.30	
Solid ground floor	M2	45.82	4M2	183.28	**1056.39**	6M2	274.92	**1272.76**	8M2	366.56	**1489.13**	10M2	458.20	**1705.50**
ROOF														
Flat roof construction 50 x 150 mm joists	M2	50.06	8M2	400.48		10M2	500.60		13M2	650.78		15M2	750.90	
Work to top of external wall	M	23.71	7M	165.97		8M	189.68		9M	213.39		10M	237.10	
Three layer felt roofing	M2	36.43	8M2	291.44		10M2	364.30		13M2	473.59		15M2	546.45	
Fascia and eaves soffit	M	42.61	8M	340.88		9M	383.49		10M	426.10		11M	468.71	
Gutters and fittings	M	18.68	3M	56.04		4M	74.72		5M	93.40		6M	112.08	
Flashings	M	24.70	3M	74.10		4M	98.80		5M	123.50		6M	148.20	
Abutment to existing wall	M	61.52	3M	184.56	**1513.47**	4M	246.08	**1857.67**	5M	307.60	**2288.36**	6M	369.12	**2632.56**
EXTERNAL WALLS														
Brick and block cavity wall	M2	106.91	13M2	1389.83	**1389.83**	15M2	1603.65	**1603.65**	18M2	1924.38	**1924.38**	20M2	2138.20	**2138.20**

Specification B 12 m2 - 18 m2

Element	Unit	Unit Rate £	Ref B/1F 2x6 Size 2.00 x 6.00 m Area 12 m2 Qty	Total £	Element Total £	Ref B/1F 2x7 Size 2.00 x 7.00 m Area 14 m2 Qty	Total £	Element Total £	Ref B/1F 2x8 Size 2.00 x 8.00 m Area 16 m2 Qty	Total £	Element Total £	Ref B/1F 2x9 Size 2.00 x 9.00 m Area 18 m2 Qty	Total £	Element Total £
SINGLE STOREY														
FLAT ROOF Continued/.....														
	M	124.73	11M	1372.03		12M	1496.76		13M	1621.49		14M	1746.22	
	M2	45.82	12M2	549.84	**1921.87**	14M2	641.48	**2138.24**	16M2	733.12	**2354.61**	18M2	824.76	**2570.98**
	M2	50.06	18M2	901.08		20M2	1001.20		23M2	1151.38		25M2	1251.50	
	M	23.71	11M	260.81		12M	284.52		13M	308.23		14M	331.94	
	M2	36.43	18M2	655.74		20M2	728.60		23M2	837.89		25M2	910.75	
	M	42.61	12M	511.32		13M	553.93		14M	596.54		15M	639.15	
	M	18.68	7M	130.76		8M	149.44		9M	168.12		10M	186.80	
	M	24.70	7M	172.90		8M	197.60		9M	222.30		10M	247.00	
	M	61.52	7M	430.64	**3063.25**	8M	492.16	**3407.45**	9M	553.68	**3838.14**	10M	615.20	**4182.34**
	M2	106.91	21M2	2245.11	**2245.11**	23M2	2458.93	**2458.93**	26M2	2779.66	**2779.66**	28M2	2993.48	**2993.48**

Specification B
4 m2 - 10 m2

Element	Unit	Unit Rate £	Ref B/1F 2x2 Size 2.00 x 2.00 m Area 4 m2 Qty	Total £	Element Total £	Ref B/1F 2x3 Size 2.00 x 3.00 m Area 6 m2 Qty	Total £	Element Total £	Ref B/1F 2x4 Size 2.00 x 4.00 m Area 8 m2 Qty	Total £	Element Total £	Ref B/1F 2x5 Size 2.00 x 5.00 m Area 10 m2 Qty	Total £	Element Total £
SINGLE STOREY														
FLAT ROOF														
EXTERNAL DOORS AND WINDOWS														
External door	NR	478.42	1NR	478.42		1NR	478.42		1NR	478.42		1NR	478.42	
Windows	NR	518.08	1NR	518.08		1NR	518.08		1NR	518.08		1NR	518.08	
Opening in cavity wall for door	NR	179.51	1NR	179.51		1NR	179.51		1NR	179.51		1NR	179.51	
Opening in cavity wall for window	NR	150.89	1NR	150.89	**1326.90**	1NR	150.89	**1326.90**	1NR	150.89	**1326.90**	1NR	150.89	**1326.90**
INTERNAL WALLS AND PARTITIONS														
Stud partitions	M2	51.63												
INTERNAL DOORS														
Softwood flush door	NR	251.11												
WALL FINISHES														
Plaster & decoration	M2	19.58	20M2	391.60	**391.60**	25M2	489.50	**489.50**	30M2	587.40	**587.40**	35M2	685.30	**685.30**
FLOOR FINISHES														
Thermoplastic tiles on screed	M2	35.42	4M2	141.68		6M2	212.52		8M2	283.36		10M2	354.20	
Softwood skirting	M	11.09	8M	88.72	**230.40**	10M	110.90	**323.42**	12M	133.08	**416.44**	14M	155.26	**509.46**
CEILING FINISHES														
Plasterboard and Artex	M2	16.34	4M2	65.36	**65.36**	6M2	98.04	**98.04**	8M2	130.72	**130.72**	10M2	163.40	**163.40**

Specification B
12 m2 - 18 m2

SINGLE STOREY

FLAT ROOF Continued/.....

Element	Unit	Unit Rate £	Ref B/1F 2x6 Size 2.00 x 6.00 m Area 12 m2 Qty	Total £	Element Total £	Ref B/1F 2x7 Size 2.00 x 7.00 m Area 14 m2 Qty	Total £	Element Total £	Ref B/1F 2x8 Size 2.00 x 8.00 m Area 16 m2 Qty	Total £	Element Total £	Ref B/1F 2x9 Size 2.00 x 9.00 m Area 18 m2 Qty	Total £	Element Total £
	NR	478.42	1NR	478.42		1NR	478.42		1NR	478.42		1NR	478.42	
	NR	518.08	2NR	1036.16		2NR	1036.16		2NR	1036.16		2NR	1036.16	
	NR	179.51	1NR	179.51		1NR	179.51		1NR	179.51		1NR	179.51	
	NR	150.89	2NR	301.78	**1995.87**	2NR	301.78	**1995.87**	2NR	301.78	**1995.87**	2NR	301.78	**1995.87**
	M2	51.63	5M2	258.15	**258.15**	5M2	258.15	**258.15**	5M2	258.15	**258.15**	5M2	258.15	**258.15**
	NR	251.11	1NR	251.11	**251.11**	1NR	251.11	**251.11**	1NR	251.11	**251.11**	1NR	251.11	**251.11**
	M2	19.58	40M2	783.20	**783.20**	45M2	881.10	**881.10**	50M2	979.00	**979.00**	55M2	1076.90	**1076.90**
	M2	35.42	12M2	425.04		14M2	495.88		16M2	566.72		18M2	637.56	
	M	11.09	16M	177.44	**602.48**	18M	199.62	**695.50**	20M	221.80	**788.52**	22M	243.98	**881.54**
	M2	16.34	12M2	196.08	**196.08**	14M2	228.76	**228.76**	16M2	261.44	**261.44**	18M2	294.12	**294.12**

Specification B
4 m2 - 10 m2

Element	Unit	Unit Rate £	Ref B/1F 2x2 Size 2.00 x 2.00 m Area 4 m2 Qty	Total £	Element Total £	Ref B/1F 2x3 Size 2.00 x 3.00 m Area 6 m2 Qty	Total £	Element Total £	Ref B/1F 2x4 Size 2.00 x 4.00 m Area 8 m2 Qty	Total £	Element Total £	Ref B/1F 2x5 Size 2.00 x 5.00 m Area 10 m2 Qty	Total £	Element Total £
SINGLE STOREY														
FLAT ROOF														
SERVICES														
Rainwater pipes	M	26.64	3M	79.92		3M	79.92		3M	79.92		3M	79.92	
Cold water service point	NR	110.52	1NR	110.52		1NR	110.52		1NR	110.52		1NR	110.52	
Hot water service point	NR	191.67	1NR	191.67		1NR	191.67		1NR	191.67		1NR	191.67	
Central heating service point	NR	386.51	1NR	386.51		1NR	386.51		1NR	386.51		1NR	386.51	
Electrical installation	NR	286.50	1NR	286.50	**1055.12**	1NR	286.50	**1055.12**	1NR	286.50	**1055.12**	1NR	286.50	**1055.12**
ALTERATIONS TO EXISTING BUILDINGS														
Opening in existing wall 1.80 m wide 2.00 m high	NR	689.44	1NR	689.44	**689.44**									
Opening in existing wall 2.40 m wide 2.00 m high	NR	865.59												
Opening in existing wall 3.00 m wide 2.00 m high	NR	921.26				1NR	921.26	**921.26**						
Opening in existing wall 4.00 m wide 2.00 m high	NR	1131.22							1NR	1131.22	**1131.22**			
Opening in existing wall 5.00 m wide 2.00 m high	NR	1341.19										1NR	1341.19	**1341.19**

Specification B 12 m2 - 18 m2			**Ref B/1F 2x6 Size 2.00 x 6.00 m Area 12 m2**			**Ref B/1F 2x7 Size 2.00 x 7.00 m Area 14 m2**			**Ref B/1F 2x8 Size 2.00 x 8.00 m Area 16 m2**			**Ref B/1F 2x9 Size 2.00 x 9.00 m Area 18 m2**		
			Qty	**Total £**	**Element Total £**	**Qty**	**Total £**	**Element Total £**	**Qty**	**Total £**	**Element Total £**	**Qty**	**Total £**	**Element Total £**
SINGLE STOREY FLAT ROOF Continued/.....														
Element	Unit	Unit Rate £												
	M	26.64	3M	79.92		3M	79.92		3M	79.92		3M	79.92	
	NR	110.52	1NR	110.52		1NR	110.52		1NR	110.52		1NR	110.52	
	NR	191.67	1NR	191.67		1NR	191.67		1NR	191.67		1NR	191.67	
	NR	386.51	2NR	773.02		2NR	773.02		2NR	773.02		2NR	773.02	
	NR	286.50	2NR	573.00	**1728.13**	2NR	573.00	**1728.13**	2NR	573.00	**1728.13**	2NR	573.00	**1728.13**
	NR	689.44												
	NR	865.59	2NR	1731.18	**1731.18**									
	NR	921.26				2NR	1842.52	**1842.52**	2NR	1842.52	**1842.52**			
	NR	1131.22										2NR	2262.44	**2262.44**
	NR	1341.19												

Specification B 4 m2 - 10 m2	Ref B/1F 2x2 Size 2.00 x 2.00 m Area 4 m2 Element Total £	Ref B/1F 2x3 Size 2.00 x 3.00 m Area 6 m2 Element Total £	Ref B/1F 2x4 Size 2.00 x 4.00 m Area 8 m2 Element Total £	Ref B/1F 2x5 Size 2.00 x 5.00 m Area 10 m2 Element Total £
SINGLE STOREY				
FLAT ROOF				
SUMMARY				
SUBSTRUCTURE	1056.39	1272.76	1489.13	1705.50
UPPER FLOORS	-	-	-	-
ROOF	1513.47	1857.67	2288.36	2632.56
EXTERNAL WALLS	1389.83	1603.65	1924.38	2138.20
EXTERNAL DOORS AND WINDOWS	1326.90	1326.90	1326.90	1326.90
INTERNAL WALLS AND PARTITIONS	-	-	-	-
INTERNAL DOORS	-	-	-	-
WALL FINISHES	391.60	489.50	587.40	685.30
FLOOR FINISHES	230.40	323.42	416.44	509.46
CEILING FINISHES	65.36	98.04	130.72	163.40
SERVICES	1055.12	1055.12	1055.12	1055.12
ALTERATIONS TO EXISTING BUILDINGS	689.44	921.26	1131.22	1341.19
Sub Total	7718.51	8948.32	10349.67	11557.63
Allowance for unmeasured items and sundries 5%	385.93	447.42	517.48	577.88
NET TOTAL excluding Preliminaries, Profit and Overheads	**8104.44**	**9395.74**	**10867.15**	**12135.51**

Specification B 12 m2 - 18 m2	**Ref B/1F 2x6 Size 2.00 x 6.00 m Area 12 m2**	**Ref B/1F 2x7 Size 2.00 x 7.00 m Area 14 m2**	**Ref B/1F 2x8 Size 2.00 x 8.00 m Area 16 m2**	**Ref B/1F 2x9 Size 2.00 x 9.00 m Area 18 m2**
	Element Total £	**Element Total £**	**Element Total £**	**Element Total £**
SINGLE STOREY				
FLAT ROOF				
SUMMARY Continued/.....				
	1921.87	2138.24	2354.61	2570.98
	-	-	-	-
	3063.25	3407.45	3838.14	4182.34
	2245.11	2458.93	2779.66	2993.48
	1995.87	1995.87	1995.87	1995.87
	258.15	258.15	258.15	258.15
	251.11	251.11	251.11	251.11
	783.20	881.10	979.00	1076.90
	602.48	695.50	788.52	881.54
	196.08	228.76	261.44	294.12
	1728.13	1728.13	1728.13	1728.13
	1731.18	1842.52	1842.52	2262.44
Sub Total	14776.43	15885.76	17077.15	18495.06
Allowance for unmeasured items and sundries 5%	738.82	794.29	853.86	924.75
NET TOTAL excluding Preliminaries, Profit and Overheads	**15515.25**	**16680.05**	**17931.01**	**19419.81**

Specification B 6 m2 - 15 m2

SINGLE STOREY

FLAT ROOF

Element	Unit	Unit Rate £	Ref B/1F 3x2 Size 3.00 x 2.00 m Area 6 m2 Qty	Total £	Element Total £	Ref B/1F 3x3 Size 3.00 x 3.00 m Area 9 m2 Qty	Total £	Element Total £	Ref B/1F 3x4 Size 3.00 x 4.00 m Area 12 m2 Qty	Total £	Element Total £	Ref B/1F 3x5 Size 3.00 x 5.00 m Area 15 m2 Qty	Total £	Element Total £
SUBSTRUCTURE														
Strip footings	M	124.73	9M	1122.57		10M	1247.30		11M	1372.03		12M	1496.76	
Solid ground floor	M2	45.82	6M2	274.92	**1397.49**	9M2	412.38	**1659.68**	12M2	549.84	**1921.87**	15M2	687.30	**2184.06**
ROOF														
Flat roof construction 50 x 150 mm joists	M2	50.06	11M2	550.66		14M2	700.84		18M2	901.08		21M2	1051.26	
Work to top of external wall	M	23.71	9M	213.39		10M	237.10		11M	260.81		12M	284.52	
Three layer felt roofing	M2	36.43	11M2	400.73		14M2	510.02		18M2	655.74		21M2	765.03	
Fascia and eaves soffit	M	42.61	10M	426.10		11M	468.71		12M	511.32		13M	553.93	
Gutters and fittings	M	18.68	3M	56.04		4M	74.72		5M	93.40		6M	112.08	
Flashings	M	24.70	3M	74.10		4M	98.80		5M	123.50		6M	148.20	
Abutment to existing wall	M	61.52	3M	184.56	**1905.58**	4M	246.08	**2336.27**	5M	307.60	**2853.45**	6M	369.12	**3284.14**
EXTERNAL WALLS														
Brick and block cavity wall	M2	106.91	18M2	1924.38	**1924.38**	20M2	2138.20	**2138.20**	23M2	2458.93	**2458.93**	25M2	2672.75	**2672.75**

Specification B 18 m2 - 27 m2

SINGLE STOREY

FLAT ROOF Continued/.....

Element	Unit	Unit Rate £	Ref B/1F 3x6 Size 3.00 x 6.00 m Area 18 m2 Qty	Total £	Element Total £	Ref B/1F 3x7 Size 3.00 x 7.00 m Area 21 m2 Qty	Total £	Element Total £	Ref B/1F 3x8 Size 3.00 x 8.00 m Area 24 m2 Qty	Total £	Element Total £	Ref B/1F 3x9 Size 3.00 x 9.00 m Area 27 m2 Qty	Total £	Element Total £
	M	124.73	13M	1621.49		14M	1746.22		15M	1870.95		16M	1995.68	
	M2	45.82	18M2	824.76	**2446.25**	21M2	962.22	**2708.44**	24M2	1099.68	**2970.63**	27M2	1237.14	**3232.82**
	M2	50.06	25M2	1251.50		28M2	1401.68		32M2	1601.92		35M2	1752.10	
	M	23.71	13M	308.23		14M	331.94		15M	355.65		16M	379.36	
	M2	36.43	25M2	910.75		28M2	1020.04		32M2	1165.76		35M2	1275.05	
	M	42.61	14M	596.54		15M	639.15		16M	681.76		17M	724.37	
	M	18.68	7M	130.76		8M	149.44		9M	168.12		10M	186.80	
	M	24.70	7M	172.90		8M	197.60		9M	222.30		10M	247.00	
	M	61.52	7M	430.64	**3801.32**	8M	492.16	**4232.01**	9M	553.68	**4749.19**	10M	615.20	**5179.88**
	M2	106.91	26M2	2779.66	**2779.66**	27M2	2886.57	**2886.57**	31M2	3314.21	**3314.21**	33M2	3528.03	**3528.03**

Specification B 6 m2 - 15 m2

SINGLE STOREY FLAT ROOF			Ref B/1F 3x2 Size 3.00 x 2.00 m Area 6 m2			Ref B/1F 3x3 Size 3.00 x 3.00 m Area 9 m2			Ref B/1F 3x4 Size 3.00 x 4.00 m Area 12 m2			Ref B/1F 3x5 Size 3.00 x 5.00 m Area 15 m2		
Element	Unit	Unit Rate £	Qty	Total £	Element Total £	Qty	Total £	Element Total £	Qty	Total £	Element Total £	Qty	Total £	Element Total £
EXTERNAL DOORS AND WINDOWS														
External door	NR	478.42	1NR	478.42		1NR	478.42		1NR	478.42		1NR	478.42	
Windows	NR	518.08	1NR	518.08		1NR	518.08		1NR	518.08		1NR	518.08	
Opening in cavity wall for door	NR	179.51	1NR	179.51		1NR	179.51		1NR	179.51		1NR	179.51	
Opening in cavity wall for window	NR	150.89	1NR	150.89	**1326.90**	1NR	150.89	**1326.90**	1NR	150.89	**1326.90**	1NR	150.89	**1326.90**
INTERNAL WALLS AND PARTITIONS														
Stud partitions	M2	51.63												
INTERNAL DOORS														
Softwood flush door	NR	251.11												
WALL FINISHES														
Plaster & decoration	M2	19.58	25M2	489.50	**489.50**	30M2	587.40	**587.40**	35M2	685.30	**685.30**	40M2	783.20	**783.20**
FLOOR FINISHES														
Thermoplastic tiles on screed	M2	35.42	6M2	212.52		9M2	318.78		12M2	425.04		15M2	531.30	
Softwood skirting	M	11.09	10M	110.90	**323.42**	12M	133.08	**451.86**	14M	155.26	**580.30**	16M	177.44	**708.74**
CEILING FINISHES														
Plasterboard and Artex	M2	16.34	6M2	98.04	**98.04**	9M2	147.06	**147.06**	12M2	196.08	**196.08**	15M2	245.10	**245.10**

Specification B
18 m2 - 27 m2

SINGLE STOREY FLAT ROOF Continued/.....			Ref B/1F 3x6 Size 3.00 x 6.00 m Area 18 m2			Ref B/1F 3x7 Size 3.00 x 7.00 m Area 21 m2			Ref B/1F 3x8 Size 3.00 x 8.00 m Area 24 m2			Ref B/1F 3x9 Size 3.00 x 9.00 m Area 27 m2		
Element	Unit	Unit Rate £	Qty	Total £	Element Total £	Qty	Total £	Element Total £	Qty	Total £	Element Total £	Qty	Total £	Element Total £
	NR	478.42	1NR	478.42		1NR	478.42		1NR	478.42		1NR	478.42	
	NR	518.08	2NR	1036.16		2NR	1036.16		2NR	1036.16		2NR	1036.16	
	NR	179.51	1NR	179.51		1NR	179.51		1NR	179.51		1NR	179.51	
	NR	150.89	2NR	301.78	**1995.87**	2NR	301.78	**1995.87**	2NR	301.78	**1995.87**	2NR	301.78	**1995.87**
	M2	51.63	8M2	413.04	**413.04**	8M2	413.04	**413.04**	8M2	413.04	**413.04**	8M2	413.04	**413.04**
	NR	251.11	1NR	251.11	**251.11**	1NR	251.11	**251.11**	1NR	251.11	**251.11**	1NR	251.11	**251.11**
	M2	19.58	45M2	881.10	**881.10**	50M2	979.00	**979.00**	55M2	1076.90	**1076.90**	60M2	1174.80	**1174.80**
	M2	35.42	18M2	637.56		21M2	743.82		24M2	850.08		27M2	956.34	
	M	11.09	18M	199.62	**837.18**	20M	221.80	**965.62**	22M	243.98	**1094.06**	24M	266.16	**1222.50**
	M2	16.34	18M2	294.12	**294.12**	21M2	343.14	**343.14**	24M2	392.16	**392.16**	27M2	441.18	**441.18**

Specification B 6 m2 - 15 m2

SINGLE STOREY FLAT ROOF			Ref B/1F 3x2 Size 3.00 x 2.00 m Area 6 m2			Ref B/1F 3x3 Size 3.00 x 3.00 m Area 9 m2			Ref B/1F 3x4 Size 3.00 x 4.00 m Area 12 m2			Ref B/1F 3x5 Size 3.00 x 5.00 m Area 15 m2		
Element	Unit	Unit Rate £	Qty	Total £	Element Total £	Qty	Total £	Element Total £	Qty	Total £	Element Total £	Qty	Total £	Element Total £
SERVICES														
Rainwater pipes	M	26.64	3M	79.92		3M	79.92		3M	79.92		3M	79.92	
Cold water service point	NR	110.52	1NR	110.52		1NR	110.52		1NR	110.52		1NR	110.52	
Hot water service point	NR	191.67	1NR	191.67		1NR	191.67		1NR	191.67		1NR	191.67	
Central heating service point	NR	386.51	1NR	386.51		1NR	386.51		1NR	386.51		1NR	386.51	
Electrical installation	NR	286.50	1NR	286.50	**1055.12**	1NR	286.50	**1055.12**	1NR	286.50	**1055.12**	1NR	286.50	**1055.12**
ALTERATIONS TO EXISTING BUILDINGS														
Opening in existing wall 1.80 m wide 2.00 m high	NR	689.44	1NR	689.44	**689.44**									
Opening in existing wall 2.40 m wide 2.00 m high	NR	865.59												
Opening in existing wall 3.00 m wide 2.00 m high	NR	921.26				1NR	921.26	**921.26**						
Opening in existing wall 4.00 m wide 2.00 m high	NR	1131.22							1NR	1131.22	**1131.22**			
Opening in existing wall 5.00 m wide 2.00 m high	NR	1341.19										1NR	1341.19	**1341.19**

Specification B
18 m2 - 27 m2

SINGLE STOREY

FLAT ROOF Continued/.....

Element	Unit	Unit Rate £	Ref B/1F 3x6 Size 3.00 x 6.00 m Area 18 m2 Qty	Total £	Element Total £	Ref B/1F 3x7 Size 3.00 x 7.00 m Area 21 m2 Qty	Total £	Element Total £	Ref B/1F 3x8 Size 3.00 x 8.00 m Area 24 m2 Qty	Total £	Element Total £	Ref B/1F 3x9 Size 3.00 x 9.00 m Area 27 m2 Qty	Total £	Element Total £
	M	26.64	3M	79.92		3M	79.92		3M	79.92		3M	79.92	
	NR	110.52	1NR	110.52		1NR	110.52		1NR	110.52		1NR	110.52	
	NR	191.67	1NR	191.67		1NR	191.67		1NR	191.67		1NR	191.67	
	NR	386.51	2NR	773.02		2NR	773.02		2NR	773.02		2NR	773.02	
	NR	286.50	2NR	573.00	**1728.13**	2NR	573.00	**1728.13**	2NR	573.00	**1728.13**	2NR	573.00	**1728.13**
	NR	689.44												
	NR	865.59	2NR	1731.18	**1731.18**									
	NR	921.26				2NR	1842.52	**1842.52**	2NR	1842.52	**1842.52**			
	NR	1131.22										2NR	2262.44	**2262.44**
	NR	1341.19												

Specification B 6 m2 - 15 m2	Ref B/1F 3x2 Size 3.00 x 2.00 m Area 6 m2 Element Total £	Ref B/1F 3x3 Size 3.00 x 3.00 m Area 9 m2 Element Total £	Ref B/1F 3x4 Size 3.00 x 4.00 m Area 12 m2 Element Total £	Ref B/1F 3x5 Size 3.00 x 5.00 m Area 15 m2 Element Total £
SINGLE STOREY				
FLAT ROOF				
SUMMARY				
SUBSTRUCTURE	1397.49	1659.68	1921.87	2184.06
UPPER FLOORS	-	-	-	-
ROOF	1905.58	2336.27	2853.45	3284.14
EXTERNAL WALLS	1924.38	2138.20	2458.93	2672.75
EXTERNAL DOORS AND WINDOWS	1326.90	1326.90	1326.90	1326.90
INTERNAL WALLS AND PARTITIONS	-	-	-	-
INTERNAL DOORS	-	-	-	-
WALL FINISHES	489.50	587.40	685.30	783.20
FLOOR FINISHES	323.42	451.86	580.30	708.74
CEILING FINISHES	98.04	147.06	196.08	245.10
SERVICES	1055.12	1055.12	1055.12	1055.12
ALTERATIONS TO EXISTING BUILDINGS	689.44	921.26	1131.22	1341.19
Sub Total	9209.87	10623.75	12209.17	13601.20
Allowance for unmeasured items and sundries 5%	460.49	531.19	610.46	680.06
NET TOTAL excluding Preliminaries, Profit and Overheads	**9670.36**	**11154.94**	**12819.63**	**14281.26**

Specification B 18 m2 - 27 m2	Ref B/1F 3x6 Size 3.00 x 6.00 m Area 18 m2 Element Total £	Ref B/1F 3x7 Size 3.00 x 7.00 m Area 21 m2 Element Total £	Ref B/1F 3x8 Size 3.00 x 8.00 m Area 24 m2 Element Total £	Ref B/1F 3x9 Size 3.00 x 9.00 m Area 27 m2 Element Total £
SINGLE STOREY				
FLAT ROOF				
SUMMARY Continued/.....				
	2446.25	2708.44	2970.63	3232.82
	-	-	-	-
	3801.32	4232.01	4749.19	5179.88
	2779.66	2886.57	3314.21	3528.03
	1995.87	1995.87	1995.87	1995.87
	413.04	413.04	413.04	413.04
	251.11	251.11	251.11	251.11
	881.10	979.00	1076.90	1174.80
	837.18	965.62	1094.06	1222.50
	294.12	343.14	392.16	441.18
	1728.13	1728.13	1728.13	1728.13
	1731.18	1842.52	1842.52	2262.44
Sub Total	17158.96	18345.45	19827.82	21429.80
Allowance for unmeasured items and sundries 5%	857.95	917.27	991.39	1071.49
NET TOTAL excluding Preliminaries, Profit and Overheads	**18016.91**	**19262.72**	**20819.21**	**22501.29**

Specification B 8 m2 - 20 m2

Element	Unit	Unit Rate £	Ref B/1F 4x2 Size 4.00 x 2.00 m Area 8 m2 Qty	Total £	Element Total £	Ref B/1F 4x3 Size 4.00 x 3.00 m Area 12 m2 Qty	Total £	Element Total £	Ref B/1F 4x4 Size 4.00 x 4.00 m Area 16 m2 Qty	Total £	Element Total £	Ref B/1F 4x5 Size 4.00 x 5.00 m Area 20 m2 Qty	Total £	Element Total £
SINGLE STOREY														
FLAT ROOF														
SUBSTRUCTURE														
Strip footings	M	124.73	11M	1372.03		12M	1496.76		13M	1621.49		14M	1746.22	
Solid ground floor	M2	45.82	8M2	366.56	**1738.59**	12M2	549.84	**2046.60**	16M2	733.12	**2354.61**	20M2	916.40	**2662.62**
ROOF														
Flat roof construction 50 x 150 mm joists	M2	50.06	14M2	700.84		18M2	901.08							
Flat roof construction 50 x 200 mm joists	M2	52.26							23M2	1201.98		27M2	1411.02	
Work to top of external wall	M	23.71	11M	260.81		12M	284.52		13M	308.23		14M	331.94	
Three layer felt roofing	M2	36.43	14M2	510.02		18M2	655.74		23M2	837.89		27M2	983.61	
Fascia and eaves soffit	M	42.61	12M	511.32		13M	553.93		14M	596.54		15M	639.15	
Gutters and fittings	M	18.68	3M	56.04		4M	74.72		5M	93.40		6M	112.08	
Flashings	M	24.70	3M	74.10		4M	98.80		5M	123.50		6M	148.20	
Abutment to existing wall	M	61.52	3M	184.56	**2297.69**	4M	246.08	**2814.87**	5M	307.60	**3469.14**	6M	369.12	**3995.12**
EXTERNAL WALLS														
Brick and block cavity wall	M2	106.91	23M2	2458.93	**2458.93**	25M2	2672.75	**2672.75**	28M2	2993.48	**2993.48**	29M2	3100.39	**3100.39**

Specification B
24 m2 - 36 m2

SINGLE STOREY

FLAT ROOF Continued/.....

Element	Unit	Unit Rate £	Ref B/1F 4x6 Size 4.00 x 6.00 m Area 24 m2 Qty	Total £	Element Total £	Ref B/1F 4x7 Size 4.00 x 7.00 m Area 28 m2 Qty	Total £	Element Total £	Ref B/1F 4x8 Size 4.00 x 8.00 m Area 32 m2 Qty	Total £	Element Total £	Ref B/1F 4x9 Size 4.00 x 9.00 m Area 36 m2 Qty	Total £	Element Total £
	M	124.73	15M	1870.95		16M	1995.68		17M	2120.41		18M	2245.14	
	M2	45.82	24M2	1099.68	**2970.63**	28M2	1282.96	**3278.64**	32M2	1466.24	**3586.65**	36M2	1649.52	**3894.66**
	M2	50.06	32M2	1601.92		36M2	1802.16							
	M2	52.26							41M2	2142.66		45M2	2351.70	
	M	23.71	15M	355.65		16M	379.36		17M	403.07		18M	426.78	
	M2	36.43	32M2	1165.76		36M2	1311.48		41M2	1493.63		45M2	1639.35	
	M	42.61	16M	681.76		17M	724.37		18M	766.98		19M	809.59	
	M	18.68	7M	130.76		8M	149.44		9M	168.12		10M	186.80	
	M	24.70	7M	172.90		8M	197.60		9M	222.30		10M	247.00	
	M	61.52	7M	430.64	**4539.39**	8M	492.16	**5056.57**	9M	553.68	**5750.44**	10M	615.20	**6276.42**
	M2	106.91	31M2	3314.21	**3314.21**	33M2	3528.03	**3528.03**	36M2	3848.76	**3848.76**	38M2	4062.58	**4062.58**

Specification B 8 m2 - 20 m2

SINGLE STOREY

FLAT ROOF

Element	Unit	Unit Rate £	Ref B/1F 4x2 Size 4.00 x 2.00 m Area 8 m2 Qty	Total £	Element Total £	Ref B/1F 4x3 Size 4.00 x 3.00 m Area 12 m2 Qty	Total £	Element Total £	Ref B/1F 4x4 Size 4.00 x 4.00 m Area 16 m2 Qty	Total £	Element Total £	Ref B/1F 4x5 Size 4.00 x 5.00 m Area 20 m2 Qty	Total £	Element Total £
EXTERNAL DOORS AND WINDOWS														
External door	NR	478.42	1NR	478.42		1NR	478.42		1NR	478.42		1NR	478.42	
Windows	NR	518.08	1NR	518.08		1NR	518.08		1NR	518.08		1NR	518.08	
Opening in cavity wall for door	NR	179.51	1NR	179.51		1NR	179.51		1NR	179.51		1NR	179.51	
Opening in cavity wall for window	NR	150.89	1NR	150.89	**1326.90**	1NR	150.89	**1326.90**	1NR	150.89	**1326.90**	1NR	150.89	**1326.90**
INTERNAL WALLS AND PARTITIONS														
Stud partitions	M2	51.63												
INTERNAL DOORS														
Softwood flush door	NR	251.11												
WALL FINISHES														
Plaster & decoration	M2	19.58	30M2	587.40	**587.40**	35M2	685.30	**685.30**	40M2	783.20	**783.20**	45M2	881.10	**881.10**
FLOOR FINISHES														
Thermoplastic tiles on screed	M2	35.42	8M2	283.36		12M2	425.04		16M2	566.72		20M2	708.40	
Softwood skirting	M	11.09	12M	133.08	**416.44**	14M	155.26	**580.30**	16M	177.44	**744.16**	18M	199.62	**908.02**
CEILING FINISHES														
Plasterboard and Artex	M2	16.34	8M2	130.72	**130.72**	12M2	196.08	**196.08**	16M2	261.44	**261.44**	20M2	326.80	**326.80**

Specification B
24 m2 - 36 m2

SINGLE STOREY

FLAT ROOF Continued/.....

Element	Unit	Unit Rate £	Ref B/1F 4x6 Size 4.00 x 6.00 m Area 24 m2			Ref B/1F 4x7 Size 4.00 x 7.00 m Area 28 m2			Ref B/1F 4x8 Size 4.00 x 8.00 m Area 32 m2			Ref B/1F 4x9 Size 4.00 x 9.00 m Area 36 m2		
			Qty	Total £	Element Total £	Qty	Total £	Element Total £	Qty	Total £	Element Total £	Qty	Total £	Element Total £
	NR	478.42	1NR	478.42		1NR	478.42		1NR	478.42		1NR	478.42	
	NR	518.08	2NR	1036.16		2NR	1036.16		2NR	1036.16		2NR	1036.16	
	NR	179.51	1NR	179.51		1NR	179.51		1NR	179.51		1NR	179.51	
	NR	150.89	2NR	301.78	**1995.87**	2NR	301.78	**1995.87**	2NR	301.78	**1995.87**	2NR	301.78	**1995.87**
	M2	51.63	10M2	516.30	**516.30**	10M2	516.30	**516.30**	10M2	516.30	**516.30**	10M2	516.30	**516.30**
	NR	251.11	1NR	251.11	**251.11**	1NR	251.11	**251.11**	1NR	251.11	**251.11**	1NR	251.11	**251.11**
	M2	19.58	50M2	979.00	**979.00**	55M2	1076.90	**1076.90**	60M2	1174.80	**1174.80**	65M2	1272.70	**1272.70**
	M2	35.42	24M2	850.08		28M2	991.76		32M2	1133.44		36M2	1275.12	
	M	11.09	20M	221.80	**1071.88**	22M	243.98	**1235.74**	24M	266.16	**1399.60**	26M	288.34	**1563.46**
	M2	16.34	24M2	392.16	**392.16**	28M2	457.52	**457.52**	32M2	522.88	**522.88**	36M2	588.24	**588.24**

Specification B 8 m2 - 20 m2

SINGLE STOREY

FLAT ROOF

Element	Unit	Unit Rate £	Ref B/1F 4x2 Size 4.00 x 2.00 m Area 8 m2 Qty	Total £	Element Total £	Ref B/1F 4x3 Size 4.00 x 3.00 m Area 12 m2 Qty	Total £	Element Total £	Ref B/1F 4x4 Size 4.00 x 4.00 m Area 16 m2 Qty	Total £	Element Total £	Ref B/1F 4x5 Size 4.00 x 5.00 m Area 20 m2 Qty	Total £	Element Total £
SERVICES														
Rainwater pipes	M	26.64	3M	79.92		3M	79.92		3M	79.92		3M	79.92	
Cold water service point	NR	110.52	1NR	110.52		1NR	110.52		1NR	110.52		1NR	110.52	
Hot water service point	NR	191.67	1NR	191.67		1NR	191.67		1NR	191.67		1NR	191.67	
Central heating service point	NR	386.51	1NR	386.51		1NR	386.51		1NR	386.51		1NR	386.51	
Electrical installation	NR	286.50	1NR	286.50	**1055.12**	1NR	286.50	**1055.12**	1NR	286.50	**1055.12**	1NR	286.50	**1055.12**
ALTERATIONS TO EXISTING BUILDINGS														
Opening in existing wall 1.80 m wide 2.00 m high	NR	689.44	1NR	689.44	**689.44**									
Opening in existing wall 2.40 m wide 2.00 m high	NR	865.59												
Opening in existing wall 3.00 m wide 2.00 m high	NR	921.26				1NR	921.26	**921.26**						
Opening in existing wall 4.00 m wide 2.00 m high	NR	1131.22							1NR	1131.22	**1131.22**			
Opening in existing wall 5.00 m wide 2.00 m high	NR	1341.19										1NR	1341.19	**1341.19**

Specification B
24 m2 - 36 m2

			Ref B/1F 4x6 Size 4.00 x 6.00 m Area 24 m2			Ref B/1F 4x7 Size 4.00 x 7.00 m Area 28 m2			Ref B/1F 4x8 Size 4.00 x 8.00 m Area 32 m2			Ref B/1F 4x9 Size 4.00 x 9.00 m Area 36 m2		
Element	Unit	Unit Rate £	Qty	Total £	Element Total £	Qty	Total £	Element Total £	Qty	Total £	Element Total £	Qty	Total £	Element Total £
SINGLE STOREY FLAT ROOF Continued/.....														
	M	26.64	3M	79.92		3M	79.92		3M	79.92		3M	79.92	
	NR	110.52	1NR	110.52		1NR	110.52		1NR	110.52		1NR	110.52	
	NR	191.67	1NR	191.67		1NR	191.67		1NR	191.67		1NR	191.67	
	NR	386.51	2NR	773.02		2NR	773.02		2NR	773.02		2NR	773.02	
	NR	286.50	2NR	573.00	**1728.13**	2NR	573.00	**1728.13**	2NR	573.00	**1728.13**	2NR	573.00	**1728.13**
	NR	689.44												
	NR	865.59	2NR	1731.18	**1731.18**									
	NR	921.26				2NR	1842.52	**1842.52**	2NR	1842.52	**1842.52**			
	NR	1131.22										2NR	2262.44	**2262.44**
	NR	1341.19												

Specification B 8 m2 - 20 m2	Ref B/1F 4x2 Size 4.00 x 2.00 m Area 8 m2	Ref B/1F 4x3 Size 4.00 x 3.00 m Area 12 m2	Ref B/1F 4x4 Size 4.00 x 4.00 m Area 16 m2	Ref B/1F 4x5 Size 4.00 x 5.00 m Area 20 m2
	Element Total £	Element Total £	Element Total £	Element Total £
SINGLE STOREY				
FLAT ROOF				
SUMMARY				
SUBSTRUCTURE	1738.59	2046.60	2354.61	2662.62
UPPER FLOORS	-	-	-	-
ROOF	2297.69	2814.87	3469.14	3995.12
EXTERNAL WALLS	2458.93	2672.75	2993.48	3100.39
EXTERNAL DOORS AND WINDOWS	1326.90	1326.90	1326.90	1326.90
INTERNAL WALLS AND PARTITIONS	-	-	-	-
INTERNAL DOORS	-	-	-	-
WALL FINISHES	587.40	685.30	783.20	881.10
FLOOR FINISHES	416.44	580.30	744.16	908.02
CEILING FINISHES	130.72	196.08	261.44	326.80
SERVICES	1055.12	1055.12	1055.12	1055.12
ALTERATIONS TO EXISTING BUILDINGS	689.44	921.26	1131.22	1341.19
Sub Total	10701.23	12299.18	14119.27	15597.26
Allowance for unmeasured items and sundries 5%	535.06	614.96	705.96	779.86
NET TOTAL excluding Preliminaries, Profit and Overheads	**11236.29**	**12914.14**	**14825.23**	**16377.12**

Specification B 24 m2 - 36 m2

	Ref B/1F 4x6 Size 4.00 x 6.00 m Area 24 m2	Ref B/1F 4x7 Size 4.00 x 7.00 m Area 28 m2	Ref B/1F 4x8 Size 4.00 x 8.00 m Area 32 m2	Ref B/1F 4x9 Size 4.00 x 9.00 m Area 36 m2
	Element Total £	Element Total £	Element Total £	Element Total £
SINGLE STOREY				
FLAT ROOF				
SUMMARY Continued/.....				
	2970.63	3278.64	3586.65	3894.66
	-	-	-	-
	4539.39	5056.57	5750.44	6276.42
	3314.21	3528.03	3848.76	4062.58
	1995.87	1995.87	1995.87	1995.87
	516.30	516.30	516.30	516.30
	251.11	251.11	251.11	251.11
	979.00	1076.90	1174.80	1272.70
	1071.88	1235.74	1399.60	1563.46
	392.16	457.52	522.88	588.24
	1728.13	1728.13	1728.13	1728.13
	1731.18	1842.52	1842.52	2262.44
Sub Total	19489.86	20967.33	22617.06	24411.91
Allowance for unmeasured items and sundries 5%	974.49	1048.37	1130.85	1220.60
NET TOTAL excluding Preliminaries, Profit and Overheads	**20464.35**	**22015.70**	**23747.91**	**25632.51**

Specification B 10 m2 - 25 m2

SINGLE STOREY

FLAT ROOF

Element	Unit	Unit Rate £	Ref B/1F 5x2 Size 5.00 x 2.00 m Area 10 m2 Qty	Total £	Element Total £	Ref B/1F 5x3 Size 5.00 x 3.00 m Area 15 m2 Qty	Total £	Element Total £	Ref B/1F 5x4 Size 5.00 x 4.00 m Area 20 m2 Qty	Total £	Element Total £	Ref B/1F 5x5 Size 5.00 x 5.00 m Area 25 m2 Qty	Total £	Element Total £
SUBSTRUCTURE														
Strip footings	M	124.73	13M	1621.49		14M	1746.22		15M	1870.95		16M	1995.68	
Solid ground floor	M2	45.82	10M2	458.20	**2079.69**	15M2	687.30	**2433.52**	20M2	916.40	**2787.35**	25M2	1145.50	**3141.18**
ROOF														
Flat roof construction 50 x 150 mm joists	M2	50.06	17M2	851.02		22M2	1101.32							
Flat roof construction 50 x 200 mm joists	M2	52.26							28M2	1463.28		33M2	1724.58	
Work to top of external wall	M	23.71	13M	308.23		14M	331.94		15M	355.65		16M	379.36	
Three layer felt roofing	M2	36.43	17M2	619.31		22M2	801.46		28M2	1020.04		33M2	1202.19	
Fascia and eaves soffit	M	42.61	14M	596.54		15M	639.15		16M	681.76		17M	724.37	
Gutters and fittings	M	18.68	3M	56.04		4M	74.72		5M	93.40		6M	112.08	
Flashings	M	24.70	3M	74.10		4M	98.80		5M	123.50		6M	148.20	
Abutment to existing wall	M	61.52	3M	184.56	**2689.80**	4M	246.08	**3293.47**	5M	307.60	**4045.23**	6M	369.12	**4659.90**
EXTERNAL WALLS														
Brick and block cavity wall	M2	106.91	28M2	2993.48	**2993.48**	30M2	3207.30	**3207.30**	33M2	3528.03	**3528.03**	35M2	3741.85	**3741.85**

Specification B
30 m2 - 45 m2

SINGLE STOREY

FLAT ROOF Continued/.....

Element	Unit	Unit Rate £	Ref B/1F 5x6 Size 5.00 x 6.00 m Area 30 m2			Ref B/1F 5x7 Size 5.00 x 7.00 m Area 35 m2			Ref B/1F 5x8 Size 5.00 x 8.00 m Area 40 m2			Ref B/1F 5x9 Size 5.00 x 9.00 m Area 45 m2		
			Qty	Total £	Element Total £	Qty	Total £	Element Total £	Qty	Total £	Element Total £	Qty	Total £	Element Total £
	M	124.73	17M	2120.41		18M	2245.14		19M	2369.87		20M	2494.60	
	M2	45.82	30M2	1374.60	**3495.01**	35M2	1603.70	**3848.84**	40M2	1832.80	**4202.67**	45M2	2061.90	**4556.50**
	M2	50.06	39M2	1952.34		44M2	2202.64							
	M2	52.26							50M2	2613.00		55M2	2874.30	
	M	23.71	17M	403.07		18M	426.78		19M	450.49		20M	474.20	
	M2	36.43	39M2	1420.77		44M2	1602.92		50M2	1821.50		55M2	2003.65	
	M	42.61	18M	766.98		19M	809.59		20M	852.20		21M	894.81	
	M	18.68	7M	130.76		8M	149.44		9M	168.12		10M	186.80	
	M	24.70	7M	172.90		8M	197.60		9M	222.30		10M	247.00	
	M	61.52	7M	430.64	**5277.46**	8M	492.16	**5881.13**	9M	553.68	**6681.29**	10M	615.20	**7295.96**
	M2	106.91	36M2	3848.76	**3848.76**	38M2	4062.58	**4062.58**	41M2	4383.31	**4383.31**	45M2	4810.95	**4810.95**

Specification B
10 m2 - 25 m2

SINGLE STOREY

FLAT ROOF

Element	Unit	Unit Rate £	Ref B/1F 5x2 Size 5.00 x 2.00 m Area 10 m2 Qty	Total £	Element Total £	Ref B/1F 5x3 Size 5.00 x 3.00 m Area 15 m2 Qty	Total £	Element Total £	Ref B/1F 5x4 Size 5.00 x 4.00 m Area 20 m2 Qty	Total £	Element Total £	Ref B/1F 5x5 Size 5.00 x 5.00 m Area 25 m2 Qty	Total £	Element Total £
EXTERNAL DOORS AND WINDOWS														
External door	NR	478.42	1NR	478.42		1NR	478.42		1NR	478.42		1NR	478.42	
Windows	NR	518.08	1NR	518.08		1NR	518.08		1NR	518.08		1NR	518.08	
Opening in cavity wall for door	NR	179.51	1NR	179.51		1NR	179.51		1NR	179.51		1NR	179.51	
Opening in cavity wall for window	NR	150.89	1NR	150.89	**1326.90**	1NR	150.89	**1326.90**	1NR	150.89	**1326.90**	1NR	150.89	**1326.90**
INTERNAL WALLS AND PARTITIONS														
Stud partitions	M2	51.63												
INTERNAL DOORS														
Softwood flush door	NR	251.11												
WALL FINISHES														
Plaster & decoration	M2	19.58	35M2	685.30	**685.30**	40M2	783.20	**783.20**	45M2	881.10	**881.10**	50M2	979.00	**979.00**
FLOOR FINISHES														
Thermoplastic tiles on screed	M2	35.42	10M2	354.20		15M2	531.30		20M2	708.40		25M2	885.50	
Softwood skirting	M	11.09	14M	155.26	**509.46**	16M	177.44	**708.74**	18M	199.62	**908.02**	20M	221.80	**1107.30**
CEILING FINISHES														
Plasterboard and Artex	M2	16.34	10M2	163.40	**163.40**	15M2	245.10	**245.10**	20M2	326.80	**326.80**	25M2	408.50	**408.50**

Specification B 30 m2 - 45 m2

SINGLE STOREY

FLAT ROOF Continued/.....

Element	Unit	Unit Rate £	Ref B/1F 5x6 Size 5.00 x 6.00 m Area 30 m2			Ref B/1F 5x7 Size 5.00 x 7.00 m Area 35 m2			Ref B/1F 5x8 Size 5.00 x 8.00 m Area 40 m2			Ref B/1F 5x9 Size 5.00 x 9.00 m Area 45 m2		
			Qty	Total £	Element Total £	Qty	Total £	Element Total £	Qty	Total £	Element Total £	Qty	Total £	Element Total £
	NR	478.42	1NR	478.42		1NR	478.42		1NR	478.42		1NR	478.42	
	NR	518.08	2NR	1036.16		2NR	1036.16		2NR	1036.16		2NR	1036.16	
	NR	179.51	1NR	179.51		1NR	179.51		1NR	179.51		1NR	179.51	
	NR	150.89	2NR	301.78	**1995.87**	2NR	301.78	**1995.87**	2NR	301.78	**1995.87**	2NR	301.78	**1995.87**
	M2	51.63	13M2	671.19	**671.19**	13M2	671.19	**671.19**	13M2	671.19	**671.19**	13M2	671.19	**671.19**
	NR	251.11	1NR	251.11	**251.11**	1NR	251.11	**251.11**	1NR	251.11	**251.11**	1NR	251.11	**251.11**
	M2	19.58	55M2	1076.90	**1076.90**	60M2	1174.80	**1174.80**	65M2	1272.70	**1272.70**	70M2	1370.60	**1370.60**
	M2	35.42	30M2	1062.60		35M2	1239.70		40M2	1416.80		45M2	1593.90	
	M	11.09	22M	243.98	**1306.58**	24M	266.16	**1505.86**	26M	288.34	**1705.14**	28M	310.52	**1904.42**
	M2	16.34	30M2	490.20	**490.20**	35M2	571.90	**571.90**	40M2	653.60	**653.60**	45M2	735.30	**735.30**

Specification B 10 m2 - 25 m2

SINGLE STOREY

FLAT ROOF

Element	Unit	Unit Rate £	Ref B/1F 5x2 Size 5.00 x 2.00 m Area 10 m2 Qty	Total £	Element Total £	Ref B/1F 5x3 Size 5.00 x 3.00 m Area 15 m2 Qty	Total £	Element Total £	Ref B/1F 5x4 Size 5.00 x 4.00 m Area 20 m2 Qty	Total £	Element Total £	Ref B/1F 5x5 Size 5.00 x 5.00 m Area 25 m2 Qty	Total £	Element Total £
SERVICES														
Rainwater pipes	M	26.64	3M	79.92		3M	79.92		3M	79.92		3M	79.92	
Cold water service point	NR	110.52	1NR	110.52		1NR	110.52		1NR	110.52		1NR	110.52	
Hot water service point	NR	191.67	1NR	191.67		1NR	191.67		1NR	191.67		1NR	191.67	
Central heating service point	NR	386.51	1NR	386.51		1NR	386.51		1NR	386.51		1NR	386.51	
Electrical installation	NR	286.50	1NR	286.50	**1055.12**	1NR	286.50	**1055.12**	1NR	286.50	**1055.12**	1NR	286.50	**1055.12**
ALTERATIONS TO EXISTING BUILDINGS														
Opening in existing wall 1.80 m wide 2.00 m high	NR	689.44	1NR	689.44	**689.44**									
Opening in existing wall 2.40 m wide 2.00 m high	NR	865.59												
Opening in existing wall 3.00 m wide 2.00 m high	NR	921.26				1NR	921.26	**921.26**						
Opening in existing wall 4.00 m wide 2.00 m high	NR	1131.22							1NR	1131.22	**1131.22**			
Opening in existing wall 5.00 m wide 2.00 m high	NR	1341.19										1NR	1341.19	**1341.19**

Specification B 30 m2 - 45 m2

SINGLE STOREY

FLAT ROOF Continued/.....

Element	Unit	Unit Rate £	Ref B/1F 5x6 Size 5.00 x 6.00 m Area 30 m2 Qty	Total £	Element Total £	Ref B/1F 5x7 Size 5.00 x 7.00 m Area 35 m2 Qty	Total £	Element Total £	Ref B/1F 5x8 Size 5.00 x 8.00 m Area 40 m2 Qty	Total £	Element Total £	Ref B/1F 5x9 Size 5.00 x 9.00 m Area 45 m2 Qty	Total £	Element Total £
	M	26.64	3M	79.92		3M	79.92		3M	79.92		3M	79.92	
	NR	110.52	1NR	110.52		1NR	110.52		1NR	110.52		1NR	110.52	
	NR	191.67	1NR	191.67		1NR	191.67		1NR	191.67		1NR	191.67	
	NR	386.51	2NR	773.02		2NR	773.02		2NR	773.02		2NR	773.02	
	NR	286.50	2NR	573.00	**1728.13**	2NR	573.00	**1728.13**	2NR	573.00	**1728.13**	2NR	573.00	**1728.13**
	NR	689.44												
	NR	865.59	2NR	1731.18	**1731.18**									
	NR	921.26				2NR	1842.52	**1842.52**	2NR	1842.52	**1842.52**			
	NR	1131.22										2NR	2262.44	**2262.44**
	NR	1341.19												

Specification B 10 m2 - 25 m2	Ref B/1F 5x2 Size 5.00 x 2.00 m Area 10 m2	Ref B/1F 5x3 Size 5.00 x 3.00 m Area 15 m2	Ref B/1F 5x4 Size 5.00 x 4.00 m Area 20 m2	Ref B/1F 5x5 Size 5.00 x 5.00 m Area 25 m2
	Element Total £	Element Total £	Element Total £	Element Total £
SINGLE STOREY				
FLAT ROOF				
SUMMARY				
SUBSTRUCTURE	2079.69	2433.52	2787.35	3141.18
UPPER FLOORS	-	-	-	-
ROOF	2689.80	3293.47	4045.23	4659.90
EXTERNAL WALLS	2993.48	3207.30	3528.03	3741.85
EXTERNAL DOORS AND WINDOWS	1326.90	1326.90	1326.90	1326.90
INTERNAL WALLS AND PARTITIONS	-	-	-	-
INTERNAL DOORS	-	-	-	-
WALL FINISHES	685.30	783.20	881.10	979.00
FLOOR FINISHES	509.46	708.74	908.02	1107.30
CEILING FINISHES	163.40	245.10	326.80	408.50
SERVICES	1055.12	1055.12	1055.12	1055.12
ALTERATIONS TO EXISTING BUILDINGS	689.44	921.26	1131.22	1341.19
Sub Total	12192.59	13974.61	15989.77	17760.94
Allowance for unmeasured items and sundries 5%	609.63	698.73	799.49	888.05
NET TOTAL excluding Preliminaries, Profit and Overheads	**12802.22**	**14673.34**	**16789.26**	**18648.99**

Specification B 30 m2 - 45 m2	Ref B/1F 5x6 Size 5.00 x 6.00 m Area 30 m2	Ref B/1F 5x7 Size 5.00 x 7.00 m Area 35 m2	Ref B/1F 5x8 Size 5.00 x 8.00 m Area 40 m2	Ref B/1F 5x9 Size 5.00 x 9.00 m Area 45 m2
	Element Total £	Element Total £	Element Total £	Element Total £
SINGLE STOREY				
FLAT ROOF				
SUMMARY Continued/.....				
	3495.01	3848.84	4202.67	4556.50
	-	-	-	-
	5277.46	5881.13	6681.29	7295.96
	3848.76	4062.58	4383.31	4810.95
	1995.87	1995.87	1995.87	1995.87
	671.19	671.19	671.19	671.19
	251.11	251.11	251.11	251.11
	1076.90	1174.80	1272.70	1370.60
	1306.58	1505.86	1705.14	1904.42
	490.20	571.90	653.60	735.30
	1728.13	1728.13	1728.13	1728.13
	1731.18	1842.52	1842.52	2262.44
Sub Total	21872.39	23533.93	25387.53	27582.47
Allowance for unmeasured items and sundries 5%	1093.62	1176.70	1269.38	1379.12
NET TOTAL excluding Preliminaries, Profit and Overheads	**22966.01**	**24710.63**	**26656.91**	**28961.59**

Specification B

Single storey pitch roof

[1P] 2×2/3/4.

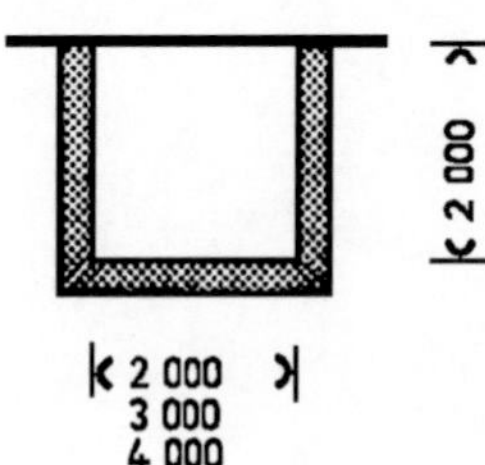

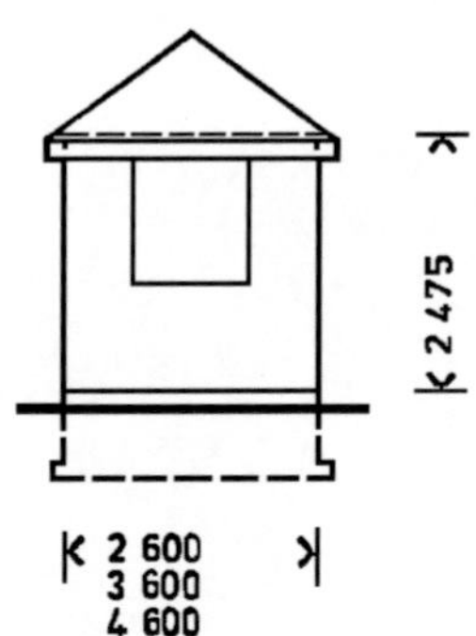

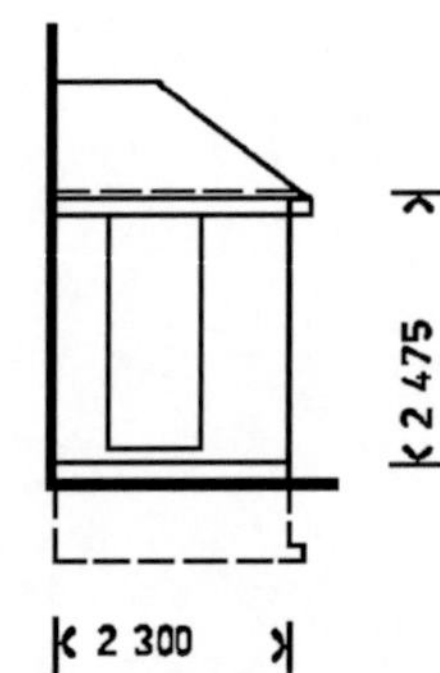

[1P] 2×5.

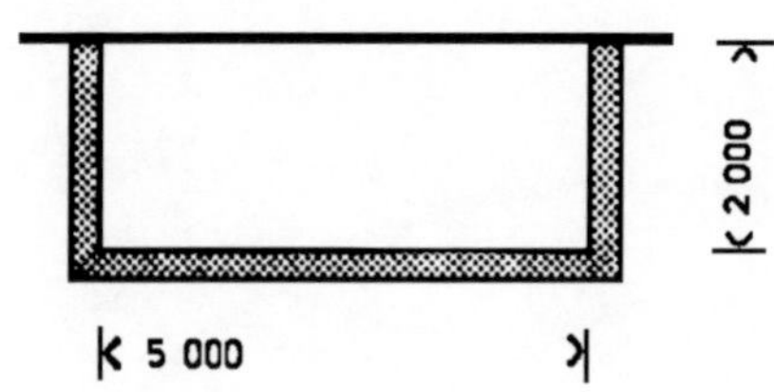

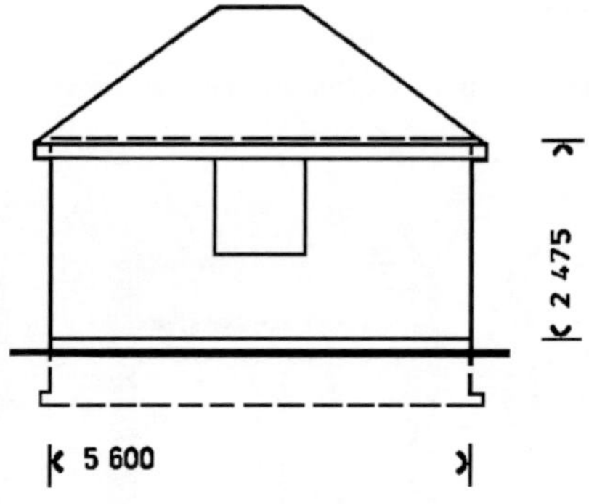

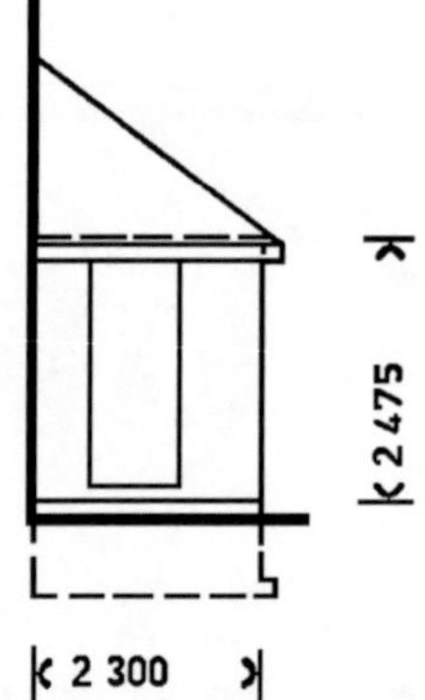

[1P] 2×6/7/8/9.

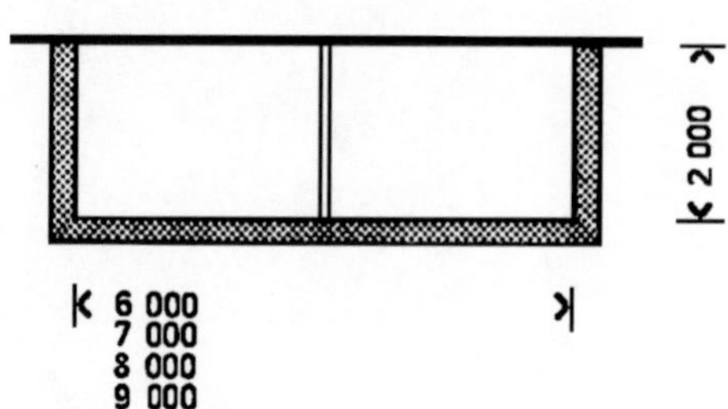

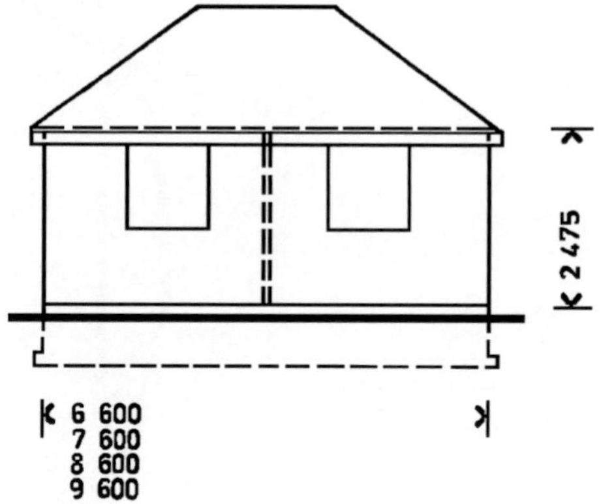

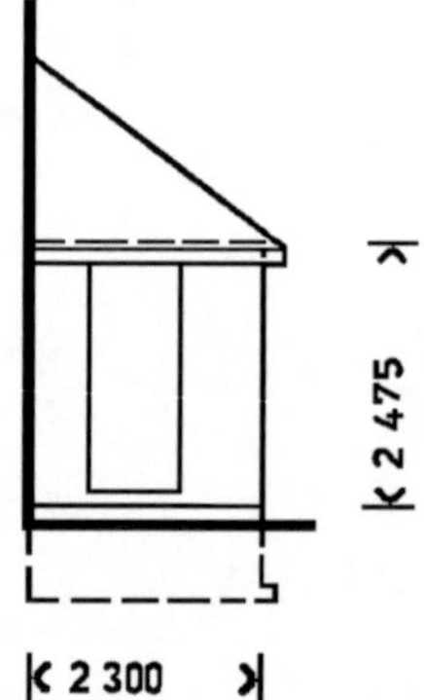

[1P] 3×2/3/4/5.

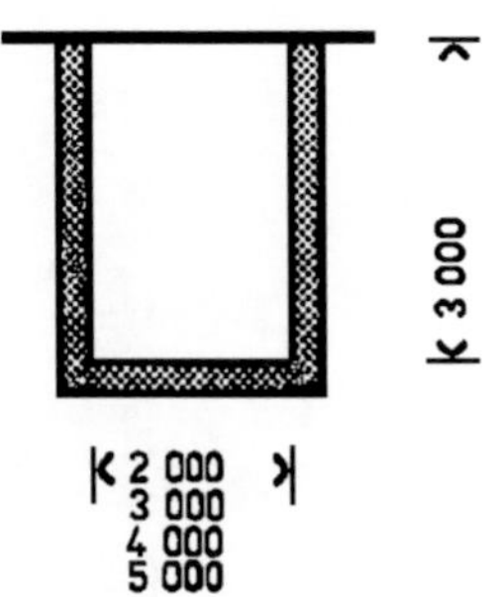

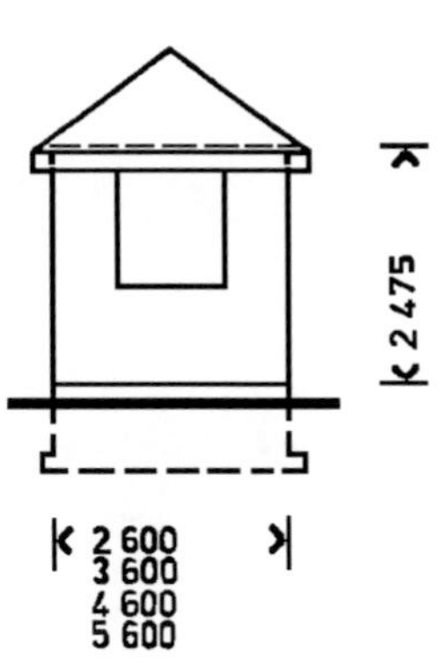

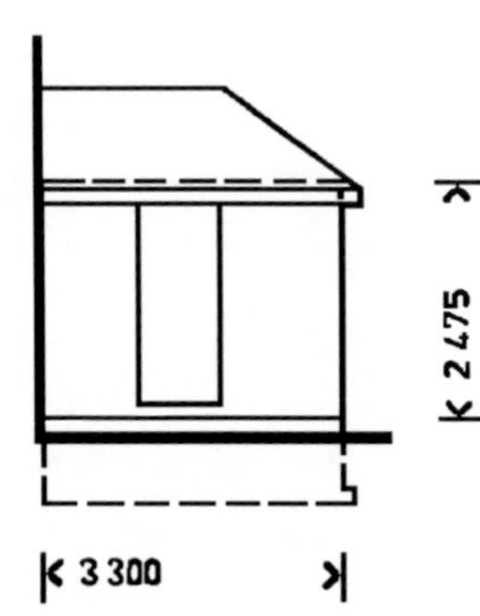

[1P] 3×6.

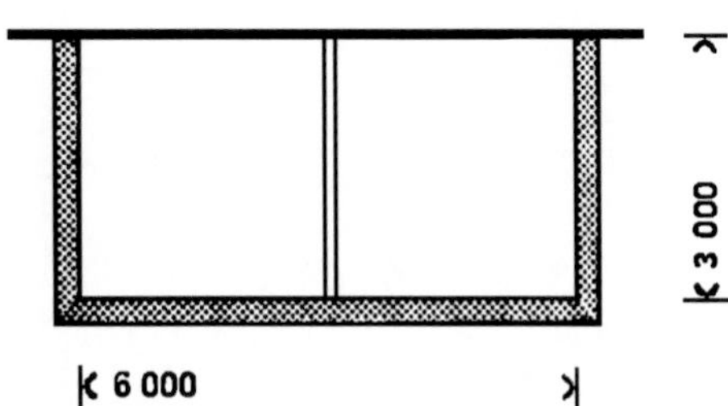

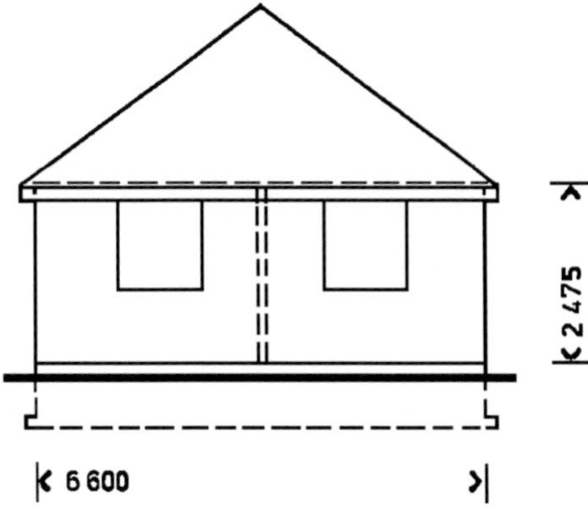

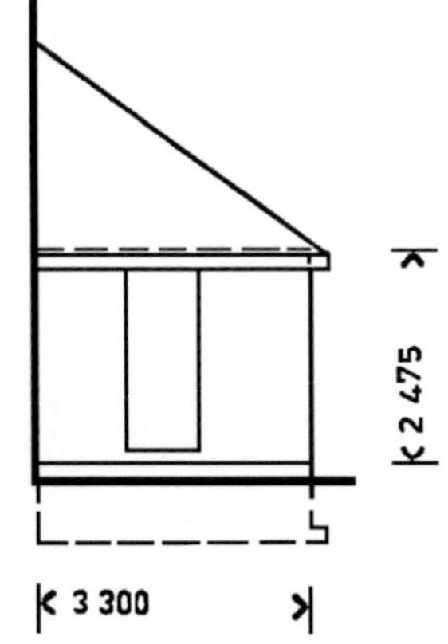

[1P] 3×7/8/9.

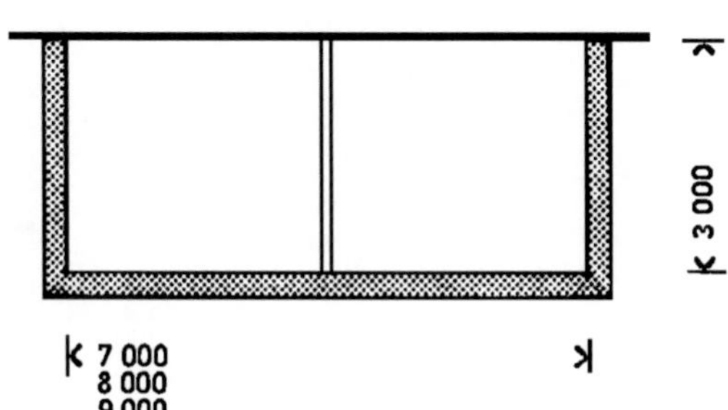

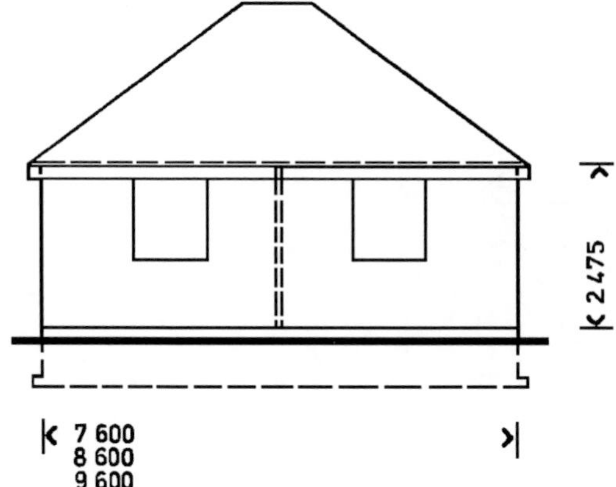

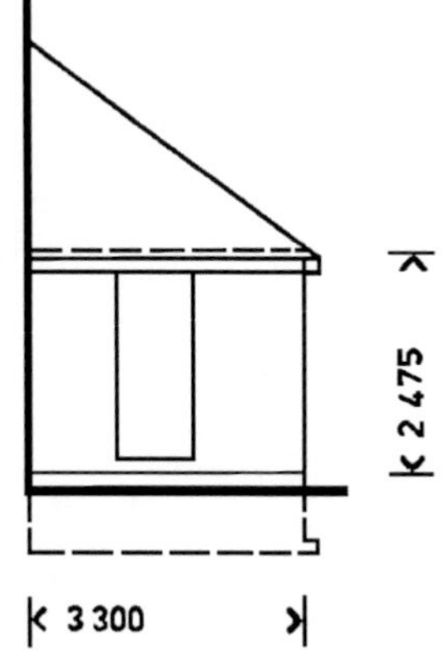

[1P] 4×2/3/4/5.

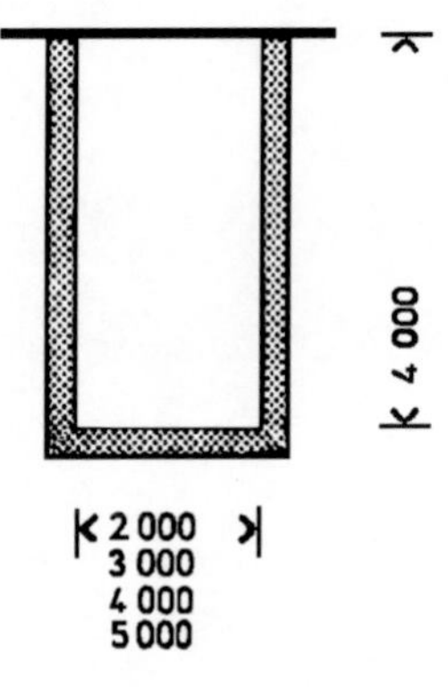

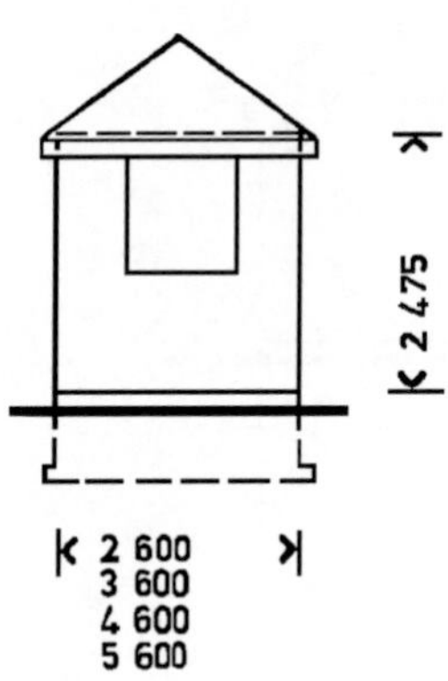

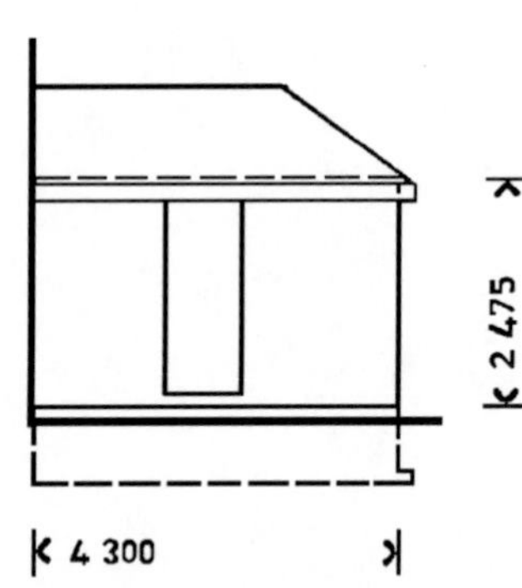

[1P] 4×6/7/8.

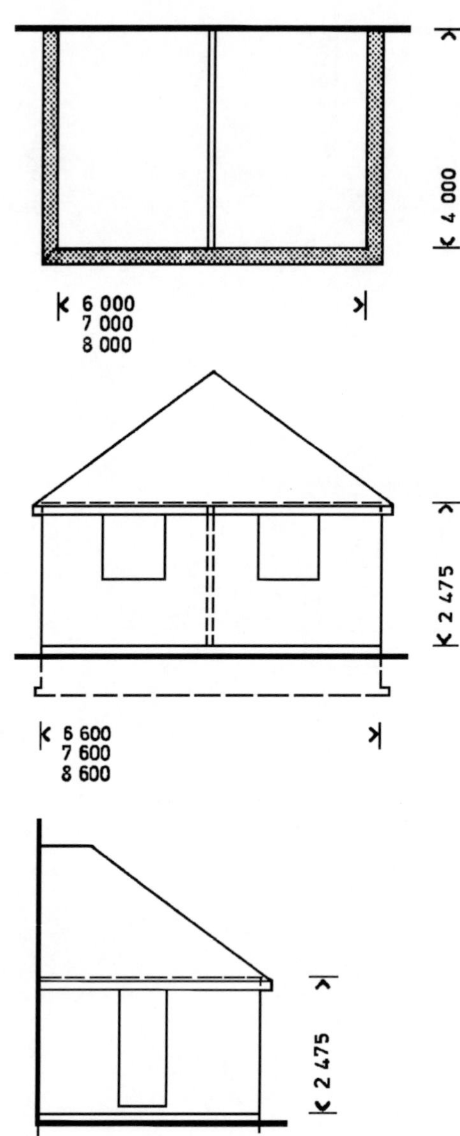

[1P] 4×9.

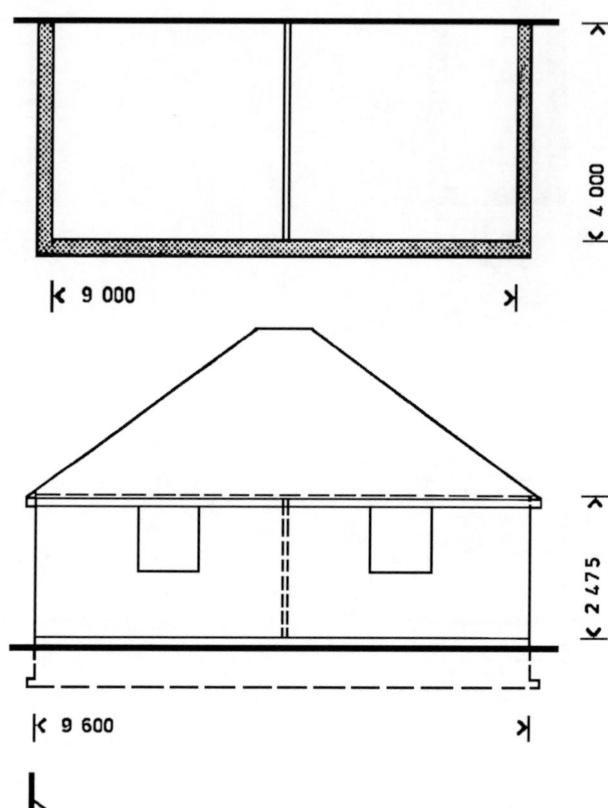

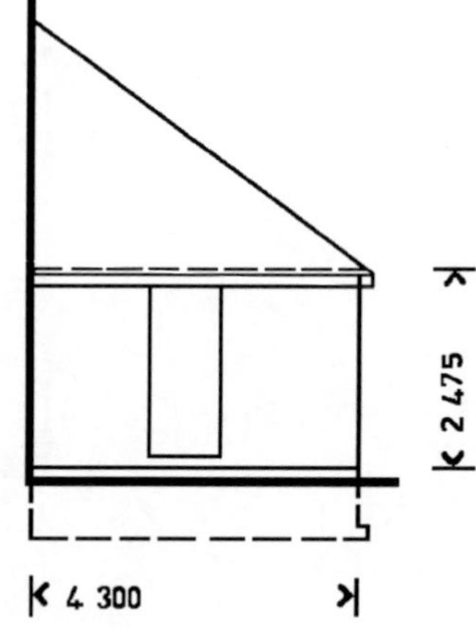

[1P] 5×2/3/4/5.

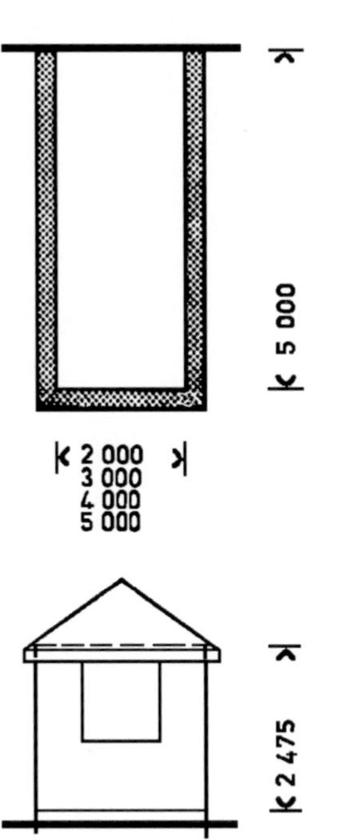

2 600
3 600
4 600
5 600

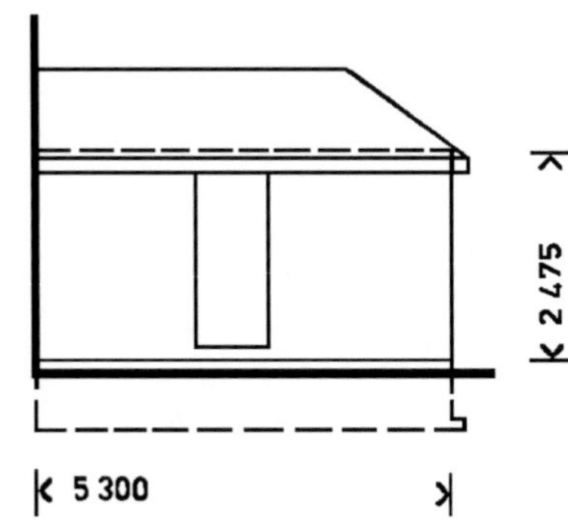

[1P] 5×6/7/8/9.

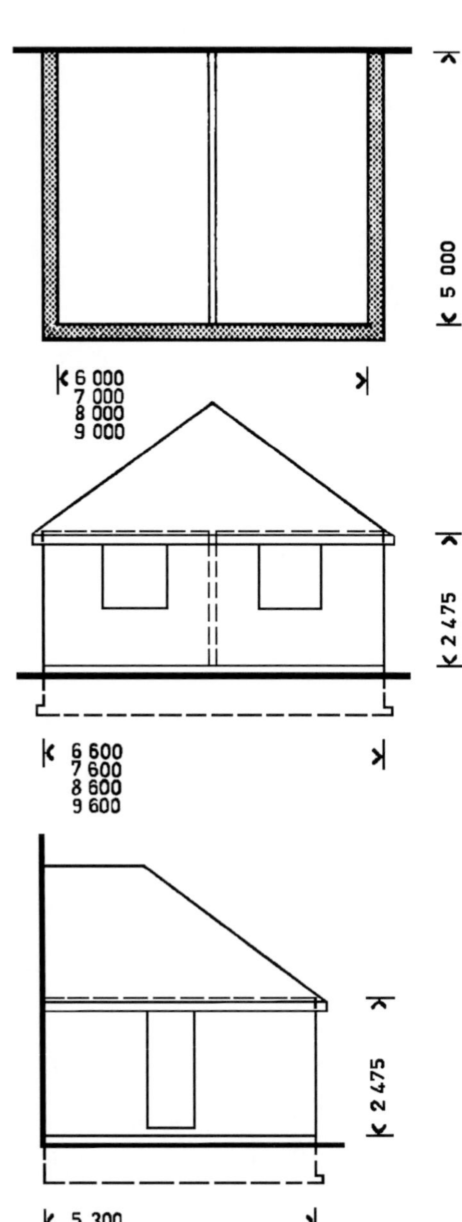

Specification B
4 m2 - 10 m2

Element	Unit	Unit Rate £	Ref B/1P 2x2 Size 2.00 x 2.00 m Area 4 m2 Qty	Total £	Element Total £	Ref B/1P 2x3 Size 2.00 x 3.00 m Area 6 m2 Qty	Total £	Element Total £	Ref B/1P 2x4 Size 2.00 x 4.00 m Area 8 m2 Qty	Total £	Element Total £	Ref B/1P 2x5 Size 2.00 x 5.00 m Area 10 m2 Qty	Total £	Element Total £
SINGLE STOREY														
PITCHED ROOF														
SUBSTRUCTURE														
Strip footings	M	124.73	7M	873.11		8M	997.84		9M	1122.57		10M	1247.30	
Solid ground floor	M2	45.82	4M2	183.28	**1056.39**	6M2	274.92	**1272.76**	8M2	366.56	**1489.13**	10M2	458.20	**1705.50**
ROOF														
Pitched roof construction	M2	55.42	8M2	443.36		10M2	554.20		13M2	720.46		15M2	831.30	
Work to top of external wall	M	23.71	7M	165.97		8M	189.68		9M	213.39		10M	237.10	
Concrete tile roofing	M2	23.48	9M2	211.32		12M2	281.76		15M2	352.20		18M2	422.64	
Work to verge	M	11.58	4M	46.32		5M	57.90		6M	69.48		7M	81.06	
Work to hip	M	41.73	6M	250.38		7M	292.11		8M	333.84		8M	333.84	
Work to eaves	M	23.22	8M	185.76		9M	208.98		10M	232.20		11M	255.42	
Fascia and eaves soffit	M	42.61	8M	340.88		9M	383.49		10M	426.10		11M	468.71	
Gutters and fittings	M	18.68	8M	149.44		9M	168.12		10M	186.80		11M	205.48	
Flashings	M	69.52	4M	278.08	**2071.51**	5M	347.60	**2483.84**	6M	417.12	**2951.59**	7M	486.64	**3322.19**
EXTERNAL WALLS														
Brick and block cavity wall	M2	106.91	13M2	1389.83	**1389.83**	15M2	1603.65	**1603.65**	18M2	1924.38	**1924.38**	20M2	2138.20	**2138.20**

Specification B 12 m2 - 18 m2			Ref B/1P 2x6 Size 2.00 x 6.00 m Area 12 m2			Ref B/1P 2x7 Size 2.00 x 7.00 m Area 14 m2			Ref B/1P 2x8 Size 2.00 x 8.00 m Area 16 m2			Ref B/1P 2x9 Size 2.00 x 9.00 m Area 18 m2		
SINGLE STOREY PITCHED ROOF Continued/.....			Qty	Total £	Element Total £	Qty	Total £	Element Total £	Qty	Total £	Element Total £	Qty	Total £	Element Total £
Element	Unit	Unit Rate £												
	M	124.73	11M	1372.03		12M	1496.76		13M	1621.49		14M	1746.22	
	M2	45.82	12M2	549.84	**1921.87**	14M2	641.48	**2138.24**	16M2	733.12	**2354.61**	18M2	824.76	**2570.98**
	M2	55.42	18M2	997.56		20M2	1108.40		23M2	1274.66		25M2	1385.50	
	M	23.71	11M	260.81		12M	284.52		13M	308.23		14M	331.94	
	M2	23.48	22M2	516.56		25M2	587.00		28M2	657.44		31M2	727.88	
	M	11.58	8M	92.64		9M	104.22		10M	115.80		11M	127.38	
	M	41.73	8M	333.84		8M	333.84		8M	333.84		8M	333.84	
	M	23.22	12M	278.64		13M	301.86		14M	325.08		15M	348.30	
	M	42.61	12M	511.32		13M	553.93		14M	596.54		15M	639.15	
	M	18.68	12M	224.16		13M	242.84		14M	261.52		15M	280.20	
	M	69.52	8M	556.16	**3771.69**	9M	625.68	**4142.29**	10M	695.20	**4568.31**	11M	764.72	**4938.91**
	M2	106.91	21M2	2245.11	**2245.11**	23M2	2458.93	**2458.93**	26M2	2779.66	**2779.66**	28M2	2993.48	**2993.48**

Specification B
4 m2 - 10 m2

SINGLE STOREY

PITCHED ROOF

Element	Unit	Unit Rate £	Ref B/1P 2x2 Size 2.00 x 2.00 m Area 4 m2 Qty	Total £	Element Total £	Ref B/1P 2x3 Size 2.00 x 3.00 m Area 6 m2 Qty	Total £	Element Total £	Ref B/1P 2x4 Size 2.00 x 4.00 m Area 8 m2 Qty	Total £	Element Total £	Ref B/1P 2x5 Size 2.00 x 5.00 m Area 10 m2 Qty	Total £	Element Total £
EXTERNAL DOORS AND WINDOWS														
External door	NR	478.42	1NR	478.42		1NR	478.42		1NR	478.42		1NR	478.42	
Windows	NR	518.08	1NR	518.08		1NR	518.08		1NR	518.08		1NR	518.08	
Opening in cavity wall for door	NR	179.51	1NR	179.51		1NR	179.51		1NR	179.51		1NR	179.51	
Opening in cavity wall for window	NR	150.89	1NR	150.89	**1326.90**	1NR	150.89	**1326.90**	1NR	150.89	**1326.90**	1NR	150.89	**1326.90**
INTERNAL WALLS AND PARTITIONS														
Stud partitions	M2	51.63												
INTERNAL DOORS														
Softwood flush door	NR	251.11												
WALL FINISHES														
Plaster & decoration	M2	19.58	20M2	391.60	**391.60**	25M2	489.50	**489.50**	30M2	587.40	**587.40**	35M2	685.30	**685.30**
FLOOR FINISHES														
Thermoplastic tiles on screed	M2	35.42	4M2	141.68		6M2	212.52		8M2	283.36		10M2	354.20	
Softwood skirting	M	11.09	8M	88.72	**230.40**	10M	110.90	**323.42**	12M	133.08	**416.44**	14M	155.26	**509.46**
CEILING FINISHES														
Plasterboard and Artex	M2	16.34	4M2	65.36	**65.36**	6M2	98.04	**98.04**	8M2	130.72	**130.72**	10M2	163.40	**163.40**

Specification B 12 m2 - 18 m2

SINGLE STOREY

PITCHED ROOF Continued/.....

Element	Unit	Unit Rate £	Ref B/1P 2x6 Size 2.00 x 6.00 m Area 12 m2			Ref B/1P 2x7 Size 2.00 x 7.00 m Area 14 m2			Ref B/1P 2x8 Size 2.00 x 8.00 m Area 16 m2			Ref B/1P 2x9 Size 2.00 x 9.00 m Area 18 m2		
			Qty	Total £	Element Total £	Qty	Total £	Element Total £	Qty	Total £	Element Total £	Qty	Total £	Element Total £
	NR	478.42	1NR	478.42		1NR	478.42		1NR	478.42		1NR	478.42	
	NR	518.08	2NR	1036.16		2NR	1036.16		2NR	1036.16		2NR	1036.16	
	NR	179.51	1NR	179.51		1NR	179.51		1NR	179.51		1NR	179.51	
	NR	150.89	2NR	301.78	**1995.87**	2NR	301.78	**1995.87**	2NR	301.78	**1995.87**	2NR	301.78	**1995.87**
	M2	51.63	5M2	258.15	**258.15**	5M2	258.15	**258.15**	5M2	258.15	**258.15**	5M2	258.15	**258.15**
	NR	251.11	1NR	251.11	**251.11**	1NR	251.11	**251.11**	1NR	251.11	**251.11**	1NR	251.11	**251.11**
	M2	19.58	40M2	783.20	**783.20**	45M2	881.10	**881.10**	50M2	979.00	**979.00**	55M2	1076.90	**1076.90**
	M2	35.42	12M2	425.04		14M2	495.88		16M2	566.72		18M2	637.56	
	M	11.09	16M	177.44	**602.48**	18M	199.62	**695.50**	20M	221.80	**788.52**	22M	243.98	**881.54**
	M2	16.34	12M2	196.08	**196.08**	14M2	228.76	**228.76**	16M2	261.44	**261.44**	18M2	294.12	**294.12**

Specification B 4 m2 - 10 m2

SINGLE STOREY

PITCHED ROOF

Element	Unit	Unit Rate £	Ref B/1P 2x2 Size 2.00 x 2.00 m Area 4 m2 Qty	Total £	Element Total £	Ref B/1P 2x3 Size 2.00 x 3.00 m Area 6 m2 Qty	Total £	Element Total £	Ref B/1P 2x4 Size 2.00 x 4.00 m Area 8 m2 Qty	Total £	Element Total £	Ref B/1P 2x5 Size 2.00 x 5.00 m Area 10 m2 Qty	Total £	Element Total £
SERVICES														
Rainwater pipes	M	26.64	3M	79.92		3M	79.92		3M	79.92		3M	79.92	
Cold water service point	NR	110.52	1NR	110.52		1NR	110.52		1NR	110.52		1NR	110.52	
Hot water service point	NR	191.67	1NR	191.67		1NR	191.67		1NR	191.67		1NR	191.67	
Central heating service point	NR	386.51	1NR	386.51		1NR	386.51		1NR	386.51		1NR	386.51	
Electrical installation	NR	286.50	1NR	286.50	**1055.12**	1NR	286.50	**1055.12**	1NR	286.50	**1055.12**	1NR	286.50	**1055.12**
ALTERATIONS TO EXISTING BUILDINGS														
Opening in existing wall 1.80 m wide 2.00 m high	NR	689.44	1NR	689.44	**689.44**									
Opening in existing wall 2.40 m wide 2.00 m high	NR	865.59												
Opening in existing wall 3.00 m wide 2.00 m high	NR	921.26				1NR	921.26	**921.26**						
Opening in existing wall 4.00 m wide 2.00 m high	NR	1131.22							1NR	1131.22	**1131.22**			
Opening in existing wall 5.00 m wide 2.00 m high	NR	1341.19										1NR	1341.19	**1341.19**

Specification B 12 m2 - 18 m2

			Ref B/1P 2x6 Size 2.00 x 6.00 m Area 12 m2			Ref B/1P 2x7 Size 2.00 x 7.00 m Area 14 m2			Ref B/1P 2x8 Size 2.00 x 8.00 m Area 16 m2			Ref B/1P 2x9 Size 2.00 x 9.00 m Area 18 m2		
			Qty	Total £	Element Total £	Qty	Total £	Element Total £	Qty	Total £	Element Total £	Qty	Total £	Element Total £
SINGLE STOREY														
PITCHED ROOF Continued/.....														
Element	Unit	Unit Rate £												
	M	26.64	3M	79.92		3M	79.92		3M	79.92		3M	79.92	
	NR	110.52	1NR	110.52		1NR	110.52		1NR	110.52		1NR	110.52	
	NR	191.67	1NR	191.67		1NR	191.67		1NR	191.67		1NR	191.67	
	NR	386.51	2NR	773.02		2NR	773.02		2NR	773.02		2NR	773.02	
	NR	286.50	2NR	573.00	**1728.13**	2NR	573.00	**1728.13**	2NR	573.00	**1728.13**	2NR	573.00	**1728.13**
	NR	689.44												
	NR	865.59	2NR	1731.18	**1731.18**									
	NR	921.26				2NR	1842.52	**1842.52**	2NR	1842.52	**1842.52**			
	NR	1131.22										2NR	2262.44	**2262.44**
	NR	1341.19												

Specification B 4 m2 - 10 m2	Ref B/1P 2x2 Size 2.00 x 2.00 m Area 4 m2	Ref B/1P 2x3 Size 2.00 x 3.00 m Area 6 m2	Ref B/1P 2x4 Size 2.00 x 4.00 m Area 8 m2	Ref B/1P 2x5 Size 2.00 x 5.00 m Area 10 m2
	Element Total £	Element Total £	Element Total £	Element Total £
SINGLE STOREY				
PITCHED ROOF				
SUMMARY				
SUBSTRUCTURE	1056.39	1272.76	1489.13	1705.50
UPPER FLOORS	-	-	-	-
ROOF	2071.51	2483.84	2951.59	3322.19
EXTERNAL WALLS	1389.83	1603.65	1924.38	2138.20
EXTERNAL DOORS AND WINDOWS	1326.90	1326.90	1326.90	1326.90
INTERNAL WALLS AND PARTITIONS	-	-	-	-
INTERNAL DOORS	-	-	-	-
WALL FINISHES	391.60	489.50	587.40	685.30
FLOOR FINISHES	230.40	323.42	416.44	509.46
CEILING FINISHES	65.36	98.04	130.72	163.40
SERVICES	1055.12	1055.12	1055.12	1055.12
ALTERATIONS TO EXISTING BUILDINGS	689.44	921.26	1131.22	1341.19
Sub Total	8276.55	9574.49	11012.90	12247.26
Allowance for unmeasured items and sundries 5%	413.83	478.72	550.65	612.36
NET TOTAL excluding Preliminaries, Profit and Overheads	**8690.38**	**10053.21**	**11563.55**	**12859.62**

Specification B 12 m2 - 18 m2	Ref B/1P 2x6 Size 2.00 x 6.00 m Area 12 m2	Ref B/1P 2x7 Size 2.00 x 7.00 m Area 14 m2	Ref B/1P 2x8 Size 2.00 x 8.00 m Area 16 m2	Ref B/1P 2x9 Size 2.00 x 9.00 m Area 18 m2
	Element Total £	Element Total £	Element Total £	Element Total £
SINGLE STOREY				
PITCHED ROOF				
SUMMARY Continued/.....				
	1921.87	2138.24	2354.61	2570.98
	-	-	-	-
	3771.69	4142.29	4568.31	4938.91
	2245.11	2458.93	2779.66	2993.48
	1995.87	1995.87	1995.87	1995.87
	258.15	258.15	258.15	258.15
	251.11	251.11	251.11	251.11
	783.20	881.10	979.00	1076.90
	602.48	695.50	788.52	881.54
	196.08	228.76	261.44	294.12
	1728.13	1728.13	1728.13	1728.13
	1731.18	1842.52	1842.52	2262.44
Sub Total	15484.87	16620.60	17807.32	19251.63
Allowance for unmeasured items and sundries 5%	774.24	831.03	890.37	962.58
NET TOTAL excluding Preliminaries, Profit and Overheads	**16259.11**	**17451.63**	**18697.69**	**20214.21**

Specification B 6 m2 - 15 m2

SINGLE STOREY

PITCHED ROOF

Element	Unit	Unit Rate £	Ref B/1P 3x2 Size 3.00 x 2.00 m Area 6 m2 Qty	Total £	Element Total £	Ref B/1P 3x3 Size 3.00 x 3.00 m Area 9 m2 Qty	Total £	Element Total £	Ref B/1P 3x4 Size 3.00 x 4.00 m Area 12 m2 Qty	Total £	Element Total £	Ref B/1P 3x5 Size 3.00 x 5.00 m Area 15 m2 Qty	Total £	Element Total £
SUBSTRUCTURE														
Strip footings	M	124.73	9M	1122.57		10M	1247.30		11M	1372.03		12M	1496.76	
Solid ground floor	M2	45.82	6M2	274.92	**1397.49**	9M2	412.38	**1659.68**	12M2	549.84	**1921.87**	15M2	687.30	**2184.06**
ROOF														
Pitched roof construction	M2	55.42	11M2	609.62		14M2	775.88		18M2	997.56		21M2	1163.82	
Work to top of external wall	M	23.71	9M	213.39		10M	237.10		11M	260.81		12M	284.52	
Concrete tile roofing	M2	23.48	13M2	305.24		17M2	399.16		22M2	516.56		26M2	610.48	
Work to verge	M	11.58	4M	46.32		5M	57.90		6M	69.48		7M	81.06	
Work to hip	M	41.73	7M	292.11		8M	333.84		9M	375.57		10M	417.30	
Work to eaves	M	23.22	10M	232.20		11M	255.42		12M	278.64		13M	301.86	
Fascia and eaves soffit	M	42.61	10M	426.10		11M	468.71		12M	511.32		13M	553.93	
Gutters and fittings	M	18.68	10M	186.80		11M	205.48		12M	224.16		13M	242.84	
Flashings	M	69.52	4M	278.08	**2589.86**	5M	347.60	**3081.09**	6M	417.12	**3651.22**	7M	486.64	**4142.45**
EXTERNAL WALLS														
Brick and block cavity wall	M2	106.91	18M2	1924.38	**1924.38**	20M2	2138.20	**2138.20**	23M2	2458.93	**2458.93**	25M2	2672.75	**2672.75**

Specification B 18 m2 - 27 m2

			Ref B/1P 3x6 Size 3.00 x 6.00 m Area 18 m2			Ref B/1P 3x7 Size 3.00 x 7.00 m Area 21 m2			Ref B/1P 3x8 Size 3.00 x 8.00 m Area 24 m2			Ref B/1P 3x9 Size 3.00 x 9.00 m Area 27 m2		
SINGLE STOREY PITCHED ROOF Continued/.....			Qty	Total £	Element Total £	Qty	Total £	Element Total £	Qty	Total £	Element Total £	Qty	Total £	Element Total £
Element	Unit	Unit Rate £												
	M	124.73	13M	1621.49		14M	1746.22		15M	1870.95		16M	1995.68	
	M2	45.82	18M2	824.76	**2446.25**	21M2	962.22	**2708.44**	24M2	1099.68	**2970.63**	27M2	1237.14	**3232.82**
	M2	55.42	25M2	1385.50		28M2	1551.76		32M2	1773.44		35M2	1939.70	
	M	23.71	13M	308.23		14M	331.94		15M	355.65		16M	379.36	
	M2	23.48	30M2	704.40		34M2	798.32		39M2	915.72		43M2	1009.64	
	M	11.58	9M	104.22		10M	115.80		11M	127.38		12M	138.96	
	M	41.73	11M	459.03		11M	459.03		11M	459.03		11M	459.03	
	M	23.22	14M	325.08		15M	348.30		16M	371.52		17M	394.74	
	M	42.61	14M	596.54		15M	639.15		16M	681.76		17M	724.37	
	M	18.68	14M	261.52		15M	280.20		16M	298.88		17M	317.56	
	M	69.52	9M	625.68	**4770.20**	10M	695.20	**5219.70**	11M	764.72	**5748.10**	12M	834.24	**6197.60**
	M2	106.91	26M2	2779.66	**2779.66**	27M2	2886.57	**2886.57**	31M2	3314.21	**3314.21**	33M2	3528.03	**3528.03**

Specification B 6 m2 - 15 m2

Element	Unit	Unit Rate £	Ref B/1P 3x2 Size 3.00 x 2.00 m Area 6 m2 Qty	Total £	Element Total £	Ref B/1P 3x3 Size 3.00 x 3.00 m Area 9 m2 Qty	Total £	Element Total £	Ref B/1P 3x4 Size 3.00 x 4.00 m Area 12 m2 Qty	Total £	Element Total £	Ref B/1P 3x5 Size 3.00 x 5.00 m Area 15 m2 Qty	Total £	Element Total £
SINGLE STOREY														
PITCHED ROOF														
EXTERNAL DOORS AND WINDOWS														
External door	NR	478.42	1NR	478.42		1NR	478.42		1NR	478.42		1NR	478.42	
Windows	NR	518.08	1NR	518.08		1NR	518.08		1NR	518.08		1NR	518.08	
Opening in cavity wall for door	NR	179.51	1NR	179.51		1NR	179.51		1NR	179.51		1NR	179.51	
Opening in cavity wall for window	NR	150.89	1NR	150.89	**1326.90**	1NR	150.89	**1326.90**	1NR	150.89	**1326.90**	1NR	150.89	**1326.90**
INTERNAL WALLS AND PARTITIONS														
Stud partitions	M2	51.63												
INTERNAL DOORS														
Softwood flush door	NR	251.11												
WALL FINISHES														
Plaster & decoration	M2	19.58	25M2	489.50	**489.50**	30M2	587.40	**587.40**	35M2	685.30	**685.30**	40M2	783.20	**783.20**
FLOOR FINISHES														
Thermoplastic tiles on screed	M2	35.42	6M2	212.52		9M2	318.78		12M2	425.04		15M2	531.30	
Softwood skirting	M	11.09	10M	110.90	**323.42**	12M	133.08	**451.86**	14M	155.26	**580.30**	16M	177.44	**708.74**
CEILING FINISHES														
Plasterboard and Artex	M2	16.34	6M2	98.04	**98.04**	9M2	147.06	**147.06**	12M2	196.08	**196.08**	15M2	245.10	**245.10**

Specification B
18 m2 - 27 m2

SINGLE STOREY

PITCHED ROOF Continued/.....

Element	Unit	Unit Rate £	Ref B/1P 3x6 Size 3.00 x 6.00 m Area 18 m2 Qty	Total £	Element Total £	Ref B/1P 3x7 Size 3.00 x 7.00 m Area 21 m2 Qty	Total £	Element Total £	Ref B/1P 3x8 Size 3.00 x 8.00 m Area 24 m2 Qty	Total £	Element Total £	Ref B/1P 3x9 Size 3.00 x 9.00 m Area 27 m2 Qty	Total £	Element Total £
	NR	478.42	1NR	478.42		1NR	478.42		1NR	478.42		1NR	478.42	
	NR	518.08	2NR	1036.16		2NR	1036.16		2NR	1036.16		2NR	1036.16	
	NR	179.51	1NR	179.51		1NR	179.51		1NR	179.51		1NR	179.51	
	NR	150.89	2NR	301.78	**1995.87**	2NR	301.78	**1995.87**	2NR	301.78	**1995.87**	2NR	301.78	**1995.87**
	M2	51.63	8M2	413.04	**413.04**	8M2	413.04	**413.04**	8M2	413.04	**413.04**	8M2	413.04	**413.04**
	NR	251.11	1NR	251.11	**251.11**	1NR	251.11	**251.11**	1NR	251.11	**251.11**	1NR	251.11	**251.11**
	M2	19.58	45M2	881.10	**881.10**	50M2	979.00	**979.00**	55M2	1076.90	**1076.90**	60M2	1174.80	**1174.80**
	M2	35.42	18M2	637.56		21M2	743.82		24M2	850.08		27M2	956.34	
	M	11.09	18M	199.62	**837.18**	20M	221.80	**965.62**	22M	243.98	**1094.06**	24M	266.16	**1222.50**
	M2	16.34	18M2	294.12	**294.12**	21M2	343.14	**343.14**	24M2	392.16	**392.16**	27M2	441.18	**441.18**

Specification B 6 m2 - 15 m2

SINGLE STOREY

PITCHED ROOF

Element	Unit	Unit Rate £	Ref B/1P 3x2 Size 3.00 x 2.00 m Area 6 m2 Qty	Total £	Element Total £	Ref B/1P 3x3 Size 3.00 x 3.00 m Area 9 m2 Qty	Total £	Element Total £	Ref B/1P 3x4 Size 3.00 x 4.00 m Area 12 m2 Qty	Total £	Element Total £	Ref B/1P 3x5 Size 3.00 x 5.00 m Area 15 m2 Qty	Total £	Element Total £
SERVICES														
Rainwater pipes	M	26.64	3M	79.92		3M	79.92		3M	79.92		3M	79.92	
Cold water service point	NR	110.52	1NR	110.52		1NR	110.52		1NR	110.52		1NR	110.52	
Hot water service point	NR	191.67	1NR	191.67		1NR	191.67		1NR	191.67		1NR	191.67	
Central heating service point	NR	386.51	1NR	386.51		1NR	386.51		1NR	386.51		1NR	386.51	
Electrical installation	NR	286.50	1NR	286.50	**1055.12**	1NR	286.50	**1055.12**	1NR	286.50	**1055.12**	1NR	286.50	**1055.12**
ALTERATIONS TO EXISTING BUILDINGS														
Opening in existing wall 1.80 m wide 2.00 m high	NR	689.44	1NR	689.44	**689.44**									
Opening in existing wall 2.40 m wide 2.00 m high	NR	865.59												
Opening in existing wall 3.00 m wide 2.00 m high	NR	921.26				1NR	921.26	**921.26**						
Opening in existing wall 4.00 m wide 2.00 m high	NR	1131.22							1NR	1131.22	**1131.22**			
Opening in existing wall 5.00 m wide 2.00 m high	NR	1341.19										1NR	1341.19	**1341.19**

Specification B 18 m2 - 27 m2			Ref B/1P 3x6 Size 3.00 x 6.00 m Area 18 m2			Ref B/1P 3x7 Size 3.00 x 7.00 m Area 21 m2			Ref B/1P 3x8 Size 3.00 x 8.00 m Area 24 m2			Ref B/1P 3x9 Size 3.00 x 9.00 m Area 27 m2		
			Qty	Total £	Element Total £	Qty	Total £	Element Total £	Qty	Total £	Element Total £	Qty	Total £	Element Total £
SINGLE STOREY														
PITCHED ROOF Continued/.....														
Element	Unit	Unit Rate £												
	M	26.64	3M	79.92		3M	79.92		3M	79.92		3M	79.92	
	NR	110.52	1NR	110.52		1NR	110.52		1NR	110.52		1NR	110.52	
	NR	191.67	1NR	191.67		1NR	191.67		1NR	191.67		1NR	191.67	
	NR	386.51	2NR	773.02		2NR	773.02		2NR	773.02		2NR	773.02	
	NR	286.50	2NR	573.00	**1728.13**	2NR	573.00	**1728.13**	2NR	573.00	**1728.13**	2NR	573.00	**1728.13**
	NR	689.44												
	NR	865.59	2NR	1731.18	**1731.18**									
	NR	921.26				2NR	1842.52	**1842.52**	2NR	1842.52	**1842.52**			
	NR	1131.22										2NR	2262.44	**2262.44**
	NR	1341.19												

Specification B 6 m2 - 15 m2

	Ref B/1P 3x2 Size 3.00 x 2.00 m Area 6 m2	Ref B/1P 3x3 Size 3.00 x 3.00 m Area 9 m2	Ref B/1P 3x4 Size 3.00 x 4.00 m Area 12 m2	Ref B/1P 3x5 Size 3.00 x 5.00 m Area 15 m2
	Element Total £	Element Total £	Element Total £	Element Total £
SINGLE STOREY				
PITCHED ROOF				
SUMMARY				
SUBSTRUCTURE	1397.49	1659.68	1921.87	2184.06
UPPER FLOORS	-	-	-	-
ROOF	2589.86	3081.09	3651.22	4142.45
EXTERNAL WALLS	1924.38	2138.20	2458.93	2672.75
EXTERNAL DOORS AND WINDOWS	1326.90	1326.90	1326.90	1326.90
INTERNAL WALLS AND PARTITIONS	-	-	-	-
INTERNAL DOORS	-	-	-	-
WALL FINISHES	489.50	587.40	685.30	783.20
FLOOR FINISHES	323.42	451.86	580.30	708.74
CEILING FINISHES	98.04	147.06	196.08	245.10
SERVICES	1055.12	1055.12	1055.12	1055.12
ALTERATIONS TO EXISTING BUILDINGS	689.44	921.26	1131.22	1341.19
Sub Total	9894.15	11368.57	13006.94	14459.51
Allowance for unmeasured items and sundries 5%	494.71	568.43	650.35	722.98
NET TOTAL excluding Preliminaries, Profit and Overheads	**10388.86**	**11937.00**	**13657.29**	**15182.49**

Specification B 18 m2 - 27 m2	Ref B/1P 3x6 Size 3.00 x 6.00 m Area 18 m2 Element Total £	Ref B/1P 3x7 Size 3.00 x 7.00 m Area 21 m2 Element Total £	Ref B/1P 3x8 Size 3.00 x 8.00 m Area 24 m2 Element Total £	Ref B/1P 3x9 Size 3.00 x 9.00 m Area 27 m2 Element Total £
SINGLE STOREY				
PITCHED ROOF				
SUMMARY Continued/.....				
	2446.25	2708.44	2970.63	3232.82
	-	-	-	-
	4770.20	5219.70	5748.10	6197.60
	2779.66	2886.57	3314.21	3528.03
	1995.87	1995.87	1995.87	1995.87
	413.04	413.04	413.04	413.04
	251.11	251.11	251.11	251.11
	881.10	979.00	1076.90	1174.80
	837.18	965.62	1094.06	1222.50
	294.12	343.14	392.16	441.18
	1728.13	1728.13	1728.13	1728.13
	1731.18	1842.52	1842.52	2262.44
Sub Total	18127.84	19333.14	20826.73	22447.52
Allowance for unmeasured items and sundries 5%	906.39	966.66	1041.34	1122.38
NET TOTAL excluding Preliminaries, Profit and Overheads	**19034.23**	**20299.80**	**21868.07**	**23569.90**

Specification B 8 m2 - 20 m2

Element	Unit	Unit Rate £	Ref B/1P 4x2 Size 4.00 x 2.00 m Area 8 m2 Qty	Total £	Element Total £	Ref B/1P 4x3 Size 4.00 x 3.00 m Area 12 m2 Qty	Total £	Element Total £	Ref B/1P 4x4 Size 4.00 x 4.00 m Area 16 m2 Qty	Total £	Element Total £	Ref B/1P 4x5 Size 4.00 x 5.00 m Area 20 m2 Qty	Total £	Element Total £
SINGLE STOREY														
PITCHED ROOF														
SUBSTRUCTURE														
Strip footings	M	124.73	11M	1372.03		12M	1496.76		13M	1621.49		14M	1746.22	
Solid ground floor	M2	45.82	8M2	366.56	**1738.59**	12M2	549.84	**2046.60**	16M2	733.12	**2354.61**	20M2	916.40	**2662.62**
ROOF														
Pitched roof construction	M2	55.42	14M2	775.88		18M2	997.56		23M2	1274.66		27M2	1496.34	
Work to top of external wall	M	23.71	11M	260.81		12M	284.52		13M	308.23		14M	331.94	
Concrete tile roofing	M2	23.48	17M2	399.16		22M2	516.56		28M2	657.44		33M2	774.84	
Work to verge	M	11.58	4M	46.32		5M	57.90		6M	69.48		7M	81.06	
Work to hip	M	41.73	8M	333.84		9M	375.57		10M	417.30		11M	459.03	
Work to eaves	M	23.22	12M	278.64		13M	301.86		14M	325.08		15M	348.30	
Fascia and eaves soffit	M	42.61	12M	511.32		13M	553.93		14M	596.54		15M	639.15	
Gutters and fittings	M	18.68	12M	224.16		13M	242.84		14M	261.52		15M	280.20	
Flashings	M	69.52	4M	278.08	**3108.21**	5M	347.60	**3678.34**	6M	417.12	**4327.37**	7M	486.64	**4897.50**
EXTERNAL WALLS														
Brick and block cavity wall	M2	106.91	23M2	2458.93	**2458.93**	25M2	2672.75	**2672.75**	28M2	2993.48	**2993.48**	29M2	3100.39	**3100.39**

Specification B
24 m2 - 36 m2

			Ref B/1P 4x6 Size 4.00 x 6.00 m Area 24 m2			Ref B/1P 4x7 Size 4.00 x 7.00 m Area 28 m2			Ref B/1P 4x8 Size 4.00 x 8.00 m Area 32 m2			Ref B/1P 4x9 Size 4.00 x 9.00 m Area 36 m2		
			Qty	Total £	Element Total £	Qty	Total £	Element Total £	Qty	Total £	Element Total £	Qty	Total £	Element Total £
SINGLE STOREY														
PITCHED ROOF Continued/.....														
Element	Unit	Unit Rate £												
	M	124.73	15M	1870.95		16M	1995.68		17M	2120.41		18M	2245.14	
	M2	45.82	24M2	1099.68	**2970.63**	28M2	1282.96	**3278.64**	32M2	1466.24	**3586.65**	36M2	1649.52	**3894.66**
	M2	55.42	32M2	1773.44		36M2	1995.12		41M2	2272.22		45M2	2493.90	
	M	23.71	15M	355.65		16M	379.36		17M	403.07		18M	426.78	
	M2	23.48	39M2	915.72		44M2	1033.12		50M2	1174.00		55M2	1291.40	
	M	11.58	9M	104.22		10M	115.80		11M	127.38		12M	138.96	
	M	41.73	12M	500.76		13M	542.49		14M	584.22		14M	584.22	
	M	23.22	16M	371.52		17M	394.74		18M	417.96		19M	441.18	
	M	42.61	16M	681.76		17M	724.37		18M	766.98		19M	809.59	
	M	18.68	16M	298.88		17M	317.56		18M	336.24		19M	354.92	
	M	69.52	9M	625.68	**5627.63**	10M	695.20	**6197.76**	11M	764.72	**6846.79**	12M	834.24	**7375.19**
	M2	106.91	31M2	3314.21	**3314.21**	33M2	3528.03	**3528.03**	36M2	3848.76	**3848.76**	38M2	4062.58	**4062.58**

Specification B
8 m2 - 20 m2

SINGLE STOREY

PITCHED ROOF

Element	Unit	Unit Rate £	Ref B/1P 4x2 Size 4.00 x 2.00 m Area 8 m2 Qty	Total £	Element Total £	Ref B/1P 4x3 Size 4.00 x 3.00 m Area 12 m2 Qty	Total £	Element Total £	Ref B/1P 4x4 Size 4.00 x 4.00 m Area 16 m2 Qty	Total £	Element Total £	Ref B/1P 4x5 Size 4.00 x 5.00 m Area 20 m2 Qty	Total £	Element Total £
EXTERNAL DOORS AND WINDOWS														
External door	NR	478.42	1NR	478.42		1NR	478.42		1NR	478.42		1NR	478.42	
Windows	NR	518.08	1NR	518.08		1NR	518.08		1NR	518.08		1NR	518.08	
Opening in cavity wall for door	NR	179.51	1NR	179.51		1NR	179.51		1NR	179.51		1NR	179.51	
Opening in cavity wall for window	NR	150.89	1NR	150.89	**1326.90**	1NR	150.89	**1326.90**	1NR	150.89	**1326.90**	1NR	150.89	**1326.90**
INTERNAL WALLS AND PARTITIONS														
Stud partitions	M2	51.63												
INTERNAL DOORS														
Softwood flush door	NR	251.11												
WALL FINISHES														
Plaster & decoration	M2	19.58	30M2	587.40	**587.40**	35M2	685.30	**685.30**	40M2	783.20	**783.20**	45M2	881.10	**881.10**
FLOOR FINISHES														
Thermoplastic tiles on screed	M2	35.42	8M2	283.36		12M2	425.04		16M2	566.72		20M2	708.40	
Softwood skirting	M	11.09	12M	133.08	**416.44**	14M	155.26	**580.30**	16M	177.44	**744.16**	18M	199.62	**908.02**
CEILING FINISHES														
Plasterboard and Artex	M2	16.34	8M2	130.72	**130.72**	12M2	196.08	**196.08**	16M2	261.44	**261.44**	20M2	326.80	**326.80**

Specification B
24 m2 - 36 m2

SINGLE STOREY

PITCHED ROOF Continued/.....

Element	Unit	Unit Rate £	Ref B/1P 4x6 Size 4.00 x 6.00 m Area 24 m2			Ref B/1P 4x7 Size 4.00 x 7.00 m Area 28 m2			Ref B/1P 4x8 Size 4.00 x 8.00 m Area 32 m2			Ref B/1P 4x9 Size 4.00 x 9.00 m Area 36 m2		
			Qty	Total £	Element Total £	Qty	Total £	Element Total £	Qty	Total £	Element Total £	Qty	Total £	Element Total £
	NR	478.42	1NR	478.42		1NR	478.42		1NR	478.42		1NR	478.42	
	NR	518.08	2NR	1036.16		2NR	1036.16		2NR	1036.16		2NR	1036.16	
	NR	179.51	1NR	179.51		1NR	179.51		1NR	179.51		1NR	179.51	
	NR	150.89	2NR	301.78	**1995.87**	2NR	301.78	**1995.87**	2NR	301.78	**1995.87**	2NR	301.78	**1995.87**
	M2	51.63	10M2	516.30	**516.30**	10M2	516.30	**516.30**	10M2	516.30	**516.30**	10M2	516.30	**516.30**
	NR	251.11	1NR	251.11	**251.11**	1NR	251.11	**251.11**	1NR	251.11	**251.11**	1NR	251.11	**251.11**
	M2	19.58	50M2	979.00	**979.00**	55M2	1076.90	**1076.90**	60M2	1174.80	**1174.80**	65M2	1272.70	**1272.70**
	M2	35.42	24M2	850.08		28M2	991.76		32M2	1133.44		36M2	1275.12	
	M	11.09	20M	221.80	**1071.88**	22M	243.98	**1235.74**	24M	266.16	**1399.60**	26M	288.34	**1563.46**
	M2	16.34	24M2	392.16	**392.16**	28M2	457.52	**457.52**	32M2	522.88	**522.88**	36M2	588.24	**588.24**

Specification B 8 m2 - 20 m2

SINGLE STOREY

PITCHED ROOF

Element	Unit	Unit Rate £	Ref B/1P 4x2 Size 4.00 x 2.00 m Area 8 m2 Qty	Total £	Element Total £	Ref B/1P 4x3 Size 4.00 x 3.00 m Area 12 m2 Qty	Total £	Element Total £	Ref B/1P 4x4 Size 4.00 x 4.00 m Area 16 m2 Qty	Total £	Element Total £	Ref B/1P 4x5 Size 4.00 x 5.00 m Area 20 m2 Qty	Total £	Element Total £
SERVICES														
Rainwater pipes	M	26.64	3M	79.92		3M	79.92		3M	79.92		3M	79.92	
Cold water service point	NR	110.52	1NR	110.52		1NR	110.52		1NR	110.52		1NR	110.52	
Hot water service point	NR	191.67	1NR	191.67		1NR	191.67		1NR	191.67		1NR	191.67	
Central heating service point	NR	386.51	1NR	386.51		1NR	386.51		1NR	386.51		1NR	386.51	
Electrical installation	NR	286.50	1NR	286.50	**1055.12**	1NR	286.50	**1055.12**	1NR	286.50	**1055.12**	1NR	286.50	**1055.12**
ALTERATIONS TO EXISTING BUILDINGS														
Opening in existing wall 1.80 m wide 2.00 m high	NR	689.44	1NR	689.44	**689.44**									
Opening in existing wall 2.40 m wide 2.00 m high	NR	865.59												
Opening in existing wall 3.00 m wide 2.00 m high	NR	921.26				1NR	921.26	**921.26**						
Opening in existing wall 4.00 m wide 2.00 m high	NR	1131.22							1NR	1131.22	**1131.22**			
Opening in existing wall 5.00 m wide 2.00 m high	NR	1341.19										1NR	1341.19	**1341.19**

Specification B
24 m2 - 36 m2

SINGLE STOREY

PITCHED ROOF Continued/.....

Element	Unit	Unit Rate £	Ref B/1P 4x6 Size 4.00 x 6.00 m Area 24 m2 Qty	Total £	Element Total £	Ref B/1P 4x7 Size 4.00 x 7.00 m Area 28 m2 Qty	Total £	Element Total £	Ref B/1P 4x8 Size 4.00 x 8.00 m Area 32 m2 Qty	Total £	Element Total £	Ref B/1P 4x9 Size 4.00 x 9.00 m Area 36 m2 Qty	Total £	Element Total £
	M	26.64	3M	79.92		3M	79.92		3M	79.92		3M	79.92	
	NR	110.52	1NR	110.52		1NR	110.52		1NR	110.52		1NR	110.52	
	NR	191.67	1NR	191.67		1NR	191.67		1NR	191.67		1NR	191.67	
	NR	386.51	2NR	773.02		2NR	773.02		2NR	773.02		2NR	773.02	
	NR	286.50	2NR	573.00	**1728.13**	2NR	573.00	**1728.13**	2NR	573.00	**1728.13**	2NR	573.00	**1728.13**
	NR	689.44												
	NR	865.59	2NR	1731.18	**1731.18**									
	NR	921.26				2NR	1842.52	**1842.52**	2NR	1842.52	**1842.52**			
	NR	1131.22										2NR	2262.44	**2262.44**
	NR	1341.19												

Specification B 8 m2 - 20 m2	Ref B/1P 4x2 Size 4.00 x 2.00 m Area 8 m2	Ref B/1P 4x3 Size 4.00 x 3.00 m Area 12 m2	Ref B/1P 4x4 Size 4.00 x 4.00 m Area 16 m2	Ref B/1P 4x5 Size 4.00 x 5.00 m Area 20 m2
	Element Total £	**Element Total £**	**Element Total £**	**Element Total £**
SINGLE STOREY				
PITCHED ROOF				
SUMMARY				
SUBSTRUCTURE	1738.59	2046.60	2354.61	2662.62
UPPER FLOORS	-	-	-	-
ROOF	3108.21	3678.34	4327.37	4897.50
EXTERNAL WALLS	2458.93	2672.75	2993.48	3100.39
EXTERNAL DOORS AND WINDOWS	1326.90	1326.90	1326.90	1326.90
INTERNAL WALLS AND PARTITIONS	-	-	-	-
INTERNAL DOORS	-	-	-	-
WALL FINISHES	587.40	685.30	783.20	881.10
FLOOR FINISHES	416.44	580.30	744.16	908.02
CEILING FINISHES	130.72	196.08	261.44	326.80
SERVICES	1055.12	1055.12	1055.12	1055.12
ALTERATIONS TO EXISTING BUILDINGS	689.44	921.26	1131.22	1341.19
Sub Total	11511.75	13162.65	14977.50	16499.64
Allowance for unmeasured items and sundries 5%	575.59	658.13	748.88	824.98
NET TOTAL excluding Preliminaries, Profit and Overheads	**12087.34**	**13820.78**	**15726.38**	**17324.62**

Specification B 24 m2 - 36 m2	Ref B/1P 4x6 Size 4.00 x 6.00 m Area 24 m2 Element Total £	Ref B/1P 4x7 Size 4.00 x 7.00 m Area 28 m2 Element Total £	Ref B/1P 4x8 Size 4.00 x 8.00 m Area 32 m2 Element Total £	Ref B/1P 4x9 Size 4.00 x 9.00 m Area 36 m2 Element Total £
SINGLE STOREY				
PITCHED ROOF				
SUMMARY Continued/.....				
	2970.63	3278.64	3586.65	3894.66
	-	-	-	-
	5627.63	6197.76	6846.79	7375.19
	3314.21	3528.03	3848.76	4062.58
	1995.87	1995.87	1995.87	1995.87
	516.30	516.30	516.30	516.30
	251.11	251.11	251.11	251.11
	979.00	1076.90	1174.80	1272.70
	1071.88	1235.74	1399.60	1563.46
	392.16	457.52	522.88	588.24
	1728.13	1728.13	1728.13	1728.13
	1731.18	1842.52	1842.52	2262.44
Sub Total	20578.10	22108.52	23713.41	25510.68
Allowance for unmeasured items and sundries 5%	1028.91	1105.43	1185.67	1275.53
NET TOTAL excluding Preliminaries, Profit and Overheads	**21607.01**	**23213.95**	**24899.08**	**26786.21**

Specification B 10 m2 - 25 m2

SINGLE STOREY

PITCHED ROOF

Element	Unit	Unit Rate £	Ref B/1P 5x2 Size 5.00 x 2.00 m Area 10 m2 Qty	Total £	Element Total £	Ref B/1P 5x3 Size 5.00 x 3.00 m Area 15 m2 Qty	Total £	Element Total £	Ref B/1P 5x4 Size 5.00 x 4.00 m Area 20 m2 Qty	Total £	Element Total £	Ref B/1P 5x5 Size 5.00 x 5.00 m Area 25 m2 Qty	Total £	Element Total £
SUBSTRUCTURE														
Strip footings	M	124.73	13M	1621.49		14M	1746.22		15M	1870.95		16M	1995.68	
Solid ground floor	M2	45.82	10M2	458.20	**2079.69**	15M2	687.30	**2433.52**	20M2	916.40	**2787.35**	25M2	1145.50	**3141.18**
ROOF														
Pitched roof construction	M2	55.42	17M2	942.14		22M2	1219.24		28M2	1551.76		33M2	1828.86	
Work to top of external wall	M	23.71	13M	308.23		14M	331.94		15M	355.65		16M	379.36	
Concrete tile roofing	M2	23.48	20M2	469.60		27M2	633.96		34M2	798.32		41M2	962.68	
Work to verge	M	11.58	4M	46.32		5M	57.90		6M	69.48		7M	81.06	
Work to hip	M	41.73	9M	375.57		10M	417.30		11M	459.03		12M	500.76	
Work to eaves	M	23.22	14M	325.08		15M	348.30		16M	371.52		17M	394.74	
Fascia and eaves soffit	M	42.61	14M	596.54		15M	639.15		16M	681.76		17M	724.37	
Gutters and fittings	M	18.68	14M	261.52		15M	280.20		16M	298.88		17M	317.56	
Flashings	M	69.52	4M	278.08	**3603.08**	5M	347.60	**4275.59**	6M	417.12	**5003.52**	7M	486.64	**5676.03**
EXTERNAL WALLS														
Brick and block cavity wall	M2	106.91	28M2	2993.48	**2993.48**	30M2	3207.30	**3207.30**	33M2	3528.03	**3528.03**	35M2	3741.85	**3741.85**

Specification B
30 m2 - 45 m2

SINGLE STOREY

PITCHED ROOF Continued/.....

Element	Unit	Unit Rate £	Ref B/1P 5x6 Size 5.00 x 6.00 m Area 30 m2 Qty	Total £	Element Total £	Ref B/1P 5x7 Size 5.00 x 7.00 m Area 35 m2 Qty	Total £	Element Total £	Ref B/1P 5x8 Size 5.00 x 8.00 m Area 40 m2 Qty	Total £	Element Total £	Ref B/1P 5x9 Size 5.00 x 9.00 m Area 45 m2 Qty	Total £	Element Total £
	M	124.73	17M	2120.41		18M	2245.14		19M	2369.87		20M	2494.60	
	M2	45.82	30M2	1374.60	**3495.01**	35M2	1603.70	**3848.84**	40M2	1832.80	**4202.67**	45M2	2061.90	**4556.50**
	M2	55.42	39M2	2161.38		44M2	2438.48		50M2	2771.00		55M2	3048.10	
	M	23.71	17M	403.07		18M	426.78		19M	450.49		20M	474.20	
	M2	23.48	47M2	1103.56		54M2	1267.92		61M2	1432.28		68M2	1596.64	
	M	11.58	9M	104.22		10M	115.80		11M	127.38		12M	138.96	
	M	41.73	13M	542.49		14M	584.22		15M	625.95		16M	667.68	
	M	23.22	18M	417.96		19M	441.18		20M	464.40		21M	487.62	
	M	42.61	18M	766.98		19M	809.59		20M	852.20		21M	894.81	
	M	18.68	18M	336.24		19M	354.92		20M	373.60		21M	392.28	
	M	69.52	9M	625.68	**6461.58**	10M	695.20	**7134.09**	11M	764.72	**7862.02**	12M	834.24	**8534.53**
	M2	106.91	36M2	3848.76	**3848.76**	38M2	4062.58	**4062.58**	41M2	4383.31	**4383.31**	43M2	4597.13	**4597.13**

Specification B 10 m2 - 25 m2

SINGLE STOREY

PITCHED ROOF

Element	Unit	Unit Rate £	Ref B/1P 5x2 Size 5.00 x 2.00 m Area 10 m2 Qty	Total £	Element Total £	Ref B/1P 5x3 Size 5.00 x 3.00 m Area 15 m2 Qty	Total £	Element Total £	Ref B/1P 5x4 Size 5.00 x 4.00 m Area 20 m2 Qty	Total £	Element Total £	Ref B/1P 5x5 Size 5.00 x 5.00 m Area 25 m2 Qty	Total £	Element Total £
EXTERNAL DOORS AND WINDOWS														
External door	NR	478.42	1NR	478.42		1NR	478.42		1NR	478.42		1NR	478.42	
Windows	NR	518.08	1NR	518.08		1NR	518.08		1NR	518.08		1NR	518.08	
Opening in cavity wall for door	NR	179.51	1NR	179.51		1NR	179.51		1NR	179.51		1NR	179.51	
Opening in cavity wall for window	NR	150.89	1NR	150.89	**1326.90**	1NR	150.89	**1326.90**	1NR	150.89	**1326.90**	1NR	150.89	**1326.90**
INTERNAL WALLS AND PARTITIONS														
Stud partitions	M2	51.63												
INTERNAL DOORS														
Softwood flush door	NR	251.11												
WALL FINISHES														
Plaster & decoration	M2	19.58	35M2	685.30	**685.30**	40M2	783.20	**783.20**	45M2	881.10	**881.10**	50M2	979.00	**979.00**
FLOOR FINISHES														
Thermoplastic tiles on screed	M2	35.42	10M2	354.20		15M2	531.30		20M2	708.40		25M2	885.50	
Softwood skirting	M	11.09	14M	155.26	**509.46**	16M	177.44	**708.74**	18M	199.62	**908.02**	20M	221.80	**1107.30**
CEILING FINISHES														
Plasterboard and Artex	M2	16.34	10M2	163.40	**163.40**	15M2	245.10	**245.10**	20M2	326.80	**326.80**	25M2	408.50	**408.50**

Specification B 30 m2 - 45 m2

Element	Unit	Unit Rate £	Ref B/1P 5x6 Size 5.00 x 6.00 m Area 30 m2 Qty	Total £	Element Total £	Ref B/1P 5x7 Size 5.00 x 7.00 m Area 35 m2 Qty	Total £	Element Total £	Ref B/1P 5x8 Size 5.00 x 8.00 m Area 40 m2 Qty	Total £	Element Total £	Ref B/1P 5x9 Size 5.00 x 9.00 m Area 45 m2 Qty	Total £	Element Total £
SINGLE STOREY														
PITCHED ROOF Continued/.....														
	NR	478.42	1NR	478.42		1NR	478.42		1NR	478.42		1NR	478.42	
	NR	518.08	2NR	1036.16		2NR	1036.16		2NR	1036.16		2NR	1036.16	
	NR	179.51	1NR	179.51		1NR	179.51		1NR	179.51		1NR	179.51	
	NR	150.89	2NR	301.78	**1995.87**	2NR	301.78	**1995.87**	2NR	301.78	**1995.87**	2NR	301.78	**1995.87**
	M2	51.63	13M2	671.19	**671.19**	13M2	671.19	**671.19**	13M2	671.19	**671.19**	13M2	671.19	**671.19**
	NR	251.11	1NR	251.11	**251.11**	1NR	251.11	**251.11**	1NR	251.11	**251.11**	1NR	251.11	**251.11**
	M2	19.58	55M2	1076.90	**1076.90**	60M2	1174.80	**1174.80**	65M2	1272.70	**1272.70**	70M2	1370.60	**1370.60**
	M2	35.42	30M2	1062.60		35M2	1239.70		40M2	1416.80		45M2	1593.90	
	M	11.09	22M	243.98	**1306.58**	24M	266.16	**1505.86**	26M	288.34	**1705.14**	28M	310.52	**1904.42**
	M2	16.34	30M2	490.20	**490.20**	35M2	571.90	**571.90**	40M2	653.60	**653.60**	45M2	735.30	**735.30**

Specification B 10 m2 - 25 m2

SINGLE STOREY PITCHED ROOF			Ref B/1P 5x2 Size 5.00 x 2.00 m Area 10 m2			Ref B/1P 5x3 Size 5.00 x 3.00 m Area 15 m2			Ref B/1P 5x4 Size 5.00 x 4.00 m Area 20 m2			Ref B/1P 5x5 Size 5.00 x 5.00 m Area 25 m2		
Element	Unit	Unit Rate £	Qty	Total £	Element Total £	Qty	Total £	Element Total £	Qty	Total £	Element Total £	Qty	Total £	Element Total £
SERVICES														
Rainwater pipes	M	26.64	3M	79.92		3M	79.92		3M	79.92		3M	79.92	
Cold water service point	NR	110.52	1NR	110.52		1NR	110.52		1NR	110.52		1NR	110.52	
Hot water service point	NR	191.67	1NR	191.67		1NR	191.67		1NR	191.67		1NR	191.67	
Central heating service point	NR	386.51	1NR	386.51		1NR	386.51		1NR	386.51		1NR	386.51	
Electrical installation	NR	286.50	1NR	286.50	**1055.12**	1NR	286.50	**1055.12**	1NR	286.50	**1055.12**	1NR	286.50	**1055.12**
ALTERATIONS TO EXISTING BUILDINGS														
Opening in existing wall 1.80 m wide 2.00 m high	NR	689.44	1NR	689.44	**689.44**									
Opening in existing wall 2.40 m wide 2.00 m high	NR	865.59												
Opening in existing wall 3.00 m wide 2.00 m high	NR	921.26				1NR	921.26	**921.26**						
Opening in existing wall 4.00 m wide 2.00 m high	NR	1131.22							1NR	1131.22	**1131.22**			
Opening in existing wall 5.00 m wide 2.00 m high	NR	1341.19										1NR	1341.19	**1341.19**

Specification B
30 m2 - 45 m2

SINGLE STOREY

PITCHED ROOF Continued/.....

Element	Unit	Unit Rate £	Ref B/1P 5x6 Size 5.00 x 6.00 m Area 30 m2 Qty	Total £	Element Total £	Ref B/1P 5x7 Size 5.00 x 7.00 m Area 35 m2 Qty	Total £	Element Total £	Ref B/1P 5x8 Size 5.00 x 8.00 m Area 40 m2 Qty	Total £	Element Total £	Ref B/1P 5x9 Size 5.00 x 9.00 m Area 45 m2 Qty	Total £	Element Total £
	M	26.64	3M	79.92		3M	79.92		3M	79.92		3M	79.92	
	NR	110.52	1NR	110.52		1NR	110.52		1NR	110.52		1NR	110.52	
	NR	191.67	1NR	191.67		1NR	191.67		1NR	191.67		1NR	191.67	
	NR	386.51	2NR	773.02		2NR	773.02		2NR	773.02		2NR	773.02	
	NR	286.50	2NR	573.00	**1728.13**	2NR	573.00	**1728.13**	2NR	573.00	**1728.13**	2NR	573.00	**1728.13**
	NR	689.44												
	NR	865.59	2NR	1731.18	**1731.18**									
	NR	921.26				2NR	1842.52	**1842.52**	2NR	1842.52	**1842.52**			
	NR	1131.22										2NR	2262.44	**2262.44**
	NR	1341.19												

Specification B 10 m2 - 25 m2	Ref B/1P 5x2 Size 5.00 x 2.00 m Area 10 m2	Ref B/1P 5x3 Size 5.00 x 3.00 m Area 15 m2	Ref B/1P 5x4 Size 5.00 x 4.00 m Area 20 m2	Ref B/1P 5x5 Size 5.00 x 5.00 m Area 25 m2
	Element Total £	Element Total £	Element Total £	Element Total £
SINGLE STOREY				
PITCHED ROOF				
SUMMARY				
SUBSTRUCTURE	2079.69	2433.52	2787.35	3141.18
UPPER FLOORS	-	-	-	-
ROOF	3603.08	4275.59	5003.52	5676.03
EXTERNAL WALLS	2993.48	3207.30	3528.03	3741.85
EXTERNAL DOORS AND WINDOWS	1326.90	1326.90	1326.90	1326.90
INTERNAL WALLS AND PARTITIONS	-	-	-	-
INTERNAL DOORS	-	-	-	-
WALL FINISHES	685.30	783.20	881.10	979.00
FLOOR FINISHES	509.46	708.74	908.02	1107.30
CEILING FINISHES	163.40	245.10	326.80	408.50
SERVICES	1055.12	1055.12	1055.12	1055.12
ALTERATIONS TO EXISTING BUILDINGS	689.44	921.26	1131.22	1341.19
Sub Total	13105.87	14956.73	16948.06	18777.07
Allowance for unmeasured items and sundries 5%	655.29	747.84	847.40	938.85
NET TOTAL excluding Preliminaries, Profit and Overheads	**13761.16**	**15704.57**	**17795.46**	**19715.92**

Specification B 30 m2 - 45 m2

	Ref B/1P 5x6 Size 5.00 x 6.00 m Area 30 m2	Ref B/1P 5x7 Size 5.00 x 7.00 m Area 35 m2	Ref B/1P 5x8 Size 5.00 x 8.00 m Area 40 m2	Ref B/1P 5x9 Size 5.00 x 9.00 m Area 45 m2
	Element Total £	Element Total £	Element Total £	Element Total £
SINGLE STOREY				
PITCHED ROOF				
SUMMARY Continued/.....				
	3495.01	3848.84	4202.67	4556.50
	-	-	-	-
	6461.58	7134.09	7862.02	8534.53
	3848.76	4062.58	4383.31	4597.13
	1995.87	1995.87	1995.87	1995.87
	671.19	671.19	671.19	671.19
	251.11	251.11	251.11	251.11
	1076.90	1174.80	1272.70	1370.60
	1306.58	1505.86	1705.14	1904.42
	490.20	571.90	653.60	735.30
	1728.13	1728.13	1728.13	1728.13
	1731.18	1842.52	1842.52	2262.44
Sub Total	23056.51	24786.89	26568.26	28607.22
Allowance for unmeasured items and sundries 5%	1152.83	1239.34	1328.41	1430.36
NET TOTAL excluding Preliminaries, Profit and Overheads	**24209.34**	**26026.23**	**27896.67**	**30037.58**

Specification B

Two storey flat roof

[2F] 2×2/3/4/5.

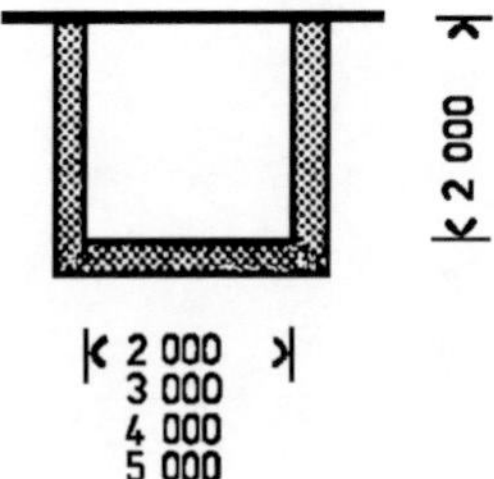

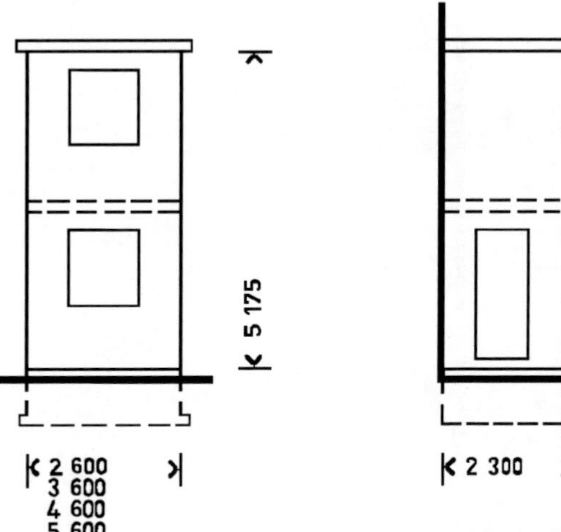

[2F] 2×6/7/8/9.

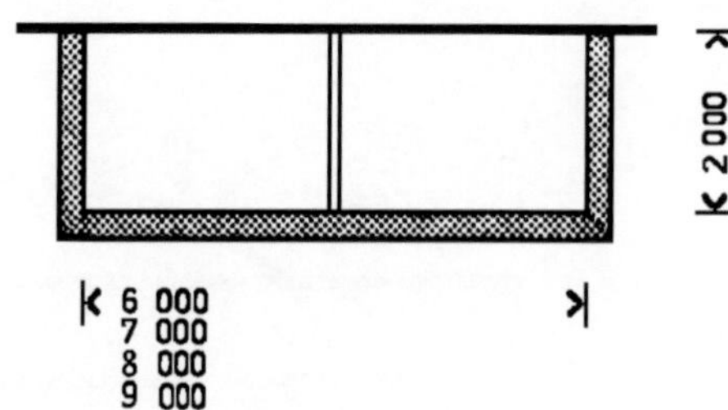

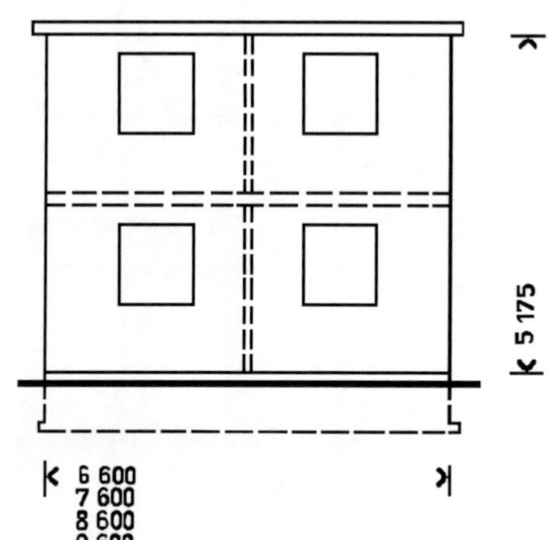

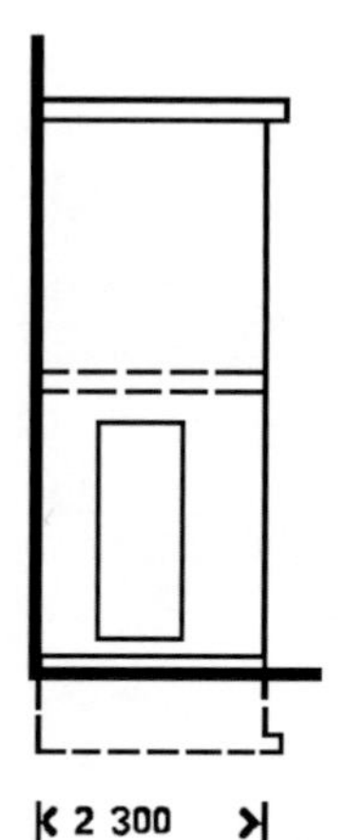

[2F] 3×2/3/4/5.

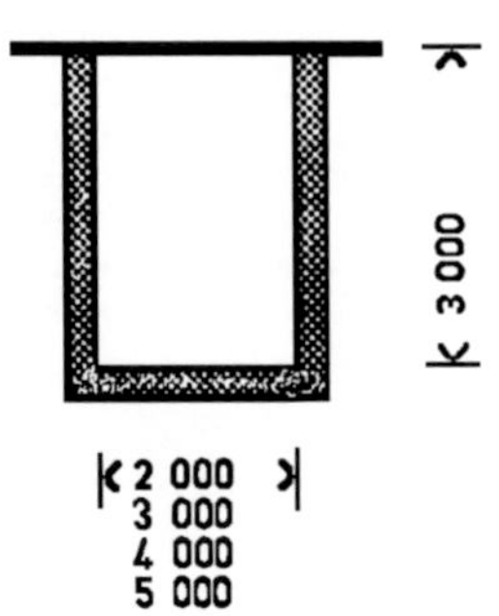

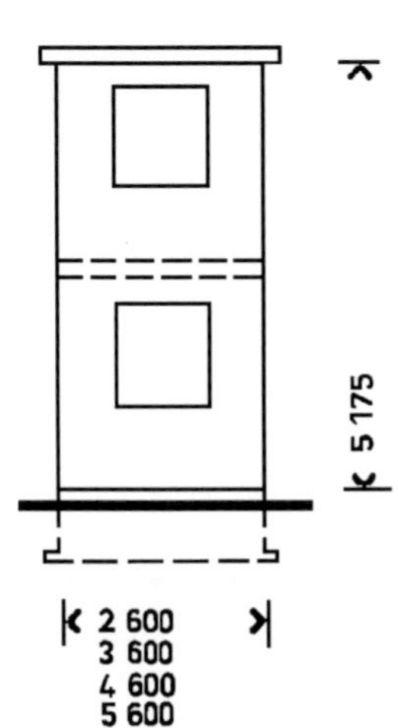

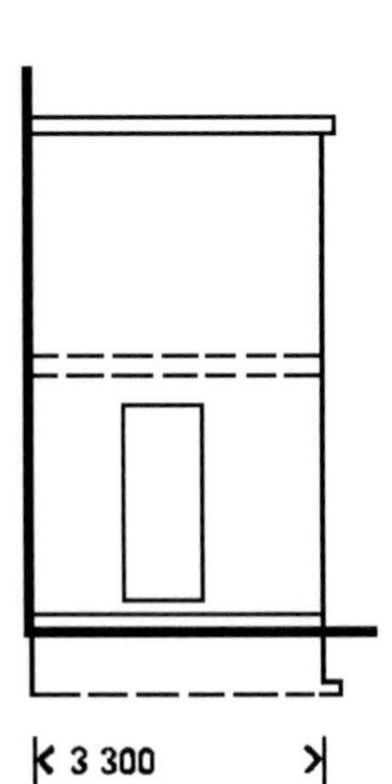

[2F] 3×6/7/8/9.

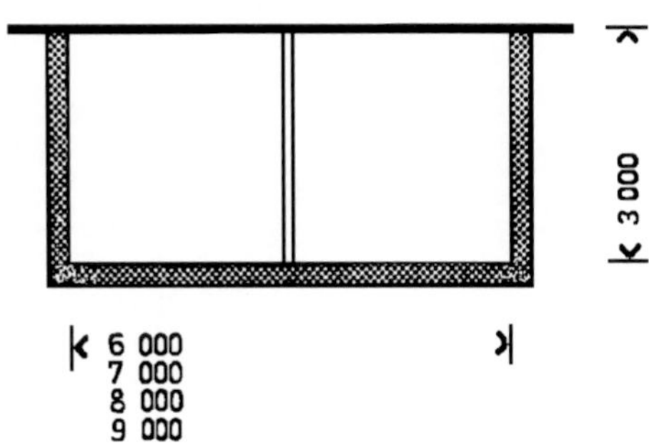

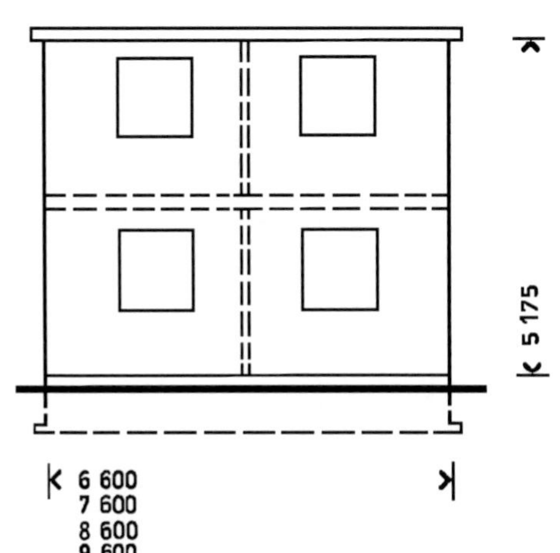

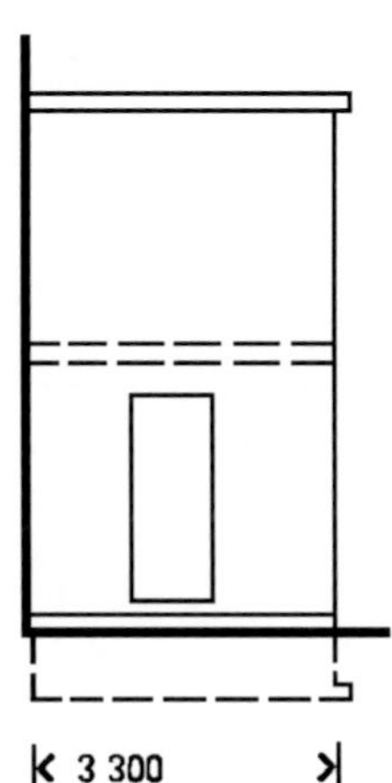

[2F] 4×2/3/4/5.

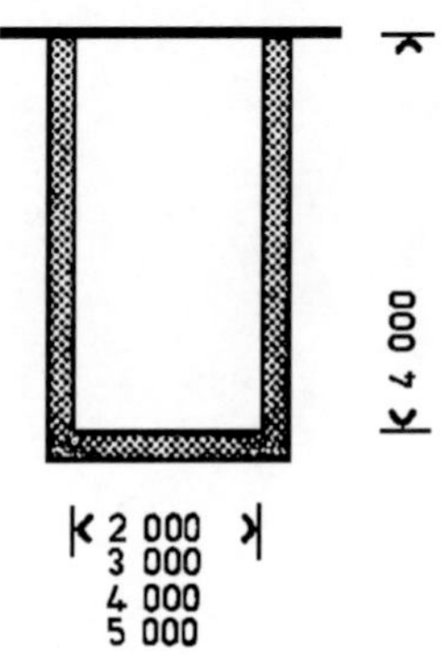

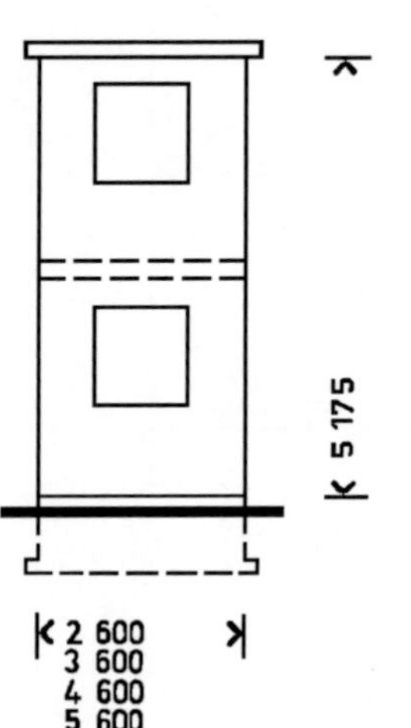

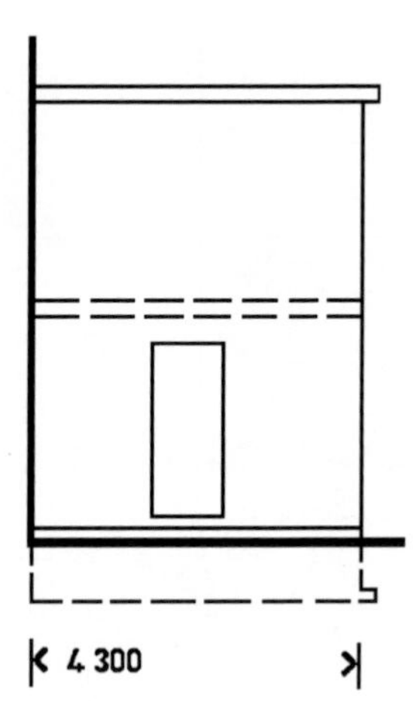

[2F] 4×6/7/8/9.

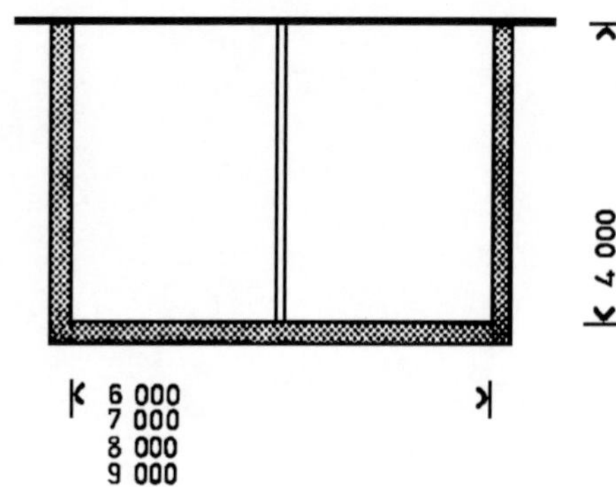

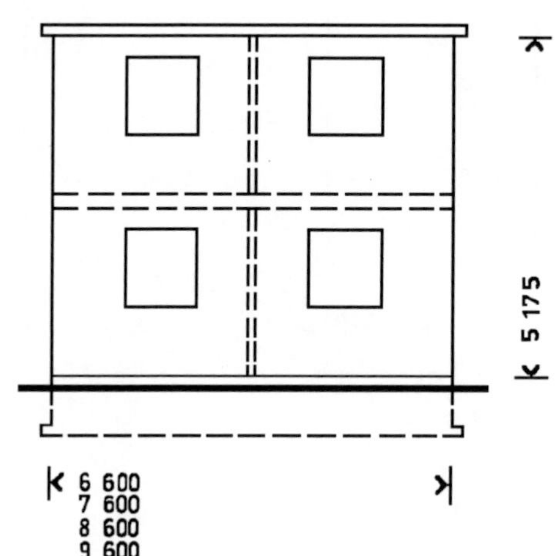

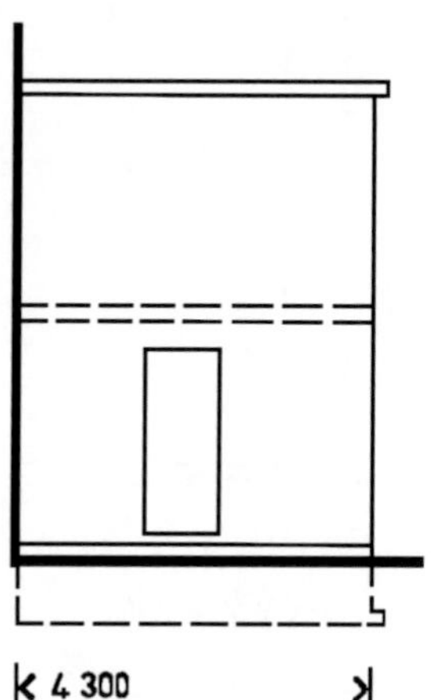

[2F] 5×2/3/4/5.

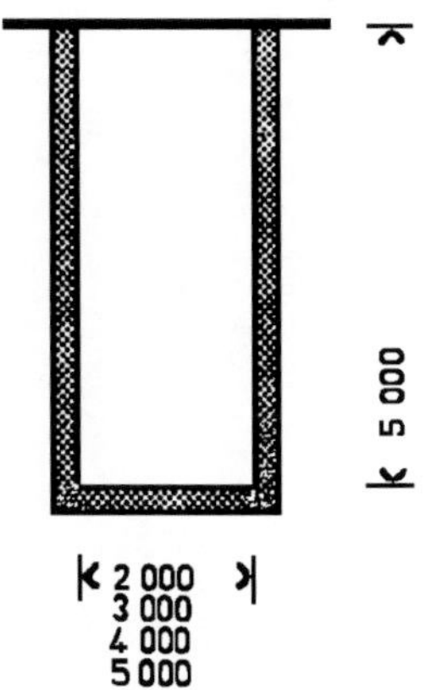

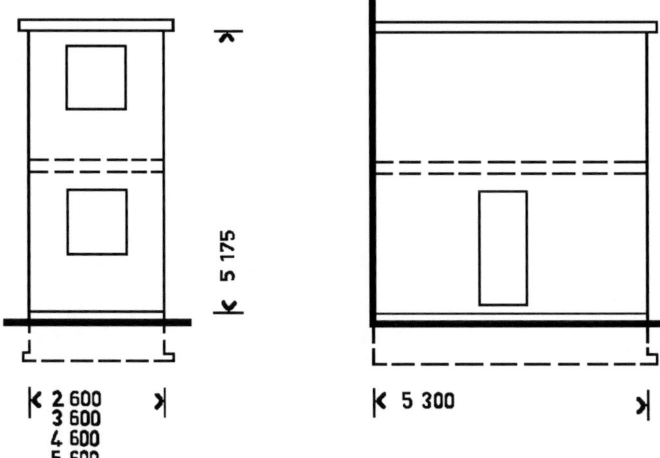

[2F] 5×6/7/8/9.

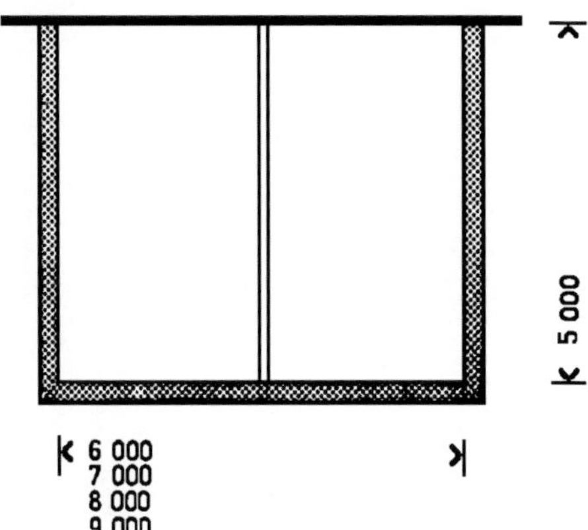

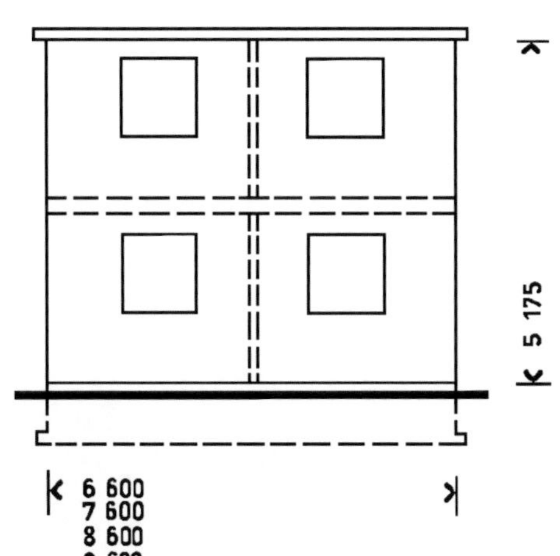

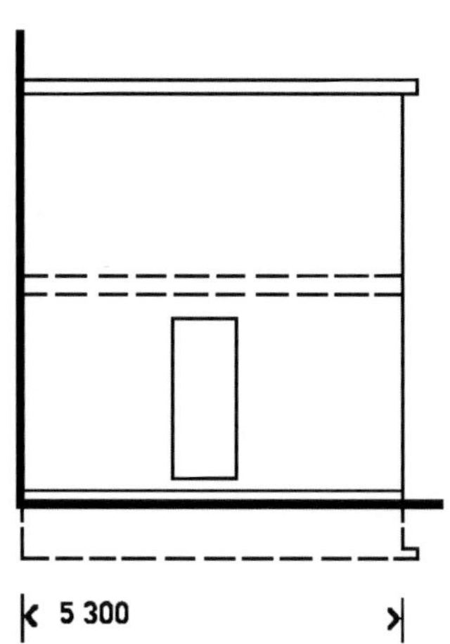

Specification B 4 m2 - 10 m2

TWO STOREY

FLAT ROOF

Element	Unit	Unit Rate £	Ref B/2F 2x2 Size 2.00 x 2.00 m Area 4 m2 Qty	Total £	Element Total £	Ref B/2F 2x3 Size 2.00 x 3.00 m Area 6 m2 Qty	Total £	Element Total £	Ref B/2F 2x4 Size 2.00 x 4.00 m Area 8 m2 Qty	Total £	Element Total £	Ref B/2F 2x5 Size 2.00 x 5.00 m Area 10 m2 Qty	Total £	Element Total £
SUBSTRUCTURE														
Strip footings	M	124.73	7M	873.11		8M	997.84		9M	1122.57		10M	1247.30	
Solid ground floor	M2	45.82	4M2	183.28	**1056.39**	6M2	274.92	**1272.76**	8M2	366.56	**1489.13**	10M2	458.20	**1705.50**
UPPER FLOORS														
Timber floor construction 50 x 150 mm joists	M2	41.30	4M2	165.20	**165.20**	6M2	247.80	**247.80**	8M2	330.40	**330.40**	10M2	413.00	**413.00**
ROOF														
Flat roof construction 50 x 150 mm joists	M2	50.06	8M2	400.48		10M2	500.60		13M2	650.78		15M2	750.90	
Work to top of external wall	M	23.71	7M	165.97		8M	189.68		9M	213.39		10M	237.10	
Three layer felt roofing	M2	36.43	8M2	291.44		10M2	364.30		13M2	473.59		15M2	546.45	
Fascia and eaves soffit	M	42.61	8M	340.88		9M	383.49		10M	426.10		11M	468.71	
Gutters and fittings	M	18.68	3M	56.04		4M	74.72		5M	93.40		6M	112.08	
Flashings	M	24.70	3M	74.10		4M	98.80		5M	123.50		6M	148.20	
Abutment to existing wall	M	61.52	3M	184.56	**1513.47**	4M	246.08	**1857.67**	5M	307.60	**2288.36**	6M	369.12	**2632.56**
EXTERNAL WALLS														
Brick and block cavity wall	M2	106.91	27M2	2886.57	**2886.57**	32M2	3421.12	**3421.12**	37M2	3955.67	**3955.67**	42M2	4490.22	**4490.22**

Specification B 12 m2 - 18 m2

Element	Unit	Unit Rate £	Ref B/2F 2x6 Size 2.00 x 6.00 m Area 12 m2			Ref B/2F 2x7 Size 2.00 x 7.00 m Area 14 m2			Ref B/2F 2x8 Size 2.00 x 8.00 m Area 16 m2			Ref B/2F 2x9 Size 2.00 x 9.00 m Area 18 m2		
			Qty	Total £	Element Total £	Qty	Total £	Element Total £	Qty	Total £	Element Total £	Qty	Total £	Element Total £
TWO STOREY														
FLAT ROOF Continued\.....														
	M	124.73	11M	1372.03		12M	1496.76		13M	1621.49		14M	1746.22	
	M2	45.82	12M2	549.84	**1921.87**	14M2	641.48	**2138.24**	16M2	733.12	**2354.61**	18M2	824.76	**2570.98**
	M2	41.30	12M2	495.60	**495.60**	14M2	578.20	**578.20**	16M2	660.80	**660.80**	18M2	743.40	**743.40**
	M2	50.06	18M2	901.08		20M2	1001.20		23M2	1151.38		25M2	1251.50	
	M	23.71	11M	260.81		12M	284.52		13M	308.23		14M	331.94	
	M2	36.43	18M2	655.74		20M2	728.60		23M2	837.89		25M2	910.75	
	M	42.61	12M	511.32		13M	553.93		14M	596.54		15M	639.15	
	M	18.68	7M	130.76		8M	149.44		9M	168.12		10M	186.80	
	M	24.70	7M	172.90		8M	197.60		9M	222.30		10M	247.00	
	M	61.52	7M	430.64	**3063.25**	8M	492.16	**3407.45**	9M	553.68	**3838.14**	10M	615.20	**4182.34**
	M2	106.91	43M2	4597.13	**4597.13**	48M2	5131.68	**5131.68**	53M2	5666.23	**5666.23**	58M2	6200.78	**6200.78**

Specification B 4 m2 - 10 m2

TWO STOREY

FLAT ROOF

Element	Unit	Unit Rate £	Ref B/2F 2x2 Size 2.00 x 2.00 m Area 4 m2 Qty	Total £	Element Total £	Ref B/2F 2x3 Size 2.00 x 3.00 m Area 6 m2 Qty	Total £	Element Total £	Ref B/2F 2x4 Size 2.00 x 4.00 m Area 8 m2 Qty	Total £	Element Total £	Ref B/2F 2x5 Size 2.00 x 5.00 m Area 10 m2 Qty	Total £	Element Total £
EXTERNAL DOORS AND WINDOWS														
External door	NR	478.42	1NR	478.42		1NR	478.42		1NR	478.42		1NR	478.42	
Windows	NR	518.08	2NR	1036.16		2NR	1036.16		2NR	1036.16		2NR	1036.16	
Opening in cavity wall for door	NR	179.51	1NR	179.51		1NR	179.51		1NR	179.51		1NR	179.51	
Opening in cavity wall for window	NR	150.89	2NR	301.78	**1995.87**	2NR	301.78	**1995.87**	2NR	301.78	**1995.87**	2NR	301.78	**1995.87**
INTERNAL WALLS AND PARTITIONS														
Stud partitions	M2	51.63												
INTERNAL DOORS														
Softwood flush door	NR	251.11												
WALL FINISHES														
Plaster & decoration	M2	19.58	40M2	783.20	**783.20**	50M2	979.00	**979.00**	60M2	1174.80	**1174.80**	70M2	1370.60	**1370.60**
FLOOR FINISHES														
Thermoplastic tiles on screed	M2	35.42	4M2	141.68		6M2	212.52		8M2	283.36		10M2	354.20	
Softwood skirting	M	11.09	16M	177.44	**319.12**	20M	221.80	**434.32**	24M	266.16	**549.52**	28M	310.52	**664.72**
CEILING FINISHES														
Plasterboard and Artex	M2	16.34	8M2	130.72	**130.72**	12M2	196.08	**196.08**	16M2	261.44	**261.44**	20M2	326.80	**326.80**

Specification B
12 m2 - 18 m2

TWO STOREY

FLAT ROOF Continued\.....

Element	Unit	Unit Rate £	Ref B/2F 2x6 Size 2.00 x 6.00 m Area 12 m2 Qty	Total £	Element Total £	Ref B/2F 2x7 Size 2.00 x 7.00 m Area 14 m2 Qty	Total £	Element Total £	Ref B/2F 2x8 Size 2.00 x 8.00 m Area 16 m2 Qty	Total £	Element Total £	Ref B/2F 2x9 Size 2.00 x 9.00 m Area 18 m2 Qty	Total £	Element Total £
	NR	478.42	1NR	478.42		1NR	478.42		1NR	478.42		1NR	478.42	
	NR	518.08	4NR	2072.32		4NR	2072.32		4NR	2072.32		4NR	2072.32	
	NR	179.51	1NR	179.51		1NR	179.51		1NR	179.51		1NR	179.51	
	NR	150.89	4NR	603.56	**3333.81**	4NR	603.56	**3333.81**	4NR	603.56	**3333.81**	4NR	603.56	**3333.81**
	M2	51.63	10M2	516.30	**516.30**	10M2	516.30	**516.30**	10M2	516.30	**516.30**	10M2	516.30	**516.30**
	NR	251.11	2NR	502.22	**502.22**	2NR	502.22	**502.22**	2NR	502.22	**502.22**	2NR	502.22	**502.22**
	M2	19.58	80M2	1566.40	**1566.40**	90M2	1762.20	**1762.20**	100M2	1958.00	**1958.00**	110M2	2153.80	**2153.80**
	M2	35.42	12M2	425.04		14M2	495.88		16M2	566.72		18M2	637.56	
	M	11.09	32M	354.88	**779.92**	36M	399.24	**895.12**	40M	443.60	**1010.32**	44M	487.96	**1125.52**
	M2	16.34	24M2	392.16	**392.16**	28M2	457.52	**457.52**	32M2	522.88	**522.88**	36M2	588.24	**588.24**

Specification B 4 m2 - 10 m2

Element	Unit	Unit Rate £	Ref B/2F 2x2 Size 2.00 x 2.00 m Area 4 m2 Qty	Total £	Element Total £	Ref B/2F 2x3 Size 2.00 x 3.00 m Area 6 m2 Qty	Total £	Element Total £	Ref B/2F 2x4 Size 2.00 x 4.00 m Area 8 m2 Qty	Total £	Element Total £	Ref B/2F 2x5 Size 2.00 x 5.00 m Area 10 m2 Qty	Total £	Element Total £
TWO STOREY														
FLAT ROOF														
SERVICES														
Rainwater pipes	M	26.64	6M	159.84		6M	159.84		6M	159.84		6M	159.84	
Cold water service point	NR	110.52	1NR	110.52		1NR	110.52		1NR	110.52		1NR	110.52	
Hot water service point	NR	191.67	1NR	191.67		1NR	191.67		1NR	191.67		1NR	191.67	
Central heating service point	NR	386.51	2NR	773.02		2NR	773.02		2NR	773.02		2NR	773.02	
Electrical installation	NR	286.50	2NR	573.00	**1808.05**	2NR	573.00	**1808.05**	2NR	573.00	**1808.05**	2NR	573.00	**1808.05**
ALTERATIONS TO EXISTING BUILDINGS														
Opening in existing wall 1.80 m wide 2.00 m high	NR	689.44	2NR	1378.88	**1378.88**									
Opening in existing wall 2.40 m wide 2.00 m high	NR	865.59												
Opening in existing wall 3.00 m wide 2.00 m high	NR	921.26				2NR	1842.52	**1842.52**						
Opening in existing wall 4.00 m wide 2.00 m high	NR	1131.22							2NR	2262.44	**2262.44**			
Opening in existing wall 5.00 m wide 2.00 m high	NR	1341.19										2NR	2682.38	**2682.38**

Specification B 12 m2 - 18 m2

TWO STOREY

FLAT ROOF Continued\.....

Element	Unit	Unit Rate £	Ref B/2F 2x6 Size 2.00 x 6.00 m Area 12 m2 Qty	Total £	Element Total £	Ref B/2F 2x7 Size 2.00 x 7.00 m Area 14 m2 Qty	Total £	Element Total £	Ref B/2F 2x8 Size 2.00 x 8.00 m Area 16 m2 Qty	Total £	Element Total £	Ref B/2F 2x9 Size 2.00 x 9.00 m Area 18 m2 Qty	Total £	Element Total £
	M	26.64	6M	159.84		6M	159.84		6M	159.84		6M	159.84	
	NR	110.52	1NR	110.52		1NR	110.52		1NR	110.52		1NR	110.52	
	NR	191.67	1NR	191.67		1NR	191.67		1NR	191.67		1NR	191.67	
	NR	386.51	4NR	1546.04		4NR	1546.04		4NR	1546.04		4NR	1546.04	
	NR	286.50	4NR	1146.00	**3154.07**	4NR	1146.00	**3154.07**	4NR	1146.00	**3154.07**	4NR	1146.00	**3154.07**
	NR	689.44												
	NR	865.59	4NR	3462.36	**3462.36**									
	NR	921.26				4NR	3685.04	**3685.04**	4NR	3685.04	**3685.04**			
	NR	1131.22										4NR	4524.88	**4524.88**
	NR	1341.19												

Specification B 4 m2 - 10 m2	Ref B/2F 2x2 Size 2.00 x 2.00 m Area 4 m2	Ref B/2F 2x3 Size 2.00 x 3.00 m Area 6 m2	Ref B/2F 2x4 Size 2.00 x 4.00 m Area 8 m2	Ref B/2F 2x5 Size 2.00 x 5.00 m Area 10 m2
	Element Total £	Element Total £	Element Total £	Element Total £
TWO STOREY				
FLAT ROOF				
SUMMARY				
SUBSTRUCTURE	1056.39	1272.76	1489.13	1705.50
UPPER FLOORS	165.20	247.80	330.40	413.00
ROOF	1513.47	1857.67	2288.36	2632.56
EXTERNAL WALLS	2886.57	3421.12	3955.67	4490.22
EXTERNAL DOORS AND WINDOWS	1995.87	1995.87	1995.87	1995.87
INTERNAL WALLS AND PARTITIONS	-	-	-	-
INTERNAL DOORS	-	-	-	-
WALL FINISHES	783.20	979.00	1174.80	1370.60
FLOOR FINISHES	319.12	434.32	549.52	664.72
CEILING FINISHES	130.72	196.08	261.44	326.80
SERVICES	1808.05	1808.05	1808.05	1808.05
ALTERATIONS TO EXISTING BUILDINGS	1378.88	1842.52	2262.44	2682.38
Sub Total	12037.47	14055.19	16115.68	18089.70
Allowance for unmeasured items and sundries 5%	601.87	702.76	805.78	904.49
NET TOTAL excluding Preliminaries, Profit and Overheads	**12639.34**	**14757.95**	**16921.46**	**18994.19**

Specification B 12 m2 - 18 m2	Ref B/2F 2x6 Size 2.00 x 6.00 m Area 12 m2 Element Total £	Ref B/2F 2x7 Size 2.00 x 7.00 m Area 14 m2 Element Total £	Ref B/2F 2x8 Size 2.00 x 8.00 m Area 16 m2 Element Total £	Ref B/2F 2x9 Size 2.00 x 9.00 m Area 18 m2 Element Total £
TWO STOREY				
FLAT ROOF				
SUMMARY Continued/.....				
	1921.87	2138.24	2354.61	2570.98
	495.60	578.20	660.80	743.40
	3063.25	3407.45	3838.14	4182.34
	4597.13	5131.68	5666.23	6200.78
	3333.81	3333.81	3333.81	3333.81
	516.30	516.30	516.30	516.30
	502.22	502.22	502.22	502.22
	1566.40	1762.20	1958.00	2153.80
	779.92	895.12	1010.32	1125.52
	392.16	457.52	522.88	588.24
	3154.07	3154.07	3154.07	3154.07
	3462.36	3685.04	3685.04	4524.88
Sub Total	23785.09	25561.85	27202.42	29596.34
Allowance for unmeasured items and sundries 5%	1189.25	1278.09	1360.12	1479.82
NET TOTAL excluding Preliminaries, Profit and Overheads	**24974.34**	**26839.94**	**28562.54**	**31076.16**

Specification B 6 m2 - 15 m2

TWO STOREY

FLAT ROOF

Element	Unit	Unit Rate £	Ref B/2F 3x2 Size 3.00 x 2.00 m Area 6 m2 Qty	Total £	Element Total £	Ref B/2F 3x3 Size 3.00 x 3.00 m Area 9 m2 Qty	Total £	Element Total £	Ref B/2F 3x4 Size 3.00 x 4.00 m Area 12 m2 Qty	Total £	Element Total £	Ref B/2F 3x5 Size 3.00 x 5.00 m Area 15 m2 Qty	Total £	Element Total £
SUBSTRUCTURE														
Strip footings	M	124.73	9M	1122.57		10M	1247.30		11M	1372.03		12M	1496.76	
Solid ground floor	M2	45.82	6M2	274.92	**1397.49**	9M2	412.38	**1659.68**	12M2	549.84	**1921.87**	15M2	687.30	**2184.06**
UPPER FLOORS														
Timber floor construction 50 x 150 mm joists	M2	41.30	6M2	247.80	**247.80**									
Timber floor construction 50 x 200 mm joists	M2	44.82				9M2	403.38	**403.38**	12M2	537.84	**537.84**	15M2	672.30	**672.30**
ROOF														
Flat roof construction 50 x 150 mm joists	M2	50.06	11M2	550.66		14M2	700.84		18M2	901.08		21M2	1051.26	
Work to top of external wall	M	23.71	9M	213.39		10M	237.10		11M	260.81		12M	284.52	
Three layer felt roofing	M2	36.43	11M2	400.73		14M2	510.02		18M2	655.74		21M2	765.03	
Fascia and eaves soffit	M	42.61	10M	426.10		11M	468.71		12M	511.32		13M	553.93	
Gutters and fittings	M	18.68	3M	56.04		4M	74.72		5M	93.40		6M	112.08	
Flashings	M	24.70	3M	74.10		4M	98.80		5M	123.50		6M	148.20	
Abutment to existing wall	M	61.52	3M	184.56	**1905.58**	4M	246.08	**2336.27**	5M	307.60	**2853.45**	6M	369.12	**3284.14**
EXTERNAL WALLS														
Brick and block cavity wall	M2	106.91	37M2	3955.67	**3955.67**	42M2	4490.22	**4490.22**	47M2	5024.77	**5024.77**	52M2	5559.32	**5559.32**

Specification B
18 m2 - 27 m2

TWO STOREY

FLAT ROOF Continued\.....

Element	Unit	Unit Rate £	Ref B/2F 3x6 Size 3.00 x 6.00 m Area 18 m2 Qty	Total £	Element Total £	Ref B/2F 3x7 Size 3.00 x 7.00 m Area 21 m2 Qty	Total £	Element Total £	Ref B/2F 3x8 Size 3.00 x 8.00 m Area 24 m2 Qty	Total £	Element Total £	Ref B/2F 3x9 Size 3.00 x 9.00 m Area 27 m2 Qty	Total £	Element Total £
	M	124.73	13M	1621.49		14M	1746.22		15M	1870.95		16M	1995.68	
	M2	45.82	18M2	824.76	**2446.25**	21M2	962.22	**2708.44**	24M2	1099.68	**2970.63**	27M2	1237.14	**3232.82**
	M2	41.30												
	M2	44.82	18M2	806.76	**806.76**	21M2	941.22	**941.22**	24M2	1075.68	**1075.68**	27M2	1210.14	**1210.14**
	M2	50.06	25M2	1251.50		28M2	1401.68		32M2	1601.92		35M2	1752.10	
	M	23.71	13M	308.23		14M	331.94		15M	355.65		16M	379.36	
	M2	36.43	25M2	910.75		28M2	1020.04		32M2	1165.76		35M2	1275.05	
	M	42.61	14M	596.54		15M	639.15		16M	681.76		17M	724.37	
	M	18.68	7M	130.76		8M	149.44		9M	168.12		10M	186.80	
	M	24.70	7M	172.90		8M	197.60		9M	222.30		10M	247.00	
	M	61.52	7M	430.64	**3801.32**	8M	492.16	**4232.01**	9M	553.68	**4749.19**	10M	615.20	**5179.88**
	M2	106.91	53M2	5666.23	**5666.23**	55M2	5880.05	**5880.05**	63M2	6735.33	**6735.33**	68M2	7269.88	**7269.88**

Specification B
6 m2 - 15 m2

TWO STOREY

FLAT ROOF

Element	Unit	Unit Rate £	Ref B/2F 3x2 Size 3.00 x 2.00 m Area 6 m2 Qty	Total £	Element Total £	Ref B/2F 3x3 Size 3.00 x 3.00 m Area 9 m2 Qty	Total £	Element Total £	Ref B/2F 3x4 Size 3.00 x 4.00 m Area 12 m2 Qty	Total £	Element Total £	Ref B/2F 3x5 Size 3.00 x 5.00 m Area 15 m2 Qty	Total £	Element Total £
EXTERNAL DOORS AND WINDOWS														
External door	NR	478.42	1NR	478.42		1NR	478.42		1NR	478.42		1NR	478.42	
Windows	NR	518.08	2NR	1036.16		2NR	1036.16		2NR	1036.16		2NR	1036.16	
Opening in cavity wall for door	NR	179.51	1NR	179.51		1NR	179.51		1NR	179.51		1NR	179.51	
Opening in cavity wall for window	NR	150.89	2NR	301.78	**1995.87**	2NR	301.78	**1995.87**	2NR	301.78	**1995.87**	2NR	301.78	**1995.87**
INTERNAL WALLS AND PARTITIONS														
Stud partitions	M2	51.63												
INTERNAL DOORS														
Softwood flush door	NR	251.11												
WALL FINISHES														
Plaster & decoration	M2	19.58	50M2	979.00	**979.00**	60M2	1174.80	**1174.80**	70M2	1370.60	**1370.60**	80M2	1566.40	**1566.40**
FLOOR FINISHES														
Thermoplastic tiles on screed	M2	35.42	6M2	212.52		9M2	318.78		12M2	425.04		15M2	531.30	
Softwood skirting	M	11.09	20M	221.80	**434.32**	24M	266.16	**584.94**	28M	310.52	**735.56**	32M	354.88	**886.18**
CEILING FINISHES														
Plasterboard and Artex	M2	16.34	12M2	196.08	**196.08**	18M2	294.12	**294.12**	24M2	392.16	**392.16**	30M2	490.20	**490.20**

Specification B 18 m2 - 27 m2

TWO STOREY

FLAT ROOF Continued\.....

Element	Unit	Unit Rate £	Ref B/2F 3x6 Size 3.00 x 6.00 m Area 18 m2 Qty	Total £	Element Total £	Ref B/2F 3x7 Size 3.00 x 7.00 m Area 21 m2 Qty	Total £	Element Total £	Ref B/2F 3x8 Size 3.00 x 8.00 m Area 24 m2 Qty	Total £	Element Total £	Ref B/2F 3x9 Size 3.00 x 9.00 m Area 27 m2 Qty	Total £	Element Total £
	NR	478.42	1NR	478.42		1NR	478.42		1NR	478.42		1NR	478.42	
	NR	518.08	4NR	2072.32		4NR	2072.32		4NR	2072.32		4NR	2072.32	
	NR	179.51	1NR	179.51		1NR	179.51		1NR	179.51		1NR	179.51	
	NR	150.89	4NR	603.56	**3333.81**	4NR	603.56	**3333.81**	4NR	603.56	**3333.81**	4NR	603.56	**3333.81**
	M2	51.63	16M2	826.08	**826.08**	16M2	826.08	**826.08**	16M2	826.08	**826.08**	16M2	826.08	**826.08**
	NR	251.11	2NR	502.22	**502.22**	2NR	502.22	**502.22**	2NR	502.22	**502.22**	2NR	502.22	**502.22**
	M2	19.58	90M2	1762.20	**1762.20**	100M2	1958.00	**1958.00**	110M2	2153.80	**2153.80**	120M2	2349.60	**2349.60**
	M2	35.42	18M2	637.56		21M2	743.82		24M2	850.08		27M2	956.34	
	M	11.09	36M	399.24	**1036.80**	40M	443.60	**1187.42**	44M	487.96	**1338.04**	48M	532.32	**1488.66**
	M2	16.34	36M2	588.24	**588.24**	42M2	686.28	**686.28**	48M2	784.32	**784.32**	54M2	882.36	**882.36**

Specification B 6 m2 - 15 m2

Element	Unit	Unit Rate £	Ref B/2F 3x2 Size 3.00 x 2.00 m Area 6 m2 Qty	Total £	Element Total £	Ref B/2F 3x3 Size 3.00 x 3.00 m Area 9 m2 Qty	Total £	Element Total £	Ref B/2F 3x4 Size 3.00 x 4.00 m Area 12 m2 Qty	Total £	Element Total £	Ref B/2F 3x5 Size 3.00 x 5.00 m Area 15 m2 Qty	Total £	Element Total £
TWO STOREY														
FLAT ROOF														
SERVICES														
Rainwater pipes	M	26.64	6M	159.84		6M	159.84		6M	159.84		6M	159.84	
Cold water service point	NR	110.52	1NR	110.52		1NR	110.52		1NR	110.52		1NR	110.52	
Hot water service point	NR	191.67	1NR	191.67		1NR	191.67		1NR	191.67		1NR	191.67	
Central heating service point	NR	386.51	2NR	773.02		2NR	773.02		2NR	773.02		2NR	773.02	
Electrical installation	NR	286.50	2NR	573.00	**1808.05**	2NR	573.00	**1808.05**	2NR	573.00	**1808.05**	2NR	573.00	**1808.05**
ALTERATIONS TO EXISTING BUILDINGS														
Opening in existing wall 1.80 m wide 2.00 m high	NR	689.44	2NR	1378.88	**1378.88**									
Opening in existing wall 2.40 m wide 2.00 m high	NR	865.59												
Opening in existing wall 3.00 m wide 2.00 m high	NR	921.26				2NR	1842.52	**1842.52**						
Opening in existing wall 4.00 m wide 2.00 m high	NR	1131.22							2NR	2262.44	**2262.44**			
Opening in existing wall 5.00 m wide 2.00 m high	NR	1341.19										2NR	2682.38	**2682.38**

Specification B 18 m2 - 27 m2

TWO STOREY

FLAT ROOF Continued\.....

Element	Unit	Unit Rate £	Ref B/2F 3x6 Size 3.00 x 6.00 m Area 18 m2 Qty	Total £	Element Total £	Ref B/2F 3x7 Size 3.00 x 7.00 m Area 21 m2 Qty	Total £	Element Total £	Ref B/2F 3x8 Size 3.00 x 8.00 m Area 24 m2 Qty	Total £	Element Total £	Ref B/2F 3x9 Size 3.00 x 9.00 m Area 27 m2 Qty	Total £	Element Total £
	M	26.64	6M	159.84		6M	159.84		6M	159.84		6M	159.84	
	NR	110.52	1NR	110.52		1NR	110.52		1NR	110.52		1NR	110.52	
	NR	191.67	1NR	191.67		1NR	191.67		1NR	191.67		1NR	191.67	
	NR	386.51	4NR	1546.04		4NR	1546.04		4NR	1546.04		4NR	1546.04	
	NR	286.50	4NR	1146.00	**3154.07**	4NR	1146.00	**3154.07**	4NR	1146.00	**3154.07**	4NR	1146.00	**3154.07**
	NR	689.44												
	NR	865.59	4NR	3462.36	**3462.36**									
	NR	921.26				4NR	3685.04	**3685.04**	4NR	3685.04	**3685.04**			
	NR	1131.22										4NR	4524.88	**4524.88**
	NR	1341.19												

Specification B 6 m2 - 15 m2	Ref B/2F 3x2 Size 3.00 x 2.00 m Area 6 m2 Element Total £	Ref B/2F 3x3 Size 3.00 x 3.00 m Area 9 m2 Element Total £	Ref B/2F 3x4 Size 3.00 x 4.00 m Area 12 m2 Element Total £	Ref B/2F 3x5 Size 3.00 x 5.00 m Area 15 m2 Element Total £
TWO STOREY				
FLAT ROOF				
SUMMARY				
SUBSTRUCTURE	1397.49	1659.68	1921.87	2184.06
UPPER FLOORS	247.80	403.38	537.84	672.30
ROOF	1905.58	2336.27	2853.45	3284.14
EXTERNAL WALLS	3955.67	4490.22	5024.77	5559.32
EXTERNAL DOORS AND WINDOWS	1995.87	1995.87	1995.87	1995.87
INTERNAL WALLS AND PARTITIONS	-	-	-	-
INTERNAL DOORS	-	-	-	-
WALL FINISHES	979.00	1174.80	1370.60	1566.40
FLOOR FINISHES	434.32	584.94	735.56	886.18
CEILING FINISHES	196.08	294.12	392.16	490.20
SERVICES	1808.05	1808.05	1808.05	1808.05
ALTERATIONS TO EXISTING BUILDINGS	1378.88	1842.52	2262.44	2682.38
Sub Total	14298.74	16589.85	18902.61	21128.90
Allowance for unmeasured items and sundries 5%	714.94	829.49	945.13	1056.45
NET TOTAL excluding Preliminaries, Profit and Overheads	**15013.68**	**17419.34**	**19847.74**	**22185.35**

Specification B 18 m2 - 27 m2	Ref B/2F 3x6 Size 3.00 x 6.00 m Area 18 m2 Element Total £	Ref B/2F 3x7 Size 3.00 x 7.00 m Area 21 m2 Element Total £	Ref B/2F 3x8 Size 3.00 x 8.00 m Area 24 m2 Element Total £	Ref B/2F 3x9 Size 3.00 x 9.00 m Area 27 m2 Element Total £
TWO STOREY				
FLAT ROOF				
SUMMARY Continued/.....				
	2446.25	2708.44	2970.63	3232.82
	806.76	941.22	1075.68	1210.14
	3801.32	4232.01	4749.19	5179.88
	5666.23	5880.05	6735.33	7269.88
	3333.81	3333.81	3333.81	3333.81
	826.08	826.08	826.08	826.08
	502.22	502.22	502.22	502.22
	1762.20	1958.00	2153.80	2349.60
	1036.80	1187.42	1338.04	1488.66
	588.24	686.28	784.32	882.36
	3154.07	3154.07	3154.07	3154.07
	3462.36	3685.04	3685.04	4524.88
Sub Total	27386.34	29094.64	31308.21	33954.40
Allowance for unmeasured items and sundries 5%	1369.32	1454.73	1565.41	1697.72
NET TOTAL excluding Preliminaries, Profit and Overheads	**28755.66**	**30549.37**	**32873.62**	**35652.12**

Specification B 8 m2 - 20 m2

Element	Unit	Unit Rate £	Ref B/2F 4x2 Size 4.00 x 2.00 m Area 8 m2 Qty	Total £	Element Total £	Ref B/2F 4x3 Size 4.00 x 3.00 m Area 12 m2 Qty	Total £	Element Total £	Ref B/2F 4x4 Size 4.00 x 4.00 m Area 16 m2 Qty	Total £	Element Total £	Ref B/2F 4x5 Size 4.00 x 5.00 m Area 20 m2 Qty	Total £	Element Total £
TWO STOREY														
FLAT ROOF														
SUBSTRUCTURE														
Strip footings	M	124.73	11M	1372.03		12M	1496.76		13M	1621.49		14M	1746.22	
Solid ground floor	M2	45.82	8M2	366.56	**1738.59**	12M2	549.84	**2046.60**	16M2	733.12	**2354.61**	20M2	916.40	**2662.62**
UPPER FLOORS														
Timber floor construction 50 x 150 mm joists	M2	41.30	8M2	330.40	**330.40**									
Timber floor construction 50 x 200 mm joists	M2	44.82				12M2	537.84	**537.84**	16M2	717.12	**717.12**	20M2	896.40	**896.40**
ROOF														
Flat roof construction 50 x 150 mm joists	M2	50.06	14M2	700.84		18M2	901.08							
Flat roof construction 50 x 200 mm joists	M2	52.26							23M2	1201.98		27M2	1411.02	
Work to top of external wall	M	23.71	11M	260.81		12M	284.52		13M	308.23		14M	331.94	
Three layer felt roofing	M2	36.43	14M2	510.02		18M2	655.74		23M2	837.89		27M2	983.61	
Fascia and eaves soffit	M	42.61	12M	511.32		13M	553.93		14M	596.54		15M	639.15	
Gutters and fittings	M	18.68	3M	56.04		4M	74.72		5M	93.40		6M	112.08	
Flashings	M	24.70	3M	74.10		4M	98.80		5M	123.50		6M	148.20	
Abutment to existing wall	M	61.52	3M	184.56	**2297.69**	4M	246.08	**2814.87**	5M	307.60	**3469.14**	6M	369.12	**3995.12**

Specification B
24 m2 - 36 m2

			Ref B/2F 4x6 Size 4.00 x 6.00 m Area 24 m2			Ref B/2F 4x7 Size 4.00 x 7.00 m Area 28 m2			Ref B/2F 4x8 Size 4.00 x 8.00 m Area 32 m2			Ref B/2F 4x9 Size 4.00 x 9.00 m Area 36 m2		
			Qty	Total £	Element Total £	Qty	Total £	Element Total £	Qty	Total £	Element Total £	Qty	Total £	Element Total £
TWO STOREY FLAT ROOF Continued\.....														
Element	Unit	Unit Rate £												
	M	124.73	15M	1870.95		16M	1995.68		17M	2120.41		18M	2245.14	
	M2	45.82	24M2	1099.68	**2970.63**	28M2	1282.96	**3278.64**	32M2	1466.24	**3586.65**	36M2	1649.52	**3894.66**
	M2	41.30												
	M2	44.82	24M2	1075.68	**1075.68**	28M2	1254.96	**1254.96**	32M2	1434.24	**1434.24**	36M2	1613.52	**1613.52**
	M2	50.06	32M2	1601.92		36M2	1802.16							
	M2	52.26							41M2	2142.66		45M2	2351.70	
	M	23.71	15M	355.65		16M	379.36		17M	403.07		18M	426.78	
	M2	36.43	32M2	1165.76		36M2	1311.48		41M2	1493.63		45M2	1639.35	
	M	42.61	16M	681.76		17M	724.37		18M	766.98		19M	809.59	
	M	18.68	7M	130.76		8M	149.44		9M	168.12		10M	186.80	
	M	24.70	7M	172.90		8M	197.60		9M	222.30		10M	247.00	
	M	61.52	7M	430.64	**4539.39**	8M	492.16	**5056.57**	9M	553.68	**5750.44**	10M	615.20	**6276.42**

Specification B 8 m2 - 20 m2

TWO STOREY FLAT ROOF			Ref B/2F 4x2 Size 4.00 x 2.00 m Area 8 m2			Ref B/2F 4x3 Size 4.00 x 3.00 m Area 12 m2			Ref B/2F 4x4 Size 4.00 x 4.00 m Area 16 m2			Ref B/2F 4x5 Size 4.00 x 5.00 m Area 20 m2		
Element	Unit	Unit Rate £	Qty	Total £	Element Total £	Qty	Total £	Element Total £	Qty	Total £	Element Total £	Qty	Total £	Element Total £
EXTERNAL WALLS														
Brick and block cavity wall	M2	106.91	47M2	5024.77	**5024.77**	52M2	5559.32	**5559.32**	57M2	6093.87	**6093.87**	59M2	6307.69	**6307.69**
EXTERNAL DOORS AND WINDOWS														
External door	NR	478.42	1NR	478.42		1NR	478.42		1NR	478.42		1NR	478.42	
Windows	NR	518.08	2NR	1036.16		2NR	1036.16		2NR	1036.16		2NR	1036.16	
Opening in cavity wall for door	NR	179.51	1NR	179.51		1NR	179.51		1NR	179.51		1NR	179.51	
Opening in cavity wall for window	NR	150.89	2NR	301.78	**1995.87**	2NR	301.78	**1995.87**	2NR	301.78	**1995.87**	2NR	301.78	**1995.87**
INTERNAL WALLS AND PARTITIONS														
Stud partitions	M2	51.63												
INTERNAL DOORS														
Softwood flush door	NR	251.11												
WALL FINISHES														
Plaster & decoration	M2	19.58	60M2	1174.80	**1174.80**	70M2	1370.60	**1370.60**	80M2	1566.40	**1566.40**	90M2	1762.20	**1762.20**
FLOOR FINISHES														
Thermoplastic tiles on screed	M2	35.42	8M2	283.36		12M2	425.04		16M2	566.72		20M2	708.40	
Softwood skirting	M	11.09	24M	266.16	**549.52**	28M	310.52	**735.56**	32M	354.88	**921.60**	36M	399.24	**1107.64**

Specification B 24 m2 - 36 m2

			Ref B/2F 4x6 Size 4.00 x 6.00 m Area 24 m2			Ref B/2F 4x7 Size 4.00 x 7.00 m Area 28 m2			Ref B/2F 4x8 Size 4.00 x 8.00 m Area 32 m2			Ref B/2F 4x9 Size 4.00 x 9.00 m Area 36 m2		
			Qty	Total £	Element Total £	Qty	Total £	Element Total £	Qty	Total £	Element Total £	Qty	Total £	Element Total £
TWO STOREY FLAT ROOF Continued\.....														
Element	Unit	Unit Rate £												
	M2	106.91	63M2	6735.33	**6735.33**	68M2	7269.88	**7269.88**	73M2	7804.43	**7804.43**	78M2	8338.98	**8338.98**
	NR	478.42	1NR	478.42		1NR	478.42		1NR	478.42		1NR	478.42	
	NR	518.08	4NR	2072.32		4NR	2072.32		4NR	2072.32		4NR	2072.32	
	NR	179.51	1NR	179.51		1NR	179.51		1NR	179.51		1NR	179.51	
	NR	150.89	4NR	603.56	**3333.81**	4NR	603.56	**3333.81**	4NR	603.56	**3333.81**	4NR	603.56	**3333.81**
	M2	51.63	20M2	1032.60	**1032.60**	20M2	1032.60	**1032.60**	20M2	1032.60	**1032.60**	20M2	1032.60	**1032.60**
	NR	251.11	2NR	502.22	**502.22**	2NR	502.22	**502.22**	2NR	502.22	**502.22**	2NR	502.22	**502.22**
	M2	19.58	100M2	1958.00	**1958.00**	110M2	2153.80	**2153.80**	120M2	2349.60	**2349.60**	130M2	2545.40	**2545.40**
	M2	35.42	24M2	850.08		28M2	991.76		32M2	1133.44		36M2	1275.12	
	M	11.09	40M	443.60	**1293.68**	44M	487.96	**1479.72**	48M	532.32	**1665.76**	52M	576.68	**1851.80**

Specification B 8 m2 - 20 m2

Element	Unit	Unit Rate £	Ref B/2F 4x2 Size 4.00 x 2.00 m Area 8 m2 Qty	Total £	Element Total £	Ref B/2F 4x3 Size 4.00 x 3.00 m Area 12 m2 Qty	Total £	Element Total £	Ref B/2F 4x4 Size 4.00 x 4.00 m Area 16 m2 Qty	Total £	Element Total £	Ref B/2F 4x5 Size 4.00 x 5.00 m Area 20 m2 Qty	Total £	Element Total £
TWO STOREY														
FLAT ROOF														
CEILING FINISHES														
Plasterboard and Artex	M2	16.34	16M2	261.44	**261.44**	24M2	392.16	**392.16**	32M2	522.88	**522.88**	40M2	653.60	**653.60**
SERVICES														
Rainwater pipes	M	26.64	6M	159.84		6M	159.84		6M	159.84		6M	159.84	
Cold water service point	NR	110.52	1NR	110.52		1NR	110.52		1NR	110.52		1NR	110.52	
Hot water service point	NR	191.67	1NR	191.67		1NR	191.67		1NR	191.67		1NR	191.67	
Central heating service point	NR	386.51	2NR	773.02		2NR	773.02		2NR	773.02		2NR	773.02	
Electrical installation	NR	286.50	2NR	573.00	**1808.05**	2NR	573.00	**1808.05**	2NR	573.00	**1808.05**	2NR	573.00	**1808.05**
ALTERATIONS TO EXISTING BUILDINGS														
Opening in existing wall 1.80 m wide 2.00 m high	NR	689.44	2NR	1378.88	**1378.88**									
Opening in existing wall 2.40 m wide 2.00 m high	NR	865.59												
Opening in existing wall 3.00 m wide 2.00 m high	NR	921.26				2NR	1842.52	**1842.52**						
Opening in existing wall 4.00 m wide 2.00 m high	NR	1131.22							2NR	2262.44	**2262.44**			
Opening in existing wall 5.00 m wide 2.00 m high	NR	1341.19										2NR	2682.38	**2682.38**

Specification B
24 m2 - 36 m2

TWO STOREY

FLAT ROOF Continued\.....

Element	Unit	Unit Rate £	Ref B/2F 4x6 Size 4.00 x 6.00 m Area 24 m2 Qty	Total £	Element Total £	Ref B/2F 4x7 Size 4.00 x 7.00 m Area 28 m2 Qty	Total £	Element Total £	Ref B/2F 4x8 Size 4.00 x 8.00 m Area 32 m2 Qty	Total £	Element Total £	Ref B/2F 4x9 Size 4.00 x 9.00 m Area 36 m2 Qty	Total £	Element Total £
	M2	16.34	48M2	784.32	**784.32**	56M2	915.04	**915.04**	64M2	1045.76	**1045.76**	72M2	1176.48	**1176.48**
	M	26.64	6M	159.84		6M	159.84		6M	159.84		6M	159.84	
	NR	110.52	1NR	110.52		1NR	110.52		1NR	110.52		1NR	110.52	
	NR	191.67	1NR	191.67		1NR	191.67		1NR	191.67		1NR	191.67	
	NR	386.51	4NR	1546.04		4NR	1546.04		4NR	1546.04		4NR	1546.04	
	NR	286.50	4NR	1146.00	**3154.07**	4NR	1146.00	**3154.07**	4NR	1146.00	**3154.07**	4NR	1146.00	**3154.07**
	NR	689.44												
	NR	865.59	4NR	3462.36	**3462.36**									
	NR	921.26				4NR	3685.04	**3685.04**	4NR	3685.04	**3685.04**			
	NR	1131.22										4NR	4524.88	**4524.88**
	NR	1341.19												

Specification B 8 m2 - 20 m2	Ref B/2F 4x2 Size 4.00 x 2.00 m Area 8 m2 Element Total £	Ref B/2F 4x3 Size 4.00 x 3.00 m Area 12 m2 Element Total £	Ref B/2F 4x4 Size 4.00 x 4.00 m Area 16 m2 Element Total £	Ref B/2F 4x5 Size 4.00 x 5.00 m Area 20 m2 Element Total £
TWO STOREY				
FLAT ROOF				
SUMMARY				
SUBSTRUCTURE	1738.59	2046.60	2354.61	2662.62
UPPER FLOORS	330.40	537.84	717.12	896.40
ROOF	2297.69	2814.87	3469.14	3995.12
EXTERNAL WALLS	5024.77	5559.32	6093.87	6307.69
EXTERNAL DOORS AND WINDOWS	1995.87	1995.87	1995.87	1995.87
INTERNAL WALLS AND PARTITIONS	-	-	-	-
INTERNAL DOORS	-	-	-	-
WALL FINISHES	1174.80	1370.60	1566.40	1762.20
FLOOR FINISHES	549.52	735.56	921.60	1107.64
CEILING FINISHES	261.44	392.16	522.88	653.60
SERVICES	1808.05	1808.05	1808.05	1808.05
ALTERATIONS TO EXISTING BUILDINGS	1378.88	1842.52	2262.44	2682.38
Sub Total	16560.01	19103.39	21711.98	23871.57
Allowance for unmeasured items and sundries 5%	828.00	955.17	1085.60	1193.58
NET TOTAL excluding Preliminaries, Profit and Overheads	**17388.01**	**20058.56**	**22797.58**	**25065.15**

Specification B 24 m2 - 36 m2	Ref B/2F 4x6 Size 4.00 x 6.00 m Area 24 m2	Ref B/2F 4x7 Size 4.00 x 7.00 m Area 28 m2	Ref B/2F 4x8 Size 4.00 x 8.00 m Area 32 m2	Ref B/2F 4x9 Size 4.00 x 9.00 m Area 36 m2
	Element Total £	**Element Total £**	**Element Total £**	**Element Total £**
TWO STOREY				
FLAT ROOF				
SUMMARY continued/…				
	2970.63	3278.64	3586.65	3894.66
	1075.68	1254.96	1434.24	1613.52
	4539.39	5056.57	5750.44	6276.42
	6735.33	7269.88	7804.43	8338.98
	3333.81	3333.81	3333.81	3333.81
	1032.60	1032.60	1032.60	1032.60
	502.22	502.22	502.22	502.22
	1958.00	2153.80	2349.60	2545.40
	1293.68	1479.72	1665.76	1851.80
	784.32	915.04	1045.76	1176.48
	3154.07	3154.07	3154.07	3154.07
	3462.36	3685.04	3685.04	4524.88
Sub Total	30842.09	33116.35	35344.62	38244.84
Allowance for unmeasured items and sundries 5%	1542.10	1655.82	1767.23	1912.24
NET TOTAL excluding Preliminaries, Profit and Overheads	**32384.19**	**34772.17**	**37111.85**	**40157.08**

Specification B 10 m2 - 25 m2

TWO STOREY

FLAT ROOF

Element	Unit	Unit Rate £	Ref B/2F 5x2 Size 5.00 x 2.00 m Area 10 m2 Qty	Total £	Element Total £	Ref B/2F 5x3 Size 5.00 x 3.00 m Area 15 m2 Qty	Total £	Element Total £	Ref B/2F 5x4 Size 5.00 x 4.00 m Area 20 m2 Qty	Total £	Element Total £	Ref B/2F 5x5 Size 5.00 x 5.00 m Area 25 m2 Qty	Total £	Element Total £
SUBSTRUCTURE														
Strip footings	M	124.73	13M	1621.49		14M	1746.22		15M	1870.95		16M	1995.68	
Solid ground floor	M2	45.82	10M2	458.20	**2079.69**	15M2	687.30	**2433.52**	20M2	916.40	**2787.35**	25M2	1145.50	**3141.18**
UPPER FLOORS														
Timber floor construction 50 x 150 mm joists	M2	41.30	10M2	413.00	**413.00**									
Timber floor construction 50 x 200 mm joists	M2	44.82				15M2	672.30	**672.30**	20M2	896.40	**896.40**			
Timber floor construction 75 x 250 mm joists	M2	66.47										25M2	1661.75	**1661.75**
ROOF														
Flat roof construction 50 x 150 mm joists	M2	50.06	17M2	851.02		22M2	1101.32							
Flat roof construction 50 x 200 mm joists	M2	52.26							28M2	1463.28		33M2	1724.58	
Work to top of external wall	M	23.71	13M	308.23		14M	331.94		15M	355.65		16M	379.36	
Three layer felt roofing	M2	36.43	17M2	619.31		22M2	801.46		28M2	1020.04		33M2	1202.19	
Fascia and eaves soffit	M	42.61	14M	596.54		15M	639.15		16M	681.76		17M	724.37	
Gutters and fittings	M	18.68	3M	56.04		4M	74.72		5M	93.40		6M	112.08	
Flashings	M	24.70	3M	74.10		4M	98.80		5M	123.50		6M	148.20	
Abutment to existing wall	M	61.52	3M	184.56	**2689.80**	4M	246.08	**3293.47**	5M	307.60	**4045.23**	6M	369.12	**4659.90**

Specification B 30 m2 - 45 m2

TWO STOREY

FLAT ROOF Continued\.....

Element	Unit	Unit Rate £	Ref B/2F 5x6 Size 5.00 x 6.00 m Area 30 m2 Qty	Total £	Element Total £	Ref B/2F 5x7 Size 5.00 x 7.00 m Area 35 m2 Qty	Total £	Element Total £	Ref B/2F 5x8 Size 5.00 x 8.00 m Area 40 m2 Qty	Total £	Element Total £	Ref B/2F 5x9 Size 5.00 x 9.00 m Area 45 m2 Qty	Total £	Element Total £
	M	124.73	17M	2120.41		18M	2245.14		19M	2369.87		20M	2494.60	
	M2	45.82	30M2	1374.60	**3495.01**	35M2	1603.70	**3848.84**	40M2	1832.80	**4202.67**	45M2	2061.90	**4556.50**
	M2	41.30												
	M2	44.82	30M2	1344.60	**1344.60**	35M2	1568.70	**1568.70**	40M2	1792.80	**1792.80**			
	M2	66.47										45M2	2991.15	**2991.15**
	M2	50.06	39M2	1952.34		44M2	2202.64							
	M2	52.26							50M2	2613.00		55M2	2874.30	
	M	23.71	17M	403.07		18M	426.78		19M	450.49		20M	474.20	
	M2	36.43	39M2	1420.77		44M2	1602.92		50M2	1821.50		55M2	2003.65	
	M	42.61	18M	766.98		19M	809.59		20M	852.20		21M	894.81	
	M	18.68	7M	130.76		8M	149.44		9M	168.12		10M	186.80	
	M	24.70	7M	172.90		8M	197.60		9M	222.30		10M	247.00	
	M	61.52	7M	430.64	**5277.46**	8M	492.16	**5881.13**	9M	553.68	**6681.29**	10M	615.20	**7295.96**

Specification B 10 m2 - 25 m2

TWO STOREY FLAT ROOF			Ref B/2F 5x2 Size 5.00 x 2.00 m Area 10 m2			Ref B/2F 5x3 Size 5.00 x 3.00 m Area 15 m2			Ref B/2F 5x4 Size 5.00 x 4.00 m Area 20 m2			Ref B/2F 5x5 Size 5.00 x 5.00 m Area 25 m2		
Element	Unit	Unit Rate £	Qty	Total £	Element Total £	Qty	Total £	Element Total £	Qty	Total £	Element Total £	Qty	Total £	Element Total £
EXTERNAL WALLS														
Brick and block cavity wall	M2	106.91	57M2	6093.87	**6093.87**	62M2	6628.42	**6628.42**	67M2	7162.97	**7162.97**	72M2	7697.52	**7697.52**
EXTERNAL DOORS AND WINDOWS														
External door	NR	478.42	1NR	478.42		1NR	478.42		1NR	478.42		1NR	478.42	
Windows	NR	518.08	2NR	1036.16		2NR	1036.16		2NR	1036.16		2NR	1036.16	
Opening in cavity wall for door	NR	179.51	1NR	179.51		1NR	179.51		1NR	179.51		1NR	179.51	
Opening in cavity wall for window	NR	150.89	2NR	301.78	**1995.87**	2NR	301.78	**1995.87**	2NR	301.78	**1995.87**	2NR	301.78	**1995.87**
INTERNAL WALLS AND PARTITIONS														
Stud partitions	M2	51.63												
INTERNAL DOORS														
Softwood flush door	NR	251.11												
WALL FINISHES														
Plaster & decoration	M2	19.58	70M2	1370.60	**1370.60**	80M2	1566.40	**1566.40**	90M2	1762.20	**1762.20**	100M2	1958.00	**1958.00**

Specification B 30 m2 - 45 m2

TWO STOREY

FLAT ROOF Continued\.....

Element	Unit	Unit Rate £	Ref B/2F 5x6 Size 5.00 x 6.00 m Area 30 m2 Qty	Total £	Element Total £	Ref B/2F 5x7 Size 5.00 x 7.00 m Area 35 m2 Qty	Total £	Element Total £	Ref B/2F 5x8 Size 5.00 x 8.00 m Area 40 m2 Qty	Total £	Element Total £	Ref B/2F 5x9 Size 5.00 x 9.00 m Area 45 m2 Qty	Total £	Element Total £
	M2	106.91	73M2	7804.43	**7804.43**	78M2	8338.98	**8338.98**	83M2	8873.53	**8873.53**	88M2	9408.08	**9408.08**
	NR	478.42	1NR	478.42		1NR	478.42		1NR	478.42		1NR	478.42	
	NR	518.08	4NR	2072.32		4NR	2072.32		4NR	2072.32		4NR	2072.32	
	NR	179.51	1NR	179.51		1NR	179.51		1NR	179.51		1NR	179.51	
	NR	150.89	4NR	603.56	**3333.81**	4NR	603.56	**3333.81**	4NR	603.56	**3333.81**	4NR	603.56	**3333.81**
	M2	51.63	26M2	1342.38	**1342.38**	26M2	1342.38	**1342.38**	26M2	1342.38	**1342.38**	26M2	1342.38	**1342.38**
	NR	251.11	2NR	502.22	**502.22**	2NR	502.22	**502.22**	2NR	502.22	**502.22**	2NR	502.22	**502.22**
	M2	19.58	110M2	2153.80	**2153.80**	120M2	2349.60	**2349.60**	130M2	2545.40	**2545.40**	140M2	2741.20	**2741.20**

Specification B
10 m2 - 25 m2

TWO STOREY

FLAT ROOF

Element	Unit	Unit Rate £	Ref B/2F 5x2 Size 5.00 x 2.00 m Area 10 m2 Qty	Total £	Element Total £	Ref B/2F 5x3 Size 5.00 x 3.00 m Area 15 m2 Qty	Total £	Element Total £	Ref B/2F 5x4 Size 5.00 x 4.00 m Area 20 m2 Qty	Total £	Element Total £	Ref B/2F 5x5 Size 5.00 x 5.00 m Area 25 m2 Qty	Total £	Element Total £
FLOOR FINISHES														
Thermoplastic tiles on screed	M2	35.42	10M2	354.20		15M2	531.30		20M2	708.40		25M2	885.50	
Softwood skirting	M	11.09	28M	310.52	**664.72**	32M	354.88	**886.18**	36M	399.24	**1107.64**	40M	443.60	**1329.10**
CEILING FINISHES														
Plasterboard and Artex	M2	16.34	20M2	326.80	**326.80**	30M2	490.20	**490.20**	40M2	653.60	**653.60**	50M2	817.00	**817.00**
SERVICES														
Rainwater pipes	M	26.64	6M	159.84		6M	159.84		6M	159.84		6M	159.84	
Cold water service point	NR	110.52	1NR	110.52		1NR	110.52		1NR	110.52		1NR	110.52	
Hot water service point	NR	191.67	1NR	191.67		1NR	191.67		1NR	191.67		1NR	191.67	
Central heating service point	NR	386.51	2NR	773.02		2NR	773.02		2NR	773.02		2NR	773.02	
Electrical installation	NR	286.50	2NR	573.00	**1808.05**	2NR	573.00	**1808.05**	2NR	573.00	**1808.05**	2NR	573.00	**1808.05**

Specification B
30 m2 - 45 m2

TWO STOREY

FLAT ROOF Continued\.....

Element	Unit	Unit Rate £	Ref B/2F 5x6 Size 5.00 x 6.00 m Area 30 m2 Qty	Total £	Element Total £	Ref B/2F 5x7 Size 5.00 x 7.00 m Area 35 m2 Qty	Total £	Element Total £	Ref B/2F 5x8 Size 5.00 x 8.00 m Area 40 m2 Qty	Total £	Element Total £	Ref B/2F 5x9 Size 5.00 x 9.00 m Area 45 m2 Qty	Total £	Element Total £
	M2	35.42	30M2	1062.60		35M2	1239.70		40M2	1416.80		45M2	1593.90	
	M	11.09	44M	487.96	**1550.56**	48M	532.32	**1772.02**	52M	576.68	**1993.48**	56M	621.04	**2214.94**
	M2	16.34	60M2	980.40	**980.40**	70M2	1143.80	**1143.80**	80M2	1307.20	**1307.20**	90M2	1470.60	**1470.60**
	M	26.64	6M	159.84		6M	159.84		6M	159.84		6M	159.84	
	NR	110.52	1NR	110.52		1NR	110.52		1NR	110.52		1NR	110.52	
	NR	191.67	1NR	191.67		1NR	191.67		1NR	191.67		1NR	191.67	
	NR	386.51	4NR	1546.04		4NR	1546.04		4NR	1546.04		4NR	1546.04	
	NR	286.50	4NR	1146.00	**3154.07**	4NR	1146.00	**3154.07**	4NR	1146.00	**3154.07**	4NR	1146.00	**3154.07**

Specification B 10 m2 - 25 m2

			Ref B/2F 5x2 Size 5.00 x 2.00 m Area 10 m2			Ref B/2F 5x3 Size 5.00 x 3.00 m Area 15 m2			Ref B/2F 5x4 Size 5.00 x 4.00 m Area 20 m2			Ref B/2F 5x5 Size 5.00 x 5.00 m Area 25 m2		
			Qty	Total £	Element Total £	Qty	Total £	Element Total £	Qty	Total £	Element Total £	Qty	Total £	Element Total £
TWO STOREY														
FLAT ROOF														
Element	Unit	Unit Rate £												
ALTERATIONS TO EXISTING BUILDINGS														
Opening in existing wall 1.80 m wide 2.00 m high	NR	689.44	2NR	1378.88	**1378.88**									
Opening in existing wall 2.40 m wide 2.00 m high	NR	865.59												
Opening in existing wall 3.00 m wide 2.00 m high	NR	921.26				2NR	1842.52	**1842.52**						
Opening in existing wall 4.00 m wide 2.00 m high	NR	1131.22							2NR	2262.44	**2262.44**			
Opening in existing wall 5.00 m wide 2.00 m high	NR	1341.19										2NR	2682.38	**2682.38**

Specification B
30 m2 - 45 m2

TWO STOREY

FLAT ROOF Continued\.....

Element	Unit	Unit Rate £	Ref B/2F 5x6 Size 5.00 x 6.00 m Area 30 m2 Qty	Total £	Element Total £	Ref B/2F 5x7 Size 5.00 x 7.00 m Area 35 m2 Qty	Total £	Element Total £	Ref B/2F 5x8 Size 5.00 x 8.00 m Area 40 m2 Qty	Total £	Element Total £	Ref B/2F 5x9 Size 5.00 x 9.00 m Area 45 m2 Qty	Total £	Element Total £
	NR	689.44												
	NR	865.59	4NR	3462.36	**3462.36**									
	NR	921.26				4NR	3685.04	**3685.04**	4NR	3685.04	**3685.04**			
	NR	1131.22										4NR	4524.88	**4524.88**
	NR	1341.19												

Specification B 10 m2 - 25 m2	Ref B/2F 5x2 Size 5.00 x 2.00 m Area 10 m2	Ref B/2F 5x3 Size 5.00 x 3.00 m Area 15 m2	Ref B/2F 5x4 Size 5.00 x 4.00 m Area 20 m2	Ref B/2F 5x5 Size 5.00 x 5.00 m Area 25 m2
	Element Total £	Element Total £	Element Total £	Element Total £
TWO STOREY				
FLAT ROOF				
SUMMARY				
SUBSTRUCTURE	2079.69	2433.52	2787.35	3141.18
UPPER FLOORS	413.00	672.30	896.40	1661.75
ROOF	2689.80	3293.47	4045.23	4659.90
EXTERNAL WALLS	6093.87	6628.42	7162.97	7697.52
EXTERNAL DOORS AND WINDOWS	1995.87	1995.87	1995.87	1995.87
INTERNAL WALLS AND PARTITIONS	-	-	-	-
INTERNAL DOORS	-	-	-	-
WALL FINISHES	1370.60	1566.40	1762.20	1958.00
FLOOR FINISHES	664.72	886.18	1107.64	1329.10
CEILING FINISHES	326.80	490.20	653.60	817.00
SERVICES	1808.05	1808.05	1808.05	1808.05
ALTERATIONS TO EXISTING BUILDINGS	1378.88	1842.52	2262.44	2682.38
Sub Total	18821.28	21616.93	24481.75	27750.75
Allowance for unmeasured items and sundries 5%	941.06	1080.85	1224.09	1387.54
NET TOTAL excluding Preliminaries, Profit and Overheads	**19762.34**	**22697.78**	**25705.84**	**29138.29**

Specification B 30 m2 - 45 m2	**Ref B/2F 5x6 Size 5.00 x 6.00 m Area 30 m2**	**Ref B/2F 5x7 Size 5.00 x 7.00 m Area 35 m2**	**Ref B/2F 5x8 Size 5.00 x 8.00 m Area 40 m2**	**Ref B/2F 5x9 Size 5.00 x 9.00 m Area 45 m2**
	Element Total £	**Element Total £**	**Element Total £**	**Element Total £**
TWO STOREY				
FLAT ROOF				
SUMMARY Continued/.....				
	3495.01	3848.84	4202.67	4556.50
	1344.60	1568.70	1792.80	2991.15
	5277.46	5881.13	6681.29	7295.96
	7804.43	8338.98	8873.53	9408.08
	3333.81	3333.81	3333.81	3333.81
	1342.38	1342.38	1342.38	1342.38
	502.22	502.22	502.22	502.22
	2153.80	2349.60	2545.40	2741.20
	1550.56	1772.02	1993.48	2214.94
	980.40	1143.80	1307.20	1470.60
	3154.07	3154.07	3154.07	3154.07
	3462.36	3685.04	3685.04	4524.88
Sub Total	34401.10	36920.59	39413.89	43535.79
Allowance for unmeasured items and sundries 5%	1720.06	1846.03	1970.69	2176.79
NET TOTAL excluding Preliminaries, Profit and Overheads	**36121.16**	**38766.62**	**41384.58**	**45712.58**

Specification B

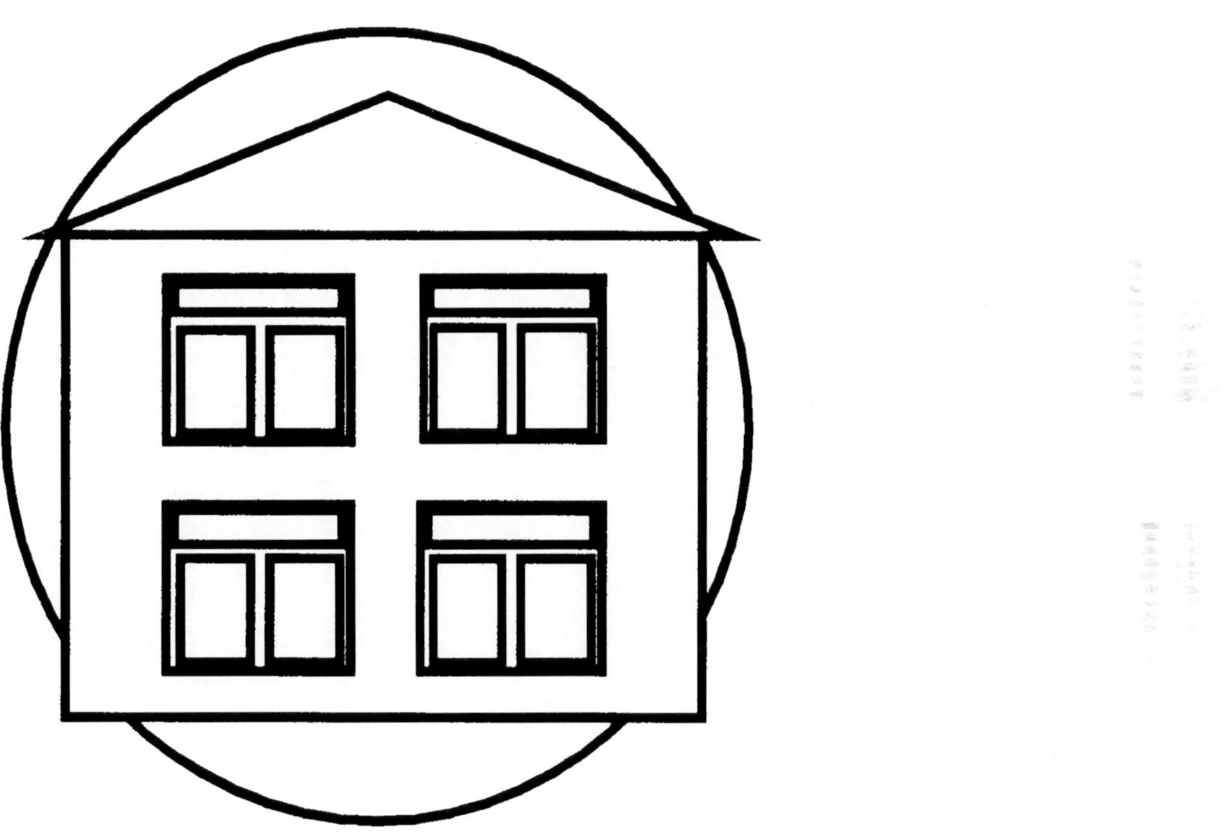

Two storey pitch roof

[2P] 2×2/3/4/5.

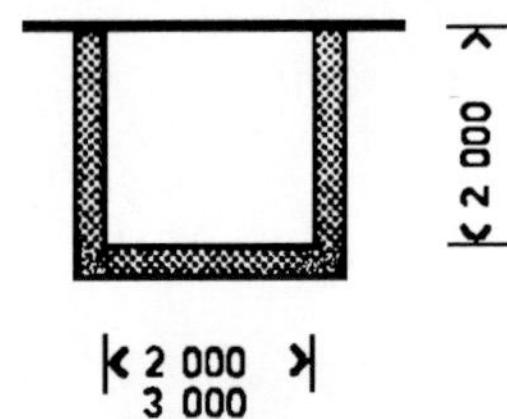

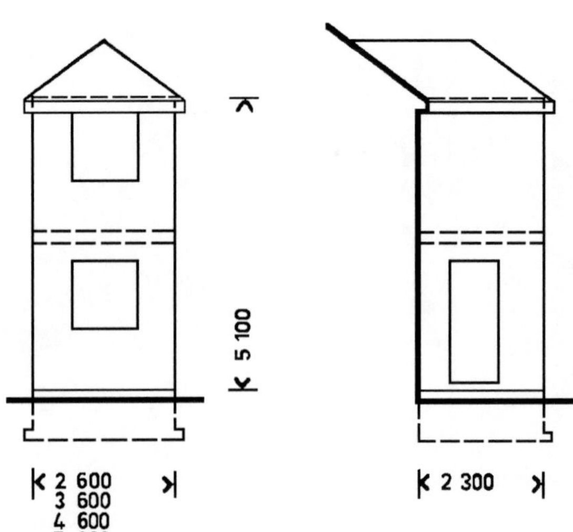

[2P] 2×6/7/8/9.

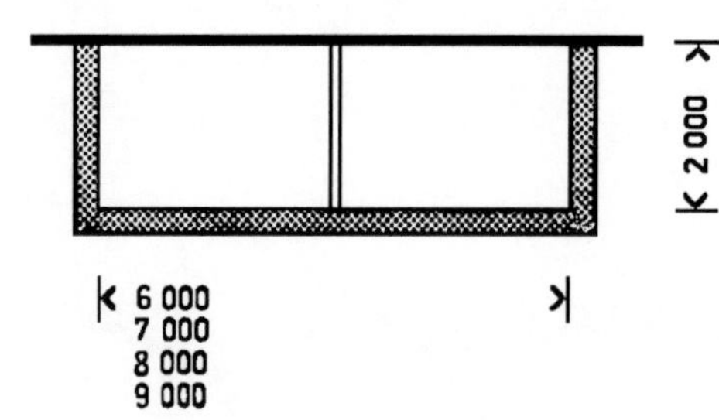

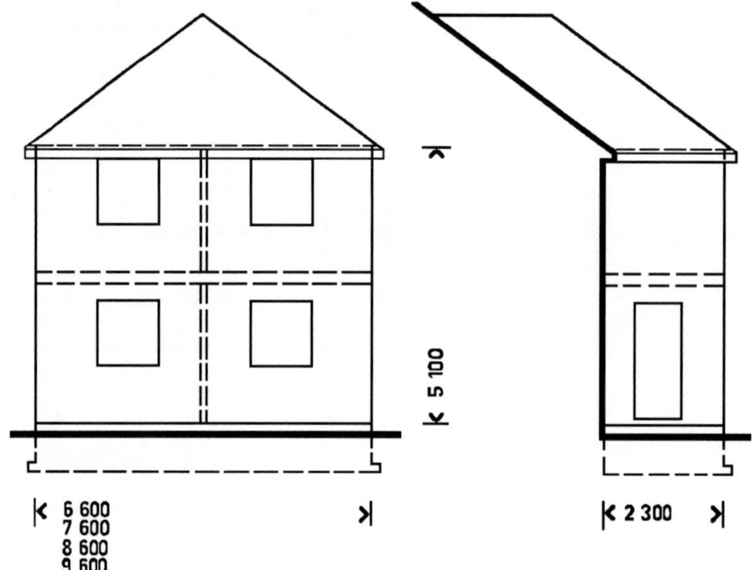

[2P] 3 × 2/3/4/5.

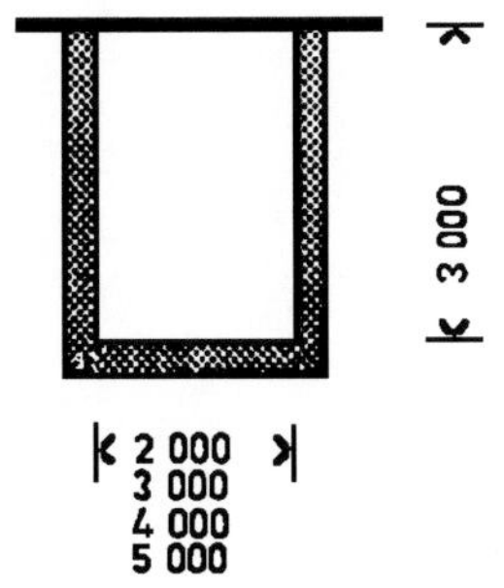

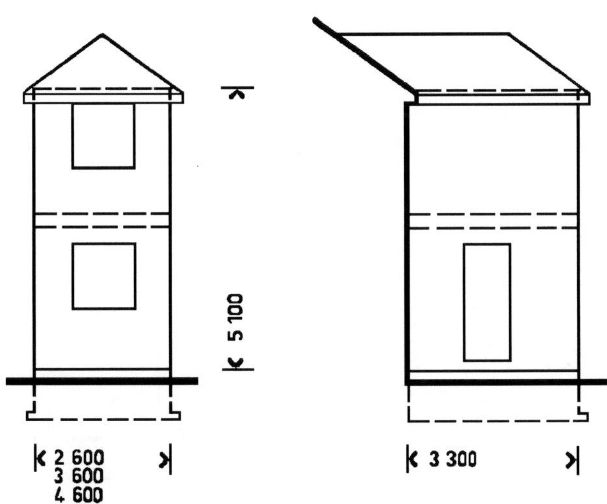

[2P] 3 × 6/7/8/9.

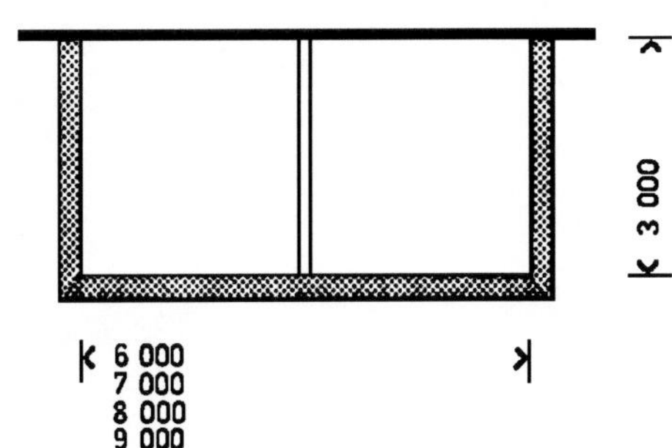

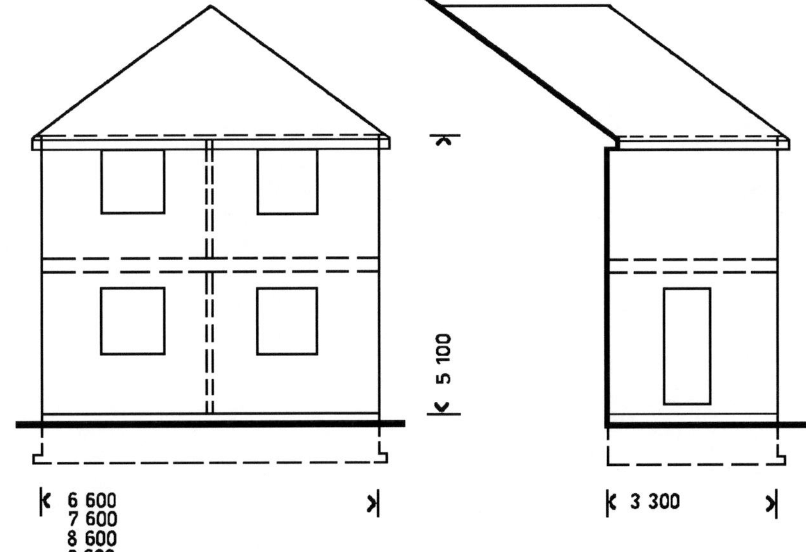

[2P] 4× 2/3/4/5.

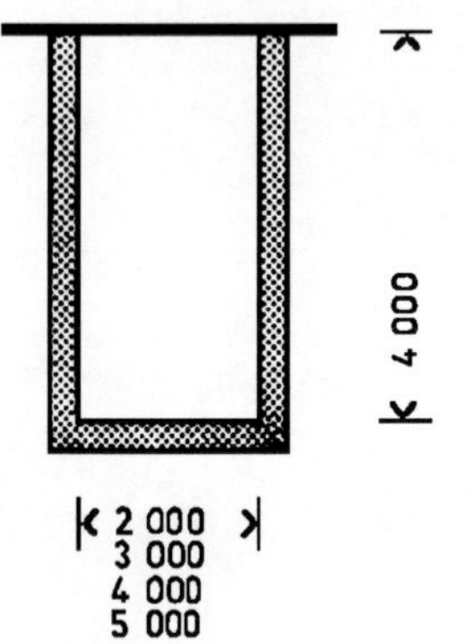

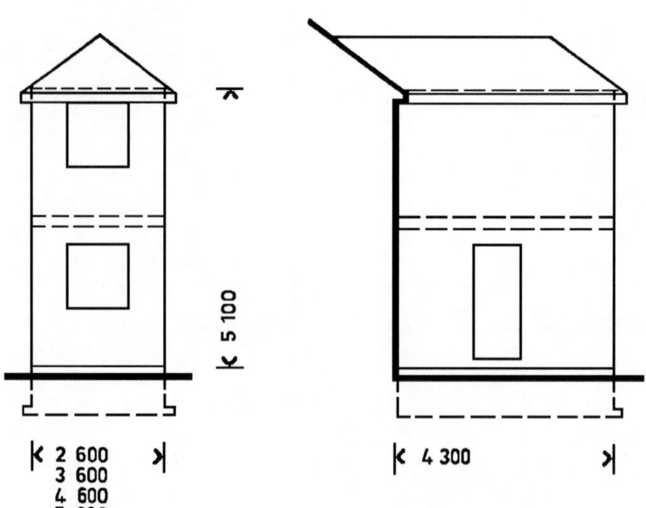

[2P] 4×6/7/8/9.

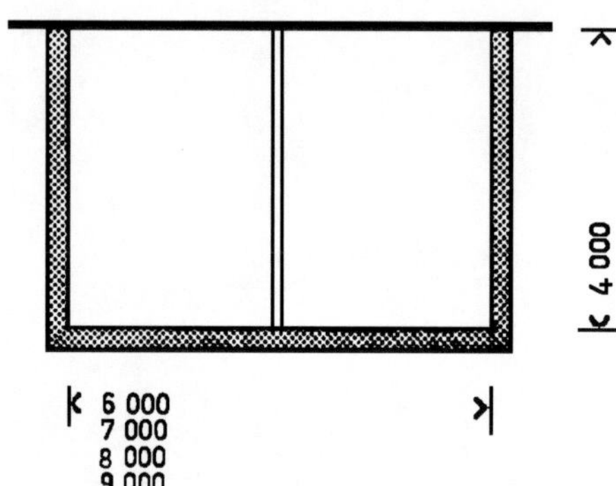

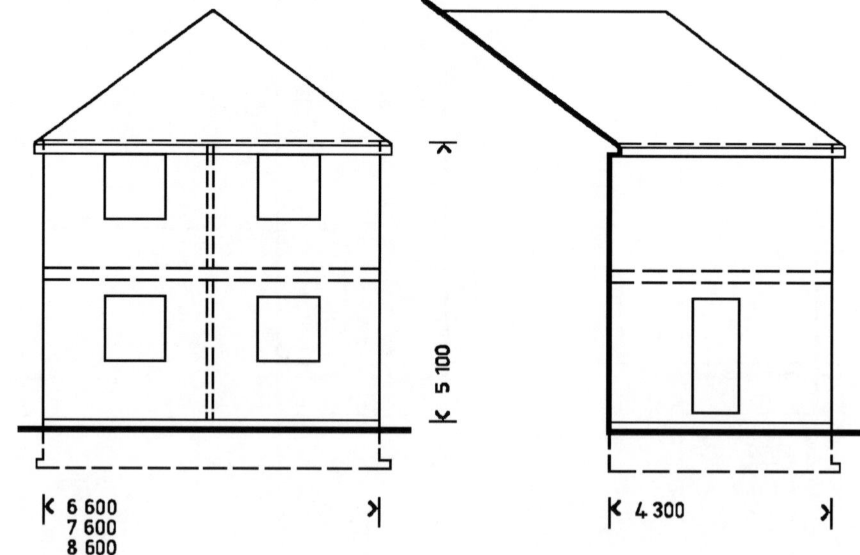

[2P] 5 × 2/3/4/5.

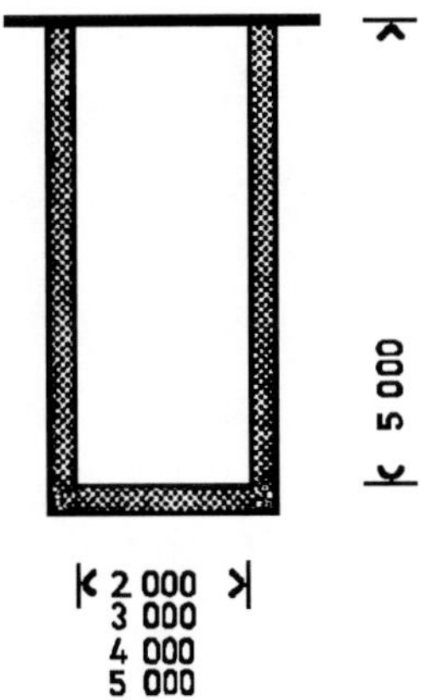

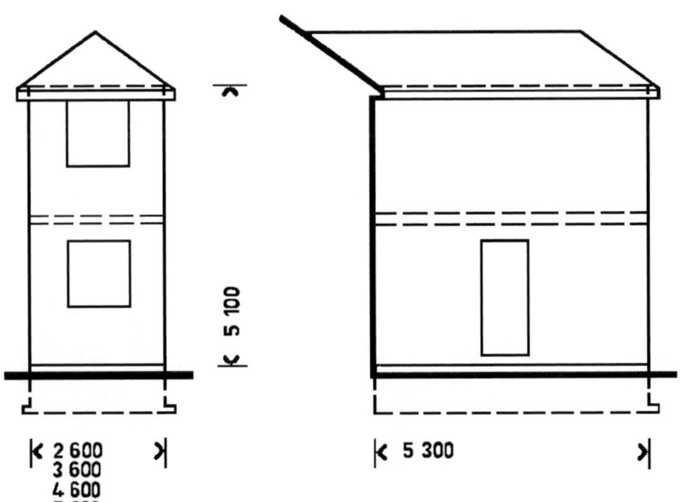

[2P] 5 × 6/7/8/9.

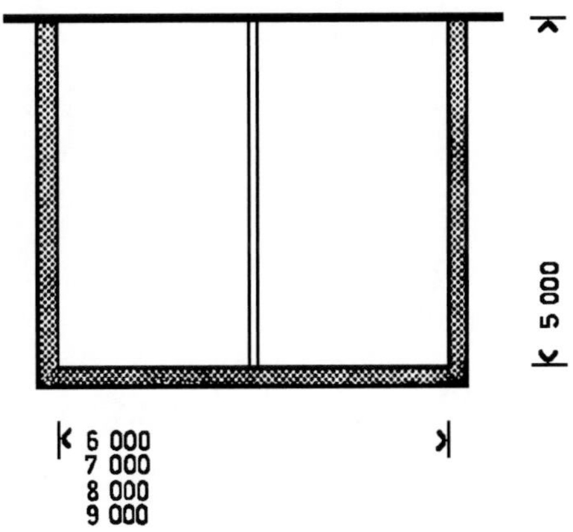

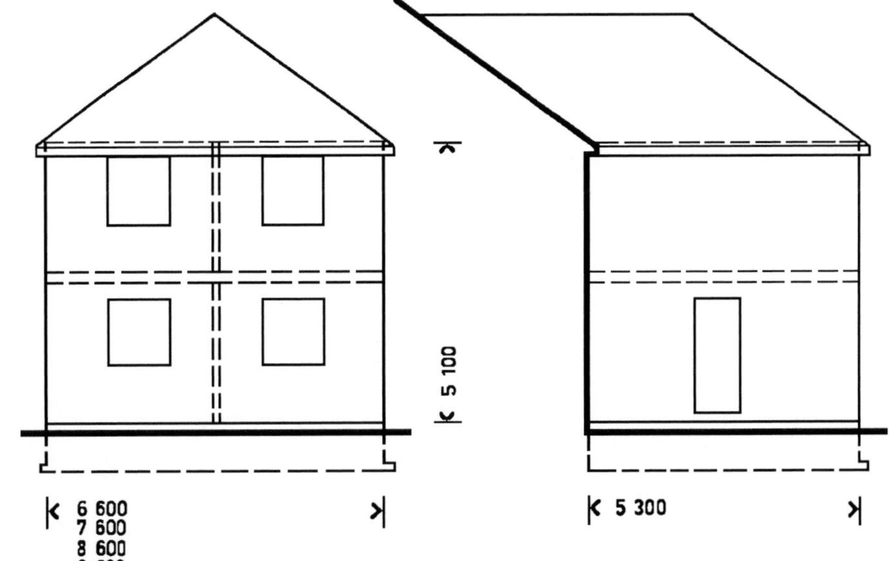

Specification B 4 m2 - 10 m2

TWO STOREY

PITCHED ROOF

Element	Unit	Unit Rate £	Ref B/2P 2x2 Size 2.00 x 2.00 m Area 4 m2 Qty	Total £	Element Total £	Ref B/2P 2x3 Size 2.00 x 3.00 m Area 6 m2 Qty	Total £	Element Total £	Ref B/2P 2x4 Size 2.00 x 4.00 m Area 8 m2 Qty	Total £	Element Total £	Ref B/2P 2x5 Size 2.00 x 5.00 m Area 10 m2 Qty	Total £	Element Total £
SUBSTRUCTURE														
Strip footings	M	124.73	7M	873.11		8M	997.84		9M	1122.57		10M	1247.30	
Solid ground floor	M2	45.82	4M2	183.28	**1056.39**	6M2	274.92	**1272.76**	8M2	366.56	**1489.13**	10M2	458.20	**1705.50**
UPPER FLOORS														
Timber floor construction 50 x 150 mm joists	M2	41.30	4M2	165.20	**165.20**	6M2	247.80	**247.80**	8M2	330.40	**330.40**	10M2	413.00	**413.00**
ROOF														
Pitched roof construction	M2	55.42	10M2	554.20		14M2	775.88		19M2	1052.98		24M2	1330.08	
Work to top of external wall	M	23.71	7M	165.97		8M	189.68		9M	213.39		10M	237.10	
Concrete tile roofing	M2	23.48	12M2	281.76		17M2	399.16		23M2	540.04		29M2	680.92	
Work to hip	M	41.73	7M	292.11		9M	375.57		11M	459.03		11M	459.03	
Work to eaves	M	23.22	8M	185.76		9M	208.98		10M	232.20		11M	255.42	
Fascia and eaves soffit	M	42.61	8M	340.88		9M	383.49		10M	426.10		11M	468.71	
Gutters and fittings	M	18.68	8M	149.44	**1970.12**	9M	168.12	**2500.88**	10M	186.80	**3110.54**	11M	205.48	**3636.74**
EXTERNAL WALLS														
Brick and block cavity wall	M2	106.91	27M2	2886.57	**2886.57**	32M2	3421.12	**3421.12**	37M2	3955.67	**3955.67**	42M2	4490.22	**4490.22**

Specification B
12 m2 - 18 m2

Element	Unit	Unit Rate £	Ref B/2P 2x6 Size 2.00 x 6.00 m Area 12 m2 Qty	Total £	Element Total £	Ref B/2P 2x7 Size 2.00 x 7.00 m Area 14 m2 Qty	Total £	Element Total £	Ref B/2P 2x8 Size 2.00 x 8.00 m Area 16 m2 Qty	Total £	Element Total £	Ref B/2P 2x9 Size 2.00 x 9.00 m Area 18 m2 Qty	Total £	Element Total £
TWO STOREY														
PITCHED ROOF Continued\.....														
	M	124.73	11M	1372.03		12M	1496.76		13M	1621.49		14M	1746.22	
	M2	45.82	12M2	549.84	**1921.87**	14M2	641.48	**2138.24**	16M2	733.12	**2354.61**	18M2	824.76	**2570.98**
	M2	41.30	12M2	495.60	**495.60**	14M2	578.20	**578.20**	16M2	660.80	**660.80**	18M2	743.40	**743.40**
	M2	55.42	30M2	1662.60		36M2	1995.12		43M2	2383.06		50M2	2771.00	
	M	23.71	11M	260.81		12M	284.52		13M	308.23		14M	331.94	
	M2	23.48	37M2	868.76		45M2	1056.60		53M2	1244.44		62M2	1455.76	
	M	41.73	13M	542.49		15M	625.95		16M	667.68		19M	792.87	
	M	23.22	12M	278.64		13M	301.86		14M	325.08		15M	348.30	
	M	42.61	12M	511.32		13M	553.93		14M	596.54		15M	639.15	
	M	18.68	12M	224.16	**4348.78**	13M	242.84	**5060.82**	14M	261.52	**5786.55**	15M	280.20	**6619.22**
	M2	106.91	43M2	4597.13	**4597.13**	48M2	5131.68	**5131.68**	53M2	5666.23	**5666.23**	58M2	6200.78	**6200.78**

Specification B 4 m2 - 10 m2

TWO STOREY

PITCHED ROOF

Element	Unit	Unit Rate £	Ref B/2P 2x2 Size 2.00 x 2.00 m Area 4 m2 Qty	Total £	Element Total £	Ref B/2P 2x3 Size 2.00 x 3.00 m Area 6 m2 Qty	Total £	Element Total £	Ref B/2P 2x4 Size 2.00 x 4.00 m Area 8 m2 Qty	Total £	Element Total £	Ref B/2P 2x5 Size 2.00 x 5.00 m Area 10 m2 Qty	Total £	Element Total £
EXTERNAL DOORS AND WINDOWS														
External door	NR	478.42	1NR	478.42		1NR	478.42		1NR	478.42		1NR	478.42	
Windows	NR	518.08	2NR	1036.16		2NR	1036.16		2NR	1036.16		2NR	1036.16	
Opening in cavity wall for door	NR	179.51	1NR	179.51		1NR	179.51		1NR	179.51		1NR	179.51	
Opening in cavity wall for window	NR	150.89	2NR	301.78	**1995.87**	2NR	301.78	**1995.87**	2NR	301.78	**1995.87**	2NR	301.78	**1995.87**
INTERNAL WALLS AND PARTITIONS														
Stud partitions	M2	51.63												
INTERNAL DOORS														
Softwood flush door	NR	251.11												
WALL FINISHES														
Plaster & decoration	M2	19.58	40M2	783.20	**783.20**	50M2	979.00	**979.00**	60M2	1174.80	**1174.80**	70M2	1370.60	**1370.60**
FLOOR FINISHES														
Thermoplastic tiles on screed	M2	35.42	4M2	141.68		6M2	212.52		8M2	283.36		10M2	354.20	
Softwood skirting	M	11.09	16M	177.44	**319.12**	20M	221.80	**434.32**	24M	266.16	**549.52**	28M	310.52	**664.72**
CEILING FINISHES														
Plasterboard and Artex	M2	16.34	8M2	130.72	**130.72**	12M2	196.08	**196.08**	16M2	261.44	**261.44**	20M2	326.80	**326.80**

Specification B 12 m2 - 18 m2

TWO STOREY

PITCHED ROOF Continued\.....

Element	Unit	Unit Rate £	Ref B/2P 2x6 Size 2.00 x 6.00 m Area 12 m2 Qty	Total £	Element Total £	Ref B/2P 2x7 Size 2.00 x 7.00 m Area 14 m2 Qty	Total £	Element Total £	Ref B/2P 2x8 Size 2.00 x 8.00 m Area 16 m2 Qty	Total £	Element Total £	Ref B/2P 2x9 Size 2.00 x 9.00 m Area 18 m2 Qty	Total £	Element Total £
	NR	478.42	1NR	478.42		1NR	478.42		1NR	478.42		1NR	478.42	
	NR	518.08	4NR	2072.32		4NR	2072.32		4NR	2072.32		4NR	2072.32	
	NR	179.51	1NR	179.51		1NR	179.51		1NR	179.51		1NR	179.51	
	NR	150.89	4NR	603.56	**3333.81**	4NR	603.56	**3333.81**	4NR	603.56	**3333.81**	4NR	603.56	**3333.81**
	M2	51.63	10M2	516.30	**516.30**	10M2	516.30	**516.30**	10M2	516.30	**516.30**	10M2	516.30	**516.30**
	NR	251.11	2NR	502.22	**502.22**	2NR	502.22	**502.22**	2NR	502.22	**502.22**	2NR	502.22	**502.22**
	M2	19.58	80M2	1566.40	**1566.40**	90M2	1762.20	**1762.20**	100M2	1958.00	**1958.00**	110M2	2153.80	**2153.80**
	M2	35.42	12M2	425.04		14M2	495.88		16M2	566.72		18M2	637.56	
	M	11.09	32M	354.88	**779.92**	36M	399.24	**895.12**	40M	443.60	**1010.32**	44M	487.96	**1125.52**
	M2	16.34	24M2	392.16	**392.16**	28M2	457.52	**457.52**	32M2	522.88	**522.88**	36M2	588.24	**588.24**

Specification B 4 m2 - 10 m2

TWO STOREY

PITCHED ROOF

Element	Unit	Unit Rate £	Ref B/2P 2x2 Size 2.00 x 2.00 m Area 4 m2 Qty	Total £	Element Total £	Ref B/2P 2x3 Size 2.00 x 3.00 m Area 6 m2 Qty	Total £	Element Total £	Ref B/2P 2x4 Size 2.00 x 4.00 m Area 8 m2 Qty	Total £	Element Total £	Ref B/2P 2x5 Size 2.00 x 5.00 m Area 10 m2 Qty	Total £	Element Total £
SERVICES														
Rainwater pipes	M	26.64	6M	159.84		6M	159.84		6M	159.84		6M	159.84	
Cold water service point	NR	110.52	1NR	110.52		1NR	110.52		1NR	110.52		1NR	110.52	
Hot water service point	NR	191.67	1NR	191.67		1NR	191.67		1NR	191.67		1NR	191.67	
Central heating service point	NR	386.51	2NR	773.02		2NR	773.02		2NR	773.02		2NR	773.02	
Electrical installation	NR	286.50	2NR	573.00	**1808.05**	2NR	573.00	**1808.05**	2NR	573.00	**1808.05**	2NR	573.00	**1808.05**
ALTERATIONS TO EXISTING BUILDINGS														
Opening in existing wall 1.80 m wide 2.00 m high	NR	689.44	2NR	1378.88	**1378.88**									
Opening in existing wall 2.40 m wide 2.00 m high	NR	865.59												
Opening in existing wall 3.00 m wide 2.00 m high	NR	921.26				2NR	1842.52	**1842.52**						
Opening in existing wall 4.00 m wide 2.00 m high	NR	1131.22							2NR	2262.44	**2262.44**			
Opening in existing wall 5.00 m wide 2.00 m high	NR	1341.19										2NR	2682.38	**2682.38**

Specification B 12 m2 - 18 m2

TWO STOREY

PITCHED ROOF Continued\.....

Element	Unit	Unit Rate £	Ref B/2P 2x6 Size 2.00 x 6.00 m Area 12 m2			Ref B/2P 2x7 Size 2.00 x 7.00 m Area 14 m2			Ref B/2P 2x8 Size 2.00 x 8.00 m Area 16 m2			Ref B/2P 2x9 Size 2.00 x 9.00 m Area 18 m2		
			Qty	Total £	Element Total £	Qty	Total £	Element Total £	Qty	Total £	Element Total £	Qty	Total £	Element Total £
	M	26.64	6M	159.84		6M	159.84		6M	159.84		6M	159.84	
	NR	110.52	1NR	110.52		1NR	110.52		1NR	110.52		1NR	110.52	
	NR	191.67	1NR	191.67		1NR	191.67		1NR	191.67		1NR	191.67	
	NR	386.51	4NR	1546.04		4NR	1546.04		4NR	1546.04		4NR	1546.04	
	NR	286.50	4NR	1146.00	**3154.07**	4NR	1146.00	**3154.07**	4NR	1146.00	**3154.07**	4NR	1146.00	**3154.07**
	NR	689.44												
	NR	865.59	4NR	3462.36	**3462.36**									
	NR	921.26				4NR	3685.04	**3685.04**	4NR	3685.04	**3685.04**			
	NR	1131.22										4NR	4524.88	**4524.88**
	NR	1341.19												

Specification B 4 m2 - 10 m2	Ref B/2P 2x2 Size 2.00 x 2.00 m Area 4 m2 Element Total £	Ref B/2P 2x3 Size 2.00 x 3.00 m Area 6 m2 Element Total £	Ref B/2P 2x4 Size 2.00 x 4.00 m Area 8 m2 Element Total £	Ref B/2P 2x5 Size 2.00 x 5.00 m Area 10 m2 Element Total £
TWO STOREY				
PITCHED ROOF				
SUMMARY				
SUBSTRUCTURE	1056.39	1272.76	1489.13	1705.50
UPPER FLOORS	165.20	247.80	330.40	413.00
ROOF	1970.12	2500.88	3110.54	3636.74
EXTERNAL WALLS	2886.57	3421.12	3955.67	4490.22
EXTERNAL DOORS AND WINDOWS	1995.87	1995.87	1995.87	1995.87
INTERNAL WALLS AND PARTITIONS	-	-	-	-
INTERNAL DOORS	-	-	-	-
WALL FINISHES	783.20	979.00	1174.80	1370.60
FLOOR FINISHES	319.12	434.32	549.52	664.72
CEILING FINISHES	130.72	196.08	261.44	326.80
SERVICES	1808.05	1808.05	1808.05	1808.05
ALTERATIONS TO EXISTING BUILDINGS	1378.88	1842.52	2262.44	2682.38
Sub Total	12494.12	14698.40	16937.86	19093.88
Allowance for unmeasured items and sundries 5%	624.71	734.92	846.89	954.69
NET TOTAL excluding Preliminaries, Profit and Overheads	**13118.83**	**15433.32**	**17784.75**	**20048.57**

Specification B 12 m2 - 18 m2	Ref B/2P 2x6 Size 2.00 x 6.00 m Area 12 m2	Ref B/2P 2x7 Size 2.00 x 7.00 m Area 14 m2	Ref B/2P 2x8 Size 2.00 x 8.00 m Area 16 m2	Ref B/2P 2x9 Size 2.00 x 9.00 m Area 18 m2
	Element Total £	Element Total £	Element Total £	Element Total £
TWO STOREY				
PITCHED ROOF				
SUMMARY Continued/.....				
	1921.87	2138.24	2354.61	2570.98
	495.60	578.20	660.80	743.40
	4348.78	5060.82	5786.55	6619.22
	4597.13	5131.68	5666.23	6200.78
	3333.81	3333.81	3333.81	3333.81
	516.30	516.30	516.30	516.30
	502.22	502.22	502.22	502.22
	1566.40	1762.20	1958.00	2153.80
	779.92	895.12	1010.32	1125.52
	392.16	457.52	522.88	588.24
	3154.07	3154.07	3154.07	3154.07
	3462.36	3685.04	3685.04	4524.88
Sub Total	25070.62	27215.22	29150.83	32033.22
Allowance for unmeasured items and sundries 5%	1253.53	1360.76	1457.54	1601.66
NET TOTAL excluding Preliminaries, Profit and Overheads	**26324.15**	**28575.98**	**30608.37**	**33634.88**

Specification B 6 m2 - 15 m2

			Ref B/2P 3x2 Size 3.00 x 2.00 m Area 6 m2			Ref B/2P 3x3 Size 3.00 x 3.00 m Area 9 m2			Ref B/2P 3x4 Size 3.00 x 4.00 m Area 12 m2			Ref B/2P 3x5 Size 3.00 x 5.00 m Area 15 m2		
TWO STOREY PITCHED ROOF			Qty	Total £	Element Total £	Qty	Total £	Element Total £	Qty	Total £	Element Total £	Qty	Total £	Element Total £
Element	Unit	Unit Rate £												
SUBSTRUCTURE														
Strip footings	M	124.73	9M	1122.57		10M	1247.30		11M	1372.03		12M	1496.76	
Solid ground floor	M2	45.82	6M2	274.92	**1397.49**	9M2	412.38	**1659.68**	12M2	549.84	**1921.87**	15M2	687.30	**2184.06**
UPPER FLOORS														
Timber floor construction 50 x 150 mm joists	M2	41.30	6M2	247.80	**247.80**									
Timber floor construction 50 x 200 mm joists	M2	44.82				9M2	403.38	**403.38**	12M2	537.84	**537.84**	15M2	672.30	**672.30**
ROOF														
Pitched roof construction	M2	55.42	13M2	720.46		18M2	997.56		24M2	1330.08		30M2	1662.60	
Work to top of external wall	M	23.71	9M	213.39		10M	237.10		11M	260.81		12M	284.52	
Concrete tile roofing	M2	23.48	16M2	375.68		22M2	516.56		30M2	704.40		37M2	868.76	
Work to hip	M	41.73	9M	375.57		10M	417.30		11M	459.03		13M	542.49	
Work to eaves	M	23.22	10M	232.20		11M	255.42		12M	278.64		13M	301.86	
Fascia and eaves soffit	M	42.61	10M	426.10		11M	468.71		12M	511.32		13M	553.93	
Gutters and fittings	M	18.68	10M	186.80	**2530.20**	11M	205.48	**3098.13**	12M	224.16	**3768.44**	13M	242.84	**4457.00**
EXTERNAL WALLS														
Brick and block cavity wall	M2	106.91	37M2	3955.67	**3955.67**	42M2	4490.22	**4490.22**	47M2	5024.77	**5024.77**	52M2	5559.32	**5559.32**

Specification B 18 m2 - 27 m2

TWO STOREY

PITCHED ROOF Continued\.....

Element	Unit	Unit Rate £	Ref B/2P 3x6 Size 3.00 x 6.00 m Area 18 m2 Qty	Total £	Element Total £	Ref B/2P 3x7 Size 3.00 x 7.00 m Area 21 m2 Qty	Total £	Element Total £	Ref B/2P 3x8 Size 3.00 x 8.00 m Area 24 m2 Qty	Total £	Element Total £	Ref B/2P 3x9 Size 3.00 x 9.00 m Area 27 m2 Qty	Total £	Element Total £
	M	124.73	13M	1621.49		14M	1746.22		15M	1870.95		16M	1995.68	
	M2	45.82	18M2	824.76	**2446.25**	21M2	962.22	**2708.44**	24M2	1099.68	**2970.63**	27M2	1237.14	**3232.82**
	M2	41.30												
	M2	44.82	18M2	806.76	**806.76**	21M2	941.22	**941.22**	24M2	1075.68	**1075.68**	27M2	1210.14	**1210.14**
	M2	55.42	37M2	2050.54		44M2	2438.48		52M2	2881.84		60M2	3325.20	
	M	23.71	13M	308.23		14M	331.94		15M	355.65		16M	379.36	
	M2	23.48	45M2	1056.60		54M2	1267.92		64M2	1502.72		74M2	1737.52	
	M	41.73	15M	625.95		16M	667.68		17M	709.41		19M	792.87	
	M	23.22	14M	325.08		15M	348.30		16M	371.52		17M	394.74	
	M	42.61	14M	596.54		15M	639.15		16M	681.76		17M	724.37	
	M	18.68	14M	261.52	**5224.46**	15M	280.20	**5973.67**	16M	298.88	**6801.78**	17M	317.56	**7671.62**
	M2	106.91	53M2	5666.23	**5666.23**	55M2	5880.05	**5880.05**	63M2	6735.33	**6735.33**	68M2	7269.88	**7269.88**

Specification B 6 m2 - 15 m2

TWO STOREY

PITCHED ROOF

Element	Unit	Unit Rate £	Ref B/2P 3x2 Size 3.00 x 2.00 m Area 6 m2 Qty	Total £	Element Total £	Ref B/2P 3x3 Size 3.00 x 3.00 m Area 9 m2 Qty	Total £	Element Total £	Ref B/2P 3x4 Size 3.00 x 4.00 m Area 12 m2 Qty	Total £	Element Total £	Ref B/2P 3x5 Size 3.00 x 5.00 m Area 15 m2 Qty	Total £	Element Total £
EXTERNAL DOORS AND WINDOWS														
External door	NR	478.42	1NR	478.42		1NR	478.42		1NR	478.42		1NR	478.42	
Windows	NR	518.08	2NR	1036.16		2NR	1036.16		2NR	1036.16		2NR	1036.16	
Opening in cavity wall for door	NR	179.51	1NR	179.51		1NR	179.51		1NR	179.51		1NR	179.51	
Opening in cavity wall for window	NR	150.89	2NR	301.78	**1995.87**	2NR	301.78	**1995.87**	2NR	301.78	**1995.87**	2NR	301.78	**1995.87**
INTERNAL WALLS AND PARTITIONS														
Stud partitions	M2	51.63												
INTERNAL DOORS														
Softwood flush door	NR	251.11												
WALL FINISHES														
Plaster & decoration	M2	19.58	50M2	979.00	**979.00**	60M2	1174.80	**1174.80**	70M2	1370.60	**1370.60**	80M2	1566.40	**1566.40**
FLOOR FINISHES														
Thermoplastic tiles on screed	M2	35.42	6M2	212.52		9M2	318.78		12M2	425.04		15M2	531.30	
Softwood skirting	M	11.09	20M	221.80	**434.32**	24M	266.16	**584.94**	28M	310.52	**735.56**	32M	354.88	**886.18**
CEILING FINISHES														
Plasterboard and Artex	M2	16.34	12M2	196.08	**196.08**	18M2	294.12	**294.12**	24M2	392.16	**392.16**	30M2	490.20	**490.20**

Specification B 18 m2 - 27 m2

TWO STOREY

PITCHED ROOF Continued\.....

Element	Unit	Unit Rate £	Ref B/2P 3x6 Size 3.00 x 6.00 m Area 18 m2 Qty	Total £	Element Total £	Ref B/2P 3x7 Size 3.00 x 7.00 m Area 21 m2 Qty	Total £	Element Total £	Ref B/2P 3x8 Size 3.00 x 8.00 m Area 24 m2 Qty	Total £	Element Total £	Ref B/2P 3x9 Size 3.00 x 9.00 m Area 27 m2 Qty	Total £	Element Total £
	NR	478.42	1NR	478.42		1NR	478.42		1NR	478.42		1NR	478.42	
	NR	518.08	4NR	2072.32		4NR	2072.32		4NR	2072.32		4NR	2072.32	
	NR	179.51	1NR	179.51		1NR	179.51		1NR	179.51		1NR	179.51	
	NR	150.89	4NR	603.56	**3333.81**	4NR	603.56	**3333.81**	4NR	603.56	**3333.81**	4NR	603.56	**3333.81**
	M2	51.63	16M2	826.08	**826.08**	16M2	826.08	**826.08**	16M2	826.08	**826.08**	16M2	826.08	**826.08**
	NR	251.11	2NR	502.22	**502.22**	2NR	502.22	**502.22**	2NR	502.22	**502.22**	2NR	502.22	**502.22**
	M2	19.58	90M2	1762.20	**1762.20**	100M2	1958.00	**1958.00**	110M2	2153.80	**2153.80**	120M2	2349.60	**2349.60**
	M2	35.42	18M2	637.56		21M2	743.82		24M2	850.08		27M2	956.34	
	M	11.09	36M	399.24	**1036.80**	40M	443.60	**1187.42**	44M	487.96	**1338.04**	48M	532.32	**1488.66**
	M2	16.34	36M2	588.24	**588.24**	42M2	686.28	**686.28**	48M2	784.32	**784.32**	54M2	882.36	**882.36**

Specification B
6 m2 - 15 m2

TWO STOREY

PITCHED ROOF

Element	Unit	Unit Rate £	Ref B/2P 3x2 Size 3.00 x 2.00 m Area 6 m2 Qty	Total £	Element Total £	Ref B/2P 3x3 Size 3.00 x 3.00 m Area 9 m2 Qty	Total £	Element Total £	Ref B/2P 3x4 Size 3.00 x 4.00 m Area 12 m2 Qty	Total £	Element Total £	Ref B/2P 3x5 Size 3.00 x 5.00 m Area 15 m2 Qty	Total £	Element Total £
SERVICES														
Rainwater pipes	M	26.64	6M	159.84		6M	159.84		6M	159.84		6M	159.84	
Cold water service point	NR	110.52	1NR	110.52		1NR	110.52		1NR	110.52		1NR	110.52	
Hot water service point	NR	191.67	1NR	191.67		1NR	191.67		1NR	191.67		1NR	191.67	
Central heating service point	NR	386.51	2NR	773.02		2NR	773.02		2NR	773.02		2NR	773.02	
Electrical installation	NR	286.50	2NR	573.00	**1808.05**	2NR	573.00	**1808.05**	2NR	573.00	**1808.05**	2NR	573.00	**1808.05**
ALTERATIONS TO EXISTING BUILDINGS														
Opening in existing wall 1.80 m wide 2.00 m high	NR	689.44	2NR	1378.88	**1378.88**									
Opening in existing wall 2.40 m wide 2.00 m high	NR	865.59												
Opening in existing wall 3.00 m wide 2.00 m high	NR	921.26				2NR	1842.52	**1842.52**						
Opening in existing wall 4.00 m wide 2.00 m high	NR	1131.22							2NR	2262.44	**2262.44**			
Opening in existing wall 5.00 m wide 2.00 m high	NR	1341.19										2NR	2682.38	**2682.38**

Specification B
18 m2 - 27 m2

TWO STOREY

PITCHED ROOF Continued\.....

Element	Unit	Unit Rate £	Ref B/2P 3x6 Size 3.00 x 6.00 m Area 18 m2			Ref B/2P 3x7 Size 3.00 x 7.00 m Area 21 m2			Ref B/2P 3x8 Size 3.00 x 8.00 m Area 24 m2			Ref B/2P 3x9 Size 3.00 x 9.00 m Area 27 m2		
			Qty	Total £	Element Total £	Qty	Total £	Element Total £	Qty	Total £	Element Total £	Qty	Total £	Element Total £
	M	26.64	6M	159.84		6M	159.84		6M	159.84		6M	159.84	
	NR	110.52	1NR	110.52		1NR	110.52		1NR	110.52		1NR	110.52	
	NR	191.67	1NR	191.67		1NR	191.67		1NR	191.67		1NR	191.67	
	NR	386.51	4NR	1546.04		4NR	1546.04		4NR	1546.04		4NR	1546.04	
	NR	286.50	4NR	1146.00	**3154.07**	4NR	1146.00	**3154.07**	4NR	1146.00	**3154.07**	4NR	1146.00	**3154.07**
	NR	689.44												
	NR	865.59	4NR	3462.36	**3462.36**									
	NR	921.26				4NR	3685.04	**3685.04**	4NR	3685.04	**3685.04**			
	NR	1131.22										4NR	4524.88	**4524.88**
	NR	1341.19												

Specification B 6 m2 - 15 m2	Ref B/2P 3x2 Size 3.00 x 2.00 m Area 6 m2	Ref B/2P 3x3 Size 3.00 x 3.00 m Area 9 m2	Ref B/2P 3x4 Size 3.00 x 4.00 m Area 12 m2	Ref B/2P 3x5 Size 3.00 x 5.00 m Area 15 m2
	Element Total £	**Element Total £**	**Element Total £**	**Element Total £**
TWO STOREY				
PITCHED ROOF				
SUMMARY				
SUBSTRUCTURE	1397.49	1659.68	1921.87	2184.06
UPPER FLOORS	247.80	403.38	537.84	672.30
ROOF	2530.20	3098.13	3768.44	4457.00
EXTERNAL WALLS	3955.67	4490.22	5024.77	5559.32
EXTERNAL DOORS AND WINDOWS	1995.87	1995.87	1995.87	1995.87
INTERNAL WALLS AND PARTITIONS	-	-	-	-
INTERNAL DOORS	-	-	-	-
WALL FINISHES	979.00	1174.80	1370.60	1566.40
FLOOR FINISHES	434.32	584.94	735.56	886.18
CEILING FINISHES	196.08	294.12	392.16	490.20
SERVICES	1808.05	1808.05	1808.05	1808.05
ALTERATIONS TO EXISTING BUILDINGS	1378.88	1842.52	2262.44	2682.38
Sub Total	14923.36	17351.71	19817.60	22301.76
Allowance for unmeasured items and sundries 5%	746.17	867.59	990.88	1115.09
NET TOTAL excluding Preliminaries, Profit and Overheads	**15669.53**	**18219.30**	**20808.48**	**23416.85**

Specification B 18 m2 - 27 m2

	Ref B/2P 3x6 Size 3.00 x 6.00 m Area 18 m2	Ref B/2P 3x7 Size 3.00 x 7.00 m Area 21 m2	Ref B/2P 3x8 Size 3.00 x 8.00 m Area 24 m2	Ref B/2P 3x9 Size 3.00 x 9.00 m Area 27 m2
	Element Total £	Element Total £	Element Total £	Element Total £
TWO STOREY				
PITCHED ROOF				
SUMMARY Continued/.....				
	2446.25	2708.44	2970.63	3232.82
	806.76	941.22	1075.68	1210.14
	5224.46	5973.67	6801.78	7671.62
	5666.23	5880.05	6735.33	7269.88
	3333.81	3333.81	3333.81	3333.81
	826.08	826.08	826.08	826.08
	502.22	502.22	502.22	502.22
	1762.20	1958.00	2153.80	2349.60
	1036.80	1187.42	1338.04	1488.66
	588.24	686.28	784.32	882.36
	3154.07	3154.07	3154.07	3154.07
	3462.36	3685.04	3685.04	4524.88
Sub Total	28809.48	30836.30	33360.80	36446.14
Allowance for unmeasured items and sundries 5%	1440.47	1541.82	1668.04	1822.31
NET TOTAL excluding Preliminaries, Profit and Overheads	**30249.95**	**32378.12**	**35028.84**	**38268.45**

Specification B 8 m2 - 20 m2

TWO STOREY

PITCHED ROOF

Element	Unit	Unit Rate £	Ref B/2P 4x2 Size 4.00 x 2.00 m Area 8 m2 Qty	Total £	Element Total £	Ref B/2P 4x3 Size 4.00 x 3.00 m Area 12 m2 Qty	Total £	Element Total £	Ref B/2P 4x4 Size 4.00 x 4.00 m Area 16 m2 Qty	Total £	Element Total £	Ref B/2P 4x5 Size 4.00 x 5.00 m Area 20 m2 Qty	Total £	Element Total £
SUBSTRUCTURE														
Strip footings	M	124.73	11M	1372.03		12M	1496.76		13M	1621.49		14M	1746.22	
Solid ground floor	M2	45.82	8M2	366.56	**1738.59**	12M2	549.84	**2046.60**	16M2	733.12	**2354.61**	20M2	916.40	**2662.62**
UPPER FLOORS														
Timber floor construction 50 x 150 mm joists	M2	41.30	8M2	330.40	**330.40**									
Timber floor construction 50 x 200 mm joists	M2	44.82				12M2	537.84	**537.84**	16M2	717.12	**717.12**	20M2	896.40	**896.40**
ROOF														
Pitched roof construction	M2	55.42	16M2	886.72		22M2	1219.24		29M2	1607.18		36M2	1995.12	
Work to top of external wall	M	23.71	11M	260.81		12M	284.52		13M	308.23		14M	331.94	
Concrete tile roofing	M2	23.48	20M2	469.60		27M2	633.96		34M2	798.32		44M2	1033.12	
Work to hip	M	41.73	9M	375.57		11M	459.03		13M	542.49		14M	584.22	
Work to eaves	M	23.22	12M	278.64		13M	301.86		14M	325.08		15M	348.30	
Fascia and eaves soffit	M	42.61	12M	511.32		13M	553.93		14M	596.54		15M	639.15	
Gutters and fittings	M	18.68	12M	224.16	**3006.82**	13M	242.84	**3695.38**	14M	261.52	**4439.36**	15M	280.20	**5212.05**
EXTERNAL WALLS														
Brick and block cavity wall	M2	106.91	47M2	5024.77	**5024.77**	52M2	5559.32	**5559.32**	57M2	6093.87	**6093.87**	59M2	6307.69	**6307.69**

Specification B 24 m2 - 36 m2

TWO STOREY

PITCHED ROOF Continued\.....

Element	Unit	Unit Rate £	Ref B/2P 4x6 Size 4.00 x 6.00 m Area 24 m2 Qty	Total £	Element Total £	Ref B/2P 4x7 Size 4.00 x 7.00 m Area 28 m2 Qty	Total £	Element Total £	Ref B/2P 4x8 Size 4.00 x 8.00 m Area 32 m2 Qty	Total £	Element Total £	Ref B/2P 4x9 Size 4.00 x 9.00 m Area 36 m2 Qty	Total £	Element Total £
	M	124.73	15M	1870.95		16M	1995.68		17M	2120.41		18M	2245.14	
	M2	45.82	24M2	1099.68	**2970.63**	28M2	1282.96	**3278.64**	32M2	1466.24	**3586.65**	36M2	1649.52	**3894.66**
	M2	41.30												
	M2	44.82	24M2	1075.68	**1075.68**	28M2	1254.96	**1254.96**	32M2	1434.24	**1434.24**	36M2	1613.52	**1613.52**
	M2	55.42	44M2	2438.48		52M2	2881.84		61M2	3380.62		70M2	3879.40	
	M	23.71	15M	355.65		16M	379.36		17M	403.07		18M	426.78	
	M2	23.48	54M2	1267.92		64M2	1502.72		75M2	1761.00		86M2	2019.28	
	M	41.73	16M	667.68		17M	709.41		19M	792.87		20M	834.60	
	M	23.22	16M	371.52		17M	394.74		18M	417.96		19M	441.18	
	M	42.61	16M	681.76		17M	724.37		18M	766.98		19M	809.59	
	M	18.68	16M	298.88	**6081.89**	17M	317.56	**6910.00**	18M	336.24	**7858.74**	19M	354.92	**8765.75**
	M2	106.91	63M2	6735.33	**6735.33**	68M2	7269.88	**7269.88**	73M2	7804.43	**7804.43**	78M2	8338.98	**8338.98**

Specification B 8 m2 - 20 m2

TWO STOREY

PITCHED ROOF

Element	Unit	Unit Rate £	Ref B/2P 4x2 Size 4.00 x 2.00 m Area 8 m2			Ref B/2P 4x3 Size 4.00 x 3.00 m Area 12 m2			Ref B/2P 4x4 Size 4.00 x 4.00 m Area 16 m2			Ref B/2P 4x5 Size 4.00 x 5.00 m Area 20 m2		
			Qty	Total £	Element Total £	Qty	Total £	Element Total £	Qty	Total £	Element Total £	Qty	Total £	Element Total £
EXTERNAL DOORS AND WINDOWS														
External door	NR	478.42	1NR	478.42		1NR	478.42		1NR	478.42		1NR	478.42	
Windows	NR	518.08	2NR	1036.16		2NR	1036.16		2NR	1036.16		2NR	1036.16	
Opening in cavity wall for door	NR	179.51	1NR	179.51		1NR	179.51		1NR	179.51		1NR	179.51	
Opening in cavity wall for window	NR	150.89	2NR	301.78	**1995.87**	2NR	301.78	**1995.87**	2NR	301.78	**1995.87**	2NR	301.78	**1995.87**
INTERNAL WALLS AND PARTITIONS														
Stud partitions	M2	51.63												
INTERNAL DOORS														
Softwood flush door	NR	251.11												
WALL FINISHES														
Plaster & decoration	M2	19.58	60M2	1174.80	**1174.80**	70M2	1370.60	**1370.60**	80M2	1566.40	**1566.40**	90M2	1762.20	**1762.20**
FLOOR FINISHES														
Thermoplastic tiles on screed	M2	35.42	8M2	283.36		12M2	425.04		16M2	566.72		20M2	708.40	
Softwood skirting	M	11.09	24M	266.16	**549.52**	28M	310.52	**735.56**	32M	354.88	**921.60**	36M	399.24	**1107.64**
CEILING FINISHES														
Plasterboard and Artex	M2	16.34	16M2	261.44	**261.44**	24M2	392.16	**392.16**	32M2	522.88	**522.88**	40M2	653.60	**653.60**

Specification B 24 m2 - 36 m2

Element	Unit	Unit Rate £	Ref B/2P 4x6 Size 4.00 x 6.00 m Area 24 m2 Qty	Total £	Element Total £	Ref B/2P 4x7 Size 4.00 x 7.00 m Area 28 m2 Qty	Total £	Element Total £	Ref B/2P 4x8 Size 4.00 x 8.00 m Area 32 m2 Qty	Total £	Element Total £	Ref B/2P 4x9 Size 4.00 x 9.00 m Area 36 m2 Qty	Total £	Element Total £
TWO STOREY														
PITCHED ROOF Continued\.....														
	NR	478.42	1NR	478.42		1NR	478.42		1NR	478.42		1NR	478.42	
	NR	518.08	4NR	2072.32		4NR	2072.32		4NR	2072.32		4NR	2072.32	
	NR	179.51	1NR	179.51		1NR	179.51		1NR	179.51		1NR	179.51	
	NR	150.89	4NR	603.56	**3333.81**	4NR	603.56	**3333.81**	4NR	603.56	**3333.81**	4NR	603.56	**3333.81**
	M2	51.63	20M2	1032.60	**1032.60**	20M2	1032.60	**1032.60**	20M2	1032.60	**1032.60**	20M2	1032.60	**1032.60**
	NR	251.11	2NR	502.22	**502.22**	2NR	502.22	**502.22**	2NR	502.22	**502.22**	2NR	502.22	**502.22**
	M2	19.58	100M2	1958.00	**1958.00**	110M2	2153.80	**2153.80**	120M2	2349.60	**2349.60**	130M2	2545.40	**2545.40**
	M2	35.42	24M2	850.08		28M2	991.76		32M2	1133.44		36M2	1275.12	
	M	11.09	40M	443.60	**1293.68**	44M	487.96	**1479.72**	48M	532.32	**1665.76**	52M	576.68	**1851.80**
	M2	16.34	48M2	784.32	**784.32**	56M2	915.04	**915.04**	64M2	1045.76	**1045.76**	72M2	1176.48	**1176.48**

Specification B
8 m2 - 20 m2

			Ref B/2P 4x2 Size 4.00 x 2.00 m Area 8 m2			Ref B/2P 4x3 Size 4.00 x 3.00 m Area 12 m2			Ref B/2P 4x4 Size 4.00 x 4.00 m Area 16 m2			Ref B/2P 4x5 Size 4.00 x 5.00 m Area 20 m2		
TWO STOREY PITCHED ROOF			Qty	Total £	Element Total £	Qty	Total £	Element Total £	Qty	Total £	Element Total £	Qty	Total £	Element Total £
Element	Unit	Unit Rate £												
SERVICES														
Rainwater pipes	M	26.64	6M	159.84		6M	159.84		6M	159.84		6M	159.84	
Cold water service point	NR	110.52	1NR	110.52		1NR	110.52		1NR	110.52		1NR	110.52	
Hot water service point	NR	191.67	1NR	191.67		1NR	191.67		1NR	191.67		1NR	191.67	
Central heating service point	NR	386.51	2NR	773.02		2NR	773.02		2NR	773.02		2NR	773.02	
Electrical installation	NR	286.50	2NR	573.00	**1808.05**	2NR	573.00	**1808.05**	2NR	573.00	**1808.05**	2NR	573.00	**1808.05**
ALTERATIONS TO EXISTING BUILDINGS														
Opening in existing wall 1.80 m wide 2.00 m high	NR	689.44	2NR	1378.88	**1378.88**									
Opening in existing wall 2.40 m wide 2.00 m high	NR	865.59												
Opening in existing wall 3.00 m wide 2.00 m high	NR	921.26				2NR	1842.52	**1842.52**						
Opening in existing wall 4.00 m wide 2.00 m high	NR	1131.22							2NR	2262.44	**2262.44**			
Opening in existing wall 5.00 m wide 2.00 m high	NR	1341.19										2NR	2682.38	**2682.38**

Specification B 24 m2 - 36 m2

TWO STOREY

PITCHED ROOF Continued\.....

Element	Unit	Unit Rate £	Ref B/2P 4x6 Size 4.00 x 6.00 m Area 24 m2 Qty	Total £	Element Total £	Ref B/2P 4x7 Size 4.00 x 7.00 m Area 28 m2 Qty	Total £	Element Total £	Ref B/2P 4x8 Size 4.00 x 8.00 m Area 32 m2 Qty	Total £	Element Total £	Ref B/2P 4x9 Size 4.00 x 9.00 m Area 36 m2 Qty	Total £	Element Total £
	M	26.64	6M	159.84		6M	159.84		6M	159.84		6M	159.84	
	NR	110.52	1NR	110.52		1NR	110.52		1NR	110.52		1NR	110.52	
	NR	191.67	1NR	191.67		1NR	191.67		1NR	191.67		1NR	191.67	
	NR	386.51	4NR	1546.04		4NR	1546.04		4NR	1546.04		4NR	1546.04	
	NR	286.50	4NR	1146.00	**3154.07**	4NR	1146.00	**3154.07**	4NR	1146.00	**3154.07**	4NR	1146.00	**3154.07**
	NR	689.44												
	NR	865.59	4NR	3462.36	**3462.36**									
	NR	921.26				4NR	3685.04	**3685.04**	4NR	3685.04	**3685.04**			
	NR	1131.22										4NR	4524.88	**4524.88**
	NR	1341.19												

Specification B 8 m2 - 20 m2	Ref B/2P 4x2 Size 4.00 x 2.00 m Area 8 m2 Element Total £	Ref B/2P 4x3 Size 4.00 x 3.00 m Area 12 m2 Element Total £	Ref B/2P 4x4 Size 4.00 x 4.00 m Area 16 m2 Element Total £	Ref B/2P 4x5 Size 4.00 x 5.00 m Area 20 m2 Element Total £
TWO STOREY				
PITCHED ROOF				
SUMMARY				
SUBSTRUCTURE	1738.59	2046.60	2354.61	2662.62
UPPER FLOORS	330.40	537.84	717.12	896.40
ROOF	3006.82	3695.38	4439.36	5212.05
EXTERNAL WALLS	5024.77	5559.32	6093.87	6307.69
EXTERNAL DOORS AND WINDOWS	1995.87	1995.87	1995.87	1995.87
INTERNAL WALLS AND PARTITIONS	-	-	-	-
INTERNAL DOORS	-	-	-	-
WALL FINISHES	1174.80	1370.60	1566.40	1762.20
FLOOR FINISHES	549.52	735.56	921.60	1107.64
CEILING FINISHES	261.44	392.16	522.88	653.60
SERVICES	1808.05	1808.05	1808.05	1808.05
ALTERATIONS TO EXISTING BUILDINGS	1378.88	1842.52	2262.44	2682.38
Sub Total	17269.14	19983.90	22682.20	25088.50
Allowance for unmeasured items and sundries 5%	863.46	999.20	1134.11	1254.43
NET TOTAL excluding Preliminaries, Profit and Overheads	**18132.60**	**20983.10**	**23816.31**	**26342.93**

Specification B 24 m2 - 36 m2	Ref B/2P 4x6 Size 4.00 x 6.00 m Area 24 m2	Ref B/2P 4x7 Size 4.00 x 7.00 m Area 28 m2	Ref B/2P 4x8 Size 4.00 x 8.00 m Area 32 m2	Ref B/2P 4x9 Size 4.00 x 9.00 m Area 36 m2
	Element Total £	Element Total £	Element Total £	Element Total £
TWO STOREY				
PITCHED ROOF				
SUMMARY Continued/.....				
	2970.63	3278.64	3586.65	3894.66
	1075.68	1254.96	1434.24	1613.52
	6081.89	6910.00	7858.74	8765.75
	6735.33	7269.88	7804.43	8338.98
	3333.81	3333.81	3333.81	3333.81
	1032.60	1032.60	1032.60	1032.60
	502.22	502.22	502.22	502.22
	1958.00	2153.80	2349.60	2545.40
	1293.68	1479.72	1665.76	1851.80
	784.32	915.04	1045.76	1176.48
	3154.07	3154.07	3154.07	3154.07
	3462.36	3685.04	3685.04	4524.88
Sub Total	32384.59	34969.78	37452.92	40734.17
Allowance for unmeasured items and sundries 5%	1619.23	1748.49	1872.65	2036.71
NET TOTAL excluding Preliminaries, Profit and Overheads	**34003.82**	**36718.27**	**39325.57**	**42770.88**

Specification B 10 m2 - 25 m2

Element	Unit	Unit Rate £	Ref B/2P 5x2 Size 5.00 x 2.00 m Area 10 m2 Qty	Total £	Element Total £	Ref B/2P 5x3 Size 5.00 x 3.00 m Area 15 m2 Qty	Total £	Element Total £	Ref B/2P 5x4 Size 5.00 x 4.00 m Area 20 m2 Qty	Total £	Element Total £	Ref B/2P 5x5 Size 5.00 x 5.00 m Area 25 m2 Qty	Total £	Element Total £
TWO STOREY														
PITCHED ROOF														
SUBSTRUCTURE														
Strip footings	M	124.73	13M	1621.49		14M	1746.22		15M	1870.95		16M	1995.68	
Solid ground floor	M2	45.82	10M2	458.20	**2079.69**	15M2	687.30	**2433.52**	20M2	916.40	**2787.35**	25M2	1145.50	**3141.18**
UPPER FLOORS														
Timber floor construction 50 x 150 mm joists	M2	41.30	10M2	413.00	**413.00**									
Timber floor construction 50 x 200 mm joists	M2	44.82				15M2	672.30	**672.30**	20M2	896.40	**896.40**			
Timber floor construction 75 x 250 mm joists	M2	66.47										25M2	1661.75	**1661.75**
ROOF														
Pitched roof construction	M2	55.42	19M2	1052.98		26M2	1440.92		34M2	1884.28		42M2	2327.64	
Work to top of external wall	M	23.71	13M	308.23		14M	331.94		15M	355.65		16M	379.36	
Concrete tile roofing	M2	23.48	23M2	540.04		32M2	751.36		44M2	1033.12		52M2	1220.96	
Work to hip	M	41.73	10M	417.30		12M	500.76		14M	584.22		15M	625.95	
Work to eaves	M	23.22	14M	325.08		15M	348.30		16M	371.52		17M	394.74	
Fascia and eaves soffit	M	42.61	14M	596.54		15M	639.15		16M	681.76		17M	724.37	
Gutters and fittings	M	18.68	14M	261.52	**3501.69**	15M	280.20	**4292.63**	16M	298.88	**5209.43**	17M	317.56	**5990.58**

Specification B 30 m2 - 45 m2			Ref B/2P 5x6 Size 5.00 x 6.00 m Area 30 m2			Ref B/2P 5x7 Size 5.00 x 7.00 m Area 35 m2			Ref B/2P 5x8 Size 5.00 x 8.00 m Area 40 m2			Ref B/2P 5x9 Size 5.00 x 9.00 m Area 45 m2		
			Qty	Total £	Element Total £	Qty	Total £	Element Total £	Qty	Total £	Element Total £	Qty	Total £	Element Total £
TWO STOREY														
PITCHED ROOF Continued\.....														
Element	Unit	Unit Rate £												
	M	124.73	17M	2120.41		18M	2245.14		19M	2369.87		20M	2494.60	
	M2	45.82	30M2	1374.60	**3495.01**	35M2	1603.70	**3848.84**	40M2	1832.80	**4202.67**	45M2	2061.90	**4556.50**
	M2	41.30												
	M2	44.82	30M2	1344.60	**1344.60**	35M2	1568.70	**1568.70**	40M2	1792.80	**1792.80**			
	M2	66.47										45M2	2991.15	**2991.15**
	M2	55.42	51M2	2826.42		60M2	3325.20		70M2	3879.40		80M2	4433.60	
	M	23.71	17M	403.07		18M	426.78		19M	450.49		20M	474.20	
	M2	23.48	62M2	1455.76		74M2	1737.52		86M2	2019.28		99M2	2324.52	
	M	41.73	17M	709.41		18M	751.14		20M	834.60		21M	876.33	
	M	23.22	18M	417.96		19M	441.18		20M	464.40		21M	487.62	
	M	42.61	18M	766.98		19M	809.59		20M	852.20		21M	894.81	
	M	18.68	18M	336.24	**6915.84**	19M	354.92	**7846.33**	20M	373.60	**8873.97**	21M	392.28	**9883.36**

Specification B 10 m2 - 25 m2			Ref B/2P 5x2 Size 5.00 x 2.00 m Area 10 m2			Ref B/2P 5x3 Size 5.00 x 3.00 m Area 15 m2			Ref B/2P 5x4 Size 5.00 x 4.00 m Area 20 m2			Ref B/2P 5x5 Size 5.00 x 5.00 m Area 25 m2		
			Qty	Total £	Element Total £	Qty	Total £	Element Total £	Qty	Total £	Element Total £	Qty	Total £	Element Total £
TWO STOREY														
PITCHED ROOF														
Element	Unit	Unit Rate £												
EXTERNAL WALLS														
Brick and block cavity wall	M2	106.91	57M2	6093.87	**6093.87**	62M2	6628.42	**6628.42**	67M2	7162.97	**7162.97**	72M2	7697.52	**7697.52**
EXTERNAL DOORS AND WINDOWS														
External door	NR	478.42	1NR	478.42		1NR	478.42		1NR	478.42		1NR	478.42	
Windows	NR	518.08	2NR	1036.16		2NR	1036.16		2NR	1036.16		2NR	1036.16	
Opening in cavity wall for door	NR	179.51	1NR	179.51		1NR	179.51		1NR	179.51		1NR	179.51	
Opening in cavity wall for window	NR	150.89	2NR	301.78	**1995.87**	2NR	301.78	**1995.87**	2NR	301.78	**1995.87**	2NR	301.78	**1995.87**
INTERNAL WALLS AND PARTITIONS														
Stud partitions	M2	51.63												
INTERNAL DOORS														
Softwood flush door	NR	251.11												
WALL FINISHES														
Plaster & decoration	M2	19.58	70M2	1370.60	**1370.60**	80M2	1566.40	**1566.40**	90M2	1762.20	**1762.20**	100M2	1958.00	**1958.00**

Specification B 30 m2 - 45 m2

TWO STOREY

PITCHED ROOF Continued\.....

Element	Unit	Unit Rate £	Ref B/2P 5x6 Size 5.00 x 6.00 m Area 30 m2 Qty	Total £	Element Total £	Ref B/2P 5x7 Size 5.00 x 7.00 m Area 35 m2 Qty	Total £	Element Total £	Ref B/2P 5x8 Size 5.00 x 8.00 m Area 40 m2 Qty	Total £	Element Total £	Ref B/2P 5x9 Size 5.00 x 9.00 m Area 45 m2 Qty	Total £	Element Total £
	M2	106.91	73M2	7804.43	**7804.43**	78M2	8338.98	**8338.98**	83M2	8873.53	**8873.53**	88M2	9408.08	**9408.08**
	NR	478.42	1NR	478.42		1NR	478.42		1NR	478.42		1NR	478.42	
	NR	518.08	4NR	2072.32		4NR	2072.32		4NR	2072.32		4NR	2072.32	
	NR	179.51	1NR	179.51		1NR	179.51		1NR	179.51		1NR	179.51	
	NR	150.89	4NR	603.56	**3333.81**	4NR	603.56	**3333.81**	4NR	603.56	**3333.81**	4NR	603.56	**3333.81**
	M2	51.63	26M2	1342.38	**1342.38**	26M2	1342.38	**1342.38**	26M2	1342.38	**1342.38**	26M2	1342.38	**1342.38**
	NR	251.11	2NR	502.22	**502.22**	2NR	502.22	**502.22**	2NR	502.22	**502.22**	2NR	502.22	**502.22**
	M2	19.58	110M2	2153.80	**2153.80**	120M2	2349.60	**2349.60**	130M2	2545.40	**2545.40**	140M2	2741.20	**2741.20**

Specification B 10 m2 - 25 m2			Ref B/2P 5x2 Size 5.00 x 2.00 m Area 10 m2			Ref B/2P 5x3 Size 5.00 x 3.00 m Area 15 m2			Ref B/2P 5x4 Size 5.00 x 4.00 m Area 20 m2			Ref B/2P 5x5 Size 5.00 x 5.00 m Area 25 m2		
			Qty	Total £	Element Total £	Qty	Total £	Element Total £	Qty	Total £	Element Total £	Qty	Total £	Element Total £
TWO STOREY														
PITCHED ROOF														
Element	Unit	Unit Rate £												
FLOOR FINISHES														
Thermoplastic tiles on screed	M2	35.42	10M2	354.20		15M2	531.30		20M2	708.40		25M2	885.50	
Softwood skirting	M	11.09	28M	310.52	**664.72**	32M	354.88	**886.18**	36M	399.24	**1107.64**	40M	443.60	**1329.10**
CEILING FINISHES														
Plasterboard and Artex	M2	16.34	20M2	326.80	**326.80**	30M2	490.20	**490.20**	40M2	653.60	**653.60**	50M2	817.00	**817.00**
SERVICES														
Rainwater pipes	M	26.64	6M	159.84		6M	159.84		6M	159.84		6M	159.84	
Cold water service point	NR	110.52	1NR	110.52		1NR	110.52		1NR	110.52		1NR	110.52	
Hot water service point	NR	191.67	1NR	191.67		1NR	191.67		1NR	191.67		1NR	191.67	
Central heating service point	NR	386.51	2NR	773.02		2NR	773.02		2NR	773.02		2NR	773.02	
Electrical installation	NR	286.50	2NR	573.00	**1808.05**	2NR	573.00	**1808.05**	2NR	573.00	**1808.05**	2NR	573.00	**1808.05**

Specification B
30 m2 - 45 m2

Element	Unit	Unit Rate £	Ref B/2P 5x6 Size 5.00 x 6.00 m Area 30 m2 Qty	Total £	Element Total £	Ref B/2P 5x7 Size 5.00 x 7.00 m Area 35 m2 Qty	Total £	Element Total £	Ref B/2P 5x8 Size 5.00 x 8.00 m Area 40 m2 Qty	Total £	Element Total £	Ref B/2P 5x9 Size 5.00 x 9.00 m Area 45 m2 Qty	Total £	Element Total £
TWO STOREY														
PITCHED ROOF Continued\.....														
	M2	35.42	30M2	1062.60		35M2	1239.70		40M2	1416.80		45M2	1593.90	
	M	11.09	44M	487.96	**1550.56**	48M	532.32	**1772.02**	52M	576.68	**1993.48**	56M	621.04	**2214.94**
	M2	16.34	60M2	980.40	**980.40**	70M2	1143.80	**1143.80**	80M2	1307.20	**1307.20**	90M2	1470.60	**1470.60**
	M	26.64	6M	159.84		6M	159.84		6M	159.84		6M	159.84	
	NR	110.52	1NR	110.52		1NR	110.52		1NR	110.52		1NR	110.52	
	NR	191.67	1NR	191.67		1NR	191.67		1NR	191.67		1NR	191.67	
	NR	386.51	4NR	1546.04		4NR	1546.04		4NR	1546.04		4NR	1546.04	
	NR	286.50	4NR	1146.00	**3154.07**	4NR	1146.00	**3154.07**	4NR	1146.00	**3154.07**	4NR	1146.00	**3154.07**

Specification B 10 m2 - 25 m2

TWO STOREY

PITCHED ROOF

Element	Unit	Unit Rate £	Ref B/2P 5x2 Size 5.00 x 2.00 m Area 10 m2 Qty	Total £	Element Total £	Ref B/2P 5x3 Size 5.00 x 3.00 m Area 15 m2 Qty	Total £	Element Total £	Ref B/2P 5x4 Size 5.00 x 4.00 m Area 20 m2 Qty	Total £	Element Total £	Ref B/2P 5x5 Size 5.00 x 5.00 m Area 25 m2 Qty	Total £	Element Total £
ALTERATIONS TO EXISTING BUILDINGS														
Opening in existing wall 1.80 m wide 2.00 m high	NR	689.44	2NR	1378.88	**1378.88**									
Opening in existing wall 2.40 m wide 2.00 m high	NR	865.59												
Opening in existing wall 3.00 m wide 2.00 m high	NR	921.26				2NR	1842.52	**1842.52**						
Opening in existing wall 4.00 m wide 2.00 m high	NR	1131.22							2NR	2262.44	**2262.44**			
Opening in existing wall 5.00 m wide 2.00 m high	NR	1341.19										2NR	2682.38	**2682.38**

Specification B 30 m2 - 45 m2

TWO STOREY

PITCHED ROOF Continued\.....

Element	Unit	Unit Rate £	Ref B/2P 5x6 Size 5.00 x 6.00 m Area 30 m2 Qty	Total £	Element Total £	Ref B/2P 5x7 Size 5.00 x 7.00 m Area 35 m2 Qty	Total £	Element Total £	Ref B/2P 5x8 Size 5.00 x 8.00 m Area 40 m2 Qty	Total £	Element Total £	Ref B/2P 5x9 Size 5.00 x 9.00 m Area 45 m2 Qty	Total £	Element Total £
	NR	689.44												
	NR	865.59	4NR	3462.36	**3462.36**									
	NR	921.26				4NR	3685.04	**3685.04**	4NR	3685.04	**3685.04**			
	NR	1131.22										4NR	4524.88	**4524.88**
	NR	1341.19												

Specification B 10 m2 - 25 m2	Ref B/2P 5x2 Size 5.00 x 2.00 m Area 10 m2	Ref B/2P 5x3 Size 5.00 x 3.00 m Area 15 m2	Ref B/2P 5x4 Size 5.00 x 4.00 m Area 20 m2	Ref B/2P 5x5 Size 5.00 x 5.00 m Area 25 m2
	Element Total £	Element Total £	Element Total £	Element Total £
TWO STOREY				
PITCHED ROOF				
SUMMARY				
SUBSTRUCTURE	2079.69	2433.52	2787.35	3141.18
UPPER FLOORS	413.00	672.30	896.40	1661.75
ROOF	3501.69	4292.63	5209.43	5990.58
EXTERNAL WALLS	6093.87	6628.42	7162.97	7697.52
EXTERNAL DOORS AND WINDOWS	1995.87	1995.87	1995.87	1995.87
INTERNAL WALLS AND PARTITIONS	-	-	-	-
INTERNAL DOORS	-	-	-	-
WALL FINISHES	1370.60	1566.40	1762.20	1958.00
FLOOR FINISHES	664.72	886.18	1107.64	1329.10
CEILING FINISHES	326.80	490.20	653.60	817.00
SERVICES	1808.05	1808.05	1808.05	1808.05
ALTERATIONS TO EXISTING BUILDINGS	1378.88	1842.52	2262.44	2682.38
Sub Total	19633.17	22616.09	25645.95	29081.43
Allowance for unmeasured items and sundries 5%	981.66	1130.80	1282.30	1454.07
NET TOTAL excluding Preliminaries, Profit and Overheads	**20614.83**	**23746.89**	**26928.25**	**30535.50**

Specification B 30 m2 - 45 m2	Ref B/2P 5x6 Size 5.00 x 6.00 m Area 30 m2	Ref B/2P 5x7 Size 5.00 x 7.00 m Area 35 m2	Ref B/2P 5x8 Size 5.00 x 8.00 m Area 40 m2	Ref B/2P 5x9 Size 5.00 x 9.00 m Area 45 m2
	Element Total £	Element Total £	Element Total £	Element Total £
TWO STOREY				
PITCHED ROOF				
SUMMARY Continued/.....				
	3495.01	3848.84	4202.67	4556.50
	1344.60	1568.70	1792.80	2991.15
	6915.84	7846.33	8873.97	9883.36
	7804.43	8338.98	8873.53	9408.08
	3333.81	3333.81	3333.81	3333.81
	1342.38	1342.38	1342.38	1342.38
	502.22	502.22	502.22	502.22
	2153.80	2349.60	2545.40	2741.20
	1550.56	1772.02	1993.48	2214.94
	980.40	1143.80	1307.20	1470.60
	3154.07	3154.07	3154.07	3154.07
	3462.36	3685.04	3685.04	4524.88
Sub Total	36039.48	38885.79	41606.57	46123.19
Allowance for unmeasured items and sundries 5%	1801.97	1944.29	2080.33	2306.16
NET TOTAL excluding Preliminaries, Profit and Overheads	**37841.45**	**40830.08**	**43686.90**	**48429.35**

STANDARD ESTIMATES

WHAT IF THE STANDARD ESTIMATE DOES NOT FIT YOUR REQUIREMENT?

Even with 256 fully priced standard estimates, it is possible that you will not be able to locate an estimate which exactly matches your requirements. In this case, you should refer to the following chapter. Chapter 5 contains details of all the prices used in the standard estimates including drawings giving details and sections of the building extension types.

An important feature of Chapter 5 is the selection of worked examples which show clearly and concisely how to modify the standard estimates for your own needs.

5

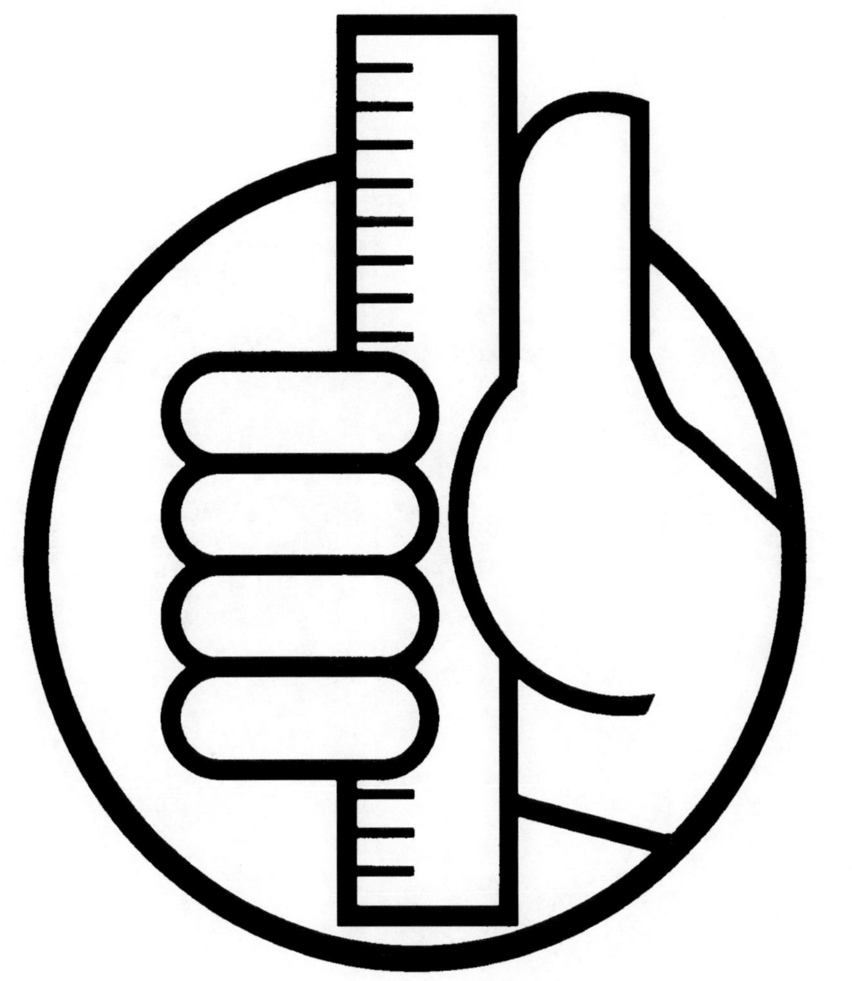

Cost details and adjustments

CHAPTER 5

COST DETAILS AND ADJUSTMENTS

COST DETAILS

This chapter provides the detailed costs of all the items listed in the Standard Estimates. Whereas the standard estimates show all-up items with their total price per m, m2 or Nr the detailed cost breakdowns included in this chapter provides a full analysis of those all-up items.

For example, the standard estimates include an item of Fascia and Eaves Soffit with a total price per metre run of £48.27 (Specification A). The detailed cost breakdown shows every item of work required and how the unit rate of £48.27 has been built up.

The example below reproduces the full analysis of the Fascia and Eaves Soffit item. The columns are numbered 1-14 and lines of text lettered A-J so that the function of each one may be explained.

	1	2	3	4	5	6	7	8	9	10	11	12	13	14
		Qty	Hours per unit L=Labour P=Plant	Total Labour Time	Labour Rate Per Hour	Total Value of Labour £	Total Plant Time	Plant Rate Per Hour	Total Value of Plant £	Mat Unit Rate	Total Value of Material £	S/c Unit Rate	Total Value of s/c spec. £	**TOTAL £**
A	Fascia and eaves soffit													
B	**12 mm Supalux soffit 200 mm wide; 25 mm exterior grade plywood fascia 250 mm high; sawn softwood bearers; painted finish.**													
C	**1 METRE RUN OF FASCIA INCLUDES (A)**													
D	25 mm exterior grade plywood fascia 250 mm wide	1.000m	L=0.43	0.43	15.43	6.63				6.29	6.29			**12.92**
E	12 mm 'Supalux' soffit 200 mm wide	1.000m	L=0.50	0.50	15.43	7.72				6.53	6.53			**14.25**
F	Sawn softwood bearers 38 x 50 mm	1.540m	L=0.08	0.12	15.43	1.85				0.81	1.25			**3.10**
G	Prepare, knot, prime, stop, one undercoat and one coat alkyd based paint to wood surfaces externally	0.490m2	L=0.61	0.30	15.43	4.63				2.18	1.07			**5.70**
H	PVCu one piece soffit ventilator	2.000Nr	L=0.26	0.53	15.43	8.18				2.06	4.12			**12.30**
J	**TOTALS**			**1.88**		**£29.01**					**£19.26**			**£48.27**

Column 1

Line A	identifies the item as "Fascia and Eaves soffit"
Line B	gives a more detailed description
Line C	shows that the analysis and cost is for a metre run - Specification A
Lines D-H	lists the 5 items of work included in Fascia and Eaves soffits
Line J	shows the totals ie

Col 4	- Total labour time	=	1.88 hours
Col 6	- Total labour cost	=	£29.01
Col 11	- Total material cost	=	£19.26
Col 14	- Total cost of item ie £29.01 plus £19.26	=	£48.27

Column 2 Shows the quantity required of each of the 5 items D-H.

Column 3 Indicates the labour or plant time per m, m2 or Nr.

Column 4 Gives the total labour time required ie the quantity (Col 2) multiplied by the time per unit (Col 3).

Column 5 Shows the labour hourly rate used.

Column 6 Shows the total value of labour ie the total labour time (Col 4) multiplied by the labour hourly rate (Col 5).

Column 7 Gives the total plant time required ie the quantity (Col 2) multiplied by the time per unit (Col 3).

Column 8 Shows the plant hire rate per hour.

Column 9 Shows the total value of plant ie the total plant time (Col 7) multiplied by the plant hire rate per hour (Col 8).

Column 10 Shows the value of material required per m, m2 or Nr.

Column 11 Shows the total value of material ie the quantity (Col 2) multiplied by the value of material required per m, m2 or Nr (Col 10).

Column 12 Gives the unit rate for any work to be undertaken by sub-contractors.

Column 13 Shows the total value of work undertaken by sub-contractors ie quantity (Col 2) multiplied by sub-contractor unit rate (Col 12).

Column 14 Shows total value of columns 6, 9, 11 and 13.

The detailed cost breakdown of each item provides the builder with two essential facilities. Firstly he can easily identify the total cost of labour, plant, materials and subcontractors. Secondly, he has the opportunity to compare these costs with previous contracts and, if necessary, adjust all or any of these costs to suit his own particular circumstances.

The detailed cost breakdowns follow. Where appropriate, detailed drawings and sections have been provided to illustrate and compliment the item description.

IMPORTANT NOTE: Some differences in prices will be noticed between unit costs shown in the standard estimates and those shown in the detailed breakdowns. These differences result from rounding up of calculations on the Database from 3 to 2 decimal places.

Item Build Ups	Qty	Hours per unit L=Labour P=Plant	Total Labour Time	Labour Rate Per Hour	Total Value of Labour £	Total Plant Time	Plant Rate Per Hour	Total Value of Plant £	Mat Unit Rate	Total Value of Material £	S/c Unit Rate	Total Value of s/c spec. £	TOTAL £
SUBSTRUCTURE Strip footings													
Hand excavation; concrete bed 300 mm thick; brick and block cavity wall 750 mm high; cavity filled with concrete; damp proof course.													
1 METRE RUN OF STRIP FOOTING INCLUDES (A)													
Excavate topsoil by hand, average 150 mm	0.625m2	L=0.32	0.20	11.39	2.28								**2.28**
Excavate trench by hand	0.470m3	L=3.47	1.63	11.39	18.57								**18.57**
Disposal of excavated material on site	0.543m3	P=0.06				0.03	47.06	1.41					**1.41**
Support to sides of excavation	1.500m2	L=0.17	0.25	14.24	3.56				0.55	0.83			**4.39**
Level and compact bottom of excavation	0.600m2	L=0.08	0.05	11.39	0.57								**0.57**
Part refill trench by hand using "Whacker"	0.020m3	L=1.26 P=0.22	0.03	11.39	0.34		3.61						**0.34**
Hardcore filling in trench	0.130m3	L=2.05 P=0.28	0.27	11.39	3.08	0.04	3.61	0.14	23.54	3.06			**6.28**
Plain concrete grade C20/25 in trench	0.180m3	L=1.43	0.26	11.39	2.96				94.94	17.09			**20.05**
Concrete in filling to cavity wall	0.045m3	L=4.18	0.19	11.39	2.16				94.89	4.27			**6.43**
Class A engineering brick PC £493.42/1000 in cement mortar 1:3 in skin of hollow wall	0.750m2	L=1.55	1.16	21.13	24.51				33.43	25.07			**49.58**
Form cavity 75 mm wide with 5 Nr 200 mm galvanised butterfly ties per m2	0.750m2	L=0.04	0.03	21.13	0.63				0.35	0.26			**0.89**
140 mm solid concrete blocks in cement mortar 1:3 in skin of hollow wall	0.750m2	L=1.16	0.87	23.97	20.85				13.13	9.85			**30.70**
Terracotta air brick size 215 x 65 mm	0.500Nr	L=0.07	0.03	21.13	0.63				0.94	0.47			**1.10**
Polythene horizontal DPC 100 mm wide	1.000m	L=0.02	0.02	21.13	0.42				0.29	0.29			**0.71**
Polythene horizontal DPC 150 mm wide	1.000m	L=0.03	0.03	21.13	0.63				0.46	0.46			**1.09**
			5.02		**£81.19**	**0.07**		**£1.55**		**£61.65**			**£144.39**

[A] Substructure

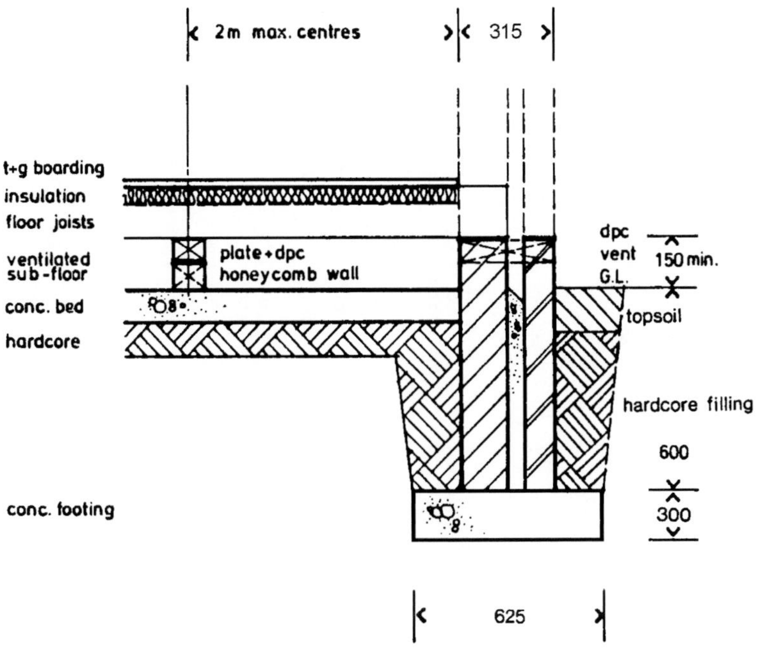
2m max. centres
315
t+g boarding
insulation
floor joists
ventilated sub-floor
conc. bed
hardcore
plate+dpc
honeycomb wall
dpc
vent
G.L.
150 min.
topsoil
hardcore filling
600
300
conc. footing
625

[A] Upper Floor

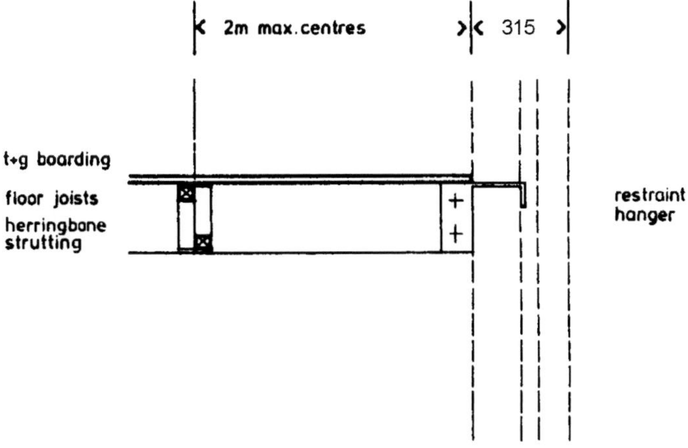
2m max. centres
315
t+g boarding
floor joists
herringbone strutting
restraint hanger

Item Build Ups	Qty	Hours per unit L=Labour P=Plant	Total Labour Time	Labour Rate Per Hour	Total Value of Labour £	Total Plant Time	Plant Rate Per Hour	Total Value of Plant £	Mat Unit Rate	Total Value of Material £	S/c Unit Rate	Total Value of s/c spec. £	TOTAL £
SUBSTRUCTURE cont/... Strip footings cont/...													
Hand excavation; concrete bed 300 mm thick; brick and block cavity wall 750 mm high; cavity filled with concrete; damp proof course.													
1 METRE RUN OF STRIP FOOTING INCLUDES (B)													
Excavate topsoil by hand, average 150 mm	0.575m2	L=0.32	0.18	11.39	2.05								**2.05**
Excavate trench by hand	0.430m3	L=3.47	1.49	11.39	16.97								**16.97**
Disposal of excavated material on site	0.496m3	P=0.06				0.03	47.06	1.41					**1.41**
Support to sides of excavation	1.500m2	L=0.17	0.25	14.24	3.56				0.55	0.83			**4.39**
Level and compact bottom of excavation	0.580m2	L=0.08	0.05	11.39	0.57								**0.57**
Part refill trench by hand using "Whacker"	0.020m3	L=1.26 P=0.22	0.03	11.39	0.34		3.61						**0.34**
Hardcore filling in trench	0.135m3	L=2.05 P=0.28	0.28	11.39	3.19	0.04	3.61	0.14	23.56	3.18			**6.51**
Plain concrete grade C20/25 in trench	0.173m3	L=1.43	0.25	11.39	2.85				94.97	16.43			**19.28**
Concrete in filling to cavity wall	0.045m3	L=4.18	0.19	11.39	2.16				94.89	4.27			**6.43**
Common bricks PC £311.01/1000 in cement mortar 1:3 in skin of hollow wall	0.750m2	L=1.44	1.08	21.13	22.82				21.92	16.44			**39.26**
Form cavity 75 mm wide with 5 Nr 200 mm galvanised butterfly ties per m2	0.750m2	L=0.04	0.03	21.13	0.63				0.35	0.26			**0.89**
100 mm Solid concrete blocks in gauged mortar 1:2:9 in skin of hollow wall	0.750m2	L=1.05	0.79	23.97	18.94				8.76	6.57			**25.51**
Polythene horizontal DPC 100 mm wide	2.000m	L=0.02	0.04	21.13	0.85				0.29	0.58			**1.43**
			4.66		**£74.93**	**0.07**		**£1.55**		**£48.56**			**£125.04**

[B] Substructure

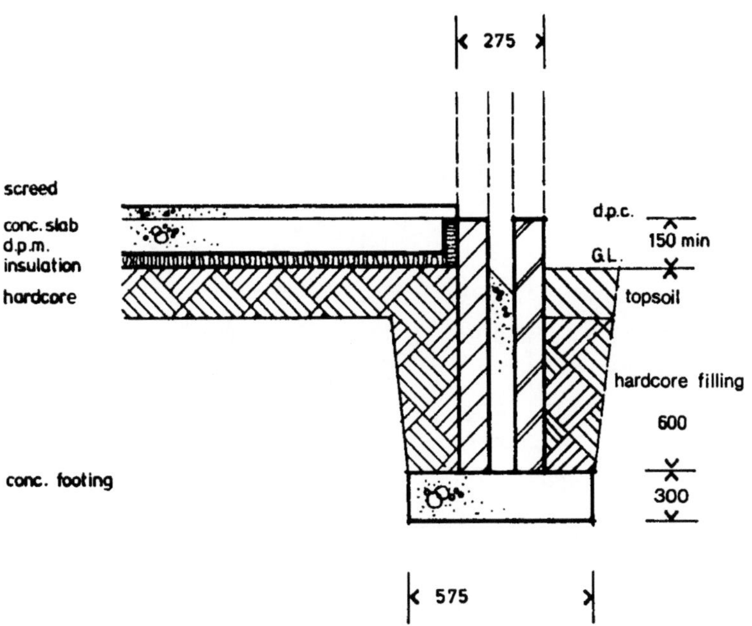

[B] Upper Floor

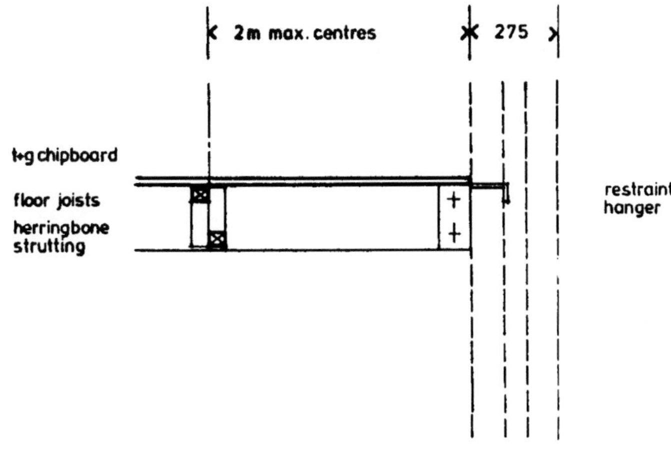

Item Build Ups	Qty	Hours per unit L=Labour P=Plant	Total Labour Time	Labour Rate Per Hour	Total Value of Labour £	Total Plant Time	Plant Rate Per Hour	Total Value of Plant £	Mat Unit Rate	Total Value of Material £	S/c Unit Rate	Total Value of s/c spec. £	TOTAL £
SUBSTRUCTURE cont/... Solid ground floor													
Compacting ground; hardcore filling 150 mm thick; concrete bed 100 mm thick; 1200 gauge polythene sheet; insulation.													
1 SQUARE METRE OF SOLID FLOOR INCLUDES (B)													
Excavate topsoil by hand, average 150 mm	1.000m2	L=0.32	0.32	11.39	3.64								**3.64**
Disposal of excavated material on site	0.150m3	P=0.06				0.01	47.06	0.47					**0.47**
Level and compact ground with a vibrating roller	2.000m2	L=0.14 P=0.06	0.27	11.39	3.08	0.11	17.67	1.94					**5.02**
Hardcore filling by hand 150 mm average thick	1.000m2	L=0.48 P=0.08	0.48	11.39	5.47	0.08	17.67	1.41	3.53	3.53			**10.41**
Blind surfaces of hardcore with sand 25 mm thick	1.000m2	L=0.09 P=0.03	0.09	11.39	1.03	0.03	17.67	0.53	1.50	1.50			**3.06**
Plain concrete grade C20/25 in 100 - 150 mm bed	0.100m3	L=1.65	0.17	11.39	1.94				95.00	9.50			**11.44**
1200 Gauge polythene sheet	1.000m2	L=0.03	0.03	11.39	0.34				0.30	0.30			**0.64**
65 mm Polyfoam insulation board	1.000m2	L=0.16	0.16	18.76	3.00				10.20	10.20			**13.20**
			1.52		**£18.50**	**0.23**		**£4.35**		**£25.03**			**£47.88**

Item Build Ups

Item Build Ups	Qty	Hours per unit L=Labour P=Plant	Total Labour Time	Labour Rate Per Hour	Total Value of Labour £	Total Plant Time	Plant Rate Per Hour	Total Value of Plant £	Mat Unit Rate	Total Value of Material £	S/c Unit Rate	Total Value of s/c spec. £	TOTAL £
SUBSTRUCTURE cont/... Hollow ground floor													
Compacting ground; hardcore filling 100 mm thick; concrete bed 150 mm thick; half brick honeycomb wall 300 mm high; damp proof course; softwood wall plates bedded on brick wall; softwood floor joists at 400 mm centres; 70 mm insulation wedged between joists; 19 mm thick tongued and grooved boarding.													
1 SQUARE METRE OF HOLLOW FLOOR INCLUDES (A)													
Excavate topsoil by hand, average 150 mm	1.000m2	L=0.32	0.32	11.39	3.64								**3.64**
Disposal of excavated material on site	0.150m3	P=0.06				0.01	47.06	0.47					**0.47**
Level and compact ground with a vibrating roller	2.000m2	L=0.14 P=0.06	0.27	11.39	3.08	0.11	17.67	1.94					**5.02**
Hardcore filling by hand 100 mm average thick	1.000m2	L=0.35 P=0.08	0.35	11.39	3.99	0.08	17.67	1.41	2.35	2.35			**7.75**
Plain concrete grade C20/25 in 100 - 150 mm bed	0.150m3	L=1.65	0.25	11.39	2.85				94.93	14.24			**17.09**
Common bricks PC £311.01/1000 in cement mortar 1:3 in half brick honeycomb wall	0.100m2	L=1.76	0.18	21.13	3.80				21.90	2.19			**5.99**
Polythene horizontal DPC 100 mm wide	0.400m	L=0.02	0.01	21.13	0.21				0.28	0.11			**0.32**
Bed wallplate 100 mm wide in cement mortar 1:3	0.400m	L=0.08	0.03	21.13	0.63				0.13	0.05			**0.68**
Sawn softwood wallplate 50 x 100 mm	0.400m	L=0.20	0.08	15.43	1.23				1.48	0.59			**1.82**
Sawn softwood floor joists 50 x 150 mm	3.000m	L=0.15	0.45	15.43	6.94				2.23	6.69			**13.63**
Insulation 70 mm thick, wedged between joists	1.000m2	L=0.18	0.18	15.43	2.78				4.65	4.65			**7.43**
Wrought softwood tongued and grooved floor boarding 19 mm thick	1.000m2	L=0.86	0.86	15.43	13.27				14.72	14.72			**27.99**
			2.98		**£42.42**	**0.20**		**£3.82**		**£45.59**			**£91.83**

Item Build Ups	Qty	Hours per unit L=Labour P=Plant	Total Labour Time	Labour Rate Per Hour	Total Value of Labour £	Total Plant Time	Plant Rate Per Hour	Total Value of Plant £	Mat Unit Rate	Total Value of Material £	S/c Unit Rate	Total Value of s/c spec. £	TOTAL £
UPPER FLOORS Suspended timber floors													
N.B. The size of floor joist will depend on the span. Three examples of suspended floor are shown below each with a different size floor joist. The standard estimates will clearly show which of these examples has been used.													
25 mm thick tongued and grooved boarding; 50 x 50 mm herring bone strutting; sawn softwood floor joists at 400 mm centres; metal hangers built in.													
1 SQUARE METRE OF SUSPENDED FLOOR WITH 50 X 150 MM JOISTS INCLUDES (A)													
Sawn softwood floor joists 50 x 150 mm	2.800m	L=0.15	0.42	15.43	6.48				2.23	6.24			**12.72**
Sawn softwood herring bone strutting 50 x 50 mm to 150 mm deep joists at mid span	0.420m	L=0.45	0.19	15.43	2.93				1.52	0.64			**3.57**
Wrought softwood tongued and grooved floor boarding 25 mm thick	1.000m2	L=0.86	0.86	15.43	13.27				20.15	20.15			**33.42**
15 mm wallboard underlay	1.000m2	L=0.33	0.33	15.43	5.09				3.09	3.09			**8.18**
Expanded Metal Co. SPH Joist hangers type 'S' for 50 mm joists 150 mm deep built in	2.000Nr	L=0.09	0.18	15.43	2.78				3.13	6.26			**9.04**
100 mm acoustic insulation laid between joists	1.000m2	L=0.35	0.35	15.43	5.40				5.49	5.49			**10.89**
			2.33		**£35.95**					**£41.87**			**£77.82**

Item Build Ups	Qty	Hours per unit L=Labour P=Plant	Total Labour Time	Labour Rate Per Hour	Total Value of Labour £	Total Plant Time	Plant Rate Per Hour	Total Value of Plant £	Mat Unit Rate	Total Value of Material £	S/c Unit Rate	Total Value of s/c spec. £	TOTAL £
UPPER FLOORS cont/... Suspended timber floors cont/...													
1 SQUARE METRE OF SUSPENDED FLOOR WITH 50 X 200 MM JOISTS INCLUDES (A)													
Sawn softwood floor joists 50 x 200 mm	2.800m	L=0.16	0.45	15.43	6.94				2.96	8.29			**15.23**
Sawn softwood herring bone strutting 50 x 50 mm to 250 mm deep joists at mid span	0.420m	L=0.45	0.19	15.43	2.93				1.52	0.64			**3.57**
Wrought softwood tongued and grooved floor boarding 25 mm thick	1.000m2	L=0.86	0.86	15.43	13.27				20.15	20.15			**33.42**
15 mm wallboard underlay	1.000m2	L=0.33	0.33	15.43	5.09				3.09	3.09			**8.18**
Expanded Metal Co. SPH Joist hangers type 'S' for 50 mm joists 200 mm deep built in	2.000Nr	L=0.09	0.18	15.43	2.78				3.63	7.26			**10.04**
100 mm acoustic insulation laid between joists	1.000m2	L=0.35	0.35	15.43	5.40				5.49	5.49			**10.89**
			2.36		**£36.41**					**£44.92**			**£81.33**
1 SQUARE METRE OF SUSPENDED FLOOR WITH 75 X 250 MM JOISTS INCLUDES (A)													
Sawn softwood floor joists 75 x 250 mm	2.800m	L=0.29	0.81	15.43	12.50				7.16	20.05			**32.55**
Sawn softwood herring bone strutting 50 x 50 mm to 250 mm deep joists at mid span	0.420m	L=0.45	0.19	15.43	2.93				1.52	0.64			**3.57**
Wrought softwood tongued and grooved floor boarding 25 mm thick	1.000m2	L=0.86	0.86	15.43	13.27				20.15	20.15			**33.42**
15 mm wallboard underlay	1.000m2	L=0.33	0.33	15.43	5.09				3.09	3.09			**8.18**
Expanded Metal Co. SPH Joist hangers type 'S' for 75 mm joists 250 mm deep built in	2.000Nr	L=0.12	0.23	15.43	3.55				5.47	10.94			**14.49**
100 mm acoustic insulation laid between joists	1.000m2	L=0.35	0.35	15.43	5.40				5.49	5.49			**10.89**
			2.77		**£42.74**					**£60.36**			**£103.10**

Item Build Ups	Qty	Hours per unit L=Labour P=Plant	Total Labour Time	Labour Rate Per Hour	Total Value of Labour £	Total Plant Time	Plant Rate Per Hour	Total Value of Plant £	Mat Unit Rate	Total Value of Material £	S/c Unit Rate	Total Value of s/c spec. £	TOTAL £
UPPER FLOORS cont/... Suspended timber floors cont/...													
N.B. The size of the floor joist will depend on the span. Three examples of suspended floor are shown below each with a different size floor joist. The standard estimates will clearly show which one of these examples has been used.													
22 mm thick tongued and grooved chipboard; 50 x 50 mm herring bone strutting; sawn softwood floor joists at 400 mm centres; metal hangers built in.													
1 SQUARE METRE OF SUSPENDED FLOOR WITH 50 X 150 MM JOISTS INCLUDES (B)													
Sawn softwood floor joists 50 x 150 mm	2.800m	L=0.15	0.42	15.43	6.48				2.23	6.24			**12.72**
Sawn softwood herring bone strutting 50 x 50 mm to 150 mm deep joists at mid span	0.420m	L=0.45	0.19	15.43	2.93				1.52	0.64			**3.57**
Chipboard tongued and grooved floor boarding 22 mm thick	1.000m2	L=0.44	0.44	15.43	6.79				9.14	9.14			**15.93**
Expanded Metal Co. SPH Joist hangers type 'S' for 50 mm joists 150 mm deep built in	2.000Nr	L=0.09	0.18	15.43	2.78				3.13	6.26			**9.04**
			1.23		**£18.98**					**£22.28**			**£41.26**

Item Build Ups	Qty	Hours per unit L=Labour P=Plant	Total Labour Time	Labour Rate Per Hour	Total Value of Labour £	Total Plant Time	Plant Rate Per Hour	Total Value of Plant £	Mat Unit Rate	Total Value of Material £	S/c Unit Rate	Total Value of s/c spec. £	TOTAL £
UPPER FLOORS cont/... Suspended timber floors cont/...													
1 SQUARE METRE OF SUSPENDED FLOOR WITH 50 X 200 MM JOISTS INCLUDES (B)													
Sawn softwood floor joists 50 x 200 mm	2.800m	L=0.16	0.45	15.43	6.94				2.96	8.29			**15.23**
Sawn softwood herring bone strutting 50 x 50 mm to 200 mm deep joists at mid span	0.420m	L=0.45	0.19	15.43	2.93				1.52	0.64			**3.57**
Chipboard tongued and grooved floor boarding 22 mm thick	1.000m2	L=0.44	0.44	15.43	6.79				9.14	9.14			**15.93**
Expanded Metal Co. SPH Joist hangers type 'S' for 50 mm joists 200 mm deep built in	2.000Nr	L=0.09	0.18	15.43	2.78				3.63	7.26			**10.04**
			1.26		**£19.44**					**£25.33**			**£44.77**
1 SQUARE METRE OF SUSPENDED FLOOR WITH 75 X 250 MM JOISTS INCLUDES (B)													
Sawn softwood floor joists 75 x 250 mm	2.800m	L=0.29	0.81	15.43	12.50				7.16	20.05			**32.55**
Sawn softwood herring bone strutting 50 x 50 mm to 250 mm deep joists at mid span	0.420m	L=0.45	0.19	15.43	2.93				1.52	0.64			**3.57**
Chipboard tongued and grooved floor boarding 22 mm thick	1.000m2	L=0.44	0.44	15.43	6.79				9.14	9.14			**15.93**
Expanded Metal Co. SPH Joist hangers type 'S' for 75 mm joists 250 mm deep built in	2.000Nr	L=0.12	0.23	15.43	3.55				5.47	10.94			**14.49**
			1.67		**£25.77**					**£40.77**			**£66.54**

Item Build Ups	Qty	Hours per unit L=Labour P=Plant	Total Labour Time	Labour Rate Per Hour	Total Value of Labour £	Total Plant Time	Plant Rate Per Hour	Total Value of Plant £	Mat Unit Rate	Total Value of Material £	S/c Unit Rate	Total Value of s/c spec. £	TOTAL £
ROOFS Flat roof construction													
N.B. The size of the roof joist required will depend on the width of the span. Two examples of flat roof construction are shown below each with a different size roof joist. The standard estimate will clearly show which of these examples has been used.													
18 mm Plywood decking; sawn softwood roof joists; herring bone strutting, firring pieces, insulation.													
1 SQUARE METRE OF FLAT ROOF CONSTRUCTION WITH 50 X 150 MM JOISTS INCLUDES (A)													
Sawn softwood roof joists 50 x 150 mm	3.300m	L=0.16	0.51	15.43	7.87				2.23	7.36			**15.23**
Sawn softwood herring bone strutting 50 x 50 mm to 150 mm deep joists at mid span	0.370m	L=0.45	0.17	15.43	2.62				1.54	0.57			**3.19**
Exterior grade plywood boarding 18 mm thick	1.000m2	L=0.38	0.38	15.43	5.86				19.34	19.34			**25.20**
50 mm Sawn softwood firring pieces 75 mm average depth	2.180m	L=0.06	0.14	15.43	2.16				0.93	2.03			**4.19**
PIR Polyisocyanurate foam sheet insulation 100mm thick, between joists and 35mm insulation under joists	0.900m2	L=0.20	0.18	15.43	2.78				17.44	15.70			**18.48**
			1.38		**£21.29**					**£45.00**			**£66.29**
1 SQUARE METRE OF FLAT ROOF CONSTRUCTION WITH 50 X 200 MM JOISTS INCLUDES (A)													
Sawn softwood roof joists 50 x 200 mm	3.300m	L=0.17	0.55	15.43	8.49				2.96	9.77			**18.26**
Sawn softwood herring bone strutting 50 x 50 mm to 200 mm deep joists at mid span	0.370m	L=0.45	0.17	15.43	2.62				1.54	0.57			**3.19**
Exterior grade plywood boarding 18 mm thick	1.000m2	L=0.38	0.38	15.43	5.86				19.34	19.34			**25.20**
50 mm Sawn softwood firring pieces 75 mm average depth	2.180m	L=0.06	0.14	15.43	2.16				0.93	2.03			**4.19**
PIR Polyisocyanurate foam sheet insulation 130mm thick, between joists	0.900m2	L=0.20	0.18	15.43	2.78				16.52	14.87			**17.65**
			1.42		**£21.91**					**£46.58**			**£68.49**

[A] Flat Roof

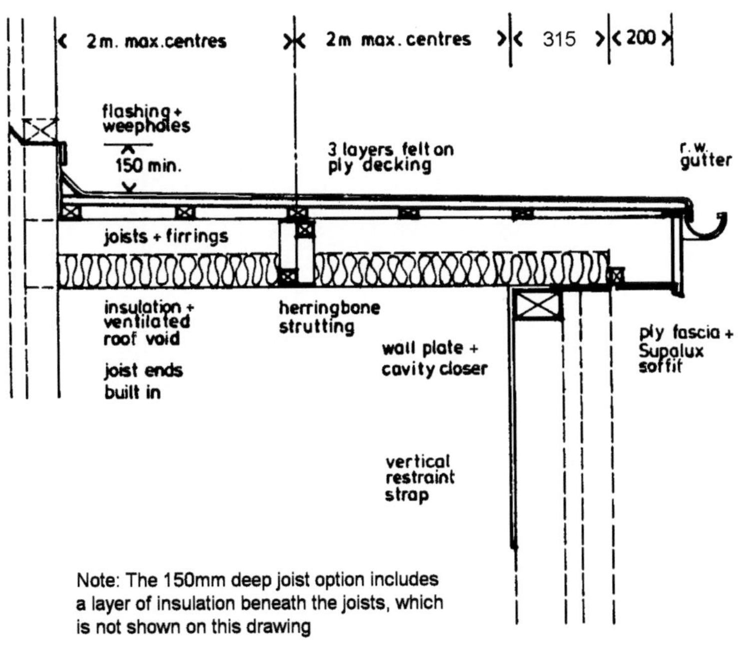

Note: The 150mm deep joist option includes a layer of insulation beneath the joists, which is not shown on this drawing

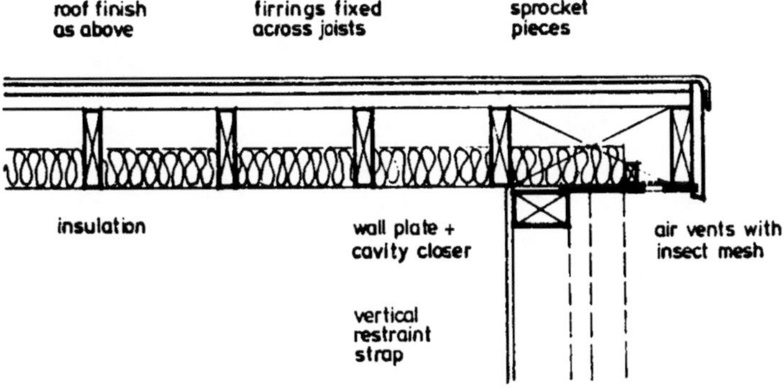

[A] Pitched Roof

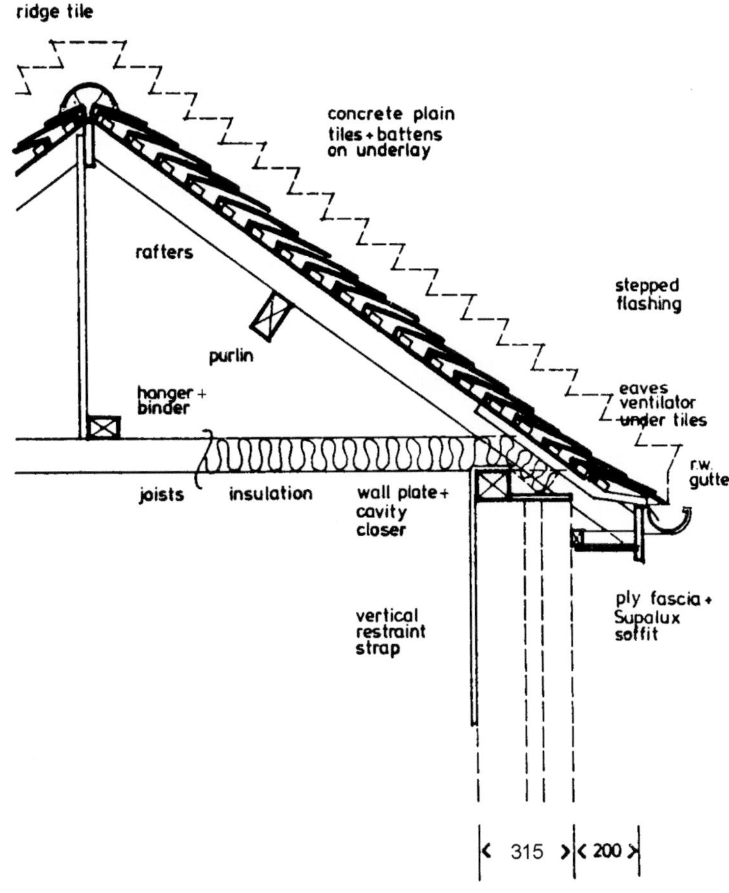

Item Build Ups	Qty	Hours per unit L=Labour P=Plant	Total Labour Time	Labour Rate Per Hour	Total Value of Labour £	Total Plant Time	Plant Rate Per Hour	Total Value of Plant £	Mat Unit Rate	Total Value of Material £	S/c Unit Rate	Total Value of s/c spec. £	TOTAL £
ROOFS cont/... Flat roof construction cont/...													
N.B. The size of the roof joist required will depend on the width of the span. Two examples of flat roof construction are shown below each with a different size roof joist. The standard estimate will clearly show which of these examples has been used.													
18 mm Chipboard decking; sawn softwood roof joists; herring bone strutting; firring pieces, insulation.													
1 SQUARE METRE OF FLAT ROOF CONSTRUCTION WITH 50 X 150 MM JOISTS INCLUDES (B)													
Sawn softwood roof joists 50 x 150 mm	3.300m	L=0.16	0.51	15.43	7.87				2.23	7.36			**15.23**
Sawn softwood herring bone strutting 50 x 50 mm to 150 mm deep joists at mid span	0.370m	L=0.45	0.17	15.43	2.62				1.54	0.57			**3.19**
Chipboard tongued and grooved decking 18 mm thick	1.000m2	L=0.32	0.32	15.43	4.94				4.02	4.02			**8.96**
50 mm Sawn softwood firring pieces 75 mm average depth	2.180m	L=0.06	0.14	15.43	2.16				0.93	2.03			**4.19**
PIR Polyisocyanurate foam sheet insulation 100mm thick, between joists and 35mm insulation under joists	0.900m2	L=0.20	0.18	15.43	2.78				17.44	15.70			**18.48**
			1.32		**£20.37**					**£29.68**			**£50.05**
1 SQUARE METRE OF FLAT ROOF CONSTRUCTION WITH 50 X 200 MM JOISTS INCLUDES (B)													
Sawn softwood roof joists 50 x 200 mm	3.300m	L=0.17	0.55	15.43	8.49				2.96	9.77			**18.26**
Sawn softwood herring bone strutting 50 x 50 mm to 200 mm deep joists at mid span	0.370m	L=0.45	0.17	15.43	2.62				1.54	0.57			**3.19**
Chipboard tongued and grooved decking 18 mm thick	1.000m2	L=0.32	0.32	15.43	4.94				4.02	4.02			**8.96**
50 mm Sawn softwood firring pieces 75 mm average depth	2.180m	L=0.06	0.14	15.43	2.16				0.93	2.03			**4.19**
PIR Polyisocyanurate foam sheet insulation 130mm thick, between joists	0.900m2	L=0.20	0.18	15.43	2.78				16.52	14.87			**17.65**
			1.36		**£20.99**					**£31.26**			**£52.25**

[B] Flat Roof

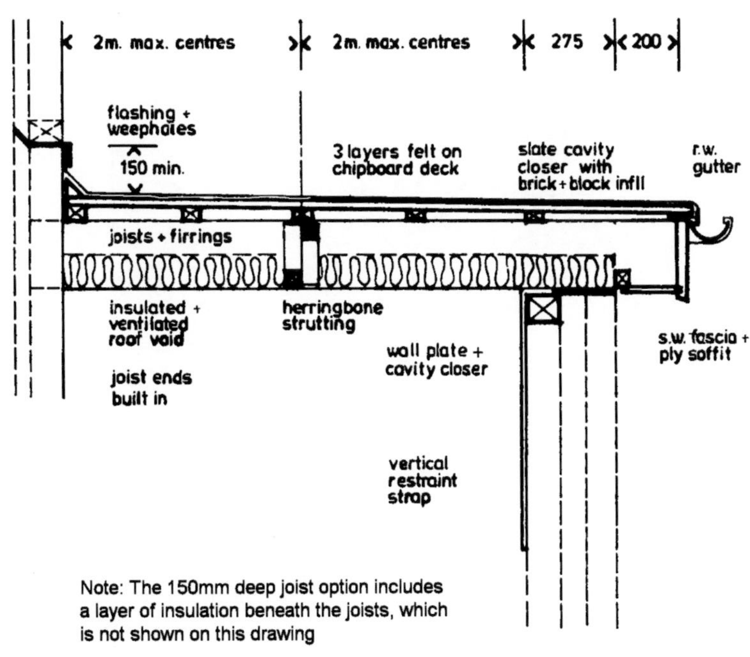

Note: The 150mm deep joist option includes a layer of insulation beneath the joists, which is not shown on this drawing

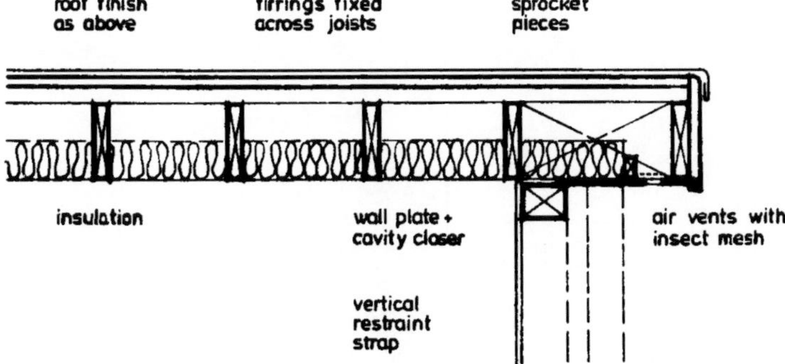

[B] Pitched Roof

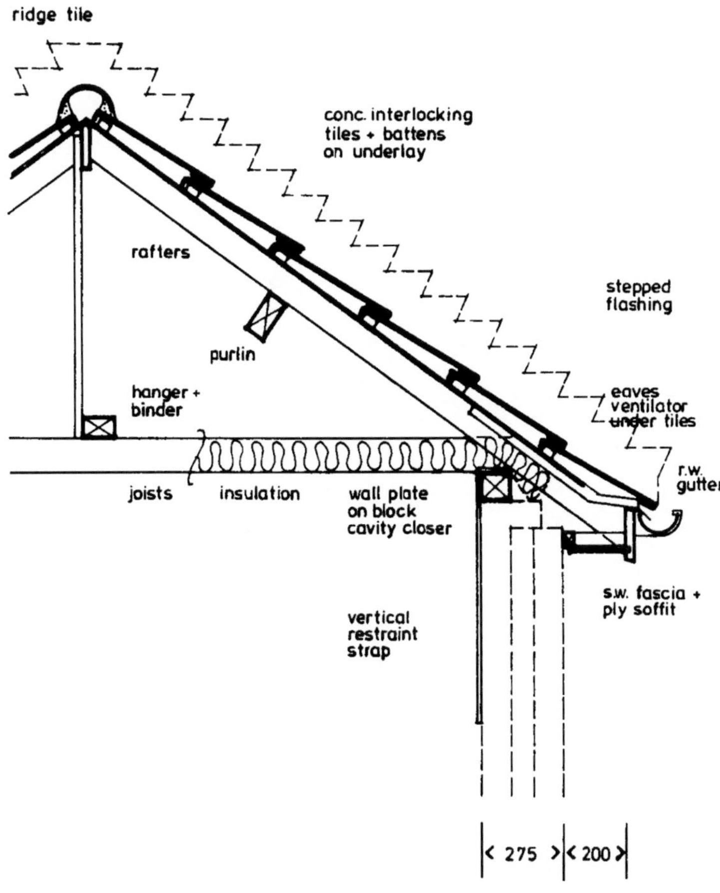

Item Build Ups

Item Build Ups	Qty	Hours per unit L=Labour P=Plant	Total Labour Time	Labour Rate Per Hour	Total Value of Labour £	Total Plant Time	Plant Rate Per Hour	Total Value of Plant £	Mat Unit Rate	Total Value of Material £	S/c Unit Rate	Total Value of s/c spec. £	TOTAL £
ROOFS cont/... Pitched roof construction													
Timber traditional framed construction with hips; rafters, joists, binders, hangers, ties, struts, purlins, ridgeboard, rafters at 450 mm centres; roof pitch 35 degrees.													
1 SQUARE METRE OF ROOF CONSTRUCTION (MEASURED ON PLAN AREA) INCLUDES (A+B)													
Sawn softwood roof timbers 25 x 100 mm	0.380m	L=0.14	0.05	15.43	0.77				0.95	0.36			**1.13**
Sawn softwood roof timbers 25 x 175 mm	0.070m	L=0.25	0.02	15.43	0.31				1.71	0.12			**0.43**
Sawn softwood roof timbers 38 x 100 mm	7.290m	L=0.17	1.26	15.43	19.44				1.55	11.30			**30.74**
Sawn softwood roof timbers 50 x 100 mm	0.480m	L=0.21	0.10	15.43	1.54				1.48	0.71			**2.25**
Sawn softwood bearers 75 x 100 mm	0.340m	L=0.29	0.10	15.43	1.54				2.56	0.87			**2.41**
Galvanised steel restraint strap 1000 mm long	0.500Nr	L=0.21	0.10	15.43	1.54				4.04	2.02			**3.56**
Glassfibre insulation quilt 100 mm thick, between rafters	0.900m2	L=0.18	0.17	15.43	2.62				3.27	2.94			**5.56**
Glassfibre insulation quilt 200 mm thick, over rafters	1.000m2	L=0.20	0.20	15.43	3.09				6.16	6.16			**9.25**
			2.00		**£30.85**					**£24.48**			**£55.33**
Work to top of external wall													
Close top of external wall, sawn softwood wallplate, steel strap.													
1 METRE RUN INCLUDES (A+B)													
Sawn softwood wallplate 50 x 100 mm	1.000m	L=0.14	0.14	15.43	2.16				1.48	1.48			**3.64**
Bed wallplate 100 mm wide in cement mortar 1:3	1.000m	L=0.08	0.08	21.13	1.69								**1.82**
Galvanised mild steel strap 800 mm long	1.000Nr	L=0.44	0.44	15.43	6.79				2.41	2.41			**9.20**
Supalux cavity closer 150 mm wide	1.000m	L=0.41	0.41	15.43	6.33				2.77	2.77			**9.10**
			1.07		**£16.97**					**£6.79**			**£23.76**

Item Build Ups	Qty	Hours per unit L=Labour P=Plant	Total Labour Time	Labour Rate Per Hour	Total Value of Labour £	Total Plant Time	Plant Rate Per Hour	Total Value of Plant £	Mat Unit Rate	Total Value of Material £	S/c Unit Rate	Total Value of s/c spec. £	TOTAL £
ROOFS cont/... Roof coverings													
Built up felt roofing will be carried out by a Specialist or Sub-Contractor.													
1 SQUARE METRE OF ROOF COVERING INCLUDES (A)													
Three layer built up felt roofing to plywood deck as follows:- First layer Type 3G perforated BS747 Second layer Ruberglas GP120 Third layer Ruberglas GP120 Solar reflective paint	1.000m2										51.19	51.19	**51.19**
												£51.19	**£51.19**
Underfelt; plain tiling with aluminium nails on sawn softwood battens; 35 degree pitch.													
1 SQUARE METRE OF ROOF COVERING (MEASURED ON SLOPE) INCLUDES (A)													
Starex high performance slaters felt, 150 laps	1.150m2	L=0.02	0.03	26.82	0.80				2.55	2.93			**3.73**
Redland concrete plain tiles 265 x 165 mm, 100 gauge, 65 mm lap, aluminium nails to each fifth course and perimeter, 38 x 19 mm sawn softwood battens	1.150m2	L=0.93	1.06	26.82	28.43				32.23	37.06			**65.49**
			1.09		**£29.23**					**£39.99**			**£69.22**
Built up felt roofing will be carried out by a Specialist or Sub-Contractor.													
1 SQUARE METRE OF ROOF COVERING INCLUDES (B)													
Three layer built up felt roofing to plywood deck as follows:- First layer Type 3G perforated BS747 Second layer Ruberglas GP120 Third layer Ruberglas GP120 mineral surfaced felt	1.000m2										36.43	36.43	**36.43**
												£36.43	**£36.43**

Item Build Ups	Qty	Hours per unit L=Labour P=Plant	Total Labour Time	Labour Rate Per Hour	Total Value of Labour £	Total Plant Time	Plant Rate Per Hour	Total Value of Plant £	Mat Unit Rate	Total Value of Material £	S/c Unit Rate	Total Value of s/c spec. £	TOTAL £
ROOFS cont/... Roof coverings cont/...													
Underfelt; plain tiling with aluminium nails on sawn softwood battens; 35 degree pitch.													
1 SQUARE METRE OF ROOF COVERING (MEASURED ON SLOPE) INCLUDES (B)													
Starex high performance slaters felt, 150 laps	1.150m2	L=0.02	0.03	26.82	0.80				2.55	2.93			**3.73**
Redland Renown granular faced tiles 418 x 330 mm, 75 mm lap, all perimeter tiles fixed, 38 x 24 mm sawn softwood battens	1.150m2	L=0.19	0.22	26.82	5.90				12.05	13.86			**19.76**
			0.25		**£6.70**					**£16.79**			**£23.49**
Work to verge													
1 METRE RUN OF VERGE INCLUDES (A+B)													
Verge tile, bed and point on fibre cement undercloak strip 150 mm wide	1.000m	L=0.28	0.28	26.82	7.51				4.15	4.15			**11.66**
			0.28		**£7.51**					**£4.15**			**£11.66**
Work to hip													
1 METRE RUN OF HIP INCLUDES (A+B)													
Half round hip tile, pointed in cement mortar	1.000m	L=0.50	0.50	26.82	13.41				18.45	18.45			**31.86**
Cut roof tiles at hip	2.000m	L=0.15	0.30	26.82	8.05				0.93	1.86			**9.91**
			0.80		**£21.46**					**£20.31**			**£41.77**
Work to eaves													
1 METRE RUN OF EAVES INCLUDES (A)													
Redvent eaves ventilation in black PVC comprising air conducting tray 740 mm wide with gutter skirt, 60 mm apron 203 mm wide and fascia grille unit; fixing with aluminium nails	1.000m	L=0.18	0.18	26.82	4.83				12.55	12.55			**17.38**
Double course of tiles at eaves	1.000m	L=0.08	0.08	26.82	2.15				3.18	3.18			**5.33**
			0.26		**£6.98**					**£15.73**			**£22.71**

Item Build Ups	Qty	Hours per unit L=Labour P=Plant	Total Labour Time	Labour Rate Per Hour	Total Value of Labour £	Total Plant Time	Plant Rate Per Hour	Total Value of Plant £	Mat Unit Rate	Total Value of Material £	S/c Unit Rate	Total Value of s/c spec. £	TOTAL £
ROOFS cont/... Roof coverings cont/...													
Work to eaves													
1 METRE RUN OF EAVES INCLUDES (B)													
Redvent eaves ventilation in black PVC comprising air conducting tray 740 mm wide with gutter skirt, 60 mm apron 203 mm wide and fascia grille unit; fixing with aluminium nails	1.000m	L=0.18	0.18	26.82	4.83				12.55	12.55			**17.38**
Double course of tiles at eaves	1.000m	L=0.08	0.08	26.82	2.15				3.67	3.67			**5.82**
			0.26		**£6.98**					**£16.22**			**£23.20**
Fascia and eaves soffit													
12 mm Supalux soffit 200 mm wide; 25 mm exterior grade plywood fascia 250 mm high; sawn softwood bearers; painted finish.													
1 METRE RUN OF FASCIA INCLUDES (A)													
25 mm exterior grade plywood fascia 250 mm wide	1.000m	L=0.43	0.43	15.43	6.63				6.29	6.29			**12.92**
12 mm Supalux soffit 200 mm wide	1.000m	L=0.50	0.50	15.43	7.72				6.53	6.53			**14.25**
Sawn softwood bearers 38 x 50 mm	1.540m	L=0.08	0.12	15.43	1.85				0.81	1.25			**3.10**
Prepare, knot, prime, stop; one undercoat and one coat alkyd based paint to wood surfaces; externally	0.490m2	L=0.61	0.30	15.43	4.63				2.18	1.07			**5.70**
PVCu one piece soffit ventilator	2.000Nr	L=0.26	0.53	15.43	8.18				2.06	4.12			**12.30**
			1.88		**£29.01**					**£19.26**			**£48.27**

Item Build Ups	Qty	Hours per unit L=Labour P=Plant	Total Labour Time	Labour Rate Per Hour	Total Value of Labour £	Total Plant Time	Plant Rate Per Hour	Total Value of Plant £	Mat Unit Rate	Total Value of Material £	S/c Unit Rate	Total Value of s/c spec. £	TOTAL £
ROOFS cont/... Roof coverings cont/...													
12 mm Plywood soffit 200 mm wide; 25 mm wrought softwood fascia 250 mm high; sawn softwood bearers; painted finish.													
1 METRE RUN OF FASCIA INCLUDES (B)													
25 mm wrought softwood fascia 250 mm wide	1.000m	L=0.50	0.50	15.43	7.72				6.83	6.83			**14.55**
12 mm exterior grade plywood soffit 200 mm wide	1.000m	L=0.29	0.29	15.43	4.47				2.66	2.66			**7.13**
Sawn softwood bearers 38 x 50 mm	1.540m	L=0.08	0.12	15.43	1.85				0.81	1.25			**3.10**
Prepare, knot, prime, stop; one undercoat and one coat alkyd based paint to wood surfaces; externally	0.490m2	L=0.61	0.30	15.43	4.63				2.18	1.07			**5.70**
PVCu one piece soffit ventilator	2.000Nr	L=0.26	0.53	15.43	8.18				2.06	4.12			**12.30**
			1.74		**£26.85**					**£15.93**			**£42.78**
Gutters and fittings													
112 mm diameter half round PVCu gutter fixed with standard brackets.													
1 METRE RUN OF GUTTER INCLUDES (A+B)													
112 mm half round gutter	1.000m	L=0.31	0.31	32.03	9.93				3.01	3.01			**12.94**
Stopped end	0.375Nr	L=0.13	0.05	32.03	1.60				1.23	0.46			**2.06**
90 degree angle	0.080Nr	L=0.31	0.02	32.03	0.64				3.25	0.26			**0.90**
Outlet	0.211Nr	L=0.31	0.06	32.03	1.92				2.94	0.62			**2.54**
			0.44		**£14.09**					**£4.35**			**£18.44**

Item Build Ups	Qty	Hours per unit L=Labour P=Plant	Total Labour Time	Labour Rate Per Hour	Total Value of Labour £	Total Plant Time	Plant Rate Per Hour	Total Value of Plant £	Mat Unit Rate	Total Value of Material £	S/c Unit Rate	Total Value of s/c spec. £	TOTAL £
ROOFS cont/... Flashings													
Milled lead sheet code 4													
1 METRE RUN OF FLASHINGS INCLUDES (A+B)													
Lead flashing 200 mm girth	1.000m										23.16	23.16	**23.16**
Rake out joint of brickwork	1.000m	L=0.01	0.01	21.13	0.21								**0.21**
Point edges in cement mortar 1:3	1.000m	L=0.06	0.06	21.13	1.27				0.13	0.13			**1.40**
			0.07		**£1.48**							**£23.16**	**£24.77**
Milled lead sheet code 4													
1 METRE RUN OF STEPPED FLASHINGS INCLUDES (A+B)													
Lead stepped flashing 400 mm girth	1.000m										67.44	67.44	**67.44**
Rake out joint of brickwork	1.350m	L=0.01	0.01	21.13	0.21								**0.21**
Point edges in cement mortar 1:3	1.350m	L=0.06	0.08	21.13	1.69				0.13	0.18			**1.87**
			0.09		**£1.90**							**£67.44**	**£69.52**
Abutment to existing wall													
Cavity tray fitted to existing wall.													
1 METRE RUN INCLUDES (A+B)													
Cut out brick course in short lengths, insert cavity tray, insert cavity weep/ventilators, replace bricks and make good	1.000m	L=2.02	1.67	21.13	35.29				18.91	18.91			**54.20**
			1.67		**£35.29**					**£18.91**			**£54.20**

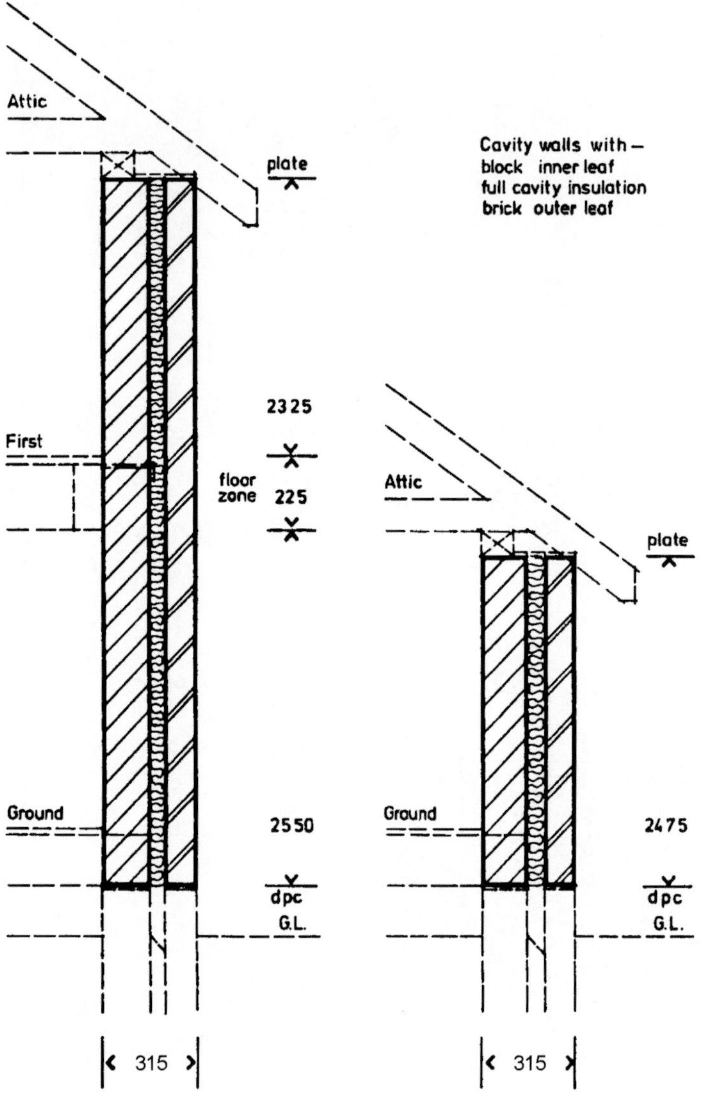
[A] External Walls
PITCHED ROOF
Attic
plate
Cavity walls with –
block inner leaf
full cavity insulation
brick outer leaf
2325
First
floor zone
225
Attic
plate
Ground
2550
dpc
G.L.
Ground
2475
dpc
G.L.
315
315

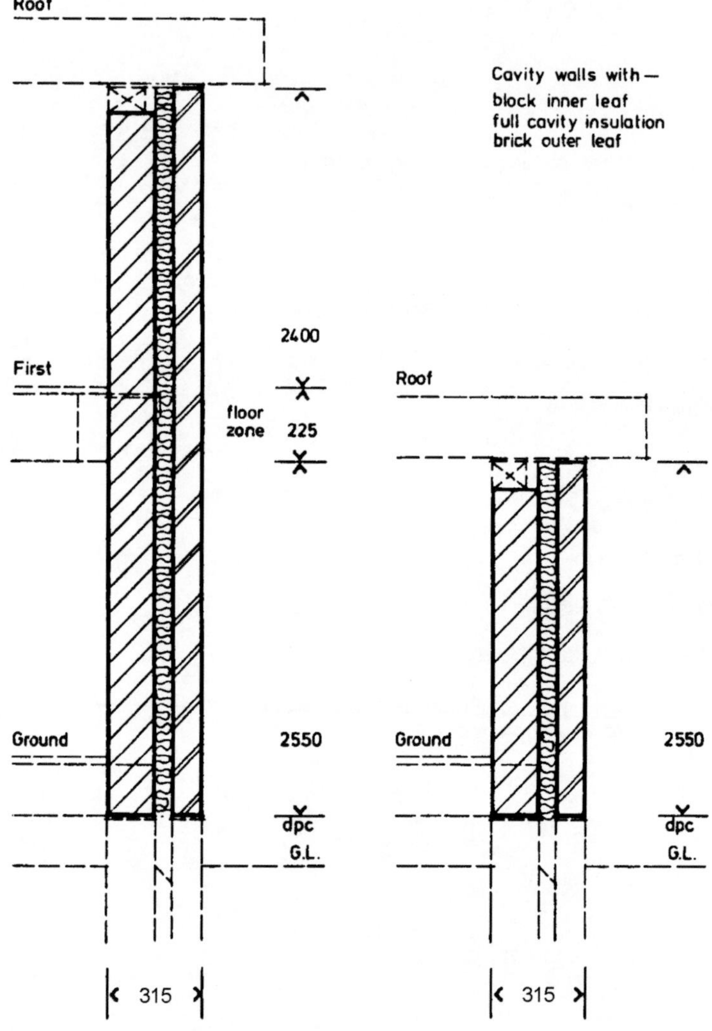
[A] External Walls
FLAT ROOF
Roof
Cavity walls with –
block inner leaf
full cavity insulation
brick outer leaf
2400
First
floor zone
225
Roof
Ground
2550
dpc
G.L.
Ground
2550
dpc
G.L.
315
315

[B] External Walls
PITCHED ROOF

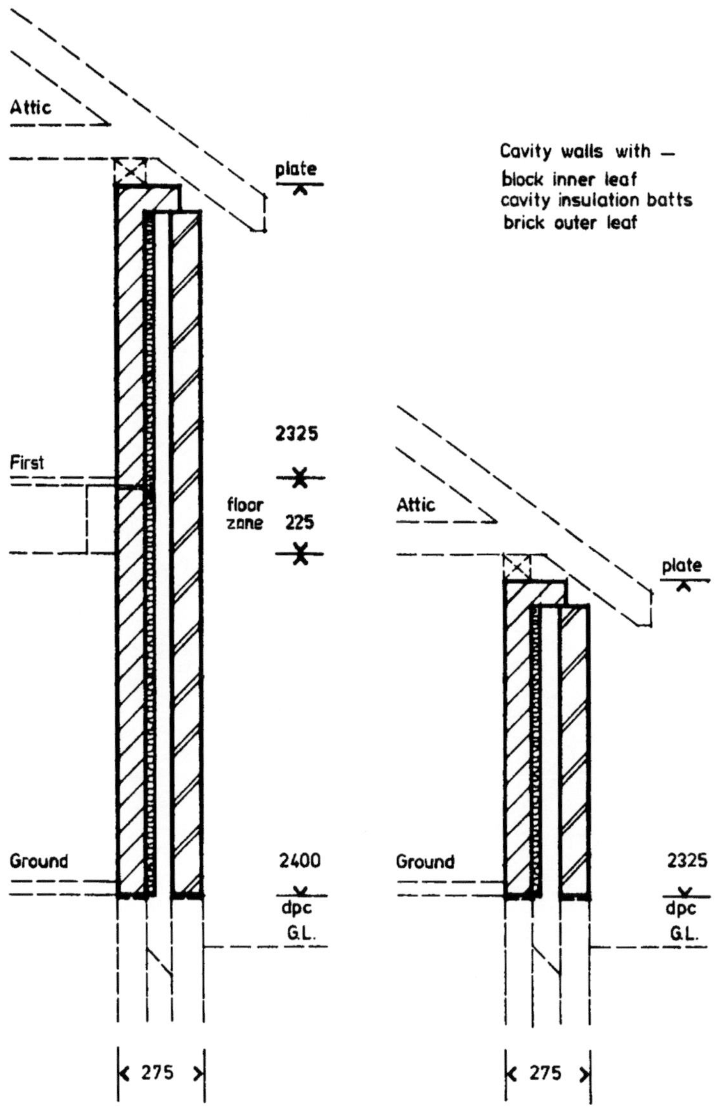

[B] External Walls
FLAT ROOF

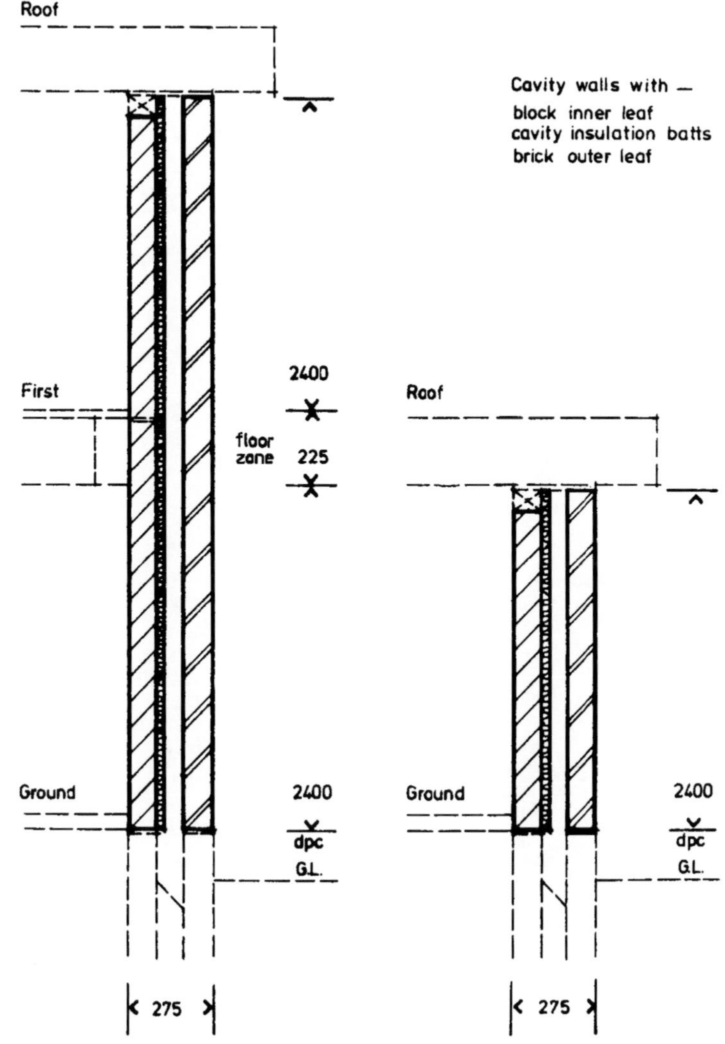

Item Build Ups	Qty	Hours per unit L=Labour P=Plant	Total Labour Time	Labour Rate Per Hour	Total Value of Labour £	Total Plant Time	Plant Rate Per Hour	Total Value of Plant £	Mat Unit Rate	Total Value of Material £	S/c Unit Rate	Total Value of s/c spec. £	TOTAL £
EXTERNAL WALLS Brick and block cavity wall including ties													
1 SQUARE METRE OF EXTERNAL WALL INCLUDES (A)													
Facing bricks PC £351.38/1000 in gauged mortar 1:2:9 in 102.5 mm skin of hollow wall, flush pointing	1.000m2	L=1.99	1.99	21.13	42.05				24.43	24.43			**66.48**
Form cavity 75 mm wide with 5 Nr 200 mm galvanised butterfly ties per m2	1.000m2	L=0.04	0.04	21.13	0.85				0.34	0.34			**1.19**
Thermalite shield blocks 440 x 215 mm in gauged mortar 1:2:9 in 140 mm skin of hollow wall	1.000m2	L=0.83	0.83	23.97	19.90				18.76	18.76			**38.66**
75 mm Dritherm cavity batts	1.000m2	L=0.13	0.13	21.13	2.75				5.07	5.07			**7.82**
			2.99		**£65.55**					**£48.60**			**£114.15**
1 SQUARE METRE OF EXTERNAL WALL INCLUDES (B)													
Facing bricks PC £351.38/1000 in gauged mortar 1:2:9 in 102.5 mm skin of hollow wall, flush pointing	1.000m2	L=1.99	1.99	21.13	42.05				24.43	24.43			**66.48**
Form cavity 75 mm wide with 5 Nr 200 mm galvanised butterfly ties per m2	1.000m2	L=0.04	0.04	21.13	0.85				0.34	0.34			**1.19**
Thermalite shield blocks 440 x 215 mm in gauged mortar 1:2:9 in 100 mm skin of hollow wall	1.000m2	L=0.72	0.72	23.97	17.26				13.31	13.31			**30.57**
35 mm PIR Polyisocyanurate foam sheet insulation	1.000m2	L=0.13	0.13	21.13	2.75				5.82	5.82			**8.57**
			2.88		**£62.91**					**£43.90**			**£106.81**

Item Build Ups	Qty	Hours per unit L=Labour P=Plant	Total Labour Time	Labour Rate Per Hour	Total Value of Labour £	Total Plant Time	Plant Rate Per Hour	Total Value of Plant £	Mat Unit Rate	Total Value of Material £	S/c Unit Rate	Total Value of s/c spec. £	TOTAL £
EXTERNAL DOORS AND WINDOWS External doors													
Hardwood period door, including frame, ironmongery and finishings.													
1 NR EXTERNAL DOOR INCLUDES (A)													
Premdoor 44 mm hardwood four panel pre-glazed door	1.000Nr	L=1.32	1.32	15.43	20.37				99.91	99.91			**120.28**
Premdor Meranti weatherboard	1.000Nr	L=0.46	0.46	15.43	7.10				17.14	17.14			**24.24**
Wrought hardwood once rebated, once grooved door jamb and head 56 x 143 mm	5.250m	L=0.44	2.29	15.43	35.33				21.61	113.45			**148.78**
Wrought hardwood once sunk-weathered, once rebated, three times grooved door sill 56 x 168 mm	1.090m	L=0.41	0.45	15.43	6.94				42.90	46.76			**53.70**
Hardwood moulded architrave 25 x 75 mm	5.340m	L=0.35	1.84	15.43	28.39				5.90	31.51			**59.90**
Bed frame in cement mortar 1:3	6.340m	L=0.22	1.40	21.13	29.58				0.13	0.82			**30.40**
Point edge in polysulphide mastic one side	6.340m	L=0.22	1.40	21.13	29.58				1.30	8.24			**37.82**
Prepare; two coats polyurethane varnish on wood surfaces internally	1.790m2	L=0.41	0.73	15.43	11.26				1.91	3.42			**14.68**
Prepare; two coats polyurethane varnish to frames and linings 150 - 300 mm girth; internally	6.080m	L=0.19	1.13	15.43	17.44				0.67	4.07			**21.51**
Prepare; one preservative basecoat and two coats external grade varnish to wood surfaces	1.790m2	L=0.56	1.01	15.43	15.58				3.57	6.39			**21.97**
Prepare; one preservative basecoat and two coats external grade varnish to frames and linings not exceeding 150 mm girth; externally	6.080m	L=0.17	1.03	15.43	15.89				0.66	4.01			**19.90**
Fix only heavy steel butts	1.500Pair	L=0.35	0.52	15.43	8.02								**8.02**
Fix only mortice deadlock	1.000Nr	L=1.27	1.26	15.43	19.44								**19.44**
Fix only lever lock / latch furniture	1.000Set	L=0.58	0.57	15.43	8.80								**8.80**
P.C. £65.00 for door ironmongery	1.000Set								65.00	65.00			**65.00**
			15.41		**£253.72**					**£400.72**			**£654.44**

[A] External Door

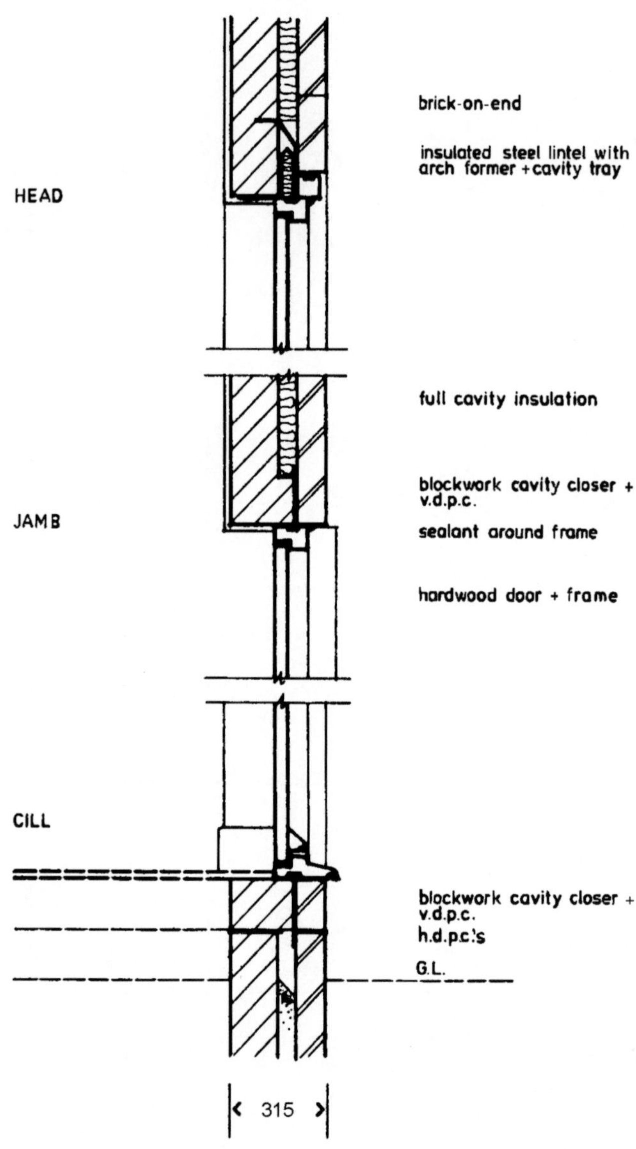
HEAD
JAMB
CILL
brick-on-end
insulated steel lintel with arch former + cavity tray
full cavity insulation
blockwork cavity closer + v.d.p.c.
sealant around frame
hardwood door + frame
blockwork cavity closer + v.d.p.c.
h.d.p.c.'s
G.L.
315

[A] Window

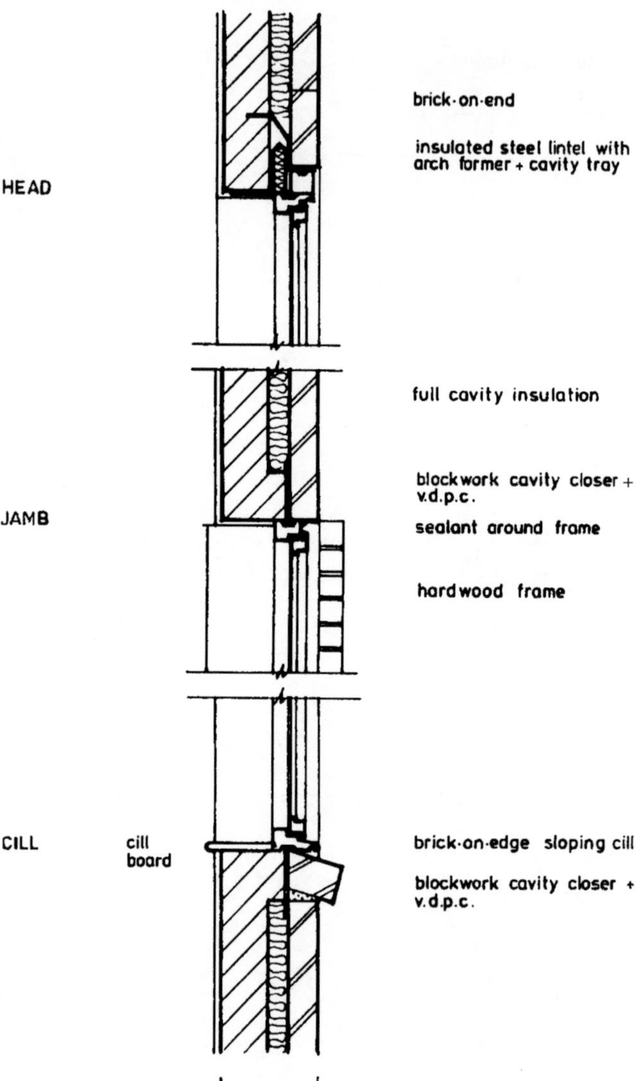
HEAD
JAMB
CILL
cill board
brick-on-end
insulated steel lintel with arch former + cavity tray
full cavity insulation
blockwork cavity closer + v.d.p.c.
sealant around frame
hardwood frame
brick-on-edge sloping cill
blockwork cavity closer + v.d.p.c.
315

[B] External Door

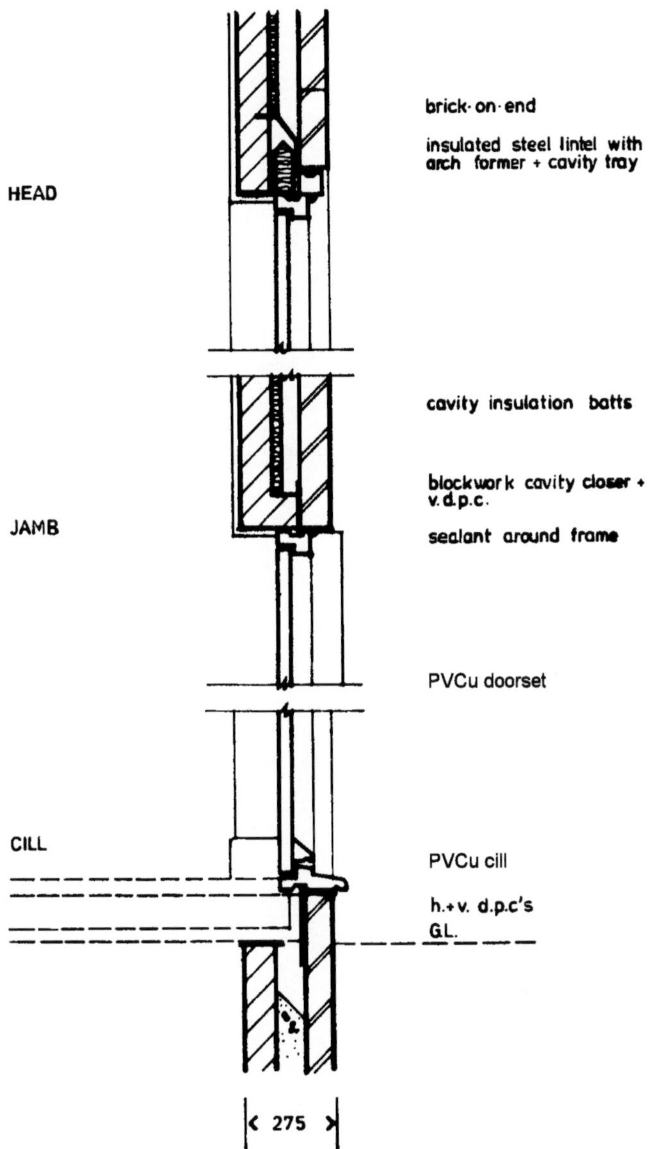
HEAD
JAMB
CILL
brick·on·end
insulated steel lintel with arch former + cavity tray
cavity insulation batts
blockwork cavity closer + v.d.p.c.
sealant around frame
PVCu doorset
PVCu cill
h.+v. d.p.c's
G.L.
275

[B] Window

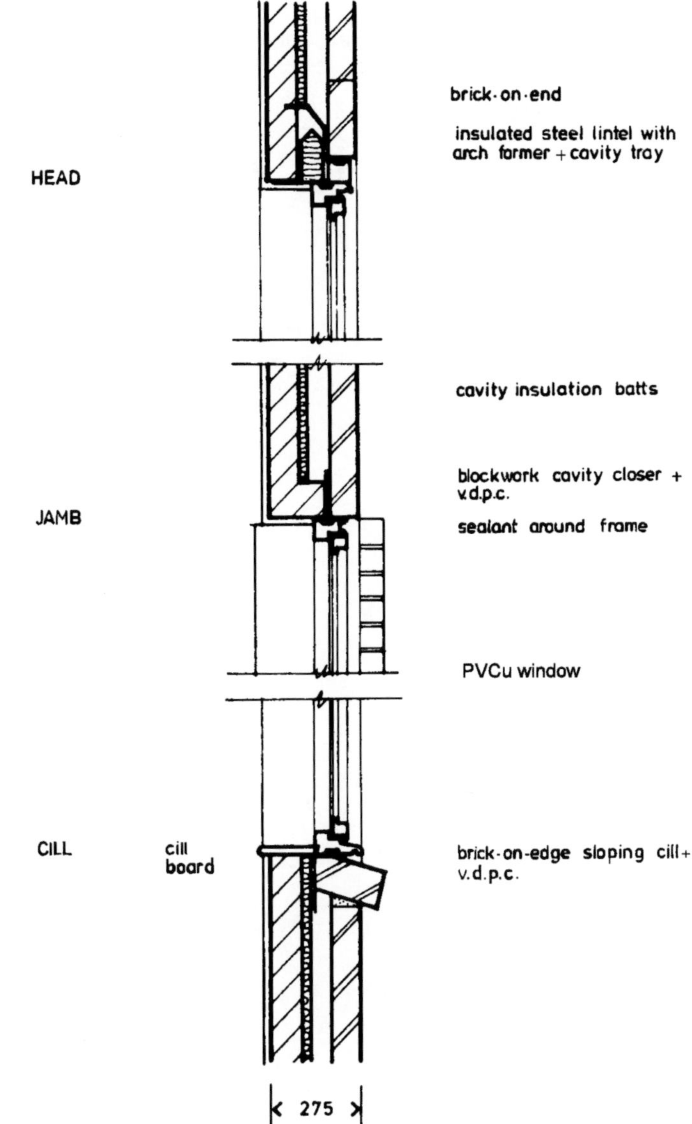
HEAD
JAMB
CILL
cill board
brick·on·end
insulated steel lintel with arch former + cavity tray
cavity insulation batts
blockwork cavity closer + v.d.p.c.
sealant around frame
PVCu window
brick·on·edge sloping cill+ v.d.p.c.
275

Item Build Ups	Qty	Hours per unit L=Labour P=Plant	Total Labour Time	Labour Rate Per Hour	Total Value of Labour £	Total Plant Time	Plant Rate Per Hour	Total Value of Plant £	Mat Unit Rate	Total Value of Material £	S/c Unit Rate	Total Value of s/c spec. £	TOTAL £
EXTERNAL DOORS AND WINDOWS cont/... External doors cont/...													
Solid PVCu door including frame, ironmongery and finishings.													
1 NR EXTERNAL DOOR INCLUDES (B)													
900 x 2100 mm PVCu door and frame, white, complete with lock and lever furniture	1.000Nr	L=2.30	2.30	15.43	35.49				291.50	291.50			**326.99**
Wrought softwood twice rounded architrave 25 x 125 mm	5.340m	L=0.21	1.11	15.43	17.13				7.74	41.33			**58.46**
Bed frame in cement mortar 1:3	6.340m	L=0.22	1.40	21.13	29.58				0.13	0.82			**30.40**
Point edge in polysulphide mastic one side	6.340m	L=0.22	1.40	21.13	29.58				1.30	8.24			**37.82**
Prepare, knot, prime, stop; one undercoat and one coat alkyd based paint to window boards 150 - 300 mm girth; internally	5.340m	L=0.26	1.39	15.43	21.45				0.60	3.20			**24.65**
			7.60		**£133.23**					**£345.09**			**£478.32**

Item Build Ups	Qty	Hours per unit L=Labour P=Plant	Total Labour Time	Labour Rate Per Hour	Total Value of Labour £	Total Plant Time	Plant Rate Per Hour	Total Value of Plant £	Mat Unit Rate	Total Value of Material £	S/c Unit Rate	Total Value of s/c spec. £	TOTAL £
EXTERNAL DOORS AND WINDOWS cont/... Windows													
Standard hardwood window 1200 x 1200 mm, including glazing, ironmongery, window board and decoration.													
1 NR WINDOW COMPLETE INCLUDES (A)													
Hardwood window 1200 x 1200 mm, preservative treated, factory double glazed, complete with stays and fasteners	1.000Nr	L=1.74	1.74	15.43	26.85				457.37	457.37			**484.22**
32 x 225 mm Hardwood window board	1.500m	L=0.92	1.38	15.43	21.29				27.98	41.97			**63.26**
Returned notched end to window board	2.000Nr	L=0.29	0.58	15.43	8.95								**8.95**
Galvanised mild steel frame ties 200 x 25 x 3 mm	4.000Nr	L=0.14	0.55	15.43	8.49				0.72	2.88			**11.37**
Bed frame in cement mortar 1:3	4.800m	L=0.22	1.06	21.13	22.40				0.13	0.62			**23.02**
Point edge in polysulphide mastic one side	4.800m	L=0.22	1.06	21.13	22.40				1.30	6.24			**28.64**
Prepare; two coats polyurethane varnish to skirtings 150 - 300 mm girth; internally	1.500m	L=0.21	0.31	15.43	4.78				0.67	1.01			**5.79**
Prepare; two coats polyurethane varnish to glazed windows in medium panes; internally	1.440m2	L=0.74	1.07	15.43	16.51				1.36	1.96			**18.47**
Prepare; one preservative basecoat and two coats external grade varnish to glazed windows in medium panes; externally	1.440m2	L=1.14	1.65	15.43	25.46				2.55	3.67			**29.13**
			9.40		**£157.13**					**£515.72**			**£672.85**

Item Build Ups	Qty	Hours per unit L=Labour P=Plant	Total Labour Time	Labour Rate Per Hour	Total Value of Labour £	Total Plant Time	Plant Rate Per Hour	Total Value of Plant £	Mat Unit Rate	Total Value of Material £	S/c Unit Rate	Total Value of s/c spec. £	TOTAL £
EXTERNAL DOORS AND WINDOWS cont/... Windows cont/...													
Standard PVCu window 1200 x 1200 mm including glazing, ironmongery, window board and decoration.													
1 NR WINDOW COMPLETE INCLUDES (B)													
PVCu window 1200 x 1200 mm, factory double glazed, complete with stays and fasteners	1.000Nr	L=1.50	1.50	15.43	23.15				390.50	390.50			**413.65**
25 x 200 mm Wrought softwood window board	1.500m	L=0.75	1.12	15.43	17.28				6.67	10.01			**27.29**
Returned notched end to window board	2.000Nr	L=0.23	0.46	15.43	7.10								**7.10**
Galvanised mild steel frame ties 200 x 25 x 3 mm	4.000Nr	L=0.14	0.55	15.43	8.49				0.72	2.88			**11.37**
Bed frame in cement mortar 1:3	4.800m	L=0.22	1.06	21.13	22.40				0.13	0.62			**23.02**
Point edge in polysulphide mastic one side	4.800m	L=0.22	1.06	21.13	22.40				1.30	6.24			**28.64**
Prepare, knot, prime, stop; one undercoat and one coat alkyd based paint to window boards 150 - 300 mm girth; internally	1.500m	L=0.26	0.39	15.43	6.02				0.60	0.90			**6.92**
			6.14		**£106.84**					**£411.15**			**£517.99**

Item Build Ups	Qty	Hours per unit L=Labour P=Plant	Total Labour Time	Labour Rate Per Hour	Total Value of Labour £	Total Plant Time	Plant Rate Per Hour	Total Value of Plant £	Mat Unit Rate	Total Value of Material £	S/c Unit Rate	Total Value of s/c spec. £	TOTAL £
EXTERNAL DOORS AND WINDOWS cont/... Opening in cavity wall for Door													
Lintel, cavity tray, work to jambs and sills including DPC's.													
1 NR OPENING FOR DOOR INCLUDES (A)													
Catnic lintel type CG50/100; 1200 mm long	1.000Nr	L=0.13	0.13	21.13	2.75				39.38	39.38			**42.13**
Cavity gutter	0.540m2	L=0.55	0.30	21.13	6.34				8.54	4.61			**10.95**
Close cavity at jambs	4.000m	L=0.20	0.80	21.13	16.90				1.67	6.68			**23.58**
Vertical DPC at jambs 150 mm wide	4.400m	L=0.06	0.25	21.13	5.28				0.46	2.02			**7.30**
Close cavity at sills	1.090m	L=0.25	0.27	21.13	5.71				1.67	1.82			**7.53**
Polythene horizontal DPC 150 mm wide	1.090m	L=0.03	0.04	21.13	0.85				0.46	0.50			**1.35**
Fair return on facings at head and jambs	4.900m	L=0.11	0.54	21.13	11.41								**11.41**
Expamet angle bead	4.900m	L=0.15	0.74	23.97	17.74				0.97	4.75			**22.49**
13 mm Two coat plaster to walls not exceeding 300 mm wide	0.740m2	L=0.89	0.66	23.97	15.82				2.91	2.15			**17.97**
			3.73		**£82.80**					**£61.91**			**£144.71**

Item Build Ups	Qty	Hours per unit L=Labour P=Plant	Total Labour Time	Labour Rate Per Hour	Total Value of Labour £	Total Plant Time	Plant Rate Per Hour	Total Value of Plant £	Mat Unit Rate	Total Value of Material £	S/c Unit Rate	Total Value of s/c spec. £	TOTAL £
EXTERNAL DOORS AND WINDOWS cont/... Opening in cavity wall for Door cont/...													
Lintel, cavity tray, work to jambs and sills including DPC's.													
1 NR OPENING FOR DOOR INCLUDES (B)													
Catnic lintel type CG70/100; 1200 mm long	1.000Nr	L=0.14	0.14	21.13	2.96				39.35	39.35			**42.31**
Cavity gutter	0.540m2	L=0.55	0.30	21.13	6.34				8.54	4.61			**10.95**
Close cavity at jambs	4.000m	L=0.17	0.66	21.13	13.95				1.14	4.56			**18.51**
Vertical DPC at jambs 100 mm wide	4.400m	L=0.04	0.19	21.13	4.01				0.29	1.28			**5.29**
Close cavity at sills	1.090m	L=0.22	0.24	21.13	5.07				1.14	1.24			**6.31**
Polythene horizontal DPC 100 mm wide	1.090m	L=0.02	0.02	21.13	0.42				0.28	0.31			**0.73**
Fair return on facings at head and jambs	4.900m	L=0.11	0.54	21.13	11.41								**11.41**
Expamet angle bead	4.900m	L=0.15	0.74	23.97	17.74				0.97	4.75			**22.49**
13 mm Two coat plaster to walls not exceeding 300 mm wide	0.490m2	L=0.89	0.44	23.97	10.55				2.92	1.43			**11.98**
1200 mm Arch former to lintel	1.000Nr	L=0.08	0.08	21.13	1.69				47.80	47.80			**49.49**
			3.35		**£74.14**					**£105.33**			**£179.47**

Item Build Ups	Qty	Hours per unit L=Labour P=Plant	Total Labour Time	Labour Rate Per Hour	Total Value of Labour £	Total Plant Time	Plant Rate Per Hour	Total Value of Plant £	Mat Unit Rate	Total Value of Material £	S/c Unit Rate	Total Value of s/c spec. £	TOTAL £
EXTERNAL DOORS AND WINDOWS cont/... Opening in cavity wall for Window													
Lintel, cavity tray, work to jambs and sills including brick on edge sill and DPC.													
1 NR OPENING FOR WINDOW INCLUDES (A)													
Catnic lintel type CG50/100; 1500 mm long	1.000Nr	L=0.14	0.14	21.13	2.96				50.91	50.91			**53.87**
Cavity gutter	0.680m2	L=0.55	0.38	21.13	8.03				8.53	5.80			**13.83**
Close cavity at jambs	2.400m	L=0.20	0.48	21.13	10.14				1.67	4.01			**14.15**
Vertical DPC at jambs 150 mm wide	2.800m	L=0.06	0.16	21.13	3.38				0.46	1.29			**4.67**
Close cavity at sills	1.300m	L=0.25	0.33	21.13	6.97				1.67	2.17			**9.14**
Polythene horizontal DPC 150 mm wide	1.200m	L=0.03	0.04	21.13	0.85				0.46	0.55			**1.40**
Fair return on facings at head and jambs	3.600m	L=0.11	0.40	21.13	8.45								**8.45**
Brick on edge sill in facing bricks	1.200m	L=0.83	0.99	21.13	20.92				6.08	7.30			**28.22**
Expamet angle bead	3.600m	L=0.15	0.54	23.97	12.94				0.97	3.49			**16.43**
13 mm Two coat plaster to walls not exceeding 300 mm wide	0.540m2	L=0.89	0.48	23.97	11.51				2.91	1.57			**13.08**
			3.94		**£86.15**					**£77.09**			**£163.24**

Item Build Ups	Qty	Hours per unit L=Labour P=Plant	Total Labour Time	Labour Rate Per Hour	Total Value of Labour £	Total Plant Time	Plant Rate Per Hour	Total Value of Plant £	Mat Unit Rate	Total Value of Material £	S/c Unit Rate	Total Value of s/c spec. £	TOTAL £
EXTERNAL DOORS AND WINDOWS cont/... Opening in cavity wall for Window cont/...													
Lintel, cavity tray, work to jambs and sills including brick on edge sill and DPC's.													
1 NR OPENING FOR WINDOW INCLUDES (B)													
Catnic lintel type CG70/100; 1500 mm long	1.000Nr	L=0.15	0.15	21.13	3.17				49.16	49.16			**52.33**
Cavity gutter	0.680m2	L=0.55	0.38	21.13	8.03				8.53	5.80			**13.83**
Close cavity at jambs	2.400m	L=0.17	0.40	21.13	8.45				1.14	2.74			**11.19**
Vertical DPC at jambs 100 mm wide	2.800m	L=0.04	0.12	21.13	2.54				0.29	0.81			**3.35**
Close cavity at sills	1.300m	L=0.22	0.29	21.13	6.13				1.14	1.48			**7.61**
Polythene horizontal DPC 100 mm wide	1.200m	L=0.02	0.03	21.13	0.63				0.29	0.35			**0.98**
Fair return on facings at head and jambs	3.600m	L=0.11	0.40	21.13	8.45								**8.45**
Brick on edge sill in facing bricks	1.200m	L=0.83	0.99	21.13	20.92				6.08	7.30			**28.22**
Expamet angle bead	3.600m	L=0.15	0.54	23.97	12.94				0.97	3.49			**16.43**
13 mm Two coat plaster to walls not exceeding 300 mm wide	0.360m2	L=0.89	0.32	23.97	7.67				2.92	1.05			**8.72**
			3.62		**£78.93**					**£72.18**			**£151.11**
INTERNAL WALLS AND PARTITIONS Stud partitions													
Internal stud partition; sawn softwood studding and noggings; gypsum plasterboard both sides.													
1 SQUARE METRE OF PARTITION INCLUDES (A+B)													
Sawn softwood studding and nogging 50 x 75 mm	4.170m	L=0.28	1.15	15.43	17.74				1.11	4.63			**22.37**
Fixing with 75 mm clasp nails to brickwork	0.700m	L=0.09	0.06	15.43	0.93				0.19	0.13			**1.06**
12.5 mm Gypsum plasterboard, tapered edges, galvanised nails to softwood, joints filled, taped and finished flush, holes filled with joint filler	2.000m2	L=0.51	1.01	21.13	21.34				3.37	6.74			**28.08**
			2.22		**£40.01**					**£11.50**			**£51.51**

[A] Stud Partition

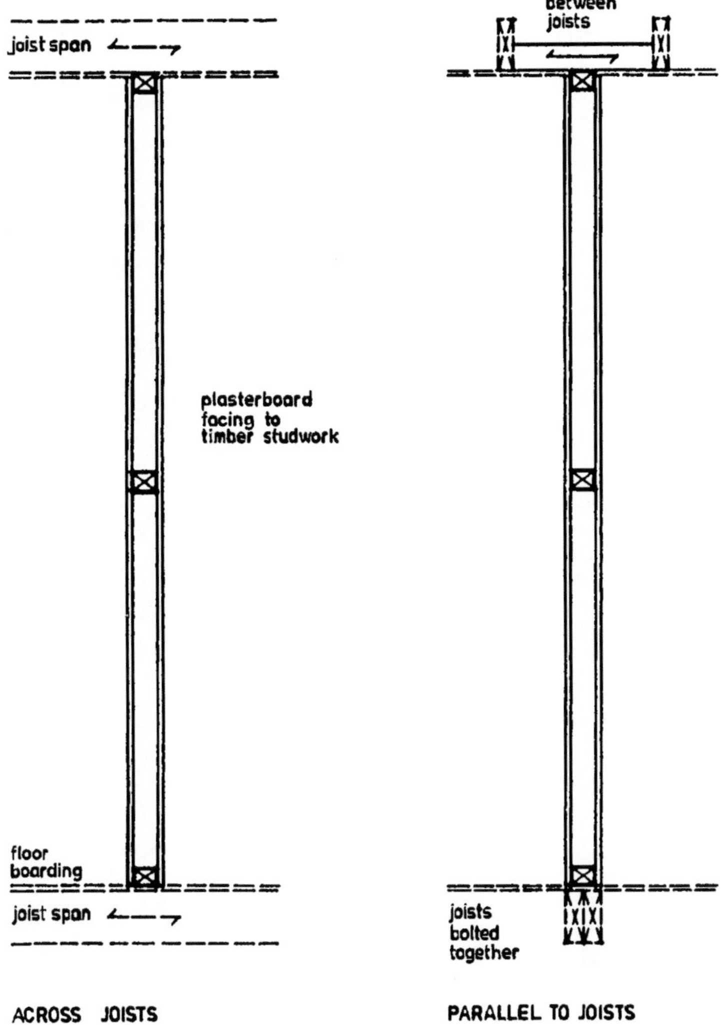

[A] Alterations

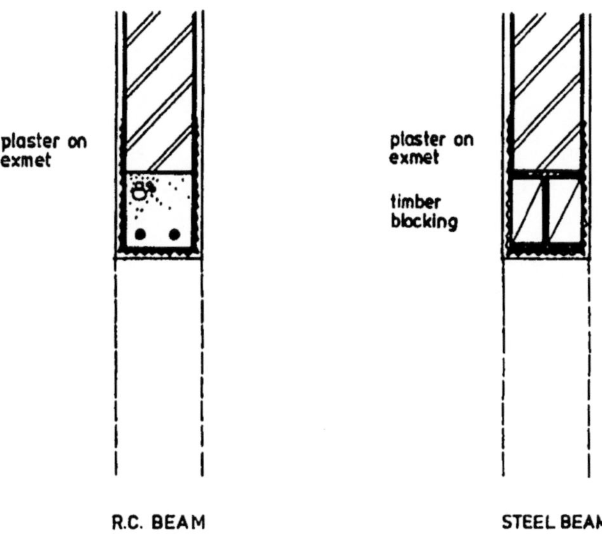

[B] Stud Partition

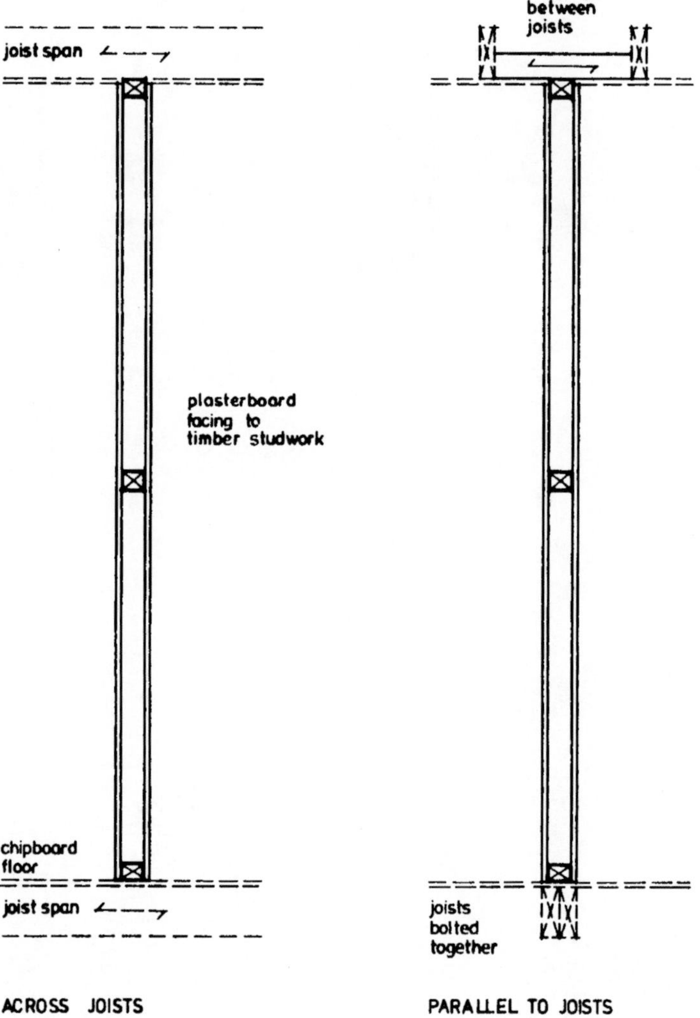

[B] Alterations

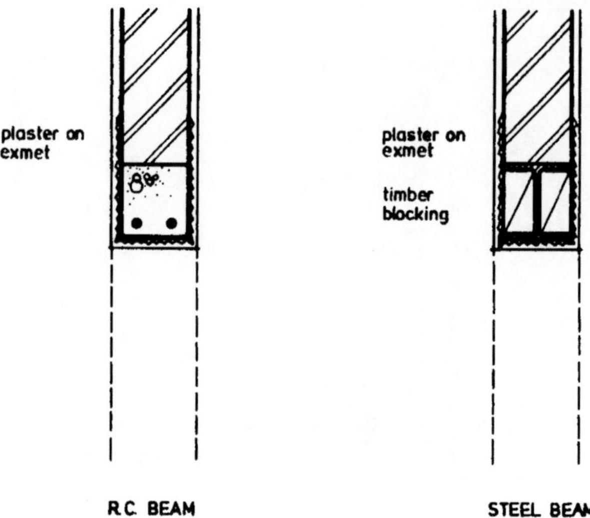

Item Build Ups	Qty	Hours per unit L=Labour P=Plant	Total Labour Time	Labour Rate Per Hour	Total Value of Labour £	Total Plant Time	Plant Rate Per Hour	Total Value of Plant £	Mat Unit Rate	Total Value of Material £	S/c Unit Rate	Total Value of s/c spec. £	TOTAL £
INTERNAL DOORS Hardwood flush door													
Door complete including frame, ironmongery and finishings.													
1 NR FLUSH DOOR INCLUDES (A)													
Premdor De-Luxe Ash veneered, factory finished flush door, shrink wrapped, 762 x 1981 mm	1.000Nr	L=1.04	1.03	15.43	15.89				55.40	55.40			**71.29**
Hardwood door frame and lining, tongued at angles, 20 x 143 mm	4.820m	L=0.28	1.33	15.43	20.52				8.58	41.36			**61.88**
Hardwood stop fillet 13 x 38 mm	4.700m	L=0.27	1.25	15.43	19.29				3.15	14.81			**34.10**
Hardwood moulded architrave 25 x 75 mm	10.180m	L=0.35	3.51	15.43	54.16				5.90	60.06			**114.22**
Prepare; two coats polyurethane varnish to frames and linings; internally	1.850m2	L=0.41	0.76	15.43	11.73				2.07	3.83			**15.56**
Prepare; two coats polyurethane varnish on wood surfaces internally	3.210m2	L=0.41	1.32	15.43	20.37				1.91	6.13			**26.50**
Fix only medium steel butts	1.500Pair	L=0.31	0.47	15.43	7.25								**7.25**
Fix only mortice latch	1.000Nr	L=1.15	1.15	15.43	17.74								**17.74**
Fix only lever lock / latch furniture	1.000Set	L=0.58	0.57	15.43	8.80								**8.80**
P.C. £55.00 for door ironmongery	1.000Set								55.00	55.00			**55.00**
			11.39		**£175.75**					**£236.59**			**£412.34**

Item Build Ups	Qty	Hours per unit L=Labour P=Plant	Total Labour Time	Labour Rate Per Hour	Total Value of Labour £	Total Plant Time	Plant Rate Per Hour	Total Value of Plant £	Mat Unit Rate	Total Value of Material £	S/c Unit Rate	Total Value of s/c spec. £	TOTAL £
INTERNAL DOORS cont/... Softwood flush door													
Door complete including frame, ironmongery and finishing.													
1 NR FLUSH DOOR INCLUDES (B)													
Premdor interior flush door, primed, size 762 x 1981 mm	1.000Nr	L=0.92	0.92	15.43	14.20				20.03	20.03			**34.23**
Wrought softwood linings tongued at angles, 25 x 150 mm	4.820m	L=0.23	1.11	15.43	17.13				2.90	13.98			**31.11**
Wrought softwood stop fillet 13 x 38 mm	4.700m	L=0.15	0.70	15.43	10.80				1.09	5.12			**15.92**
Wrought softwood architrave 19 x 50 mm, chamfered and rounded	9.990m	L=0.17	1.73	15.43	26.69				0.84	8.39			**35.08**
Prepare, knot, prime, stop; one coat primer; one undercoat, one coat alkyd based gloss to wood surfaces	3.210m2	L=0.58	1.86	15.43	28.70				2.19	7.03			**35.73**
Prepare, knot, prime, stop; one undercoat and one coat alkyd based paint to frames and linings	1.650m2	L=0.58	0.95	15.43	14.66				2.19	3.61			**18.27**
Fix only medium steel butts	1.500Pair	L=0.23	0.35	15.43	5.40								**5.40**
Fix only mortice latch	1.000Nr	L=0.86	0.86	15.43	13.27								**13.27**
Fix only lever lock / latch furniture	1.000Set	L=0.46	0.46	15.43	7.10								**7.10**
P.C. £55.00 for door ironmongery	1.000Set								55.00	55.00			**55.00**
			8.94		**£137.95**					**£113.16**			**£251.11**
WALL FINISHES Plaster and decoration													
Thistle plaster and emulsion paint to brick or block walls.													
1 SQUARE METRE WALL FINISH INCLUDES (A+B)													
2 mm Thistle plaster finish on 11 mm Thistle Browning coat to brick or block wall	1.000m2	L=0.44	0.44	23.97	10.55				2.91	2.91			**13.46**
One mist and two full coats vinyl silk emulsion paint to walls internally	1.000m2	L=0.30	0.30	15.43	4.63				1.49	1.49			**6.12**
			0.74		**£15.18**					**£4.40**			**£19.58**

Item Build Ups	Qty	Hours per unit L=Labour P=Plant	Total Labour Time	Labour Rate Per Hour	Total Value of Labour £	Total Plant Time	Plant Rate Per Hour	Total Value of Plant £	Mat Unit Rate	Total Value of Material £	S/c Unit Rate	Total Value of s/c spec. £	TOTAL £
FLOOR FINISHES Laminate													
1 SQUARE METRE FLOOR FINISH INCLUDES (A)													
10mm laminate flooring, oak plank, microbevelled edges, lacquered finish	1.000m2	L=0.38	0.38	15.43	5.86				18.19	18.19			**24.05**
5mm underlay to strip flooring, laid loose	1.000m2	L=0.20	0.20	15.43	3.09				3.23	3.23			**6.32**
			0.58		**£8.95**					**£21.42**			**£30.37**
Thermoplastic tiles on screed													
1 SQUARE METRE FLOOR FINISH INCLUDES (B)													
38 mm Cement and sand screed 1:3 to floor	1.000m2	L=0.31	0.31	23.97	7.43				5.01	5.01			**12.44**
Marley Econoflex Series 4 thermoplastic tiles 300 x 300 x 2 mm	1.000m2	L=0.44	0.44	21.13	9.30				13.77	13.77			**23.07**
			0.75		**£16.73**					**£18.78**			**£35.51**
Skirtings													
Hardwood moulded skirting													
1 METRE RUN OF SKIRTING INCLUDES (A)													
25 x 125 mm Hardwood moulded skirting	1.000m	L=0.55	0.55	15.43	8.49				8.53	8.53			**17.02**
Prepare; two coats polyurethane varnish to skirtings 150 mm girth; internally	1.000m	L=0.14	0.14	15.43	2.16				0.37	0.37			**2.53**
			0.69		**£10.65**					**£8.90**			**£19.55**
Softwood skirting, decoration													
1 METRE RUN OF SKIRTING INCLUDES (B)													
Wrought softwood bullnosed skirting 19 x 100 mm	1.000m	L=0.40	0.40	15.43	6.17				1.64	1.64			**7.81**
Prepare, knot, prime, stop; one undercoat and one coat alkyd based paint to skirtings 150 mm girth	1.000m	L=0.19	0.19	15.43	2.93				0.30	0.30			**3.23**
			0.59		**£9.10**					**£1.94**			**£11.04**

Item Build Ups	Qty	Hours per unit L=Labour P=Plant	Total Labour Time	Labour Rate Per Hour	Total Value of Labour £	Total Plant Time	Plant Rate Per Hour	Total Value of Plant £	Mat Unit Rate	Total Value of Material £	S/c Unit Rate	Total Value of s/c spec. £	TOTAL £
CEILING FINISHES Plasterboard, plaster and decoration													
Gypsum plasterboard, thistleboard finish plaster and emulsion paint to ceilings.													
1 SQUARE METRE OF CEILING FINISH INCLUDES (A)													
9.5 mm Gypsum plasterboard fixed with galvanised nails to softwood ceilings	1.000m2	L=0.24	0.24	21.13	5.07				3.79	3.79			**8.86**
5 mm Thistle board finish plaster to plasterboard in two coats, including scrimming joints	1.000m2	L=0.38	0.38	23.97	9.11				1.81	1.81			**10.92**
One mist coat, two full coats vinyl silk emulsion paint to ceilings internally	1.000m2	L=0.35	0.35	15.43	5.40				1.49	1.49			**6.89**
			0.97		**£19.58**					**£7.09**			**£26.67**
Plasterboard and Artex finish													
Gypsum plasterboard; scrimming joints; Artex stipple finish.													
1 SQUARE METRE OF CEILING FINISH INCLUDES (B)													
9.5 mm Gypsum plasterboard fixed with galvanised nails to softwood ceilings	1.000m2	L=0.24	0.24	21.13	5.07				3.79	3.79			**8.86**
One coat Artex sealer and one coat Artex standard compound with stipple finish to ceilings, including scrimming joints	1.000m2	L=0.39	0.39	15.43	6.02				1.54	1.54			**7.56**
			0.63		**£11.09**					**£5.33**			**£16.42**

Item Build Ups	Qty	Hours per unit L=Labour P=Plant	Total Labour Time	Labour Rate Per Hour	Total Value of Labour £	Total Plant Time	Plant Rate Per Hour	Total Value of Plant £	Mat Unit Rate	Total Value of Material £	S/c Unit Rate	Total Value of s/c spec. £	TOTAL £
SERVICES Rainwater pipes													
68 mm Diameter PVCu pipes fixed with standard brackets.													
1 METRE RUN OF RAINWATER PIPE INCLUDES (A+B)													
68 mm pipe	1.000m	L=0.42	0.42	32.03	13.45				2.35	2.35			**15.80**
Shoe	0.330Nr	L=0.44	0.15	32.03	4.80				2.55	0.84			**5.64**
Offset 150 mm projection	0.660Nr	L=0.17	0.11	32.03	3.52				2.92	1.93			**5.45**
			0.68		**£21.77**					**£5.12**			**£26.89**
Water service													
Cold water service per point including pipe fittings, bends, elbows, tees, stop valves, draw off cocks; pipework in copper.													
1 NR COLD WATER SERVICE POINT INCLUDES (A+B)													
22 mm Copper pipes BS EN1057 Part 1 Table X, capillary fittings, two piece spacing clips at 1500 mm centres	0.400m	L=0.31	0.12	32.03	3.84				5.05	2.02			**5.86**
22 mm Tees	0.200Nr	L=0.31	0.06	32.03	1.92				3.10	0.62			**2.54**
22 mm Elbows	0.100Nr	L=0.28	0.03	32.03	0.96				1.40	0.14			**1.10**
22 mm Gunmetal and brass stop valve	0.100Nr	L=0.30	0.03	32.03	0.96				19.30	1.93			**2.89**
15 mm Copper pipes BS EN1057 Part 1 Table X, capillary fittings, two piece spacing clips at 1500 mm centres	3.600m	L=0.29	1.03	32.03	32.99				2.56	9.22			**42.21**
15 mm Elbow	3.400Nr	L=0.24	0.82	32.03	26.26				0.51	1.73			**27.99**
15 mm Tee	0.600Nr	L=0.28	0.17	32.03	5.45				0.98	0.59			**6.04**
15 mm Straight tap connector	1.000Nr	L=0.24	0.24	32.03	7.69				2.52	2.52			**10.21**
15 mm Gunmetal and brass stop valve	0.600Nr	L=0.26	0.16	32.03	5.12				10.97	6.58			**11.70**
			2.66		**£85.19**					**£25.35**			**£110.54**

Item Build Ups	Qty	Hours per unit L=Labour P=Plant	Total Labour Time	Labour Rate Per Hour	Total Value of Labour £	Total Plant Time	Plant Rate Per Hour	Total Value of Plant £	Mat Unit Rate	Total Value of Material £	S/c Unit Rate	Total Value of s/c spec. £	TOTAL £
SERVICES cont/... Water service cont/...													
Hot water service per point including pipe fittings, bends, elbows, tees, stop valves, draw off cocks; pipework in copper.													
1 NR HOT WATER SERVICE POINT INCLUDES (A+B)													
22 mm Copper pipes BS EN1057 Part 1 Table X, capillary fittings, two piece spacing clips at 1500 mm centres	0.670m	L=0.31	0.21	32.03	6.73				5.04	3.38			**10.11**
22 mm Straight tap connector	0.330Nr	L=0.28	0.09	32.03	2.88				3.00	0.99			**3.87**
22 mm Elbow	0.330Nr	L=0.28	0.09	32.03	2.88				1.36	0.45			**3.33**
22 mm Tank connector	0.170Nr	L=0.35	0.06	32.03	1.92				14.18	2.41			**4.33**
15 mm Copper pipes BS EN1057 Part 1 Table X, capillary fittings, two piece spacing clips at 1500 mm centres	6.000m	L=0.29	1.72	32.03	55.09				2.56	15.36			**70.45**
15 mm Elbow	5.670Nr	L=0.24	1.37	32.03	43.88				0.51	2.89			**46.77**
15 mm Tee	1.000Nr	L=0.28	0.28	32.03	8.97				0.98	0.98			**9.95**
15 mm Tank connector	1.000Nr	L=0.33	0.33	32.03	10.57				9.32	9.32			**19.89**
15 mm Gunmetal and brass stop valve	1.000Nr	L=0.26	0.26	32.03	8.33				10.96	10.96			**19.29**
22 mm Preformed sectional pipe insulation, jointed with adhesive, secured with tape	0.670m	L=0.09	0.06	32.03	1.92				2.93	1.96			**3.88**
			4.47		**£143.17**					**£48.70**			**£191.87**

Item Build Ups	Qty	Hours per unit L=Labour P=Plant	Total Labour Time	Labour Rate Per Hour	Total Value of Labour £	Total Plant Time	Plant Rate Per Hour	Total Value of Plant £	Mat Unit Rate	Total Value of Material £	S/c Unit Rate	Total Value of s/c spec. £	TOTAL £
SERVICES cont/... Water service cont/...													
Central Heating service per point including pipe fittings, bends, elbows, tees, stop valves, draw off cocks; pipework in copper.													
1 NR C.H. SERVICE POINT INCLUDES (A+B)													
15 mm Copper pipes BS EN1057 Part 1 Table X, capillary fittings, two piece spacing clips at 1500 mm centres	9.000m	L=0.29	2.57	32.03	82.32				2.56	23.04			**105.36**
15 mm Elbow	4.000Nr	L=0.24	0.97	32.03	31.07				0.51	2.04			**33.11**
15 mm Tee	2.000Nr	L=0.28	0.55	32.03	17.62				0.98	1.96			**19.58**
15 mm Straight tap connector	2.000Nr	L=0.24	0.48	32.03	15.37				2.52	5.04			**20.41**
15 mm Preformed sectional pipe insulation, jointed with adhesive, secured with tape	6.000m	L=0.09	0.53	32.03	16.98				2.04	12.24			**29.22**
22 mm Copper pipes BS EN1057 Part 1 Table X, capillary fittings, two piece spacing clips at 1500 mm centres	6.000m	L=0.31	1.85	32.03	59.26				5.05	30.30			**89.56**
22 mm Tee	2.000Nr	L=0.31	0.62	32.03	19.86				3.12	6.24			**26.10**
22 mm Gunmetal and brass stop valve	1.000Nr	L=0.30	0.30	32.03	9.61				19.26	19.26			**28.87**
22 mm Preformed sectional pipe insulation, jointed with adhesive, secured with tape	6.000m	L=0.09	0.53	32.03	16.98				2.92	17.52			**34.50**
			8.40		**£269.07**					**£117.64**			**£386.71**
Electrical services													
Installations with concealed wiring, prices per point including cable, switchplates, socket outlets but excluding appliances and luminaires.													
ELECTRICAL SERVICES INCLUDE (A+B)													
Lighting point, one way switch	1.000NR										74.00	74.00	**74.00**
Socket point, double, 13amp	1.000NR										82.50	82.50	**82.50**
Cooker outlet	1.000NR										130.00	130.00	**130.00**
												£286.50	**£286.50**

Item Build Ups	Qty	Hours per unit L=Labour P=Plant	Total Labour Time	Labour Rate Per Hour	Total Value of Labour £	Total Plant Time	Plant Rate Per Hour	Total Value of Plant £	Mat Unit Rate	Total Value of Material £	S/c Unit Rate	Total Value of s/c spec. £	TOTAL £
ALTERATIONS TO EXISTING BUILDINGS Cutting opening in wall													
Cutting opening in existing cavity wall, brick outer skin, block inner skin, including needling and propping; insert lintel, cavity tray, make good jamb, DPC's, work to reveals, make good plasterwork.													
1 NR OPENING SIZE 1.80 M WIDE 2.00 M HIGH INCLUDES (A+B)													
Cut hole through cavity wall for needle, insert needle and pair of props, remove afterwards and make good wall	2.000Nr	L=2.51 P=2.00	5.01	21.13	105.86	4.00	2.20	8.80	7.87	15.74			**130.40**
Cut out 100 mm blockwork walling	3.600m2	L=0.37	1.34	21.13	28.31								**28.31**
Cut out half brick facing brickwork walling	3.600m2	L=0.84	3.01	21.13	63.60								**63.60**
Cut and pin end of new lintel in 100 mm blockwork	2.000Nr	L=0.25	0.50	21.13	10.57								**10.57**
Cut and pin end of new lintel in half brick wall	2.000Nr	L=0.33	0.67	21.13	14.16								**14.16**
Make good jamb and cill, close cavity and build in DPC	5.800m	L=1.67	9.69	21.13	204.75				4.87	28.25			**233.00**
Insert lintel, including bedding ends in c.m. 1:3, precast reinforced concrete lintel size 327.5 x 215 mm	2.100m	L=0.79	1.66	21.13	35.08				48.95	102.80			**137.88**
Wedge and pin with slates in c.m. 1:3	4.200m	L=0.24	1.01	21.13	21.34				5.26	22.09			**43.43**
Build in horizontal fibre based bitumen felt DPC with cavity gutter in cavity wall	0.630m2	L=0.28	0.18	21.13	3.80				7.75	4.88			**8.68**
Make good reveals and surrounds with Thistle gypsum plaster 300 mm wide	0.580m2	L=1.30	0.75	23.97	17.98				2.95	1.71			**19.69**
			23.82		**£505.45**	**4.00**		**£8.80**		**£175.47**			**£689.72**

Item Build Ups	Qty	Hours per unit L=Labour P=Plant	Total Labour Time	Labour Rate Per Hour	Total Value of Labour £	Total Plant Time	Plant Rate Per Hour	Total Value of Plant £	Mat Unit Rate	Total Value of Material £	S/c Unit Rate	Total Value of s/c spec. £	TOTAL £
ALTERATIONS TO EXISTING BUILDINGS cont/... Cutting opening in wall cont/...													
1 NR OPENING SIZE 2.40 M WIDE 2.00 M HIGH INCLUDES (A+B)													
Cut hole through cavity wall for needle, insert needle and pair of props, remove afterwards and make good wall	3.000Nr	L=2.51 P=2.00	7.52	21.13	158.90	6.00	2.20	13.20	7.87	23.61			**195.71**
Cut out 100 mm blockwork walling	4.800m2	L=0.37	1.78	21.13	37.61								**37.61**
Cut out half brick facing brickwork walling	4.800m2	L=0.84	4.01	21.13	84.73								**84.73**
Cut and pin end of new lintel in 100 mm blockwork	2.000Nr	L=0.25	0.50	21.13	10.57								**10.57**
Cut and pin end of new lintel in half brick wall	2.000Nr	L=0.33	0.67	21.13	14.16								**14.16**
Make good jamb and cill, close cavity and build in DPC	6.400m	L=1.67	10.69	21.13	225.88				4.87	31.17			**257.05**
Insert lintel, including bedding ends in c.m. 1:3, precast reinforced concrete lintel size 327.5 x 215 mm	2.700m	L=0.79	2.13	21.13	45.01				48.95	132.17			**177.18**
Wedge and pin with slates in c.m. 1:3	5.400m	L=0.24	1.30	21.13	27.47				5.26	28.40			**55.87**
Build in horizontal fibre based bitumen felt DPC with cavity gutter in cavity wall	0.810m2	L=0.28	0.23	21.13	4.86				7.75	6.28			**11.14**
Make good reveals and surrounds with Thistle gypsum plaster 300 mm wide	0.640m2	L=1.30	0.83	23.97	19.90				2.94	1.88			**21.78**
			29.66		**£629.09**	**6.00**		**£13.20**		**£223.51**			**£865.80**

Item Build Ups	Qty	Hours per unit L=Labour P=Plant	Total Labour Time	Labour Rate Per Hour	Total Value of Labour £	Total Plant Time	Plant Rate Per Hour	Total Value of Plant £	Mat Unit Rate	Total Value of Material £	S/c Unit Rate	Total Value of s/c spec. £	TOTAL £
ALTERATIONS TO EXISTING BUILDINGS cont/... Cutting opening in wall cont/...													
1 NR OPENING SIZE 3.00 M WIDE 2.00 M HIGH INCLUDES (A+B)													
Cut hole through cavity wall for needle, insert needle and pair of props, remove afterwards and make good wall	4.000Nr	L=2.51 P=2.00	10.02	21.13	211.72	8.00	2.20	17.60	7.87	31.48			**260.80**
Cut out 100 mm blockwork walling	6.000m2	L=0.37	2.23	21.13	47.12								**47.12**
Cut out half brick facing brickwork walling	6.000m2	L=0.84	5.01	21.13	105.86								**105.86**
Cut and pin end of new lintel in 100 mm blockwork	2.000Nr	L=0.25	0.50	21.13	10.57								**10.57**
Cut and pin end of new lintel in half brick wall	2.000Nr	L=0.33	0.67	21.13	14.16								**14.16**
Make good jamb and cill, close cavity and build in DPC	4.000m	L=1.67	6.68	21.13	141.15				4.87	19.48			**160.63**
Insert lintel, including bedding ends in c.m. 1:3, precast reinforced concrete lintel size 327.5 x 215 mm	3.300m	L=0.79	2.61	21.13	55.15				48.95	161.54			**216.69**
Wedge and pin with slates in c.m. 1:3	6.600m	L=0.24	1.58	21.13	33.39				5.26	34.72			**68.11**
Build in horizontal fibre based bitumen felt DPC with cavity gutter in cavity wall	0.990m2	L=0.28	0.28	21.13	5.92				7.76	7.68			**13.60**
Make good reveals and surrounds with Thistle gypsum plaster 300 mm wide	0.700m2	L=1.30	0.91	23.97	21.81				2.94	2.06			**23.87**
			30.49		**£646.85**	**8.00**		**£17.60**		**£256.96**			**£921.41**

Item Build Ups	Qty	Hours per unit L=Labour P=Plant	Total Labour Time	Labour Rate Per Hour	Total Value of Labour £	Total Plant Time	Plant Rate Per Hour	Total Value of Plant £	Mat Unit Rate	Total Value of Material £	S/c Unit Rate	Total Value of s/c spec. £	TOTAL £
ALTERATIONS TO EXISTING BUILDINGS cont/... Cutting opening in wall cont/...													
1 NR OPENING SIZE 4.00 M WIDE 2.00 M HIGH INCLUDES (A+B)													
Cut hole through cavity wall for needle, insert needle and pair of props, remove afterwards and make good wall	5.000Nr	L=2.51 P=2.00	12.53	21.13	264.76	10.00	2.20	22.00	7.87	39.35			**326.11**
Cut out 100 mm blockwork walling	8.000m2	L=0.37	2.97	21.13	62.76								**62.76**
Cut out half brick facing brickwork walling	8.000m2	L=0.84	6.68	21.13	141.15								**141.15**
Cut and pin end of new lintel in 100 mm blockwork	2.000Nr	L=0.25	0.50	21.13	10.57								**10.57**
Cut and pin end of new lintel in half brick wall	2.000Nr	L=0.33	0.67	21.13	14.16								**14.16**
Make good jamb and cill, close cavity and build in DPC	4.000m	L=1.67	6.68	21.13	141.15				4.87	19.48			**160.63**
Insert lintel, including bedding ends in c.m. 1:3, precast reinforced concrete lintel size 327.5 x 215 mm	4.300m	L=0.79	3.40	21.13	71.84				48.95	210.49			**282.33**
Wedge and pin with slates in c.m. 1:3	8.600m	L=0.24	2.06	21.13	43.53				5.26	45.24			**88.77**
Build in horizontal fibre based bitumen felt DPC with cavity gutter in cavity wall	1.290m2	L=0.28	0.36	21.13	7.61				7.75	10.00			**17.61**
Make good reveals and surrounds with Thistle gypsum plaster 300 mm wide	0.800m2	L=1.30	1.04	23.97	24.93				2.94	2.35			**27.28**
			36.89		**£782.46**	**10.00**		**£22.00**		**£326.91**			**£1131.37**

Item Build Ups	Qty	Hours per unit L=Labour P=Plant	Total Labour Time	Labour Rate Per Hour	Total Value of Labour £	Total Plant Time	Plant Rate Per Hour	Total Value of Plant £	Mat Unit Rate	Total Value of Material £	S/c Unit Rate	Total Value of s/c spec. £	TOTAL £
ALTERATIONS TO EXISTING BUILDINGS cont/... Cutting opening in wall cont/...													
1 NR OPENING SIZE 5.00 M WIDE 2.00 M HIGH INCLUDES (A+B)													
Cut hole through cavity wall for needle, insert needle and pair of props, remove afterwards and make good wall	6.000Nr	L=2.51 P=2.00	15.04	21.13	317.80	12.00	2.20	26.40	7.87	47.22			**391.42**
Cut out 100 mm blockwork walling	10.000m2	L=0.37	3.71	21.13	78.39								**78.39**
Cut out half brick facing brickwork walling	10.000m2	L=0.84	8.35	21.13	176.44								**176.44**
Cut and pin end of new lintel in 100 mm blockwork	2.000Nr	L=0.25	0.50	21.13	10.57								**10.57**
Cut and pin end of new lintel in half brick wall	2.000Nr	L=0.33	0.67	21.13	14.16								**14.16**
Make good jamb and cill, close cavity and build in DPC	4.000m	L=1.67	6.68	21.13	141.15				4.87	19.48			**160.63**
Insert lintel, including bedding ends in c.m. 1:3, precast reinforced concrete lintel size 327.5 x 215 mm	5.300m	L=0.79	4.19	21.13	88.53				48.95	259.44			**347.97**
Wedge and pin with slates in c.m. 1:3	10.600m	L=0.24	2.54	21.13	53.67				5.26	55.76			**109.43**
Build in horizontal fibre based bitumen felt DPC with cavity gutter in cavity wall	1.590m2	L=0.28	0.44	21.13	9.30				7.75	12.32			**21.62**
Make good reveals and surrounds with Thistle gypsum plaster 300 mm wide	0.900m2	L=1.30	1.17	23.97	28.04				2.94	2.65			**30.69**
			43.29		**£918.05**	**12.00**		**£26.40**		**£396.87**			**£1341.32**

CALCULATING THE TOTAL LABOUR TIME

As has been shown, the detailed cost breakdowns display the total labour time for each item (Column 4). These times may be used to establish the overall total labour time for the whole project. Note: this total would assume only one productive person carrying out the tasks.

This is achieved by using both the standard estimate and the detailed cost breakdown. A worked example of the calculation of the total labour time for a typical standard estimate is shown below.

If we assume an extension to Specification A Single Storey Pitched Roof Plan size 3.00 x 3.00m, then referring to standard estimated A/1P 3 x 3 together with the detailed cost breakdowns, the following may be calculated:

	Detailed Costs Time Allowance (Col 4) Hours	Quantity in Standard Estimate A/1P 3 x 3	Total Time Required Hours	
Strip Footings	5.02	10M	50.20	
Hollow Ground Floor	2.98	9M2	26.82	
Pitched Roof Construction	2.00	14M2	28.00	
Work to Top of External Wall	1.07	10M	10.70	
Plain Tile Roofing	1.09	17M2	18.53	
Work to Verge	0.28	5M	1.40	
Work to Hip	0.80	8M	6.40	
Work to Eaves	0.26	11M	2.86	
Fascia and Eaves Soffit	1.88	11M	20.68	
Gutters and Fittings	0.44	11M	4.84	
Flashings	0.09	5M	0.45	
Brick and Block cavity wall	2.99	20M2	59.80	
External Door	15.41	1NR	15.41	
Windows	9.40	1NR	9.40	
Opening for Door	3.73	1NR	3.73	
Opening for Window	3.94	1NR	3.94	
Plaster and Decoration	0.74	30M2	22.20	
Laminate	0.58	9M2	5.22	
Hardwood Skirting	0.69	12M	8.28	
Plasterboard Ceiling	0.97	9M2	8.73	
Rainwater Pipes	0.68	3M	2.04	
Cold Water Service Point	2.66	1NR	2.66	
Hot Water Service Point	4.47	1NR	4.47	
Central Heating Service Point	8.40	1NR	8.40	
Electrical Installation	-	1NR	0.00	
Opening in Existing Walls	30.49	1NR	30.49	
TOTAL NR OF LABOUR HOURS TO CONSTRUCT STANDARD ESTIMATE A/1P 3 x 3			355.65	**Hours**

NB: No allowance for Electrical Work and lead flashing. It is anticipated that these will be carried out by a sub-contractor.

ADJUSTING THE COSTS TO MODIFY THE STANDARD ESTIMATES

The following paragraphs provide a number of worked examples to explain clearly and concisely how to adjust the detailed cost breakdowns in order to modify the standard estimates.

The changes considered are:

a) Plan size different to standard estimate.

b) Depth of foundation brickwork increased from 750 mm to 950 mm.

c) Cost of facing bricks adjusted from £351.38/1000 to £396.23/1000.

d) Window changed in size from 1200 x 1200 mm to 1800 x 1300 mm.

e) External door and frame changed from PVCu to hardwood.

To illustrate the worked examples and their effect on a standard estimate, use has been made of standard estimate ref A/1P 4 x 4 which is for a single storey pitched roof extension constructed to specification A and having a plan size of 4.00 x 4.00m.

Plan Size Different to Standard Estimate

For this example it is assumed that the Builder's specification requires a plan size of 4.00m projection 4.50m wide. This modification will result in the adjustment of many of the items contained in the standard estimate for a 4.00 x 4.00m extension.

The following table shows the standard estimate A/1P 4 x 4 from Chapter 4, the modifications required and the resultant modified estimate. In this first adjustment, all the modifications are to quantity and not price.

Briefly, the modifications affect strip footings, ground floor, roof structure, roof coverings, external walls and structure.

SPECIFICATION A SINGLE STOREY PITCHED ROOF Element	Unit	Unit Rate £	Ref. A/1P 4x4 Size 4.00 x 4.00m Area 16m2 Qty	Total £	Element Total £	Modification	Modified Estimate Size 4.00 x 4.50m Area 18m2 Qty	Total £	Element Total £
SUBSTRUCTURE									
Strip footings	M	144.41.	13M	1877.33		Quantity adjusted to	15M	2166.15	
Hollow ground floor	M2	91.57	16M2	1465.12	**3342.45**	Quantity adjusted to	18M2	1648.26	**3814.41**
ROOF									
Pitched roof construction	M2	55.42	23M2	1274.66		Quantity adjusted to	26M2	1440.92	
Work to top of external wall	M	23.71	13M	308.23		Quantity adjusted to	14M	331.94	
Plain tile roofing	M2	69.30	28M2	1940.40		Quantity adjusted to	32M2	2217.60	
Work to verge	M	11.58	6M	69.48		No change	6M	69.48	
Work to hip	M	41.73	10M	417.30		No change	10M	417.30	
Work to eaves	M	22.73	14M	318.22		Quantity adjusted to	15M	340.95	
Fascia and eaves soffit	M	48.01	14M	672.14		Quantity adjusted to	15M	720.15	
Gutters and fittings	M	18.68	14M	261.52		Quantity adjusted to	15M	280.20	
Flashings	M	69.52	6M	417.12	**5679.07**	No change	6M	417.12	**6235.66**
EXTERNAL WALLS									
Brick and block cavity wall	M2	114.25	28M2	3199.00	**3199.00**	Quantity adjusted to	31M2	3541.75	**3541.75**

SPECIFICATION A SINGLE STOREY PITCHED ROOF Element	Unit	Unit Rate £	Ref. A/1P 4x4 Size 4.00 x 4.00m Area 16m2 Qty	Total £	Element Total £	Modification	Modified Estimate Size 4.00 x 4.50m Area 18m2 Qty	Total £	Element Total £
EXTERNAL DOORS AND WINDOWS									
External door	NR	655.02	1NR	655.02		No change	1NR	655.02	
Windows	NR	672.89	1NR	672.89		No change	1NR	672.89	
Opening in cavity wall for door	NR	144.37	1NR	144.37		No change	1NR	144.37	
Opening in cavity wall for window	NR	162.98	1NR	162.98	**1635.26**	No change	1NR	162.98	**1635.26**
WALL FINISHES									
Plaster and decoration	M2	19.58	40M2	783.20	**783.20**	Quantity adjusted to	43M2	841.94	**841.94**
FLOOR FINISHES									
Laminate	M2	30.30	16M2	484.80		Quantity adjusted to	18M2	545.40	
Hardwood skirting	M	19.52	16M	312.32	**797.12**	Quantity adjusted to	18M	351.36	**896.76**
CEILING FINISHES									
Plasterboard, plaster and decoration	M2	26.68	16M2	426.88	**426.88**	Quantity adjusted to	18M2	480.24	**480.24**

SPECIFICATION A SINGLE STOREY PITCHED ROOF Element	Unit	Unit Rate £	Ref. A/1P 4x4 Size 4.00 x 4.00m Area 16m2 Qty	Total £	Element Total £	Modification	Modified Estimate Size 4.00 x 4.50m Area 18m2 Qty	Total £	Element Total £
SERVICES									
Rainwater pipes	M	26.64	3M	79.92		No change	3M	79.92	
Cold water service point	NR	110.52	1NR	110.52		No change	1NR	110.52	
Hot water service point	NR	191.67	1NR	191.67		No change	1NR	191.67	
Central heating service point	NR	386.51	1NR	386.51		No change	1NR	386.51	
Electrical installation	NR	286.50	1NR	286.50	**1055.12**	No change	1NR	286.50	**1055.12**
ALTERATIONS TO EXISTING BUILDINGS									
Opening in existing wall 4.00m wide 2.00m high	NR	1131.22	1NR	1131.22	**1131.22**	No change	1NR	1131.22	**1131.22**

NB: The modified estimate is not totalled here, but after the worked examples on the following pages have been dealt with.

ADJUSTING THE COSTS TO MODIFY THE STANDARD ESTIMATES cont/...

Depth of Foundation Brickwork Increased
In this example, the depth of the foundation brickwork is increased from 750 mm to 950 mm ie an increase of 200 mm. This will affect the quantities of the majority of the items included in a metre run.

By referring to the detailed cost breakdown of the strip footings, the quantities may be identified as follows. (Refer to section through foundations shown opposite detailed cost breakdown).

Strip footings
Hand excavation; concrete bed 300 mm thick; brick and block cavity wall 750 mm high; cavity filled with concrete; damp proof course.

1 METRE RUN OF STRIP FOOTING INCLUDES (A)	Qty	Modifications	New Quantities
Excavate topsoil by hand, average 150 mm	0.625m2	no change	0.625m2
Excavate trench by hand	0.470m3	0.625x0.20x1.00 = 0.13m3 thus 0.47+0.13	0.600m3
Disposal of excavated material on site	0.543m3	200 mm extra depth	0.600m3
Support to sides of excavation	1.500m2	200 mm extra depth each side	1.900m2
Level and compact bottom of excavation	0.600m2	no change	0.600m2
Part refill trench by hand using "Whacker"	0.020m3	no change	0.020m3
Plain concrete grade C20/25 in trench	0.180m3	no change	0.180m3
Hardcore filling in trench	0.130m3	200 mm extra depth	0.190m3
Concrete in filling to cavity wall	0.045m3	200 mm extra depth	0.060m3
Class A engineering brick PC£493.42/1000 in cement mortar 1:3 in skin of hollow wall	0.750m2	200 mm extra depth	0.950m2
Form cavity 75 mm wide with 5 Nr 200 mm galvanised butterfly ties per m2	0.750m2	200 mm extra depth	0.950m2
140 mm solid concrete blocks in cement mortar 1:3 in skin of hollow wall	0.750m2	200 mm extra depth	0.950m2
Terracotta air brick size 215x65 mm	0.500Nr	No change	0.500Nr
Polythene horizontal DPC 100 mm wide	1.000m	No change	1.000m
Polythene horizontal DPC 150 mm wide	1.000m	No change	1.000m

The following page shows the detailed cost breakdown recalculated using the new quantities.

Item Build Ups

Item Build Ups	Qty	Hours per unit L=Labour P=Plant	Total Labour Time	Labour Rate Per Hour	Total Value of Labour £	Total Plant Time	Plant Rate Per Hour	Total Value of Plant £	Mat Unit Rate	Total Value of Material £	S/c Unit Rate	Total Value of s/c spec. £	TOTAL £
SUBSTRUCTURE Strip footings (recalculated)													
Hand excavation; concrete bed 300 mm thick; brick and block cavity wall 950 mm high; cavity filled with concrete; damp proof course.													
1 METRE RUN OF STRIP FOOTING INCLUDES (A)													
Excavate topsoil by hand, average 150 mm	0.625m2	L=0.32	0.20	11.39	2.28								**2.28**
Excavate trench by hand	0.600m3	L=3.47	2.08	11.39	23.69								**23.69**
Disposal of excavated material on site	0.600m3	P=0.06				0.03	47.06	1.41					**1.41**
Support to sides of excavation	1.900m2	L=0.17	0.31	14.24	4.41				0.55	1.05			**5.46**
Level and compact bottom of excavation	0.600m2	L=0.08	0.05	11.39	0.57								**0.57**
Part refill trench by hand using "Whacker"	0.020m3	L=1.26 P=0.22	0.03	11.39	0.34		3.61						**0.34**
Plain concrete grade C20/25 in trench	0.180m3	L=1.43	0.26	11.39	2.96				94.94	17.09			**20.05**
Hardcore filling in trench	0.190m3	L=2.05 P=0.28	0.39	11.39	4.44	0.05	3.61	0.18	23.53	4.47			**9.09**
Concrete in filling to cavity wall	0.060m3	L=4.18	0.25	11.39	2.85				95.00	5.70			**8.55**
Class A engineering brick PC £493.42/1000 in cement mortar 1:3 in skin of hollow wall	0.950m2	L=1.55	1.47	21.13	31.06				33.42	31.75			**62.81**
Form cavity 75 mm wide with 5 Nr 200 mm galvanised butterfly ties per m2	0.950m2	L=0.04	0.04	21.13	0.85				0.34	0.32			**1.17**
140 mm solid concrete blocks in cement mortar 1:3 in skin of hollow wall	0.950m2	L=1.16	1.10	23.97	26.37				13.13	12.47			**38.84**
Terracotta air brick size 215 x 65 mm	0.500Nr	L=0.07	0.03	21.13	0.63				0.94	0.47			**1.10**
Polythene horizontal DPC 100 mm wide	1.000m	L=0.02	0.02	21.13	0.42				0.29	0.29			**0.71**
Polythene horizontal DPC 150 mm wide	1.000m	L=0.03	0.03	21.13	0.63				0.46	0.46			**1.09**
			6.26		**£101.50**	**0.08**		**£1.59**		**£74.07**			**£177.16**

ADJUSTING THE COSTS TO MODIFY THE STANDARD ESTIMATES cont/...

Adjusting the Cost of Facing Bricks

In this worked example it is assumed that the Builder's client has chosen an expensive facing brick. The detailed cost breakdown shows a cost of £351.38/1000 for facing bricks. The Builder's client has chosen a facing brick costing say £396.23/1000.

In the Memoranda section (Chapter 10) under Brickwork and Blockwork, a table is included which lists the number of bricks required per m2 for various thicknesses of wall. For a half brick wall, the table shows that 59.25 bricks are required excluding waste.

Allowing a waste factor of 5%, 59.25 becomes 62.21 say 63 bricks per m2.

The cost of the bricks may now be identified as follows:

a) At £351.38/1000 the cost of a square metre is

$$\frac{351.38}{1000.00} \times 63 = £22.14$$

b) At £396.23/1000 the cost of a square metre is

$$\frac{396.23}{1000.00} \times 63 = £24.96$$

This is an increase of £2.82 per m2. The material cost indicated in the detailed cost breakdown is £24.43. However, this includes the mortar.

To adjust the cost for bricks at £396.23/1000 simply increase the unit rate of £66.48 by £2.82 to **£69.30**.

Using the revised unit cost of £69.30 per m2 the total cost per m2 of external wall is recalculated as shown below.

1 SQUARE METRE OF EXTERNAL WALL INCLUDES (A)	TOTAL £
Facing bricks PC £396.23/1000 in gauged mortar 1:2:9 in 102.5 mm skin of hollow wall, flush pointing	69.30
Form cavity 75 mm wide with 5 Nr 200 mm galvanised butterfly ties per m2	1.19
Thermalite shield blocks 440 x 215 mm in gauged mortar1:2:9 in 140 mm skin of hollow wall	38.66
75 mm Dritherm cavity batts	7.82
ADJUSTED COST PER M2	**116.97**

ADJUSTING THE COSTS TO MODIFY THE STANDARD ESTIMATES cont/...

Change of Window Size

In this example, it is assumed that the Builder has to provide a larger window than is included in the standard estimate i.e. 1800 x 1300 mm rather than 1200 x 1200 mm. This adjustment will affect two of the items on the standard estimate.

a) The window
b) The opening in the cavity wall.

To adjust the window, refer to the detailed cost breakdown, the following adjustments must be made:

Windows

Standard hardwood window 1200 x 1200 mm, including glazing ironmongery, window board and decoration **1 NR WINDOW COMPLETE INCLUDES (A)**	**Qty**	**Modification**	**New Quantities**
Hardwood window 1200 x 1200 mm, preservative treated, factory double glazed, complete with stays and fasteners	1.000Nr	Replace with 1800 x 1300 mm hardwood window Cost say £542.76 new lab time 2.11	1.000Nr
32 x 230 mm hardwood window board	1.500m	Extra width	2.100m
Returned notched end to window board	2.000Nr	No change	2.000Nr
Galvanised mild steel frame ties 200 x 25 x 3 mm	4.000Nr	No change	4.000Nr
Bed frame in cement mortar 1:3	4.800m	Extra width and height	6.200m
Point edge in polysulphide mastic one side	4.800m	Extra width and height	6.200m
Prepare two coats polyurethane varnish to window board 150-300 mm girth internally	1.500m	To longer window board	2.100m
Prepare two coats polyurethane varnish to glazed windows in medium panes internally	1.440m2	Larger area	2.340m2
Prepare, one preservative basecoat and two coats external grade varnish to glazed windows in medium panes externally	1.440m2	Larger area	2.340m2

The following page shows the detailed cost breakdown recalculated using the new quantities and new window.

Item Build Ups	Qty	Hours per unit L=Labour P=Plant	Total Labour Time	Labour Rate Per Hour	Total Value of Labour £	Total Plant Time	Plant Rate Per Hour	Total Value of Plant £	Mat Unit Rate	Total Value of Material £	S/c Unit Rate	Total Value of s/c spec. £	TOTAL £
EXTERNAL DOORS AND WINDOWS Windows (recalculated)													
Standard hardwood window 1800 x 1300 mm, including glazing, ironmongery, window board and decoration.													
1 NR WINDOW COMPLETE INCLUDES (A)													
Hardwood window 1800 x 1300 mm, preservative treated, factory double glazed, complete with stays and fasteners	1.000Nr	L=2.11	2.11	15.43	32.56				542.76	542.76			**575.32**
32 x 225 mm Hardwood window board	2.100m	L=0.92	1.93	15.43	29.78				27.98	58.76			**88.54**
Returned notched end to window board	2.000Nr	L=0.29	0.58	15.43	8.95								**8.95**
Galvanised mild steel frame ties 200 x 25 x 3 mm	4.000Nr	L=0.14	0.55	15.43	8.49				0.72	2.88			**11.37**
Bed frame in cement mortar 1:3	6.200m	L=0.22	1.37	21.13	28.95				0.13	0.81			**29.76**
Point edge in polysulphide mastic one side	6.200m	L=0.22	1.37	21.13	28.95				1.30	8.06			**37.01**
Prepare; two coats polyurethane varnish to skirtings 150 - 300 mm girth; internally	2.100m	L=0.21	0.43	15.43	6.63				0.67	1.41			**8.04**
Prepare; two coats polyurethane varnish to glazed windows in medium panes; internally	2.340m2	L=0.74	1.74	15.43	26.85				1.36	3.18			**30.03**
Prepare; one preservative basecoat and two coats external grade varnish to glazed windows in medium panes; externally	2.340m2	L=1.14	2.68	15.43	41.35				2.55	5.97			**47.32**
			12.76		**£212.51**					**£623.83**			**£836.34**

ADJUSTING THE COSTS TO MODIFY THE STANDARD ESTIMATES cont/...

Change to Window Size cont/...

The second adjustment to provide for the larger window is that to the window opening. The replacement window is wider than the one in the standard estimate, which means that the opening will also be wider. This requires a longer lintel. In addition, the quantities of the other items of work to the window opening will increase.

Refer to the detailed cost breakdown for the window opening and make the following adjustments.

Opening in cavity wall for window

Lintel, cavity tray, work to jambs and sills including brick on edge sill and DPC **1 NR OPENING FOR WINDOW INCLUDES (A)**	**Qty**	**Modification**	**New Quantities**
Catnic lintel type CG50/100 1500 mm long	1.000Nr	Replace with 2100 mm long lintel cost £70.40. New lab time 0.72	1.000Nr
Cavity gutter	0.680m2	Extra length	1.020m2
Close cavity at jambs	2.400m	Extra height	2.600m
Vertical DPC at jambs 150 mm wide	2.800m	Extra height	3.000m
Close cavity at sills	1.300m	Extra length	1.900m
Polythene horizontal DPC 150 mm wide	1.200m	Extra length	1.800m
Fair return on facings at head and jambs	3.600m	Extra length and height	4.900m
Brick on edge sill in facing bricks	1.200m	Extra length	1.800m
Expamet angle bead	3.600m	Extra length	4.900m
13 mm Two coat plaster to walls not exceeding 300 mm wide	0.540m2	Extra area	0.735m2

The following page shows the detailed cost breakdown recalculated.

Item Build Ups	Qty	Hours per unit L=Labour P=Plant	Total Labour Time	Labour Rate Per Hour	Total Value of Labour £	Total Plant Time	Plant Rate Per Hour	Total Value of Plant £	Mat Unit Rate	Total Value of Material £	S/c Unit Rate	Total Value of s/c spec. £	TOTAL £
EXTERNAL DOORS AND WINDOWS cont/... Opening in cavity wall for Window (recalculated)													
Lintel, cavity tray, work to jambs and sills including brick on edge sill and DPC.													
1 NR OPENING FOR WINDOW INCLUDES (A)													
Catnic lintel type CG70/100; 2100 mm long	1.000Nr	L=0.72	0.72	21.13	15.21				70.40	70.40			**85.61**
Cavity gutter	1.020m2	L=0.55	0.56	21.13	11.83				8.53	8.70			**20.53**
Close cavity at jambs	2.600m	L=0.20	0.52	21.13	10.99				1.67	4.34			**15.33**
Vertical DPC at jambs 150 mm wide	3.000m	L=0.06	0.17	21.13	3.59				0.46	1.38			**4.97**
Close cavity at sills	1.900m	L=0.25	0.48	21.13	10.14				1.67	3.17			**13.31**
Polythene horizontal DPC 150 mm wide	1.800m	L=0.03	0.06	21.13	1.27				0.46	0.83			**2.10**
Fair return on facings at head and jambs	4.900m	L=0.11	0.54	21.13	11.41								**11.41**
Brick on edge sill in facing bricks	1.800m	L=0.83	1.49	21.13	31.48				6.08	10.94			**42.42**
Expamet angle bead	4.900m	L=0.15	0.74	23.97	17.74				0.97	4.75			**22.49**
13 mm Two coat plaster to walls not exceeding 300 mm wide	0.735m2	L=0.89	0.65	23.97	15.58				2.91	2.14			**17.72**
			5.93		**£129.24**					**£106.65**			**£235.89**

ADJUSTING THE COSTS TO MODIFY THE STANDARD ESTIMATES cont/...

External Door and Frame Changed to Softwood

This is a fairly straightforward modification. It is assumed that the Builder's client requires a PVCu doorset in lieu of a hardwood door. Referring to the Specifications A and B we see that Specification B contains a PVCu doorset.

The standard estimate used in these worked examples is A/1P 4 x 4. To find a PVCu doorset we refer to standard estimates B/1P 4 x 4. Here we see the cost price of an external door complete is £478.42. Standard estimate A/1P 4 x 4 shows a cost for a hardwood external door of £655.02. Simply delete this price and substitute £478.42.

Modifying the Standard Estimate

As we have seen, the first adjustment has to accommodate a change of plan size from 4.00 x 4.00m to 4.00 x 4.50m. Using standard estimate A/1P 4 x 4 a modified estimate was prepared. Now we adjust the modified estimate to include the changes made in this Chapter, i.e.

- Depth of foundation brickwork increased from 750 mm to 950 mm
- Cost of facing brickwork adjusted from £351.38/1000 to £396.23/1000
- Change of window size from 1200 x 1200 mm to 1800 x 1300 mm
- External door and frame changed from hardwood to PVCu.

The following table shows the modified estimate for plan size 4.00 x 4.50 mm, the adjustments to be made and the resultant final estimate for the Builder's own project. The total labour time calculation is also included.

SPECIFICATION A
SINGLE STOREY
PITCHED ROOF

Element	Unit	Unit Rate	Ref A/1P 4 x 4 as Modified for Plan Size 4.00 x 4.50m				Estimate for Plan Size 4.00 x 4.50m including Worked Examples of Specification Changes				
			Qty	Total £	Element Total £		Qty	Total £	Element Total £	Lab Time in Cost Breakdown	Total Lab Time Hrs
SUBSTRUCTURE											
Strip footings	M	144.41	15M	2166.15		New unit rate £177.16	15M	2657.40		6.26	93.90
Hollow ground floor	M2	91.57	18M2	1648.26	**3814.41**	No change	18M2	1648.26	**4305.66**	2.98	53.64
ROOF											
Pitched roof construction	M2	55.42	26M2	1440.92		No change	26M2	1440.92		2.00	52.00
Work to top of external wall	M	23.71	14M	331.94		No change	14M	331.94		1.07	14.98
Plain tile roofing	M2	69.30	32M2	2217.60		No change	32M2	2217.60		1.09	34.88
Work to verge	M	11.58	6M	69.48		No change	6M	69.48		0.28	1.68
Work to hip	M	41.73	10M	417.30		No change	10M	417.30		0.80	8.00
Work to eaves	M	22.73	15M	340.95		No change	15M	340.95		0.26	3.90
Fascia and eaves soffit	M	48.01	15M	720.15		No change	15M	720.15		1.88	28.20
Gutters and fittings	M	18.68	15M	280.20		No change	15M	280.20		0.44	6.60
Flashings	M	69.52	6 m	417.12	**6235.66**	No change	6 m	417.12	**6235.66**	0.09	0.54
EXTERNAL WALLS											
Brick and block cavity wall	M2	114.25	31M2	3541.75	**3541.75**	New unit rate £116.97	31M2	3626.07	**3626.07**	2.99	92.69
EXTERNAL DOORS AND WINDOWS											
External door	NR	655.02	1 Nr	655.02		New unit rate £478.32	1 Nr	478.32		7.60	7.60
Window	NR	672.89	1 Nr	672.89		New unit rate £836.34	1 Nr	836.34		12.76	12.76
Opening for door	NR	144.37	1 Nr	144.37		No change	1 Nr	144.37		3.73	3.73
Opening for window	NR	162.98	1 Nr	162.98	**1635.26**	New unit rate £235.89	1 Nr	235.89	**1694.92**	5.93	5.93
										Total Carried Forward	421.03

SPECIFICATION A SINGLE STOREY PITCHED ROOF			Ref A/1P 4 x 4 as Modified for Plan Size 4.00 x 4.50m				Estimate for Plan Size 4.00 x 4.50m including Worked Examples of Specification Changes				
Element	**Unit**	**Unit Rate**	**Qty**	**Total £**	**Element Total £**		**Qty**	**Total £**	**Element Total £**	**Lab Time in Cost Breakdown**	**Total Lab Time Hrs**
WALL FINISHES											
Plaster and decoration	M2	19.58	43M2	841.94	**841.94**	No change	43M2	841.94	**841.94**	0.74	31.82
FLOOR FINISHES											
Laminate	M2	30.30	18M2	545.40		No change	18M2	545.40		0.58	10.44
Hardwood skirting	M	19.52	18M	351.36	**896.76**	No change	18M	351.36	**896.76**	0.69	12.42
CEILING FINISHES											
Plasterboard, plaster and decoration	M2	26.68	18M2	480.24	**480.24**	No change	18M2	480.24	**480.24**	0.97	17.46
SERVICES											
Rainwater pipes	M	26.64	3 m	79.92		No change	3 m	79.92		0.68	2.04
Cold water service point	NR	110.52	1 Nr	110.52		No change	1 Nr	110.52		2.66	2.66
Hot water service point	NR	191.67	1 Nr	191.67		No change	1 Nr	191.67		4.47	4.47
Central heating service point	NR	386.51	1 Nr	386.51		No change	1 Nr	386.51		8.40	8.40
Electrical installation	NR	286.50	1 Nr	286.50	**1055.12**	No change	1 Nr	286.50	**1055.12**	-	-
ALTERATIONS TO EXISTING BUILDING											
Opening in existing wall 4.00m wide 2.00m high	NR	1131.22	1 Nr	1131.22	**1131.22**	No change	1 Nr	1131.22	**1131.22**	36.89	36.89

TOTAL COST OF ESTIMATE FOR PLAN SIZE 4.00 X 4.50M INCLUDING WORKED EXAMPLES OF SPECIFICATION CHANGES AS ILLUSTRATED IN THIS CHAPTER — **£20267.59**

TOTAL LABOUR TIME — 547.63

NB: Total cost of estimate **excludes** Contractor's overheads and profit, Preliminaries (see Chapter 3) and VAT

6

Alteration work

Unit Rates

		Man-Hours	Plant Hours	Net Labour Price £	Net Plant Price £	Net Mats Price £	Net Unit Price £	Unit
GENERALLY								
	This chapter is in two sections. The first section comprises a selection of unit rates for typical items of cutting openings in walling and filling in openings in walls. The second section comprises a fully measured and priced estimate for a roof space conversion. A detailed drawing is provided and the estimate is intended to illustrate all the typical items of work associated with a roof space conversion.							
CN	**CUTTING OPENINGS ETC. IN WALLING**							
	In order to provide flexible pricing for the infinite variation in cutting openings of different sizes, wall thicknesses finishes etc., the prices have been broken down into operations to allow composite prices to be built up. The total net price should be composed of some or all of the following component operations: 1 Needling propping and supports 2 Cutting out walling 3 Making good jambs 4 Inserting lintels, arch bars and forming arches 5 Forming sills to openings cut in old walls 6 Building in damp proof courses 7 Making good wall finishes and extending to jambs							
	NEEDLING, PROPPING AND SUPPORTS							
	Note: net materials price allows for 6 uses of timber							
001	**Sawn timber needles and props (not exceeding 3000 mm above floor level); cutting holes for needles and making good wall after removal (per needle and pair of props) for**							
002	Brick walls:							
	Half brick thick	1.11	2.00	23.53	4.40	3.72	**31.65**	Nr
	one brick thick	1.67	2.00	35.30	4.40	5.59	**45.29**	Nr
	one-and-a-half brickwall	2.28	2.00	48.06	4.40	9.00	**61.46**	Nr
003	Blockwork walls:							
	75 mm thick	1.02	2.00	21.57	4.40	3.29	**29.26**	Nr
	100 mm thick	1.21	2.00	25.50	4.40	3.31	**33.21**	Nr
	150 mm thick	1.49	2.00	31.37	4.40	4.65	**40.42**	Nr
004	Stone rubble walling:							
	300 mm thick	1.72	2.00	46.08	4.40	12.41	**62.89**	Nr
	450 mm thick	2.23	2.00	59.75	4.40	18.15	**82.30**	Nr
	600 mm thick	2.60	2.00	69.71	4.40	21.52	**95.63**	Nr
005	Stone ashlar walling:							
	150 mm thick	1.67	2.00	35.30	4.40	8.75	**48.45**	Nr
	200 mm thick	2.18	2.00	46.09	4.40	13.73	**64.22**	Nr

Unit Rates

	Unit Rates	Man-Hours	Plant Hours	Net Labour Price £	Net Plant Price £	Net Mats Price £	Net Unit Price £	Unit
	300 mm thick	2.74	2.00	57.86	4.40	17.49	**79.75**	Nr
006	Cavity walling comprising facing brick outer skin and concrete block inner skin:							
	250 mm thick (100 mm inner skin)	2.51	2.00	52.94	4.40	8.03	**65.37**	Nr
	300 mm thick (150 mm inner skin)	2.69	2.00	56.87	4.40	2.02	**63.29**	Nr
	CUTTING OUT WALLING							
007	**Cutting out walling to form new openings and for new lintels, removing debris and loading into skips**							
008	Common brickwork:							
	Half brick thick	0.63	-	13.35	-	-	**13.35**	m2
	one brick thick	0.84	-	17.64	-	-	**17.64**	m2
	one-and-a-half brick thick	1.25	-	26.49	-	-	**26.49**	m2
009	Engineering brickwork:							
	Half brick thick	1.00	-	21.19	-	-	**21.19**	m2
	one brick thick	1.42	-	30.02	-	-	**30.02**	m2
	one-and-a-half brick thick	2.05	-	43.31	-	-	**43.31**	m2
010	Facing brickwork:							
	Half brick thick	0.84	-	17.64	-	-	**17.64**	m2
	one brick thick	1.25	-	26.49	-	-	**26.49**	m2
	one-and-a-half brick thick	1.70	-	35.91	-	-	**35.91**	m2
011	Blockwork walls:							
	75 mm thick	0.23	-	4.92	-	-	**4.92**	m2
	100 mm thick	0.37	-	7.84	-	-	**7.84**	m2
	150 mm thick	0.46	-	9.72	-	-	**9.72**	m2
012	Stone rubble walling:							
	300 mm thick	0.42	-	11.24	-	-	**11.24**	m2
	450 mm thick	0.55	-	14.70	-	-	**14.70**	m2
	600 mm thick	0.84	-	22.39	-	-	**22.39**	m2
013	Stone ashlar walling:							
	150 mm thick	0.42	-	8.85	-	-	**8.85**	m2
	200 mm thick	0.55	-	11.58	-	-	**11.58**	m2
	300 mm thick	0.67	-	14.11	-	-	**14.11**	m2
014	Reinforced concrete wall:							
	100 mm thick	2.09	0.92	23.79	12.24	-	**36.03**	m2
	150 mm thick	3.14	1.36	35.74	18.13	-	**53.87**	m2
	200 mm thick	4.18	1.83	47.58	24.37	-	**71.95**	m2
015	Cavity walling comprising facing brick outer skin and concrete block inner skin:							
	250 mm thick (100 mm inner skin)	1.15	-	24.29	-	-	**24.29**	m2
	300 mm thick (150 mm inner skin)	1.35	-	28.52	-	-	**28.52**	m2

	Unit Rates	Man-Hours	Plant Hours	Net Labour Price £	Net Plant Price £	Net Mats Price £	Net Unit Price £	Unit
016	**Cutting away walling at jambs, sills and heads of existing opening to enlarge openings; removing debris and loading into skips**							
017	Common brickwork:							
	Half brick thick	1.26	-	26.66	-	-	**26.66**	m2
	one brick thick	1.67	-	35.30	-	-	**35.30**	m2
	one-and-a-half brick thick	2.51	-	52.94	-	-	**52.94**	m2
018	Engineering brickwork:							
	Half brick thick	2.01	-	42.36	-	-	**42.36**	m2
	one brick thick	2.84	-	60.00	-	-	**60.00**	m2
	one-and-a-half brick thick	4.10	-	86.61	-	-	**86.61**	m2
019	Facing brickwork:							
	Half brick thick	1.67	-	35.30	-	-	**35.30**	m2
	one brick thick	2.51	-	52.94	-	-	**52.94**	m2
	one-and-a-half brick thick	3.40	-	71.83	-	-	**71.83**	m2
020	Blockwork walls:							
	75 mm thick	0.46	-	9.72	-	-	**9.72**	m2
	100 mm thick	0.74	-	15.63	-	-	**15.63**	m2
	150 mm thick	0.92	-	19.44	-	-	**19.44**	m2
021	Stone rubble walling:							
	300 mm thick	0.84	-	22.39	-	-	**22.39**	m2
	450 mm thick	1.09	-	29.15	-	-	**29.15**	m2
	600 mm thick	1.67	-	44.82	-	-	**44.82**	m2
022	Stone ashlar walling:							
	150 mm thick	0.84	-	17.64	-	-	**17.64**	m2
	200 mm thick	1.09	-	22.96	-	-	**22.96**	m2
	300 mm thick	1.34	-	28.24	-	-	**28.24**	m2
023	Reinforced concrete wall:							
	100 mm thick	2.32	1.06	26.44	14.17	-	**40.61**	m2
	150 mm thick	3.34	1.53	38.07	20.39	-	**58.46**	m2
	200 mm thick	4.46	2.04	50.74	27.19	-	**77.93**	m2
024	Cavity walling comprising facing brick outer skin and concrete block inner skin:							
	250 mm thick (100 mm inner skin)	2.30	-	48.59	-	-	**48.59**	m2
	300 mm thick (150 mm inner skin)	2.70	-	57.04	-	-	**57.04**	m2
	CUTTING AND PINNING							
025	**Cut and pin ends of new lintels and arch bars to openings cut in old walls**							
026	Common brickwork:							
	Half brick thick	0.25	-	5.30	-	-	**5.30**	Nr
	one brick thick	0.33	-	7.06	-	-	**7.06**	Nr

	Unit Rates	Man-Hours	Plant Hours	Net Labour Price £	Net Plant Price £	Net Mats Price £	Net Unit Price £	Unit
	one-and-a-half brick thick	0.50	-	10.58	-	-	**10.58**	Nr
027	Engineering brickwork:							
	Half brick thick	0.40	-	8.43	-	-	**8.43**	Nr
	one brick thick	0.57	-	11.98	-	-	**11.98**	Nr
	one-and-a-half brick thick	1.07	-	22.56	-	-	**22.56**	Nr
028	Facing brickwork:							
	Half brick thick	0.33	-	7.06	-	-	**7.06**	Nr
	one brick thick	0.50	-	10.58	-	-	**10.58**	Nr
	one-and-a-half brick thick	1.00	-	21.19	-	-	**21.19**	Nr
029	Blockwork walls:							
	75 mm thick	0.17	-	3.53	-	-	**3.53**	Nr
	100 mm thick	0.25	-	5.30	-	-	**5.30**	Nr
	150 mm thick	0.42	-	8.85	-	-	**8.85**	Nr
030	Stone rubble walling:							
	300 mm thick	0.33	-	7.06	-	-	**7.06**	Nr
	450 mm thick	0.42	-	8.85	-	-	**8.85**	Nr
	600 mm thick	0.67	-	14.11	-	-	**14.11**	Nr
031	Stone ashlar walling:							
	150 mm thick	0.25	-	5.30	-	-	**5.30**	Nr
	200 mm thick	0.59	-	12.36	-	-	**12.36**	Nr
	300 mm thick	1.00	-	21.19	-	-	**21.19**	Nr
	MAKING GOOD JAMBS							
032	**Making good jambs of openings cut in old brick walls with new brickwork in mortar to match existing; bonding to existing**							
033	Common brickwork (P.C. £311.01 per 1000) in gauged mortar (1:2:9):							
	prepared for plastering:							
	half brick thick	0.28	-	5.87	-	3.46	**9.33**	m
	one brick thick	0.51	-	10.79	-	6.83	**17.62**	m
	one-and-a-half brick thick	0.70	-	14.72	-	10.25	**24.97**	m
	finished fair and flush pointed:							
	half brick thick	0.59	-	12.36	-	3.46	**15.82**	m
	one brick thick	1.09	-	22.96	-	6.83	**29.79**	m
	one-and-a-half brick thick	1.42	-	30.02	-	10.25	**40.27**	m
034	Class B Engineering brickwork (P.C. £391.75 per 1000) in cement mortar (1:3):							
	prepared for plastering:							
	half brick thick	0.42	-	8.85	-	4.36	**13.21**	m
	one brick thick	0.70	-	14.72	-	8.60	**23.32**	m
	one-and-a-half brick thick	1.02	-	21.57	-	12.92	**34.49**	m

	Unit Rates	Man-Hours	Plant Hours	Net Labour Price £	Net Plant Price £	Net Mats Price £	Net Unit Price £	Unit
	finished fair and flush pointed:							
	half brick thick	0.84	-	17.64	-	4.36	**22.00**	m
	one brick thick	1.59	-	33.55	-	8.60	**42.15**	m
	one-and-a-half brick thick	2.01	-	42.36	-	12.92	**55.28**	m
035	Facing brickwork (P.C. £351.38 per 1000) in gauged mortar(1:2:9):							
	flush pointed:							
	half brick thick	0.59	-	12.36	-	3.91	**16.27**	m
	one brick thick	1.09	-	22.96	-	7.71	**30.67**	m
	one-and-a-half brick thick	1.42	-	30.02	-	11.58	**41.60**	m
036	**Making good jambs and sills of openings cut in cavity walling comprising facing brick outer skins and concrete block inner skins, with new facing bricks, blocks and mortar to match existing**							
037	Facing bricks (P.C. £351.38 per 1000) and natural aggregate concrete blocks in gauged mortar (1:2:9); returning inner skin to close cavity; building in Hyload or similar vertical damp proof course:							
	pointing with a flush joint externally and prepared for plastering internally:							
	250 mm thick (100 mm inner skin)	1.67	-	35.30	-	4.87	**40.17**	m
	300 mm thick (150 mm inner skin)	2.01	-	42.36	-	5.31	**47.67**	m
	pointing with a flush joint internally and externally:							
	250 mm thick (100 mm inner skin)	2.09	-	44.13	-	4.87	**49.00**	m
	300 mm thick (150 mm inner skin)	2.42	-	51.19	-	5.31	**56.50**	m
038	**Making good jambs of openings cut in old concrete blockwork walls with new blockwork in mortar to match existing; bonding to existing**							
039	Natural aggregate solid concrete blocks in gauged mortar (1:2:9):							
	prepared for plastering:							
	60 mm thick	0.42	-	8.85	-	1.59	**10.44**	m
	100 mm thick	0.59	-	12.36	-	2.31	**14.67**	m
	150 mm thick	0.84	-	17.64	-	4.63	**22.27**	m
	finished fair and flush pointed:							
	60 mm thick	0.50	-	10.58	-	1.59	**12.17**	m
	100 mm thick	0.67	-	14.11	-	2.31	**16.42**	m
	150 mm thick	1.00	-	21.19	-	4.63	**25.82**	m
040	**Making good jambs of openings cut in old random rubble stone walling**							
041	With common brickwork (P.C. £311.01 per 1000) in gauged mortar (1:2:9) block bonded; prepared for plastering:							
	300 mm thick	1.00	-	21.19	-	6.66	**27.85**	m
	450 mm thick	1.34	-	28.24	-	9.93	**38.17**	m
	600 mm thick	1.67	-	35.30	-	13.19	**48.49**	m
	With random rubble stone salvaged from demolition in gauged mortar (1:2:9) finished fair & flush pointed:							
	300 mm thick	1.17	-	24.70	-	6.78	**31.48**	m
	450 mm thick	1.50	-	31.75	-	10.05	**41.80**	m
	600 mm thick	1.75	-	36.86	-	13.31	**50.17**	m

	Unit Rates	Man-Hours	Plant Hours	Net Labour Price £	Net Plant Price £	Net Mats Price £	Net Unit Price £	Unit
042	**Making good jambs of openings cut in old ashlar masonry stone walling with stone salvaged from demolition in gauged mortar**							
043	Prepared for plastering one side; finished fair and flush pointed one side:							
	50 mm thick	1.67	-	35.30	-	0.13	**35.43**	m
	200 mm thick	2.01	-	42.36	-	0.13	**42.49**	m
	300 mm thick	2.34	-	49.41	-	0.13	**49.54**	m
	Finish fair and flush pointed both sides:							
	150 mm thick	1.75	-	36.86	-	0.13	**36.99**	m
	200 mm thick	2.17	-	45.88	-	0.13	**46.01**	m
	300 mm thick	2.51	-	52.94	-	0.13	**53.07**	m
044	**Making good jambs of openings cut in old reinforced concrete walls**							
045	With cement mortar (1:3) average 25 mm thick; wall:							
	100 mm thick	0.23	-	4.92	-	0.32	**5.24**	m
	150 mm thick	0.28	-	5.87	-	0.49	**6.36**	m
	200 mm thick	0.33	-	6.89	-	0.65	**7.54**	m
	Fair cutting with carborundum wheel both sides of wall prior to demolition:							
	100 mm thick	0.37	0.34	4.23	0.41	-	**4.64**	m
	150 mm thick	0.46	0.43	5.29	0.51	-	**5.80**	m
	200 mm thick	0.56	0.51	6.35	0.61	-	**6.96**	m
	INSERTING LINTELS, ARCH BARS AND FORMING ARCHES							
046	**In situ reinforced concrete grade (1:2:4) x 19 mm aggregate filled into formwork**							
047	Lintels, cross-sectional area:							
	not exceeding 0.03 m3	6.96	-	130.57	-	137.84	**268.41**	m3
	0.03 - 0.10 m2	5.11	-	95.76	-	137.84	**233.60**	m3
	0.10 - 0.25 m2	4.41	-	82.72	-	137.84	**220.56**	m3
	exceeding 0.25 m2	3.71	-	69.65	-	137.84	**207.49**	m3
048	**Steel bar reinforcement**							
049	High yield steel, BS 4449:							
	12 mm diameter	0.08	-	1.16	-	0.83	**1.99**	m
	16 mm diameter	0.11	-	1.71	-	1.52	**3.23**	m
	8 mm diameter in links and stirrups	0.07	-	1.02	-	0.39	**1.41**	m

	Unit Rates	Man-Hours	Plant Hours	Net Labour Price £	Net Plant Price £	Net Mats Price £	Net Unit Price £	Unit
052	**Formwork to sides and soffit of lintels (NB 'making' price allows for ONE use of timber)**							
053	Soffit of lintel not exceeding 3.5 m high:							
	not exceeding 200 mm wide:							
	making	2.65	-	40.83	-	10.51	**51.34**	m
	fixing	1.39	-	25.44	-	1.80	**27.24**	m
	200 - 400 mm wide:							
	making	2.93	-	45.13	-	21.01	**66.14**	m
	fixing	1.67	-	30.54	-	3.52	**34.06**	m
	400 - 600 mm wide:							
	making	4.04	-	62.32	-	31.51	**93.83**	m
	fixing	2.23	-	40.72	-	5.27	**45.99**	m
054	Sides of lintels:							
	not exceeding 200 mm wide:							
	making	1.53	-	23.64	-	16.81	**40.45**	m
	fixing	0.98	-	17.84	-	2.77	**20.61**	m
	200 - 400 mm wide:							
	making	1.95	-	30.07	-	27.30	**57.37**	m
	fixing	1.25	-	22.92	-	4.67	**27.59**	m
	400 - 600 mm wide:							
	making	2.51	-	38.67	-	37.80	**76.47**	m
	fixing	1.53	-	28.00	-	6.37	**34.37**	m
055	ADD to **'making'** prices for fair face finish formed with oil tempered hardboard lining:							
	soffits:							
	not exceeding 200 mm wide	-	-	-	-	0.63	**0.63**	m
	200 - 400 mm wide	-	-	-	-	1.26	**1.26**	m
	400 - 600 mm wide	-	-	-	-	1.89	**1.89**	m
	sides:							
	not exceeding 200 mm wide	-	-	-	-	1.01	**1.01**	m
	200 - 400 mm wide	-	-	-	-	1.64	**1.64**	m
	400 - 600 mm wide	-	-	-	-	2.27	**2.27**	m
056	**Prestressed precast concrete lintels; reinforced with steel bars as necessary; bedding and pointing in cement mortar (1:3)**							
057	Concrete Lintels:							
	Prestressed, precast:							
	150 x 65 mm	0.28	-	5.87	-	8.87	**14.74**	m
	220 x 65 mm	0.37	-	7.84	-	13.38	**21.22**	m
	Precast, reinforced:							
	150 x 100 mm	0.42	-	8.85	-	16.42	**25.27**	m
	150 x 140 mm	0.49	-	10.37	-	14.31	**24.68**	m
	215 x 215 mm	0.70	-	14.72	-	38.01	**52.73**	m
	327.5 x 215 mm	0.79	-	16.69	-	48.95	**65.64**	m

	Unit Rates	Man-Hours	Plant Hours	Net Labour Price £	Net Plant Price £	Net Mats Price £	Net Unit Price £	Unit
058	**Wedging and pinning up with slates in cement mortar (1:3) between top of new lintels and underside of old construction**							
059	Thickness of wall:							
	50 mm	0.24	-	5.07	-	4.34	**9.41**	m
	100 and 102.5 mm	0.24	-	5.07	-	5.26	**10.33**	m
	150 mm	0.34	-	7.18	-	6.18	**13.36**	m
	200 mm	0.43	-	9.08	-	7.10	**16.18**	m
	215 mm	0.48	-	10.14	-	7.98	**18.12**	m
	300 mm	0.67	-	14.15	-	8.95	**23.10**	m
	327.5 mm	0.72	-	15.21	-	8.99	**24.20**	m
	450 mm	0.95	-	20.07	-	9.99	**30.06**	m
	600 mm	1.29	-	27.25	-	11.05	**38.30**	m
060	**Catnic lintels; bedding ends in cement mortar (1:3)**							
061	Type CG50/100 for use in cavity walls with 50-65 mm cavity; 100 mm inner skin:							
	900 mm long	0.38	-	8.05	-	30.38	**38.43**	Nr
	1200 mm long	0.42	-	8.85	-	39.38	**48.23**	Nr
	1500 mm long	0.46	-	9.80	-	50.91	**60.71**	Nr
062	Type CH70/100 for use in cavity walls with 70-85 mm cavity; 100 mm inner skin:							
	2400 mm long	0.66	-	13.94	-	135.77	**149.71**	Nr
063	Type CX70/100 for use in cavity walls with 70-85 mm cavity; 100 mm inner skin:							
	2700 mm long	0.70	-	14.72	-	178.07	**192.79**	Nr
	3000 mm long	0.74	-	15.70	-	198.01	**213.71**	Nr
064	Type CN5XA for use in internal 100 mm walls; 100 x 143 mm deep:							
	1050 mm long	0.27	-	5.68	-	36.53	**42.21**	Nr
	1200 mm long	0.31	-	6.49	-	37.58	**44.07**	Nr
	1500 mm long	0.35	-	7.46	-	42.23	**49.69**	Nr
	2400 mm long	0.47	-	10.01	-	79.95	**89.96**	Nr
065	Type CN6XB for use in internal 100 mm walls; 100 x 219 mm deep:							
	2700 mm long	0.52	-	10.99	-	148.01	**159.00**	Nr
	3000 mm long	0.56	-	11.77	-	158.70	**170.47**	Nr
066	Type CN56XA for use in internal 150 mm walls; 150 x 143 mm deep:							
	1050 mm long	0.33	-	7.06	-	33.44	**40.50**	Nr
	1200 mm long	0.38	-	8.05	-	39.57	**47.62**	Nr
	1500 mm long	0.42	-	8.85	-	49.38	**58.23**	Nr
	2400 mm long	0.55	-	11.58	-	88.61	**100.19**	Nr
067	**Steel arch bars; cutting and pinning ends**							
068	75 x 20 mm flat arch bar	0.08	-	1.58	-	15.74	**17.32**	m
069	100 x 75 x 10 mm angle arch bar	0.11	-	2.34	-	14.22	**16.56**	m
070	150 x 90 x 12 mm angle arch bar	0.14	-	2.96	-	24.37	**27.33**	m

	Unit Rates	Man-Hours	Plant Hours	Net Labour Price £	Net Plant Price £	Net Mats Price £	Net Unit Price £	Unit
071	**Arches built of facing bricks (P.C. £351.38 per 1000) in gauged mortar; flush pointing where exposed; centering and support**							
072	Flat arches:							
	brick-on-edge; 225 mm soffit 112.5 mm high	2.79	-	58.83	-	12.66	**71.49**	m
	brick-on-end; 112.5 mm soffit 225 mm high	2.01	-	42.36	-	9.29	**51.65**	m
073	Segmental arches:							
	brick-on-edge; 225 mm soffit 112.5 mm high:							
	single course	2.83	-	59.83	-	12.66	**72.49**	m
	two courses	3.06	-	64.71	-	18.60	**83.31**	m
	brick-on-end; 112.5 mm soffit 225 mm high	2.01	-	42.36	-	9.29	**51.65**	m
074	Semi-circular arches:							
	brick-on-edge; 225 mm soffit 112.5 mm high:							
	single course	5.48	-	115.68	-	12.66	**128.34**	m
	two courses	5.71	-	120.60	-	18.60	**139.20**	m
	brick-on-end; 112.5 mm soffit 225 mm high	4.92	-	103.91	-	9.29	**113.20**	m
075	**Arches built of salvaged random rubble stone in gauged mortar (1:2:9) flush pointing where exposed; centering and supports**							
076	Flat arches formed of stones on edge:							
	150 mm soffit 150 mm high	2.23	-	59.75	-	5.23	**64.98**	m
	200 mm soffit 300 mm high	3.25	-	87.14	-	9.19	**96.33**	m
077	Segmental arches formed of stones on edge:							
	150 mm soffit 150 mm high	2.28	-	61.02	-	5.23	**66.25**	m
	200 mm soffit 300 mm high	3.30	-	88.40	-	9.19	**97.59**	m
078	Semi-circular arches formed of stones on edge:							
	150 mm soffit 150 mm high	4.55	-	96.08	-	5.23	**101.31**	m
	200 mm soffit 300 mm high	6.13	-	164.30	-	9.19	**173.49**	m
	600 mm soffit 300 mm high	9.93	-	266.38	-	27.56	**293.94**	m
	FORMING SILLS TO OPENINGS CUT IN OLD WALLS							
079	**Sills formed of facing bricks (P.C. £351.38 per 1000) in cement mortar (1:3)**							
080	Brick-on-edge sills pointing on top and front edges and soffits where projecting:							
	112.5 x 112.5 mm snapped headers set flush with wall face	0.56	-	11.77	-	3.34	**15.11**	m
	250 x 112.5 mm weathered sill set to project 25 mm	1.39	-	29.41	-	8.80	**38.21**	m
081	**Sills formed of granular faced concrete plain roofing tiles (P.C. £633.00 per 1000) bedded, jointed and pointed in cement mortar (1:3)**							
082	Double course tiles laid breaking joint:							
	150 mm wide set to project 25 mm	0.70	-	14.72	-	4.11	**18.83**	m
	265 mm wide set to project 50 mm	0.70	-	14.72	-	6.70	**21.42**	m

	Unit Rates	Man-Hours	Plant Hours	Net Labour Price £	Net Plant Price £	Net Mats Price £	Net Unit Price £	Unit
083	**Precast reconstructed stone weathered and throated sills bedded, jointed and pointed in gauged mortar (1:2:9)**							
084	150 x 75 mm	0.28	-	5.87	-	63.25	**69.12**	m
	200 x 75 mm	0.37	-	7.84	-	80.18	**88.02**	m
	BUILDING IN DAMP PROOF COURSES							
085	**Hyload or similar damp proof course to BS 8215 bedded in gauged mortar (1:2:9)**							
086	Horizontal damp proof courses:							
	150 mm girth behind sills	0.05	-	0.99	-	1.22	**2.21**	m
	200 mm girth behind sills	0.08	-	1.58	-	1.55	**3.13**	m
087	Horizontal damp proof courses with cavity gutters in hollow walls:							
	over 225 mm girth	0.28	-	5.87	-	7.75	**13.62**	m2
	MAKING GOOD WALL FINISHINGS AND EXTENDING TO JAMBS							
088	**Making good reveals or surrounds to opening cut in old walls with Thistle gypsum plaster and with flush joints to existing plasterwork on**							
089	Brickwork:							
	not exceeding 300 mm wide	1.30	-	31.14	-	2.94	**34.08**	m2
	exceeding 300 mm wide	0.65	-	15.58	-	2.94	**18.52**	m2
090	Blockwork:							
	not exceeding 300 mm wide	1.30	-	31.14	-	2.94	**34.08**	m2
	exceeding 300 mm wide	0.65	-	15.58	-	2.94	**18.52**	m2
091	Rubble stonework:							
	not exceeding 300 mm wide	1.49	-	35.60	-	3.08	**38.68**	m2
	exceeding 300 mm wide	0.74	-	17.81	-	3.08	**20.89**	m2
092	Ashlar stonework:							
	not exceeding 300 mm wide	1.30	-	31.14	-	2.94	**34.08**	m2
	exceeding 300 mm wide	0.65	-	15.58	-	2.94	**18.52**	m2
093	Reinforced concrete:							
	not exceeding 300 mm wide	0.93	-	22.25	-	2.80	**25.05**	m2
	exceeding 300 mm wide	0.46	-	11.12	-	2.80	**13.92**	m2
094	Extra for dubbing out plasterwork for each additional 12 mm thickness:							
	not exceeding 300 mm wide	0.46	-	11.12	-	2.02	**13.14**	m2
	exceeding 300 mm wide	0.23	-	5.59	-	2.02	**7.61**	m2

Unit Rates		Man-Hours	Plant Hours	Net Labour Price £	Net Plant Price £	Net Mats Price £	Net Unit Price £	Unit
095	**Making good reveals or surrounds to opening cut in old walls with cement and sand render and with flush joints to existing plasterwork on**							
096	Brickwork:							
	not exceeding 300 mm wide	1.54	-	36.94	-	2.33	**39.27**	m2
	exceeding 300 mm wide	0.77	-	18.48	-	2.33	**20.81**	m2
097	Blockwork:							
	not exceeding 300 mm wide	1.54	-	36.94	-	2.33	**39.27**	m2
	exceeding 300 mm wide	0.77	-	18.48	-	2.33	**20.81**	m2
098	Rubble stonework:							
	not exceeding 300 mm wide	1.67	-	40.06	-	2.46	**42.52**	m2
	exceeding 300 mm wide	0.84	-	20.02	-	2.46	**22.48**	m2
099	Ashlar stonework:							
	not exceeding 300 mm wide	1.54	-	36.94	-	2.33	**39.27**	m2
	exceeding 300 mm wide	0.77	-	18.48	-	2.33	**20.81**	m2
100	Reinforced concrete:							
	not exceeding 300 mm wide	1.54	-	36.94	-	2.33	**39.27**	m2
	exceeding 300 mm wide	0.77	-	18.48	-	2.33	**20.81**	m2
CP	**FILLING IN OPENINGS ETC. IN WALLING**							
	In order to provide flexible pricing for the large number of variations possible in filling up openings of different sizes, the prices have been broken down into operations to allow composite prices to be built up. The total net price should be composed of some or all of the following component operations:							
	1 Preparing for raising including cutting out sills 2 Building in damp proof courses 3 Filling in openings 4 Cutting, toothing and bonding at jambs 5 Wedging and pinning to work over 6 Making good and extending in situ finishings PREPARING FOR RAISING (including cutting out sills)							
001	**Preparing for raising**							
002	Concrete surfaces:							
	not exceeding 250 mm wide	0.09	-	1.96	-	-	**1.96**	m
	250 - 500 mm wide	0.09	-	1.96	-	-	**1.96**	m
	500 - 1000 mm wide	0.11	-	2.34	-	-	**2.34**	m
003	Brickwork surfaces:							
	half brick wide	0.05	-	0.99	-	-	**0.99**	m
	one brick wide	0.07	-	1.39	-	-	**1.39**	m
	one-and-a-half brick wide	0.09	-	1.96	-	-	**1.96**	m

Unit Rates

	Unit Rates	Man-Hours	Plant Hours	Net Labour Price £	Net Plant Price £	Net Mats Price £	Net Unit Price £	Unit
	two brick wide	0.12	-	2.56	-	-	**2.56**	m
004	Concrete blockwork surfaces:							
	not exceeding 150 mm wide	0.05	-	0.99	-	-	**0.99**	m
	150 - 300 mm wide	0.09	-	1.96	-	-	**1.96**	m
005	Random rubble walling surfaces:							
	300 mm wide	0.14	-	2.96	-	-	**2.96**	m
	450 mm wide	0.19	-	3.93	-	-	**3.93**	m
	600 mm wide	0.23	-	4.92	-	-	**4.92**	m
006	Ashlar masonry surfaces:							
	100 mm wide	0.05	-	0.99	-	-	**0.99**	m
	150 mm wide	0.06	-	1.18	-	-	**1.18**	m
	200 mm wide	0.07	-	1.39	-	-	**1.39**	m
007	**Cutting out sills, loading into skips**							
008	Precast concrete or reconstructed stone 150 mm thick:							
	not exceeding 150 mm wide	0.25	-	5.30	-	-	**5.30**	m
	150 - 300 mm wide	0.42	-	8.85	-	-	**8.85**	m
	300 - 600 mm wide	0.67	-	14.11	-	-	**14.11**	m
009	Flush brick-on-edge sills:							
	common brickwork or facing brickwork in gauged mortar:							
	not exceeding half brick wide	0.33	-	7.06	-	-	**7.06**	m
	half brick to one brick wide	0.50	-	10.58	-	-	**10.58**	m
	one brick to one-and-a-half brick wide	0.84	-	17.64	-	-	**17.64**	m
	engineering brickwork in cement mortar:							
	not exceeding half brick wide	0.50	-	10.58	-	-	**10.58**	m
	half brick to one brick wide	0.75	-	15.91	-	-	**15.91**	m
	one brick to one-and-a-half brick wide	1.25	-	26.49	-	-	**26.49**	m
010	Projecting brick-on-edge sills:							
	common brickwork or facing brickwork in gauged mortar:							
	not exceeding 250 mm wide	0.25	-	5.30	-	-	**5.30**	m
	250 - 500 mm wide	0.42	-	8.85	-	-	**8.85**	m
	engineering brickwork in cement mortar:							
	not exceeding 250 mm wide	0.42	-	8.85	-	-	**8.85**	m
	250 - 500 mm wide	0.59	-	12.36	-	-	**12.36**	m
011	Flush stone sills:							
	150 x 150 mm	0.67	-	14.11	-	-	**14.11**	m
	150 x 250 mm	0.84	-	17.64	-	-	**17.64**	m
012	Projecting stone sills:							
	200 x 100 mm	0.50	-	10.58	-	-	**10.58**	m
	300 x 150 mm	0.67	-	14.11	-	-	**14.11**	m

Unit Rates

		Man-Hours	Plant Hours	Net Labour Price £	Net Plant Price £	Net Mats Price £	Net Unit Price £	Unit
	BUILDING IN DAMP PROOF COURSES							
013	**Bitumen damp proof courses, BS 743 Table 1; 100 mm laps; in cement mortar (1:3) pointing where exposed**							
014	Hessian base, ref. A; horizontal:							
	over 225 mm wide	0.28	-	5.87	-	11.00	**16.87**	m2
	50 mm wide	0.03	-	0.59	-	0.62	**1.21**	m
	100 mm wide	0.03	-	0.59	-	1.10	**1.69**	m
	102.5 mm wide	0.03	-	0.59	-	1.20	**1.79**	m
	150 mm wide	0.04	-	0.78	-	1.72	**2.50**	m
	225 mm wide	0.08	-	1.58	-	2.49	**4.07**	m
015	Fibre base, ref. B; horizontal:							
	over 225 mm wide	0.28	-	5.87	-	8.93	**14.80**	m2
	50 mm wide	0.03	-	0.59	-	0.51	**1.10**	m
	100 mm wide	0.03	-	0.59	-	0.89	**1.48**	m
	102.5 mm wide	0.03	-	0.59	-	0.97	**1.56**	m
	150 mm wide	0.04	-	0.78	-	1.41	**2.19**	m
	225 mm wide	0.08	-	1.58	-	2.02	**3.60**	m
	Note 016 not used							
	FILLING IN OPENINGS							
017	**Common bricks (P.C. £311.01 per 1000) in gauged mortar (1:2:9) in filling to openings**							
018	Half brickwall:							
	prepared for plastering	1.81	-	38.26	-	22.54	**60.80**	m2
	finished fair and flush pointed:							
	one side	2.23	-	47.07	-	22.54	**69.61**	m2
	both sides	2.65	-	55.90	-	22.54	**78.44**	m2
019	One brickwall:							
	prepared for plastering	3.06	-	64.71	-	45.70	**110.41**	m2
	finished fair and flush pointed:							
	one side	3.48	-	73.56	-	45.70	**119.26**	m2
	both sides	3.90	-	82.35	-	45.70	**128.05**	m2
020	One-and-a-half brickwall:							
	prepared for plastering	3.62	-	76.47	-	69.07	**145.54**	m2
	finished fair and flush pointed:							
	one side	4.04	-	85.32	-	69.07	**154.39**	m2
	both sides	4.46	-	94.11	-	69.07	**163.18**	m2

Unit Rates

		Man-Hours	Plant Hours	Net Labour Price £	Net Plant Price £	Net Mats Price £	Net Unit Price £	Unit
021	**Class B Engineering bricks (P.C. £391.75 per 1000) in cement mortar (1:3) in filling to openings**							
022	Half brickwall:							
	prepared for plastering	1.95	-	41.17	-	27.83	**69.00**	m2
	finished fair and flush pointed:							
	one side	2.37	-	50.02	-	27.83	**77.85**	m2
	both sides	2.79	-	58.83	-	27.83	**86.66**	m2
023	One brickwall:							
	prepared for plastering	3.14	-	66.29	-	56.13	**122.42**	m2
	finished fair and flush pointed:							
	one side	3.56	-	75.10	-	56.13	**131.23**	m2
	both sides	3.97	-	83.93	-	56.13	**140.06**	m2
024	One-and-a-half brickwall:							
	prepared for plastering	3.76	-	79.43	-	84.71	**164.14**	m2
	finished fair and flush pointed:							
	one side	4.18	-	88.34	-	84.71	**173.05**	m2
	both sides	4.60	-	97.09	-	84.71	**181.80**	m2
025	**Facing bricks (P.C. £351.38 per 1000) in gauged mortar (1:2:9) in filling to openings**							
026	Half brickwall flush pointed one side	2.51	-	52.94	-	25.16	**78.10**	m2
027	One brickwall flush pointed both sides	4.60	-	97.09	-	50.87	**147.96**	m2
028	**Extra over for flush pointing for pointing with a weathered or struck joint**							
029	Common brickwork:							
	one side	0.08	-	1.58	-	-	**1.58**	m2
	both sides	0.15	-	3.13	-	-	**3.13**	m2
030	Engineering brickwork:							
	one side	0.08	-	1.58	-	-	**1.58**	m2
	both sides	0.15	-	3.13	-	-	**3.13**	m2
031	Facing brickwork:							
	one side	0.08	-	1.58	-	-	**1.58**	m2
	both sides	0.15	-	3.13	-	-	**3.13**	m2

Unit Rates

		Man-Hours	Plant Hours	Net Labour Price £	Net Plant Price £	Net Mats Price £	Net Unit Price £	Unit
032	**Precast concrete blocks BS 6073, natural aggregates, compressive strength 7N/mm2, face size 440 x 215 mm in gauged mortar (1:2:9)**							
033	75 mm walls in solid blocks:							
	prepared for plastering	1.05	-	22.16	-	8.01	**30.17**	m2
	finished fair and flush pointed:							
	one side	1.19	-	25.10	-	8.01	**33.11**	m2
	both sides	1.33	-	28.05	-	8.01	**36.06**	m2
034	100 mm walls in solid blocks:							
	prepared for plastering	1.25	-	26.49	-	8.76	**35.25**	m2
	finished fair and flush pointed:							
	one side	1.39	-	29.41	-	8.76	**38.17**	m2
	both sides	1.53	-	32.36	-	8.76	**41.12**	m2
035	150 mm walls in solid blocks:							
	prepared for plastering	1.53	-	32.36	-	13.13	**45.49**	m2
	finished fair and flush pointed:							
	one side	1.67	-	35.30	-	13.13	**48.43**	m2
	both sides	1.81	-	38.26	-	13.13	**51.39**	m2
036	200 mm walls in solid blocks:							
	prepared for plastering	1.86	-	39.21	-	26.39	**65.60**	m2
	finished fair and flush pointed:							
	one side	2.02	-	42.67	-	26.39	**69.06**	m2
	both sides	2.20	-	46.37	-	26.39	**72.76**	m2
037	**Cotswold limestone, Guiting quarry, uncoursed random rubble walling; 100 - 180 mm high with natural exposed faces; in cement lime mortar (1:2:9); joints recessed 12 mm deep as the work proceeds**							
038	Walls; facing and pointing both sides:							
	300 mm thick	2.60	-	69.71	-	112.64	**182.35**	m2
	450 mm thick	4.46	-	119.48	-	171.36	**290.84**	m2
	600 mm thick	7.24	-	194.18	-	227.77	**421.95**	m2
039	EXTRA FOR:							
	bringing to courses at average 500 mm intervals; each exposed face	0.35	-	9.47	-	-	**9.47**	m2
	coursed random rubble walling in minimum 100 mm, maximum 180 mm courses; each exposed face	0.98	-	26.18	-	-	**26.18**	m2
040	**Natural stonework (P.C. £2122.78 per m3) in plain blocks; exposed faces having smooth or rubbed finish; in white cement-lime-putty mortar (2:5:7) with crushed stone dust; flush pointing as the work proceeds in filling openings**							
041	Walls:							
	150 mm thick	4.64	-	98.04	-	348.60	**446.64**	m2
	200 mm thick	6.03	-	127.45	-	463.60	**591.05**	m2

	Unit Rates	Man-Hours	Plant Hours	Net Labour Price £	Net Plant Price £	Net Mats Price £	Net Unit Price £	Unit
042	Facework tied to backing with stainless steel wire ties:							
	75 mm thick	2.79	-	58.83	-	174.30	**233.13**	m2
	100 mm thick	3.71	-	78.44	-	231.80	**310.24**	m2
043	**Cavity walling comprising outer skin in facing bricks (P.C. £351.38 per 1000) in gauged mortar (1:2:9); inner skin in natural aggregate concrete blocks in gauged mortar and twisted wire ties, five per m2**							
044	250 mm Cavity wall comprising half brick outer skin and 100 mm solid block inner skin prepared for plastering	3.81	-	80.40	-	34.58	**114.98**	m2
045	300 mm Cavity wall comprising half brick outer skin and 150 mm solid block inner skin prepared for plastering	4.08	-	86.27	-	38.95	**125.22**	m2
046	EXTRA FOR fair face and flush pointing to inner skin	0.14	-	2.96	-	-	**2.96**	m2
	CUTTING, TOOTHING AND BONDING JAMBS							
047	**Bonding ends of brick walls to existing; 112.5 mm deep in alternate courses; cutting pockets in existing structure; extra material for bonding**							
048	Common brickwork in gauged mortar (1:2:9):							
	half brick thick	0.56	-	11.77	-	1.11	**12.88**	m
	one brick thick	0.79	-	16.69	-	2.21	**18.90**	m
	one-and-a-half brick thick	1.11	-	23.53	-	3.45	**26.98**	m
049	Engineering brickwork in cement mortar (1:3):							
	half brick thick	0.74	-	15.70	-	1.36	**17.06**	m
	one brick thick	1.07	-	22.56	-	2.73	**25.29**	m
	one-and-a-half brick thick	1.49	-	31.37	-	4.22	**35.59**	m
050	Facing brickwork in gauged mortar (1:2:9):							
	half brick thick	0.70	-	14.72	-	1.24	**15.96**	m
	one brick thick	1.02	-	21.57	-	2.46	**24.03**	m
051	**Bonding ends of precast concrete block walls to existing; 150 mm deep in alternate block courses; cutting pockets in existing structure; extra material for bonding**							
052	Walls:							
	75 mm thick	0.24	-	5.09	-	0.38	**5.47**	m
	100 mm thick	0.30	-	6.27	-	0.41	**6.68**	m
	150 mm thick	0.35	-	7.46	-	0.61	**8.07**	m
	200 mm thick	0.46	-	9.80	-	1.38	**11.18**	m

	Unit Rates	Man-Hours	Plant Hours	Net Labour Price £	Net Plant Price £	Net Mats Price £	Net Unit Price £	Unit
053	**Bonding ends of Cotswold limestone uncoursed random rubble walling to existing; 100 mm deep in average 140 mm alternate stone courses; cutting pockets in existing structure; extra material for bonding**							
054	Walls:							
	300 mm thick	0.70	-	18.69	-	5.74	**24.43**	m
	450 mm thick	1.07	-	28.64	-	8.68	**37.32**	m
	600 mm thick	1.39	-	37.33	-	11.48	**48.81**	m
055	**Bonding ends of natural stone walls to existing; average 100 mm deep in average 150 mm high alternate courses; cutting pockets in existing structure; extra material for bonding**							
056	Walls:							
	150 mm thick	0.60	-	12.76	-	6.24	**19.00**	m
	200 mm thick	0.79	-	16.69	-	8.47	**25.16**	m
057	Facework:							
	75 mm thick	0.42	-	8.85	-	5.35	**14.20**	m
	100 mm thick	0.51	-	10.79	-	7.05	**17.84**	m
	WEDGING AND PINNING TO WORK OVER							
058	**Wedging and pinning up concealed work with slates in cement mortar (1:3)**							
059	Brick walls and concrete block walls:							
	half brick	0.26	-	5.58	-	5.26	**10.84**	m
	one brick	0.44	-	9.30	-	7.98	**17.28**	m
	one-and-a-half-brick	0.68	-	14.41	-	8.99	**23.40**	m
	75 mm walls	0.22	-	4.65	-	4.34	**8.99**	m
	100 mm walls	0.26	-	5.58	-	5.26	**10.84**	m
	150 mm walls	0.36	-	7.67	-	6.18	**13.85**	m
	200 mm walls	0.47	-	9.99	-	7.10	**17.09**	m
060	**Wedging and pinning up exposed work**							
061	Fair faced brickwork or blockwork:							
	half brick	0.37	-	7.90	-	5.26	**13.16**	m
	one brick	0.55	-	11.62	-	7.98	**19.60**	m
	one-and-a-half-brick	0.79	-	16.73	-	8.99	**25.72**	m
	50 mm walls	0.33	-	6.97	-	4.34	**11.31**	m
	100 mm walls	0.37	-	7.90	-	5.26	**13.16**	m
	150 mm walls	0.47	-	9.99	-	6.18	**16.17**	m
	200 mm walls	0.58	-	12.32	-	7.10	**19.42**	m
062	Facing brick:							
	half brick	0.39	-	8.13	-	5.26	**13.39**	m
	one brick	0.56	-	11.85	-	7.98	**19.83**	m

	Unit Rates	Man-Hours	Plant Hours	Net Labour Price £	Net Plant Price £	Net Mats Price £	Net Unit Price £	Unit
063	Uncoursed random rubble walling:							
	300 mm thick	0.81	-	21.83	-	8.95	**30.78**	m
	450 mm thick	1.27	-	33.93	-	15.98	**49.91**	m
	600 mm thick	1.82	-	48.68	-	21.31	**69.99**	m
064	Natural stonework:							
	75 mm thick	0.47	-	9.99	-	4.41	**14.40**	m
	100 mm thick	0.50	-	10.46	-	5.26	**15.72**	m
	150 mm thick	0.53	-	11.15	-	6.18	**17.33**	m
	200 mm thick	0.55	-	11.62	-	7.10	**18.72**	m
	MAKING GOOD AND EXTENDING IN SITU FINISHINGS							
065	**Thistle plaster finish; browning undercoat to brick, block or stonework**							
066	13 mm Two coat work to walls:							
	over 300 mm wide	0.65	-	15.58	-	2.94	**18.52**	m2
	fair flush joint to existing finishings	0.05	-	1.13	-	-	**1.13**	m
067	Dubbing out, if required, per 10 mm thickness:							
	over 300 mm wide	0.23	-	5.59	-	2.63	**8.22**	m2
068	**Cement and sand (1:3) trowelled finish to brickwork, blockwork or stonework**							
069	12 mm One coat work:							
	over 300 mm wide	0.52	-	12.47	-	1.55	**14.02**	m2
070	18 mm Two coat work:							
	over 300 mm wide	0.77	-	18.48	-	2.33	**20.81**	m2
071	Fair flush joint to existing finishes	0.05	-	1.13	-	-	**1.13**	m
072	Dubbing out, if required, per 12 mm thickness	0.25	-	6.02	-	1.55	**7.57**	m2
	EXTENDING SKIRTINGS TO MATCH EXISTING							
073	**Wrought softwood; fixing direct with hardened steel masonry nails**							
074	Skirtings:							
	19 x 100 mm once rounded	0.28	-	4.29	-	1.58	**5.87**	m
	25 x 125 mm moulded	0.33	-	5.03	-	2.15	**7.18**	m
	25 x 250 mm moulded	0.46	-	7.16	-	12.74	**19.90**	m
075	**In situ skirtings**							
076	19 x 150 mm Granolithic skirting; square top edge coved joint with existing floor finish	0.93	-	14.32	-	0.61	**14.93**	m

	Unit Rates	Man-Hours	Plant Hours	Net Labour Price £	Net Plant Price £	Net Mats Price £	Net Unit Price £	Unit
077	19 x 150 mm Cement and sand (1:3) trowelled skirting; rounded top edge, square joint onto floor finish	0.74	-	11.47	-	0.39	**11.86**	m
078	**Tiled skirtings**							
	Note 079 not used							
080	152 x 127 x 9.5 mm Ceramic tile skirting; rounded top edge, coved joint to existing floor finish	0.46	-	7.16	-	24.83	**31.99**	m
	TYING IN NEW WALLING TO EXISTING							
081	Expamet stainless steel wall starters; plugging to existing brickwork with plugs and screws provided; bending out tie arms at 225 mm centres and building in to joints of new walls:							
	60 - 75 mm	0.14	-	2.96	-	12.92	**15.88**	m
	110 - 115 mm	0.14	-	2.96	-	10.05	**13.01**	m
	125 - 180 mm	0.26	-	5.49	-	17.57	**23.06**	m
	190 - 260 mm	0.26	-	5.49	-	21.80	**27.29**	m

ROOF SPACE CONVERSION

This section contains a fully measured and priced estimate for a typical roof space conversion. Each part of the work is priced in detail so that the cost of every building activity involved in such a conversion can be identified.

The estimate is based on the drawing as shown, but this is provided for **guidance only,** the configuration of a roof space conversion will vary considerably depending on the age and method of construction of the existing roof structure. When planning and executing such work a qualified Structural Engineer and/or Building Surveyor should be closely involved.

Loft Conversion

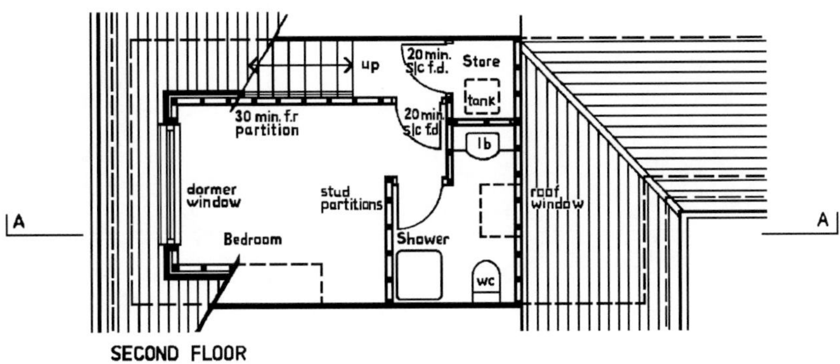

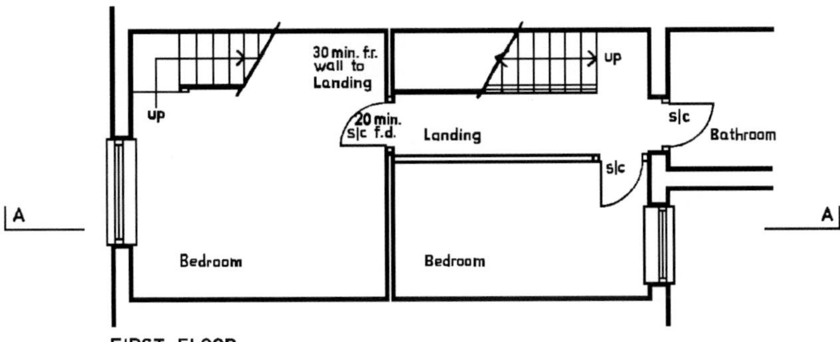

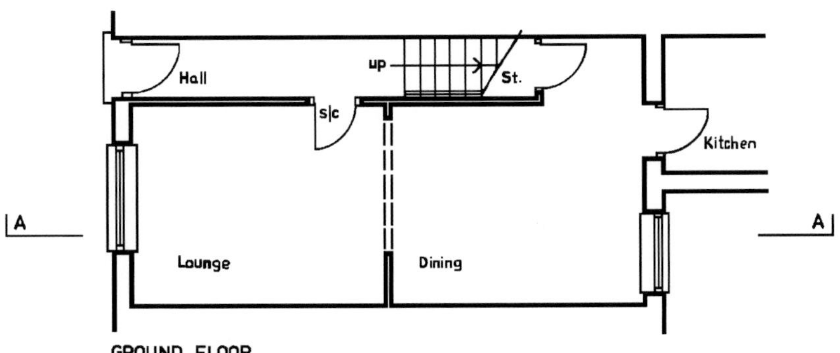

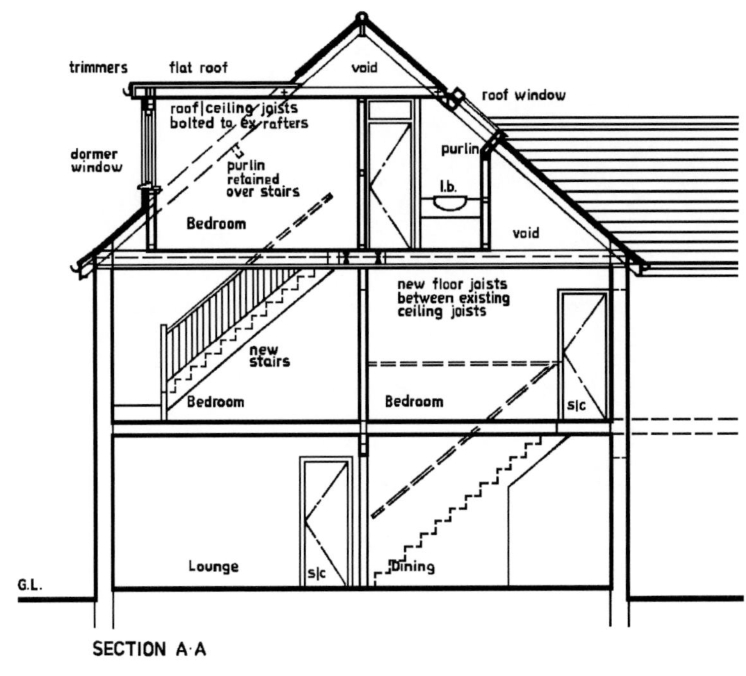

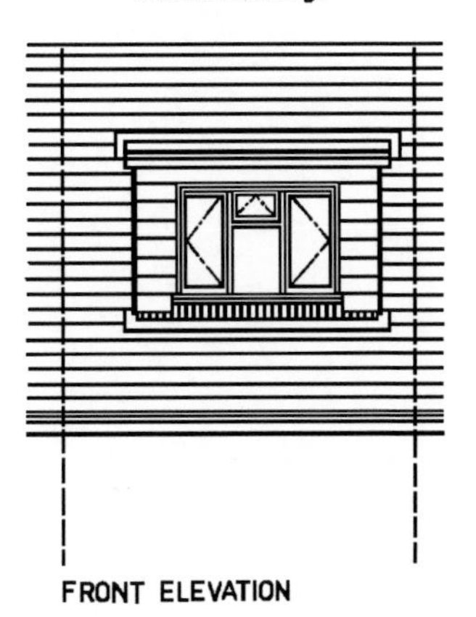

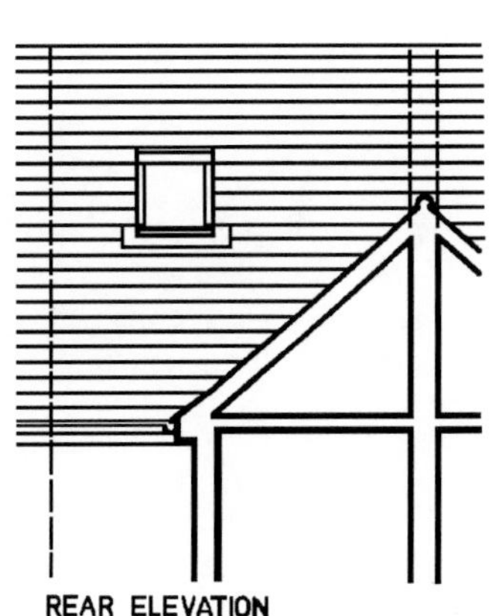

Item Build Ups	Qty	Hours per unit L=Labour P=Plant	Total Labour Time	Labour Rate Per Hour	Total Value of Labour £	Total Plant Time	Plant Rate Per Hour	Total Value of Plant £	Mat Unit Rate	Total Value of Material £	S/c Unit Rate	Total Value of s/c spec. £	TOTAL £
ROOF SPACE CONVERSION Preliminaries													
Scaffolding to front elevation 4000 mm wide x 5200 mm high to eaves. obtain all necessary licences and approvals, allow for all necessary measures to safeguard the public.													
Sub Contractor quotation	1.000 Item											745.00	**745.00**
												£745.00	**£745.00**
Extra for extending scaffold over roof and providing tarpaulins as weather protection.													
Sub Contractor quotation	1.000 Item											970.00	**970.00**
												£970.00	**£970.00**
Scaffolding, trestles, staging etc inside the building.													
Sub Contractor quotation	1.000 Item											270.00	**270.00**
												£270.00	**£270.00**
Provide skip for rubbish disposal.													
Cost of skip	3.000 Nr											480.00	**480.00**
												£480.00	**£480.00**
Clean up site on completion of work.													
Allowance for labour	1.000Item	L=8.40	8.40	11.39	95.68								**95.68**
			8.40		**£95.68**								**£95.68**
Preparation Work													
Strip out existing carpets, furnishings and fittings from first floor bedroom and landing,set aside for re use, provide protection.													
Strip out carpet, furniture and fittings, set aside for re use.	1.000Item	L=4.20	4.20	11.39	47.84								**47.84**
Polythene sheet protection	32.000m2	L=0.32	10.08	11.39	114.81				0.39	12.48			**127.29**
			14.28		**£162.65**					**£12.48**			**£175.13**

Item Build Ups	Qty	Hours per unit L=Labour P=Plant	Total Labour Time	Labour Rate Per Hour	Total Value of Labour £	Total Plant Time	Plant Rate Per Hour	Total Value of Plant £	Mat Unit Rate	Total Value of Material £	S/c Unit Rate	Total Value of s/c spec. £	TOTAL £
ROOF SPACE CONVERSION cont/… Remove Roof Coverings													
Remove gutter and fascia, remove tiles, battens and felt, set aside for re use, load remaining material into skips, leave lead flashings in place for re use.													
Remove gutter and fascia	5.000m	L=0.13	0.66	11.39	7.52								**7.52**
Strip tiles and set aside	25.000m2	L=0.19	4.65	26.82	124.71								**124.71**
Strip battens	25.000m2	L=0.05	1.18	26.82	31.65								**31.65**
Strip underfelt	25.000m2	L=0.02	0.45	26.82	12.07								**12.07**
			6.94		**£175.95**								**£175.95**
Work to junction with adjacent roof.													
Remove tiling, cut back felt and battens	12.000m	L=0.29	3.53	11.39	40.21								**40.21**
			3.53		**£40.21**								**£40.21**
Second Floor Joists and Flooring													
Prepare for insertion of new joists by cutting out existing studding etc, including protecting existing ceiling.													
Cutting out and preparation	1.000Item	L=2.63	2.63	11.39	29.96								**29.96**
			2.63		**£29.96**								**£29.96**
22 mm Tongued and grooved flooring grade chipboard on new 50 x 200 mm joists at 400 mm centres between existing ceiling joists, bottom of new joists to be 10 mm above top face of existing ceiling.													
Sawn softwood floor joists 50 x 200 mm	101.000m	L=0.16	16.26	15.43	250.89				2.96	298.96			**549.85**
Sawn softwood solid strutting to 50 x 200 mm joists	12.000m	L=0.38	4.54	15.43	70.05				2.96	35.52			**105.57**
22 mm Chipboard flooring	20.000m2	L=0.44	8.74	15.43	134.86				9.14	182.80			**317.66**
			29.54		**£455.80**					**£517.28**			**£973.08**

Item Build Ups	Qty	Hours per unit L=Labour P=Plant	Total Labour Time	Labour Rate Per Hour	Total Value of Labour £	Total Plant Time	Plant Rate Per Hour	Total Value of Plant £	Mat Unit Rate	Total Value of Material £	S/c Unit Rate	Total Value of s/c spec. £	TOTAL £
ROOF SPACE CONVERSION cont/... Ridge Beam													
4500 mm Long 254 x 146 x 37 kg/m universal beam,build in both ends to brickwork, including all necessary hoisting and temporary support.													
254 x 146 x 37 kg/m Universal beam	0.170tonne	L=2.75	0.47	62.37	29.31					278.60			**307.91**
Cut and pin ends	2.000Nr	L=0.33	0.67	21.13	14.16								**14.16**
Wedge and pin	4.500m	L=0.48	2.16	21.13	45.64				7.98	35.91			**81.55**
			3.30		**£89.11**					**£314.51**			**£403.62**
Dormer structure													
Form new dormer overall size 2800 mm long 2000 mm high 2500 mm deep in existing roof, 50 x 150 mm roof joists at 400 mm centres, 50 x 100 mm studs to front and sides, 50 x 100 mm additional rafters at sides, pressure impregnated timber, including cutting out existing roof timbers and disposal.													
Sawn softwood joists 50 x 150 mm	40.000m	L=0.25	10.12	15.43	156.15				2.23	89.20			**245.35**
Galvanised mild steel strap 800 mm long	20.000Nr	L=0.44	8.74	15.43	134.86				2.41	48.20			**183.06**
Sawn softwood roof timbers 50 x 100 mm	50.000m	L=0.21	10.65	15.43	164.33				1.48	74.00			**238.33**
M10 x 100 Bolt	4.000Nr	L=0.14	0.55	15.43	8.49				0.22	0.88			**9.37**
Cut out rafter	6.000Nr	L=0.50	3.02	11.39	34.40								**34.40**
Cut out purlin	1.000Nr	L=0.53	0.53	11.39	6.04								**6.04**
			33.61		**£504.27**					**£212.28**			**£716.55**

Item Build Ups	Qty	Hours per unit L=Labour P=Plant	Total Labour Time	Labour Rate Per Hour	Total Value of Labour £	Total Plant Time	Plant Rate Per Hour	Total Value of Plant £	Mat Unit Rate	Total Value of Material £	S/c Unit Rate	Total Value of s/c spec. £	TOTAL £
ROOF SPACE CONVERSION cont/... Dormer Roof													
Three layer mineral finish felt on 18 mm chipboard on 50 mm firrings, 100 mm fibreglass insulation, vapour barrier, 12.5 mm plasterboard and skim ceiling.													
Three layer built up felt roofing to plywood deck as follows:- First layer Type 3G perforated BS747 Second layer Ruberglas GP120 Third layer Ruberglas GP120 mineral surfaced felt	8.000m2										36.43	291.44	**291.44**
Chipboard tongued and grooved decking 18 mm thick	8.000m2	L=0.32	2.58	15.43	39.81				4.02	32.16			**71.97**
Firrings 50 mm average depth	21.000m	L=0.04	0.92	15.43	14.20				0.63	13.23			**27.43**
Glassfibre insulation quilt 100 mm thick	8.000m2	L=0.18	1.47	15.43	22.68				3.27	26.16			**48.84**
12.5 mm Plasterboard duplex grade fixed with galvanised nails to softwood	8.000m2	L=0.29	2.32	21.13	49.02				3.84	30.72			**79.74**
5 mm Thistle board finish plaster to plasterboard in two coats, including scrimming joints	8.000m2	L=0.38	3.02	23.97	72.39				1.81	14.48			**86.87**
			10.31		**£198.10**					**£116.75**		**£291.44**	**£606.29**
12 mm Supalux soffit 200 mm wide; 25 mm exterior grade plywood fascia 250 mm high; sawn softwood bearers; painted finish.													
25 mm BS 5268 PT2, WBP BB/BB, exterior grade plywood fascia 250 mm wide	9.200m	L=0.43	3.92	15.43	60.49				6.29	57.87			**118.36**
12 mm Supalux soffit 200 mm wide	9.200m	L=0.50	4.55	15.43	70.21				6.53	60.08			**130.29**
Sawn softwood bearers 38 x 50 mm	13.840m	L=0.08	1.04	15.43	16.05				0.81	11.21			**27.26**
Prepare, knot, prime, stop; one undercoat and one coat alkyd based paint to wood surfaces; externally	3.920m2	L=0.61	2.40	15.43	37.03				2.19	8.58			**45.61**
PVCu one piece soffit ventilator	16.000Nr	L=0.26	4.21	15.43	64.96				2.06	32.96			**97.92**
			16.12		**£248.74**					**£170.70**			**£419.44**

Item Build Ups	Qty	Hours per unit L=Labour P=Plant	Total Labour Time	Labour Rate Per Hour	Total Value of Labour £	Total Plant Time	Plant Rate Per Hour	Total Value of Plant £	Mat Unit Rate	Total Value of Material £	S/c Unit Rate	Total Value of s/c spec. £	TOTAL £
ROOF SPACE CONVERSION cont/... Dormer Roof cont/...													
112 mm diameter half round PVCu gutter fixed with standard brackets.													
112 mm half round gutter	3.000m	L=0.31	0.92	32.03	29.47				3.01	9.03			**38.50**
Stopped end	1.000Nr	L=0.13	0.13	32.03	4.16				1.23	1.23			**5.39**
90 degree angle	1.000Nr	L=0.31	0.31	32.03	9.93				3.27	3.27			**13.20**
Outlet	1.000Nr	L=0.31	0.31	32.03	9.93				2.94	2.94			**12.87**
			1.67		**£53.49**					**£16.47**			**£69.96**
68 mm Diameter PVCu pipes fixed with standard brackets.													
68 mm pipe	2.000m	L=0.42	0.84	32.03	26.91				2.35	4.70			**31.61**
Shoe	1.000Nr	L=0.44	0.44	32.03	14.09				2.55	2.55			**16.64**
Offset 150 mm projection	1.000Nr	L=0.17	0.17	32.03	5.45				2.92	2.92			**8.37**
			1.45		**£46.45**					**£10.17**			**£56.62**

Item Build Ups	Qty	Hours per unit L=Labour P=Plant	Total Labour Time	Labour Rate Per Hour	Total Value of Labour £	Total Plant Time	Plant Rate Per Hour	Total Value of Plant £	Mat Unit Rate	Total Value of Material £	S/c Unit Rate	Total Value of s/c spec. £	TOTAL £
ROOF SPACE CONVERSION cont/... Dormer Sides and Front													
265 x 165 mm Plain concrete tiles 114 mm gauge 38 mm lap to vertical faces on 38 x 19 mm battens, underfelt, 100 mm fibreglas insulation, 12 mm Supalux board to inside faces, code 4 lead flashings.													
Vertical tiles	8.000m2	L=1.43	11.44	26.82	306.82				30.30	242.40			**549.22**
Angle tiles	4.000m	L=0.23	0.94	26.82	25.21				34.93	139.72			**164.93**
Top edge	7.000m	L=0.16	1.13	26.82	30.31				2.84	19.88			**50.19**
Raking cutting	6.000m	L=0.14	0.86	26.82	23.07				3.77	22.62			**45.69**
Lead flashing 200 mm girth	6.000m										23.16	138.96	**138.96**
100 mm Thick insulation	8.000m2	L=0.35	2.76	15.43	42.59				3.27	26.16			**68.75**
12 mm Supalux	8.000m2	L=0.81	6.44	21.13	136.08				32.78	262.24			**398.32**
Raking cutting on Supalux	6.000m	L=0.08	0.48	21.13	10.14				4.90	29.40			**39.54**
			24.05		**£574.22**					**£742.42**		**£138.96**	**£1455.60**

Item Build Ups	Qty	Hours per unit L=Labour P=Plant	Total Labour Time	Labour Rate Per Hour	Total Value of Labour £	Total Plant Time	Plant Rate Per Hour	Total Value of Plant £	Mat Unit Rate	Total Value of Material £	S/c Unit Rate	Total Value of s/c spec. £	TOTAL £
ROOF SPACE CONVERSION cont/... Dormer Sides and Front cont/...													
Standard softwood window 1800 x 1300 mm including glazing, ironmongery, window board and decoration.													
PVCu window 1800 x 1300 mm, factory double glazed, complete with stays and fasteners	1.000Nr	L=2.25	2.25	15.43	34.72				630.19	630.19			**664.91**
25 x 200 mm Wrought softwood window board	2.100m	L=0.75	1.57	15.43	24.23				6.67	14.01			**38.24**
Returned notched end to window board	2.000Nr	L=0.23	0.46	15.43	7.10								**7.10**
Galvanised mild steel frame ties 200 x 25 x 3 mm	4.000Nr	L=0.14	0.55	15.43	8.49				0.72	2.88			**11.37**
Point edge in polysulphide mastic one side	6.200m	L=0.22	1.37	21.13	28.95				1.30	8.06			**37.01**
Prepare, knot, prime, stop; one undercoat and one coat alkyd based paint to window boards 150 - 300 mm girth; internally	2.100m	L=0.26	0.55	15.43	8.49				0.60	1.26			**9.75**
			6.75		**£111.98**					**£656.40**			**£768.38**

Item Build Ups	Qty	Hours per unit L=Labour P=Plant	Total Labour Time	Labour Rate Per Hour	Total Value of Labour £	Total Plant Time	Plant Rate Per Hour	Total Value of Plant £	Mat Unit Rate	Total Value of Material £	S/c Unit Rate	Total Value of s/c spec. £	TOTAL £
ROOF SPACE CONVERSION cont/... Main Roof													
Plain tiles on 38 x 19 mm battens, underfelt, on existing roof timbers.													
Redland concrete plain tiles 265 x 165 mm, 100 gauge, 65 mm lap, aluminium nails to each fifth course and perimeter, 38 x 19 mm sawn softwood battens	18.000m2	L=0.93	16.67	26.82	447.09				32.23	580.14			**1027.23**
			16.67		**£447.09**					**£580.14**			**£1027.23**
12 mm Supalux soffit 200 mm wide; 25 mm exterior grade plywood fascia 250 mm high; sawn softwood bearers; painted finish.													
25 mm BS 5268 PT2, WBP BB/BB, exterior grade plywood fascia 250 mm wide	5.750m	L=0.43	2.45	15.43	37.80				6.29	36.17			**73.97**
12 mm Supalux soffit 200 mm wide	5.750m	L=0.50	2.85	15.43	43.98				6.53	37.55			**81.53**
Sawn softwood bearers 38 x 50 mm	8.650m	L=0.08	0.65	15.43	10.03				0.81	7.01			**17.04**
Prepare, knot, prime, stop; one undercoat and one coat alkyd based paint to wood surfaces; externally	2.450m2	L=0.61	1.50	15.43	23.15				2.19	5.37			**28.52**
PVCu one piece soffit ventilator	10.000Nr	L=0.26	2.63	15.43	40.58				2.06	20.60			**61.18**
			10.08		**£155.54**					**£106.70**			**£262.24**
112 mm diameter half round PVCu gutter fixed with standard brackets.													
112 mm half round gutter	5.000m	L=0.31	1.54	32.03	49.33				3.01	15.05			**64.38**
Stopped end	2.000Nr	L=0.13	0.26	32.03	8.33				1.23	2.46			**10.79**
90 degree angle	1.000Nr	L=0.31	0.31	32.03	9.93				3.27	3.27			**13.20**
Outlet	1.000Nr	L=0.31	0.31	32.03	9.93				2.94	2.94			**12.87**
			2.42		**£77.52**					**£23.72**			**£101.24**
68 mm Diameter PVCu pipes fixed with standard brackets.													
68 mm pipe	5.000m	L=0.42	2.09	32.03	66.94				2.35	11.75			**78.69**
Shoe	1.000Nr	L=0.44	0.44	32.03	14.09				2.55	2.55			**16.64**
Offset 300 mm projection	1.000Nr	L=0.17	0.17	32.03	5.45				2.92	2.92			**8.37**
			2.70		**£86.48**					**£17.22**			**£103.70**

Item Build Ups	Qty	Hours per unit L=Labour P=Plant	Total Labour Time	Labour Rate Per Hour	Total Value of Labour £	Total Plant Time	Plant Rate Per Hour	Total Value of Plant £	Mat Unit Rate	Total Value of Material £	S/c Unit Rate	Total Value of s/c spec. £	TOTAL £
ROOF SPACE CONVERSION cont/... Roof Light													
Remove existing roof tiles battens and felt and form opening for Velux rooflight 660 x 1180 mm, trim rafters, insert rooflight, flashings, reinstate roof coverings.													
Velux window type GGL-206, 660 x 1180 mm	1.000Nr	L=1.15	1.15	15.43	17.74				240.29	240.29			**258.03**
Velux flashing	1.000Nr	L=1.15	1.15	15.43	17.74				45.00	45.00			**62.74**
Sawn softwood joists 50 x 150 mm	12.400m	L=0.25	3.14	15.43	48.45				2.23	27.65			**76.10**
Strip tiles and set aside	3.000m2	L=0.19	0.56	26.82	15.02								**15.02**
Strip battens	1.000m2	L=0.05	0.05	26.82	1.34								**1.34**
Strip underfelt	1.000m2	L=0.02	0.02	26.82	0.54								**0.54**
Refix tiles	11.000Nr	L=0.30	3.27	26.82	87.70				0.12	1.32			**89.02**
			9.34		**£188.53**					**£314.26**			**£502.79**
Stairwell Opening													
Form new opening 2800 x 1100 mm in existing ceiling, trimming opening with 50 x 200 mm joists (joists measured with second floor), cutting out ceiling joists, making good plasterboard ceiling and skim, including temporary supports.													
Temporary supports	2.000Nr	L=1.11 P=2.00	2.23	21.13	47.12	4.00	2.20	8.80	3.65	7.30			**63.22**
Cut out plasterboard	3.080m2	L=0.37	1.14	11.39	12.98								**12.98**
Cut out joists	3.080m2	L=0.19	0.59	11.39	6.72								**6.72**
Making good	8.000m2	L=1.19	9.50	23.97	227.72				6.63	53.04			**280.76**
12 mm Plywood lining	4.000m	L=0.22	0.87	15.43	13.42				2.06	8.24			**21.66**
			14.33		**£307.96**	**4.00**		**£8.80**		**£68.58**			**£385.34**

Item Build Ups	Qty	Hours per unit L=Labour P=Plant	Total Labour Time	Labour Rate Per Hour	Total Value of Labour £	Total Plant Time	Plant Rate Per Hour	Total Value of Plant £	Mat Unit Rate	Total Value of Material £	S/c Unit Rate	Total Value of s/c spec. £	TOTAL £
ROOF SPACE CONVERSION cont/... Staircase													
Wrought softwood straight flight staircase 3000 mm rise, 3112 mm going, 14 Nr treads, 15 Nr risers, extra 800 x 800 mm tread at bottom, 900 mm balustrade.													
Straight stairs	1.000Nr	L=19.55	19.55	15.43	301.66				515.09	515.09			**816.75**
Extra tread	1.000Nr	L=1.26	1.26	15.43	19.44				55.46	55.46			**74.90**
Balustrade	4.000m	L=3.62	14.49	15.43	223.58				42.50	170.00			**393.58**
Newel post	2.000Nr	L=0.58	1.15	15.43	17.74				35.07	70.14			**87.88**
			36.45		**£562.42**					**£810.69**			**£1373.11**
Doors													
Remove existing door and load into skip, replace with new half hour fire check door and 38 x 25 mm stops screwed to frame, new ironmongery.													
Remove door	1.000Nr	L=0.70	0.70	15.43	10.80				0.95	0.95			**11.75**
Wrought softwood stop fillet 25 x 38 mm	5.000m	L=0.29	1.44	15.43	22.22				1.07	5.35			**27.57**
838 x 1981 mm Half hour fire check door	1.000Nr	L=1.38	1.38	15.43	21.29				140.48	140.48			**161.77**
Fix only medium steel butts	1.000Pair	L=0.31	0.31	15.43	4.78								**4.78**
Fix only lever lock / latch furniture	1.000Set	L=0.58	0.57	15.43	8.80								**8.80**
Fix only door closer	1.000Nr	L=1.73	1.73	15.43	26.69								**26.69**
P.C. £65.00 for door ironmongery	1.000Set								65.00	65.00			**65.00**
			6.13		**£94.58**					**£211.78**			**£306.36**

Item Build Ups	Qty	Hours per unit L=Labour P=Plant	Total Labour Time	Labour Rate Per Hour	Total Value of Labour £	Total Plant Time	Plant Rate Per Hour	Total Value of Plant £	Mat Unit Rate	Total Value of Material £	S/c Unit Rate	Total Value of s/c spec. £	TOTAL £
ROOF SPACE CONVERSION cont/... Doors cont/...													
Door complete including frame and ironmongery.													
Premdor interior flush door, primed, size 762 x 1981 mm	1.000Nr	L=0.92	0.92	15.43	14.20				20.03	20.03			**34.23**
Wrought softwood linings tongued at angles, 25 x 150 mm	4.820m	L=0.23	1.11	15.43	17.13				2.90	13.98			**31.11**
Wrought softwood stop fillet 13 x 38 mm	4.520m	L=0.15	0.68	15.43	10.49				1.09	4.93			**15.42**
Wrought softwood architrave 19 x 50 mm, chamfered and rounded	9.920m	L=0.17	1.72	15.43	26.54				0.84	8.33			**34.87**
Fix only medium steel butts	1.500Pair	L=0.23	0.35	15.43	5.40								**5.40**
Fix only mortice latch	1.000Nr	L=0.86	0.86	15.43	13.27								**13.27**
Fix only lever lock / latch furniture	1.000Set	L=0.46	0.46	15.43	7.10								**7.10**
P.C. £55.00 for door ironmongery	1.000Set								55.00	55.00			**55.00**
			6.10		**£94.13**					**£102.27**			**£196.40**
Fire check door complete with frame and ironmongery.													
838 x 1981 mm Half hour fire check door	1.000Nr	L=1.38	1.38	15.43	21.29				140.48	140.48			**161.77**
Wrought softwood linings tongued at angles, 25 x 150 mm	4.820m	L=0.23	1.11	15.43	17.13				2.90	13.98			**31.11**
Wrought softwood stop fillet 25 x 38 mm	4.520m	L=0.29	1.30	15.43	20.06				1.07	4.84			**24.90**
Wrought softwood architrave 19 x 50 mm, chamfered and rounded	9.920m	L=0.17	1.72	15.43	26.54				0.84	8.33			**34.87**
Fix only medium steel butts	1.500Pair	L=0.23	0.35	15.43	5.40								**5.40**
Fix only mortice latch	1.000Nr	L=0.86	0.86	15.43	13.27								**13.27**
Fix only lever lock / latch furniture	1.000Set	L=0.46	0.46	15.43	7.10								**7.10**
P.C. £55.00 for door ironmongery	1.000Set								55.00	55.00			**55.00**
			7.18		**£110.79**					**£222.63**			**£333.42**

Item Build Ups	Qty	Hours per unit L=Labour P=Plant	Total Labour Time	Labour Rate Per Hour	Total Value of Labour £	Total Plant Time	Plant Rate Per Hour	Total Value of Plant £	Mat Unit Rate	Total Value of Material £	S/c Unit Rate	Total Value of s/c spec. £	TOTAL £
ROOF SPACE CONVERSION cont/... Partitions													
Uprate existing partition to provide half hour fire resistance by fixing 12.5 mm plasterboard both sides, joints taped and filled, emulsion paint													
9.5 mm Plasterboard fixed with galvanised nails to softwood	7.000m2	L=0.96	6.69	23.97	160.36				6.63	46.41			**206.77**
Extra over cost of 12.5 mm plasterboard	7.000m2	L=0.06	0.39	23.97	9.35				0.04	0.28			**9.63**
One mist and two full coats vinyl silk emulsion paint to walls internally	7.000m2	L=0.30	2.10	15.43	32.40				1.49	10.43			**42.83**
			9.18		**£202.11**					**£57.12**			**£259.23**
Internal stud partition; sawn softwood studding and noggings; gypsum plasterboard both sides, emulsion paint													
Sawn softwood studding and nogging 50 x 75 mm	83.400m	L=0.28	23.02	15.43	355.20				1.11	92.57			**447.77**
Fixing with 75 mm clasp nails to brickwork	13.400m	L=0.09	1.23	15.43	18.98				0.18	2.41			**21.39**
12.5 mm Gypsum plasterboard, tapered edges, galvanised nails to softwood, joints filled, taped and finished flush, holes filled with joint filler	40.000m2	L=0.51	20.24	21.13	427.67				3.37	134.80			**562.47**
One mist and two full coats vinyl silk emulsion paint to walls internally	35.000m2	L=0.30	10.50	15.43	162.02				1.49	52.15			**214.17**
			54.99		**£963.87**					**£281.93**			**£1245.80**
Internal stud partition; sawn softwood studding and noggings; gypsum plasterboard one side, emulsion paint													
Sawn softwood studding and nogging 50 x 75 mm	41.700m	L=0.28	11.51	15.43	177.60				1.11	46.29			**223.89**
Fixing with 75 mm clasp nails to brickwork	6.700m	L=0.09	0.62	15.43	9.57				0.18	1.21			**10.78**
12.5 mm Gypsum plasterboard, tapered edges, galvanised nails to softwood, joints filled, taped and finished flush, holes filled with joint filler	10.000m2	L=0.51	5.06	21.13	106.92				3.37	33.70			**140.62**
One mist and two full coats vinyl silk emulsion paint to walls internally	7.000m2	L=0.30	2.10	15.43	32.40				1.49	10.43			**42.83**
			19.29		**£326.49**					**£91.63**			**£418.12**

Item Build Ups	Qty	Hours per unit L=Labour P=Plant	Total Labour Time	Labour Rate Per Hour	Total Value of Labour £	Total Plant Time	Plant Rate Per Hour	Total Value of Plant £	Mat Unit Rate	Total Value of Material £	S/c Unit Rate	Total Value of s/c spec. £	TOTAL £
ROOF SPACE CONVERSION cont/... Wall Finishes													
108 x 108 x 4 mm Glazed wall tiling fixed with adhesive to floated backing and grouted with white cement.													
Wall tiling	8.000m2	L=1.95	15.60	15.43	240.71				16.81	134.48			**375.19**
			15.60		**£240.71**					**£134.48**			**£375.19**
Floor Finishes													
6 mm Hardboard, flameproof to BS 476 Class 1 to existing floor boarding, including all necessary cutting and jointing.													
6 mm Hardboard	30.000m2	L=0.58	17.25	15.43	266.17				4.17	125.10			**391.27**
Prepare boarding to receive hardboard	30.000m2	L=0.12	3.63	15.43	56.01								**56.01**
			20.88		**£322.18**					**£125.10**			**£447.28**
Softwood skirting, decoration													
Wrought softwood bullnosed skirting 19 x 100 mm	25.000m	L=0.40	10.05	15.43	155.07				1.64	41.00			**196.07**
Prepare, knot, prime, stop; one undercoat and one coat alkyd based paint to skirtings 150 mm girth	25.000m	L=0.19	4.78	15.43	73.76				0.30	7.50			**81.26**
			14.83		**£228.83**					**£48.50**			**£277.33**
Ceiling Finishes													
12.5 mm Plasterboard and skim, emulsion paint, vapour barrier, 100 mm fibreglass insulation between rafters													
Glassfibre insulation quilt 100 mm thick	25.000m2	L=0.18	4.60	15.43	70.98				3.27	81.75			**152.73**
12.5 mm Plasterboard duplex grade fixed with galvanised nails to softwood	25.000m2	L=0.29	7.25	21.13	153.19				3.84	96.00			**249.19**
5 mm Thistle board finish plaster to plasterboard in two coats, including scrimming joints	25.000m2	L=0.38	9.45	23.97	226.52				1.81	45.25			**271.77**
One mist coat, two full coats vinyl silk emulsion paint to ceilings internally	25.000m2	L=0.35	8.85	15.43	136.56				1.49	37.25			**173.81**
			30.15		**£587.25**					**£260.25**			**£847.50**

Item Build Ups	Qty	Hours per unit L=Labour P=Plant	Total Labour Time	Labour Rate Per Hour	Total Value of Labour £	Total Plant Time	Plant Rate Per Hour	Total Value of Plant £	Mat Unit Rate	Total Value of Material £	S/c Unit Rate	Total Value of s/c spec. £	TOTAL £
ROOF SPACE CONVERSION cont/... Services													
W.C. suite coloured vitreous china close coupled syphonic P trap, 9 litre cistern flushing bend and connector, plastic ring seat, fixing pan with screws to floor, fixing cistern with screws to softwood.													
W.C. suite	1.000Nr	L=2.75	2.75	32.03	88.08				173.54	173.54			**261.62**
			2.75		**£88.08**					**£173.54**			**£261.62**
Vanity unit with worktop and cupboard, coloured lavatory basin vitreous china, 32 mm chromium plated waste plug, chain and stay, pair 13 mm chromium plated pillar taps.													
Lavatory basin	1.000Nr	L=2.86	2.86	32.03	91.61				83.95	83.95			**175.56**
P.C. £410.00 for vanity unit	1.000Item								410.00	410.00			**410.00**
			2.86		**£91.61**					**£493.95**			**£585.56**
Shower enclosure and electric instant shower.													
P.C. £815.00 for shower enclosure and electric instant shower	1.000Item								815.00	815.00			**815.00**
										£815.00			**£815.00**
Alterations to existing plumbing system and all connections and new pipework to new fittings, including builders work.													
P.C. £720.00 for alteration work	1.000Item								720.00	720.00			**720.00**
										£720.00			**£720.00**

ROOF SPACE CONVERSION Continued/.....

SUMMARY

	£
Scaffolding	**745.00**
Extend scaffolding	**970.00**
Trestles etc.	**270.00**
Skips	**480.00**
Clean up on completion	**95.68**
Preparation work	**175.13**
Remove roof coverings	**175.95**
Work to junction with adjacent roof	**40.21**
Second floor joists cut out	**29.96**
Flooring and joists	**973.08**
Ridge beam	**403.62**
Dormer structure	**716.55**
Dormer roof covering and construction	**606.29**
Eaves, fascia and soffit	**419.44**
PVCu gutter	**69.96**
PVCu rainwater pipe	**56.62**
Dormer sides and front	**1455.60**
Window	**768.38**
Main roof covering	**1027.23**
Eaves and fascia soffit	**262.24**
PVCu gutter	**101.24**
PVCu rainwater pipe	**103.70**

Roof lights	**502.79**
Stairwell opening	**385.34**
Staircase	**1373.11**
Doors, remove existing and replace	**306.36**
New door	**196.40**
New fire check door	**333.42**
Uprate partition	**259.23**
Stud partition plasterboard both sides	**1245.80**
Stud partition plasterboard one side	**418.12**
Wall finishes	**375.19**
Floor finishes	**447.28**
Skirtings	**277.33**
Ceiling finishes	**847.50**
W C Suite	**261.62**
Vanity unit	**585.56**
Shower enclosure	**815.00**
Alterations to plumbing system	**720.00**
TOTAL FOR THIS EXAMPLE	**£19295.93**

N.B Exclusive of Preliminaries, profit and overheads.

7

External works

Composites

TYPICAL ITEMS

		Paving complete: £	Unit
	SITE WORKS		
	The following is a selection of average all-up rates for typical items of external work associated with the construction of building extensions.		
200	**Pavings, stripping vegetable soil 150 mm thick; excavating to reduce levels average 300 mm deep and removing from site; hard-core bed 150 mm thick to falls; surface paving**		
201	Plain in situ concrete laid in bays; trowel smooth finish; expansion joints between bays; formwork to edges; thickness:		
	75 mm	41.46	m2
	100 mm	45.58	m2
	150 mm	52.66	m2
	200 mm	74.05	m2
202	Reinforced in situ grass-concrete paving including soil filling and grass seeding; thickness:		
	100 mm	53.97	m2
	150 mm	63.68	m2
203	Precast grass-concrete paving including soil filling and grass seeding; thickness:		
	73 mm	49.43	m2
	103 mm	52.93	m2
204	Precast paving; 10 mm open joints; pointing joints with cement, lime, mortar (1:1:6):		
	600 x 900 x 50 mm precast concrete flags	35.90	m2
	600 x 450 x 40 mm reconstructed stone; weathered York grey finish; coloured mortar pointing	80.39	m2
205	Charcon Europa 200 x 100 mm concrete blocks laid on screeded bed of sand and compacted with vibrating plate:		
	65 mm thick	47.62	m2
	80 mm thick	50.52	m2
206	Facing bricks P.C. £351.38 per 1000 bedding and grouting joints with cement mortar (1:3); herringbone pattern:		
	75 mm thick, bricks laid flat	69.30	m2
	112.5 mm thick, bricks laid on edge	85.84	m2
207	Bitumen macadam paving 75 mm thick in two coats laid by machine, comprising 28 mm nominal size bitumen base course and various wearing courses:		
	paving of 50 mm thick base course and 25 mm thick wearing course of 14 mm nominal size open textured bitumen macadam	41.32	m2
	paving of 50 mm thick base course and 25 mm thick wearing course of 10 mm nominal size dense bitumen macadam	42.60	m2

Composites

		Paving complete: £	Unit
	paving of 60 mm thick base course and 15 mm thick wearing course of fine cold asphalt	42.70	m2
208	**Edgings, Kerbs and Channels**		
209	Precast concrete edgings, kerbs and channels including excavating trenches and concrete foundations:		
	51 x 152 mm edging on 150 x 75 mm foundation:		
	straight	9.92	m
	127 x 254 mm half battered kerb on 450 x 150 mm foundation:		
	straight	25.47	m
	curved	31.00	m
	127 x 254 mm half battered kerb and 254 x 127 mm channel on 600 x 200 mm foundation:		
	straight	47.14	m
	curved	58.05	m

		Road width between kerbs: 3.00 m £	4.50 m £	6.00 m £	7.50 m £	Unit
210	**Roads and footpaths comprising roads of bitumen macadam surfacing on Type 1 granular road base material with 12 x 25 mm half battered kerbs both sides and pavements 2000 mm wide**					
	Note: Prices allow for 500 mm reduced level excavation in addition to excavation for construction					
211	Road construction 500 mm thick overall comprising 300 mm granular sub-base, 105 mm dense bitumen macadam road base, 60 mm dense bitumen macadam base course and 35 mm wearing course with:					
	pavement comprising 60 mm dense bitumen macadam base course and 15 mm cold asphalt wearing course on 100 mm hard-core:					
	one side of road	548.48	711.82	874.29	1037.33	m
	both sides of road	677.29	839.77	1002.80	1165.28	m
	pavement comprising 100 mm in situ concrete paving on 100 mm hard-core:					
	one side of road	541.80	591.27	639.88	689.05	m
	both sides of road	663.92	712.53	761.70	810.31	m
	pavement comprising 50 mm precast concrete paving flags on 100 mm hard-core:					
	one side of road	528.62	578.09	626.70	675.87	m
	both sides of road	637.57	686.18	735.35	783.96	m
212	EXTRA FOR road construction being 650 mm thick overall with 450 mm granular sub-base	64.91	91.05	116.90	143.03	m

Composites

		All Road widths: £	Unit
213	EXTRA FOR 254 x 127 mm precast concrete channel:		
	one side of road	8.69	m
	both sides of road	17.37	m

		Trenches average depth: 1000 mm £	1500 mm £	2000 mm £	2500 mm £	3000 mm £	Unit
	DRAINAGE						
214	**Drain pipes with allowance for bends, junctions, saddles, tapers and the like; excavating trenches by machine; removing surplus spoil to tip within 10 km of site**						
215	Land drains formed of perforated or porous pipes; trenches completely filled with gravel 19 mm down:						
	Hepline pipes and fittings; nominal size:						
	100 mm	50.34	76.35	98.60	129.45	153.05	m
	150 mm	54.21	80.22	102.49	135.48	156.92	m
	225 mm	83.92	116.03	144.97	182.54	213.20	m
216	Drainpipes laid directly on trench bottoms; no special backfilling:						
	Supersleve pipes and fittings; nominal size:						
	100 mm	25.14	36.03	43.84	59.57	68.72	m
	150 mm	30.27	41.16	48.97	64.70	73.85	m
	vitrified clay pipes and fittings; BS65 normal quality; nominal size:						
	100 mm	30.20	41.09	48.90	64.63	73.78	m
	150 mm	35.12	46.01	53.82	69.55	58.74	m
	225 mm	51.03	63.43	72.68	90.54	101.48	m
217	Drainpipes laid on 150 mm granular bed with granular filling to half height of pipe; backfilling of excavated material:						
	vitrified clay pipes and fittings; BS65 normal quality; nominal size:						
	100 mm	40.06	50.95	58.76	74.49	83.64	m
	150 mm	48.09	58.98	66.79	82.52	91.67	m
	225 mm	67.07	79.47	88.72	106.58	90.69	m
	concrete pipes and fittings; BS5911 part 1; nominal size:						
	225 mm	90.22	102.62	111.87	129.73	140.67	m
	300 mm	106.38	120.23	130.94	150.15	162.35	m
	375 mm	130.11	145.68	157.48	178.72	192.47	m
	450 mm	160.17	178.42	197.21	217.92	234.30	m
	525 mm	196.59	216.18	231.89	259.64	277.71	m
	600 mm	250.73	269.55	294.75	318.78	323.58	m
	cast iron pipes and fittings; all spigot; mechanical joints; nominal size:						
	100 mm	68.26	79.15	86.96	102.69	111.84	m
	150 mm	139.39	150.28	158.09	173.82	182.97	m
	PVCu pipes and fittings; nominal size:						
	110 mm	35.90	43.37	54.60	70.33	79.48	m
	160 mm	48.10	58.99	66.80	82.53	91.68	m

Composites

		Trenches average depth:					
		1000 mm £	1500 mm £	2000 mm £	2500 mm £	3000 mm £	Unit
218	Drain pipes laid on 150 mm granular bed and completely surrounded with granular filling to 150 mm above top of pipe; backfilling with excavated material:						
	vitrified clay pipes and fittings; BS65 normal quality; nominal size:						
	100 mm	57.19	68.08	75.89	91.62	100.77	m
	150 mm	69.93	80.82	88.63	104.36	113.51	m
	225 mm	95.04	107.44	116.69	134.55	145.49	m
	concrete pipes and fittings; BS5911 part 1; nominal size:						
	225 mm	118.19	130.59	139.84	157.70	168.64	m
	300 mm	144.30	158.15	168.86	188.07	196.66	m
	375 mm	182.92	198.49	210.29	231.53	245.28	m
	450 mm	242.46	260.71	279.50	300.21	316.59	m
	525 mm	-	356.12	371.83	399.58	417.65	m
	600 mm	-	456.17	481.37	505.40	510.20	m
	PVCu pipes and fittings; nominal size:						
	110 mm	53.03	63.92	71.73	87.46	96.61	m
	160 mm	69.94	80.83	88.64	104.37	113.52	m
219	Drain pipes laid on 150 mm granular bed and completely surrounded with granular filling to 150 mm above top of pipe; backfilling with imported granular material:						
	vitrified clay pipes and fittings; BS65 normal quality; nominal size:						
	100 mm	84.33	119.86	152.85	193.22	227.55	m
	150 mm	98.20	138.69	175.58	220.92	259.13	m
	225 mm	122.22	167.82	210.29	261.37	305.53	m
	concrete pipes and fittings; BS5911 part 1; nominal size:						
	225 mm	145.37	190.97	233.44	284.52	328.68	m
	300 mm	170.67	226.58	278.25	339.54	392.71	m
	375 mm	206.56	271.94	333.57	404.63	468.20	m
	450 mm	249.52	325.62	402.82	481.37	556.16	m
	525 mm	-	441.25	523.38	617.56	702.07	m
	600 mm	-	512.00	602.71	708.55	802.49	m

Composites

	Description	600 x 450 £	900 x 600 £	1200 x 750 £	1500 x 900 £	Unit
		Internal size; mm :				
	BRICK MANHOLES					
220	**The following prices allow for excavation, backfilling 150 mm working space with excavated material, removing surplus spoil from site; in situ concrete base; one brick wall in Class B engineering bricks, struck pointed internally; 200 mm in situ reinforced concrete cover slabs (where required); cast in light duty inspection cover and frames; step irons at 300 mm vertical centres; curved main channel and 2 Nr branch channel bends and benching finished with cement and sand (1:3)** NB: manholes over 2000 mm deep have shaft 600 x 450 mm in Class B engineering bricks					
221	Manholes depth from cover to invert:					
	500 mm	470.92	669.31	-	-	Nr
	750 mm	608.57	-	-	-	Nr
	1000 mm	746.28	1027.82	1317.37	1683.84	Nr
	1250 mm	893.71	-	-	-	Nr
	1500 mm	1017.78	1387.03	1761.22	2214.99	Nr
	2000 mm	-	1757.28	-	-	Nr
	2500 mm	-	2080.07	2547.54	3110.75	Nr
	3000 mm	-	-	2855.49	3432.80	Nr
	4000 mm	-	-	3534.12	4063.60	Nr

	Description	1050 mm £	1500 mm £	Unit
		Internal size; diameter:		
	PRECAST CONCRETE MANHOLES			
222	**The following prices for precast concrete manholes to BS 5911, Part 1 include for excavation; backfilling 150 mm working space with weak concrete; removing surplus spoil from site; in situ concrete base; precast concrete chamber rings and light duty concrete cover slabs; cast iron light duty inspection covers and frames; step irons at 300 mm vertical centres; curved main channel and 2 Nr branch channel bends and benching finished with cement and sand (1:3)** NB: manholes over 2000 mm deep have taper section and 675 mm diameter shaft to ground level			
223	Manhole depth from cover to invert:			
	500 mm	618.01	-	Nr
	750 mm	-	-	Nr
	1000 mm	760.85	1293.97	Nr
	1250 mm	-	-	Nr
	1500 mm	971.07	1627.68	Nr
	2000 mm	1121.71	-	Nr

8

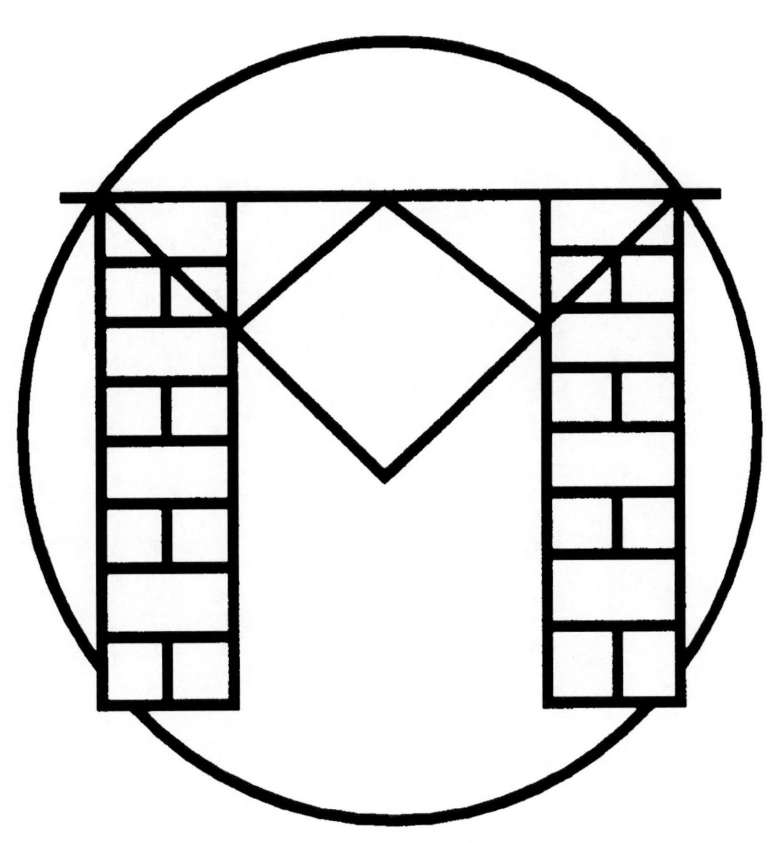

Basic Prices, Labour, Plant, Materials

BASIC PRICES, LABOUR, PLANT AND MATERIALS

LABOUR

The following hourly rates have been used in the trades as shown. The detailed calculations of these hourly rates are shown in Chapter 1.

Please note: The labour hours throughout this book are representative of the time required for one productive man to carry out the unit of work.
Gang rates are calculated as follows by obtaining the overall gang cost and then dividing this by the number of productive members in the gang. The resulting rate is the Gang Cost per **Man - hour.** By using the same principle, any size gang may be built-up and used against the standard labour hours in this section.

EXCAVATION AND EARTHWORK	Excavation	**Labourers (standard rate)**	**£11.39 per hour**
	Labourers using air or electric percussion drills, hammers, rammers etc.	**Labourers (skill rate A)**	**£12.01 per hour**
	Earthwork support	**Labourers (semi-skill rate A)**	**£14.24 per hour**
CONCRETE WORK	Plain concrete	**Labourers (standard rate)**	**£11.39 per hour**
	Reinforcement	**Craftsman**	**£15.43 per hour**
	Formwork (making)	**Craftsman**	**£15.43 per hour**

A0201 Reinforced concrete - Gang rate of 4 labourers with one carpenter in attendance

Shuttering Carpenter	1.00	x	15.43	=	15.43
Concretor	4.00	x	11.39	=	45.56
Poker vibrator	3.00	x	4.68	=	14.04

Total hourly cost of gang				=	75.03

Gang rate (divided by 4) = £18.76 per Man-hour

A0202 Precast concrete - gang rate of 2 craftsmen and one labourer

Ganger/Craftsman	2.00	x	15.43	=	30.86
Precast Concrete Labourer	1.00	x	11.39	=	11.39

Total hourly cost of gang				=	42.25

Gang rate (divided by 2) = £21.13 per Man-hour

A0203 Formwork fix and strike gang - gang rate of 4 craftsmen and one labourer

Shuttering Carpenter	4.00	x	15.43	=	61.72
Formwork Labourer	1.00	x	11.39	=	11.39

Total hourly cost of gang				=	73.11

Gang rate (divided by 4) = £18.28 per Man-hour

BRICKWORK AND BLOCKWORK	A0204 Brickwork:					
	Brick/Block Layer	2.00	x	15.43	=	30.86
	Brick/Blockwork Labourer	1.00	x	11.39	=	11.39

	Total hourly cost of gang				=	42.25

	Gang rate (divided by 2) = £21.13 per Man-hour					
	A0205 Blocklaying					
	Brick/Block Layer	4.00	x	15.43	=	61.72
	Brick/Blockwork Labourer	3.00	x	11.39	=	34.17

	Total hourly cost of gang				=	95.89

	Gang rate (divided by 4) = £23.97 per Man-hour					
ROOFING	A0208 Roof slating and tiling					
	Roof Slater/Tiler	1.00	x	15.43	=	15.43
	Roof Slating/Tiling Labourer	1.00	x	11.39	=	11.39

	Total hourly cost of gang				=	26.82

	Gang rate (divided by 1) = £26.82 per Man-hour					
	A0209 Roof decking					
	Carpenter	1.00	x	15.43	=	15.43
	Roof Decking Labourer	1.00	x	11.39	=	11.39

	Total hourly cost of gang				=	26.82

	Gang rate (divided by 1) = £26.82 per Man-hour					
WOODWORK	Woodwork		**Craftsman**			**£15.43 per hour**
METALWORK	Fixing steel and aluminium windows to timber surrounds		**Craftsman**			**£15.43 per hour**
	A0204 Fixing arch bars, lintels and the like					
	Brick/Block Layer	2.00	x	15.43	=	30.86
	Brick/Blockwork Labourer	1.00	x	11.39	=	11.39

	Total hourly cost of gang				=	42.25

	Gang rate (divided by 2) = £21.13 per Man-hour					

Section	Description	Qty		Rate		Total
PLUMBING AND MECHANICAL ENGINEERING INSTALLATIONS	A0211 General plumbing work					
	Advanced PHMES Operative	1.00	x	19.86	=	19.86
	Apprentice Plumber (3rd Year)	1.00	x	12.17	=	12.17

	Total hourly cost of gang				=	32.03

	Gang rate (divided by 1) = £32.03 per Man-hour					
	A0204 Builders work in connection with plumbing installations					
	Brick/Block Layer	2.00	x	15.43	=	30.86
	Brick/Blockwork Labourer	1.00	x	11.39	=	11.39

	Total hourly cost of gang				=	42.25

	Gang rate (divided by 2) = £21.13 per Man-hour					
FLOOR, WALL AND CEILING FINISHES	Clay and ceramic wall and floor tiling		**Craftsman**			**£15.43 per hour**
	A0212 Solid plasterwork, screeds, in situ flooring					
	Plasterer	4.00	x	15.43	=	61.72
	Plastering Labourer	3.00	x	11.39	=	34.17

	Total hourly cost of gang				=	95.89

	Gang rate (divided by 4) = £23.97 per Man-hour					
	A0213 Wallboard, drylinings, partitions:					
	Plasterboard Tacker	2.00	x	15.43	=	30.86
	Plasterboard Tacking Labourer	1.00	x	11.39	=	11.39

	Total hourly cost of gang				=	42.25

	Gang rate (divided by 2) = £21.13 per Man-hour					
	A0218 Sheet and tile PVC floor coverings:					
	Sheet/Flex. Tile Floorlayer	2.00	x	15.43	=	30.86
	Floorlaying Labourer	1.00	x	11.39	=	11.39

	Total hourly cost of gang				=	42.25

	Gang rate (divided by 2) = £21.13 per Man-hour					
PAINTING AND DECORATING	Painting		**Craftsman**			**£15.43 per hour**
	Paperhanging		**Craftsman**			**£15.43 per hour**

DRAINAGE	Laying pipes up to but not including 300 mm diameter		**Labourer (skill rate B)**			**£12.31 per hour**
	Laying pipes 300 mm diameter and over		**Labourer (skill rate C)**			**£12.65 per hour**
	A0216 Brickwork in manholes and the like					
	Brick/Block Layer	1.00	x	15.43	=	15.43
	Brick/Blockwork Labourer	1.00	x	11.39	=	11.39

	Total hourly cost of gang				=	26.82

	Gang rate (divided by 1) = £26.82 per Man-hour					
	A0211 Laying and jointing cast iron pipes and fittings					
	Advanced PHMES Operative	1.00	x	19.86	=	19.86
	Apprentice Plumber (3rd Year)	1.00	x	12.17	=	12.17

	Total hourly cost of gang				=	32.03

	Gang rate (divided by 1) = £32.03 per Man-hour					
EXTERNAL WORKS	Generally		**Labourers (standard rate)**			**£11.39 per hour**
	A0202 Precast concrete screen walling blocks, brick pavings, brick kerbs and the like					
	Ganger/Craftsman	2.00	x	15.43	=	30.86
	Precast Concrete Labourer	1.00	x	11.39	=	11.39

	Total hourly cost of gang				=	42.25

	Gang rate (divided by 2) = £21.13 per Man-hour					
	A0211 Pipework in external servcices					
	Advanced PHMES Operative	1.00	x	19.86	=	19.86
	Apprentice Plumber (3rd Year)	1.00	x	12.17	=	12.17

	Total hourly cost of gang				=	32.03

	Gang rate (divided by 1) = £32.03 per Man-hour					

Plant Hire Charges

		Daily Hire Charge £	Productive Hours Hrs	Cost Per Hour £	Operator Per Hour £	Fuel Per Hour £	Total Cost Per Hour £
PLANT	The hire charges shown exclude the cost of operators and fuel but are inclusive of oil, grease and the like. Fuel costs have been added in the following table as appropriate. The operator costs are either added in the table below or, where no operator shown, have been allowed for in the rates given in the individual items of work. The cost of delivery to, or collection from site is EXCLUDED and allowance for this should be made in Preliminaries (see Chapter 3). The following are a selection of typical items of plant which could be used in connection with the type and scope of work covered in this book.						
A0021	JCB 3C	85.00	6.00	14.17	14.60	5.63	**34.40**
A0022	Cat D5 1CY	145.00	6.00	24.17	14.60	8.29	**47.06**
A0023	Hymac 580	154.00	6.00	25.67	14.60	7.49	**47.76**
A0024	Hymac 580 with breaker hammer and 230 cfm compressor	230.00	7.00	32.86	14.60	9.15	**56.61**
A0031	Dumper 2000 Kg capacity, hydraulic tip	45.00	6.00	7.50	12.01	2.52	**22.03**
A0041	16 Tonne tipper truck (inclusive)	224.00	8.00	28.00	-	-	**28.00**
A0051	8 Tonne roller	80.00	6.00	13.33	12.01	6.63	**31.97**
A0052	Vibrating roller, 400 Kg	24.00	6.00	4.00	12.01	1.66	**17.67**
A0061	Whacker	16.50	6.00	2.75	-	0.86	**3.61**
A0063	Compressor 100 cfm and one breaker	32.00	6.00	5.33	-	0.86	**6.19**
A0064	250 cfm compressor	54.00	6.00	9.00	-	1.33	**10.33**
A0065	600 cfm compressor	102.00	6.00	17.00	-	2.52	**19.52**
A0066	Compressor 250 cfm and two hammers	72.00	6.00	12.00	-	1.33	**13.33**
A0071	Compressor hose	2.75	6.00	0.46	-	-	**0.46**
A0073	70 lb hammer	2.50	6.00	0.42	-	-	**0.42**
A0074	Concrete scabbler	21.00	6.00	3.50	-	-	**3.50**
A0075	Kango hammer	25.00	6.00	4.17	-	-	**4.17**
A0081	Power float (helicopter)	20.00	6.00	3.33	-	0.86	**4.19**
A0091	Grinder and cutting discs	7.20	6.00	1.20	-	-	**1.20**
A0101	Bar bending and shearing machine (diesel)	16.50	6.00	2.75	-	1.66	**4.41**
A0141	Bitumen melting pot	4.00	6.00	0.67	-	3.84	**4.51**
A0191	Oxy-acetylene equipment and gas	19.50	4.00	4.88	-	4.6	**9.48**

Basic Prices of Materials

MATERIALS

EXCAVATION AND EARTHWORK

Code	Description	Supply Price £	Waste Factor %	Unload. Labour £	Unload. Plant £	Total Unit Cost £	Unit
	Basic prices of materials include an allowance for waste and, where appropriate, the cost of labour and plant in unloading. Where materials are supplied on pallets or other returnable containers, any costs or surcharges are excluded. The following are a selection of basic prices of materials which have either been used in the standard estimates or will be useful for price adjustments to the standard estimates. Note that the code numbers shown on the left hand side of each item, refer to the main BCIS Database. The prices are for materials supplied in full loads to sites within 30 miles of the point of supply.						
A0321	Building sand	24.16	10%	-	-	26.57	tonne
A0351	Hardcore	18.11	-	-	-	18.11	m3
A0347	Gravel 20 mm down	32.38	10%	-	-	35.62	tonne
A0361	Timber for earthwork support	280.30	5%	11.39	-	306.27	m3
A0301	Portland cement delivered in bags	137.81	5%	11.39	-	156.66	tonne
A0331	Fine aggregate	29.64	10%	-	-	32.60	tonne
A0343	20 mm Aggregate	30.95	10%	-	-	34.05	tonne
A0342	40 mm Aggregate	31.05	10%	-	-	34.15	tonne

CONCRETE WORK

Code	Description	Supply Price £	Waste Factor %	Unload. Labour £	Unload. Plant £	Total Unit Cost £	Unit
	Hot rolled deformed high tensile steel reinforcement bars to BS 4449 in standard lengths (not exceeding 12 m) cut, bent, bundled and labelled (25 to under 100 tonnes):						
F0322	8 mm .395 kg per metre	875.00	2.5%	22.78	-	920.22	tonne
F0323	10 mm .616 kg per metre	854.00	2.5%	22.78	-	898.70	tonne
F0324	12 mm .888 kg per metre	831.00	2.5%	22.78	-	875.12	tonne
F0325	16 mm 1.579 kg per metre	788.00	2.5%	22.78	-	831.05	tonne
F0326	20 mm 2.466 kg per metre	766.00	2.5%	22.78	-	808.50	tonne
F0327	25 mm 3.854 kg per metre	750.00	2.5%	22.78	-	792.10	tonne
F0443	32 mm 6.313 kg per metre	750.00	2.5%	22.78	-	792.10	tonne
F0444	40 mm 9.864 kg per metre	750.00	2.5%	22.78	-	792.10	tonne
	Steel fabric reinforcement to BS 4483, supplied in standard sheets, 8 to under 20 tonne loads, reference:						
F0462	A 142 2.22 kg per m2	2.05	2.5%	0.03	-	2.13	m2
F0463	A 193 3.02 kg per m2	2.60	2.5%	0.08	-	2.75	m2
F0464	A 252 3.95 kg per m2	3.47	2.5%	0.08	-	3.64	m2
F0465	A 393 6.16 kg per m2	5.21	2.5%	0.11	-	5.45	m2
F0466	B 196 3.05 kg per m2	2.90	2.5%	0.08	-	3.05	m2
F0467	B 283 3.73 kg per m2	3.54	2.5%	0.08	-	3.71	m2
F0468	B 385 4.53 kg per m2	3.91	2.5%	0.08	-	4.09	m2
F0469	B 503 5.93 kg per m2	4.95	2.5%	0.11	-	5.19	m2
F0470	B 785 8.14 kg per m2	7.73	2.5%	0.15	-	8.08	m2
F0336	B 1131 10.90 kg per m2	9.08	2.5%	0.23	-	9.54	m2

Basic Prices of Materials

Code	Description	Supply Price £	Waste Factor %	Unload. Labour £	Unload. Plant £	Total Unit Cost £	Unit
F0337	C 283 2.61 kg per m2	2.48	2.5%	0.03	-	2.57	m2
F0338	C 385 3.41 kg per m2	3.24	2.5%	0.08	-	3.40	m2
F0339	C 503 4.34 kg per m2	4.12	2.5%	0.08	-	4.31	m2
F0472	C 636 5.55 kg per m2	5.27	2.5%	0.11	-	5.51	m2
F0340	C 785 6.72 kg per m2	6.38	2.5%	0.15	-	6.69	m2
F0341	D 49 .77 kg per m2	1.83	2.5%	0.03	-	1.91	m2
F0260	Sawn softwood for formwork	295.00	12.5%	11.39	-	344.69	m3
F0261	18 mm Plywood for formwork	8.60	10%	2.85	-	12.60	m2
F0263	Nails (mixed)	2.90	10%	-	-	3.19	kg
F0345	Oil Tempered hardboard 3.2 mm	2.82	7.5%	0.11	-	3.15	m2
F0347	25 mm Wrought face boarding	13.82	5%	0.26	-	14.78	m2
F0348	50 x 38 mm twice splayed timber fillets P.A.R.	0.86	5%	0.02	-	0.93	m
F0349	100 x 50 mm twice splayed timber fillets P.A.R.	1.78	5%	0.06	-	1.93	m
F0266	Formwork oil	1.54	20%	-	-	1.85	ltr
F0350	Release agent Febstrike	4.57	10%	-	-	5.03	ltr
F0955	Protective polythene sheet	0.37	5%	-	-	0.39	m2
	Prestressed precast concrete lintels:						
F0702	100 x 65 mm	5.95	-	0.21	-	6.16	m
F0703	150 x 65 mm	8.59	-	0.28	-	8.87	m
F0705	220 x 65 mm	12.94	-	0.44	-	13.38	m
F0706	265 x 65 mm	17.36	-	0.51	-	17.87	m
	Ready mixed concrete - Dense natural aggregate CP 110; grade:						
F0451	15 N/mm2	84.52	5%	-	-	88.75	m3
F0452	20 N/mm2	87.45	5%	-	-	91.82	m3
F0453	25 N/mm2 20 mm Aggregate	90.43	5%	-	-	94.95	m3
F0454	30 N/mm2	93.79	5%	-	-	98.48	m3
F0455	35 N/mm2	93.93	5%	-	-	98.63	m3
F0456	1 - 3 - 6	84.99	5%	-	-	89.24	m3
F0457	1 - 2 - 4	90.50	5%	-	-	95.03	m3
	Ready Mixed Concrete - Lightweight aggregate (Lytag) CP 110; grade:						
F0500	15 N/mm2	143.81	5%	-	-	151.00	m3
F0501	20 N/mm2	147.40	5%	-	-	154.77	m3
F0502	25 N/mm2	152.93	5%	-	-	160.57	m3
F0503	30 N/mm2	156.30	5%	-	-	164.11	m3
F0504	35 N/mm2	163.73	5%	-	-	171.91	m3

BRICKWORK & BLOCKWORK

Code	Description	Supply Price £	Waste Factor %	Unload. Labour £	Unload. Plant £	Total Unit Cost £	Unit
	NOTE: All bricks are 215 x 102.5 x 65 mm; where no 'Labour unloading' prices are shown the materials are supplied palletised for crane unloading (surcharge for pallets excluded). Due to the wide range of facing bricks, special bricks etc., which are available, the following P.C. prices have been included to provide representative costs for these items.						
G0102	Common bricks	311.01	5%	-	-	326.56	1000

Basic Prices of Materials

		Supply Price £	Waste Factor %	Unload. Labour £	Unload. Plant £	Total Unit Cost £	Unit
G0103	Class A engineering bricks	493.42	5%	-	-	518.09	1000
G0104	Class B engineering bricks	391.75	5%	-	-	411.33	1000
G0105	Facing bricks	351.38	5%	-	-	368.95	1000
	Precast concrete blocks, BS 6073, furnace clinker aggregate, compressive strength 3.5 N/mm2 , face size 440 x 215 mm delivered to sites within about 25 miles of point of supply in 19 tonne loads:						
	solid blocks:						
G0134	100 mm	8.07	5%	-	-	8.48	m2
G0136	140 mm	12.46	5%	-	-	13.08	m2
G0194	Extra for smooth face blocks, any thickness	1.44	5%	-	-	1.51	m2
	Thermalite blocks, co-ordinating face size 440 x 215 mm delivered to sites within about 40 miles of point of supply in 15 tonne loads:						
	Shield 2000:						
G0153	100 mm	11.79	7.5%	-	-	12.67	m2
G0155	140 mm	16.50	7.5%	-	-	17.74	m2
G0157	190 mm	22.40	7.5%	-	-	24.08	m2
G0158	200 mm	23.58	7.5%	-	-	25.34	m2
	Trenchblocks:						
G0159	275 mm	32.42	7.5%	-	-	34.86	m2
G0160	300 mm	35.36	7.5%	-	-	38.02	m2
	Smooth face Paint Grade blocks:						
G0163	100 mm	18.96	7.5%	-	-	20.38	m2
G0164	140 mm	26.53	7.5%	-	-	28.52	m2
G0167	200 mm	37.91	7.5%	-	-	40.75	m2
	Turbo blocks:						
G0614	100 mm	11.72	7.5%	-	-	12.60	m2
G0619	190 mm	22.26	7.5%	-	-	23.93	m2
G0620	200 mm	23.44	7.5%	-	-	25.19	m2
	Lignacite blocks, compressive strength 3.5 N/mm2, face size 440 x 215 mm delivered to sites within about 100-150 miles of point of supply in 15 tonne loads:						
	solid blocks:						
G0169	75 mm	11.81	7.5%	-	-	12.69	m2
G0170	100 mm	15.32	7.5%	-	-	16.47	m2
G0171	140 mm	19.78	7.5%	-	-	21.26	m2
G0172	150 mm	23.77	7.5%	-	-	25.55	m2
G0181	190 mm	28.46	7.5%	-	-	30.60	m2
G0182	200 mm (special)	30.48	7.5%	-	-	32.77	m2
	hollow blocks:						
G0173	140 mm (special)	17.99	10%	-	-	19.79	m2
G0174	190 mm (special)	24.79	10%	-	-	27.27	m2
G0175	200 mm (special)	24.79	10%	-	-	27.27	m2
G0176	215 mm (special)	26.56	10%	-	-	29.21	m2
	cellular blocks:						
G0178	100 mm	12.40	10%	-	-	13.64	m2
G0179	150 mm (special)	17.01	10%	-	-	18.71	m2
G0180	Extra for Fair Face blocks, any thickness	0.96	10%	-	-	1.06	m2

Basic Prices of Materials

Code	Description	Supply Price £	Waste Factor %	Unload. Labour £	Unload. Plant £	Total Unit Cost £	Unit
A0301	Portland cement delivered in bags	137.81	5%	11.39	-	156.66	tonne
A0311	Hydrated lime delivered in bags	216.00	5%	11.39	-	238.76	tonne
A0302	White Portland cement delivered in bags	314.16	5%	11.39	-	341.83	tonne
G0205	Colouring pigment (red, brown, yellow)	8.96	5%	-	-	9.41	kg
A0321	Building sand BS 1200	24.16	10%	-	-	26.57	tonne
A0331	Concreting sand (fine aggregate)	29.64	10%	-	-	32.60	tonne
A0342	19 mm Aggregate	31.05	10%	-	-	34.15	tonne
G0208	Refractory aggregate (crushed firebrick)	237.27	5%	11.39	-	261.10	tonne
G0209	Flue joint compound	4.92	10%	-	-	5.41	nr
	Ready mixed mortars (***guide prices*** *based on London pricing levels)* from RMC Readymix Ltd:						
G0611	lime sand mortar (1:12)	44.98	5%	-	-	47.22	tonne
G0612	lime sand mortar (1:6)	46.09	5%	-	-	48.40	tonne
G0613	lime sand mortar (1:4.5)	47.21	5%	-	-	49.57	tonne
	Damp proof courses to BS 6398, any standard width:						
G0269	Hessian base, ref A	9.25	5%	-	-	9.71	m2
G0270	Fibre base, ref B	7.28	5%	-	-	7.64	m2
	Cavity wall ties:						
G0311	200 mm stainless steel flat bar tie with expanded ends, type 1	0.27	10%	-	-	0.30	nr
G0312	200 mm stainless steel general purpose wire tie, type 2	0.12	10%	-	-	0.13	nr
G0313	200 mm stainless steel housing tie, type 4	0.06	10%	-	-	0.07	nr
G0314	75 mm stainless steel brick to timber tie	0.17	10%	-	-	0.18	nr
	PIR Polyisocyanurate foam sheet insulation (1200 x 450mm):						
G0315	40 mm	5.29	10%	-	-	5.82	m2
G0316	50 mm	6.48	15%	-	-	7.45	m2
	Fibreglass Dritherm cavity wall insulation (1200 x 455 mm) :						
G0317	75 mm	4.61	10%	-	-	5.07	m2
G0318	Gun-grade polysulphide mastic (100 ml cart.)	4.08	10%	-	-	4.49	nr
G0319	Fillcrete joint filler, 19 mm thick, cut to size	14.47	10%	-	-	15.92	m2
	Exmet galvanised brickwork reinforcement:						
G0320	65 mm wide (100 metres)	62.64	10%	-	-	68.90	coil
G0321	115 mm wide (100 metres)	107.84	10%	-	-	118.62	coil
G0322	175 mm wide (100 metres)	169.02	10%	-	-	185.92	coil
G0323	Lead for running in mortices	2.15	5%	0.01	-	2.27	kg
	Terracotta cavity wall liners for 275 mm wall:						
G0324	215 x 65 mm	1.49	5%	-	-	1.56	nr
G0325	215 x 140 mm	1.65	5%	-	-	1.73	nr
G0326	215 x 215 mm	4.57	5%	-	-	4.80	nr

Basic Prices of Materials

Code	Description	Supply Price £	Waste Factor %	Unload. Labour £	Unload. Plant £	Total Unit Cost £	Unit
	Terracotta air bricks, square hole pattern:						
G0327	215 x 65 mm	0.89	5%	-	-	0.93	nr
G0328	215 x 140 mm	1.23	5%	-	-	1.29	nr
G0329	215 x 215 mm	3.31	5%	-	-	3.48	nr

ROOFING WORK

Code	Description	Supply Price £	Waste Factor %	Unload. Labour £	Unload. Plant £	Total Unit Cost £	Unit
	NOTE: Where no 'Labour Unloading' prices are shown the materials are supplied palletised for crane unloading (surcharge for pallets excluded). The cost of hoisting roofing materials to roof level is allowed in Preliminaries.						
	Burlington slates (quarry prices plus average £45.00 per tonne delivery):						
	Blue/grey slates Type 1 - Patterns of uniform length and width:						
M0021	610 x 305 mm	4945.50	5%	-	-	5192.78	1000
M0022	510 x 255 mm	2110.50	5%	-	-	2216.03	1000
M0023	405 x 205 mm	1354.50	5%	-	-	1422.23	1000
	Blue/grey slates Type 2 - Sized of uniform length and random widths:						
M0024	610 mm long	1176.00	5%	-	-	1234.80	tonne
M0025	510 mm long	887.25	5%	-	-	931.61	tonne
M0026	405 mm long	845.25	5%	-	-	887.51	tonne
	Blue/grey random slates, random lengths, proportionate and random widths:						
M0027	1200 - 765 mm lengths (best mixed)	2021.25	5%	-	-	2122.31	tonne
M0028	710 - 560 mm lengths (best mixed)	1097.25	5%	-	-	1152.11	tonne
M0029	550 - 305 mm lengths (best mixed)	887.25	5%	-	-	931.61	tonne
M0030	355 - 255 mm lengths (best mixed)	651.00	5%	-	-	683.55	tonne
	Westmorland light green Patterns; uniform length and widths:						
M0031	610 x 305 mm	17099.25	5%	-	-	17954.21	1000
M0032	405 x 255 mm	6478.50	5%	-	-	6802.43	1000
M0033	355 x 205 mm	3895.50	5%	-	-	4090.28	1000
	Westmorland light green Sized; uniform length and random widths:						
M0034	610 mm long	4026.75	5%	-	-	4228.09	tonne
M0035	510 mm long	3186.75	5%	-	-	3346.09	tonne
M0036	405 mm long	2394.00	5%	-	-	2513.70	tonne
	Westmorland light green Randoms; random lengths, proportionate and random widths:						
M0037	610 - 305 mm lengths	2730.00	5%	-	-	2866.50	tonne
M0038	510 - 305 mm lengths	2320.50	5%	-	-	2436.53	tonne
M0039	460 - 230 mm lengths	1659.00	5%	-	-	1741.95	tonne
	undercloak slates 305 x 150 mm and other special sizes slate-and-a-half etc.:						
M0040	blue/grey	110.25	5%	-	-	115.76	m2
M0041	light green	222.60	5%	-	-	233.73	m2
	Marley Eternit 2000 slates and accessories delivered to sites:						
M0050	Garsdale 600 x 300 mm: blue/black	1104.00	2.5%	-	2.33	1133.99	1000
M0051	Birkdale 600 x 300 mm: blue/black, heather, green	1434.00	2.5%	-	2.33	1472.24	1000
M0053	Garsdale 500 x 250 mm: blue/black	914.00	2.5%	-	1.46	938.35	1000

Basic Prices of Materials

		Supply Price £	Waste Factor %	Unload. Labour £	Unload. Plant £	Total Unit Cost £	Unit
	Marley Eternit roof tiles and accessories delivered to sites in the Greater London area:						
M0103	Ludlow Major granule and smooth	946.00	5%	-	-	993.30	1000
M0105	Mendip granule and smooth	962.00	5%	-	-	1010.10	1000
M0107	Modern smooth	982.00	5%	-	-	1031.10	1000
M0108	Wessex smooth	1459.00	5%	-	-	1531.95	1000
M0109	Malvern smooth	1055.00	5%	-	-	1107.75	1000
M0110	Melbourn smooth slates	2109.00	5%	-	-	2214.45	1000
M0111	Ludlow Plus granule and smooth	664.94	5%	-	-	698.18	1000
M0165	Anglia Plus granule and smooth	698.18	5%	-	-	733.09	1000
M0113	Pascoll roll granule	3.90	5%	-	-	4.09	nr
M0114	segmental ridge granule or smooth	4.39	5%	-	-	4.61	nr
M0115	Modern ridge granule or smooth	4.61	5%	-	-	4.84	nr
M0116	Modern mono ridge granule or smooth	8.23	5%	-	-	8.64	nr
M0117	segmental mono ridge granule or smooth	8.23	5%	-	-	8.64	nr
M0118	trough valleys smooth	8.23	5%	-	-	8.64	nr
M0119	dentil slips and verge slips	0.22	5%	-	-	0.23	nr
	Redland roof tiles and accessories delivered to sites in the Greater London area:						
M0201	49 Interlocking	737.10	5%	-	-	773.96	1000
M0202	Norfolk pantiles	765.45	5%	-	-	803.72	1000
M0204	50 Double Roman or Renown	1056.30	5%	-	-	1109.12	1000
M0205	Redland Cambrian interlocking slates	2461.20	5%	-	-	2584.26	1000
M0209	Regent or Grovebury	1075.20	5%	-	-	1128.96	1000
M0212	Stonewold MK2 slates	2724.75	5%	-	-	2860.99	1000
M0214	Plain tiles	443.10	5%	-	-	465.26	1000
M0216	Ornamental tiles	821.10	5%	-	-	862.16	1000
	Sandtoft clay roofing tiles delivered to sites in the North London area:						
M0321	Old English pantiles - Natural Red	1283.31	5%	-	12.23	1360.32	1000
M0322	Old English pantiles - Mixed Russet	1283.31	5%	-	12.23	1360.32	1000
M0323	Gaelic tiles - Natural Red	2427.70	5%	-	12.23	2561.93	1000
M0324	Koramic Romulus tiles - Natural Red	1296.54	5%	-	12.23	1374.21	1000
M0325	County pantiles - Natural Red	1248.03	5%	-	20.09	1331.53	1000
M0326	County pantiles - Mixed Russet	1248.03	5%	-	20.09	1331.53	1000
M0327	Goxhill (hand-made) Red Plain tiles	1047.38	5%	-	7.28	1107.39	1000
	Underslating:						
M0371	Rubershield – Pro breathable membrane (50 m2 roll)	97.54	12.5%	1.14	-	111.01	nr
M0372	Zylex reinforced felt - standard (15 m2 roll)	32.68	12.5%	1.14	-	38.05	nr
M0373	Roofguard SB non-breathable membrane (45 m2 roll)	62.14	12.5%	1.14	-	71.19	nr

Basic Prices of Materials

WOODWORK

		Supply Price £	Waste Factor %	Unload. Labour £	Unload. Plant £	Total Unit Cost £	Unit
	Ancillary materials, (e.g. nails, screws, glue)						
	Prices of materials include for ordinary wire nails, glue and the like according to description and waste allowances etc. All items are deemed fixed with ordinary nails; extra over prices are given in the SUNDRIES section, for fixing with other types of nail, screws, plugs etc.						
	Material						
	Sawn softwood, Building quality, untreated:						
N0001	13 x 25 mm	0.15	7.5%	-	-	0.16	m
N0002	13 x 38 mm	0.22	7.5%	0.01	-	0.24	m
N0003	13 x 50 mm	0.24	7.5%	0.01	-	0.26	m
N0004	13 x 75 mm	0.36	7.5%	0.01	-	0.40	m
N0005	13 x 100 mm	0.48	7.5%	0.01	-	0.53	m
N0006	19 x 100 mm	0.73	7.5%	0.02	-	0.80	m
N0007	19 x 150 mm	1.09	7.5%	0.03	-	1.20	m
N0008	25 x 25 mm	0.24	7.5%	0.01	-	0.27	m
N0009	25 x 38 mm	0.37	7.5%	0.01	-	0.41	m
N0010	25 x 50 mm	0.49	7.5%	0.01	-	0.53	m
N0011	25 x 63 mm	0.61	7.5%	0.02	-	0.68	m
N0012	25 x 75 mm	0.72	7.5%	0.02	-	0.80	m
N0013	25 x 100 mm	0.86	7.5%	0.03	-	0.96	m
N0056	25 x 150 mm	1.30	7.5%	0.04	-	1.44	m
N0057	25 x 175 mm	1.55	7.5%	0.05	-	1.72	m
N0058	32 x 150 mm	2.09	7.5%	0.05	-	2.30	m
N0059	32 x 200 mm	2.79	7.5%	0.07	-	3.08	m
N0014	38 x 38 mm	0.55	7.5%	0.02	-	0.61	m
N0015	38 x 50 mm	0.73	7.5%	0.02	-	0.81	m
N0016	38 x 63 mm	0.92	7.5%	0.03	-	1.02	m
N0017	38 x 75 mm	1.09	7.5%	0.03	-	1.20	m
N0018	38 x 100 mm	1.40	7.5%	0.04	-	1.55	m
N0019	38 x 150 mm	2.09	7.5%	0.06	-	2.31	m
N0021	50 x 50 mm	0.68	7.5%	0.03	-	0.76	m
N0022	50 x 63 mm	0.92	7.5%	0.04	-	1.03	m
N0023	50 x 75 mm	0.99	7.5%	0.04	-	1.11	m
N0024	50 x 100 mm	1.32	7.5%	0.06	-	1.48	m
N0025	50 x 125 mm	1.65	7.5%	0.07	-	1.85	m
N0026	50 x 150 mm	1.98	7.5%	0.09	-	2.23	m
N0027	50 x 175 mm	2.31	7.5%	0.10	-	2.59	m
N0028	50 x 200 mm	2.64	7.5%	0.11	-	2.96	m
N0029	50 x 225 mm	2.97	7.5%	0.13	-	3.33	m
N0030	50 x 250 mm	4.04	7.5%	0.14	-	4.50	m
N0031	50 x 275 mm	4.61	7.5%	0.16	-	5.13	m
N0032	50 x 300 mm	5.03	7.5%	0.17	-	5.59	m

Basic Prices of Materials

		Supply Price £	Waste Factor %	Unload. Labour £	Unload. Plant £	Total Unit Cost £	Unit
N0033	75 x 75 mm	1.71	7.5%	0.06	-	1.90	m
N0034	75 x 100 mm	2.28	7.5%	0.09	-	2.55	m
N0035	75 x 125 mm	2.85	7.5%	0.11	-	3.18	m
N0036	75 x 150 mm	3.42	7.5%	0.13	-	3.82	m
N0037	75 x 175 mm	3.99	7.5%	0.15	-	4.45	m
N0038	75 x 200 mm	4.56	7.5%	0.17	-	5.09	m
N0039	75 x 225 mm	5.13	7.5%	0.19	-	5.72	m
N0040	75 x 250 mm	6.45	7.5%	0.21	-	7.16	m
N0041	75 x 275 mm	7.10	7.5%	0.23	-	7.88	m
N0042	75 x 300 mm	7.75	7.5%	0.26	-	8.61	m
N0043	100 x 100 mm	3.36	7.5%	0.11	-	3.73	m
N0044	100 x 150 mm	5.04	7.5%	0.17	-	5.60	m
N0045	100 x 200 mm	6.72	7.5%	0.23	-	7.47	m
N0046	100 x 225 mm	7.56	7.5%	0.26	-	8.41	m
N0047	100 x 250 mm	8.93	7.5%	0.28	-	9.91	m
N0048	100 x 300 mm	10.71	7.5%	0.34	-	11.88	m
N0049	38 x 38 mm angle fillets	0.34	7.5%	0.02	-	0.39	m
N0050	50 x 50 mm angle fillets	0.70	7.5%	0.03	-	0.78	m
N0051	75 x 75 mm angle fillets	1.11	7.5%	0.06	-	1.26	m
N0052	25 x 50 mm tilting fillets	0.53	7.5%	0.01	-	0.59	m
N0053	38 x 75 mm tilting fillets	1.25	7.5%	0.03	-	1.38	m
N0054	50 x 50 mm rolls	1.11	7.5%	0.03	-	1.23	m
N0055	50 x 75 mm rolls	1.67	7.5%	0.04	-	1.83	m
N0081	19 mm square edge boarding 150 mm wide	1.10	7.5%	0.03	-	1.21	m
N0082	25 mm square edge boarding 150 mm wide	1.29	7.5%	0.04	-	1.43	m
	Wrought softwood, untreated:						
N0083	13 x 19 mm	0.30	7.5%	0.03	-	0.36	m
N0084	13 x 25 mm	0.41	7.5%	-	-	0.44	m
N0085	13 x 32 mm	0.54	7.5%	-	-	0.58	m
N0091	13 x 50 mm	0.53	7.5%	0.01	-	0.58	m
N0092	19 x 25 mm	0.58	7.5%	0.01	-	0.63	m
N0086	19 x 32 mm	0.75	7.5%	0.01	-	0.81	m
N0093	19 x 38 mm	0.73	7.5%	0.01	-	0.79	m
N0094	19 x 50 mm	0.82	7.5%	0.01	-	0.90	m
N0095	19 x 75 mm	1.22	7.5%	0.02	-	1.33	m
N0096	19 x 100 mm	1.62	7.5%	0.02	-	1.76	m
N0097	19 x 125 mm	2.02	7.5%	0.03	-	2.21	m
N0098	19 x 150 mm	2.43	7.5%	0.03	-	2.65	m
N0099	19 x 175 mm	2.84	7.5%	0.04	-	3.09	m
N0100	19 x 200 mm	3.24	7.5%	0.04	-	3.53	m
N0101	22 x 75 mm	1.42	7.5%	0.02	-	1.55	m
N0102	25 x 38 mm	0.92	7.5%	0.01	-	1.00	m
N0103	25 x 50 mm	0.95	7.5%	0.01	-	1.03	m

	Basic Prices of Materials	Supply Price £	Waste Factor %	Unload. Labour £	Unload. Plant £	Total Unit Cost £	Unit
N0104	25 x 75 mm	1.42	7.5%	0.02	-	1.55	m
N0105	25 x 100 mm	1.77	7.5%	0.03	-	1.93	m
N0106	25 x 125 mm	2.22	7.5%	0.04	-	2.43	m
N0107	25 x 150 mm	2.66	7.5%	0.04	-	2.90	m
N0108	25 x 175 mm	3.10	7.5%	0.05	-	3.39	m
N0109	25 x 200 mm	4.18	7.5%	0.06	-	4.56	m
N0110	25 x 225 mm	4.89	7.5%	0.06	-	5.32	m
N0111	25 x 250 mm	4.92	7.5%	0.07	-	5.36	m
N0112	32 x 63 mm	1.47	7.5%	0.02	-	1.60	m
N0113	32 x 75 mm	1.76	7.5%	0.03	-	1.92	m
N0114	32 x 100 mm	2.20	7.5%	0.04	-	2.41	m
N0115	32 x 150 mm	3.30	7.5%	0.05	-	3.60	m
N0116	38 x 50 mm	1.30	7.5%	0.02	-	1.41	m
N0119	38 x 100 mm	2.36	7.5%	0.04	-	2.58	m
N0117	38 x 115 mm	2.75	7.5%	0.05	-	3.01	m
N0120	38 x 125 mm	2.95	7.5%	0.05	-	3.22	m
N0118	38 x 150 mm	3.53	7.5%	0.06	-	3.86	m
N0121	50 x 50 mm	1.40	7.5%	0.03	-	1.54	m
N0122	50 x 75 mm	2.10	7.5%	0.04	-	2.30	m
N0123	50 x 100 mm	2.70	7.5%	0.06	-	2.97	m
N0124	50 x 150 mm	5.05	7.5%	0.09	-	5.52	m
N0125	63 x 75 mm	3.35	7.5%	0.05	-	3.65	m
N0126	63 x 100 mm	4.24	7.5%	0.07	-	4.63	m
N0127	63 x 115 mm	5.01	7.5%	0.08	-	5.47	m
N0128	63 x 125 mm	5.30	7.5%	0.09	-	5.80	m
N0129	63 x 150 mm	6.36	7.5%	0.11	-	6.96	m
N0130	63 x 175 mm	7.42	7.5%	0.13	-	8.12	m
N0131	75 x 75 mm	3.00	7.5%	0.06	-	3.29	m
N0132	75 x 100 mm	5.05	7.5%	0.09	-	5.52	m
N0133	75 x 150 mm	7.57	7.5%	0.13	-	8.28	m
N0134	100 x 100 mm	6.98	7.5%	0.11	-	7.62	m
	Wrought softwood boarding, untreated, 125 mm wide:						
N0135	19 mm square edged	1.62	7.5%	0.03	-	1.77	m
N0136	22 mm square edged	1.83	7.5%	0.03	-	2.00	m
N0137	25 mm square edged	1.83	7.5%	0.04	-	2.01	m
N0138	19 mm tongued and grooved	1.62	7.5%	0.03	-	1.77	m
N0139	22 mm tongued and grooved	2.22	7.5%	0.03	-	2.42	m
N0140	25 mm tongued and grooved	2.22	7.5%	0.04	-	2.43	m
N0141	19 mm shiplap weatherboarding (150 mm wide)	2.22	7.5%	0.03	-	2.42	m
N0142	25 mm shiplap weatherboarding (150 mm wide)	2.92	7.5%	0.04	-	3.18	m

	Basic Prices of Materials	Supply Price £	Waste Factor %	Unload. Labour £	Unload. Plant £	Total Unit Cost £	Unit
N0143	13 mm tongued, grooved and V-jointed (100 mm wide)	0.97	7.5%	0.01	-	1.06	m
N0144	19 mm tongued, grooved and V-jointed (100 mm wide)	1.48	7.5%	0.02	-	1.62	m
N0145	16 mm cross-tongued (450 mm wide)	6.75	7.5%	0.08	-	7.34	m
N0146	19 mm cross-tongued (450 mm wide)	8.21	7.5%	0.11	-	8.95	m
N0147	25 mm cross-tongued (450 mm wide)	10.27	7.5%	0.11	-	11.16	m
	Hardwood, average prices; ex wharf:						
N0207	hardwood European oak kiln dried square edged, 51 mm thick board, prime quality	2240.12	7.5%	-	-	2408.12	m3
N0208	hardwood Beech European kiln dried square edged, 51 mm thick board	1120.73	7.5%	-	-	1204.78	m3
N0209	hardwood Beech European kiln dried square edged, 51 mm thick board, steamed	1038.95	7.5%	-	-	1116.87	m3
N0210	hardwood Iroko kiln dried square edged, 51 mm thick board	1173.01	7.5%	-	-	1260.99	m3
N0211	hardwood Idigbo kiln dried square edged, 51 mm thick board	911.60	7.5%	-	-	979.97	m3
N0212	hardwood Utile kiln dried square edged, 51 mm thick board	1227.97	7.5%	-	-	1320.07	m3
N0213	hardwood Sapele kiln dried square edged, 51 mm thick board	1108.66	7.5%	-	-	1191.81	m3
N0214	hardwood Meranti kiln dried square edged, 51 mm thick board	1051.02	7.5%	-	-	1129.84	m3
N0215	hardwood Douglas Fir kiln dried square edged, 51 mm thick board	931.71	7.5%	-	-	1001.58	m3
N0216	hardwood English Green Oak waney edged, 102 mm thick board	1608.70	7.5%	-	-	1729.35	m3
N0217	hardwood Sweet Chestnut air dried, 51 mm thick board	2077.90	7.5%	-	-	2233.75	m3
N0219	hardwood Western Red Cedar waney edged, 51 mm thick board	2077.90	7.5%	-	-	2233.75	m3
N0220	hardwood Western Hemlock kiln dried square edged, 51 mm thick board	1052.36	7.5%	-	-	1131.29	m3
N0221	hardwood American White Oak kiln dried square edged, 51 mm thick board	1679.75	7.5%	-	-	1805.73	m3
N0222	hardwood American Red Oak kiln dried square edged, 51 mm thick board	1541.67	7.5%	-	-	1657.30	m3
N0223	hardwood Ash kiln dried square edged, 51 mm thick board	1105.98	7.5%	-	-	1188.93	m3
N0224	hardwood American Black Walnut kiln dried square edged, 51 mm thick board	2614.14	7.5%	-	-	2810.20	m3
N0225	hardwood American Cherry kiln dried square edged, 51 mm thick board	1995.16	7.5%	-	-	2144.80	m3
	Wrought Softwood standard mouldings:						
	quadrant:						
N0241	13 mm	0.67	7.5%	-	-	0.72	m
N0242	19 mm	0.75	7.5%	-	-	0.81	m
N0243	25 mm	1.30	7.5%	-	-	1.40	m
	scotia mould:						
N0244	19 mm	0.83	7.5%	-	-	0.89	m
N0245	25 mm	1.43	7.5%	-	-	1.53	m
	half round:						
N0246	25 mm	1.43	7.5%	-	-	1.53	m
	cover strip:						
N0247	13 x 50 mm	1.28	7.5%	0.01	-	1.39	m
	picture rail, moulded:						
N0248	19 x 50 mm	1.87	7.5%	0.01	-	2.02	m
	architrave:						
N0249	19 x 50 mm, bullnosed	0.77	7.5%	0.01	-	0.84	m
N0250	19 x 50 mm, chamfered and rounded	0.77	7.5%	0.01	-	0.84	m
N0251	25 x 75 mm, ogee or torus	1.57	7.5%	0.02	-	1.71	m
	skirting:						
N0252	19 x 75 mm, bullnosed	1.16	7.5%	0.02	-	1.27	m

	Basic Prices of Materials	Supply Price £	Waste Factor %	Unload. Labour £	Unload. Plant £	Total Unit Cost £	Unit
N0253	19 x 100 mm, bullnosed	1.51	7.5%	0.02	-	1.64	m
N0254	19 x 75 mm, chamfered or rounded	1.16	7.5%	0.02	-	1.27	m
N0255	19 x 100 mm, chamfered or rounded	1.51	7.5%	0.02	-	1.64	m
N0256	19 x 100 mm, ogee or torus	1.51	7.5%	0.02	-	1.64	m
N0257	25 x 175 mm, ogee or torus	3.44	7.5%	0.05	-	3.75	m
	handrails:						
N0258	50 x 50 mm, mopstick	3.03	7.5%	0.03	-	3.29	m
N0259	50 x 75 mm, toad's back	4.54	7.5%	0.04	-	4.92	m
N0260	50 x 100 mm, sow's ear	6.44	7.5%	0.06	-	6.99	m
	weatherboard; throated:						
N0261	50 x 50 mm	3.02	7.5%	-	-	3.25	m
N0262	50 x 75 mm	4.54	7.5%	-	-	4.88	m
N0263	63 x 75 mm	5.45	7.5%	-	-	5.86	m
	windowboards, rebated and rounded:						
N0264	25 x 150 mm	5.25	7.5%	0.04	-	5.69	m
N0265	25 x 200 mm	6.14	7.5%	0.06	-	6.67	m
N0266	25 x 225 mm	9.75	7.5%	0.06	-	10.54	m
	Wrought hardwood standard mouldings:						
N0281	architrave, moulded, 25 x 75 mm	5.47	7.5%	0.02	-	5.90	m
N0282	skirting, moulded, 25 x 125 mm	7.89	7.5%	0.04	-	8.53	m
N0283	weatherboard, moulded, 50 x 63 mm	7.82	-	-	-	7.82	m
N0284	windowboard, nosed and tongued, 32 x 225 mm	25.95	7.5%	0.08	-	27.98	m
	Sheet products, delivered in full pallets						
	Standard quality hardboard:						
	plain:						
N0301	3.2 mm	1.56	5%	0.03	-	1.67	m2
N0302	4.8 mm	2.75	5%	0.06	-	2.95	m2
N0303	6.0 mm	3.90	5%	0.08	-	4.17	m2
	perforated:						
N0304	3.2 mm	2.41	5%	0.03	-	2.56	m2
N0305	6.0 mm	5.14	5%	0.08	-	5.48	m2
	tempered:						
N0306	3.2 mm	2.66	5%	0.03	-	2.83	m2
N0308	6.0 mm	3.80	5%	0.08	-	4.07	m2
	Class 1 flame retardant quality hardboard to BS 476:						
N0309	3.2 mm	3.96	5%	0.03	-	4.19	m2
	Painted hardboard:						
N0311	3.2 mm	2.27	5%	0.03	-	2.42	m2
	Medium quality hardboard:						
	interior quality (Sundeala K):						
N0312	6.4 mm	5.14	5%	0.02	-	5.42	m2
N0313	9.5 mm	7.58	5%	0.02	-	7.98	m2
	exterior quality (Sundeala A):						
N0317	12.7 mm	14.53	5%	0.05	-	15.31	m2

Basic Prices of Materials

		Supply Price £	Waste Factor %	Unload. Labour £	Unload. Plant £	Total Unit Cost £	Unit
	Flame retardant to BS 476 - class 1:						
N0318	6.4 mm	8.38	5%	0.03	-	8.83	m2
N0319	9.5 mm	10.38	5%	0.03	-	10.93	m2
	Building board (Monolux 40):						
	natural finish:						
N0320	12.7 mm	63.09	5%	0.05	-	66.30	m2
N0321	19.0 mm	80.20	5%	0.06	-	84.27	m2
N0322	25.0 mm	96.16	5%	0.08	-	101.05	m2
	Insulation board ivory finish (Softboard):						
N0323	12.0 mm	2.75	5%	0.05	-	2.94	m2
	Chipboard:						
	plain:						
N0324	12 mm	2.56	5%	0.08	-	2.78	m2
N0325	15 mm	3.08	5%	0.10	-	3.34	m2
N0326	18 mm	3.70	5%	0.13	-	4.02	m2
N0327	25 mm	5.12	5%	0.17	-	5.55	m2
	moisture resistant:						
N0328	18 mm	5.29	5%	0.13	-	5.69	m2
	flooring grade, square edged:						
N0329	18 mm	4.87	5%	0.13	-	5.25	m2
N0330	22 mm	6.11	5%	0.15	-	6.58	m2
	flooring grade, tongued and grooved:						
N0331	18 mm	5.50	5%	0.13	-	5.91	m2
N0332	22 mm	8.55	5%	0.15	-	9.14	m2
	melamine faced both sides; white, unlipped:						
N0333	15 mm	5.01	5%	0.10	-	5.37	m2
N0334	18 mm	5.29	5%	0.13	-	5.69	m2
	Blockboard:						
	Finnish Birch faced:						
N0336	18 mm	15.31	5%	0.13	-	16.21	m2
N0338	25 mm	19.71	5%	0.17	-	20.88	m2
	Brazilian Virola faced:						
N0339	18 mm	9.90	5%	0.08	-	10.48	m2
N0341	25 mm	14.60	5%	0.13	-	15.46	m2
	Plywood:						
	Internal quality, MR bonding, Far Eastern, red/white:						
N0344	4 mm	2.95	5%	0.02	-	3.11	m2
N0345	6 mm	3.28	5%	0.05	-	3.50	m2
N0346	9 mm	4.97	5%	0.06	-	5.28	m2
N0347	12 mm	6.44	5%	0.08	-	6.85	m2
	External quality, WBP bonding, Finnish Birch faced:						
N0348	4 mm	5.65	5%	0.02	-	5.95	m2
N0349	6 mm	6.63	5%	0.05	-	7.01	m2
N0350	9 mm	8.79	5%	0.06	-	9.29	m2
N0351	12 mm	10.75	5%	0.08	-	11.37	m2

	Basic Prices of Materials	Supply Price £	Waste Factor %	Unload. Labour £	Unload. Plant £	Total Unit Cost £	Unit
	Floor panels, grade BB/WG, Birch faced:						
N0356	12 mm	13.57	5%	0.08	-	14.33	m2
N0357	15 mm	16.48	5%	0.10	-	17.41	m2
N0358	18 mm	20.13	5%	0.13	-	21.27	m2
	Plywood to BS 5268 PT2:						
	WBP BB/BB, exterior grade:						
N0352	12 mm	12.61	5%	0.08	-	13.32	m2
N0353	15 mm	15.37	5%	0.10	-	16.24	m2
N0354	18 mm	18.29	5%	0.13	-	19.34	m2
N0355	25 mm	23.78	5%	0.17	-	25.15	m2
	Non-asbestos boards, fire resisting Class 0:						
	Masterboard:						
N0359	6 mm	12.43	5%	0.05	-	13.10	m2
N0360	9 mm	21.56	5%	0.06	-	22.70	m2
N0361	12 mm	27.20	5%	0.08	-	28.64	m2
	sanded finish Supalux:						
N0362	6 mm	17.55	5%	0.05	-	18.48	m2
N0363	9 mm	24.48	5%	0.06	-	25.77	m2
N0364	12 mm	31.01	5%	0.08	-	32.64	m2
	Laminboard:						
	Birch faced:						
N0365	16 mm	17.20	5%	0.11	-	18.18	m2
N0366	18 mm	19.44	5%	0.15	-	20.57	m2
N0367	25 mm	20.08	5%	0.17	-	21.26	m2
N0381	0.9 mm plastic laminate 10' x 4' sheet (standard range)	50.47	5%	-	-	53.00	nr
N0391	0.9 mm plastic laminate edging up to 18 mm wide	0.86	5%	-	-	0.90	m
	Trussed rafters, stress graded, pressure impregnated						
	'Fink' or 'W' pattern; 450 mm overhang both sides:						
	22.5 degree pitch, span:						
N0401	5000 mm	27.95	-	-	0.54	28.49	nr
N0402	6000 mm	32.28	-	-	0.54	32.82	nr
N0403	7000 mm	38.63	-	-	0.54	39.17	nr
N0404	8000 mm	48.92	-	-	0.54	49.46	nr
N0405	10000 mm	71.68	-	-	0.54	72.22	nr
	35 degree pitch, span:						
N0406	5000 mm	30.57	-	-	0.54	31.11	nr
N0407	6000 mm	34.98	-	-	0.54	35.52	nr
N0408	7000 mm	38.95	-	-	0.54	39.49	nr
N0409	8000 mm	57.40	-	-	0.54	57.94	nr
N0410	10000 mm	78.31	-	-	0.54	78.85	nr
	45 degree pitch, span:						
N0411	5000 mm	33.87	-	-	0.54	34.41	nr
N0412	6000 mm	42.93	-	-	0.54	43.47	nr
N0413	7000 mm	58.05	-	-	0.54	58.59	nr

Basic Prices of Materials

Code	Description	Supply Price £	Waste Factor %	Unload. Labour £	Unload. Plant £	Total Unit Cost £	Unit
N0414	8000 mm	73.36	-	-	0.54	73.90	nr
N0415	10000 mm	92.15	-	-	0.54	92.69	nr
	PREMDOR DOORS						
	Clear pine Casement and Panel Doors; unprimed:						
	Country half light door, 4 mm glass:						
N0511	686 x 1981 mm	103.41	2.5%	0.57	-	106.58	nr
N0512	762 x 1981 mm	103.41	2.5%	0.57	-	106.58	nr
N0513	838 x 1981 mm	103.41	2.5%	0.57	-	106.58	nr
	Embossed moulded hardboard-faced hollow core "Canterbury" doors; 6 panel:						
	35 mm thick; primed finish:						
N0537	457 x 1981 mm	26.67	2.5%	0.57	-	27.92	nr
N0538	533 x 1981 mm	26.67	2.5%	0.57	-	27.92	nr
N0539	610 x 1981 mm	26.67	2.5%	0.57	-	27.92	nr
N0540	686 x 1981 mm	26.67	2.5%	0.57	-	27.92	nr
N0541	762 x 1981 mm	26.67	2.5%	0.57	-	27.92	nr
	"Flush Veneer" Interior Flush Doors, concealed lipping two edges; pre-lacquered finish:						
	Sapele Veneered:						
	35 mm thick:						
N0661	457 x 1981 mm	38.96	5%	0.23	-	41.15	nr
N0662	533 x 1981 mm	38.96	5%	0.23	-	41.15	nr
N0663	610 x 1981 mm	38.96	5%	0.23	-	41.15	nr
N0664	686 x 1981 mm	38.96	5%	0.23	-	41.15	nr
N0665	762 x 1981 mm	38.96	5%	0.23	-	41.15	nr
N0666	838 x 1981 mm	40.30	5%	0.23	-	42.56	nr
	40 mm thick:						
N0667	526 x 2040 mm	41.75	5%	0.23	-	44.08	nr
N0668	626 x 2040 mm	41.75	5%	0.23	-	44.08	nr
N0669	726 x 2040 mm	41.75	5%	0.23	-	44.08	nr
N0670	826 x 2040 mm	41.75	5%	0.23	-	44.08	nr
	Ash Veneered:						
	35 mm thick:						
N0677	762 x 1981 mm	52.53	5%	0.23	-	55.40	nr
	Traditional hardwood, Casement and Panel Doors one coat sealer preservative; (all sizes same price); including glazing beads where applicable:						
	44 mm thick doors; pattern:						
N0574	Richmond	96.91	2.5%	0.57	-	99.91	nr
	MAGNET STOCK PATTERN DOOR AND VESTIBULE FRAMES						
	Softwood door frames, preservative treated and primed, (weatherstrip included):						
	Unassembled, no sills:						
N0901	DF26 - 762 x 1981 mm	48.13	-	0.95	-	49.08	nr
N0902	DF28 - 813 x 2032 mm	48.13	-	0.95	-	49.08	nr
N0903	DF29 - 838 x 1981 mm	48.13	-	0.95	-	49.08	nr

Basic Prices of Materials

		Supply Price £	Waste Factor %	Unload. Labour £	Unload. Plant £	Total Unit Cost £	Unit
	Assembled, untreated hardwood sill with waterbar; open in:						
N0904	FNS26 - 762 x 1981 mm	68.29	-	0.95	-	69.24	nr
N0905	FNS28 - 813 x 2032 mm	68.29	-	0.95	-	69.24	nr
N0906	FNS29 - 838 x 1981 mm	68.29	-	0.95	-	69.24	nr
	Assembled, untreated hardwood sill; open out:						
N0907	FXS26 - 762 x 1981 mm	68.29	-	0.95	-	69.24	nr
N0909	FXS29 - 838 x 1981 mm	68.29	-	0.95	-	69.24	nr
N0910	FXS310 -1168 x 1981 mm	89.10	-	0.95	-	90.05	nr
	Unassembled, no sills, 25 mm rebates with intumescent strips:						
N0911	FDF6626 - 762 x 1981 mm	87.15	-	0.95	-	88.10	nr
N0912	FDF6629 - 838 x 1981 mm	87.15	-	0.95	-	88.10	nr
	Magnet "Statesman" Windows, weather stripped, preservative treated to NHBC standard, complete with locking stays and fasteners						
	Georgian Statesman softwood side hung windows, preservative treated and stained before delivery, including beads; supplied loose:						
N1049	B107C 631 x 750 (wide x high)	141.07	-	0.38	-	141.45	nr
N1050	B110V 631 x 1050 (wide x high)	166.59	-	0.76	-	167.35	nr
N1051	B112V 631 x 1200 (wide x high)	171.59	-	0.85	-	172.44	nr
N1052	B113V 631 x 1350 (wide x high)	175.96	-	0.95	-	176.91	nr
N1053	B207C 1200 x 750 (wide x high)	203.32	-	0.95	-	204.27	nr
N1054	B209C 1200 x 900 (wide x high)	236.21	-	1.05	-	237.26	nr
N1055	B210TX 1200 x 1050 (wide x high)	276.08	-	1.14	-	277.22	nr
N1056	B212TX 1200 x 1200 (wide x high)	284.75	-	1.23	-	285.98	nr
N1057	B213TX 1200 x 1350 (wide x high)	299.30	-	1.33	-	300.63	nr
N1058	B310CVC 1769 x 1050 (wide x high)	353.28	-	1.42	-	354.70	nr
N1059	B312CVC 1769 x 1200 (wide x high)	380.93	-	1.51	-	382.44	nr
N1060	B313CVC 1769 x 1350 (wide x high)	392.19	-	1.62	-	393.81	nr
N1061	B412CVVC 2338 x 1200 (wide x high)	816.27	-	1.62	-	817.89	nr
	PURPOSE MADE DOORS AND WINDOWS						
	PVCu doorset and windows:						
	Solid door and frame, white, complete with mortice lock, lever furniture and fitting kit:						
N2430	900 x 2100 mm	291.50	-	-	-	291.50	nr
	PVCu window, 24mm double glazed units:						
N2233	1200 x 1200 mm, 1 side hung and 1 directly glazed panel	390.50	-	-	-	390.50	nr
N2234	1200 x 1350 mm, 1 side hung and 1 directly glazed panel	399.30	-	-	-	399.30	nr
N2287	1800 x 1200 mm, 2 side hung and 1 directly glazed panel	630.19	-	-	-	630.19	nr
	SUNDRIES AND INSULATION						
N1501	Proprietary plugs 'Rawlplug' plastic type; No 8 x 38 mm	0.02	10%	-	-	0.02	nr
N1502	Steel wood screws No 8 x 38 mm	0.02	10%	-	-	0.02	nr
N1503	Brass screws; self colour No 8 x 38 mm	0.03	10%	-	-	0.04	nr

Basic Prices of Materials

		Supply Price £	Waste Factor %	Unload. Labour £	Unload. Plant £	Total Unit Cost £	Unit
N1504	Brass countersunk screw cups 8 gauge, recess type	0.06	10%	-	-	0.07	nr
N1505	Cut steel clasp nails 75 mm	3.25	10%	-	-	3.58	kg
N1506	Hardened steel masonry nails 50 mm x 2.5 mm diameter	0.01	10%	-	-	0.01	nr
	Black coach screws, square head:						
N1507	1/4" x 2"	0.02	2.5%	-	-	0.02	nr
N1508	5/16" x 2"	0.04	2.5%	-	-	0.04	nr
N1509	3/8" x 2"	0.07	2.5%	-	-	0.07	nr
N1510	3/8" x 3"	0.08	2.5%	-	-	0.08	nr
N1511	3/8" x 4"	0.11	2.5%	-	-	0.11	nr
N1512	3/8" x 5"	0.12	2.5%	-	-	0.13	nr
N1513	Evomastic general purpose mastic, 370 ml C30 cartridge	2.65	2.5%	-	-	2.72	nr
N1514	Evo-stik 528 contact adhesive	11.55	2.5%	-	-	11.84	ltr
V0405	Intumescent paint	18.34	7.5%	-	-	19.71	ltr
N5001	PVCu soffit strip	1.96	5%	-	-	2.06	m
	PIR Polyisocyanurate foam sheet insulation:						
N1545	35 mm thick	4.84	5%	-	-	5.08	m2
N1539	100 mm thick	11.77	5%	-	-	12.36	m2
N1540	130 mm thick	15.73	5%	-	-	16.52	m2
	Glass fibre loft insulating mat 1200 mm wide:						
N1552	100 mm thick (split 3 x 400 mm) (9.17 m roll)	27.84	5%	0.23	-	29.47	roll
N1553	100 mm thick (split 2 x 600 mm) (9.17 m roll)	27.84	5%	0.23	-	29.47	roll

STRUCTURAL STEELWORK

		Supply Price £	Waste Factor %	Unload. Labour £	Unload. Plant £	Total Unit Cost £	Unit
	Universal Beams						
	Size 914 x 419 (mm):						
P0010	388 (kg/m)	1138.00	2.5%	2.85	16.59	1186.38	tonne
P0011	343 (kg/m)	1138.00	2.5%	2.85	16.59	1186.38	tonne
	Size 914 x 305 (mm):						
P0012	289 (kg/m)	1138.00	2.5%	2.85	16.59	1186.38	tonne
P0013	253 (kg/m)	1138.00	2.5%	2.85	16.59	1186.38	tonne
P0014	224 (kg/m)	1138.00	2.5%	2.85	16.59	1186.38	tonne
P0015	201 (kg/m)	1138.00	2.5%	2.85	16.59	1186.38	tonne
	Size 838 x 292 (mm):						
P0016	226 (kg/m)	1128.00	2.5%	2.85	16.59	1176.13	tonne
P0017	194 (kg/m)	1128.00	2.5%	2.85	16.59	1176.13	tonne
P0018	176 (kg/m)	1128.00	2.5%	2.85	16.59	1176.13	tonne
	Size 762 x 267 (mm):						
P0019	197 (kg/m)	1128.00	2.5%	2.85	16.59	1176.13	tonne
P0020	173 (kg/m)	1128.00	2.5%	2.85	16.59	1176.13	tonne
P0021	147 (kg/m)	1128.00	2.5%	2.85	16.59	1176.13	tonne
	Size 686 x 254 (mm):						
P0022	170 (kg/m)	1128.00	2.5%	2.85	16.59	1176.13	tonne
P0023	152 (kg/m)	1128.00	2.5%	2.85	16.59	1176.13	tonne

Basic Prices of Materials

		Supply Price £	Waste Factor %	Unload. Labour £	Unload. Plant £	Total Unit Cost £	Unit
P0024	140 (kg/m)	1128.00	2.5%	2.85	16.59	1176.13	tonne
P0025	125 (kg/m)	1128.00	2.5%	2.85	16.59	1176.13	tonne
	Size 610 x 305 (mm):						
P0026	238 (kg/m)	1118.00	2.5%	2.85	16.59	1165.88	tonne
P0027	179 (kg/m)	1118.00	2.5%	2.85	16.59	1165.88	tonne
P0028	149 (kg/m)	1118.00	2.5%	2.85	16.59	1165.88	tonne
	Size 610 x 229 (mm):						
P0029	140 (kg/m)	1096.00	2.5%	2.85	16.59	1143.33	tonne
P0030	125 (kg/m)	1096.00	2.5%	2.85	16.59	1143.33	tonne
P0031	113 (kg/m)	1096.00	2.5%	2.85	16.59	1143.33	tonne
P0032	101 (kg/m)	1096.00	2.5%	2.85	16.59	1143.33	tonne
	Size 533 x 210 (mm):						
P0033	122 (kg/m)	1096.00	2.5%	2.85	16.59	1143.33	tonne
P0034	109 (kg/m)	1096.00	2.5%	2.85	16.59	1143.33	tonne
P0035	101 (kg/m)	1096.00	2.5%	2.85	16.59	1143.33	tonne
P0036	92 (kg/m)	1096.00	2.5%	2.85	16.59	1143.33	tonne
P0037	82 (kg/m)	1096.00	2.5%	2.85	16.59	1143.33	tonne
	Size 457 x 191 (mm):						
P0038	98 (kg/m)	1086.00	2.5%	2.85	16.59	1133.08	tonne
P0039	89 (kg/m)	1086.00	2.5%	2.85	16.59	1133.08	tonne
P0040	82 (kg/m)	1086.00	2.5%	2.85	16.59	1133.08	tonne
P0041	74 (kg/m)	1086.00	2.5%	2.85	16.59	1133.08	tonne
P0042	67 (kg/m)	1086.00	2.5%	2.85	16.59	1133.08	tonne
	Size 457 x 152 (mm):						
P0043	82 (kg/m)	1096.00	2.5%	2.85	16.59	1143.33	tonne
P0044	74 (kg/m)	1096.00	2.5%	2.85	16.59	1143.33	tonne
P0045	67 (kg/m)	1096.00	2.5%	2.85	16.59	1143.33	tonne
P0046	60 (kg/m)	1096.00	2.5%	2.85	16.59	1143.33	tonne
P0047	52 (kg/m)	1096.00	2.5%	2.85	16.59	1143.33	tonne
	Size 406 x 178 (mm):						
P0048	74 (kg/m)	1096.00	2.5%	2.85	16.59	1143.33	tonne
P0049	67 (kg/m)	1096.00	2.5%	2.85	16.59	1143.33	tonne
P0050	60 (kg/m)	1096.00	2.5%	2.85	16.59	1143.33	tonne
P0051	54 (kg/m)	1096.00	2.5%	2.85	16.59	1143.33	tonne
	Size 406 x 140 (mm):						
P0052	46 (kg/m)	1096.00	2.5%	2.85	16.59	1143.33	tonne
P0053	39 (kg/m)	1096.00	2.5%	2.85	16.59	1143.33	tonne
	Size 356 x 171 (mm):						
P0054	67 (kg/m)	1096.00	2.5%	2.85	16.59	1143.33	tonne
P0055	57 (kg/m)	1096.00	2.5%	2.85	16.59	1143.33	tonne
P0056	51 (kg/m)	1096.00	2.5%	2.85	16.59	1143.33	tonne
P0057	45 (kg/m)	1096.00	2.5%	2.85	16.59	1143.33	tonne
	Size 356 x 127 (mm):						
P0058	39 (kg/m)	1096.00	2.5%	2.85	16.59	1143.33	tonne
P0059	33 (kg/m)	1096.00	2.5%	2.85	16.59	1143.33	tonne
	Size 305 x 165 (mm):						
P0060	54 (kg/m)	1086.00	2.5%	2.85	16.59	1133.08	tonne
P0061	46 (kg/m)	1086.00	2.5%	2.85	16.59	1133.08	tonne
P0062	40 (kg/m)	1086.00	2.5%	2.85	16.59	1133.08	tonne

Basic Prices of Materials

		Supply Price £	Waste Factor %	Unload. Labour £	Unload. Plant £	Total Unit Cost £	Unit
	Size 305 x 127 (mm):						
P0063	48 (kg/m)	1086.00	2.5%	2.85	16.59	1133.08	tonne
P0064	42 (kg/m)	1086.00	2.5%	2.85	16.59	1133.08	tonne
P0065	37 (kg/m)	1086.00	2.5%	2.85	16.59	1133.08	tonne
	Size 305 x 102 (mm):						
P0066	33 (kg/m)	1086.00	2.5%	2.85	16.59	1133.08	tonne
P0067	28 (kg/m)	1086.00	2.5%	2.85	16.59	1133.08	tonne
P0068	25 (kg/m)	1086.00	2.5%	2.85	16.59	1133.08	tonne
	Size 254 x 146 (mm):						
P0069	43 (kg/m)	1096.00	2.5%	2.85	16.59	1143.33	tonne
P0070	37 (kg/m)	1096.00	2.5%	2.85	16.59	1143.33	tonne
P0071	31 (kg/m)	1096.00	2.5%	2.85	16.59	1143.33	tonne
	Size 254 x 102 (mm):						
P0072	28 (kg/m)	1096.00	2.5%	2.85	16.59	1143.33	tonne
P0073	25 (kg/m)	1096.00	2.5%	2.85	16.59	1143.33	tonne
P0074	22 (kg/m)	1096.00	2.5%	2.85	16.59	1143.33	tonne
	Size 203 x 133 (mm):						
P0075	30 (kg/m)	1096.00	2.5%	2.85	16.59	1143.33	tonne
P0076	25 (kg/m)	1096.00	2.5%	2.85	16.59	1143.33	tonne
	Universal columns						
	Size 356 x 406 (mm):						
P0077	634 (kg/m)	1154.00	2.5%	2.85	16.59	1202.78	tonne
P0078	551 (kg/m)	1154.00	2.5%	2.85	16.59	1202.78	tonne
P0079	467 (kg/m)	1154.00	2.5%	2.85	16.59	1202.78	tonne
P0080	393 (kg/m)	1144.00	2.5%	2.85	16.59	1192.53	tonne
P0081	340 (kg/m)	1144.00	2.5%	2.85	16.59	1192.53	tonne
P0082	287 (kg/m)	1144.00	2.5%	2.85	16.59	1192.53	tonne
P0083	235 (kg/m)	1144.00	2.5%	2.85	16.59	1192.53	tonne
	Size 356 x 368 (mm):						
P0084	202 (kg/m)	1144.00	2.5%	2.85	16.59	1192.53	tonne
P0085	177 (kg/m)	1144.00	2.5%	2.85	16.59	1192.53	tonne
P0086	153 (kg/m)	1144.00	2.5%	2.85	16.59	1192.53	tonne
P0087	129 (kg/m)	1144.00	2.5%	2.85	16.59	1192.53	tonne
	Size 305 x 305 (mm):						
P0088	283 (kg/m)	1096.00	2.5%	2.85	16.59	1143.33	tonne
P0089	240 (kg/m)	1096.00	2.5%	2.85	16.59	1143.33	tonne
P0090	198 (kg/m)	1096.00	2.5%	2.85	16.59	1143.33	tonne
	Size 305 x 305 (mm):						
P0091	158 (kg/m)	1096.00	2.5%	2.85	16.59	1143.33	tonne
P0092	137 (kg/m)	1096.00	2.5%	2.85	16.59	1143.33	tonne
P0093	118 (kg/m)	1096.00	2.5%	2.85	16.59	1143.33	tonne
P0094	97 (kg/m)	1096.00	2.5%	2.85	16.59	1143.33	tonne
	Size 254 x 254 (mm):						
P0095	167 (kg/m)	1086.00	2.5%	2.85	16.59	1133.08	tonne
P0096	132 (kg/m)	1086.00	2.5%	2.85	16.59	1133.08	tonne
P0097	107 (kg/m)	1086.00	2.5%	2.85	16.59	1133.08	tonne
P0098	89 (kg/m)	1086.00	2.5%	2.85	16.59	1133.08	tonne
P0099	73 (kg/m)	1086.00	2.5%	2.85	16.59	1133.08	tonne

Basic Prices of Materials

Code	Description	Supply Price £	Waste Factor %	Unload. Labour £	Unload. Plant £	Total Unit Cost £	Unit
	Size 203 x 203 (mm):						
P0100	86 (kg/m)	1086.00	2.5%	2.85	16.59	1133.08	tonne
P0101	71 (kg/m)	1086.00	2.5%	2.85	16.59	1133.08	tonne
P0102	60 (kg/m)	1086.00	2.5%	2.85	16.59	1133.08	tonne
P0103	52 (kg/m)	1086.00	2.5%	2.85	16.59	1133.08	tonne
P0104	46 (kg/m)	1086.00	2.5%	2.85	16.59	1133.08	tonne
	Size 152 x 152 (mm):						
P0105	37 (kg/m)	1076.00	2.5%	2.85	16.59	1122.83	tonne
P0106	30 (kg/m)	1076.00	2.5%	2.85	16.59	1122.83	tonne
P0107	23 (kg/m)	1076.00	2.5%	2.85	16.59	1122.83	tonne
	Joists						
P0108	254 x 203 (mm) 81.85 (kg/m)	1250.00	2.5%	2.85	16.59	1301.18	tonne
P0109	254 x 114 (mm) 37.20 (kg/m)	1250.00	2.5%	2.85	16.59	1301.18	tonne
P0110	203 x 152 (mm) 52.09 (kg/m)	1250.00	2.5%	2.85	16.59	1301.18	tonne
P0111	203 x 102 (mm) 25.33 (kg/m)	1250.00	2.5%	2.85	16.59	1301.18	tonne
P0113	152 x 127 (mm) 37.20 (kg/m)	1250.00	2.5%	2.85	16.59	1301.18	tonne
P0114	152 x 89 (mm) 17.09 (kg/m)	1250.00	2.5%	2.85	16.59	1301.18	tonne
P0116	127 x 114 (mm) 29.76 (kg/m)	1250.00	2.5%	2.85	16.59	1301.18	tonne
P0117	127 x 114 (mm) 26.79 (kg/m)	1250.00	2.5%	2.85	16.59	1301.18	tonne
P0118	127 x 76 (mm) 16.37 (kg/m)	1250.00	2.5%	2.85	16.59	1301.18	tonne
P0120	114 x 114 (mm) 26.79 (kg/m)	1250.00	2.5%	2.85	16.59	1301.18	tonne
P0121	102 x 102 (mm) 23.06 (kg/m)	1250.00	2.5%	2.85	16.59	1301.18	tonne
P0122	89 x 89 (mm) 19.35 (kg/m)	1250.00	2.5%	2.85	16.59	1301.18	tonne
P0123	76 x 76 (mm) 12.65 (kg/m)	1250.00	2.5%	2.85	16.59	1301.18	tonne
	Channels						
P0124	430 x 100 (mm) 64.40 (kg/m)	1341.00	2.5%	2.85	15.92	1393.76	tonne
P0125	380 x 100 (mm) 54.00 (kg/m)	1203.00	2.5%	2.85	16.59	1253.00	tonne
P0126	300 x 100 (mm) 45.50 (kg/m)	1171.00	2.5%	2.85	16.59	1220.20	tonne
P0127	300 x 90 (mm) 41.40 (kg/m)	1171.00	2.5%	2.85	16.59	1220.20	tonne
P0128	260 x 90 (mm) 34.80 (kg/m)	1171.00	2.5%	2.85	16.59	1220.20	tonne
P0129	260 x 75 (mm) 27.60 (kg/m)	1171.00	2.5%	2.85	16.59	1220.20	tonne
P0130	230 x 90 (mm) 32.20 (kg/m)	1171.00	2.5%	2.85	16.59	1220.20	tonne
P0131	230 x 75 (mm) 25.70 (kg/m)	1171.00	2.5%	2.85	16.59	1220.20	tonne
P0132	200 x 90 (mm) 29.70 (kg/m)	1096.00	2.5%	2.85	16.59	1143.33	tonne
P0133	200 x 75 (mm) 23.40 (kg/m)	1060.00	2.5%	2.85	16.59	1106.43	tonne
P0134	180 x 90 (mm) 26.10 (kg/m)	1096.00	2.5%	2.85	16.59	1143.33	tonne
P0135	180 x 75 (mm) 20.30 (kg/m)	1060.00	2.5%	2.85	16.59	1106.43	tonne
P0136	150 x 90 (mm) 23.90 (kg/m)	1096.00	2.5%	2.85	16.59	1143.33	tonne
P0137	150 x 75 (mm) 17.90 (kg/m)	1060.00	2.5%	2.85	16.59	1106.43	tonne
P0138	125 x 65 (mm) 14.80 (kg/m)	1060.00	2.5%	2.85	16.59	1106.43	tonne
P0139	100 x 50 (mm) 10.20 (kg/m)	1060.00	2.5%	2.85	16.59	1106.43	tonne
P0140	75 x 50 (mm) 9.30 (kg/m)	880.09	2.5%	2.85	16.59	922.02	tonne
P0141	75 x 35 (mm) 6.60 (kg/m)	880.09	2.5%	2.85	16.59	922.02	tonne
P0143	50 x 35 (mm) 5.70 (kg/m)	880.09	2.5%	2.85	16.59	922.02	tonne
P0144	50 x 25 (mm) 4.50 (kg/m)	880.09	2.5%	2.85	16.59	922.02	tonne

Basic Prices of Materials

		Supply Price £	Waste Factor %	Unload. Labour £	Unload. Plant £	Total Unit Cost £	Unit
	Equal Angles						
	Size 200 x 200 (mm); Thickness:						
P0146	16 (mm)	1138.00	2.5%	2.85	16.59	1186.38	tonne
P0147	18 (mm)	1138.00	2.5%	2.85	16.59	1186.38	tonne
P0148	20 (mm)	1138.00	2.5%	2.85	16.59	1186.38	tonne
P0149	24 (mm)	1138.00	2.5%	2.85	16.59	1186.38	tonne
	Size 150 x 150 (mm); Thickness:						
P0150	10 (mm)	1054.00	2.5%	2.85	16.59	1100.28	tonne
P0151	12 (mm)	1054.00	2.5%	2.85	16.59	1100.28	tonne
P0152	15 (mm)	1054.00	2.5%	2.85	16.59	1100.28	tonne
P0153	18	1054.00	2.5%	2.85	16.59	1100.28	tonne
	Size 120 x 120 (mm); Thickness:						
P0154	8 (mm)	1044.00	2.5%	2.85	16.59	1090.03	tonne
P0155	10 (mm)	1044.00	2.5%	2.85	16.59	1090.03	tonne
P0156	12 (mm)	1044.00	2.5%	2.85	16.59	1090.03	tonne
P0157	15 (mm)	1044.00	2.5%	2.85	16.59	1090.03	tonne
	Size 100 x 100 (mm); Thickness:						
P0158	8 (mm)	1034.00	2.5%	2.85	16.59	1079.78	tonne
P0159	10 (mm)	1034.00	2.5%	2.85	16.59	1079.78	tonne
P0160	12 (mm)	1034.00	2.5%	2.85	16.59	1079.78	tonne
P0161	15 (mm)	1034.00	2.5%	2.85	16.59	1079.78	tonne
	Size 90 x 90 (mm); Thickness:						
P0162	6 (mm)	1034.00	2.5%	2.85	16.59	1079.78	tonne
P0163	8 (mm)	1034.00	2.5%	2.85	16.59	1079.78	tonne
P0164	10 (mm)	1034.00	2.5%	2.85	16.59	1079.78	tonne
P0165	12 (mm)	1034.00	2.5%	2.85	16.59	1079.78	tonne
	Size 80 x 80 (mm); Thickness:						
P0166	6 (mm)	825.82	2.5%	2.85	16.59	866.40	tonne
P0167	8 (mm)	825.82	2.5%	2.85	16.59	866.40	tonne
P0168	10 (mm)	825.82	2.5%	2.85	16.59	866.40	tonne
	Size 70 x 70 (mm); Thickness:						
P0169	6 (mm)	825.82	2.5%	2.85	16.59	866.40	tonne
P0170	8 (mm)	825.82	2.5%	2.85	16.59	866.40	tonne
P0171	10 (mm)	825.82	2.5%	2.85	16.59	866.40	tonne
	Size 60 x 60 (mm); Thickness:						
P0172	5 (mm)	825.82	2.5%	2.85	16.59	866.40	tonne
P0173	6 (mm)	825.82	2.5%	2.85	16.59	866.40	tonne
P0174	8 (mm)	825.82	2.5%	2.85	16.59	866.40	tonne
P0175	10 (mm)	825.82	2.5%	2.85	16.59	866.40	tonne
	Size 50 x 50 (mm); Thickness:						
P0176	5 (mm)	825.82	2.5%	2.85	16.59	866.40	tonne
P0177	6 (mm)	825.82	2.5%	2.85	16.59	866.40	tonne
P0178	8 (mm)	825.82	2.5%	2.85	16.59	866.40	tonne
	Size 45 x 45 (mm); Thickness:						
P0179	4 (mm)	825.82	2.5%	2.85	16.59	866.40	tonne
P0180	5 (mm)	825.82	2.5%	2.85	16.59	866.40	tonne
P0181	6 (mm)	825.82	2.5%	2.85	16.59	866.40	tonne
	Size 40 x 40 (mm); Thickness:						
P0182	5 (mm)	825.82	2.5%	2.85	16.59	866.40	tonne

Basic Prices of Materials

Code	Description	Supply Price £	Waste Factor %	Unload. Labour £	Unload. Plant £	Total Unit Cost £	Unit
P0183	6 (mm)	825.82	2.5%	2.85	16.59	866.40	tonne
	Size 30 x 30 (mm); Thickness:						
P0185	5 (mm)	825.82	2.5%	2.85	16.59	866.40	tonne
P0186	6 (mm)	825.82	2.5%	2.85	16.59	866.40	tonne
	Unequal Angles						
	Size200 x 150 (mm); Thickness:						
P0187	12 (mm)	1563.00	2.5%	2.85	16.59	1622.00	tonne
P0188	15 (mm)	1563.00	2.5%	2.85	16.59	1622.00	tonne
P0189	18 (mm)	1563.00	2.5%	2.85	16.59	1622.00	tonne
	Size 200 x 100 (mm); Thickness:						
P0190	10 (mm)	1138.00	2.5%	2.85	16.59	1186.38	tonne
P0191	12 (mm)	1138.00	2.5%	2.85	16.59	1186.38	tonne
P0192	15 (mm)	1138.00	2.5%	2.85	16.59	1186.38	tonne
	Size 150 x 90 (mm); Thickness:						
P0193	10 (mm)	1096.00	2.5%	2.85	16.59	1143.33	tonne
P0194	12 (mm)	1096.00	2.5%	2.85	16.59	1143.33	tonne
P0195	15 (mm)	1096.00	2.5%	2.85	16.59	1143.33	tonne
	Size 150 x 75 (mm); Thickness:						
P0196	10 (mm)	1060.00	2.5%	2.85	16.59	1106.43	tonne
P0197	12 (mm)	1060.00	2.5%	2.85	16.59	1106.43	tonne
P0198	15 (mm)	1060.00	2.5%	2.85	16.59	1106.43	tonne
	Size 125 x 75 (mm); Thickness:						
P0199	8 (mm)	1060.00	2.5%	2.85	16.59	1106.43	tonne
P0200	10 (mm)	1060.00	2.5%	2.85	16.59	1106.43	tonne
P0201	12 (mm)	1060.00	2.5%	2.85	16.59	1106.43	tonne
	Size 100 x 75 (mm); Thickness:						
P0202	8 (mm)	1060.00	2.5%	2.85	16.59	1106.43	tonne
P0203	10 (mm)	1060.00	2.5%	2.85	16.59	1106.43	tonne
P0204	12 (mm)	1060.00	2.5%	2.85	16.59	1106.43	tonne
	Size 100 x 65 (mm); Thickness:						
P0205	7 (mm)	1060.00	2.5%	2.85	16.59	1106.43	tonne
P0206	8 (mm)	1060.00	2.5%	2.85	16.59	1106.43	tonne
P0207	10 (mm)	1060.00	2.5%	2.85	16.59	1106.43	tonne
	Size 80 x 60 (mm); Thickness:						
P0208	6 (mm)	825.82	2.5%	2.85	16.59	866.40	tonne
P0209	7 (mm)	825.82	2.5%	2.85	16.59	866.40	tonne
P0210	8 (mm)	825.82	2.5%	2.85	16.59	866.40	tonne
	Size 75 x 50 (mm); Thickness:						
P0211	6 (mm)	825.82	2.5%	2.85	16.59	866.40	tonne
P0212	8 (mm)	825.82	2.5%	2.85	16.59	866.40	tonne
	Size 65 x 50 (mm); Thickness:						
P0213	5 (mm)	825.82	2.5%	2.85	16.59	866.40	tonne
P0214	6 (mm)	825.82	2.5%	2.85	16.59	866.40	tonne
P0215	8 (mm)	825.82	2.5%	2.85	16.59	866.40	tonne
	Size 60 x 30 (mm); Thickness:						
P0216	5 (mm)	825.82	2.5%	2.85	16.59	866.40	tonne
P0217	6 (mm)	825.82	2.5%	2.85	16.59	866.40	tonne

Basic Prices of Materials

		Supply Price £	Waste Factor %	Unload. Labour £	Unload. Plant £	Total Unit Cost £	Unit
	Size 50 x 40 (mm); Thickness:						
P0218	5 (mm)	825.82	2.5%	2.85	16.59	866.40	tonne
P0219	6 (mm)	825.82	2.5%	2.85	16.59	866.40	tonne
	Tees						
P0220	Size 51 x 51; thickness 6 (mm)	1761.08	2.5%	2.85	16.59	1825.04	tonne
	Extra over Basic prices for stockholders margins or small quantities:						
P0227	Up to 5 kg	594.59	-	-	-	594.59	tonne
P0228	5 - 25 kg	495.50	-	-	-	495.50	tonne
P0229	25 - 50 kg	495.50	-	-	-	495.50	tonne
P0230	50 - 100 kg	297.30	-	-	-	297.30	tonne
P0231	Over 100 kg	297.30	-	-	-	297.30	tonne
P0240	Extra for shot blasting and priming steel sections (average mix) before delivery	120.00	-	-	-	120.00	tonne

METALWORK

		Supply Price £	Waste Factor %	Unload. Labour £	Unload. Plant £	Total Unit Cost £	Unit
	Steel lintels by Catnic, **delivered to site**						
	Type CG50/100; 243 mm wide; suitable for use in external walls having a 50-65 mm wide cavity and 100 mm inner skin: length:						
Q0121	750 mm	25.25	-	0.05	-	25.30	nr
Q0122	900 mm	30.31	-	0.07	-	30.38	nr
Q0123	1200 mm	39.28	-	0.10	-	39.38	nr
Q0124	1500 mm	50.77	-	0.14	-	50.91	nr
Q0125	1800 mm	63.10	-	0.19	-	63.29	nr
Q0126	2100 mm	72.45	-	0.26	-	72.71	nr
Q0127	2400 mm	88.81	-	0.31	-	89.12	nr
Q0128	2700 mm	100.80	-	0.43	-	101.23	nr
Q0129	3000 mm	139.56	-	0.48	-	140.04	nr
Q0130	3300 mm	155.79	-	0.58	-	156.37	nr
Q0131	3600 mm	170.95	-	0.64	-	171.59	nr
Q0132	3900 mm	272.95	-	0.75	-	273.70	nr
	Type CZ50/100; 243 mm wide; suitable for use in external walls having a 50-65 mm wide cavity and 100 mm inner skin: length:						
Q0133	4200 mm	302.98	-	0.81	-	303.79	nr
Q0134	4575 mm	339.77	-	0.99	-	340.76	nr
Q0135	4800 mm	356.09	-	1.06	-	357.15	nr
Q5001	Arch former to lintel 1200 mm	47.70	-	0.10	-	47.80	Nr

Basic Prices of Materials

PLUMBING

		Supply Price £	Waste Factor %	Unload. Labour £	Unload. Plant £	Total Unit Cost £	Unit
	The cost of unloading materials is included in the price for fixing the materials.						
	Cast iron eaves gutters and fittings						
R0111	100 mm half round:	16.35	5%	-	-	17.17	m
	Extra over for:						
R0112	stopped end	4.19	2.5%	-	-	4.30	nr
R0113	angle/nozzle outlet	12.46	2.5%	-	-	12.77	nr
R0114	fascia bracket	3.51	2.5%	-	-	3.59	nr
	Cast aluminium eaves gutters and fittings; plain mill finish						
R0131	100 mm half round:	10.85	5%	-	-	11.39	m
	Extra over for:						
R0132	stopped end	3.23	2.5%	-	-	3.31	nr
R0133	angle, 90° / 135°	6.67	2.5%	-	-	6.84	nr
R0134	outlet, 63 mm drop	7.67	2.5%	-	-	7.86	nr
R0135	fascia bracket	1.92	2.5%	-	-	1.96	nr
	PVCu gutters and fittings						
R0181	112 mm half round:	2.00	5%	-	-	2.10	m
	Extra over for:						
R0182	stopped end	1.20	2.5%	-	-	1.23	nr
R0183	angle 90°	2.47	2.5%	-	-	2.53	nr
R0184	outlet	2.14	2.5%	-	-	2.19	nr
R0185	gutter jointing bracket	1.38	2.5%	-	-	1.41	nr
R0186	gutter support bracket	0.73	2.5%	-	-	0.74	nr
	Cast iron rainwater pipes and fittings						
R0231	100 mm nominal size pipes; eared	39.95	5%	-	-	41.95	m
	Extra over for:						
R0232	shoe, eared	34.67	2.5%	-	-	35.53	nr
R0233	bend	27.39	2.5%	-	-	28.08	nr
R0234	offset, 150 mm projection	46.14	2.5%	-	-	47.29	nr
R0235	offset, 300 mm projection	56.99	2.5%	-	-	58.41	nr
R0236	branch	40.35	2.5%	-	-	41.36	nr
	Cast aluminium rainwater pipes and fittings; plain mill finish						
R0264	102 mm nominal size pipes:	21.99	5%	-	-	23.09	m
	Extra over for:						
R0265	shoe, eared	10.93	2.5%	-	-	11.20	nr
R0266	bend	14.44	2.5%	-	-	14.81	nr
R0267	offset, 152 mm projection	23.09	2.5%	-	-	23.67	nr
R0268	offset, 304 mm projection	29.17	2.5%	-	-	29.90	nr
R0269	offset, 609 mm projection	43.25	2.5%	-	-	44.33	nr

Basic Prices of Materials

		Supply Price £	Waste Factor %	Unload. Labour £	Unload. Plant £	Total Unit Cost £	Unit
R0270	branch	17.09	2.5%	-	-	17.51	nr
	PVCu rainwater pipes and fittings						
R0299	110 mm nominal size ring seal pipe:	4.06	5%	-	-	4.26	m
	Extra over for:						
R0300	shoe	4.31	2.5%	-	-	4.42	nr
R0301	bend	6.30	2.5%	-	-	6.46	nr
R0302	offset bend	6.51	2.5%	-	-	6.67	nr
R0303	branch	8.60	2.5%	-	-	8.82	nr
R0304	clip	2.39	2.5%	-	-	2.45	nr
R0305	drain connector	5.19	2.5%	-	-	5.32	nr
	Copper pipes BS 2871, Part 1						
	Table X:						
R0369	15 mm nominal size pipe	2.22	5%	-	-	2.33	m
R0370	22 mm nominal size pipe	4.44	5%	-	-	4.66	m
R0371	28 mm nominal size pipe	5.60	5%	-	-	5.88	m
R0372	35 mm nominal size pipe	11.08	5%	-	-	11.63	m
R0373	42 mm nominal size pipe	13.29	5%	-	-	13.96	m
R0374	54 mm nominal size pipe	17.49	5%	-	-	18.37	m
	Capillary fittings for copper pipes, BS EN1254, Part 1						
	Straight coupling:						
R0390	15 mm	0.28	2.5%	-	-	0.29	nr
R0391	22 mm	0.75	2.5%	-	-	0.76	nr
R0392	28 mm	1.73	2.5%	-	-	1.78	nr
R0393	35 mm	5.86	2.5%	-	-	6.01	nr
R0394	42 mm	9.79	2.5%	-	-	10.03	nr
R0395	54 mm	18.05	2.5%	-	-	18.50	nr
	Tank connector with back nut:						
R0396	15 mm	9.09	2.5%	-	-	9.32	nr
R0397	22 mm	13.84	2.5%	-	-	14.19	nr
R0398	28 mm	18.20	2.5%	-	-	18.65	nr
R0399	35 mm	24.22	2.5%	-	-	24.82	nr
R0400	42 mm	31.75	2.5%	-	-	32.54	nr
R0401	54 mm	48.51	2.5%	-	-	49.72	nr
	Straight tap connector:						
R0402	15 mm	2.46	2.5%	-	-	2.52	nr
R0403	22 mm	2.92	2.5%	-	-	3.00	nr
	Elbow:						
R0404	15 mm	0.50	2.5%	-	-	0.51	nr
R0405	22 mm	1.32	2.5%	-	-	1.35	nr
R0406	28 mm	2.78	2.5%	-	-	2.85	nr
R0407	35 mm	12.55	2.5%	-	-	12.86	nr
R0408	42 mm	20.73	2.5%	-	-	21.25	nr
R0409	54 mm	42.82	2.5%	-	-	43.89	nr

Basic Prices of Materials

		Supply Price £	Waste Factor %	Unload. Labour £	Unload. Plant £	Total Unit Cost £	Unit
	Overflow bend:						
R0981	22 mm	18.83	2.5%	-	-	19.31	nr
	Tee:						
R0410	15 mm	0.96	2.5%	-	-	0.98	nr
R0411	22 mm	3.04	2.5%	-	-	3.12	nr
R0412	28 mm	7.72	2.5%	-	-	7.91	nr
R0413	35 mm	20.43	2.5%	-	-	20.95	nr
R0414	42 mm	32.77	2.5%	-	-	33.59	nr
R0415	54 mm	66.08	2.5%	-	-	67.73	nr
	Reducing tee:						
R0416	22 x 22 x 15 mm	2.42	2.5%	-	-	2.48	nr
R0417	28 x 28 x 22 mm	11.41	2.5%	-	-	11.69	nr
R0418	35 x 35 x 28 mm	27.32	2.5%	-	-	28.01	nr
R0419	42 x 42 x 35 mm	61.86	2.5%	-	-	63.40	nr
R0420	54 x 54 x 42 mm	103.94	2.5%	-	-	106.54	nr
	Gunmetal and brass stop valves, BS 1010						
	Stopcock, copper x copper, compression joints:						
R0740	15 mm nominal size	10.70	2.5%	-	-	10.96	nr
R0741	22 mm nominal size	18.79	2.5%	-	-	19.26	nr
R0742	28 mm nominal size	49.02	2.5%	-	-	50.24	nr
	Stopcock, PVC x PVC:						
R0743	3/8" nominal size	28.42	2.5%	-	-	29.13	nr
R0744	1/2" nominal size	29.31	2.5%	-	-	30.04	nr
	Stopcock, polythene x polythene:						
R0745	3/8" nominal size	28.42	2.5%	-	-	29.13	nr
R0746	1/2" nominal size	29.31	2.5%	-	-	30.04	nr
R0747	3/4" nominal size	44.00	2.5%	-	-	45.10	nr
	Stopcock, female threaded ends:						
R0749	15 mm nominal size	25.36	2.5%	-	-	25.99	nr
R0750	20 mm nominal size	35.67	2.5%	-	-	36.56	nr
R0751	28 mm nominal size	63.45	2.5%	-	-	65.04	nr
R0752	35 mm nominal size	156.73	2.5%	-	-	160.65	nr
R0753	42 mm nominal size	215.11	2.5%	-	-	220.48	nr
R0754	54 mm nominal size	338.38	2.5%	-	-	346.83	nr
	Gunmetal gatevalve, BS 5154 copper x copper, capillary ends:						
R0755	15 mm nominal size	19.66	2.5%	-	-	20.15	nr
R0756	22 mm nominal size	34.05	2.5%	-	-	34.91	nr
R0757	28 mm nominal size	57.96	2.5%	-	-	59.41	nr
R0758	35 mm nominal size	89.02	2.5%	-	-	91.24	nr
R0759	42 mm nominal size	118.21	2.5%	-	-	121.17	nr
R0760	54 mm nominal size	176.58	2.5%	-	-	180.99	nr
	Sinks						
	Fireclay sink, Belfast pattern, BS 1206:						
R0800	610 x 455 x 255 mm	205.99	-	-	-	205.99	nr
R0801	760 x 455 x 255 mm	399.77	-	-	-	399.77	nr

Basic Prices of Materials

		Supply Price £	Waste Factor %	Unload. Labour £	Unload. Plant £	Total Unit Cost £	Unit
	Stainless steel sink:						
R0802	1000 x 600 mm (single drainer)	82.69	-	-	-	82.69	nr
R0803	1500 x 600 mm (double drainer)	169.81	-	-	-	169.81	nr
	Baths, nominal sizes						
	Cast iron, porcelain enamelled, rectangular, white:						
R0805	1500 mm long	366.45	-	-	-	366.45	nr
R0806	1700 mm long	366.45	-	-	-	366.45	nr
	Pressed steel, vitreous enamelled, rectangular:						
R0807	1500 mm long, white	141.04	-	-	-	141.04	nr
R0808	1700 mm long, white	141.04	-	-	-	141.04	nr
R0809	1700 mm long, coloured	141.04	-	-	-	141.04	nr
	5 mm glass fibre reinforced acrylic:						
R0810	1700 mm long, white	139.89	-	-	-	139.89	nr
R0811	1700 mm long, coloured	139.89	-	-	-	139.89	nr
	Lavatory basins						
	Vitreous china:						
R0812	560 x 405 mm, white	39.90	-	-	-	39.90	nr
R0813	560 x 405 mm, coloured	52.50	-	-	-	52.50	nr
R0814	635 x 455 mm, white	82.69	-	-	-	82.69	nr
R0815	635 x 455 mm, coloured	82.69	-	-	-	82.69	nr
	Pedestal stand:						
R0816	white	22.16	-	-	-	22.16	nr
R0817	coloured	22.16	-	-	-	22.16	nr
	WC suites						
	Vitreous china, close coupled, washdown, dual flush syphon:						
R0820	white	150.71	-	-	-	150.71	nr
R0821	coloured	150.71	-	-	-	150.71	nr
	Vitreous china, close coupled, syphonic, double trap:						
R0822	white	160.82	-	-	-	160.82	nr
R0823	coloured	160.82	-	-	-	160.82	nr
	Solid plastic seat and cover:						
R0824	white	12.73	-	-	-	12.73	nr
R0825	coloured	12.73	-	-	-	12.73	nr
	Sundries						
	Bib tap, BS 5412, chromium plated:						
R0835	13 mm nominal size	9.90	2.5%	-	-	10.15	nr
R0836	19 mm nominal size	17.67	2.5%	-	-	18.11	nr
	Pillar tap, BS 5412, chromium plated:						
R0837	13 mm nominal size	9.79	2.5%	-	-	10.03	nr
R0838	19 mm nominal size	14.47	2.5%	-	-	14.84	nr

Basic Prices of Materials

		Supply Price £	Waste Factor %	Unload. Labour £	Unload. Plant £	Total Unit Cost £	Unit
	Cisterns and cylinders						
	Plastic water storage cistern, BS 4213, complete with lids and insulation:						
R0867	18 ltr capacity, type PC 4	41.17	-	-	-	41.17	nr
R0868	114 ltr capacity, type PC 25	45.81	-	-	-	45.81	nr
R0869	227 ltr capacity, type PC 50	71.72	-	-	-	71.72	nr
R0870	455 ltr capacity, type PC 100	148.06	-	-	-	148.06	nr
FLOOR WALL AND CEILING FINISHINGS							
A0311	Hydrated lime delivered in bags	216.00	5%	11.39	-	238.76	tonne
A0323	Plastering sand	28.52	10%	-	-	31.37	tonne
A0331	Concreting sand (fine aggregate)	29.64	10%	-	-	32.60	tonne
T0055	Coarse aggregate 10 mm nominal size	24.15	10%	-	-	26.57	tonne
T0084	Crushed stone 14 - 6 mm	18.78	5%	-	-	19.72	tonne
T0085	Derbyshire spar chippings 15 - 5 mm	63.67	5%	-	-	66.85	tonne
T0091	Leicestershire granite chippings 14 mm	46.30	10%	-	-	50.94	tonne
	Limelite plasters delivered to site:						
T0040	Tarmac High Impact Finish	268.59	5%	11.39	-	293.98	tonne
T0041	Limelite Backing	343.00	5%	11.39	-	372.11	tonne
T0042	Whitewall High Impact Backing Browning	279.89	5%	11.39	-	305.85	tonne
T0043	Limelite Renovating	435.35	5%	11.39	-	469.08	tonne
	The following prices are based on full loads (22.5 tonnes) delivered to site. Full loads of plaster only orders are classified as 22.5 tonnes or 18 full pallets whichever is the lower weight. Prices are applicable to the whole of England, Wales and Scottish mainland. - Service charges may be applied for requirements outside a 'normal full load'						
T0059	Thistle Browning	309.76	5%	11.39	-	337.21	tonne
T0061	Thistle Hardwall	275.88	5%	11.39	-	301.63	tonne
T0062	Thistle Bonding coat	307.82	5%	11.39	-	335.17	tonne
T0064	Thistle Finish	226.51	5%	11.39	-	249.80	tonne
T0056	Thistle Board finish	212.13	5%	11.39	-	234.69	tonne
T0058	Thistle Wall finish	319.65	5%	11.39	-	347.59	tonne
T0066	Thistle Universal one coat plaster	356.44	5%	11.39	-	386.22	tonne
T0116	15 mm Gyproc Fireline	4.97	5%	0.18	-	5.41	m2
T0118	9.5 mm Gyproc wallboard	2.37	5%	0.10	-	2.59	m2
T0119	9.5 mm Gyproc lath/Thistle baseboard	2.73	5%	0.10	-	2.97	m2
T0120	12.5 mm Gyproc lath/Thistle baseboard	3.65	5%	0.14	-	3.98	m2
T0121	12.5 mm Gyproc wallboard	2.37	5%	0.14	-	2.63	m2
T0122	15 mm Gyproc wallboard	2.84	5%	0.10	-	3.09	m2
T0123	12.5 mm Gyproc Fireline board	2.88	5%	0.14	-	3.17	m2
T0124	19 mm Gyproc plank	4.91	5%	0.20	-	5.37	m2
T0125	Extra cost of Duplex grade board	1.09	5%	-	-	1.15	m2
T0126	22 mm Gyproc Thermal board (loads of 500 m2)	4.61	5%	0.14	-	4.99	m2
T0127	30 mm Gyproc Thermal board (loads of 500 m2)	5.08	5%	0.14	-	5.48	m2
T0128	40 mm Gyproc Thermal board (loads of 500 - 959 m2)	5.83	5%	0.14	-	6.27	m2
T0129	50 mm Gyproc Thermal board VC (loads of 500 - 959 m2)	6.90	5%	0.14	-	7.39	m2
T0130	50 mm Gyproc thermal board super (loads of 499 m2)	13.96	5%	0.14	-	14.81	m2

Basic Prices of Materials

Code	Description	Supply Price £	Waste Factor %	Unload. Labour £	Unload. Plant £	Total Unit Cost £	Unit
T0131	60 mm Gyproc thermal board super (loads of 499 m2)	15.46	5%	0.14	-	16.38	m2
T0137	70 mm Gyproc thermal board super (loads of 499 m2)	16.75	5%	0.14	-	17.73	m2
T0147	42 mm Gyproc Tri-line (loads of 6-12 pallets)	12.81	5%	0.14	-	13.60	m2
T0148	52 mm Gyproc Tri-line (loads of 6-12 pallets)	15.18	5%	0.14	-	16.09	m2
	Expanded metal lath; galvanised:						
T0111	BB 263 9 mm mesh 0.500 mm material	5.67	10%	-	-	6.24	m2
T0113	BB 264 9 mm mesh 0.725 mm material	7.93	10%	-	-	8.73	m2
T0402	Riblath ref 269 0.300 material	10.08	10%	0.03	-	11.12	m2
T0403	Riblath ref 271 0.500 material	11.60	10%	0.03	-	12.79	m2
T0404	Spraylath ref 273 0.500 material	13.94	10%	0.03	-	15.37	m2
T0405	Red-rib lath ref 274 0.500 material	12.80	10%	-	-	14.08	m2
T0407	Strip mesh ref 584 for external use 100 mm wide	3.28	10%	-	-	3.61	m
T0409	Corner mesh ref 583 for external use 100 mm wide	1.27	10%	-	-	1.40	m
	Expanded metal lath, stainless steel:						
T0410	ref. 267 Riblath 0.300 mm material	29.97	10%	-	-	32.97	m2
T0448	ref. 95S Spec.304.S.15 0.46 mm material	30.08	10%	-	-	33.08	m2
	Stainless steel clamping system:						
T0112	standard band 1/2" wide ref RB112	1.06	10%	-	-	1.16	m
T0114	standard band 3/4" wide ref RB134	1.25	10%	-	-	1.37	m
T0406	standard buckle ref TB112	0.23	5%	-	-	0.24	nr
T0408	standard buckle ref TB134	0.34	5%	-	-	0.36	nr
	Expamet beads for plaster, plasterboard and render:						
T0070	ref 550 angle bead	0.92	5%	-	-	0.97	m
T0411	ref 558 maxicon angle bead	0.73	5%	-	-	0.77	m
T0072	ref 588 movement bead, internal use	7.66	5%	-	-	8.05	m
T0412	ref 590 movement bead, external use	8.63	5%	-	-	9.06	m
T0413	ref 562 plaster stop bead 10 mm deep	1.16	5%	-	-	1.22	m
T0068	ref 563 plaster stop bead 13 mm deep	1.13	5%	-	-	1.19	m
T0414	ref 565 plaster stop bead 16 mm deep	1.61	5%	-	-	1.69	m
T0415	ref 566 plaster stop bead 19 mm deep	1.61	5%	-	-	1.69	m
T0073	ref 579 architrave bead	2.47	5%	-	-	2.59	m
T0074	ref 580 architrave bead	2.46	5%	-	-	2.58	m
T0416	ref 585 architrave bead	2.46	5%	-	-	2.58	m
T0417	ref 586 architrave bead	2.53	5%	-	-	2.66	m
	Glazed wall tiles:						
T0151	108 x 108 x 4 mm	0.18	5%	-	-	0.19	nr
T0152	152 x 152 x 5.5 mm	0.35	5%	-	-	0.37	nr
T0154	Ceramic tile adhesive	0.70	10%	0.02	-	0.79	ltr
T0155	Ceramic tile grout	0.88	10%	0.01	-	0.98	kg
	Patterned glazed wall tiles:						
T0156	108 x 108 x 4 mm	0.23	5%	-	-	0.24	nr

	Basic Prices of Materials	Supply Price £	Waste Factor %	Unload. Labour £	Unload. Plant £	Total Unit Cost £	Unit
T0157	152 x 152 x 5.5 mm	0.42	5%	-	-	0.44	nr
T0158	200 x 150 x 6.5 mm	0.88	5%	-	-	0.92	nr
	Quarry tiles - brown:						
T0160	150 x 150 x 12.5 mm	0.55	5%	-	-	0.58	nr
	Extra for:						
T0161	rounded edge tiles	0.97	5%	-	-	1.02	nr
T0192	double rounded edge tiles	3.01	5%	-	-	3.16	nr
T0162	194 x 194 x 25 mm	2.33	5%	-	-	2.45	nr
	Extra for:						
T0163	rounded edge tiles	3.04	5%	-	-	3.19	nr
T0193	double rounded edge tiles	6.88	5%	-	-	7.22	nr
T0164	150 x 150 mm cove skirting	1.44	5%	-	-	1.51	nr
	Extra for:						
T0165	internal angle	4.25	5%	-	-	4.46	nr
T0166	external angle	4.25	5%	-	-	4.46	nr
	Porcelain floor tiles:						
T0175	150 x 150 x 8.5 mm	0.53	5%	-	-	0.56	nr
T0177	200 x 200 x 8.5 mm	0.83	5%	-	-	0.87	nr
T0180	150 x 100 x 8.5 mm round top cove skirting	1.89	5%	-	-	1.99	nr
	Extra for:						
T0181	internal angle	3.41	5%	-	-	3.58	nr
T0182	external angle	3.41	5%	-	-	3.58	nr
T0183	200 x 100 x 8.5 mm square top cove skirting	3.64	5%	-	-	3.82	nr
	Extra for:						
T0184	internal angle	3.41	5%	-	-	3.58	nr
T0185	external angle	3.41	5%	-	-	3.58	nr
	Underlay:						
T0720	Fibreboard – 5 mm thick	3.15	2.5%	-	-	3.23	m2
	Laminate flooring:						
T0721	Oak plank microbevelled edges lacquered finish 10 mm	17.32	5%	-	-	18.19	m2
T0723	Hardwood radiator pipe cover	2.63	2.5%	-	-	2.69	nr
	Isover APR 1200 acoustics rolls:						
T0758	100 mm	5.11	7.5%	-	-	5.49	m2

Basic Prices of Materials

PAINTING AND DECORATING

Code	Description	Supply Price £	Waste Factor %	Unload. Labour £	Unload. Plant £	Total Unit Cost £	Unit
	Primers:						
V0101	all purpose primer	15.43	2.5%	-	-	15.82	ltr
V0102	wood primer, white and pink	7.31	2.5%	-	-	7.49	ltr
V0103	metal primer, zinc phosphate	8.05	2.5%	-	-	8.25	ltr
V0104	metal primer, zinc chromate	7.44	2.5%	-	-	7.62	ltr
V0105	metal primer, calcium plumbate	39.37	2.5%	-	-	40.36	ltr
V0106	metal primer, red oxide	8.02	2.5%	-	-	8.22	ltr
V0107	alkali resisting primer	12.80	2.5%	-	-	13.12	ltr
V0108	aluminium wood primer	13.89	2.5%	-	-	14.24	ltr
V0109	acrylic primer undercoat (white)	7.31	2.5%	-	-	7.49	ltr
V0110	quick drying wood primer	12.48	2.5%	-	-	12.79	ltr
V0111	etching primer (2 pack)	21.00	2.5%	-	-	21.53	ltr
V0112	thinners for etching primer	11.73	2.5%	-	-	12.03	ltr
V0113	preservative primer	12.29	2.5%	-	-	12.59	ltr
	Undercoats:						
V0120	white	6.11	2.5%	-	-	6.26	ltr
V0121	brilliant white	6.11	2.5%	-	-	6.26	ltr
V0122	standard colours	6.73	2.5%	-	-	6.90	ltr
	Eggshell paints:						
V0130	white	6.67	2.5%	-	-	6.84	ltr
V0131	brilliant white	6.67	2.5%	-	-	6.84	ltr
V0132	standard colours	7.34	2.5%	-	-	7.53	ltr
	Gloss paints:						
V0140	white	6.11	2.5%	-	-	6.26	ltr
V0141	brilliant white	6.56	2.5%	-	-	6.73	ltr
V0142	standard colours	6.73	2.5%	-	-	6.90	ltr
	Emulsion paints:						
	silk:						
V0150	white	5.57	2.5%	-	-	5.71	ltr
V0151	brilliant white	5.80	2.5%	-	-	5.95	ltr
V0152	standard colours	6.11	2.5%	-	-	6.26	ltr
	matt:						
V0153	white	4.81	2.5%	-	-	4.93	ltr
V0154	brilliant white	5.08	2.5%	-	-	5.20	ltr
V0155	standard colours	9.05	2.5%	-	-	9.28	ltr
	Metal finish:						
V0160	Finnigan's 'Hammerite' metal finish	10.34	2.5%	-	-	10.60	ltr
V0161	Finnigan's 'Smoothrite' metal finish	10.34	2.5%	-	-	10.60	ltr
V0162	Finnigan's No. 1 metal primer	12.76	2.5%	-	-	13.08	ltr
V0163	Finnigan's thinners	6.70	2.5%	-	-	6.87	ltr
	Chlorinated rubber paints:						
V0170	finish	19.24	2.5%	-	-	19.72	ltr
V0171	finish, rich colours	24.37	2.5%	-	-	24.98	ltr
V0172	thick coating brushing	20.40	2.5%	-	-	20.91	ltr
V0173	thick coating airless spray	18.52	2.5%	-	-	18.98	ltr
V0174	primer undercoat, off white	19.69	2.5%	-	-	20.19	ltr
V0175	metal primer	13.61	2.5%	-	-	13.95	ltr
V0176	chlorinated thinners	7.44	2.5%	-	-	7.62	ltr

Basic Prices of Materials

Code	Description	Supply Price £	Waste Factor %	Unload. Labour £	Unload. Plant £	Total Unit Cost £	Unit
	Wood preservers:						
V0200	clear wood preserver	5.61	5%	-	-	5.89	ltr
V0201	light oak/dark oak preserver	5.61	5%	-	-	5.89	ltr
V0202	green wood preserver	5.61	5%	-	-	5.89	ltr
V0203	exterior golden brown/chestnut	3.44	5%	-	-	3.61	ltr
V0204	water repellent, clear	2.57	5%	-	-	2.70	ltr
	Decorative preservers:						
V0210	red cedar	6.55	5%	-	-	6.87	ltr
	Wood stains:						
V0211	Premier	14.89	5%	-	-	15.63	ltr
V0212	Select	14.27	5%	-	-	14.98	ltr
	Varnishes:						
V0213	clear varnish (gloss, satin or matt)	9.22	2.5%	-	-	9.45	ltr
V0214	Ultra Clear (water based)	10.79	2.5%	-	-	11.06	ltr
V0215	Yacht varnish (exterior)	9.74	2.5%	-	-	9.99	ltr
	Wood preservers and stains (Sadolin):						
V0230	'Base' timber preservative (clear)	11.18	5%	-	-	11.74	ltr
V0231	'Classic' decorative timber protection	11.18	5%	-	-	11.74	ltr
V0232	'Superdec' opaque wood protection	12.83	5%	-	-	13.47	ltr
V0233	'Extra' joinery protection	11.18	5%	-	-	11.74	ltr

DRAINAGE

Code	Description	Supply Price £	Waste Factor %	Unload. Labour £	Unload. Plant £	Total Unit Cost £	Unit
	"HepLine" vitrified clay perforated pipe and fittings; with integral PVCu couplings:						
	pipes:						
W0091	100 mm	4.22	5%	-	-	4.43	m
W0092	150 mm	7.66	5%	-	-	8.04	m
W0093	225 mm	16.22	5%	-	-	17.03	m
	NOTE: For bends and junctions see Supersleve						
	"SuperSleve" and "HepSleve" vitrified clay drainage systems to BS EN295:1991:						
	pipes:						
W0120	100 mm	2.54	5%	-	-	2.67	m
W0121	150 mm	5.13	5%	-	-	5.39	m
	couplings (polyprop.) with standard sealing rings:						
W0123	100 mm	1.87	2.5%	-	-	1.92	nr
W0124	150 mm	3.40	2.5%	-	-	3.48	nr
	bends (ref. 8,14,16,20):						
W0126	100 mm	3.43	2.5%	-	-	3.51	nr
W0127	150 mm	7.06	2.5%	-	-	7.23	nr
	junctions (oblique or curved square: ref.22 & 25):						
W0129	100 x 100 mm	7.40	2.5%	-	-	7.58	nr
W0130	150 x 150 mm	9.44	2.5%	-	-	9.68	nr
	saddle (oblique or square: ref. 37 and 38):						
W0132	100 mm	7.26	2.5%	-	-	7.45	nr
W0133	150 mm	10.81	2.5%	-	-	11.08	nr
	rest bend (ref. 19):						
W0135	100 mm	6.06	2.5%	-	-	6.22	nr
W0136	150 mm	9.06	2.5%	-	-	9.29	nr

Basic Prices of Materials		Supply Price £	Waste Factor %	Unload. Labour £	Unload. Plant £	Total Unit Cost £	Unit
	taper pipe (ref.46):						
W0138	100 to 150 mm	8.74	2.5%	-	-	8.96	nr
	socket adaptor (ref.SA):						
W0140	100 mm	3.63	2.5%	-	-	3.72	nr
W0141	150 mm	7.16	2.5%	-	-	7.33	nr
W0142	225 mm	14.75	2.5%	-	-	15.12	nr
	adaptor to Hepseal:						
W0143	100 mm	2.95	2.5%	-	-	3.03	nr
W0144	150 mm	5.08	2.5%	-	-	5.21	nr
W0145	225 mm	7.01	2.5%	-	-	7.19	nr
	low-back P-trap:						
W0146	100 mm	7.40	2.5%	-	-	7.58	nr
W0147	150 mm	11.95	2.5%	-	-	12.25	nr
	Hepworth vitrified clay unjointed spigot and socket pipes and fittings BS 65:						
	pipes:						
W0200	100 mm in 1.00m pipe lengths	5.50	5%	-	-	5.78	m
W0201	150 mm in 1.5m pipe lengths	8.47	5%	-	-	8.89	m
W0202	225 mm in 1.75m pipe lengths	16.77	5%	-	-	17.61	m
	bends, (ref 8, 14, 16 or 20):						
W0203	100 mm	5.50	2.5%	-	-	5.64	nr
W0204	150 mm	8.55	2.5%	-	-	8.76	nr
W0205	225 mm	26.77	2.5%	-	-	27.44	nr
	rest bends (ref 19):						
W0206	100 mm	9.04	2.5%	-	-	9.27	nr
W0207	150 mm	15.43	2.5%	-	-	15.81	nr
	junctions, single (ref 22 & 25):						
W0208	100 x 100 mm	10.11	2.5%	-	-	10.36	nr
W0209	150 x 100 mm	16.88	2.5%	-	-	17.30	nr
W0210	150 x 150 mm	16.88	2.5%	-	-	17.30	nr
W0211	tarred gaskin	0.26	10%	-	-	0.28	m
	UPO Plastic underground drainage pipes, fittings and accessories, generally as BS4660:						
	pipes:						
W0310	110 mm	3.68	5%	-	-	3.86	m
W0311	160 mm	8.64	5%	-	-	9.07	m
	bend 87.5 degrees:						
W0312	110 mm	9.14	-	-	-	9.14	nr
W0313	160 mm	22.33	-	-	-	22.33	nr
	bend 45 degrees:						
W0314	110 mm	9.14	-	-	-	9.14	nr
W0315	160 mm	22.33	-	-	-	22.33	nr
	junction:						
W0316	110 x 110mm x 87.5 degrees	14.99	-	-	-	14.99	nr
W0317	160 x 110mm x 45 degrees	35.24	-	-	-	35.24	nr
	double socket pipe couplers:						
W0318	110 mm	3.62	5%	-	-	3.81	nr
W0319	160 mm	8.12	5%	-	-	8.52	nr

Basic Prices of Materials

		Supply Price £	Waste Factor %	Unload. Labour £	Unload. Plant £	Total Unit Cost £	Unit
	aluminium rodding eye:						
W0320	110 mm	28.52	-	-	-	28.52	nr
	universal trap:						
W0321	110 mm	18.59	-	-	-	18.59	nr
	plain square hopper:						
W0322	110 mm	7.86	-	-	-	7.86	nr
	universal gully:						
W0323	110 mm	28.31	-	-	-	28.31	nr
	Concrete inspection chambers to BS 5911 Part 2 Brierley (Garstang) Ltd., Catterall, Garstang. Lancs:						
	small chamber sections, internal size 600 x 450 mm:						
W0701	150 mm deep	11.69	5%	0.44	-	12.73	nr
W0702	225 mm deep	13.57	5%	0.69	-	14.97	nr
W0703	300 mm deep	15.08	5%	0.90	-	16.78	nr
	small frame units, for 600 x 450 mm chamber:						
W0704	frame	23.37	5%	0.67	-	25.24	nr
W0705	lid	21.86	5%	0.67	-	23.66	nr
	medium chamber sections, internal size 800 x 600 mm:						
W0706	150 mm deep	15.46	5%	0.68	-	16.94	nr
W0707	225 mm deep	18.09	5%	0.93	-	19.98	nr
W0708	300 mm deep	22.62	5%	1.25	-	25.06	nr
	medium frame units, for 800 x 600 mm chamber:						
W0709	frame	23.37	5%	0.85	-	25.43	nr
W0710	lid	21.86	5%	0.85	-	23.85	nr
W0712	HD Frame Unit	52.02	5%	0.49	1.48	56.69	nr
W0713	HD Lid Unit	30.91	5%	0.49	1.48	34.52	nr
	large chamber sections, internal size 1000 x 800 mm:						
W0715	150 mm deep	18.47	5%	0.72	2.17	22.43	nr
W0716	225 mm deep	22.24	5%	0.97	2.92	27.44	nr
W0720	300 mm deep	29.78	5%	1.08	3.27	35.84	nr
	large frame units, for 1000 x 800 mm chamber:						
W0718	Frame Unit	30.91	5%	0.35	1.07	33.95	nr
W0722	HD Frame Unit	63.33	5%	0.67	2.03	69.33	nr
W0723	HD Frame Unit	63.33	5%	0.67	2.03	69.33	nr
W0724	HD Frame Unit	63.33	5%	0.67	2.03	69.33	nr
W0729	loose step irons	5.65	5%	-	-	5.94	nr
	Broadstel Universal access covers and frames with rubber seal and locking devices; Drainage Systems:						
	medium duty:						
W0655	600 x 450 mm (ref. DC7369B)	90.47	-	0.14	-	90.62	nr
W0656	600 x 600 mm (ref. DC7369C)	101.69	-	0.16	-	101.85	nr
	medium heavy duty:						
W0657	600 x 450 mm (ref. DC7379B)	106.00	-	0.14	-	106.14	nr
W0658	600 x 600 mm (ref. DC7379C)	120.95	-	0.16	-	121.11	nr
	the foregoing covers with brass tops to visible edges:						
W0659	600 x 450 mm (ref. DC7369B)	284.33	-	0.14	-	284.47	nr
W0660	600 x 600 mm (ref. DC7369C)	297.16	-	0.16	-	297.32	nr
W0661	600 x 450 mm (ref. DC7379B)	295.35	-	0.14	-	295.49	nr

Basic Prices of Materials

Code	Description	Supply Price £	Waste Factor %	Unload. Labour £	Unload. Plant £	Total Unit Cost £	Unit
W0662	600 x 600 mm (ref. DC7379C)	314.23	-	0.16	-	314.39	nr
	Channels and fittings, socketed, vitrified clay, Hepworth:						
	half section straight main channel:						
W0415	100 x 600 mm long	2.32	5%	-	-	2.43	nr
W0416	150 x 600 mm long	3.73	5%	-	-	3.91	nr
W0417	225 x 1000 mm long	11.76	5%	-	-	12.35	nr
W0418	300 x 1000 mm long	24.14	5%	-	-	25.35	nr
	half section main channel enlarger/reducer:						
W0423	150 - 100 mm	14.89	5%	-	-	15.63	nr
W0424	225 - 150 mm	32.86	5%	-	-	34.50	nr
W0425	300 - 225 mm	64.62	5%	-	-	67.85	nr
	half section main channel bends 15, 30, 45 & 90 degrees:						
W0419	100 mm	3.54	5%	-	-	3.71	nr
W0420	150 mm	5.84	5%	-	-	6.13	nr
W0421	225 mm	19.48	5%	-	-	20.46	nr
W0422	300 mm	39.72	5%	-	-	41.71	nr
	half section tapered main channel bend:						
W0426	150 - 100 mm	22.41	5%	-	-	23.53	nr
W0427	225 - 150 mm	64.22	5%	-	-	67.43	nr
W0428	300 - 225 mm	130.33	5%	-	-	136.85	nr
	half section branch channel bends:						
W0429	100 mm	7.31	5%	-	-	7.68	nr
W0430	150 mm	11.99	5%	-	-	12.59	nr
W0431	225 mm	39.86	5%	-	-	41.85	nr
W0432	300 mm	78.98	5%	-	-	82.92	nr
	three-quarter section branch channel bends:						
W0433	100 mm	8.07	5%	-	-	8.47	nr
W0434	150 mm	13.55	5%	-	-	14.22	nr
W0435	225 mm	49.43	5%	-	-	51.90	nr
	Glassfibre septic tank:						
W0460	7500 litres, standard grade	1536.47	-	2.85	8.60	1547.93	nr
W0461	extra for light access cover and frame	97.38	-	-	-	97.38	nr

EXTERNAL WORKS

Code	Description	Supply Price £	Waste Factor %	Unload. Labour £	Unload. Plant £	Total Unit Cost £	Unit
	Marshalls 'Keyblok' concrete block paving in blocks size 200 x 100 mm:						
Y0110	natural, 60 mm thick	8.99	2.5%	-	-	9.21	m2
Y0111	natural, 80 mm thick	10.00	2.5%	-	-	10.25	m2
Y0112	coloured, 60 mm thick	10.00	2.5%	-	-	10.25	m2
Y0113	coloured, 80 mm thick	11.55	2.5%	-	-	11.84	m2
	Precast concrete hydraulically pressed kerbs and channels BS 340:						
Y0114	150 x 305 x 915 mm Figs 1, 4, 6, 8	8.47	2.5%	-	-	8.68	nr
Y0115	125 x 255 x 915 mm Figs 2, 5, 7, 8	4.41	2.5%	-	-	4.52	nr
Y0116	125 x 150 x 915 mm Figs 2a, 5, 7a, 8, 9	3.22	2.5%	-	-	3.30	nr
	EXTRA OVER prices for:						
Y0117	standard dish channels	2.24	2.5%	-	-	2.30	nr
Y0118	radius and droppers	2.90	2.5%	-	-	2.97	nr

Basic Prices of Materials

		Supply Price £	Waste Factor %	Unload. Labour £	Unload. Plant £	Total Unit Cost £	Unit
Y0119	quadrant angles	10.90	2.5%	-	-	11.18	nr
	Precast concrete hydraulically pressed edgings BS 340:						
Y0120	50 x 150 x 915 mm Figs 11, 12, 13	1.80	2.5%	-	-	1.84	nr
Y0121	50 x 200 x 915 mm Figs 11, 13	3.07	2.5%	-	-	3.14	nr
Y0122	50 x 250 x 915 mm Figs 11, 13	3.59	2.5%	-	-	3.68	nr
	Safeticurb drainage units:						
Y0124	DBA slot unit 250 x 250 x 914 mm 125 mm bore	36.78	2.5%	-	-	37.70	nr
Y0126	DBM slot unit 250 x 250 x 414 mm 125 mm bore	65.46	2.5%	-	-	67.10	nr
	Safeticurb fittings:						
Y0133	Silt box top type A (cast iron)	256.53	2.5%	-	-	262.94	nr
Y0131	Silt box top type J (cast iron)	416.86	2.5%	-	-	427.28	nr
Y0136	Kerb inspection unit DBK SP (or HB2)	133.61	2.5%	-	-	136.95	nr
Y0138	Kerb manhole cover SP (or HB2)	480.99	2.5%	-	-	493.01	nr
Y0137	Kerb transition unit SP (or HB2)	54.06	2.5%	-	-	55.41	nr
	Precast concrete paving slabs hydraulically pressed BS 368: natural grey plain smooth face:						
Y0202	450 x 600 x 50 mm	4.10	2.5%	-	-	4.20	nr
Y0203	600 x 600 x 50 mm	4.62	2.5%	-	-	4.74	nr
Y0204	750 x 600 x 50 mm	5.71	2.5%	-	-	5.86	nr
Y0205	900 x 600 x 50 mm	6.07	2.5%	-	-	6.22	nr
Y0161	Marshalls Beany block combined kerb and drainage system	58.39	2.5%	-	-	59.85	m
	Marshalls precast concrete bollards:						
	White finish:						
Y0176	Bridgeford	97.69	2.5%	-	-	100.13	nr
Y0177	Woodhouse	81.36	2.5%	-	-	83.40	nr
Y0178	Richmond	131.36	2.5%	-	-	134.64	nr
Y0179	Wilmslow	176.40	2.5%	-	-	180.81	nr
	Exposed aggregate finish bollards:						
Y0180	Truro	263.73	2.5%	-	-	270.32	nr
Y0181	Thetford	136.11	2.5%	-	-	139.51	nr
Y0182	Wexham	152.24	2.5%	-	-	156.05	nr
	'Westminster' replica pattern:						
Y0183	Edward	185.18	2.5%	-	-	189.81	nr
Y0184	Coronet	217.72	2.5%	-	-	223.16	nr
Y0185	Regent	185.18	2.5%	-	-	189.81	nr

	Basic Prices of Materials	Supply Price £	Waste Factor %	Unload. Labour £	Unload. Plant £	Total Unit Cost £	Unit
	Marshalls boulevard range of street furniture in precast concrete:						
Y0186	1400 rectangular planter, complete unit, 1 ring high	751.80	-	-	-	751.80	nr
Y0187	1200 circular planter, complete unit, 1 ring high	634.33	-	-	-	634.33	nr
Y0188	2000 rectangular seat, complete unit	762.22	-	-	-	762.22	nr
Y0189	700 planter, complete unit, 1 ring high	549.99	-	-	-	549.99	nr
Y0190	700 circular litter bin with cover	321.21	-	-	-	321.21	nr
	2000 seat:						
Y0192	free standing	607.88	-	-	-	607.88	nr
Y0193	ground fixed	536.15	-	-	-	536.15	nr

9

Planning and Building Regulation Fees

THE TOWN & COUNTRY PLANNING (Fees for Applications and Deemed Applications) (England) REGULATIONS 2008

Fees are payable in respect of most applications for planning permission. These notes are for **guidance only** and not all fees are shown. If in doubt refer to Regulations available from HMSO or contact your local planning office.

Guide to planning fees effective 26/02/10

1 Building or Engineering Operations
Enlargement, improvement or other alteration to an existing dwelling
£150 for alterations to one dwelling
£295 for alterations to two or more dwellings
£150 for ancillary operations within the cartilage of an existing dwelling i.e. the construction or erection of gates, walls, fences, sheds, vehicular access etc

New residential buildings
£335 per dwelling erected (50 or fewer dwellings)
Where development exceeds 50 dwellings **£16,565** plus **£100** for each dwelling in excess of 50 subject to a maximum of **£250,000**

Non-residential buildings
£170 where no new floor area is created e.g. shop fronts
£170 where less than 40 sq.m of gross floor space is created
£335 where between 40 and 75 sq.m of gross floor space is created
Where the area of gross floor space exceeds 75 sq.m, **£335** for each additional 75 sq.m or part thereof up tp 3750 sq.m
Where the area of gross floor space exceeds 3750 sq.m **£16,565** plus **£100** for each additional 75 sq.m or part thereof in excess of 3750 sq.m (maximum **£250,000**)

Erection, alteration or replacement of plant and machinery
£335 per 1,000 sq.m (0.1 hectares) of site area uo to 5 hectares
Where the site area exceeds 5 hectares, **£16,565** plus **£100** for each 0.1 hectare (or part thereof) in excess of 5 hectares (maximum **£250,000**)

Outline Applications
£335 per 1000 sq.m (0.1 hectares) of site area (or part therof) where the site area does not exceed 2.5 hectares
Where the site area exceeds 2.5 hectares, **£8,285** plus **£100** for each 0.1 hectares in excess of 2.5 hectares (maximum **£125,000**)

Reserved Matters Applications
Fee is the same as for an application for Full Permission for the type and scale of development proposed in the outline application regardless of how many reserved matters are submitted at the same time for approval

Construction of car parks, service roads or other access where the development is required for a purpose incidental to the existing use of the land **£170**

2 Uses
£335 for change of use for non-residential purposes

Conversion of residential building into separate dwellings (e.g. converting a house into flats)
£335 per extra dwelling, where development is under 50 dwellings
£16,565 plus **£100** for each additional dwelling in excess of the first 50 where development is over 50 dwellings (maximum **£250,000**)

Conversion of a non-residential building into separate dwellings
£335 per extra dwelling, where development is under 50 dwellings
£16,565 plus **£100** for each additional dwelling in excess of the first 50 where development is over 50 dwellings (maximum **£250,000**)

3 Agricultural Buildings
The erection, on land used for the purpose of agriculture, of buildings to be used for agricultural purposes

Outline Applications
£335 for each 0.1 hectare of site area, where the site area does not exceed 2.5 hectares
£8,285, and a further **£100** for each 0.1 hectare, where site area exceeds 2.5 hectares (maximum **£125,000**)

Other Cases
£70 where area of gross floor space does not exceed 465 sq.m
£335 where area of gross floor space exceeds 465 sq.m but does not exceed 540 sq.m

Where the gross floor space exceeds 540 sq.m but does not exceed 4215 sq.m, **£335** for the first 540 sq.m and a further **£335** for each 75 sq.m (or part thereof) in excess of 540 sq.m

Where the gross floor space exceeds 4215 sq.m **£16,565** and a further **£100** for each 75 sq.m (or part thereof) in excess of 4215 sq.m (maximum **£250,000**)

Building Incidental to Agricultural Use (Glasshouses)
£170 where gross floor space does not exceed 465 sq.m
£1,870 where gross floor space exceeds 465 sq.m

4 Lawful Development Certificates
Certificate of lawfulness of existing use or development (CLEUD) Section 191 Application
The fee is the same as for an equivalent planning application for the use or development, except where the application is for use as separate dwellings, in which case the fee is **£335** per dwelling for up to 50 dwellings or where the use is for more than 50 dwellings, **£16,565** and an additional **£100** for each dwelling in excess of 50 (maximum **£250,000**)

Certificate of lawfulness of proposed use or development (CLOPUD) Section 192 Application
The fee is half the amount of the equivalent planning application.

5 Prior Approval
Schedule 2 of the Town & Country Planning (General permitted Development) Order 1995
£70 for application for prior approval under Part 6 (Agricultural), Part 7 (Forestry) or Part 31 (Demolition)
£335 for application for prior approval under Part 24 (Electronic Communications Code Operators)

6 Advertisement Consent
£95 Advertisement relating to a business carried out on the premises
£95 Advance signs directing the public to a business which cannot be seen from the site of the advertisement
£335 All other advertisements e.g. hoardings

7 Satellite Dishes
£150 Domestic
£335 Non-domestic

8 Conditions
£170 To vary a condition on an existing Planning Permission (other than an extension to the duration of a Planning Permission, when a fresh application is required), or, if within 12 months of a permission, refer to the Free Go note.

£25 Discharge or compliance with a condition(s) attached to a grant of planning permission for a householder* application.

*Householders developments are defined as those within the curtilage of a house which require an application for planning permission and are not a change of use. **Included** in householder developments are extensions, conservatories, loft conversions, dormer windows, alterations, garages, car ports or outbuildings, swimming pools, walls, fences, domestic vehicular accesses including footway crossovers, porches and satellite dishes.

£85 Discharge or compliance with a condition(s) attached to an application other than a householder application as detailed above

9 Non-material changes to planning permission
Alternative proposal for the Same Site
£25 if the application is a householder application
£170 in any other case

10 Grant of replacement planning permission subject to a new time limit (Time extant permission)
£50 if the application is a householder application
£500 if the application is an application for a major development
£170 in any other case

11 Exemptions/Concessions
Alternative proposal for the Same Site
The fee should be calculated separately for each proposal and then the highest fee, together with half the fee for each alternative proposal added to arrive at the total fee

Cross Authority Boundary Developments
The application and fee should be forwarded to the Authority that covers the largest part of the site. The fee is either the total of each part of the site (calculated separately) or 150% of the fee for the whole site, whichever is smaller

People with Disabilities
A No fee is payable where the proposal is to alter or extend an existing dwelling for the benefit of a disabled person living or intending to live there, or for works in the cartilage of an existing dwelling e.g. access
B No fee is payable where the proposal solely relates to works to provide a means of access for disabled people to a building to which the public are admitted
C There is no fee exemption for an application to construct a new dwelling for someone with a disability

Permitted Development
No fee is payable for applications required because of the removal of Permitted Development rights by a planning condition or by an Article 4 Direction

Listed Building Consent
No fee payable

Conservation Area Consent
No fee payable

Works to trees subject to a Tree Preservation Order
No fee payable

Playing Fields
A flat rate of **£335** for applications by non-profit making clubs or other non-profit making sporting or recreational organisations, relating to playing fields for their own use. This does not cover applications to erect buildings. Golf courses, golf driving ranges and enclosed courts are not covered by this concession.

Free Go
Application of the same character as a previous application submitted by the same applicant on the same (or part of the same) site either within 12 months of a permission or a refusal, or, where an application was withdrawn, within 12 months of the date of the making of the earlier one.

12 Notes
Floor space is taken to be the gross amount (all storeys including basements and garaging) to be created by the development. This is an external measurement, including the thickness of internal and external walls.

Building Regulations Charges (effective from 1.4.2012)

GUIDANCE NOTES FOR CLIENTS

The following notes and tables are for guidance only. Please contact your local authority. Fees are revised annually.

Before you build, extend or convert, you or your agent must advise your Local Authority either by submitting Full Plans or a Building Notice. The charge payable depends upon the type of work, the number of dwellings in a building and the total floor area. The following tables may be used in conjunction with the current scheme to calculate the charges. Please contact your local Authority Building Control office. With the exception of the Regularisation charge, all Local Authority charges are subject to VAT at the appropriate rate.

Charges are payable as follows:

- A Plan Charge, payable when plans of the building work are deposited, is for the consideration, passing or rejection of plans detailing the proposed building work.
- An Inspection Charge, payable on demand following the first inspection, is for all the inspections of the building work that is included on the plans that have been deposited.
- A Building Notice Charge, payable when the building notice is submitted, is for consideration of the building notice and associated site inspections.
- An Additional Charge may be payable where electrical work is undertaken by a person other than a Competent Person, or a person who has sufficient accreditation to install, inspect and test such work, and is set to cover any additional contractors used by the Council to determine compliance with Part P of the Building Regulations.

NOTE: *The sum of the plan charge and the inspection charge is equal to the building notice charge.*
For the charge payable in respect of any other type of Building Regulation submission please contact your local planning authority.

Exemption From Charge: Where the work is to provide disabled access and facilities to an existing public building or dwelling, or is an extension to a dwelling to store or provide medical treatment for a disabled person, no charge may be payable.

Floor Area: Means the following:-

- The floor area of a dwelling, extension, garage, carport, loft conversion, commercial extension or other similar construction, is the total floor area calculated by reference to the finished internal faces of the walls enclosing the area, or if at any point there is no enclosing wall, by reference to the outermost edge of the floor.
- The total floor area of any dwelling or extension is the total floor area of all the storeys that comprise the dwelling or are in the extension.

Multiple Works: Where multiple works are involved charges calculated by reference to more than one table might be applicable.

VAT: The charges in this scheme must be paid together with the Value Added Tax that is payable in respect of that charge. Customs and Excise advise that VAT should be added to all charges except the regularisation charge. **THIS MUST BE ADDED TO THE NET VALUES IN THE TABLES AT PREVAILING RATE OF VAT.**

Help: Please contact your local planning authority.

SCHEDULE 1 SET CHARGES FOR NEW DWELLINGS / HOUSING

Standard charges payable for the erection of small domestic dwellings (including flats) (up to 300m2 and not exceeding three storeys).
These charges also apply for those cases where housing units are created from converting an existing building.
These charges are laid out for Full Plans Applications. In the event of an application for new dwellings wishing to be paid on a Building Notice, please contact us direct.

	PLAN CHARGE (Payment with application)	INSPECTION CHARGE (Invoiced after commencement)	Additional Charge
No of Dwellings	Fee £	Fee £	incl VAT £
1	179.98	413.96	Charge is set for each dwelling when appropriate – see below.
2	239.98	575.94	
3	304.97	729.93	
4	369.96	884.91	
5	439.96	1034.90	
6	509.95	1184.88	
7	529.95	1324.87	
8	549.95	1469.85	
9	569.94	1614.84	
10	579.94	1754.82	
For charges in respect of the construction of more than 10 dwellings please contact the Building Consultancy Service			

Small domestic building means a building (including connected drainage work within the curtilage of that building):-

(a) which is used, or intended to be used wholly for the purposes of one or more dwellings, none of which has a floor area exceeding 300 m2, excluding any garage or carport

(b) which has no more than three storeys, each basement level being counted as one storey.

Including such a building which incorporates an integral garage or to which is attached a garage or carport or both which shares one or more walls with that building.

Additional Charge

In the unlikely event of the electrical installation work being undertaken by a person other than a Competent Person registered with a Competent Body, or a person who has sufficient accreditation to install, inspect and test such work, an additional charge may be made to cover any additional contractors used by the council to determine compliance with Part P. This charge is identified in the table below, and will be charged per dwelling / housing unit formed where a non competent person is used.

Additional Charge	Fee £
Additional charge (per dwelling or housing unit formed) for those cases where a non Part P electrical contractor is used. This additional fee is payable after the commencement of works.	141.65

SCHEDULE 2 TABLE B - STANDARD CHARGES FOR SMALL BUILDINGS AND EXTENSIONS

Standard charges payable for the erection of certain small domestic extensions, loft conversions, garages, garage conversions, and basement conversions, up to certain floor areas.

Type of Work (Extensions to dwellings)	PLAN CHARGE (Payment with application)	INSPECTION CHARGE (Invoiced after commencement)	BUILDING NOTICE CHARGE (Payment with application)
	Fee £	Fee £	Fee £
Single Storey Domestic Extensions not exceeding 10m2 floor area	164.30	204.46	407.17
Single Storey Domestic extensions over 10m2 but not exceeding 40m2 floor area	164.30	328.86	544.02
Single Storey Domestic extensions over 40m2 but not exceeding 100m2 floor area	208.19	431.16	703.28
Two Storey Domestic Extensions not exceeding 40m2 floor area	208.19	363.86	629.26
Two Storey Domestic Extensions over 40m2 floor area but not exceeding 200m2	208.19	498.46	777.32
Loft conversion that does not include the construction of a dormer / gable	164.30	271.74	481.20
Loft conversion that includes the construction of a dormer / gable	164.30	305.40	518.21
Erection or extension of a non exempt detached or attached domestic garage or carport or both not exceeding 100m2 floor area	164.30	191.19	392.58
Conversion of a garage to a dwelling into a habitable room(s)	164.30	170.80	370.15
Alterations to extend or create a basement up to 100m2 floor area	164.30	339.06	555.23

Additional Charge

In the event of the electrical installation work being undertaken by a person other than a Competent Person registered with a Competent Body, or a person who has sufficient accreditation to install, inspect and test such work, an additional charge may be made to cover any additional contractors used by the council to determine compliance with Part P.

Additional Charge	Fee £
Additional charge (per dwelling or housing unit formed) for those cases where a non Part P electrical contractor is used. This additional fee is payable after the commencement of works.	141.65

Individually Determined Fees:
For charges relating to any extension or alteration of a dwelling consisting of the provision of an extension in excess of the sizes given above, please contact Building Consultancy Services direct for an Individually Determined Fee Quote.

Note:
(a) Where the work in question comprises or includes the erection of more than one extension to a building used or intended to be used for the purposes of a single private dwelling, the total floor areas of all such extensions shall be aggregated in determining the charge payable in accordance with Schedule 2, Tables B and C. Alternatively an individually determined fee may be requested.
(b) In Schedule 2:-
(i) A reference to an "extension" is a reference to an extension which has no more than three storeys, each basement level counting as one storey; and
(ii) A reference to a dwelling is a reference also to a building consisting of a garage or carport or both, which is used with a house or with a building consisting of flats or maisonettes or both.
(c) Where a project includes alterations as well as an extension, the alterations will be subject to an additional charge in accordance with Schedule 2 Table C.

SCHEDULE 2 TABLE C - STANDARD CHARGES FOR SMALL DOMESTIC ALTERATIONS TO A SINGLE BUILDING
Standard charges payable for certain small domestic alterations to a single building

Type of Work (Alterations to dwellings)	FULL PLANS CHARGE	BUILDINGS NOTICE CHARGE	REDUCTION FACTORS AVAILABLE
	Fee £	Fee £	
Renovation of a thermal element to a single dwelling	131.99	145.19	Not applicable
Internal alterations, installation of fittings, drainage alteration and/or structural alterations (not electrical) – based on estimated cost of work			
up to £2,000 of estimated cost	131.99	145.19	30% reduction
over £2,000 and up to £5,000 of estimated cost	197.98	217.78	30% reduction
over £5,000 and up to £10,000 of estimated cost	263.97	290.38	30% reduction
over £10,000 and up to £25,000 of estimated cost	329.97	362.96	30% reduction
over £25,000 and up to £50,000 of estimated cost	395.70	435.70	30% reduction
Window and door replacements (non competent persons scheme) – per dwelling unit	131.99	145.19	Individually determined
Electrical work (non competent persons scheme) – re-wiring or new installation in a dwelling	263.97	290.38	Not applicable
Electrical work (non competent persons scheme) – all other work other than the re-wiring of a dwelling	197.98	217.78	Not applicable

Reduction Factors
Where work identified in Table C above is undertaken on the same application and at the same time as work identified in Table B, then an individually determined reduction of these Table C charges may be made, based on the likely savings in time being made by the council.

SCHEDULE 3 TABLE D - STANDARD CHARGES FOR NON DOMESTIC WORK – EXTENSIONS AND NEW BUILD
Standard charges payable for the erection of certain small non-domestic extensions to a single building and new build.
The amount of time to carry out the building regulation function varies, dependent on the different use catagories of building, with some categories taking additional time to check and inspect.

Building Use (Extensions and New Build)	Floor Area	FULL PLANS APPLICATIONS		REGULARISATION
		PLAN CHARGE (Payment with application)	INSPECTION CHARGE (Invoiced after commencement)	REGULARISATION CHARGE (Payment with application)
		Fee £	Fee £	Fee (VAT not payable) £
Industrial and Storage Use (i.e. Purpose Groups 6, 7(a) and 7(b) incl factories, car parks, manufacturing, and similar uses)	Floor area not exceeding 10m2	169.98	192.98	508.15
	Floor area over 10m2 but not exceeding 40m2	169.98	324.97	692.93
	Floor area over 40m2 but not exceeding 100m2	199.98	426.96	877.71

		FULL PLANS APPLICATIONS		REGULARISATION
All Other Use Classes (i.e. Purpose Groups 3 and 4 incl offices, shops and commercial premises)	Floor area not exceeding 10m2	169.98	225.98	554.35
	Floor area over 10m2 but not exceeding 40m2	169.98	357.96	739.13
	Floor area over 40m2 but not exceeding 100m2	199.98	459.95	923.91

SCHEDULE 3 TABLE E - STANDARD CHARGES FOR ALL OTHER NON DOMESTIC WORK - ALTERATIONS

Standard charges payable for certain alterations in non-domestic buildings.

		FULL PLANS APPLICATIONS	
Category of work (Alterations)		**PLAN CHARGE (Payment with application)**	**INSPECTION CHARGE (Invoiced after commencement)**
	Floor Area	**Fee £**	**Fee £**
Window replacement (non competent persons)	Per installation – up to 20 windows	164.98	Included in plan charge
	Per installation – over 20 and up to 50 windows	214.98	Included in plan charge
New shop front(s)	Per installation – up to 20 windows	164.98	Included in plan charge
	Per installation – over 20 and up to 50 windows	214.98	Included in plan charge
Alterations not described elsewhere – including structural alterations and installation of controlled fittings	Estimated cost – up to £2,000	197.98	Included in plan charge
	Estimated cost – over £2,000 and up to £5,000	263.97	Included in plan charge
	Estimated cost – over £5,000 and up to £10,000	329.97	Included in plan charge
	Estimated cost – over £10,000 and up to £25,000	395.96	Included in plan charge
	Estimated cost – over £25,000 and up to £50,000	462.18	Included in plan charge
Installation of Mezzanine floor (industrial type raised storage platform)	Floor area – up to 200m2	197.98	329.97
Office fit out	Floor area – up to 200m2	164.98	197.98
Shop fit out	Floor area – up to 200m2	164.98	197.98

10

Memoranda

METRIC CONVERSION FACTORS

	Metric	= Imperial	Imperial	= Metric
LENGTH	1 mm	= 0.0394 inches	1 inch	= 25.4 (exact) mm
	1 m	= 3.2808 feet	1 foot	= 0.3048 m
	1 m	= 1.0936 yards	1 yard	= 0.9144 m
	1 km	= 0.6214 miles	1 mile	= 1.6093 km
AREA	1 mm2	= 0.0016 square inches	1 square inch	= 645.1600 mm2
	1 m2	= 10.7639 square feet	1 square foot	= 0.0929 m2
	1 m2	= 1.1960 square yards	1 square yard	= 0.8361 m2
	1 km2	= 0.3861 square mile	1 square mile	= 2.5900 km2
	1 ha	= 2.4711 acres	1 acre	= 0.4047 ha
VOLUME	1 m3	= 35.3147 cubic feet	1 cubic foot	= 0.0283 m3
	1 m3	= 1.3080 cubic yards	1 cubic yard	= 0.7646 m3
	1 litre	= 1.7598 pints	1 pint	= 0.5683 litres
	1 litre	= 0.2200 gallons (UK)	1 gallon (UK)	= 4.5461 litres
NOTE:	1 litre	= 1000 cm3		
	1 m3	= 1000 litres		
WEIGHT	1 kg	= 2.2046 pounds	1 pound	= 0.4536 kg
	1 kg	= 0.0197 hundredweight	1 hundredweight	= 50.8024 kg
	1 tonne	= 0.9842 ton	1 ton	= 1.0161 tonnes
FORCE	1 N	= 0.2248 pdf	1 pdf	= 4.4482 N
	1 N	= 7.2330 pdl	1 pdl	= 0.1383 N
	1 kN	= 0.1004 tonf	1 tonf	= 9.9640 kN
NOTE:	Standard gravity (gn)	= 9.80665 m/s2 (exactly)		
PRESSURE	1 kpa	= 0.1450 lbf/square inch	1 lbf/square inch	= 6.8948 kpa
NOTE:	1 kpa	= 1 kN/m2	= 0.001 N/mm2	
ENERGY (work and heat)	1 kJ	= 0.9478 Btu	1 Btu	= 1.0551 kJ
POWER	1 W	= 3.4121 Btu/Hr	1 Btu	= 0.2931 W
	1 kW	= 1.3410 hp	1 hp	= 0.7457 kW

METRIC CONVERSION TABLE

Inches and fractions of inches to millimetres

	millimetres											
Inches	0	1	2	3	4	5	6	7	8	9	10	11
		25.400	50.800	76.200	101.600	127.000	152.400	177.800	203.200	228.600	254.000	279.400
1/32	0.794	26.194	51.594	76.994	102.394	127.794	153.194	178.594	203.994	229.394	254.794	280.194
1/16	1.588	26.998	52.388	77.788	103.188	128.588	153.988	179.388	204.788	230.188	255.588	280.988
3/32	2.381	27.781	53.181	78.581	103.981	129.381	154.781	180.181	205.581	230.981	256.381	281.781
1/8	3.175	28.575	53.975	79.375	104.775	130.175	155.575	180.975	206.375	231.775	257.175	282.575
5/32	3.969	29.369	54.769	80.169	105.569	130.969	156.369	181.769	207.169	232.569	257.969	283.369
3/16	4.762	30.162	55.562	80.962	106.362	131.762	157.162	182.562	207.962	233.362	258.762	284.162
7/32	5.556	30.956	56.356	81.756	107.156	132.556	157.956	183.356	208.756	234.156	259.556	284.956
1/4	6.350	31.750	57.150	82.550	107.950	133.350	158.750	184.150	209.550	234.950	260.350	285.750
9/32	7.144	32.544	57.944	83.344	108.744	134.144	159.544	184.944	210.344	235.744	261.144	286.544
5/16	7.983	33.338	58.738	84.138	109.538	134.938	160.338	185.738	211.138	236.538	261.938	287.338
11/32	8.731	34.131	59.531	84.931	110.331	135.731	161.131	186.531	211.931	237.331	262.731	288.131
3/8	9.525	34.925	60.325	85.725	111.125	136.525	161.925	187.325	212.725	238.125	263.525	228.925
13/32	10.319	35.719	61.119	86.519	111.919	137.319	162.719	188.119	213.519	238.919	264.319	289.719
7/16	11.112	36.512	61.912	87.312	112.712	138.112	163.512	188.912	214.312	239.712	265.112	290.512
15/32	11.906	37.306	62.706	88.106	113.906	138.906	164.306	189.706	215.106	240.506	265.906	291.306
1/2	12.700	38.100	63.500	88.900	114.300	139.700	165.100	190.500	215.900	241.300	266.700	292.100
17/32	13.494	38.894	64.294	89.694	115.094	140.494	165.894	191.294	216.694	242.494	267.494	292.894
9/16	14.288	39.688	65.088	90.488	115.888	141.288	166.688	192.088	217.488	242.888	268.288	293.688
19/32	15.081	40.481	65.881	91.281	116.681	142.081	167.481	192.881	218.281	243.681	269.081	294.481
5/8	15.875	41.275	66.675	92.075	117.475	142.875	168.275	193.675	219.075	244.475	269.875	295.275
21/32	16.669	42.069	67.469	92.869	118.269	143.669	169.069	194.469	219.869	245.269	270.669	296.069
11/16	17.462	42.862	68.262	93.662	119.062	144.462	169.862	195.262	220.662	246.062	271.462	296.862
23/32	18.256	43.656	69.056	94.456	119.856	145.256	170.656	196.056	221.456	246.856	272.256	297.656
3/4	19.050	44.450	69.850	95.250	120.650	146.050	171.450	196.850	222.250	247.650	273.050	298.450
25/32	19.844	45.244	70.644	96.044	121.444	146.844	172.244	197.644	223.044	248.444	273.844	299.244
13/16	20.638	46.038	71.438	96.838	122.238	147.638	173.038	198.438	223.838	249.238	274.638	300.038
27/32	21.431	46.831	72.231	97.631	123.031	148.431	173.831	199.231	224.631	250.031	275.431	300.831
7/8	22.225	47.625	73.025	98.425	123.825	149.225	174.625	200.025	225.425	250.825	276.225	301.625
29/32	23.019	48.419	73.819	99.219	124.619	150.019	175.419	200.819	226.219	251.619	277.019	302.419
15/16	23.812	49.212	74.612	100.012	125.412	150.812	176.212	201.612	227.012	252.412	277.812	303.212
31/32	24.606	50.006	75.406	100.806	126.206	151.606	177.006	202.406	227.806	253.206	278.606	304.006

THICKNESS OF SHEETING ETC

12 inches	=	304.800 mm
1000 gauge	=	250 mμ
1200 gauge	=	300 mμ

MEASUREMENT FORMULAE

Perimeters or circumferences of planes

Circle: 3.14159 x Diameter

Ellipse: 3.14159 (major axis + minor axis) / 2

Sector: Radius x Degrees in Arc / 57.3

Surface areas of planes and solids

Circle: 3.14159 x Radius Sq

Sphere: 3.14159 x Diameter Sq

Ellipse: 0.7854 (major axis x minor axis)

Cylinder: (circumference x length) + (2 x area of end)

Cone: Area of base + (circumference x slant height) / 2

Frustum of cone: 3.14159 x slant height (radius at top + radius at bottom) + area of top + area of bottom

Pyramid: (sum of base perimeters) slant height / 2 + area of base

Sector of circle: 3.14159 x Degrees in Arc x Radius Sq / 360

Segment of circle: Area of sector LESS area of triangle

Segment of arc: 2 / 3 (chord x rise) + rise3 / 2 x chord

Bellmouth at road junction: Area 'A' = 3 / 14 x Radius Sq

Volumes of solids

Sphere : 4.1888 x Radius cubed

Cone : height / 3 (area of base)

Frustum of cone: height / 2 (3.14159 x R Sq + r Sq + Rr) where R and r are radius of base and top

Pyramid: height / 3 (area of base)

Frustum of pyramid: height / 3 (A + B + square root (AB)) where A and B are areas of base and top

Lengths of rafters

To calculate the lengths of rafters:

Multiply the lengths on plan (from centre line of ridge to extreme horizontal projection of rafter) by the secant of the angle.

Pitch in degrees	Natural Secant	Pitch in degrees	Natural Secant	Pitch in degrees	Natural Secant
5.0	1.0038	25.0	1.1034	45.0	1.4142
7.5	1.0086	27.5	1.1274	50.0	1.5557
10.0	1.0154	30.0	1.1547	55.0	1.7435
12.5	1.0243	32.5	1.1857	60.0	2.0000
15.0	1.0353	35.0	1.2208	65.0	2.3662
17.5	1.0485	37.5	1.2605	70.0	2.9238
20.0	1.0642	40.0	1.3054	75.0	3.8637
22.5	1.0824	42.5	1.3563		

EXCAVATION AND EARTHWORK

Bearing capacities of soils

Nature of soil:	Approximate bearing capacity; kN/m2
Peat and bog	0 - 20
Clay, marl, loam	330 - 750
Solid chalk	110 - 450
Solid rock (unweathered)	220 - 2000
Gravel, coarse	660 - 900
Gravel, fine	450 - 660
Sand	220 - 550

Bulkage of soils after excavation

Nature of soil:	Approximate bulkage of 1 m3 after excavation:
Vegetable soil and loam	1.25 - 1.30 m3
Soft clay, marl	1.30 - 1.40 m3
Sand	1.10 - 1.15 m3
Gravel	1.20 - 1.25 m3
Chalk	1.40 - 1.50 m3
Stiff clay	1.40 - 1.50 m3
Rock, weathered	1.30 - 1.40 m3
Rock, unweathered	1.50 - 1.60 m3

CONCRETE WORK

NOTE: The following quantities allow for the increase in bulk of moist sand and moist all-in aggregate.

Quantities of materials per 1 m3 of hardened concrete			
Nominal mix by volume	Cement tonnes	Moist sand m3	Gravel m3
1:3:6	0.215	0.55	0.88
1:2:4	0.304	0.53	0.84
1:1.5:3	0.389	0.50	0.80
		Moist all-in aggregate (m3)	
1:6	0.304	1.45	
1:9	0.214	1.52	
1:12	0.167	1.55	
Nominal mix by weight	Cement tonnes	Moist sand tonnes	Gravel tonnes
1:3:6	0.216	0.81	1.31
1:2:4	0.312	0.81	1.24
1:1.5:3	0.391	0.74	1.17
	Cement tonnes	Moist all-in aggregate (tonnes)	
1:6	0.312	2.15	
1:9	0.217	2.26	
1:12	0.172	2.38	

Quantities of materials per 50 kg bag of cement			
Nominal mix by volume	Cement 50 kg bag	Moist sand kg	Gravel kg
1:3:6	1	130	205
1:2:4	1	85	140
1:1.5:3	1	65	105
		Moist all-in aggregate (kg):	
1:6	1	240	
1:9	1	355	
1:12	1	465	
Nominal mix by weight	Cement 50 kg bag	Moist sand kg	Gravel kg
1:3:6	1	190	305
1:2:4	1	130	200
1:1.5:3	1	95	150
		Moist all-in aggregate kg	
1:6	1	345	
1:9	1	520	
1:12	1	690	

Weights of steel bar reinforcement

Diameter	kg/m	m/tonne	Cross-sectional area mm2
6 mm	0.222	4505	28.3
8 mm	0.395	2532	50.3
10 mm	0.616	1624	78.5
12 mm	0.888	1126	113.1
16 mm	1.579	634	201.1
20 mm	2.466	406	314.2
25 mm	3.854	260	490.9
32 mm	6.313	158	804.2
40 mm	9.864	101	1256.6
50 mm	15.413	65	1963.3

Weights of steel bar reinforcement in various percentages of 1 m3 of concrete

Percentage of reinforcement	0.5	0.75	1.00	1.25	1.50	1.75	2.00	2.50	3.00	3.50	4.00	4.50	5.00
Weights kg per m3	39	59	79	98	118	137	157	196	236	275	314	353	393

Weights of stainless steel bar reinforcement

Diameter	kg/m	m/tonne	Cross-sectional area mm2
10 mm	0.667	1499	78.5
12 mm	0.938	1066	113.1
16 mm	1.628	614	201.1
20 mm	2.530	395	314.2
25 mm	4.000	250	490.9
32 mm	6.470	155	804.2

Weights of steel fabric reinforcement

Fabric reinforcement to BS 4483:

SQUARE MESH FABRIC	Mesh size: Main	Mesh size: Cross	Wire size: Main	Wire size: Cross	Weight per m2
BS reference	mm	mm	mm	mm	kg
A 393	200	200	10	10	6.16
A 252	200	200	8	8	3.95
A 193	200	200	7	7	3.02
A 142	200	200	6	6	2.22
A 98	200	200	5	5	1.54
STRUCTURAL MESH FABRIC					
B1131	100	200	12	8	10.90
B 785	100	200	10	8	8.14
B 503	100	200	8	8	5.93
B 385	100	200	7	7	4.53
B 283	100	200	6	7	3.73
B 196	100	200	5	7	3.05
LONG MESH FABRIC					
C 785	100	400	10	6	6.72
C 503	100	400	8	5	4.34
C 385	100	400	7	5	3.41
C 283	100	400	6	5	2.61
WRAPPING FABRIC					
D 98	200	200	5	5	1.54
D 49	100	100	2.5	2.5	0.770
CARRIAGE WAY FABRIC					
C 636	80-130	400	8-10	6	5.55

BRICKWORK AND BLOCKWORK

Bricks and mortar required per m2

Bricks 215 x 102.5 x 65 mm with 10 mm joints:

Wall thickness	Number of bricks (no waste allowance)	Mortar (m3) no frogs	Mortar (m3) one frog	Mortar (m3) two frogs
102.5 mm (half brick)	59.25	0.017	0.024	0.031
215 mm (one brick)	118.50	0.045	0.059	0.073
327.5 mm (one and a half brick)	177.75	0.072	0.093	0.114
440 mm (two brick)	237.00	0.101	0.128	0.155

Length of pointing to one face per m2:

Extra over common brickwork for facing and pointing one side in:	Number of bricks (no waste allowance)	Horizontal joints	Vertical joints	Combined
English bond	89.0	13.3 m	5.8 m	19.1 m
Flemish bond	79.0	13.3 m	5.1 m	18.4 m
English garden wall bond	74.0	13.3 m	4.8 m	18.1 m
Flemish garden wall bond	68.0	13.3 m	4.4 m	17.7m

Blocks and mortar required per m2

Blocks 440 x 215 mm on face with 10 mm joints require 9.88 blocks per m2 (exclusive of waste)

Wall thickness (mm)	50	60	70	75	90	100	115	125
Mortar (m3/m2)	0.003	0.004	0.005	0.005	0.006	0.007	0.008	0.008
Wall thickness (mm)	140	150	190	215	220	250	255	305
Mortar (m3/m2)	0.009	0.010	0.013	0.014	0.015	0.017	0.017	0.020

Analysis of mortar mixes per m3				Analysis of mortar mixes per 50 kg bag of Cement			
Nominal mix by volume	Cement tonnes	Lime tonnes	Sand (moist) m3	Nominal mix by volume	Cement 50 kg bag	Lime 25 kg bag	Sand (moist m3) kg
1:3	0.52	-	1.36	1:3	1	-	168
1:4	0.43	-	1.50	1:4	1	-	224
1:1:6	0.27	0.13	1.38	1:1:6	1	1	327
1:2:9	0.19	0.19	1.44	1:2:9	1	2	486

ROOFING

Quantities of slates, tiles etc per m2

NOTE: The quantities in the table below are net with no allowance for waste.

Type:	Size (mm)	Lap (mm)	Gauge (mm)	Number (Nr)	Battens (m/m2)	Slate or tile nails (Nr)		Batten nails (Nr)
Natural slates - uniform sizes:	610 x 305	75	268	12.26	3.75	25		10
	455 x 255	75	189	20.64	5.30	42		12
	405 x 255	75	165	23.75	6.10	48		14
	355 x 205	75	140	34.84	7.15	86		16
	305 x 205	75	115	42.42	8.70	85		20
Natural slates - uniform length Random widths:	560 long	75	243	14.73	4.12	29		10
	510 long	75	218	18.18	4.60	36		11
	405 long	75	165	29.93	6.10	60		14
	355 long	75	140	40.24	7.15	81		16
	305 long	75	115	57.02	8.70	114		20
Natural slates - random length,	1220 - 760	75	455	4.55	2.20	9		5
	760 - 560	75	294	10.36	3.40	21		8

Type:	Size (mm)	Lap (mm)	Gauge (mm)	Number (Nr)	Battens (m/m2)	Slate or tile nails (Nr)		Batten nails (Nr)
length:	510 - 305	75	165	26.35	6.10	52		14
	455 - 230	75	135	38.98	7.40	78		17
	355 - 255	75	115	58.00	8.70	116		20
						Hooks (Nr)		
Eternit slates - hook fixing:	600 x 300	110	245	13.50	4.08	14		7
		90	255	13.00	3.92	13		7
	500 x 250	110	195	20.50	5.13	21		9
		90	205	19.50	4.88	20		8
	400 x 270	110	145	25.50	6.90	26		12
		90	155	23.90	6.45	24		11
	400 x 200	110	145	34.50	6.90	35		12
		90	155	32.30	6.45	32		11
						Slate fixing nails (Nr)	Slate fixing discs (Nr)	
Eternit slates - nail and disc rivet fixing:	600 x 300	70	265	12.50	3.77	25	13	6
		76	262	12.60	3.82	25	13	6
		90	255	13.10	3.92	26	13	7
		100	250	13.30	4.00	26	13	7
		110	245	13.60	4.08	27	-	-
	500 x 250	70	215	18.60	4.65	37	19	8
		76	212	18.90	4.72	38	19	8
		90	205	19.50	4.88	39	20	8
	400 x 270	70	165	22.50	6.06	45	23	10
		76	162	22.80	6.17	46	23	10
		90	155	23.80	6.45	48	24	11
	400 x 200	70	165	30.00	6.06	60	30	10
		76	162	30.70	6.17	61	31	10
		90	155	31.90	6.45	64	32	11
Bradstone slates - Cotswold pattern	380 x 330 (average)	75	150	20.21	6.67	42		15
Moordale pattern	480 x 375 (average)	75	200	13.35	5.00	26		12
Cedar shingles - uniform lengths random widths:	400 long	210	95	1.77	10.53	84		18
		146	127	2.39	7.87	64		13
		120	140	2.63	7.14	58		12
		100	150	2.86	6.67	54		11
		70	165	3.10	6.06	48		10
		44	178	3.34	5.62	46		10
Vertical cladding		146 (av)	175 & 178	2.39	7.87	64		13
shadow coursing (double thickness)		70	165	1.60	6.06	48		11
		44	178	1.70	5.62	45		10
Marley concrete tiles	413 x 330	75	338	***10.20	2.96	10		5
		100	313	**11.00	3.20	11		5
	419 x 330	75	344	9.70	2.91	10		5
		100	319	10.50	3.14	11		5
	380 x 230	75	305	16.10	3.28	16		6
		100	280	17.50	3.57	18		6
Redland concrete	430 x 380	75	355	8.21	2.82	8		6
		100	317	10.52	3.16	11		7
	417 x 330	75	342	9.75	2.92	10		7
	381 x 229	75	306	*15.94	3.27	16		7

Type:	Size (mm)	Lap (mm)	Gauge (mm)	Number (Nr)	Battens (m/m2)	Slate fixing nails (Nr)	Slate fixing discs (Nr)	Batten nails (Nr)
** Yeoman 10.76 * Redland 49 16.34								
						Tile fixing nails (Nr)		
Sandtoft Goxhill clay tiles	470 x 285	100	370	11.50	2.70	12		6
	342 x 266	75	267	17.80	3.75	18		8
	342 x 241**	75	267	18.50	3.75	19		8
	342 x 241*	75	267	18.80	3.75	19		8
** Old English * Gaelic								
Plain tiles	265 x 165	65	100	60	10.00	24*		23
		75	95	64	10.53	26*		24
		85	90	68	11.11	28*		25
	(Vertical)	37	114	54	8.77	108		20
* Nailing 5th Courses								

Thicknesses of sheet metal

Lead BS 1178: BS Code	lbs/ft2	Thickness (mm)	kg/m2	Colour code
3	2.91	1.25	14.18	Green
4	4.19	1.80	20.41	Blue
5	5.21	2.24	25.40	Red
6	5.82	2.50	28.36	Black
7	7.33	3.15	35.72	White
8	8.26	3.55	40.26	Orange

Copper BS 2870: Thickness (mm)	Bay width Roll (mm)	Bay width Seam (mm)	Standard width to form bay	Length of each sheet (m)
0.45	500	525	600	1.80
0.60	500	525	600	1.80
0.70	650	675	750	1.80

Zinc BS 849: Zinc Gauge Nr	Thickness mm	Weight kg/m2	Weight Oz/ft2
10	0.48	3.2	11.39
11	0.56	3.8	13.18
12	0.64	4.3	14.98
13	0.71	4.8	16.78
14	0.79	5.3	18.58
15	0.91	6.2	21.57
16	1.04	7.0	24.57

Approximate numbers of copper nails per kg

	Length (mm) x Shank (mm)	Number per kg
Round lost head nails	65 x 3.75	178
	50 x 3.35	292
	40 x 2.65	474
Clout nails	65 x 3.75	170
	50 x 3.35	241
	45 x 3.35	308
	40 x 3.35	335

	Length (mm) x Shank (mm)	Number per kg
Clout nails	30 x 3.35	448
	25 x 2.65	740
	20 x 2.65	920
Cut clout nails	50 x 3.00	275
	45 x 2.65	330
	40 x 2.65	440
	30 x 2.36	627
	25 x 2.00	1298
Extra large head felt nails	25 x 3.35	440
	20 x 3.35	544
	15 x 3.00	691
	13 x 3.00	880

Approximate number of aluminium nails per kg

	Length (mm) x Shank (mm)	Number per kg		Length (mm) x Shank (mm)	Number per kg
Plain round head nails	115 x 5.00	159	Clout, slate and tile nails	65 x 3.75	504
	100 x 5.00	184		60 x 3.75	550
	90 x 4.50	246		50 x 3.75	644
	75 x 4.00	338		45 x 3.35	924
	65 x 3.75	490		40 x 3.35	980
	60 x 3.35	714		30 x 3.00	1512
	50 x 3.35	812		25 x 3.35	1540
	45 x 2.65	1428		20 x 3.00	2300
	40 x 2.65	1610			
	30 x 2.00	3276	Tile pegs	40 x 5.00	450
	25 x 2.00	4004		30 x 5.00	545
	20 x 1.60	7588		30 x 4.50	600
Round lost	75 x 3.75	448	Extra large head	25 x 3.35	1296
head nails	65 x 3.35	672	felt nails	20 x 3.35	1848
	60 x 3.35	756		15 x 3.35	1840
	50 x 3.35	860			
	40 x 2.64	1390			

WOODWORK

Approximate numbers of steel wire nails per kg

	Length (mm) x Shank (mm)	Number per kg		Length (mm) x Shank (mm)	Number per kg		Length (mm) x Shank (mm)	Number per kg
Round wire nails with plain heads	200 x 8.00	13	Cut floor brads	75 x 3.35	100	Oval brad head and oval lost head nails	150 x 7.10 x 5.00	31
	180 x 6.70	22		65 x 3.35	154		125 x 6.70 x 4.50	44
	150 x 6.00	29		60 x 3.00	198		100 x 6.00 x 4.00	64
	125 x 5.60	42		50 x 2.65	264		90 x 5.60 x 3.75	90
	115 x 5.00	57		45 x 2.36	330		75 x 5.00 x 3.35	125
	100 x 5.00	66		40 x 2.36	396		65 x 4.00 x 2.65	230
	90 x 4.50	88					60 x 3.75 x 2.36	340
	75 x 4.00	121	Cut clasp nails	200 x 6.00	11		50 x 3.35 x 2.00	470
	65 x 3.75	175		175 x 5.60	13		45 x 3.35 x 2.00	655
	60 x 3.35	255		150 x 5.60	19		40 x 2.65 x 1.60	940
	50 x 3.35	290		125 x 5.00	30		30 x 2.65 x 1.60	1480

	Length (mm) x Shank (mm)	Number per kg		Length (mm) x Shank (mm)	Number per kg		Length (mm) x Shank (mm)	Number per kg
	45 x 2.65	510		100 x 4.00	48		25 x 2.00 x 1.25	2530
	40 x 2.65	575		90 x 3.75	66		20 x 2.00 x 1.25	4500
	30 x 2.36	840		75 x 3.35	103			
	25 x 2.00	1430		65 x 3.00	171	Round lost head nails	100 x 4.50	75
	20 x 1.60	2710		60 x 2.65	202		90 x 4.50	85
				50 x 2.65	286		75 x 3.75	150
Round lost head nails	75 x 3.75	160		40 x 2.00	616		65 x 3.75	180
	65 x 3.35	240		30 x 1.80	858		50 x 3.75	230
	60 x 3.35	270		25 x 1.60	1384		45 x 3.35	330
	50 x 3.00	360					40 x 3.35	350
	40 x 2.36	760					30 x 3.00	540
	30 x 2.00	1190					25 x 2.65	815
	25 x 1.00	6100					20 x 2.65	1035
	20 x 1.00	8030					15 x 2.36	1540
	15 x 1.00	9400						

Lengths of timber per m3

mm m/m3	mm m/m3	mm m/m3	mm m/m3
16 x 16......3906	19 x 19......2770	22 x 22......2066	25 x 25......1600
19......3289	22......2392	25......1818	32......1250
22......2841	25......2105	32......1420	38......1053
25......2500	32......1645	38......1196	44........909
32......1953	38......1385	44......1033	50........800
38......1645	44......1196	50........909	63........635
44......1420	50......1053	63........722	75........533
50......1250	63........835	75........606	100........400
63........992	75........702	100........455	125........320
75........833	100........526	125........364	150........267
100........625	125........421	150........303	
125........500	150........351		
150........417			
25 x 175.......229	32 x 32.......977	38 x 38.......693	44 x 44.......517
200.......200	38.......822	44.......598	50.......455
225.......178	44.......710	50.......526	63.......361
250.......160	50.......625	63.......418	75.......303
300.......133	63.......496	75.......351	100.......227
	75.......417	100.......263	125.......182
	100.......313	125.......211	150.......152
	125.......250	150.......175	175.......130
	150.......208	175.......150	200.......114
	175.......179	200.......132	225.......101
50 x 50.......400	200.......156	225.......117	250.........91
63.......317	225.......139	250.......105	300.........76
75.......267	250.......125	300.........88	
100.......200	300.......104		
125.......160			
150.......133	63 x 63.......252	75 x 75.......178	100 x 100......100
175.......114	75.......212	100.......133	150........67
200.......100	100.......159	125.......107	200........50
225.........89	125.......127	150.........89	250........40
250.........80	150.......106	175.........76	300........33
300.........67	175.........91	200.........67	
	200.........79	225.........59	200........33
200 x 200.......25	225.........71	250.........53	250........27
250 x 250.......16	250.........63	300.........44	300........22
300 x 300.......11	300.........53		

Standard lengths of timber

1.8 m
2.1 m, 2.4 m, 2.7 m,
3.0 m, 3.3 m, 3.6 m, 3.9 m,
4.2 m, 4.5 m, 4.8 m,
5.1 m, 5.4 m, 5.7 m,
6.0 m,+ 6.3 m,+ 6.6 m,+ 6.9 m,+
7.2 m,+
+ These lengths may only be available from North American sources

Ends, angles, mitres, intersections and the like

SMM6 Clause N1.10 requires ends, angles, mitres, intersections and the like to be enumerated where the cross-sectional area of wrought timber exceeds 0.002 m2. Where the cross-sectional area is less than 0.002 m2 then ends, angles, mitres, intersections and the like are 'deemed to be included'.
The following scantlings DO NOT exceed 0.002 m3 and ends etc are 'deemed to be included'

13 mm x	16 mm x	22 mm x	25 mm x	32 mm x	38 mm x	44 mm x
13 mm	16 mm	22 mm	25 mm	32 mm	38 mm	44 mm
16 mm	19 mm	25 mm	32 mm	38 mm	44 mm	
19 mm	22 mm	32 mm	38 mm	44 mm	50 mm	
22 mm	25 mm	38 mm	44 mm	50 mm		
25 mm	32 mm	44 mm	50 mm	63 mm		
32 mm	38 mm	50 mm	63 mm			
38 mm	44 mm	63 mm	75 mm			
44 mm	50 mm	75 mm				
50 mm	63 mm					
63 mm	75 mm					
75 mm	100 mm					
100 mm	125 mm					
125 mm						
150 mm						

STRUCTURAL STEELWORK

Dimensions and weights of structural steel sections

Universal beams		Universal beams	
Size (mm)	x kg/m	Size (mm)	x kg/m
914 x 419	388	457 x 152	82
	343		74
914 x 305	289		67
	253		60
	224		52
	201	406 x 178	74
838 x 292	226		67
	194		60
	176		54
762 x 267	197	406 x 140	46
	173		39
	147	356 x 171	67
686 x 254	170		57
	152		51
	140		45
	125	356 x 127	39
610 x 305	238		33
	179	305 x 165	54

Universal columns	
Size (mm)	x kg/m
356 x 406	634
	551
	467
	393
	340
	287
	235
356 x 368	202
	177
	153
	129
305 x 305	283
	240
	198
	158
	137
	118
	97

Universal beams		Universal beams	
	149		46
610 x 229	140	305 x 127	48
	125		42
	113		37
	101	305 x 102	33
553 x 210	122		28
	109		25
	101	254 x 146	43
	92		37
	82		31
457 x 191	98	254 x 102	28
	89		25
	82		22
	74	203 x 133	30
	67		25

Universal columns	
254 x 254	167
	132
	107
	89
	73
203 x 203	86
	71
	60
203 x 203	52
	46
152 x 152	37
	30
	23

Joists	
Size (mm)	x kg/m
254 x 203	81.85
254 x 114	37.20
203 x 152	52.09
203 x 102	25.33
178 x 102	21.54
152 x 127	37.20
152 x 89	17.09
152 x 76	17.86
127 x 114	29.76
127 x 114	26.79
127 x 76	16.37
127 x 76	13.36
114 x 114	26.79
102 x 102	23.07
102 x 64	9.65
102 x 44	7.44
89 x 89	19.35
76 x 76	14.67
76 x 76	12.65

Channels	
Size (mm)	x kg/m
432 x 102	65.54
381 x 102	55.10
305 x 102	46.18
305 x 89	41.69
254 x 89	35.74
254 x 76	28.29
229 x 89	32.76
229 x 76	26.06
203 x 89	29.78
203 x 76	23.82
178 x 89	26.81
178 x 76	20.84
152 x 89	23.84
152 x 76	17.88
127 x 64	14.90
102 x 51	10.42
76 x 38	6.70

Equal angles (Imperial sizes)

Size and	thickness (mm)	x kg/m
203 x 203	25	76.00
	24	71.51
	22	67.05
	21	62.56
	19	57.95
	17	53.30
	16	48.68
152 x 152	22	49.32
	21	46.03
	19	42.75
	17	39.32
	16	36.07

Size and	thickness (mm)	x kg/m
76 x 76	14	15.50
	13	13.85
	11	12.20
	9	10.57
	8	8.93
	6	7.16
64 x 64	12	11.31
	11	10.12
	9	8.78
	8	7.45
	6	5.96
57 x 57	9	7.74

Size and	thickness (mm)	x kg/m
	14	32.62
	13	29.07
	11	25.60
	9	22.02
127 x 127	19	35.16
	17	32.47
	16	29.66
	14	26.80
	13	23.99
	11	21.14
	10	18.30
102 x 102	19	27.57
	17	25.48
	16	23.37
	14	21.17
	13	18.91
	11	16.69
	9	14.44
	8	12.06
89 x 89	16	20.10
	14	18.31
	13	16.38
	11	14.44
	9	12.50
	8	10.58
	6	8.49

Size and	thickness (mm)	x kg/m
	8	6.55
	6	5.35
	5	4.01
51 x 51	9	6.85
	8	5.80
	6	4.77
	5	3.58
44 x 44	8	5.06
	6	4.02
	5	3.13
38 x 38	8	4.24
	6	3.50
	5	2.68
32 x 32	6	2.83
	5	2.16
	3	1.49
26 x 26	6	2.23
	5	1.72
	3	1.19

Unequal angles (Imperial sizes)

Size and	thickness (mm)	x kg/m
229 x 102	22	53.77
	21	50.21
	19	46.45
	17	42.87
	16	39.20
	14	35.43
	13	31.56
203 x 152	22	58.09
	21	54.22
	19	50.32
	17	46.30
	16	42.32
	14	38.29
	13	34.10
127 x 76	14	21.17
	13	18.91
	11	16.69
	9	14.44

Size and	thickness (mm)	x kg/m
203 x 102	19	42.75
	17	39.32
	16	36.07
	14	32.62
	13	29.07
179 x 89	16	31.30
	14	28.28
	13	25.31
	11	22.36
	9	19.22
152 x 102	19	35.16
	17	32.47
	16	29.66
	14	26.80
	13	23.99
	11	21.14
	9	18.30
102 x 64	11	13.40
	9	11.61
	8	9.69
	6	7.69

Size and	thickness (mm)	x kg/m
152 x 89	16	27.99
	14	25.46
	13	22.77
	11	20.12
	9	17.26
	8	14.44
152 x 76	16	26.52
	14	23.99
	13	21.45
	11	18.92
	9	16.39
	8	13.69
127 x 89	16	24.86
	14	22.64
	13	20.26
	11	17.89
	9	15.35
	8	12.94
76 x 64	8	8.19
	6	6.65
76 x 51	11	10.12

Size and	thickness (mm)	x kg/m
	8	12.06
102 x 89	16	21.75
	14	19.67
	13	17.72
	11	15.62
	9	13.55
	8	11.31
102 x 76	14	18.31
	13	16.38
	11	14.44
	9	12.50
	8	10.58

Size and	thickness (mm)	x kg/m
89 x 76	14	16.83
	13	15.20
	11	13.40
	9	11.61
	8	9.69
	6	7.89
89 x 64	11	12.20
	9	10.57
	8	8.93
	6	7.16
76 x 64	11	11.17
	9	9.68

Size and	thickness (mm)	x kg/m
	9	8.78
	8	7.45
	6	5.96
	5	4.62
64 x 51	9	7.74
	8	6.55
	6	5.35
	5	4.01
64 x 38	8	5.80
	6	4.77
	5	3.58
51 x 38	8	5.06
	6	4.02
	5	3.13

Unequal angles (metric type)

Size and	thickness (mm)	x kg/m
200 x 150	12	32.00
	15	39.60
	18	47.10
200 x 100	10	23.00
	12	27.30
	15	33.70
150 x 90	10	18.20
	12	21.60
	15	26.60
150 x 75	10	17.00
	12	20.20
	15	24.80
125 x 75	8	12.20
	10	15.00
	12	17.80
100 x 75	8	10.60
	10	13.00
	12	15.40

Size and	thickness (mm)	x kg/m
100 x 65	7	8.77
	8	9.94
	10	12.30
80 x 60	6	6.37
	7	7.36
	8	8.34
75 x 50	6	5.65
	8	7.39
65 x 50	5	4.35
	6	5.16
	8	6.75
60 x 30	5	3.37
	6	3.99
40 x 25	4	1.93

Equal angles (metric sizes)

Size and	thickness (mm)	x kg/m
250 x 250	25	93.60
	28	104.00
	32	118.00
	35	128.00
200 x 200	16	48.50
	18	54.20
	20	59.90
	24	71.10
150 x 150	10	23.00

Size and	thickness (mm)	x kg/m
100 x 100	15	21.90
90 x 90	6	8.30
	7	9.61
	8	10.90
	10	13.40
	12	15.90
80 x 80	6	7.34
	8	9.63
	10	11.90

Size and	thickness (mm)	x kg/m
50 x 50	5	3.77
	6	4.47
	8	5.82
45 x 45	3	2.09
	4	2.74
	5	3.38
	6	4.00
40 x 40	3	1.84
	4	2.42

Size and	thickness (mm)	x kg/m	Size and	thickness (mm)	x kg/m	Size and	thickness (mm)	x kg/m
	12	27.30	70 x 70	6	6.38		5	2.97
	15	33.80		8	8.36		6	3.52
	18	40.10		10	10.30	30 x 30	3	1.36
120 x 120	8	14.70	60 x 60	5	4.57		4	1.78
	10	18.20		6	5.42		5	2.18
	12	21.60		8	7.09	25 x 25	3	1.11
	15	26.60		10	8.69		4	1.45
100 x 100	8	12.20	50 x 50	3	2.33		5	1.77
	12	17.80		4	3.06			

Circular Hollow Sections (CHS)

Outside diameter (mm)	Thickness (mm)	Weight (kg/m)
457.0	10.0	110.0
	12.5	137.0
	16.0	174.0
	20.0	216.0
	25.0	266.0
	32.0	335.0
	40.0	411.0
406.4	10.0	97.8
	12.5	121.0
	16.0	154.0
	20.0	191.0
	25.0	235.0
	32.0	295.0
355.6	8.0	68.6
	10.0	85.2
	12.5	106.0
	16.0	154.0
	20.0	166.0
	25.0	204.0
139.7	5.0	16.6
	6.3	20.7
	8.0	26.0
	10.0	32.0
114.3	3.6	9.83
	5.0	13.50
	6.3	16.80
88.9	3.2	6.76
	4.0	8.38
	5.0	10.30

Outside diameter (mm)	Thickness (mm)	Weight (kg/m)
323.9	8.0	62.3
	10.0	77.4
	12.5	96.0
	16.0	121.0
	20.0	150.0
	25.0	184.0
273.0	6.3	41.4
	8.0	52.3
	10.0	64.9
	12.5	80.3
	16.0	101.0
	20.0	125.0
	25.0	153.0
244.5	6.3	37.0
	8.0	46.7
	10.0	57.8
	12.5	71.5
	16.0	90.2
	20.0	111.0
76.1	3.2	5.75
	4.0	7.11
	5.0	8.77
60.3	3.2	4.51
	4.0	5.55
	5.0	6.82
48.3	3.2	3.56
	4.0	4.37
	5.0	5.34

Outside diameter (mm)	Thicknes s (mm)	Weight (kg/m)
219.1	6.3	33.1
	8.0	41.6
	10.0	51.6
	12.5	63.7
	16.0	80.1
	20.0	98.2
193.7	5.4	25.1
	6.3	29.1
	8.0	36.6
	10.0	45.3
	12.5	55.9
	16.0	70.1
168.3	5.0	20.1
	6.3	25.2
	8.0	31.6
	10.0	39.0
42.4	2.6	2.55
	3.2	3.09
	4.0	3.79
33.7	2.6	1.99
	3.2	2.41
	4.0	2.93
26.9	3.2	1.87
21.3	3.2	1.43

Square Hollow Sections (SHS)

Outside dimensions (mm)	Thickness (mm)	Weight (kg/m)
400x400	10.0	122.0
	12.5	152.0
350x350	10.0	106.0
	12.5	132.0
	16.0	167.0
300x300	10.0	90.7
	12.5	112.0
	16.0	142.0
250x250	6.3	48.1
	8.0	60.5
	10.0	75.0
	12.5	92.6
	16.0	117.0
200x200	6.3	38.2
	8.0	48.0
	10.0	59.3
	12.5	73.0
	16.0	91.5
180x180	6.3	34.2
	8.0	43.0
	10.0	53.0
	12.5	65.2
	16.0	81.4

Outside dimensions (mm)	Thickness (mm)	Weight (kg/m)
150x150	5.0	22.7
	6.3	28.3
	8.0	35.4
	10.0	43.6
	12.5	53.4
	16.0	66.4
120x120	5.0	18.0
	6.3	22.3
	8.0	27.9
	10.0	34.2
100x100	4.0	12.0
	5.0	14.8
	6.3	18.4
	8.0	22.9
	10.0	27.9
90x90	3.6	9.72
	5.0	13.30
	6.3	16.40
80x80	3.6	8.59
	5.0	11.70
	6.3	14.40

Outside dimensions (mm)	Thickness (mm)	Weight (kg/m)
70x70	3.6	7.46
	5.0	10.10
60x60	3.2	5.67
	4.0	6.97
	5.0	8.54
50x50	3.2	4.66
	4.0	5.72
	5.0	6.97
40x40	2.6	3.03
	3.2	3.66
	4.0	4.46
30x30	2.6	2.21
	3.2	2.65
20x20	2.0	1.12
	2.6	1.39

Rectangular Hollow Sections (RHS)

Outside dimensions (mm)	Thickness (mm)	Weight (kg/m)
450 x 250	10.0	106.0
	12.5	132.0
	16.0	167.0
400 x 200	10.0	90.7
	12.5	112.0
	16.0	142.0
300 x 200	6.3	48.1
	8.0	60.5
	10.0	75.0
	12.5	92.6
	16.0	117.0
120 x 60	3.6	9.72
	5.0	13.30
	6.3	16.40
100 x 60	3.6	8.59
	5.0	11.70
	6.3	14.40

Outside dimensions (mm)	Thickness (mm)	Weight (kg/m)
250 x 150	6.3	38.2
	8.0	48.0
	10.0	59.3
	12.5	73.0
	16.0	91.5
200 x 100	5.0	22.7
	6.3	28.3
	8.0	35.4
	10.0	43.6
	12.5	53.4
	16.0	66.4
90 x 50	3.6	7.46
	5.0	10.10
80 x 40	3.2	5.67
	4.0	6.97
60 x 40	3.2	4.66
	4.0	5.72

Outside dimensions (mm)	Thickness (mm)	Weight (kg/m)
160 x 80	5.0	18.0
	6.3	22.3
	8.0	27.9
	10.0	34.2
150 x 100	5.0	18.7
	6.3	23.3
	8.0	29.1
	10.0	35.7
120 x 80	5.0	14.8
	6.3	18.4
	8.0	22.9
	10.0	27.9

Outside dimensions (mm)	Thickness (mm)	Weight (kg/m)	Outside dimensions (mm)	Thickness (mm)	Weight (kg/m)	Outside dimensions (mm)	Thickness (mm)	Weight (kg/m)
100 x 50	3.2	7.18						
	4.0	8.86	50 x 30	2.6	3.03			
	5.0	10.90		3.2	3.66			

FLOOR WALL AND CEILING FINISHINGS

Average coverage of Gypsum plasters

Finishing plasters	Thickness (mm)	Coverage (m2/tonne)	Undercoat plasters	Thickness (mm)	Coverage (m2/tonne)
Thistle multi finish	2	350 - 450	Thistle browning	11	140 - 240
Thistle board finish	5	160 - 170	Thistle bonding coat	11	100 - 115
Thistle universal one coat	5	225 - 235	Thistle hardwood	11	115 - 130
	10	105 - 115	Thistle tough coat	11	135 - 150
	13	85 - 95			
Thistle projection one coat	5	140 - 160			
	10	70 - 80			
	13	60 - 70			

PAINTING AND DECORATING

Average coverages of paint per coat

The following table is reproduced by permission of: The Paint and Painting Industries' Liaison Committee - Constituent bodies: - British Decorators Association, National Federation of Painting and Decorating Contractors, Paintmakers Association of Great Britain and Scottish Decorators Federation.

The schedule of average coverage figures in respect of painting work is the 1974 revision (with amendments as at April 2000) of the schedule compiled and approved for the guidance of commercial organisations and professional bodies when assessing the values of materials in painting work

In this revision a range of spreading capacities is given. Figures are in square metres per litre, except for oil-bound water paint and cement-based paint which are given in square metres per kilogram.

For comparative purposes figures are given for a single coat, but users are *advised* to follow manufacturers' recommendations as to when to use single or multicoat systems.

It is emphasised that the figures quoted in the schedule are practical figures for brush application, achieved in scale painting work and take into account losses and wastage. They are not optimum figures based upon ideal conditions of surface, nor minimum figures reflecting the reverse of these conditions.

There will be instances when the figures indicated by paint manufacturers in their literature will be higher than those shown in the schedule. The committee realise that under ideal conditions of application, and depending on such factors as the skill of the applicator and the type and quality of the product, better covering figures can be achieved.

The figures given below are for application by brush and to appropriate systems on each surface. They are given for guidance and are qualified to allow for variation depending on certain factors.

Type of surface

Coating (m2 per litre)	Finishing plaster	Wood floated rendering	Smooth concrete/ cement	Fair faced brickwork	Fair faced blockwork	Roughcast/ Pebbledash	Hard board	Soft fibre insulating board
Water thinned primer/under-coat								
as primer	13-15	-	-	-	-	-	10-12	7-10
as undercoat	-	-	-	-	-	-	-	7-10
Plaster primer (including building board)	9-11	8-12	9-11	7-9	5-7	2-4	8-10	7-9
Alkali resistant primer	7-11	6-8	7-11	6-8	4-6	2-4		
External wall primer sealer	6-8	6-7	6-8	5-7	4-6	2-4		
Undercoat	11-14	7-9	7-9	6-8	6-8	3-4	11-14	7-10
Gloss finish	11-14	8-10	8-10	7-9	6-8	-	11-14	7-10
Eggshell /semi-gloss finish (oil based)	11-14	9-11	11-14	8-10	7-9	-	10-13	7-10
Emulsion paint:								
Standard	12-15	8-12	11-14	8-12	6-10	2-4	12-15	8-10
Contract	10-12	7-11	10-12	7-10	5-9	2-4	10-12	7-9
Heavy textured coating	2-4	2-4	2-4	2-4	2-4	-	2-4	2-4
Masonry paint	5-7	4-6	5-7	4-6	3-5	2-4	-	-
Cement based paint	-	4-6	6-7	3-6	3-6	2-3	-	-

Oil based thixotropic finish: Figures should be obtained from individual manufacturers

Glossy emulsion: Figures should be obtained from individual manufacturers

The texture of roughcast, Tyrolean and pebbledash can vary markedly and thus there can be significant variations in the coverage of paints applied to such surfaces. The figures given are thought to be typical but under some circumstances much lower coverage will be obtained.

Type of surface

Coating (m2 per litre)	Fire retardent fibre insulating board	Smooth paper faced board	Hard asbestos sheet	Structural steelwork	Metal sheeting	Joinery	Smooth primed surfaces	Smooth Under-coated surfaces
Woodprimer (oil based)	-	-	-	-	-	8-11	-	-
Water thinned primer undercoat								
as primer	-	8-11	7-10	-	-	10-14	-	-
as undercoat	-	10-12	-	-	-	12-15	12-15	-
Aluminium sealer:*								
spirit based	-	-	-	-	-	7-9	-	-
oil based	-	-	-	-	9-13	9-13	-	-
Metal primer:								
Conventional	-	-	-	7-10	10-13	-	-	-
Plaster primer (including building board)	8-10	10-12	10-12	-	-	-	-	-
Alkali resistant primer	-	-	8-10	-	-	-	-	-
External wall primer sealer	-	-	6-8	-	-	-	-	-
Undercoat	10-12	11-14	10-12	10-12	10-12	10-12	11-14	-
Gloss finish	10-12	11-14	10-12	10-12	10-12	10-12	11-14	11-14
Eggshell/ semi-gloss finish (oil based)	10-12	11-14	10-12	10-12	10-12	10-12	11-14	11-14
Emulsion paint:								
Standard	8-10	12-15	10-12	-	-	10-12	12-15	12-15
Contract	-	10-12	8-10	-	-	10-12	10-12	10-12
Heavy textured coating	2-4	2-4	2-4	2-4	2-4	2-4	2-4	2-4
Masonry paint	-	-	5-7	-	-	-	8-10	6-8
Cement based paint	-	-	4-6	-	-	-	-	-

*Aluminium primer/sealer is normally used over 'bitumen' painted surfaces.
Specialised: Figures should be obtained from individual manufacturers
Oil based thixotropic finish: Figures should be obtained from individual manufacturers
Glossy emulsion: Figures should be obtained from individual manufacturers
In many instances the coverages achieved will be affected by the suction and texture of the backing; for example, the suction and texture of brickwork can vary to such an extent that coverages outside those quoted may be on occasions obtained.
It is necessary to take these factors into account when using this table.

WEIGHTS OF BUILDING MATERIALS

Material	Weight	Unit
Aggregates:		
Coarse, natural materials	1500.0	kg/m3
Coarse, natural sands:		
dry	1600.0	kg/m3
moist	1280.0	kg/m3
Aluminium:		
Cast and wrought	2770.0	kg/m3
Corrugated sheets; thickness:		
0.87 mm	1.7	kg/m2
1.10 mm	2.4	kg/m2
1.42 mm	2.7	kg/m2
1.89 mm	3.7	kg/m2
flat sheets; thickness:		
0.87 mm	1.5	kg/m2
1.10 mm	2.0	kg/m2
1.42 mm	2.4	kg/m2
1.89 mm	3.4	kg/m2
Asbestos cement:		
corrugated sheets; profile:		
standard 3"	15.1	kg/m2
standard 6"	15.1	kg/m2
flat sheets 6.4 mm thick:		
wallboard	6.8	kg/m2
semi-compressed	11.2	kg/m2
fully-compressed	12.2	kg/m2
Asphalt:		
damp proofing; thickness:		
20 mm	42.4	kg/m2
25 mm	53.0	kg/m2
30 mm	63.6	kg/m2
flooring; thickness:		
20 mm	42.4	kg/m2
roofing; thickness:		
20 mm	43.9	kg/m2
Bitumen:		
damp proof courses BS, 743:		
type A, hessian base	3.8	kg/m2
type B, fibre base	3.3	kg/m2
type C, asbestos base	3.8	kg/m2
type D, hessian base and lead	4.4	kg/m2
type E, fibre base and lead	4.4	kg/m2
type F, asbestos base and lead	4.9	kg/m2
roofing felts, BS 747:		
hessian base type:		
1B	1.4,1.8,2.5	kg/m2
1E	3.8	kg/m2
1F	1.5	kg/m2
asbestos base; type:		
2B	1.8	kg/m2
2E	3.8	kg/m2
glass fibre base; type:		
3B	1.8	kg/m

Material	Weight	Unit
3E	2.8	kg/m2
3G	3.2	kg/m2
3H	1.7	kg/m2
Aggregates:		
sheathing and hair felts:		
AA(i)	1.7	kg/m2
AA(ii)		
brown Nr.1	2.5	kg/m2
brown Nr.2	2.0	kg/m2
brown	1.7	kg/m2
4B(i)	4.1	kg/m2
4B(ii)	4.1	kg/m2
Bitumen macadam:		
per 25 mm thickness	57.70	kg/m2
Blockwork, per 25 mm thickness:		
clay, hollow	25.5	kg/m2
concrete, natural aggregate:		
cellular	39.9	kg/m2
hollow	34.2	kg/m2
solid	53.8	kg/m2
concrete, lightweight aggregate:		
cellular	28.3	kg/m2
hollow	25.5	kg/m2
solid	31.7	kg/m2
Blockboard	450.0	kg/m3
Brass	8500.0	kg/m3
Brickwork, per 25 mm thickness:		
clay solid:		
low density	50.0	kg/m2
medium density	53.8	kg/m2
high density	58.2	kg/m2
clay perforated, 20% voids:		
low density	40.1	kg/m2
medium density	43.0	kg/m2
high density	46.1	kg/m2
concrete solid	57.7	kg/m2
calcium silicate, solid	50.0	kg/m2
Building boards, fibre:		
insulating, 12.7 mm thick	3.4	kg/m2
hardboard, 3.2 mm thick	3.4	kg/m2
Carpet	1.9 - 3.4	kg/m2
Cast stone	2240.0	kg/m3
Cement	1440.0	kg/m3
Concrete, plain:		
natural aggregates	2300.0	kg/m3
lightweight aggregates	1760.0	kg/m3
Concrete reinforced:		
natural aggregates	2450.0	kg/m3
lightweight aggregates	1900.0	kg/m3
Copper:		
cast	8730.0	kg/m3
wrought	8940.0	kg/m3

Material	Weight	Unit
Copper:		
sheet and strip; thickness:		
0.87 mm	4.9	kg/m2
1.10 mm	6.3	kg/m2
1.42 mm	8.3	kg/m2
1.89 mm	10.8	kg/m2
Cork:		
loose granular	120.0	kg/m3
board compressed per 25 mm thick	7.2	kg/m2
flooring per 25 mm thickness	9.7	kg/m2
Glass, float and plate:		
3 mm	7.71	kg/m2
4 mm	10.3	kg/m2
5 mm	12.8	kg/m2
6 mm	15.4	kg/m2
12 mm	30.8	kg/m2
25 mm	64.1	kg/m2
Glazing, patent:		
lead covered steel bars at 600 mm	26.0	kg/m2
centres and 6 mm wired glass		
aluminium bars at 600 mm centres	20.0	kg/m2
and 6 mm wired glass		
Lead:		
cast	11325.00	kg/m3
sheet, code:		
3	14.20	kg/m2
4	20.40	kg/m2
5	25.40	kg/m2
6	28.40	kg/m2
7	35.70	kg/m2
8	40.30	kg/m2
Lime, hydrated	720.00	kg/m3
Linoleum flooring:		
3.2 mm	4.40	kg/m2
4.5 mm	5.90	kg/m2
6.7 mm	9.80	kg/m2

Material	Weight	Unit
Plasterboard:		
9.5 mm	8.30	kg/m2
12.7 mm	11.20	kg/m2
19.1 mm	17.10	kg/m2
Plywood, per 25 mm thickness	15.00	kg/m2
Rendering, cement & sand (1:3):		
12 mm thick	27.70	kg/m2
18 mm thick	41.60	kg/m2
Sand:		
dry	1600.00	kg/m3
moist	1280.00	kg/m3
Screeds, cement and sand (1:3):		
25 mm	57.70	kg/m2
50 mm	115.40	kg/m2
Slate Westmorland	2880.00	kg/m3
Soil, compact:		
sands and gravels	2080.0	kg/m3
silts and clays	2000.0	kg/m3
Steel, mild and cast	7850.0	kg/m3
Stone, natural:		
Bath	2080.0	kg/m3
Darley Dale	2320.0	kg/m3
Granite, Cornish	2640.0	kg/m3
Mantle	2720.0	kg/m3
Portland	2240.0	kg/m3
Terrazzo paving:		
per 25 mm thickness	49.5	kg/m2
Thatch, Norfolk reed:		
per 300 mm thickness	40.9	kg/m2
Timber:		
softwoods	500.0	kg/m3
hardwoods	800.0	kg/m3
Water	1000.0	kg/m3
Wood wool slabs:		
per 25 mm thickness	14.4	kg/m2

USEFUL NAMES AND ADDRESSES

Asbestos Removal Contractors Association (ARCA)
Unit 1, Stretton Business Park
Brunel Drive
Burton Upon Trent, Staffordshire
DE13 0BY

☎: 01283 566467
🖷: 01283 505770
✉: info@arca.org.uk
Web: www.arca.org.uk

Association for Consultancy and Engineering (ACE)
Alliance House
12 Caxton Street
London
SW1H 0QL

☎: 020 7222 6557
🖷: 020 7990 9202
✉: consult@acenet.co.uk
Web: www.acenet.co.uk

Association of Plumbing and Heating Contractors (APHC)
12 The Pavilions
Cranmore Drive
Solihull
B90 4SB

☎: 0121 711 5030
🖷: 0121 705 7871
Web: www.competentpersonsscheme.co.uk

British Approvals for Fire Equipment (BAFE)
Bridges 2
The Fire Service College
London Road
Moreton in Marsh, Glos
GL56 0RH

☎: 0844 335 0897
🖷: 01608 653359
✉: info@bafe.org.uk
Web: www.bafe.org.uk

British Approvals Service for Cables (BASEC)
23 Presley Way
Crownhill
Milton Keynes
MK8 0ES

☎: 01908 267300
🖷: 01908 267255
✉: mail@basec.org.uk
Web: www.basec.org.uk

British Architectural Library
Royal Institute of British Architects (RIBA)
66 Portland Place
London
W1B 1AD

☎: 020 7580 5533
🖷: 020 7 255 1541
✉: info@inst.riba.org
Web: www.architecture.com

British Board of Agrément (BBA)
Bucknalls Lane
Garston
Herts
WD25 9BA

☎: 01923 665300
🖷: 01923 665301
✉: contact@bba.star.co.uk
Web: www.bbacerts.co.uk

British Constructional Steelwork Association Ltd (BCSA)
4 Whitehall Court
Westminster
London
SW1A 2ES

☎: 020 7839 8566
🖷: 020 7976 1634
✉: gillian.mitchell@steelconstruction.org
Web: www.steelconstruction.org

British Electrotechnical Approvals Board (BEAB)
Intertek
Intertek House
Cleeve Road
Leatherhead
KT22 7SB

☎: 01372 370 900
🖷: 01372 370 999
✉: info@intertek.com
Web: www.intertek.co.uk

British Hardware Federation (BIRA)
225 Bristol Road
Edgbaston
Birmingham
B5 7UB

☎: 0121 446 6688
🖷: 0121 446 5215
✉: information@bira.co.uk
Web: www.bira.co.uk

British Pest Control Association
4A Mallard Way
Pride Park
Derby
DE24 8GX

☎: 01332 294288
✉: enquiry@bpca.org.uk
Web: www.bpca.org.uk

British Plastics Federation (BPF)
6 Bath Place
Rivington Street
London
EC2A 3JE

☎: 020 7457 5000
🖷: 020 7457 5020
✉: reception@bpf.co.uk
Web: www.bpf.co.uk

Builders Merchants Federation (BMF)
15 Soho Square
London
W1D 3HL

☎: 020 7439 1753
🖷: 020 7734 2766
✉: info@bmf.org.uk
Web: www.bmf.org.uk

Building and Allied Trades Joint Industrial Council
Gordon Fisher House
14 - 15 Great James Street
London
WC1N 3DP

☎: 020 7242 7583
🖷: 020 7404 0296
✉: central@fmb.org.uk
Web: www.fmb.org.uk

Building Cost Information Service (BCIS)
Parliament Square
London
SW1P 3AD

☎: 0870 333 1600
🖷: 020 7334 3851
✉: contact@bcis.co.uk
Web: www.bcis.co.uk

Building Research Establishment (BRE)
Bucknalls Lane
Garston
Watford
WD25 9XX

☎:01923 664000
✉: enquiries@bre.co.uk
Web: www.bre.co.uk

Building Research Establishment : Scotland (BRE)
Orion House, Scottish Enterprise Technology Park
East Kilbride
Glasgow
G75 0RZ

☎: 01355 576200
✉: eastkilbride@bre.co.uk
Web: www.bre.co.uk

Building Services Research and Information Association
BSRIA Ltd
Old Bracknell Lane West
Bracknell
Berkshire
RG12 7AH

☎: 01344 465600
🖷: 01344 465626
✉: bsria@bsria.co.uk
Web: www.bsria.co.uk

Building & Engineering Services Association (B&ES)
Esca House
34 Palace Court
London
W2 4JG

☎: 020 7313 4900
🖷: 020 7727 9268
✉: contact@b-es.org.uk
Web: www.b-es.org.uk

Chartered Institute of Architectural Technologists (CIAT)
397 City Road
London
EC1V 1NH

☎: 020 7278 2206
🖷: 020 7837 3194
✉: info@ciat.org.uk
Web: www.ciat.org.uk

Chartered Institute of Arbitrators (CIArb)
12 Bloomsbury Square
London
WC1A 2LP

☎: 020 7421 7444
🖷: 020 7404 4023
✉: info@ciarb.org
Web: www.ciarb.org

Chartered Institute of Building (CIOB)
Englemere
Kings Ride
Ascot , Berkshire
SL5 7TB

☎:01344 630700
🖷: 01344 630777
✉: reception@ciob.org.uk
Web: www.ciob.org.uk

Chartered Institution of Building Service Engineers (CIBSE)
222 Balham High Road
London
SW12 9BS

☎: 020 8675 5211
🖷: 020 8675 5449
✉: enquiries@cibse.org
🌐: www.cibse.org

CBI
Centre Point
103 New Oxford Street
London
WC1A 1DU

☎: 020 7379 7400
🌐: www.cbi.org.uk

Construction Industry Research & Information Association (CIRIA)
Classic House
174-180 Old Street
London
EC1V 9BP

☎: 020 7395 8195
🖷: 020 7253 0523
✉: enquiries@ciria.org
🌐: www.ciria.org

Construction Industry Training Board (CITB)
Head Office
Bircham Newton
Kings Lynn
Norfolk
PE31 6RH

☎: 0344 994 4455
🖷: 0300 456 7587
✉: levy.grant@cskills.org
🌐: www.cskills.org

Construction Plant Hire Association
27 - 28 Newbury Street
Barbican
London
EC1A 7HU

☎: 020 7796 3366
🖷: 020 7796 3399
✉: enquiries@cpa.uk.net
🌐: www.cpa.uk.net

Construction Products Association
The Building Centre
26 Store Street
London
WC1E 7BT

☎: 020 7323 3770
🖷: 020 7323 0307
✉: enquiries@constructionproducts.org.uk
🌐: www.constructionproducts.org.uk

Contract Flooring Association Limited (CFA)
4c St Mary's Place
The Lace Market
Nottingham
NG1 1PH

☎: 0115 941 1126
🖷: 0115 941 2238
✉: info@cfa.org.uk
🌐: www.cfa.org.uk

Electrical Contractors Association (ECA)
ESCA House
34 Palace Court
Bayswater, London
W2 4HY

☎: 020 7313 4800
🖷: 020 7221 7344
✉: info@eca.co.uk
🌐: www.eca.co.uk

Electrical Contractors Association of Scotland (SELECT)
The Walled Garden, Bush Estate
Midlothian
EH26 0SB

☎: 0131 445 5577
🖷: 0131 445 5548
✉: admin@select.org.uk
🌐: www.select.org.uk

Federation of Master Builders (FMB)
Gordon Fisher House
14-15 Great James Street
London
WC1N 3DP

☎: 020 7242 7583
🖷: 020 7404 0296
✉: central@fmb.org.uk
🌐: www.fmb.org.uk

Fire Industry Association (FIA)
Tudor House, Kingsway Business Park
Oldfield Road
Hampton, Middlesex
TW12 2HD

☎: 0203 166 5002
🖷: 0208 941 0972
✉: info@fia.uk.com
🌐: www.fia.uk.com

Gas Safe Register
PO Box 6804
Basingstoke
RG24 4NB

☎: 0800 408 5500
✉: enquiries@gassaferegister.co.uk
🌐: www.gassaferegister.co.uk

Glass and Glazing Federation (GGF)
54 Ayres Street
London
SE1 1EU

☎: 020 7939 9101
🖷: 0870 042 4266
✉: info@ggf.org.uk
🌐: www.ggf.org.uk

Institution of Civil Engineers (ICE)
1 Great George Street
Westminster
London
SW1P 3AA

☎: 020 7222 7722
🖷: 020 7222 7500
✉: library@ice.org.uk (library Enq's only)
✵: www.ice.org.uk

Institution of Gas Engineers and Managers (IGEM)
IGEM House
High Street
Kegworth
Derbyshire
DE74 2DA

☎: 0844 375 4436
🖷: 01509 678 198
✉: general@igem.org.uk
✵: www.igem.org.uk

Intertek
Hilton House
Corporation Street
Rugby, Warwickshire
CV21 2DN

☎: 01788 578435
🖷: 01788 573605
✵: www.intertek.com

Joint Industry Board for the Electrical Contracting Industry (JIB)
Kingswood House
47-51 Sidcup Hill
Sidcup
Kent
DA14 6HP

☎: 020 8302 0031
🖷: 020 8309 1103
✉: administration@jib.org.uk
✵: www.jib.org.uk

Joint Industry Board for Plumbing and Mechanical Engineering (JIB-PMES)
PO Box 267
St Neots
Cambridgeshire
PE19 9DN

☎: 01480 476925
🖷: 01480 403081
✉: info@jib-pmes.org.uk
✵: www.jib-pmes.org.uk

National Approval Council for Security Systems (NACOSS)/National Security Inspectorate (NSI)
Sentinel House
5 Reform Road
Maidenhead, Berks
SL6 8BY

☎: 01628 637512
🖷: 01628 773367
✉: nsi@nsi.org.uk
✵: www.nsi.org.uk

National Access and Scaffolding Confederation (NASC)
4th Floor
12 Bridwell Place
London
EC4V 6AP

☎: 020 7822 7400
🖷: 020 7822 7401
✉: enquiries@nasc.org.uk
✵: www.nasc.org.uk

National Federation of Builders Limited (NFB)
B&CE Building
Manor Royal
Crawley, West Sussex
RH10 9QP

☎: 08450 578160
🖷: 08450 578161
✉: national@builders.org.uk
✵: www.builders.org.uk

National House Building Council (NHBC)
NHBC House
Davy Avenue
Knowlhill
Milton Keynes
MK5 8FP

☎: 0844 633 1000
🖷: 01908 747255
✉: cssupport@nhbc.co.uk
✵: www.nhbc.co.uk

National Inspection Council for Electrical Installation Contracting (NICEIC)
Warwick House
Houghton Hall Park
Houghton Regis, Beds
LU5 5ZX

☎: 0870 013 0382
🖷: 01582 539090
✉: enquiries@niceic.com
✵: www.niceic.com

National Statistics Library and Information Service
Government Buildings
Cardiff Road
Newport
NP10 8XG

☎:0845 601 3034
🖷: 01633 652747
✉: info@statistics.gov.uk
✵: www.statistics.gov.uk

Natural England
Foundry House
3 Millsands
Riverside Exchange
Sheffield
S3 8NH

☎: 0845 600 3078
🖷: 0300 060 1622
✉: enquiries@naturalengland.org.uk
✵: www.naturalengland.org.uk

Painting & Decorating Association
32 Coton Road
Nuneaton
Warwickshire
CV11 5TW

☎: 024 7635 3776
🖷: 024 7635 4513
✉: info@paintingdecoratingassociation.co.uk
✱: www.paintingdecoratingassociation.co.uk

Plastics Window Federation
Federation House
85-87 Wellington Street
Luton
LU1 5AF

☎: 01582 456147
🖷: 01582 412215
✉: ins@pwfed.co.uk
✱: www.pwfed.co.uk

Property Care Association (PCA)
Lakeview Court
Ermine Business Park
Huntington, Cambs
PE29 6XR

☎: 0844 375 4301
🖷: 01480 417 587
✉: pca@property-care.org
✱: www.property-care.org

Royal Incorporation of Architects in Scotland (RIAS)
15 Rutland Square
Edinburgh
EH1 2BE

☎: 0131 229 7545
🖷: 0131 228 2188
✉: info@rias.org.uk
✱: www.rias.org.uk

Royal Institute of British Architects (RIBA Enterprises)
66 Portland Place
London
W1B 1AD

☎: 020 7580 5533
🖷: 020 7255 1541
✉: info@riba.org
✱: www.architecture.com

Royal Institution of Chartered Surveyors (RICS)
Parliament Square
London
SW1P 3AD

☎: 024 7686 8555
🖷: 020 7334 3811
✉: contactrics@rics.org
✱: www.rics.org

Royal Town Planning Institute (RTPI)
41 Botolph Lane
London
EC3R 8DL

☎: 020 7929 9494
🖷: 020 7929 9490
✉: online@rtpi.org.uk
✱: www.rtpi.org.uk

Scottish Building Federation
Crichton House
4 Crichton's Close
Holyrood, Edinburgh
EH8 8DT

☎: 0131 556 8866
🖷: 0131 558 5247
✉: info@scottish-building.co.uk
✱: www.scottish-building.co.uk

Scottish Decorators Federation
Castlecraig Business Park
Players Road
Stirling
FK7 7SH

☎: 01786 448838
🖷: 01786 450541
✉: info@scottishdecorators.co.uk
✱: www.scottishdecorators.co.uk

Scottish and Northern Ireland Plumbing Employers Federation (SNIPEF)
Bellevue House
22 Hopetoun Street
Edinburgh
EH7 4GH

☎: 0131 556 0600
🖷: 0131 557 8409
✉: info@snipef.org
✱: www.snipef.org

Security Systems and Alarms Inspection Board (SSAIB)
7-11 Earsdon Road
West Monkseaton
Whitley Bay
Tyne & Wear
NE25 9SX

☎: 0191 296 3242
🖷: 0191 296 2667
✉: ssaib@ssaib.co.uk
✱: www.ssaib.co.uk

Society of Construction Law (UK)
The Cottage, Bullfurlong Lane
Burbage
Hinckley
LE10 2HQ

☎: 07730 474074
🖷: 01455 233253
✉: admin@scl.org.uk
✱: www.scl.org.uk

The British Library
St Pancras
96 Euston Road
London
NW1 2DB

☎: 0843 208 1144
✉: Customer-Services@bl.uk
✱: www.bl.uk

The Building Centre (Exhibitions and Bookshop)
26 Store Street
London
WC1E 7BT

☎: 020 7692 4000
✉: reception@buildingcentre.co.uk
www.buildingcentre.co.uk

The Guild of Master Craftsmen
166 High Street
Lewes, East Sussex
BN7 1XU

☎: 01273 478449
Fax: 01273 478606
✉: theguild@thegmcgroup.com
www.guildmc.com

The Chartered Institution Highways & Transportation (CIHT)
119 Britannia Walk
London
N1 7JE

☎: 020 7336 1555
Fax: 020 7336 1556
✉: info@ciht.org.uk
www.ciht.org.uk

The National Federation of Roofing Contractors Ltd (NFRC)
Roofing House
31 Worship Street
London
EC2A 2DY

☎: 020 7638 7663
Fax: 020 7256 2125
✉: info@nfrc.co.uk
www.nfrc.co.uk

Town and Country Planning Association (TCPA)
17 Carlton House Terrace
London
SW1Y 5AS

☎: 020 7930 8903
Fax: 020 7930 3280
✉: tcpa@tcpa.org.uk
www.tcpa.org.uk

Wood Protection Association
5C Flemming Court
Castleford
West Yorkshire
WF10 5HW

☎: 01977 558 274
✉: info@wood-protection.org
www.wood-protection.org

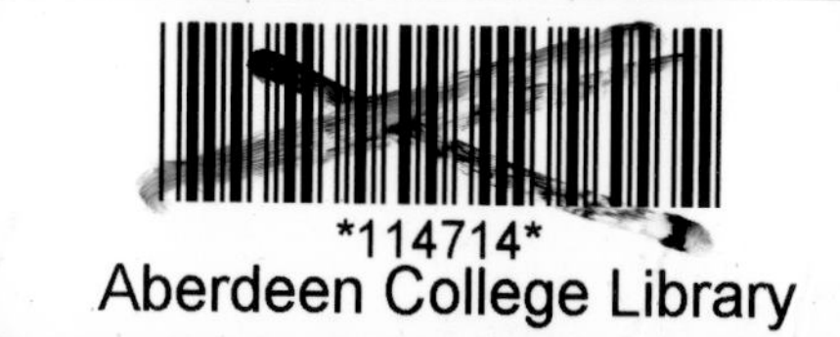